ARCHITECTURE IN BRITAIN AND IRELAND

600–1500

Lucy Archer

ARCHITECTURE
IN BRITAIN AND IRELAND
600–1500

Photographs by Edwin Smith
selected in collaboration with Olive Cook

THE HARVILL PRESS
LONDON

To Michael

First published in 1999 by
The Harvill Press
2 Aztec Row
Berners Road
London N1 0PW

www.harvill.com

First impression

Text copyright © Lucy Archer, 1999
Photographs copyright © Olive Cook, 1999

The author has asserted her moral right to be
identified as the author of this work

A CIP catalogue record for this title
is available from the British Library

ISBN 1 86046 701 6 (hbk)
ISBN 1 86046 404 1 (pbk)

Designed and typeset in Minion by
Libanus Press, Marlborough, Wiltshire

Originated by Spectrum Colour
Printed and bound in Italy by Poligrafico Dehoniano

CONTENTS

FOREWORD

In an age of indecision and disintegration in the visual arts, an age when novelty is prized above all else, it is both salutary and reassuring to look at our present and into our future out of the past. Lucy Archer's book evokes that past from the time of the great pagan sanctuary of Stonehenge, the mysterious burial mound of New Grange and the stone-built, stone-furnished houses of Skara Brae to the close of that period of unsurpassed spiritual and intellectual creativity we call the Middle Ages. So much has been written about medieval cathedrals and churches, so many photographs have been taken, that, embedded in a mass of facts, opinions and photographic imagery, our response is all too often predetermined and of the mind rather than the heart. In this book the text and illustrations combine to encourage the reader to look with his own eyes and to experience an entrancing sense of communion. Furthermore the author writes of these great ecclesiastical masterpieces not in isolation but as part of the whole fabric of the past that lives on in town and village, castle and cottage, manor house and farm and in school and collegiate buildings. It is a source of wonder that despite overpopulation and development on a scale unimaginable in the Middle Ages, despite destruction and neglect, philistinism and misguided restoration, so much survives to make its consoling and affecting visual impact.

Lucy Archer sets it all clearly before us, never descending to the purple passage, always writing with deep understanding of the history as well as of the structure and articulation of the building she is describing. Edwin Smith's photographs, taken with knowledge of architecture akin to that of the writer, complement her text. The informed and soberly expressed enthusiasm with which she unfolds her tremendous story, and of which he would have wholeheartedly approved, is counterbalanced by his warm and romantic eye. The photographs were all taken in the fifties and sixties when there were fewer cars, no motor roads and far fewer tourists, so although Stonehenge drew numbers of visitors every day and although it was already enclosed by railings, the photographer was able to experience and convey the full awesome power of the giant megaliths and their dramatic relation to the rolling expanse of their downland setting; and to enjoy a view of Salisbury unchanged since the day when Constable painted it from Walton Canonry.

The composition of each one of Edwin Smith's photographs makes an impression of such seriousness and inevitability that it is almost impossible to imagine the subject seen from another angle. And each one was of course the careful choice of a man who was both an artist and a trained architect. Sometimes the choice was prompted by the recognition and unhesitating seizure of a pregnant moment such as that which is immortalise in the picture of the Triangular Bridge at Crowland (Pl. 315) where the haunting and essentially medieval aspect of the great gaunt and decaying figure of Christ in Majesty leaning against the wall of the queer, humped structure is accentuated by the presence of two boys of our own century. More often, when confronted by an architectural subject, the photographer would consider various alternatives. After looking at Tintern, for instance, from every side, he decided to focus on the ruins of the graveyard of the parish church on the hill behind them, thus avoiding the road signs and rush of traffic that even then intruded upon the immediate vicinage of the abbey. So in the photograph of this most poetic of monastic survival we instantly recognise the source of Turner's painting and of Wordsworth's poem. The extraordinary photograph of the nave of Salisbury taken from the triforium (Pl. 141) is the result not only of delight in a deliberately selected and startling viewpoint but of an intensity of admiration – he spoke of "worshipping with the eye" and of "offering the praise of my humble craft". By making the black Purbeck marble column the pivot of the composition, the photographer concentrates our attention on the contrast between this darkest marble and the Chilmark stone of the main fabric, for it is this which infuses the flawless logic of the elevations with such overwhelming energy and spirit.

When entering and treading softly in a church or cathedral before starting to work, Edwin was not only experiencing what he described as some of the most poignant visual pleasures of his life, he was also doing what he called "rehearsing for the camera", thinking of its peculiar needs and seeking vantage points that were composed in terms of form and ·

where the source of light and shade fell within the scope of the film. He instinctively gravitated towards those parts of the building where the source of light lay diagonally in front of him and not behind. In the last year of his life his camera was a Linhof and it was with this that he took the photographs of Canterbury and those of the interior of Westminster Abbey that appear in this book. But the majority of the photographs were taken with a half-plate bellows camera made by Thorton Pickard in 1904 and called *The Ruby*. The focussing screen of course necessitated a tripod and a black cloth over the head. The exposures varied from ten to fifteen seconds to as many minutes. And every photograph was taken in existing lighting conditions.

Olive Cook

PREFACE AND ACKNOWLEDGEMENTS

Britain is extraordinarily fortunate in the astonishing number of medieval buildings and monuments which are still to be seen throughout the country, but unless one knows what to look for, these early buildings can be difficult to understand. Although they are often enjoyable simply for their picturesque qualities, they become far more interesting when one realizes why they came to be built and how they were originally used. This book aims to make them more accessible in three different ways. First, the main text traces the development of the various different building types which have survived from each period and provides a brief historical background to set them in the context of their times. Secondly, Edwin Smith's poetic and perceptive photographs complement this by providing a visual survey of the whole period, making it possible to appreciate both the salient characteristics of each style and the evolu-tionary development of architecture in Britain and Ireland from simple Celtic and Saxon beginnings to the sophisticated Gothic of the late Middle Ages. Thirdly, it is only by doing a great deal of looking that one can learn to recognize the work of different periods, and the gazetteer includes thousands of sites spread throughout the country, so that in any part of Britain readers will find a wide variety of buildings and monuments within easy reach. These include all the best-known examples and a representative selection of the many thousands more which have survived.

No one could write a book of this kind without being deeply indebted to the late Sir Nikolaus Pevsner and I should like to express my profound gratitude to him and the many other authors who have contributed to the comprehensive county guides in the *Buildings of England* series, currently being extended to Ireland, Scotland and Wales as well. These are an invaluable resource, covering the architecture of every period and all historic buildings but with a special sympathy for the earliest, since, in the words of John Newman, a contributor and now overall advisory editor of the series, "there is no doubt that for Pevsner himself it was in the Middle Ages that the awe, the thrill, and the joy of English Architecture lay." The Pevsner guides are essential for anyone exploring the architecture of a particular area in depth and they are listed under "Further Reading" at the beginning of each of the separate sections covering, England, Ireland, Scotland and Wales. It has been difficult to single out a limited number of the numerous books devoted to the architectural history of this amazingly rich period but the recommendations given here will provide a starting point for wider exploration.

Churches form the largest single category of surviving medieval buildings and there are still about 8500 of pre-Reformation date in England alone. Their contents, which are of equal interest and importance, are gradually being documented by the volunteer Church Recorders of the National Association of Decorative and Fine Arts Societies (*8a Lower Grosvenor Place, London* SW1W OEN), who have already catalogued and described hundreds of churches around the country. A great many churches are regularly open but because of the growing risk of theft and vandalism, increasing numbers are now kept locked and this makes it difficult for members of the public to know whether or when a particular church will be open. A number of schemes for opening these precious and important buildings to visitors are described on page 311. Unlike other historic monuments, churches do not charge for admission, but the cost of upkeep is a heavy burden especially for small parishes. Visitors who put a donation into the box for the Fabric Fund will be helping to safeguard the future of this vital part of our national heritage.

I am greatly indebted to everyone who has contributed to this book. First of all I want to express my gratitude to Olive Cook for allowing me to use her late husband Edwin Smith's superb photographs and for the many hours she gave up to our difficult and pleasurable task of reducing the numerous enchanting possibilities to a final selection. Her generous sharing of her formidable knowledge and experience was matched by the warmth of her welcome on my frequent visits. Emily Cole collaborated with me on the selection of buildings and monuments for the extensive gazetteer and was responsible for writing the majority of the entries. I greatly appreciated her ideal combination of patience, thoroughness and enthusiasm, which turned this daunting task into a most enjoyable undertaking. I should also like to thank Ian Chilvers for compiling the instructive glossary and Susan Wightman for her skilful design of the layout. I am extremely grateful to Christopher MacLehose for all his encouragement and to my supportive editor Sophie Henley-Price for piloting this complex book to publication. I am indebted to many people, including family and friends, for their help with the checking of facts and to all the vicars, churchwardens and others connected with church opening arrangements who have kindly found time to respond to my enquiries. Finally I want to thank my husband for more than a decade of enthusiastic and practical participation.

When I began researching this period, I had just completed my book on the work of Raymond Erith, a traditional architect of the mid twentieth century who was a committed classicist but well aware of how much the Renaissance owed to the Gothic past. He believed that far from stifling originality, the classical tradition in the broadest sense was a source of endless variety and innovation. Nothing could illustrate this more clearly than the evident continuity and the sheer diversity of architecture in Britain and Ireland over the nine centuries between 600 and 1500.

Lucy Archer

ARCHITECTURE IN BRITAIN AND IRELAND
600–1500

INTRODUCTION

Prehistoric beginnings

HOUSES AND FORTS

Most of the structures of the prehistoric period which are known only from archaeological remains and the evidence of excavations lie outside the scope of this book. These provided only the bare necessities of shelter or defence, but there are some which show a primitive architectural awareness. Well-known domestic examples include a neolithic settlement at **Skara Brae** (Mainland, Orkney, Pl. 2), which consists of stone houses with built-in stone furniture, and a late Iron Age village with pairs of courtyard houses on either side of a paved street at **Chysauster** (Cornwall, Pl. 3). Walled hill-top villages existed in Wales, especially in the north-west; an early Celtic settlement at **Tre'r Ceiri** on the Lleyn peninsula (Gwynedd), for example, had a surrounding stone rampart, up to 5 metres (16ft) thick in places but now largely collapsed, which originally protected a group of 150 stone dwellings.

As well as hill-forts of this kind, Ireland also preserves a number of ring-forts, which were first built during the Iron Age but continued to be used until the seventeenth century. The massive **Grianán of Aileach** (Co. Donegal, Pl. 4) was at one time attributed to the Middle Bronze Age (*c.*1000 B.C.) but it is now believed that it may be no earlier than the sixth century, and, like the **Staigue Fort** (Co. Kerry), which is thought to belong to the pre-Christian era, it owes its present impressive appearance to nineteenth-century restoration. **Dun Aengus**, perched on the cliffs of the Aran Island of Inishmore, has also been heavily restored, but all three give an idea of the powerful visual impact these buildings must have made in the landscape, whether on a hill-top site or, like the **Doone Fort** (Co. Donegal), on an island in a lake. The enclosing circular drystone walls of these forts are so massive that there is space within their thickness for stairs leading to passages or underground rooms, probably used for storage or perhaps for living accommodation. Access from the outside to the central space is along a passage lintelled in stone; the inner walls are stepped in terraces with flights of steps leading up to them. The more temporary structures which would have been built inside the circular enclosure are a matter for conjecture.

Circular drystone towers or fortified homesteads known as *brochs* were built in Scotland between *c.* 100 B.C. and *c.* A.D. 200, though they were previously thought to be much earlier; the famous **Broch of Mousa** in the Shetland Islands, for example, was traditionally believed to date from the Iron Age. *Brochs* were probably not built as forts, though some were surrounded with ditches and ramparts, but derived from earlier stone-

Pl. 1 *The great prehistoric stone circle at Stonehenge, Wiltshire, showing the massive sarsen stones and smaller bluestones set up in position during the third millennium B.C.*

Pl. 2 *One of a cluster of eight inter-connecting neolithic huts at Skara Brae on Mainland, Orkney; these simple dwellings, with central hearths and built-in stone furniture, were occupied from c.3100 to c.2500 B.C.*

Pl. 4 *The Grianán of Aileach, County Donegal, a huge circular stone fort of unknown date, possibly built as late as the sixth century and occupied until its partial demolition in 1101; it was reconstructed in 1870.*

Pl. 3 *The late Iron Age and Romano-British village at Chysauster, Cornwall, consisting of nine houses built round open courtyards on either side of a street; the site was inhabited from C.100 B.C.*

walled dwellings known as roundhouses. Their walls were up to 14m (45ft) high, the diameter reducing as they increased in height in the manner of a modern cooling tower, and the building could measure as much as 15m (50ft) across. These towers such as the Carloway Broch on the island of Lewis in the Outer Hebrides (Pl. 5) were constructed with two circular walls, one inside the other, the outer bonded to the inner by horizontal courses of flat stone lintels, leaving space in between for passages or galleries at each level. In order to keep strangers out, the

building could be entered only along a passageway leading from a forecourt, as at **Gurness** (Mainland, Orkney), and there were guard cells on either side of the single entrance. The interior space was divided up by stone partitions. There were no windows, but every *broch* had a hearth, and one at **Midhowe** (Rousay, Orkney) had its own water supply from a spring which is still flowing today.

The settlements which often grew up around these *brochs* show that the towers were not simply fortified places of retreat for times of emergency but safe and permanent centres where tribal groups could establish themselves. It has been suggested that the clan system originated in these small communities, where the surrounding dwellings often remained in occupation long after the towers themselves had been abandoned. In the far north these subsidiary buildings are known as "wheelhouses", because they were built with a central hearth and a series of radiating piers dividing the interior space. Their remains can still be seen in Orkney and Shetland and they are believed to have been in use from the second to the seventh or eighth centuries.

Pl. 5 *The remains of Carloway Broch on the Island of Lewis in the Outer Hebrides, a type of stone-built tower belonging to the period between* c.100 B.C. *and* c.200 A.D.; *its ruined state exposes the double-walled construction.*

SACRED STRUCTURES
AND TOMBS

The most famous and architectural of all Britain's prehistoric monuments, **Stonehenge** (Wilts, Pl. 1), the last in a sequence of monuments on the site erected between *c.*3000 and *c.*1600 B.C., is also circular in plan but differs in having apparently been built for religious rather than secular purposes. It has obvious similarities with circles of standing stones and, in its use of lintels, with Stone Age *cromlechs.* These consisted of huge upright stones or megaliths supporting horizontal capstones in order to produce a tomb chamber, which was approached along a passage through a mound of earth erected above it. One of the most magnificent examples of this kind of passage-grave, still covered by its earth mound, can be seen in Ireland at **Newgrange** (Co. Meath, Pl. 6). It has been dated to *c.*3100 B.C., and although its central chamber has a high corbelled ceiling, the smaller side chambers are roofed with capstones. Newgrange has a subtlety in its construction and in its use of spiral and other carved ornament which goes beyond the purely utilitarian. Moreover the position of the hole in its passage roof was calculated with scientific accuracy so that the first rays of the rising winter sun would shine on to the very centre of the wall of the burial chamber. A similar passage-grave at **Maes Howe** (Mainland, Orkney, begun *c.*2900–2800 B.C., Pl. 7) is also aligned on the winter solstice.

Stonehenge too was deliberately positioned and has its axis on the midsummer sunrise. The dramatic effect of this great circle of stones in the wide downland landscape is heightened by the intriguing mystery over its purpose as temple rather than tomb. In spite of innumerable delightful and fanciful theories about its possible origin and the way it was used, all that seems fairly certain is that it was some kind of religious sanctuary. It is a monument which has always inspired admiration and awe. In *c.* 2600 its builders performed the amazing feat of transporting at least eighty huge bluestones weighing up to two tons each from as far away as the Prescelly mountains in Wales. About two or three hundred years later a similar number of massive blocks of sarsen were dragged from the Marlborough Downs and set up in position. The stones are remarkable not only for their sheer size but also for the fact that they were carefully shaped with tapering uprights and curved lintels and jointed so that they are held firmly in position. In medieval times Stonehenge was thought of as the product of magic, a mythological

Pl. 6 *Looking from the entrance passage into the tall burial chamber of the magnificent prehistoric passage-grave at Newgrange, County Meath, constructed* C.3100 B.C.

interpretation providing the only apparent explanation for such an extraordinary and seemingly superhuman construction; like the Anglo-Saxon poet who described the remains of Roman fortresses as "the cunning work of giants", one fourteenth-century manuscript relates that Stonehenge was transported from Ireland by the wizard Merlin, and another illustrates his vast figure, like an outsized child playing with building blocks, casually putting it together again on Salisbury Plain. What is interesting is that it is shown not in its true circular form but as a rectangular structure, which comes far closer to the sort

Pl. 7 *The entrance passage leading into the spacious burial chamber inside the drystone cairn at Maes Howe on Mainland, Orkney, begun c.2900–2800 B.C.*

The Roman legacy

At the time when the Anglo-Saxons were establishing their earliest settlements the country must still have been scattered with the majestic and substantial buildings constructed by the Romans who had occupied Britain during the first four centuries A.D. Their occupation came to an end from about 410, but a process of decay had begun much earlier. The fortifications of many of the towns had been improved in the mid to late fourth century, but by then they were already suffering from depopulation because of the general decline in commerce brought about by the collapse of the Roman Empire as a whole. For the same reason the villas, which were essentially farms, had been gradually abandoned when farming was reduced to subsistence level because of a steady reduction in profits.

The economic consequences of the Roman withdrawal were decisive. It brought an end to state administration and military organization, both major sources of employment, and to the lucrative business of feeding, clothing and equipping the army. Large quantities of Roman coinage were no longer imported to pay the wages of the public service, though existing coins continued to circulate for some time, and trade with the rest of the Empire dried up. Towns declined rapidly but they were not all abandoned immediately. At *Verulamium* (St Albans, Herts) archaeologists have found a water-pipe laid in the mid to late fifth century, which suggests that some kind of organized urban life was being maintained then, and documentary evidence of the ninth century implies that the thermal baths of the Roman spa at *Aquae Sulis* (Bath, Avon) may still have been in use in the late sixth century. At the end of the twelfth century Giraldus Cambrensis (Gerald of Wales) was still able to describe in detail "immense palaces", "a lofty tower", hot baths and the remains of temples and an amphitheatre, all "enclosed within impressive walls" at **Caerleon** (Gwent). Conduits for water, underground passages, airvents and stoves were all clearly recognizable six centuries after the beginning of the Saxon period.

Many of the Romans' deserted buildings must have been available to the Germanic settlers in reasonably sound condition, and it may seem surprising that they apparently made so little use of them, either to live in or as a source of inspiration for their own architecture. The explanation appears to be that the invaders were forest dwellers with a completely different way of life and a well-established tradition of building in wood. They did not initially take to towns, which were irrelevant to a society

of timber-framed building the medieval chronicler would have understood. Similarly in the seventeenth century the architect Inigo Jones published his reconstruction of it as a circular Roman temple using the Tuscan order, suggesting a derivation within his own field of experience.

Stonehenge is a rare survival erected about three thousand years before our earliest extant group of religious buildings, a few modest stone churches and one wooden one, which are all that is left to us from the Anglo-Saxon period. It is these which mark the beginning of our continuous native architectural tradition.

with no central administration, where raider-bands of warriors survived by despoiling their neighbours' territory. Some Roman cities were reoccupied as time went on, but new communities often grew up nearby rather than on exactly the same sites. The early Anglo-Saxons seem to have found Roman settlements alarming; they may have suspected the presence of evil spirits in such alien places, though it is interesting to note that this did not subsequently prevent the Christian church from establishing itself at former Roman centres such as Winchester and York. Some of the missionaries even made use of Roman forts such as **Reculver** (Kent) and **Burgh** (Norfolk) as sites for their monasteries. It has been suggested that in doing so they were deliberately asserting the supremacy of their God over the pagan superstitions of the native inhabitants but they may alternatively have been motivated by a sense of continuity. Christianity had been established in Britain as early as the second century and was officially accepted throughout the Empire in the fourth. Therefore Roman settlements belonged to an earlier Christian tradition, which is unlikely to have been entirely obliterated. We know from the writings of the British monk Gildas in the mid sixth century that the British church, which continued to use the Latin language, was well established in his day, and it probably survived to some extent among the population of British extraction throughout the period of pagan domination. The Northumbrian monk Bede records that the cult of St Alban, the first British martyr, established at *Verulamium* in Roman times, was still flourishing in the early years of the eighth century.

It seems more probable, however, that in choosing the sites for their churches, the Anglo-Saxons were motivated by the purely practical advantages of solid existing defences and a plentiful supply of reusable building materials. The Anglo-Saxon invaders may have come into contact with Roman architecture in Europe before they left their homelands, but they built in wood rather than stone and would not have known how to repair masonry. When the reintroduction of Christianity brought with it a revival of forgotten Roman building methods, the first stone churches constructed by the Anglo-Saxons were built by craftsmen brought in from abroad. They sometimes made use of pillaged Roman masonry and bricks, but brick-making was not reintroduced into Britain until the early Middle Ages.

The most permanent legacy of the Romans' occupation was their network of roads, many of which have remained in use ever since, and the substantial remains of their massive defensive works, some still standing to a considerable height fifteen hundred years later. They have survived mainly because they were so solidly constructed that, even though they have almost entirely lost their stone facings, weather and time have not

been able to destroy them. The most spectacular of all is **Hadrian's Wall** (Pl. 8), begun in 122 as a boundary to protect the Romans' southern territories against the northern tribesmen they could not subdue. It stretched from coast to coast between Bowness-on-Solway, west of Carlisle, and Wallsend to the east of Newcastle upon Tyne, covering a distance of eighty Roman miles (118 km or 73 miles). At every Roman mile there was a milecastle or small fort with a gateway through the wall and between each of these there were two turrets or observation posts; further forts were built to the rear at intervals of 10–15 km (6–9 miles). The wall was about 2.3m (7ft 6ins) thick (sometimes even wider) and probably about 4.5m (15ft) high, and even now, in decay, it is a formidable sight. The Romans did not succeed in holding this northernmost frontier of their entire empire, but other fortifications were much more effective, and some continued to be used by their immediate successors, as at York, where the military headquarters building was kept in repair throughout the fifth and sixth centuries, though little is known about the town at that period.

As they retreated from the tide of the Germanic invasion, the Romano-British tended to desert the Roman military defences in favour of the traditional earlier strongholds, the Iron Age hill-forts; so the Anglo-Saxons were able to make use of these abandoned fortifications. The

Pl. 8 *A view near Housesteads, Northumberland, of the Roman Wall, which the Emperor Hadrian began to build in* A.D. *122 as a defensive barrier across Northern England.*

famous Roman forts of the Saxon shore, with their massive brick and stone walls and bastions, were built around the east and south coasts from Norfolk to the Isle of Wight towards the end of the third century. They remained impregnable while the forces garrisoned there were at full strength, but **Burgh** (Norfolk, Pl. 10) and **Portchester** (Hants, Pl. 9) must each have needed about a thousand soldiers, and when there were no longer the resources to maintain these numbers, the inadequately manned forts became vulnerable to barbarian assault. There is some evidence that the Anglo-Saxons made use of Roman fortifications, as at **Colchester** (Essex), where parts of the first-century town walls and the western Balkerne Gate are still standing, but in general the invaders seem to have avoided them, as they did the villas, and those which came into use again, especially under the Normans, were mostly not revived immediately. Portchester, the best-preserved of the Roman forts, owes its remarkable condition to the fact that it was in use sporadically from the late fifth or early sixth century onwards and during the entire Norman

Pl. 9 *The flint, tile and stone walls and hollow D-shaped bastions of Portchester Castle, Hampshire, built by the Romans in the late third century* A.D.

period. In the twelfth century a keep was built in the north-west corner, and the fort was kept in repair throughout the Middle Ages. Its flint walls bonded with courses of brick and stone slate still stand 3m (10ft) thick and 6m (20ft) high, and fourteen of its twenty-two projecting bastions have survived.

The "Dark Ages"

Until quite recently the two centuries between the withdrawal of the Romans and the Christian conversion of Kent (see p. 11) at the end of the sixth century have been dismissed as a period of impenetrable blackness when Britain reverted to barbarism. Modern studies of the historical evidence and recent archaeological discoveries present a very different picture, which shows how the waning influence of Rome was increasingly replaced by an alternative culture from the north. Excavations at Gudme on the Danish island of Fyn have revealed an important trading centre of the fourth and fifth centuries, where sophisticated gold and silver goods of local manufacture have been found, and this has clear links, both in buildings and artefacts, with a large Anglo-Saxon settlement occupied from the fifth to the eighth century which has been uncovered at **West Heslerton** (N. Yorks). Evidence of this kind indicates that Britain at this period should be seen not as an abandoned outpost of the Roman Empire but rather as an important part of an expanding Germanic world.

Change was gradual, however, and did not affect all areas of the country in the same way. When the Romans finally withdrew their troops at the beginning of the fifth century, they left it to the native population to organize its own defence. According to the British monk Gildas, writing in the mid sixth century, the Britons hired Saxon mercenaries who then rebelled against their poor conditions of service and turned to conquest. Other accounts suggest that invaders came in small bands for the express purpose of settling here and that by the second half of the sixth century they had largely succeeded in driving out the British rulers and establishing their own territories. Apart from Angles and Saxons, there were other tribes who were also attracted to Britain, including Jutes, Frisians, Suebians and Franks. They are generally thought to have begun arriving c.500, though some authorities put the date as early as c.420, seeing this as part of a general process of Germanic migration which was taking place throughout Europe in the fifth and sixth centuries.

The newcomers brought with them their pagan religion and its rites of cremation or burial, which, unlike Christian practice, involved the inclusion of grave-goods; so archaeological excavations of their cemeteries up to the time of their conversion to Christianity make it possible to differentiate between their early settlements and those of the Romano-British Christians. Although the two communities must have coexisted side by side for some considerable time, the Britons were gradually and inexorably driven westwards until they reached the wild country of Cornwall, Wales, Cumbria and Strathclyde, where they were able to establish defensible Celtic territories. In these areas the people supported themselves by primitive pastoral agriculture, with a small number of warrior lords dominating the peasant population.

In the lowland areas of central and eastern England the Germanic migrants settled permanently to a way of life based on mixed arable farming, establishing their pagan religion and their own native speech. Today we still remember their gods in the names of the days of the week, such as Wednesday, the day of *Woden*, Chief of the Gods, and Thursday, the day of *Thor*, God of Thunder. Our present-day place names, predominantly of Saxon origin, show how completely the Anglo-Saxons came to dominate, if not to outnumber, the native Britons. How many remained in these areas is not clear, and nor is their status, but they may well have been slaves rather than free men. Except in the western Celtic territories, they did not preserve a separate identity, and the supremacy of the Anglo-Saxon language, though with wide regional variations of dialect, was a strong force for unity. Once it was permanently established, all the various peoples who had settled here were irrevocably destined to become English.

Pl. 10 *The impressive walls and projecting bastions of the late third-century Roman fort at Burgh Castle in Norfolk, built with alternating bands of flint and brick.*

THE SAXON PERIOD

Historical background

Britain in Anglo-Saxon times was divided into numerous separate kingdoms, seven or possibly more of them in England alone. The shift of power between their various rulers and the scope of their authority are too complex to discuss here, but a general outline of the history of the period will provide a context for an examination of our very limited knowledge of its architecture. Among the more prominent rulers were:

Kent
Aethelbert 560–591/2

East Anglia
Redwald ?–616/27

Northumbria
Edwin 616–633
Oswald 634–642
Oswy 642–670

Mercia
Penda ?632–655
Aethelbald 716–757
Offa 757–796
Cenwulf 796–821

Wessex
Egbert 802–839
Alfred 871–900
Edward the Elder 900–925

Territorial dominance at this early stage is difficult to assess, since although one kingdom appears for a while to have been the most powerful, it may not have covered such a wide area or exercised as much control as it or its rivals did at other periods. Bede, the Northumbrian scholar

Pl. 11 *The early eleventh-century west tower of All Saints' church, Earls Barton, Northamptonshire, built c.1020, showing characteristic Saxon use of "long and short work" quoins, lesene strip decoration, blind arcading with both round and triangular arches and bell-openings separated by squat columns.*

monk whose *Ecclesiastical History of the English People* (completed *c.*731) is our main historical source, suggests, for example, that while Northumbria in the seventh century seems to have exercised authority over all areas of Britain except Kent, Mercia in the eighth does not appear to have penetrated beyond the Humber in the north or, in any permanent way, to the west of Offa's Dyke along the Welsh border. However, as a very rough guide to this confusing period it is useful to remember that Northumbria (the north and east) was predominant in the seventh century, Mercia (the Midlands) in the eighth and Wessex (the south and west) in the ninth, while by the tenth century the country had effectively been unified.

Aethelbert of Kent, who had married a Christian princess, Bertha, daughter of King Clovis of the Franks, played a key role in the introduction of Christianity direct from Rome into Britain. In 597 he agreed to receive St Augustine, who led a mission from Pope Gregory for the conversion of England, and in due course Aethelbert himself accepted the faith. As overlord of southern England he was an influential convert, and the king of Essex followed his example, setting up a see in his capital London in 604, though this did not last long. **Redwald** of East Anglia (who is of particular interest because he may well be the chieftain who was either commemorated or buried at Sutton Hoo with the famous hoard of treasure now in the British Museum) reached a pragmatic compromise, practising Christian rites alongside established pagan rituals, using two separate altars side by side in the same temple. It was he who was instrumental in helping **Edwin** of Northumbria to gain his kingdom in 616. Through his wife, who was Aethelbert's daughter and brought Christianity with her, Edwin was converted to the faith, but the Kentish mission established in his kingdom did not survive his death, in battle against Penda of Mercia, in 633. Edwin's successor, **Oswald**, a convert during his earlier exile on Irish territory, reintroduced Christianity by inviting the Irish monastery of Iona to send a mission headed by St Aidan and based on Lindisfarne. Northumbria's example, at this period of its ascendancy, influenced other rulers, and further kingdoms were converted: Wessex *c.*635, Essex (again) *c.*653, and later still Middle Anglia. Finally the Isle of Wight, the last of the pagan kingdoms, became Christian on the accession of Caedwalla, King of Wessex, *c.*686.

The two strands of Christian conversion, from Rome and from Ireland, though by no means entirely separate, left certain inconsistencies which needed to be resolved. Among other issues passionate feelings were aroused over the correct date for the celebration of Easter. Matters came to a head at the Synod of Whitby (664), where **Oswy** of Northumbria, influenced by his bishop Wilfrid, decided to follow the Kentish pattern and adhere to Roman traditions. In 668 the Pope, who had great difficulty in finding a candidate for such a remote posting, set the seal on this decision by sending Theodore (a refugee from Arab invaders in his native Asia Minor and already sixty-six years old) as a new reforming Archbishop of Canterbury. During his twenty-one years in office Theodore carried out a complete reorganization of the English church, giving it both ecclesiastical and legal authority independent of the ruling kings. By filling vacant sees and dividing up others he established many new bishoprics, and these, with a concomitant proliferation of monasteries, generated a fresh demand for works of religious art of all kinds which brought about a flowering of Christian culture. The foundations were thus laid for the rich land-owning church of the Middle Ages and the conflict it inevitably raised between religious and secular interests. The seeds of this problem are already apparent in a letter written by Bede in 734, where he expressed his anxiety about bishops and monks greedy for inflated revenues and about noblemen who had pretended to found monasteries but were actually living in them with their families on a grand scale and using the income from their endowments to support an extravagant lifestyle.

By the time of Oswy's death Northumbria had already lost much of its power in the south to the rising kingdom of Mercia. The expansion of Mercian territory had been begun in the mid seventh century by the pagan king **Penda**, when he gained control of the whole of the Midlands, to which his son added Essex, including the important trading port of London. By the early eighth century his successor **Aethelbald** dominated the whole of southern England; a contemporary document refers to him as "King of Britain". Records are scanty for this period of Mercian supremacy but Aethelbald was evidently a very powerful ruler, consolidating his territory by attacks on the Welsh, Northumbrians and West Saxons and countering the expanding wealth and influence of the church by violating ecclesiastical privileges. His exceptionally long reign of forty-one years was abruptly terminated when he was murdered by his own bodyguard. **Offa**, who followed him, was the first Anglo-Saxon king to be described in charters of the day as "King of the English". He ruled the whole of the country south of Northumbria, whose king Aethelred was his son-in-law. He raided extensively into Wales, and his surviving monument is Offa's Dyke, the embanked earthwork he built along the entire length of the Welsh border. His successor **Cenwulf**, and his brother after him, proceeded to the virtual annexation of Powys.

Egbert, the first great ruler of Wessex, was a distant relative of Offa's son-in-law Beotric of Wessex, whom he succeeded in 802. When Beornwulf of Mercia was killed suppressing an uprising of the East Anglians, Egbert took the opportunity to seize power in the south-east (829–30), thereby inheriting Offa's territorial gains. Before his death Egbert made formal arrangements to restore property appropriated from both Canterbury and Winchester in return for the unopposed succession of his son Aethelwulf. He in turn laid down that his own four sons, the youngest of whom was Alfred the Great (b. 848), should succeed him one after another. This peaceful dispensation spared Wessex dynastic strife, leaving it free to concentrate on the major threat posed by Viking invasions from Scandinavia.

The first Danish raids on the south coast, between 786 and 802, are described in the *Anglo-Saxon Chronicle* compiled in Wessex *c*.892. In the north, Norsemen (Norwegians) destroyed the church on Lindisfarne in 793, and we know that Iona and the northern Irish coast were also attacked. Regular raids are not recorded until the 830s and 40s, when Ireland and France were also targets. The year 865 saw a full-scale invasion, with reinforcements arriving in the summer of 871, the year of **Alfred**'s accession to the throne of Wessex. Northumbria fell in 867, East Anglia in 869 and the greater part of Mercia in 874–7. Alfred was put to flight by the Danish king Guthrum at Chippenham in 878 but defeated him decisively at Edington the following year and went on to capture London in 886. Another major invasion in 893–6 was successfully repelled, leaving Alfred in possession of the whole of Wessex and the south-western part of Mercia while Viking settlers established the "Danelaw", an area of Scandinavian rule in Northumbria, East Anglia and the rest of Mercia.

Alfred's success in overcoming the Danish threat was due to his use of the fifteen-year interval between his two major campaigns to carry out important naval and military reforms, which ensured that during the second war the invaders were hardly able to penetrate into Wessex at all. It also owed a great deal to the introduction of efficiently administered *burhs* or fortified garrison towns, which are thought to have been Alfred's own invention. These garrisons, which were often centres of trade and habitation as well, each had a sufficient allocation of land to support the number of men needed for the maintenance and defence of its fortifications. This was calculated by a method described in a tenth-century document called the "Burghal Hidage"; it was based on the principle of one hide (the area of land required to support one household) for every man needed, which worked out at 160 hides per furlong of wall to be defended.

In establishing a reliable system of defence rather than simply responding to random attacks, Alfred created the peaceful conditions which introduced the "Golden Age" of Anglo-Saxon art and scholarship.

He set about a deliberate revival of religion and learning which stemmed from his belief that the Viking invasions were a sign of divine displeasure. God, he thought, was punishing the English for their neglect of Christian education. Few now understood Latin; so scholars were brought in from Mercia, Wales and the Continent to translate into English the books which were needed to train young men for responsible positions in church and state. Besides scholars and scribes Alfred also employed builders, artists and craftsmen, some native and others from abroad. He founded two monasteries, one for monks and another for nuns, and others followed his example.

Alfred's son **Edward** continued this active patronage of the church, establishing two foundations at Winchester, where he built a New Minster, and carrying out a major reorganization of the diocese of Wessex. He continued with the building of fortified *burhs*, which were to become the centres of the shires he established as districts for local government. He also kept up constant pressure on the Danes, so that by the time of his death the Danelaw as far as the Humber was once again under English control.

Edward left his son in a position to dominate the entire country, and from the tenth century onwards the rulers of Wessex and their successors became the first kings to rule the whole of England. Their names include:

> Aethelstan 925–940
> Edgar 959–975
> Aethelred 978–1016
> Cnut 1016–1035
> Edward the Confessor 1042–1066
> Harold 1066

Aethelstan set about consolidating the English kingdom inherited from his father by the addition of Northumbria, which he wrested from the Vikings, and by establishing his dominance over Scotland and Wales. Marriage alliances between the royal house of Wessex and a number of continental rulers meant that his court had close links with Europe, which led to frequent political and cultural exchanges. It also ensured direct contact with the monastic reform movement already influential on the Continent, though the first "regular" or reformed Benedictine monasteries in Britain, at Glastonbury and Abingdon, were not founded until the mid tenth century. The king continued his predecessors' active patronage of the church by donating treasures from his distinguished collection of books and holy relics to religious houses throughout the country.

His nephew **Edgar**, who succeeded to the throne in 959 after the three brief reigns of his uncles and brother, made a major contribution to monastic reform through his close adviser Dunstan. His support for the church had political as well as religious motives, since the loyalty of the new foundations set up under his patronage served to extend royal influence and played an important part in establishing his political authority throughout the country. The peace and prosperity he achieved contrast sharply with the troubled reign of his son **Aethelred**, who succeeded as a child after the brief reign of his brother Edward "the Martyr", who was murdered in 975 by the opponents of the monastic party which supported him.

Aethelred's long and disastrous reign began inauspiciously with the sacking of monasteries by those who had brought him to power. He is remembered as "the Unready" (from *unraed*, ill-advised), but this gives a false impression. His early attempts to repel the Danes, whose raids began again in 980, were able and successful, while his treaty with Normandy in 991 was effective in denying them access to French ports for shelter and supplies. Disloyalty among his own nobility weakened Aethelred's position, while tribute-money or *Danegeld*, levied repeatedly in an attempt to finance defence and buy off the attackers, was a financial drain on the kingdom. The Viking leader Sweyn was aiming not just at plunder but outright conquest. In 1013 Aethelred retreated to France with his Norman wife and their children, returning after Sweyn's death the following year with Edmund Ironside, the son of his first marriage. In 1016 Aethelred died and Edmund, ceding Mercia to Sweyn's son Cnut, remained king of Wessex until his own death later that year.

Cnut was then accepted as king of England and strengthened his position by marrying Aethelred's widow, Emma of Normandy. He very soon inherited the Danish throne; so England was only a small part of his northern empire and he was obliged to make changes in the government of the country to cover his necessary absences. The kingdom was divided into four large administrative areas governed by powerful earls; Wessex, where most of the royal estates were, remained under his own control. This was administered by Earl Godwine, whose power became predominant, especially after Cnut's loss of Norway and his death in 1035. When Cnut's eldest son, Harthacnut, now king of Denmark, failed to come and claim the English throne, it passed to his half-brother Harold, who died five years later. Harthacnut then reigned for two years before the accession of **Edward** "the Confessor", son of Aethelbert, who thus restored the West Saxon monarchy.

Edward's reign was overshadowed by the continuing threat of invasion from Scandinavia. As the son of a Norman mother, brought up in exile in France, he could count on Norman support, and being childless he looked on William of Normandy as his heir. This bias caused problems with his English subjects, who resented Normans in high positions such as bishoprics. The king was powerfully opposed by Earl Godwine, who was finally driven into exile in Flanders in 1051, though he subsequently returned. In spite of these political preoccupations, Edward undertook a major and lengthy building project, the rebuilding of Westminster Abbey, which established the Norman style of architecture in Britain well before 1066 (see p. 28). The administration of the country continued within the organized framework of local and central government set up by the kings of Wessex. Shires and their subdivisions known as hundreds already existed, often centred on *burhs* established in the tenth century. Trade prospered and towns expanded, so there was no incentive for an arbitrarily imposed system of government after the Conquest, and there was in practice a considerable degree of continuity.

When Edward died, it was Godwine's son **Harold** who was chosen to succeed him. His reign lasted only a few months before the Norman **William** "the Conqueror", having landed his army in Sussex while Harold was successfully repelling a Viking invasion in Yorkshire, defeated him at the Battle of Hastings, where he met his death on 14 October 1066.

Buildings

THE ANGLO-SAXON STYLE

Since no secular architecture (see p. 35) has survived from this period, a definition of the Anglo-Saxon style must be limited to the characteristics of the very few extant ecclesiastical buildings. Saxon churches are tall and long in relation to their width. They have thick walls with small narrow doors and windows and steeply pitched roofs. Doors have flat lintels or arched heads, often made of a single piece of stone. Window openings are deeply splayed. Early mouldings are few, and square in section; columns have simple block capitals. In the later Saxon period, triangular-headed doors and windows became popular, as did multiple openings, their apertures divided from each other by short squat pillars. Crudely carved decoration appears, for example on columns and capitals, and roll mouldings are used on arches. Masonry is often of a high standard, with "long-and-short work" quoins strengthening corners and "lesenes" or pilaster-like strips used to decorate flat wall surfaces, especially on towers. These are common from the tenth century onwards and have rows of distinctive openings high up to let out the sound of the bells.

RELIGIOUS ARCHITECTURE

Continental origins

The church established in Britain under the Romans based its buildings on the early Christian churches of Rome. Some of these were circular, often to house a baptistery or a tomb, but the most popular form was the basilica or rectangular aisled hall, which had already been developed by the Romans as a secular meeting place for business or public occasions. This had a wide nave lit by windows in its upper walls, above rows of columns forming the arcades which separated the high central space from the single-storey aisles on either side. The building was entered from the east through a portico, and at the west end there was a semi-circular tribune or apse. Romano-British churches which survived into Saxon times would have been of this type, as we can see from the little fourth-century example, its interior only 6m by 8.75m (20ft by 28ft 6ins), excavated at **Silchester** (Hants). It had a short nave, side aisles and a western apse. Its plan shows a pair of short projections either side of the apse, like the incipient transepts at Old St Peter's Church in Rome, built in 326, which anticipate the later cruciform plan. Excavations of early Saxon churches, for example at **Reculver** (Kent) and **Winchester** (Hants), suggest that the main altar would have been in the nave itself, leaving the eastern space beyond it not as a sanctuary but for the use of the clergy. At Reculver there are the remains of a bench built round the apse, which may have had a bishop's seat in the centre. The name chancel (see p. 24) is derived from the screen (Latin *cancelli* – lattice-bars) which separated this part of the church from the rest of the building.

The Roman missionaries who reached Britain in the sixth and seventh centuries (see p. 11) had an uneasy relationship with the established Romano-British church. Its leaders, understandably resentful of the newcomers' criticism of their traditional practices, which differed from those of Rome, were uncooperative, easily offended and sometimes openly antagonistic. In view of this strained relationship, it is unlikely that existing churches had much influence on the newly converted Christians when they built their first places of worship. St Augustine's mission introduced a new version of Roman architecture modified by contact with Byzantium.

Late sixth-century Rome was no longer the capital of the Roman Empire, though it remained the seat of the papacy and therefore the centre of the church. The popes were the bishops of the wealthy see of

Rome, the only bishopric in the west which could claim direct descent from one of the Apostles, and from the fifth century onwards they emerged as a powerful spiritual and political force. After the death of the emperor Theodosius in 395, the Roman Empire had been divided between his two sons: the eastern part was ruled from the old Greek colony of Byzantium (modern Istanbul, Turkey), which had been named Constantinople in 330 when it was refounded as a Christian capital by the emperor Constantine the Great (306–37); the western part was based on Rome. Honorius, who ruled in the west, soon decided to move his capital to Ravenna in an attempt to escape the scourge of malaria and to evade the menace of attacks by the Goths. Like Rome, Ravenna fell to the Ostrogoths in 476, but in the sixth century it was recaptured by the emperor Justinian (527–65) and became an important Byzantine centre, with buildings which combined Roman with eastern influences. Justinian was personally responsible for commissioning a constant succession of civil, military and ecclesiastical buildings, the most magnificent being the great church of Hagia Sophia (or Santa Sophia) in Constantinople (constructed 532–7). He hoped to unite the Christian churches of the east and west under his own imperial authority, and the legislative power he granted to the bishops of Rome marked the beginning of their authority over the whole church in the west. Architectural ideas spreading from Constantinople to the west produced a Byzantine version of Roman architecture which reached England from Rome at the time of St Augustine's mission to Kent (see p. 11) and can be seen to have affected the design of early Saxon churches.

It exercised a further influence in the tenth century, as a result of the religious, cultural and architectural revival initiated by the emperor Charlemagne (768–814). The superb mosaic-ornamented church of San Vitale in Ravenna, founded by Justinian in 526, was the model for the Royal Chapel which Charlemagne built at Aix-la-Chapelle (Aachen) nearly three hundred years later. By becoming Holy Roman Emperor, a title bestowed on him by the Pope in 800 in gratitude for his defeat of the Lombards in Italy, Charlemagne re-established the idea of the western empire three centuries after it had succumbed to barbarian conquest and set about reviving the Roman Christianity of Constantine, who had first made it the state religion of the Roman Empire in 334.

The splendid churches built under Charlemagne gave rise to a new architectural style known as Carolingian, which is found throughout his empire, especially in France, Germany and the Netherlands. It looks back via Byzantium to Roman architecture but there are local variations such as the prominent west end of the church of St Riquier (c.790) at Abbeville (France) or the triangular arches of the blind arcading on the late eighth-century gatehouse at Lorsch (Germany, Pl. 12). Features like this and multiple bell-openings separated by squat columns, found on the early ninth-century tower of St Michael's Church, Fulda (Germany, Pl. 13), were later to appear on Saxon churches in Britain, for instance on the towers at Barton-upon-Humber (N. Lincs, c.990, Pl. 35) and Earls Barton (Northants, c.1020, Pl. 11). During the tenth century a further architectural revival followed under the Ottonian monarchy in Germany, and this led from the early years of the eleventh century to the development of the Romanesque style on the Continent and also in Britain.

Pl. 12 *Triangular-headed blind arcading on the Torhalle at Lorsch, Hesse, Germany, the gatehouse of a Benedictine abbey founded in the late eighth century.*

Pl. 13 *The early ninth-century tower of St Michael's church, Fulda, Hesse, Germany, showing small deeply-splayed windows and multiple bell-openings separated by squat columns.*

Pl. 14 *The small square early Saxon crypt at Repton, Derbyshire, believed to date from the eighth and ninth centuries, showing three of its four spiral-decorated columns.*

Britain was not on the fringe of the Carolingian renaissance but played a central role in it. Charlemagne's surviving correspondence with Offa of Mercia (see p. 12) shows him addressing him as an equal, respected for his Christian commitment as well as his territorial power. The other dominant English ruler he recognized was Aethelred of Northumbria. The north of England and Ireland were vitally important to Charlemagne in his revival of the lost culture of the late Roman Empire, which had been destroyed on the Continent by the barbarian invasions of the fifth century. In these Celtic areas it had been kept alive through the copying and study of ancient texts and he was able to make use of this remarkable survival of learning and scholarship in their monasteries. As one of his leading advisers, he chose the Northumbrian Alcuin of York, who spent many years at his court but never lost contact with scholars in his native country. The close political, ecclesiastical and cultural links between Britain and the Holy Roman Empire are reflected in the architecture of the later Anglo-Saxon period, in such features as the four-columned crypt at **Repton** (Derbyshire, Pl. 14) and the crypt which ran round the outside of the apse at **Brixworth** (Northants). Many aspects of design can be seen to have Carolingian antecedents., for example stripwork decoration on towers, as at **Barnack** (Cambs) or **Earls Barton** (Northants, Pl. 11) – perhaps inspired by an attempt to revive antique classical ornament – or double-splayed windows like those remodelled in the eleventh century at **Bradford-on-Avon** (Wilts, Pl. 15).

Christian conversion in Britain

It was the Irish church, directly descended from the Romano-British Christians, which brought the faith to Scotland and the north, when St Columba established his missionary headquarters on the island of Iona in the Inner Hebrides in 563. This was not the first attempt at conversion. Even earlier, St Ninian, a British Christian who had studied in Rome and under St Martin of Tours, had built a church at Whithorn on the shores of Galloway in 397 and converted many of the southern Picts. We also know that British or Irish teachers continued to establish Christian communities in Wales and the south-west of England after the Romans withdrew, but their ministries did not have the far-reaching effects of St Patrick's mission to Ireland in 405, which led to Christianity being established throughout the greater part of that country during his own lifetime. His ecclesiastical organization and the fact that Ireland, unlike England, was not troubled by Germanic invasions meant that a strong church continued to flourish. By the sixth century it was dominated by its monasteries, whose missionary activities extended as far afield as France and northern Italy. St Columba's monks, once established on Iona, moved further south to convert the heathen Anglo-Saxons and set up further religious houses, including Lindisfarne in Northumberland, founded by St Aidan in 635.

The Christian faith established in the south in the late sixth century came directly from Rome to Kent (see p. 11). King Aethelbert's Frankish Christian wife worshiped in St Martin's Church, Canterbury, whose Roman brickwork suggests that it may have been a survival from Romano-British times. It was presumably at her instigation that Aethelbert agreed in 597 to receive St Augustine and allow him to establish his mission in the city where the head of the English church, the Archbishop of Canterbury, is still based. In contrast to the north, where missionary activity was carried out from monastic centres over undefined areas, the south adopted the episcopal system of Roman

Pl. 15 *The little early Saxon church of St Lawrence at Bradford-on-Avon, Wiltshire, built c.700; both the lesene strip decoration and the upper parts of the walls with blind arcading date from the eleventh century.*

Christianity, dividing the country into dioceses presided over by bishops. The abbeys and monasteries founded by the Anglo-Saxons in southern England were the forerunners of our present cathedrals. After the Synod of Whitby in 664 (see p. 11) the diocesan system spread to the north as well, and although the numbers of bishoprics increased, the area each one covered became too large to be administered from a single centre. As a result local churches came to be built in towns and villages. Sometimes these were minsters (from Latin *monasterium*), large churches where groups of priests lived and worked together to minister to the surrounding neighbourhood. Churches were not all provided by the ecclesiastical authorities, for Bede tells of landowners building them on their estates as their own private property; here we have the origin of so many of our later parish churches.

Surviving structures

Crosses

The high stone crosses of the Celtic church are thought to mark the places where early Christian converts met for prayer before the first churches were built, and they may often have replaced earlier wooden crosses on the same sites. Although these are not strictly works of architecture, they are associated with so many of our parish churches that they ought to be

Pl. 17 *A ninth-century Celtic cross on St Cleer Common near Minions, Cornwall.*

Pl. 16 *The magnificent Anglo-Saxon cross, probably dating from the first half of the eighth century, which is housed inside the church at Ruthwell, Dumfries and Galloway; the carved scenes visible here show an archer, Mary and Martha, the penitent woman washing Christ's feet and Christ healing the blind man.*

considered here. At first they took the form of simple standing stones roughly decorated with crosses and curling lines, but they gradually adopted a cruciform shape and became much more complex and ornate. Dating is uncertain, but crosses appear to range from as early as the fifth to as late as the twelfth century. In England they can be seen in Cornwall (Pl. 17), Wales and the Midlands but are especially numerous in the north, where the Anglo-Saxon Christians were converted by missionaries from the Celtic church in Scotland and adopted its traditions. Two of the greatest surviving crosses, probably dating from the eighth century, are at **Ruthwell** (Dumfries and Galloway, Pl. 16) and **Bewcastle** (Cumbria). Both show the same eastern Mediterranean influence in their iconography and carving of vine scrolls, birds and beasts, which may be due to an influx of foreign craftsmen who arrived in England after the Synod of Whitby (see p. 12). The head of the Bewcastle Cross is missing but the surviving shaft still stands 4.3m (14ft) high above its pedestal, while the Ruthwell Cross is 5.44m (17ft 10ins) tall. The widest variety is to be found in Ireland (see p. 41), where a whole series of crosses followed a similar basic form, with a circle round the intersection of the shaft and cross-piece. They were generally decorated with biblical scenes, and we find spiral, interlace and fretwork patterns, which also occur on less sophisticated crosses in other parts of the country. The idea of the prominent central boss, which is a common feature of their design, probably derived from earlier wooden examples. The craftsmen who made these stone crosses would have had to chip away considerable quantities of stone to achieve an effect which arose naturally when two pieces of timber were fastened by a large nail where they crossed.

Over a hundred and seventy carved cross slabs have been found on the Isle of Man, which became Christian in the fifth or sixth century. They range from simple geometric designs of the period c.650–800 to low-relief representations of high crosses made during the period of Norse domination from the ninth to the thirteenth century and decorated with ornament and subject matter in both Celtic and Norse traditions.

Churches

A very few churches are the only Saxon buildings still in existence, and, with the exception of a single timber example at **Greensted** (Essex) (see p. 22, Pl. 23), they are all built of stone. When visiting them in their present-day form, one has to imagine them in their original architectural simplicity and think away the later alterations and additions, which are often substantial. On the other hand it is also important to remember the much greater richness of their original furnishings, at a time when even small churches contained valuable treasures and the more important would have been richly adorned with wall paintings, ceramic tiles, tapestries, vestments and metalwork. Battered remnants of roods or crucifixion groups survive in a number of churches, for example in Hampshire at **Breamore, Headbourne Worthy** and **Romsey** (Pl. 19), at **Langford** (Oxon) and at **Bradford-on-Avon** (Wilts), where the figures of two floating angels are all that is left. The late eighth- or early ninth-century friezes and panels at **Breedon-on-the-Hill** (Leics), the crucified

Christ at **Kedington** (Suffolk, Pl. 18), the seated Christ at **Barnack** (Cambs, Pl. 21) and the abbot with his crozier at **Sompting** (W. Sussex, Pl. 22) are rare survivals which suggest the considerable variety of Saxon sculptured decoration, seen in its architectural context at **Britford** (Wilts, Pl. 20), where there are carved slabs (probably of the ninth century) decorating the deep reveals of the entrance arch to the north porticus. A carved capital of classical design found at St Augustine's Abbey, Canterbury (perhaps early seventh-century, though possibly later), which shows traces of red, yellow and blue pigment and even

Pl. 18 *An Anglo-Saxon cross of* c.900, *carved with the crucified Christ, in the church of St Peter and St Paul at Kedington, Suffolk.*

Pl. 19 *The early eleventh-century Romsey Rood, over two metres (six feet nine inches) tall, carved on the outside wall of the south transept at Romsey Abbey, Hampshire.*

Pl. 20 *One of the tall carved slabs, probably dating from the ninth century, which decorate the deep reveals of the entrance arch to the north porticus of St Peter's church at Britford, Wiltshire.*

Pl. 21 *An early eleventh-century relief carving of the seated Christ in Majesty in the church of St John the Baptist at Barnack, Cambridgeshire.*

Pl. 22 *An eleventh-century carving in the south transept of St Mary's church at Sompting, West Sussex, showing an abbot with a crozier standing beneath an arcade.*

gilding, is a reminder of the vivid colour which has been lost.

Furnishings must also have added considerably to the richness of contemporary church interiors. A tenth-century account of the monastery at Abingdon shows the wide range of its treasures, when the writer describes how its founder "the blessed Aethelwold enriched that house . . . with the most precious adornments. For as we learn from the testimony of the ancient books he gave a golden chalice of great weight . . . He also gave three extremely beautiful crucifixes of silver and pure gold as well as with the most precious gems, with censers and cruets, cast basins and silver repoussé candelabras, and many other objects appropriate both for the monks' rites about the altar and for the comeliness of the church." Anglo-Saxon craftsmanship was admired throughout western Europe and at the time of the Norman Conquest the French historian William of Poitiers wrote that "the men of England are outstandingly skilful in all the arts."

The very small number of extant Saxon churches are merely chance survivors, and there are far too few, especially dating from the seventh and eighth centuries, for them to be fully representative of the architecture of the period. Some underwent later Saxon alterations and additions, for example St Lawrence, **Bradford-on-Avon** (Wilts, Pl. 15), where the early eighth-century plan survives but the upper walls were rebuilt *c.*950–1000. Much more survives from the tenth and eleventh centuries, but the sophistication of the artistic revival initiated by King Alfred in the late ninth century is not adequately reflected in the later Saxon buildings, or fragmentary remains of them, which are still standing. We know that in the tenth century much larger and more impressive churches were built, for instance, at Canterbury, Winchester, Worcester, Ely, Ramsey, Peterborough and Durham. These places were all major ecclesiastical centres, so it is not surprising that their earliest churches should have vanished as a result of later rebuilding, while minor churches in less important places escaped replacement.

The early Saxon period

The most remarkable survival of all is the only wooden Saxon building still in existence, the little church of St Andrew at **Greensted** near Ongar (Essex, Pl. 23). The chancel was added in the sixteenth century, but the nave still has its original walls of split oak logs set vertically in an oak sill. Another very early survival is the little stone-built St Peter's church at **Bradwell** (Essex, Pl. 24), whose nave is still standing because it continued in use as a barn. It shows traces of the characteristic plan of the churches built in Kent by St Augustine and his followers: an eastern apse, a west

Pl. 23 *The timber nave of St Andrew's church at Greensted near Ongar, Essex, built of split logs* C.1013 *or possibly even earlier; the brick plinth was inserted during restoration in 1848 and the roof was renewed in 1892; the west tower is post-medieval.*

Pl. 24 *The tiny early Saxon stone church of St Peter-on-the-Wall on the North Sea coast at Bradwell, Essex, built almost entirely of re-used Roman materials* C.654.

porch and two *porticus*, which were small low chambers opening off the nave and chancel.

The use of an apse is unusual in England, where a square-ended chancel has generally been preferred, and it reflects the Byzantine influence (see p. 15) on this early group of churches. Although they were derived from the early Christian basilica plan, they differ in this respect from contemporary churches in Rome, which have rectangular chancels; however, apses were still being built in Constantinople and Ravenna. A triple-arched opening between nave and chancel, symbolic of the Trinity, is another eastern feature which was adopted in these churches. Although none of these stone screens has survived, the one at **Reculver** (Kent, *c.*670) was not removed until the nineteenth century and is recorded in prints. Porticus seem to have had various different purposes and were sometimes two-storeyed. Those opening into the chancel were probably used as vestries or to store the vessels for Communion, while those off the nave could range from burial chambers full of tombs to places where lay people could leave their offerings or pray in private. Where there was a chamber above a porticus, it may have been used by a priest, who would have been able to look down into the church through a window or squint. Some of these openings survive in the walls of churches of Saxon origin, for example at **Deerhurst** (Glos, Pl. 37). Little is left of the other churches in this southern group apart from foundations uncovered by archaeological excavations which record their plans. We know that they made use of Roman building materials. The ruined walls of St Pancras's church, **Canterbury** (Kent), are made of Roman bricks, easily recognizable because they are much thinner and wider than later ones, sometimes even square, and look almost like very thick tiles.

The surviving seventh-century churches in Northumbria are only indirectly derived from Roman architecture. The immediate source was Gaul (France). After the Synod of Whitby had established the dominance of the Roman Christianity introduced into the south of England (see pp. 11–12), Benedict Biscop, formerly abbot of the monastery of St Peter and St Paul in Canterbury, founded two new monasteries in his native north at **Monkwearmouth** (674, Pl. 25) and **Jarrow** (685, both in Tyne and Wear). He brought in stonemasons and glassworkers from Gaul to construct the buildings, and hundreds of fragments of coloured glass and its supporting leads have been found in excavations at Jarrow. Although windows had been glazed in Roman times, the art of glass-making seems subsequently to have been lost, but it is known to have been revived in England by the tenth century. Some parts of the original buildings at Monkwearmouth and Jarrow are still visible, but the main architectural characteristics of this Northumbrian group of churches

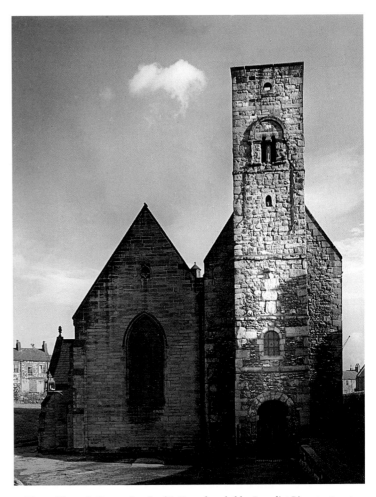

Pl. 25 *The early Saxon church of St Peter founded by Benedict Biscop c.675 at Monkwearmouth, Tyne and Wear; the upper part of the tower was added above an earlier porch in the late tenth century.*

can best be seen in the tiny parish church at **Escomb** (Co. Durham, Pl. 26, Fig. 8), built at about the same time. Except for some larger windows inserted in the thirteenth and nineteenth centuries, it has survived almost unchanged, with its original tall narrow nave, square-ended chancel and porticus. It has very small windows, splayed on the inside to let in more light and fitted with grooves either for glass in wooden frames or for shutters. It is quite possible that the windows were glazed, because fragments of glass have been found in the north porticus. The masonry shows skilled workmanship, and there is evidence that the walls were originally plastered. As in many early churches we find reused Roman masonry.

Pl. 26 *The complete surviving early Saxon church of St John the Evangelist at Escomb, County Durham, probably dating from the late seventh century, built with finely squared ashlar masonry and "long and short work" quoins; later additons include the thirteenth-century lancet windows and fourteenth-century porch.*

Presumably this was often chosen simply for convenience or economy, but here the foreign masons seem to have been deliberately and knowledgeably working with Roman materials (including the entire chancel arch, which is thought to have been brought from nearby Binchester) to produce a building recognizably in the Roman tradition. The proportions of the building are subtly worked out in relation to each other: the length of the nave is three times its width, and that in turn is the same as the diagonal measurement of the square chancel. It is interesting that in spite of the direct link between Canterbury and the earliest buildings in this Northumbrian group, these churches betray the Irish origin of northern Christianity in that they invariably have square-ended chancels rather than apses, and the arches leading into them are single rather than triple.

There are still Anglo-Saxon details to be seen in a large number of churches in Northumbria, but in Mercia the greatest of all the seventh-century churches still in existence survives almost in isolation. It belonged to the abbey of **Brixworth** (Northants, Pl. 28 and 29), founded by monks from Peterborough *c.* 680, and was built on the plan of a Roman basilica with nave aisles and a semicircular apse (destroyed by the Vikings and rebuilt in the tenth century), with an ambulatory and a crypt beneath

the altar. There is a later crypt (perhaps as early as *c.*757) beneath the ninth-century church of St Wystan at **Repton** (Derbys, Pl. 14), which was the capital of south Mercia. Two seventh-century examples of this early type of crypt, intended for the secure display of holy relics, survive at **Ripon** (N. Yorks) and **Hexham** (Northumberland, Pl. 27) and can still be visited today. There is some doubt as to how much of the surviving structure at Brixworth, which makes extensive use of salvaged Roman bricks, belongs to its earliest period, but it seems certain that the

Pl. 27 *The late seventh-century crypt beneath the medieval priory church at Hexham, Northumberland, showing reused Roman stones with carved ornament.*

Pl. 28 *The spacious nave of the monastic church of All Saints at Brixworth, Northamptonshire, built c.680, showing Roman bricks reused in the arcades and a characteristic late Saxon triple-opening into the tenth-century west tower.*

Pl. 29 *Detail of the exterior of the monastic church of All Saints at Brixworth, Northamptonshire, built c.680, showing rubble stone walls and arches of reused Roman bricks; the Norman south door was inserted in the twelfth century.*

church was completed before the Danish invasions of the ninth century which destroyed so much early Anglo-Saxon work. As a result of this wave of destruction, by far the greater number of surviving churches belong to the tenth and eleventh centuries, and it is these which are generally thought of as typical of Saxon architecture. Many features continued, however, throughout the whole period, so before considering later churches, it will be useful to summarize some of the basic characteristics of the earliest:

Plans are simple with a nave, chancel (square-ended or sometimes apsidal), projecting chambers (porticus) and sometimes a crypt under the altar. The **proportions** of the building are tall and narrow and may be geometrically subtle.

Walls are built of stone, with the single exception of the split oak logs used at Greensted (see p. 22). **Masonry** is often shaped, coursed and jointed with great care. Reused Roman stone or bricks are sometimes found.

Doors are small and narrow, with either a flat lintel or a simple arch which may be made of a single block of stone.

Windows are either square or round-headed, and both types may be found in the same building. They are set on the outer surface of the wall, their openings splayed on the inside to let in as much light as possible. The rarity of glass at this period may explain such a small window area, though it is not clear how often glazing was used, particularly in humbler churches. Alternatives were hide, horn, linen or simply wooden shutters.

Roofs were steeply pitched. Although none has survived, it is often possible to see traces on the walls which indicate their original shape. They must have been constructed in wood and were probably thatched.

The **interiors** of these very plain churches were evidently richly decorated and furnished (see pp. 19–22) but little ornament has survived. Architectural detail is simple, with **mouldings** of square section and rectangular block **capitals**. **Arches** may have voussoirs which are non-radial, i.e. made up of bricks or stones which do not taper towards the inner edge but are oblong blocks of even width fitted to the curve with wedge-shaped joints of mortar.

The later Saxon period

Church building seems almost to have ceased during the period of the Viking invasions. When it began again, from the late ninth century onwards, the native style of building was strongly influenced by Carolingian architecture (see pp. 15–16), for instance in features like the polygonal apse at **Wing** (Bucks), with its blind arcading, or the pilaster strips which cover the exterior at **Worth** (E. Sussex). A major factor was the spread from the Continent of the monastic reform movement. This called for a renewal of the ideals of the monastic way of life, which had become degenerate, and it led to the setting up of new religious houses. One of the most important of these was the Burgundian abbey of Cluny, founded in 910, which by the twelfth century had spread its influence throughout western Christendom by means of its numerous dependent houses abroad (see p. 47). The reformers' approach, with its emphasis on disciplined organization, introduced strict architectural requirements and created a demand for buildings designed for a more segregated way of life and a more formal liturgy or pattern of worship. To ensure privacy the monastic buildings which provided living accommodation for the monks were built round a cloister court, while in their churches the choir, which was at the core of their worship, was sited in the middle of the building beneath a central tower, with the main altar placed to its east in the chancel (see p. 30). These arrangements were to become standard practice from the Norman period onwards (see p. 50).

During the later Saxon period Britain was in contact with the mainstream of European culture, and the Norman Conquest was therefore far less significant architecturally than is often supposed. While a gap of a hundred years or more separates the latest of our early Saxon churches from the start of the great period of church building at the beginning of the tenth century, the later Saxon style actually overlaps with Norman from around 1050 onwards, each to some extent influencing the other. It has been argued that the late Saxon churches themselves constitute an English version of early continental Romanesque, while the first Norman work carried out in England, the rebuilding of Westminster Abbey by Edward the Confessor (c.1050), was French in both design and execution. Edward, the son of a Norman mother, was brought up in France and he imported Norman craftsmen to construct a Norman building closely related to the contemporary abbey at Jumièges (Haute-Normandie); so the Conqueror's native architecture preceded his political victory by several years. Once established in England, however, the Norman style was absorbed and modified so that it developed into a specifically English style.

Compared with the starkly simple early buildings, later Saxon churches show a growing sophistication of design, increased use of ornament and a greater feeling of space. They must still have been very dark, for windows remained small, presumably so as not to weaken the structure or to let in the weather. But it now became common to set them in the thickness of the wall, with openings splayed both to inside and outside, as at **Bradford-on-Avon** (Wilts, Pl. 15), so as to admit as much daylight as possible. Glass was still a rare and expensive commodity, to be used sparingly if at all. With the exception of **Stow** (Lincs, Pl. 30) and **Great Paxton** (Cambs), nothing has survived which suggests the vanished grandeur of the larger churches of the time, for example the New Minster at Winchester (consecrated 903), whose broad aisled nave was over 20m (65ft) wide. An aisled nave has survived at Great Paxton (*c.*1020), but most surviving churches show that the earlier unaisled type of nave continued, with three rectangular porticus at its eastern end, one central and one on each side. This arrangement gradually developed into a full cruciform plan, with the central or eastern porticus forming the chancel, those either side widening to develop into transepts, as at **Breamore** (Hants, *c.*1010, Pls 31 and 32), and a tower rising above the central space between them, as at **Norton** (Co. Durham). The crossing square, formed where the nave and transepts intersect, is an important

Pl. 30 *Looking from the nave past the crossing into the chancel of the large late Saxon church at Stow, Lincolnshire, which dates from the first half of the eleventh century; the font in the foreground is thirteenth-century.*

Pl. 31 *The crossing and narrow south transept of the early eleventh-century church of St Mary at Breamore, Hampshire, showing a stage in the emergence of a cruciform plan.*

Pl. 32 *The Saxon archway leading into the south transept of the early eleventh-century church of St Mary at Breamore, Hampshire; the inscription reads* "HERE THE COVENANT IS EXPLAINED TO THEE".

of the four arms to form a separate square on the plan. This can be seen clearly on the outside of the building, as at Stow where it forms the base of the tower. Sometimes only two corners project; at Breamore it is the eastern pair, at **Sherborne** (Dorset) the western. The choir for the monks and clergy was probably in the space beneath the tower, with the altar in the porticus or chancel to the east.

Architectural ornament

In contrast to the plainness of early Saxon work, decoration now becomes an integral part of the architecture. We begin to find roughly ornamented columns and capitals, for instance in the crypt at **Repton** (Derbys, Pl. 14) and at St Bene't's Church in **Cambridge** (Pl. 33), where there are lions crouched on the vigorously carved capitals. Sculpture is no longer confined to decorative panels or roods (see pp. 19–22) but also forms part of the actual structure of the building, as it was to do to such dramatic effect under the Normans. Mouldings of curved section are now more elaborate and are more widely used. Hood mouldings appear, both internally, where they emphasize the outer edges of arches, and externally, for the practical purpose of preventing rainwater from running on to doors and windows. We find half-shafts attached to columns and soffit rolls on the underside of arches. The effect is often rather crude but it can have great power.

Fonts

Very few baptismal fonts (from Latin *fons* – fountain) have survived from the Saxon period. They seem generally to have given way to Norman replacements, perhaps – though this is only guesswork – because the majority were made of wood. The few early fonts still in existence are all made of stone, like the tub-shaped example at **Old Radnor** (Powys), made out of a large boulder, roughly shaped, with a flat top and four stumpy legs. This is probably the oldest known and could date from the eighth century or even earlier. The particularly fine example at **Deerhurst** (Glos), which may be ninth-century work, is tall and cylindrical, carved on both bowl and base with a pattern of Celtic trumpet spirals and vine scrolls. Other early examples include one made out of the shaft of a Saxon cross at **Melbury Bubb** (Dorset) and others which were originally Roman altars, for example at **Chollerton** (Pl. 34) and in the Old Church at **Haydon Bridge** (both in Northumberland), but it is not known when any of these were turned into fonts.

feature of contemporary continental Romanesque, but except at Great Paxton, which is truly equilateral, surviving Saxon examples are not strictly correct. The transepts are not the same height or width as the nave and chancel and may vary a great deal; at **Wootton Wawen** (Warwicks, c.1020), for example, the crossing arches are of three quite different sizes. Saxon builders sometimes exercised considerable ingenuity in designing more or less equal openings, even when the spaces behind them were different, for example at Stow and Norton. A distinctive form of Saxon crossing is known as "salient" when its corners project beyond the width

Pl. 33 *One of the crudely but vigorously carved capitals and crouching beasts on the Saxon tower arch in St Bene't's church, Cambridge, which dates from the first half of the eleventh century.*

Sundials

A very practical feature which occasionally survives from late Saxon times is a dial clock, scratched on to the wall in a sunny position, for example at **Daglingworth** (Glos) and at **Kirkdale** (N. Yorks), where it is accompanied by a lengthy inscription about the founder and his rebuilding of the church. Sundials are generally found on the south side of the church and originally had a gnomon or peg projecting from the central hole. This cast a shadow on to the face, which was marked with the hours to indicate the time of Mass.

Towers

Church towers seem to have originated in Italy in the mid-ninth century, and by the tenth they had become common in England. Those found on very early churches are later additions, as at **Monkwearmouth** (Tyne and Wear, Pl. 25), where the tower (*c*.1000) was built above a two-storey porticus. At **Barton-upon-Humber** (N. Lincs, Pl. 35) the small space inside the tower was used as the nave. Many of the earliest towers were at

Pl. 34 *Two fonts in the mid twelfth-century church of St Giles at Chollerton, Northumberland; the one in the foreground was made out of a Roman altar dedicated to Jupiter which has been turned upside down and the other is thirteenth-century.*

the west end of the church and rectangular in plan. Where these have not been destroyed as a result of later widening, a Saxon tower can easily be recognized by its bell openings, which take the form of two round-headed arches with a crude stocky column between them. There may, however, be three or more openings in a row, and at **Earls Barton** (Northants, Pl. 11) there are as many as five. The arches sometimes have triangular heads, and the two different kinds may both be found together in the same building,

Pl. 36 *The Saxon tower of St Mary's church at Sompting, West Sussex, built c.1000, with the only surviving example in Britain of the "Rhenish helm" or gabled pyramidal roof which was popular in Germany.*

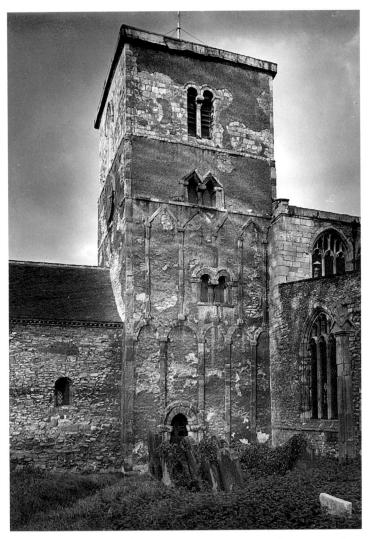

Pl. 35 *The late tenth-century tower of St Peter's church at Barton-upon-Humber, North Lincolnshire, showing the use of both round and triangular-headed arches in characteristic late Saxon bell openings and blind arcading.*

for example at **Wing** (Bucks). One can only guess how these towers would have been finished at the top, because those which survive have all been heightened or altered. Inevitably their original roofs have vanished, but the steeple at **Sompting** (W. Sussex, Pl. 36) is believed to retain its original eleventh-century form, inspired by comparable examples of the "Rhenish helm" shape then popular in the Rhineland.

Western round towers may well have been another borrowing from Germany, because they occur almost exclusively in East Anglia, which had traditional trading links with Hamburg. However, since they were built of flint, which was the readily available local material in an area which lacked any other stone, a circular form of construction was also dictated by practical considerations. Flint does not lend itself to building square corners; the rough shape of the stones demands the use of a great deal of mortar, and on a corner this is liable to crumble when exposed to rain and frost. A curved wall avoids this problem and therefore produces a much more stable structure. Most of these towers are very plain and probably date from the Norman period, but a few can be recognized as Saxon by such features as round or triangular-headed apertures and twin bell openings divided by a squat set-back column or as at **Burnham Norton** (Norfolk, Pl. 38) by the design of the doorway from the tower to the nave.

Church towers are sometimes assumed to have been places of refuge in the event of attack, but although they must have been useful as look-outs, they are unlikely to have been intended for defence. With their wooden floors and doors leading into the nave, they would have been extremely vulnerable to fire and can only have been as safe as the church as a whole. On the other hand the separate and very high towers built at about this time, or a little later, by monks in Ireland (see pp. 40–41) and Scotland (see p. 42) are very different. They are generally round, with several floors, and have their entrances between about 2m and 3m (6ft and 10ft) above the ground. Their occupants would have been in a much better position to repel an enemy, so although their old Irish name means "bell house", it seems plausible that they may also have been used as places to retreat to in time of danger.

Although the Anglo-Saxons' towers were intended primarily as belfries, openings into the naves of surviving churches show that a room lower down must sometimes have been used as an extension to the space inside the building, for example as a private chapel for a priest, who might also be able to see into the church itself. Openings into the nave vary from a small triangular squint to a full-sized window, which can be very ornate with decorative pillars or balusters, as at **Deerhurst** (Glos, Pl. 37), or a door which would have given access to a gallery. Sometimes, as at Deerhurst, one can see the stone corbels which once supported a gallery jutting out from the walls of the nave.

Two characteristic features of later Saxon architecture can readily be identified on towers. One is the use of "long-and-short" quoins to strengthen corners. This involved placing large rectangular stones one above the other, alternately vertically and horizontally, a system presumably derived from the Romans, who used it to reinforce rubble walls, and already found at **Escomb** (Co. Durham, see pp. 24–25, Pl. 26), where the Saxon church was built with reused Roman masonry. The other very recognizable feature is the use of "lesenes" or pilaster-like strips to decorate the surfaces of the walls. This also looks back to Roman architecture

Pl. 37 *The west wall of the nave inside the early Saxon church of St Mary at Deerhurst, Gloucestershire, with its surprisingly sophisticated double opening into the tenth-century tower; the Perpendicular-style roof is nineteenth-century.*

but was probably directly derived from Carolingian versions of classical decoration (see p. 17). It is sometimes thought to resemble timber-framed buildings, but this seems unlikely to have any significance; the surviving wooden church at **Greensted** (Essex, Pl. 23) has an entirely different construction, and the fact that the Saxons used triangular-headed arches would be enough to explain this unusual version of a pattern based on blind arcading. The pilaster strips are evidently intended to add visual interest to large plain areas of wall and are even used quite arbitrarily for this purpose, as on the tower at **Sompting** (W. Sussex, Pl. 36).

Pl. 38 *The round west tower of St Margaret's church at Burnham Norton, Norfolk, built of local flint; its date is uncertain but the design of the door opening into the nave suggests that it may belong to the Saxon period.*

Recognizing Saxon Churches

Plans

Tall narrow proportions; projecting chambers (porticus); square-ended or apsidal chancels; emerging cruciform plan; crossing square with "salient" corners.

Walls

Ashlar masonry, often of high quality; reused Roman materials; herringbone work; "long-and-short" quoins; lesene strip decoration and blind arcading, especially on towers.

Roofs

Traces of steeply pitched roof lines on gable end walls.

Doors

Small and narrow, with flat lintels or simple arches, sometimes made of a single stone; *later:* triangular heads as well, also hood moulds.

Windows

Very small, round, square or later triangular-headed; *early:* set on outer surface of wall and deeply splayed inwards; *later:* set in thickness of wall and splayed both inwards and outwards; also multiple windows with openings separated by squat columns.

Decoration

Early: block capitals and very plain square profile mouldings; *later:* columns and capitals roughly ornamented with crudely carved sculptured decoration; hood and roll mouldings; half shafts on columns; soffit rolls on arches.

Towers

"Long-and-short" quoins; lesene strip decoration and blind arcading; bell openings, often multiple, separated by squat columns; "salient" corners on central towers; western round towers.

SECULAR ARCHITECTURE

Visual representations

Secular architecture of this period is largely a matter for conjecture, since nothing has survived above ground. Most of the vanished buildings must have been made of wood, and for an idea of the appearance of early Saxon dwellings, we rely entirely on archaeology. The general shape of the later houses built by Viking settlers from the late ninth century onwards is reflected in the design of the "hog-backed" tombstones found mainly in eastern England, for example the fine group of these Anglo-Danish coffin covers at **Brompton-in-Allertonshire** (N. Yorks), some of which are now in the Durham Cathedral Library. Buildings of this bow-sided shape are known to have existed in Iron Age Scandinavia, and ninth-century examples have been excavated at Warendorf in Westphalia (N. Germany) and at Hamwith (**Southampton**, Hants), both probably Viking trading ports. The English hog-backed tombs which are decorated with sculptured ornament are carved with scale patterns to suggest a roof of wooden shingles, a device also found on a rare Norman tomb at **Fordwich** (Kent, Pl. 39). Even after their conversion to Christianity, the Anglo-Danes included pagan subject matter, for example the four Norse gods holding up the arch of heaven at **Heysham** (Lancs) and Brompton's crouching bears clasping the gable ends to ward off evil spirits, which are reminiscent of the grotesque animal-head finials to be seen on roofs in the Bayeux Tapestry (on display in a special gallery next to the cathedral at Bayeux in Normandy). In this great needlework record of the Conquest, made by English hands under Norman direction, we find schematic depictions of a number of ostensibly English buildings in the late eleventh century, including both a tall Germanic royal hall, with a high beamed roof and gables crested with Viking ornament, and a two-storeyed Romanesque palace with vaulted stone undercroft, external staircase and shallow-pitched roof.

ARCHAEOLOGICAL EVIDENCE

Wooden buildings

Excavations of the foundations of the Saxons' timber dwellings indicate that there were two main types, dug-out houses or *grubenhäuser* (see p. 36), which might be as small as about 3m by 4m (10ft by 13ft), and

Pl. 39 *A rare Norman stone tomb in St Mary's church at Fordwich, Kent, carved with a scale pattern representing wooden shingles on a hipped roof.*

larger post-built houses between 10m and 20m (32ft and 44ft) long and 5–8m (16–26ft) wide. These were constructed with wooden frames, the upright posts of their lower walls driven into the ground and supported by sloping props. The spaces between the posts were filled in either with palisading made of overlapping or tongued and grooved planks, plastered on the inside and possibly outside as well, or with wattle or woven branches daubed with mud or clay for weatherproofing. The roofs would have been thatched or covered with wooden shingles. Another type of timber construction, known only in a single wooden Saxon church at **Greensted** (Essex, see p. 22, Pl. 23), has a different form of palisade and it may also have been used in domestic architecture. Here the walls are made of oak logs split in half and set vertically in an oak sill. The cracks between the logs are covered on the inside with wooden battens to prevent draughts.

Much of our understanding of the appearance of Anglo-Saxon domestic architecture comes from excavations on the Continent, for example at Warendorf (Westphalia, N. Germany) where archaeologists have uncovered a settlement which includes examples of various different types of building dating from the seventh to the ninth century and ranging from small sheds to barns and houses up to 26.5m (87ft) long. In the invaders' Germanic homelands it was not unusual for humans and animals to live under the same roof, with only a partition between them, and although no Anglo-Saxon traces of this type of combined house and byre have yet been discovered, "longhouses" which fulfilled the same function later became part of the vernacular tradition in Britain. Examples still survive in remote areas of Scotland, Ireland and Wales (see p. 305) and in England on Dartmoor and in the Lake District.

Fortified royal houses, which must have existed in some numbers as the headquarters of local chieftains, are known from excavations both in Britain and on the Continent. A ninth-century hall uncovered at Elisenhof in Schleswig (Germany), near the Danish border, has the remains of the rows of externally sloping props or struts which supported its lower walls, and this arrangement is also found at **Yeavering** (Northumberland). The palace built there, for King Edwin (see p. 11) in the early seventh century, was an aisled great hall of a type which occupied the full height of the building, allowing plenty of space for the smoke from the central hearth to be drawn upwards and escape through a hole or turret in the roof. An unaisled ninth-century palace at **Cheddar** (Somerset) had its sloping struts placed inside the building, which suggests that they supported an upper floor. The existence of upper storeys is known from the familiar account of one of St Dunstan's miraculous escapes, in 978, when he was saved from falling through a collapsing floor by finding himself providentially perched on a joist. Both the Yeavering and the Cheddar halls have central doors placed opposite each other halfway along the long walls, which seems to have been characteristic of the design of such buildings. A simile which Bede uses in his *History* describes exactly this kind of communal room in use. Man's transient earthly life is compared with the flight of a swallow darting swiftly through a door into the brightness of a hall where a king is feasting with his warriors and noblemen and then out again on the other side, back into the darkness of the winter night. The Anglo-Saxon

poem *Beowulf* gives some idea of the considerable grandeur of these barn-like halls in its description of the magnificent "Heorot", "tall and wide-gabled", its lofty roof towering above the "golden tapestries that gleamed along the walls" as warriors feasted at a celebration banquet. While they slept afterwards on the floor, the hero was allotted his own quarters as a mark of respect. These were probably in a separate structure nearby but they could have been at one end of the main building, which was to become the normal arrangement in the great halls of medieval Britain (see p. 82). The foundations of seventh-century buildings excavated at Yeavering and at **Chalton** (Hants) both show cross-walls subdividing the internal space.

Archaeological reconstructions of the simple houses of humbler people have been attempted both at the Weald and Downland Museum at Singleton (W. Sussex), where one can see a wattle-walled dug-out hut and at **West Stow** near Bury St Edmunds (Suffolk), where a Saxon village occupied from the early fifth to the mid-seventh century has been rebuilt. This consists of a group of houses with walls made of vertical planks and roofs covered with thatch. They are also of the dug-out variety and have wooden floors with a hollow space underneath. There are internal hearths set on thick bases of clay, of a kind known to have remained in use in out-of-the-way places until comparatively recent times and recorded in a photograph of the interior of an Orkney croft as late as *c*.1900.

Stone buildings

Since they built stone churches, it seems likely that the Anglo-Saxons also built stone castles, but if so they have vanished, perhaps beneath more recent structures. The earliest parts of **Tintagel** Castle (Cornwall) are thought to have been Romano-British, kept up and extended by the Anglo-Saxons, and there are probably numerous cases where their work has been concealed by later building. The remains of a late Saxon stone house have been uncovered at **Northampton**. It derives from the Roman building tradition through the influence of the Carolingian revival (see pp. 15–16).

Celtic huts

In the stone country of the west and north there are traces of circular stone huts dating from the Romano-British period and much earlier. Hut circles – the archaeological remains of the foundation walls of these very simple structures, roofed with branches or turf – have been discovered in many areas, for example on Dartmoor (Devon), where the numbers found suggest that they were particularly numerous. To the same tradition belong the stone beehive-shaped dwellings which have occasionally survived in the Celtic areas of Europe. In Britain they can still be seen on the Isle of Lewis in the Outer Hebrides, while in Wales and Ireland a similar type of construction, either entirely of stone or with a thatched roof, was used for pigsties. As human housing grew more sophisticated, it is not surprising that such basic shelter should have come to be used for animals instead. These simple little buildings belong to a long tradition and are difficult to date.

Ireland

EARLY HISTORY

The Celts who had long occupied Ireland, possibly from as early as *c.*1500 B.C., were not affected by the Roman invasion of mainland Britain. Political power in Ireland fluctuated between the various local chieftains throughout the Saxon period, but it was the O'Neills of the north who were the dominant force. The church founded by the Romano-Briton St Patrick at the beginning of the fifth century was organized on episcopal lines, but during the sixth and seventh centuries bishoprics were less important than the increasing numbers of monasteries, which became cultural centres of international standing. Their missionary activities began in Scotland *c.*400 (see p. 17) and spread to England and the Continent, where further monasteries were founded in France, Switzerland, Germany, Austria and Italy. The Irish monks led lives of great hardship and their buildings were plain and simple, a typical monastery consisting of one or two very basic churches and a group of cells or beehive huts inside a walled enclosure. The only structures durable enough to have survived are in stone, for instance on the islands of **Skellig Michael** (Co. Kerry), **Inishmurray** (Co. Sligo), on the **Dingle** Peninsula (Co. Kerry, Pls 40 and 41) and on the **Aran Islands**. It is impossible to date them with any accuracy, and it is now thought that the particularly well preserved Irish group built on an island off the west coast of Co. Kerry as cells for the monks of Skellig Michael could have been built at any time between the ninth and twelfth centuries, or even earlier, while the Gallarus Oratory (Dingle), previously

Pl. 40 *Irish beehive-shaped stone huts on the Dingle Peninsula in County Kerry; these simple corbelled structures are likely to have been built some time between the ninth and the twelfth centuries but could be even earlier.*

believed to be eighth-century, could have been built three or four centuries later.

In contrast to their architectural austerity, the monks devoted themselves to producing in their simple *scriptoria* (writing rooms) illuminated manuscripts of extraordinary richness, such as the Book of Durrow (*c.*700) and the Book of Kells (*c.*800), both now preserved in the Library of Trinity College, Dublin. It was because the Irish monasteries

and, except perhaps when they were richly bound, they would have been of little interest to the invaders since they could not read. Although enormous numbers must have been destroyed, especially by fire, their lack of obvious appeal may account for the survival of those we can still see today.

As well as inflicting plunder and destruction the invaders brought benefits, such as their skills in seamanship. They also introduced coinage and brought trade to Ireland, establishing many of the present-day coastal towns, including Dublin and Waterford. Evidence of intermarriage and the blend of Irish and Norse influences in works of art both suggest that there was considerable integration with the Celtic population, even after Viking power came to an end with the defeat of their leaders by Brian (Boru) O'Neill at the Battle of Clontarf in 1014.

SURVIVING ARCHITECTURE

Architecture in Ireland during the greater part of this period developed independently of the rest of the British Isles, though through the activities of the Irish missionaries its impact was felt in both Scotland and the northern parts of England. Only in the eleventh century did Ireland begin to absorb the same continental ideas as late Saxon England, and the Norman Romanesque which took root so firmly in England had little effect here. It was the large-scale rebuilding of churches brought about by the ecclesiastical reforms of the following century that finally established English architectural influence in Ireland (see pp. 86–87).

Churches

The more substantial early architectural remains which have survived are mostly monastic and belong mainly to the period from the ninth to the twelfth century, when building in stone became widespread. Churches, tall round towers and high crosses can be seen throughout the country, sometimes together in groups, for example at **Clonmacnoise** (Co. Offaly, Pl. 43), **Glendalough** (Co. Wicklow, Pl. 42) and **Monasterboice** (Co. Louth, Pl. 44). Church architecture derives from two quite separate traditions, sometimes both combined in the same building. One is the corbelled construction which produced the beehive huts and related rectangular boat-shaped structures like the Gallarus Oratory (Co. Kerry, Pl. 41), whose walls slope inwards and join at the top to form a kind of primitive stone vault. The other is the legacy of

Pl. 41 *The Gallarus Oratory on the Dingle Peninsula, the best preserved of a number of small boat-shaped chapels in County Kerry, probably built between the ninth and the twelfth centuries.*

had used their regular contact with the Continent to make manuscript records of the learning of the late Roman Empire, before it was lost during the barbarian invasions of the fifth century, that they were able to play such an active part in Charlemagne's cultural revival four centuries later (see pp. 15–17).

The Viking invasions which began at the end of the eighth century ravaged many of the monasteries, whose treasures are still being found in excavations of warriors' graves in Scandinavia. Unlike gold and precious stones, manuscripts were not in themselves valuable artefacts,

the timber building methods of the vanished wooden architecture of the preceding period.

Although no actual buildings have survived, there are luckily a number of models which provide a reliable visual record of their appearance. Some of these miniatures were made as reliquaries, while others are stone representations surviving as tombs, for example at **Clones** (Co. Monaghan), or as the crowning features on high crosses, for example the early tenth-century Muiredach's Cross at **Monasterboice** (Co. Louth, Pl. 44), where one can even see the overlapping wooden shingles on the

Pl. 43 *The site of the great monastery at Clonmachnoise, County Offaly, founded in 548 and occupied until the sixteenth century; in the foreground is the tenth-century Cross of the Scriptures, richly carved with biblical scenes.*

Pl. 42 *The site of the sixth-century monastery at Glendalough, County Wicklow, where the latest buildings date from the thirteenth century; the eleventh or twelfth-century church with a short round belfry tower is known as St Kevin's Kitchen.*

roof, carved in minute detail. Corbelled stone roofs with the outer stones carved in imitation of these timber roofs continued in Ireland until as late as the seventeenth century. Other characteristic features derived from timber precedents are *antae*, which were formed by the projection of the side walls beyond the gable end in imitation of wooden corner posts. These appear on the restored church on **St MacDara's Island** (Co. Galway), where they are extended up the sides of the gable to meet at the top in a way that recalls cruck construction.

Pl. 44 *Detail of the east face of the ninth- or early tenth-century Cross of Muiredach at Monasterboice, County Louth; at the centre there is the Last Judgement, showing Christ standing between serried ranks of good and bad souls and St Michael waiting to weigh them in his scales.*

Churches, like three early examples at **Glendalough** (Co. Wicklow, Pl. 42) which were built before the advent of Romanesque influence, have a simple rectangular plan and, from *c*.1000 onwards, the addition of a chancel, shorter and narrower than the nave and approached from it through an arch. A trabeate or square-headed west doorway, sometimes with a filled-in relieving arch above it built flush with the wall, as at St Kevin and the Cathedral, Glendalough, is a characteristic Irish feature until *c*.1000, when round-headed arches began to be used. Windows were always small with flat or triangular tops or round heads made of

a single piece of stone. Roofs made entirely of stone (see above) were a special Irish type. Their sheer weight led to sagging halfway along their length and in order to counteract this tendency, wooden beams were used from an early date to hold the two sides apart. Their function was subsequently performed by a strainer arch halfway up the roof slope, and from this developed the type of double roof found in the twelfth century at Cormac's Chapel, **Cashel** (Co. Tipperary). This demonstrates how in buildings with a wider span roofs of corbelled construction gave way to barrel vaults. Here there is an upper arch above a half-round vault, resulting in a two-storeyed arrangement providing space which could be used to provide a small chamber above the vault, as in the church known as St Columb's House at **Kells** (Co. Meath).

Round towers

A further type of building in the round evolved when the use of lime mortar, probably introduced by Christian missionaries in the fifth century, made it possible to build much higher than with drystone masonry, using the Roman method of construction with two facing walls bound into a core of rubble and concrete. Tall round tapering towers with conical stone roofs were built on monastic sites from the tenth to the twelfth century, generally as free-standing structures but occasionally forming part of a church, as at St Kevin's church (known as St Kevin's Kitchen), **Glendalough** (Pl. 42). The fact that their doors were set high above the ground suggests that besides being belfries, they were also used by the monks as places of refuge in case of attack. Because they provided relative security, they were also used for storing valuables, as at Monasterboice; when the tower there was burnt in 1094 it was housing important monastic treasures, including the library. Accommodation inside these buildings consisted of up to four or five timber floors lit by small apertures, and access was by a rope or wooden ladder which the occupants could draw up behind them. The highest platform at the top was better lit than the others, with as many as four or even six windows. Sixty-five free-standing towers have survived at least in part; several, for example those at **Kildare** (Pl. 45) and **Monasterboice**, have been restored so that one can still climb up to the top. Round towers seldom have any carved ornament but there is sometimes a raised architrave round the windows or door, and one of the finest examples, at **Devenish Island** (Co. Fermanagh), has a frieze round the top with four human heads, one above each of the windows of its upper chamber.

Pl. 45 *The Irish Round Tower at Kildare, dated by the design of its door to the twelfth century; this tower has been restored so that it is possible to climb to the top.*

crosses is based on the fact that their decoration, which is divided into panels of interlacing, spirals and other geometrical motifs, is strongly reminiscent of the contemporary Book of Kells (see p. 37). It has been conjectured that the division of the design into small areas of intricate detail could be derived from an earlier use of panels of bronze ornament attached to a wooden cross. On ninth-century stone crosses we begin to find figures, for example in the Crucifixion on the South Cross at Clonmacnoise; by the tenth century biblical subjects of all kinds cover the surfaces of the most elaborate high crosses. The Cross of the Scriptures at **Clonmacnoise** (Pl. 43) and Muiredach's Cross at **Monasterboice** (Pl. 44) are fine examples of this period, when crosses seem to have been used for didactic purposes, to teach the whole range of Bible stories in vividly pictorial form. Around a central Crucifixion or Christ in Glory are arranged numerous carved scenes of popular Old Testament stories, from the Fall of Man to Daniel in the Lion's Den or David and Goliath, and episodes from the Life of Christ from the Adoration of the Magi to the Transfiguration. Any spare space is filled with interlacing and geometrical patterns, so that the entire surface is encrusted with ornament. The figures which appear on eleventh-century crosses are carved in higher relief, as at **Drumcliffe** (Co. Sligo), and by the twelfth century biblical scenes begin to give way to single figures of Christ or a contemporary church dignitary and patterns of interlacing animals, as at **Dysert O'Dea** (Co. Clare). Local schools of sculpture produced crosses in their own distinctive styles. The unique **Moone High Cross** (Co. Kildare) is a particularly striking and beautiful example, with its naive stylized representations of biblical subjects and serried ranks of enigmatic unidentified figures.

High crosses

High crosses (see pp. 18–19) are numerous and their design developed over a period of six hundred years from the seventh century onwards. The earliest were simple carved standing stones, for example at **Fahan** and **Carndonagh** (both in Co. Donegal), but in the eighth century we find two crosses at **Ahenny** (Co. Tipperary) which appear to hark back to wooden antecedents because of the way the design suggests that the various parts have been fastened together with nails. The dating of these

Scotland

EARLY HISTORY

The Roman occupation of Britain had little permanent effect in Scotland, for repeated attempts at subjugation were more or less unsuccessful, in spite of the fact that by the end of the first century the Lowlands had come under Roman control and the northern tribes had been defeated near Elgin (Grampian). The surviving earthworks of a large camp at **Ardoch** (Tayside), where 40,000 soldiers were based in Hadrian's time, bear witness to a substantial military presence north of the border, but the emperors' main efforts were directed towards securing the frontier with

England. In A.D. 81 Agricola established a line of camps linking the Forth and the Clyde which was subsequently refortified with a turf rampart known as the Antonine Wall. Hadrian's Wall south of the border, built after his visit in 122, followed what proved to be a more defensible line across the country from the Solway to the Tyne. A further campaign begun by Septimius Severus in 209 ended without conquest on his death two years later.

It was the Romans who gave the name Picts (*picti*, painted people) to the tribes who inhabited the wild country of the Highlands. The western coastal area of Dalriada (modern Argyllshire now divided between

Pl. 46 *The Celtic Cross of St Martin (c.950–1000) on the island of Iona in the Inner Hebrides, carved on the other side with the Virgin and Child and other biblical scenes.*

Highland and Strathclyde regions) was colonized by the Scots who migrated from Ireland in the sixth century or even earlier and eventually gave their name to the whole country. Some of the Britons driven out of their eastern territory by the Anglo-Saxons settled in Strathclyde (which also included Cumbria), while Lothian, between the Clyde and the Tweed, belonged to the English kingdom of Bernicia (later part of Northumbria). The Pictish kingdom was finally defeated by the Norsemen, who migrated from Scandinavia to establish themselves in the Orkneys, Shetlands, Hebrides and northern Highlands, while its remaining territory was united with Dalriada under the Scottish king, **Kenneth MacAlpin**, in 843. One of his successors, **Malcolm II**, also took over Lothian, defeating Cnut's attempt to retake it in 1018. After the death of the last British king of Strathclyde, the throne was claimed by Malcolm's grandson and chosen heir, **Duncan I**, who thus succeeded as ruler of the greater part of a more or less united Scotland in 1034. In 1040 he was killed by **Macbeth**, the Earl of Moray, also a grandson of Malcolm II and therefore a rival contender for the throne. Macbeth had no children and it was Duncan's son who, as a grown man, returned from exile in Northumbria to destroy him in 1057 and reign for over thirty years as **Malcolm III**.

SURVIVING ARCHITECTURE

The few architectural survivals from the Saxon period owe nothing to the Anglo-Saxons themselves but relate to the Christian conversion of Scotland begun by Irish missionaries in the sixth century (see p. 17). Monastic remains can still be seen on the west coast of Scotland at **Whithorn** (Dumfries and Galloway), which has an important group of crosses and inscribed stones dating from the fifth to the tenth century, and at **Chapel Finian** (in the same region), where beside the buttressed walls of the chapel one can identify a well and an oval enclosure. On the island of **Iona** some faint traces of the original buildings and three late tenth-century crosses (Pl. 46) survive near the later Norman and medieval buildings. At **Eilach-an-Naoimh**, also in the Inner Hebrides, there are a chapel and three monks' cells surrounded by a circular wall. Tall towers of the Irish type, built in the tenth or eleventh century, have survived in Tayside at **Brechin** and **Abernethy**, while the lower part of a square tower at **Restenneth** has been dated to the eighth century.

Wales

EARLY HISTORY

The Roman conquest of Wales, completed by A.D. 78, took the form of a military occupation controlled from *Deva* (Chester) in the north and *Isca* (Caerleon) in the south, with a series of auxiliary posts throughout the country. Excavated remains of these forts can still be seen, for example at Caerleon, Brecon and Caernarvon, as well as a few other settlements, such as a fortified town at Caerwent (Gwent) and a villa at Llantwit Major (Glamorgan); but by the beginning of the fourth century the Romans' buildings seem to have been beginning to fall into disuse. The Anglo-Saxon invaders pushed the Romano-British population westwards across England (see p. 9) but they never succeeded in conquering the various Welsh kingdoms, and Wales therefore retained its Celtic artistic traditions and a strong church with an unbroken tradition dating back to the official Christianity of the Roman Empire. A border with England was established in the eighth century, when Mercian attempts at conquest led to the construction of the still-surviving embankment known as Offa's Dyke (see p. 12), previously thought to have marked an agreed frontier but now believed to have been designed to protect English settlements from continuing Welsh attack.

The kingdom of Gwynedd, whose princes were descended from Cunedda, a Romano-Briton who migrated from Strathclyde in the fifth century, gradually came to dominate an increasing area. In the ninth century **Rhodri** *Mawr* (the Great) defeated the Vikings who had been harrying the west coast and brought the greater part of the country under his control. Wales was finally united in the mid-tenth century under **Hywel** *Dda* (the Good), who strengthened his supremacy by introducing a comprehensive legal system which included Britain's earliest known building and fire regulations. These are especially interesting for the description they provide of the vanished secular architecture of the time, simple timber or stone houses and aisled halls, and their arrangement in the type of chieftain's farmstead known as a *llys*, a group of buildings within an enclosing wall. Political unity was not maintained after Hywel's death, and the divisions which reasserted themselves were followed by the piecemeal conquests of the Normans.

SURVIVING ARCHITECTURE

No complete secular buildings survive from this period, and there are only a few fragmentary remains of ecclesiastical architecture. The Welsh church was highly ascetic, with a mainly monastic organization, and this is reflected in the simplicity of its recorded structures. Examples are the incomplete foundations of the seventh-century monastic settlement on **Ynys Seiriol**, a small island off Anglesey, which show a little church and monks' cells inside a walled enclosure, and the reconstructed Maen-du holy well at **Brecon** (Powys), a primitive hut with drystone walls and a stone roof. The early monastic foundations developed into *clas* (mother) churches, which were run on collegiate lines as important centres for learning and scholarship. Although some of these were evidently of considerable size, their buildings have not survived; but St Illtud's church at **Llanilltud Fawr** (Llantwit Major, Glamorgan), on the site of the college he founded there *c.*500, preserves a fine collection of carved Celtic crosses.

THE NORMAN PERIOD

Introduction

The architecture of this period is the English version of Romanesque, a name invented in the nineteenth century to describe the building tradition which developed in Romanized Europe after the collapse of the Roman Empire. As we have seen, influence from Normandy preceded the Conquest by some years while Anglo-Saxon workmanship continued throughout the eleventh century. Moreover since England was affected by developments on the Continent generally, English architecture under William I and his descendants does not, as its name suggests, derive exclusively from Northern France. "Norman" is simply a convenient label for describing the buildings of Britain which date from the late eleventh and twelfth centuries. After 1066 we find quite a wide range of surviving types and begin to be able to understand visually how they were used. Enough remains to make it possible to identify typical Norman design and decoration, which is so distinctive that it is very easy to recognize.

The Conquest was the last successful invasion of England by a foreign power; so unlike the buildings of their Saxon predecessors, the Normans' work was not the subject of deliberate and systematic later destruction. Since, like the Roman architecture which inspired it, it was massive and solidly made, the buildings which have survived are remarkably well preserved.

Historical background

The kings generally included in the Norman period are:

William I (the Conqueror) 1066–87
William II (Rufus) 1087–1100
Henry I 1100–1135
Stephen 1135–1154
Henry II 1154–1189

Pl. 47 Detail of the early twelfth-century nave at Waltham Abbey, Essex, showing three of the most characteristic features of the Norman period: massive drum piers with scalloped capitals, arcades with round-headed arches and extensive use of carved and incised zig-zag ornament.

The throne passed down in direct line until Henry II, who, as a great-grandson of William I, can legitimately be described as a Norman but was also the son of Geoffrey of Anjou and therefore the first of our Angevin or Plantagenet monarchs.

William I was an extremely able soldier and administrator who established Norman feudalism in England, so that the whole of society at every level depended ultimately on the king. He crushed opposition without mercy, notably in his devastation of the north of England in 1069–70. His conquest was a ruthlessly efficient and thorough take-over, but it did not greatly alter the daily life of ordinary people. Since it was an armed invasion rather than a migration, there was no large influx of foreign population; it was the leaders of society, both secular and religious, who were replaced. Many of the Saxon nobles had either died in battle or fled after the English defeat at Hastings, and William brought in a new Norman ruling class to consolidate his victory. It was made up of the barons and knights who had helped him to win the English throne and were rewarded with land in the new kingdom. His invading army of about six thousand soldiers was disbanded after four years, as soon as the subjugation of the country was assured. The many mercenary soldiers were simply sent home while the king distributed estates among his 170 most important followers, keeping a fifth of the land for himself and giving a quarter to the church. Twenty years later, when the Domesday Book survey was compiled, only two men of English descent held sizeable estates from the king, and there was only one church leader who was a Saxon rather than a Norman.

In order to ensure that none of his nobles could become too powerful, William gave each a number of small estates in different parts of the country rather than a single holding in one place, though he made exceptions for the earldoms of Chester, Shrewsbury and Hereford, where he needed strong leaders commanding large areas for the defence of the Welsh border. Those who held land did not own it outright but were tenants of the crown, and they in turn let parts of their estates to sub-tenants of their own. The basic Saxon division of the countryside into shires, hundreds and villages was not altered and the system whereby labourers gave their work and produce in return for a lord's protection continued as before. However, the Norman feudal system of land tenure brought the peasants firmly under the control of their landowner masters, just as they in turn were controlled from above. In exchange for their right to hold land, knights gave service to their superior lords who supplied money and soldiers for the king. Ownership of land was the key to power and its outward expression lay in building. The architecture which survives from this early Norman period includes churches, which are often in the transitional style, part Saxon and part Norman, and the first of the stone keeps which gradually replaced the wooden "motte and bailey" castles thrown up in haste during the early years after the Conquest.

The consolidation of Norman power continued under the Conqueror's sons. The eldest, Robert, became Duke of Normandy, while the second, **William II** (Rufus), was King of England. Astute but ruthless, he secured the support of the native English in order to suppress a rebellion of the barons who opposed his succession, and he materially strengthened his position by appropriating substantial ecclesiastical revenues to the crown. After his premature death in 1100, when he was shot by an arrow on a hunting expedition, his younger brother, **Henry I**, took advantage of their elder brother Robert's absence to seize the throne. Differences which arose between him and the church over the papal right of investiture were resolved by a compromise, whereby the Pope's spiritual authority was acknowledged but the king maintained his feudal sovereignty, thus ensuring that the enormous wealth of the church would remain within royal control. Henry's able and efficient administration brought peace. The towns expanded and there was an influx of traders from France. Jewish money-lenders, who had first come to England under William I (see p. 84) increased in number. By defeating Robert of Normandy in 1106, Henry reunited their father's two kingdoms and by marrying a princess of Saxon descent he became popular with the native English. But the harmony he achieved dissolved during the reign of his ineffectual nephew, **Stephen**, into a period of grim anarchy. Rival claimants to the throne fought over a demoralized land where, as the Anglo-Saxon chronicler records, there were castles "filled with devils and evil men" and "Christ and his saints were asleep".

Stephen's two sons predeceased him, and after his death, order was finally restored by **Henry II**, son of Henry I's daughter Matilda, who had failed to secure the throne after her father's death. He was a businesslike and powerful king who also ruled over vast French territories stretching from Brittany to the Pyrenees and by the end of his reign was overlord of Ireland as well. Henry is generally associated with the murder of Thomas à Becket, who as Archbishop of Canterbury opposed his attempts to bring the Church under some degree of state control, but one should also remember his great achievement in laying the foundation of the British legal system. During his long reign his stable administration and enforcement of justice produced conditions that favoured the vigorous development of architecture. He began by destroying hundreds of the "unlicensed" castles illegally built by the barons during Stephen's chaotic reign. The rest were brought under the authority of the crown and he improved or rebuilt all his own royal castles in Britain and throughout his French domains, often experimenting with new designs such as the polygonal keep built at **Orford** (Suffolk, Fig. 5) during the 1160s and the Round Tower at Windsor in 1180. He also lavished large sums of money on now vanished hunting lodges and palaces such as Woodstock and Clarendon.

Buildings

THE NORMAN STYLE

Norman architecture relies for its stability on solidity more than scientific calculation. It uses thick walls and massive cylindrical pillars built of rubble masonry and faced with stone. Arches are round (i.e. semicircular) and there are tunnel or groined vaults (see Fig. 11). Pointed arches and rib vaults begin to appear during the mid to late twelfth century. A wide range of bold carved patterns and vigorous but often rather crude sculptured ornament is deployed to considerable effect, for example zig-zag, beakhead or cable ornament on arches, cushion or scalloped capitals and intersecting arcading for wall decoration.

RELIGIOUS ARCHITECTURE

Historical introduction

The church in Norman Britain

To understand the ecclesiastical architecture of the Middle Ages, one needs to know something about the organization of the church at that time and in particular to understand the key role of monasticism. William I replaced all the leading Saxon churchmen with Normans, in the same way that he put secular power in the hands of his own followers. Since the church owned a quarter of all the land in his new country, ecclesiastical dignitaries were also feudal lords with considerable wealth and power. A bishop might also be the abbot of a religious house attached to his cathedral, the great church which housed his seat (Latin *cathedra*) or throne, though the day-to-day running of the community was the responsibility of a subordinate prior. Some of the Normans' cathedrals were entirely new foundations, but many were rebuildings on existing Saxon sites. It is a reflection of the fact that earlier traditions were absorbed rather than abolished that the shrines of Saxon saints, such as St Edmund at Bury St Edmunds and St Frideswide at Oxford, remained important throughout the Middle Ages, and that when the choir at

Wells was rebuilt *c*.1180, it was furnished with posthumous effigies of the cathedral's Saxon bishops. The earlier rural sees were moved to the towns for administrative reasons, with the result that the Benedictine order, the only one established in England at the time of the Conquest, came to dominate urban monastic life.

Monasticism

SAXON ANTECEDENTS

St Augustine's mission to England had established the first Benedictine house at Canterbury as early as 598, but the Danish invasions of the ninth century largely destroyed the monastic life which had grown up by that time. The major revival initiated by St Dunstan in the tenth century made monasteries not only the nation's centres of art and learning but also the source of its spiritual and intellectual leadership, attracting recruits from the highest families in the land. Statesmen therefore supported monasticism and drew on it for the leaders of public life. By the time of the Conquest there had been another decline as a result of further devastating Danish invasions from 980 onwards and the ousting of the Saxon dynasty by Cnut in the early eleventh century. This did not, however, amount to such a total obliteration as has sometimes been suggested, and we know that in 1066 there were thirty-five monasteries and nine nunneries all living according to the Benedictine rule.

NORMAN REORGANIZATION

In order to revive religious observance in their newly acquired territory, the Normans carried out a major programme of church building. The twelfth-century monk William of Malmesbury recorded that "you may see in every village, town and city churches and monasteries rising in a new style of architecture". William I's conquest coincided with a powerful movement for the reform of monastic standards in Normandy. The existing English houses were drawn into this new religious revival and brought into direct contact with the spiritual and cultural life of France. They were also drawn into the feudal system, so that instead of being on terms of equality with the secular state, they became subservient to the king. The Norman period was the beginning of a vast expansion of monasticism which was to dominate religious life in Britain throughout the Middle Ages. The number of religious houses quadrupled in the course of the twelfth century, and by the time of the Dissolution at the beginning of the sixteenth century, when the monastic population was twenty-five per cent smaller than it had been at its peak, there were about eight hundred houses in England and Wales alone. Like the

contemporary households of secular magnates, monastic communities could be very large, with several hundred dependants. Apart from those who lived in the monasteries, the Cistercian abbeys, which practised agriculture on a large scale, had lay brothers employed on outlying farms or granges, where separate living quarters with chapels were built to accommodate them. In the mid twelfth century Rievaulx had as many as 150 monks and 600 lay brothers.

There is not space here to consider all the numerous different orders which existed, but it is necessary to know about the more important ones, so as to understand how their way of life affected their architectural environment. Apart from the ruins of great churches, like those at Colchester and Castle Acre (see p. 52, Pls 51 and 52), there are not many monastic buildings which survive from the Norman period, though there are exceptions such as the mid twelfth-century chapter house at Forde Abbey (see p. 50), now the chapel. The religious houses, as we see them now, date mainly from the medieval period. Their way of life, however, was established under the Normans.

THE BENEDICTINE ORDERS

Benedictine monks, who wore black habits, were known as "black monks", while the **Augustinian** (or Austin) canons, a separate Benedictine order of priests formed to staff large non-monastic churches such as **Christchurch** Priory (Dorset) or **Waltham Abbey** (Essex, Pl. 47), were called the "black canons". These were "canons regular", so called because they lived according to a monastic rule (Latin *regula*), under the leadership of a prior. Priories were generally subservient to abbeys but not necessarily smaller or less important. In the case of the **Cluniac** order, every daughter house, whatever its size, was a priory attached to the one French abbey at Cluny. All Benedictine houses were organized round the ritual practice of their rule, but Cluny, founded in Burgundy in 910, was dedicated to restoring its strict observance, and it became increasingly influential during the eleventh century. The new Cluniac order attached great importance to liturgy and ceremonial. The first of numerous houses in Britain was founded at Lewes (E. Sussex) in 1077–8, but regrettably none of these buildings survives in use today. One can, however, study their ruins, for example at **Castle Acre** (Norfolk, Pl. 52).

Pl. 48 *The great Cistercian abbey beside the River Wye at Tintern, Gwent, founded in 1131 but rebuilt and enlarged in the thirteenth and fourteenth centuries.*

Pl. 49 *The austere Cistercian abbey set in a wooded valley at Rievaulx, North Yorkshire, which was founded in 1131, with surviving buildings dating from the thirteenth century.*

THE REFORMED ORDERS: CISTERCIAN, PREMONSTRATENSIAN, GILBERTINE, CARTHUSIAN

In the late eleventh and early twelfth centuries a further reform movement was brought about by a reaction against the growing influence of Cluny. It introduced many other more austere forms of monasticism, far the most successful of which was the **Cistercian** order founded at Cîteaux in Burgundy in 1098. This turned its back on the Benedictine emphasis on elaborate ritual and took to a life of simple manual labour in wild country, set in buildings which, at this early date, deliberately eschewed any form of architectural elaboration. In Britain the Cistercians built mainly in the north of England, where one can still visit a superb Yorkshire group of abbeys including **Fountains** (Fig. 7) and **Rievaulx** (Pl. 49), and in Wales, for instance at **Tintern** (Gwent, Pl. 48). Because their rule forbade employing outside labour, the monks had lay brothers, who lived separately within the monastic complex, to help with the work of running their abbeys and lands. They carried out every kind of practical work from baking and brewing to tanning leather and making shoes, and they also acted as masons, farm labourers and shepherds. The Cistercians, who wore habits of unbleached cloth, came to be known as "white monks", while a strict order of priests, introduced from Prémontré in France during the twelfth century and strongly influenced by the Cistercians, was the **Premonstratensian** or "white" canons. Another reformed order, for both men and women, was the **Gilbertine**, founded by St Gilbert of Sempringham *c*.1139, for nuns following both Benedictine and Cistercian rules and canons living by the Augustinian rule who acted as chaplains in their monastic churches. This gave rise to a need for separate living quarters for the two sexes. Yet stricter than the Cistercians were the **Carthusians**, who first came to England in the late twelfth century. Their order was named after the monastery of La Grande Chartreuse near Grenoble, founded by St Bruno in 1084, and their rule, which was much closer to the original concept of a hermit's existence, looked back to the early Byzantine monasteries of Egypt and Syria. Carthusian monks lived and prayed in solitude in individual cells, emerging only for church services and communal meals.

THE KNIGHTS TEMPLAR AND HOSPITALLER

Two very different orders should also be mentioned because they had a monastic presence in Britain, although they were primarily international and military organizations. These were the **Knights Templar** and **Knights Hospitaller**, orders of soldier monks established in Palestine after the First Crusade at the beginning of the twelfth century, to protect and care for the health of pilgrims on the journey to the Holy Land. Their architectural legacy is a type of circular church based on the Church of the Holy Sepulchre in Jerusalem, which was rebuilt in 1048 and greatly impressed the Crusaders with its novelty when they took the city in 1099. Several examples survive in Britain (Pls 71 and 72), including the Temple Church in **London**, where the Templars founded their first English house in 1184.

Monastic buildings

Apart from churches (see below), there are relatively few surviving buildings belonging to the monastic houses founded during the Norman period, but it was then that the plan was established which was followed, with many variations, throughout the Middle Ages. On the four sides of a central cloister were the church, the dorter (which included the monks' sleeping quarters and also the chapter house), the refectory and the storehouse, while behind them lay the infirmary and the kitchen. There is a contemporary version of this arrangement at **Castle Acre** (Norfolk, Pl. 52 and Fig. 7), where all the ruined buildings surrounding the cloister date from the twelfth century, though with later alterations. There are also cases where such buildings have been preserved because they have remained in use, as at **Forde Abbey** (Dorset, Pl. 116), converted to a house in the seventeenth century, where the mid-twelfth-century chapter house is now the chapel. However, since early timber buildings were gradually replaced in stone and a continuous process of reconstruction took place in the pursuit of greater architectural magnificence, the monastic buildings we can still see today belong predominantly to the early Middle Ages, and their design and layout are described in detail later (see pp. 112–123).

Cathedrals and abbey churches

A cathedral (see p. 46) was the most important church in its see or diocese, its name reflecting the fact that it was the bishop's seat. In some cases, for example Westminster Abbey, a monastic church might be a cathedral as well, but cathedrals were normally run by communities

Pl. 50 *The Norman west front, with portals and towers dating from the 1140s, can be seen embedded in the thirteenth-century screen façade of Lincoln Cathedral, which was consecrated in 1092; the traceried windows and upper stages of the towers are later medieval additions.*

of secular canons, administered by a Dean and Chapter. Unlike the French, the English habitually gave these great churches a monastic setting, even when they were not attached to any religious house; so instead of being set in a town square, in direct contact with the bustle of urban life, an English cathedral is surrounded by an open grassy space inside a close or walled enclosure containing the ecclesiastical buildings belonging to it. This reflects the secluded monastic pattern in which the church, whether cathedral, abbey or priory, was the focal point of the life of every religious house, with the other buildings grouped round it as conveniently as possible.

PLAN

The layout of all the greater churches was more or less the same, because those not attached to religious orders were served by bodies of lay priests in place of monks and a similar arrangement was needed. The normal plan was cruciform, with an eastern presbytery, where the priest (Latin *presbyter*) officiated, short transepts or arms and a long nave. The great length of many of these churches is a very noticeable feature and their naves were often completed over a considerable period of time, sometimes in a later style. The construction of the church always began at the east end, which was liturgically by far the most important part of the building, especially in the case of monastic foundations. Where the east end of one of these churches appears to be later than the nave, the reason will be that the original Norman presbytery was not large or imposing enough and was subsequently rebuilt; this happened, for instance, at **Peterborough** and **St Albans** in the late twelfth century and at **Exeter** and **Durham** in the thirteenth.

EXTERIOR

The external appearance of a great church was the direct outcome of its planning and construction. One can see, for example, how its walls are divided up into bays, which reflect the internal layout, and supported by buttresses to counteract the outward thrust of the arches and vaults inside the building. Wall surface decoration was common, especially blind arcading, and sculpture was used for architectural effect, for example on the tympanum above the Prior's Door at Ely (Pl. 54); but the idea of designing a façade for deliberate architectural effect emerged with the development of the west end as a formal composition.

The west front

This type of screen-façade, which had a central doorway with radiating voussoirs (see Pls 51 and 52), originated in Aquitaine in southern France, an area which came under English control during the reign of Henry II in the second half of the twelfth century (see p. 46). It became extremely popular in Britain, though the French use of column figures round the entrance was unusual here. The laity would normally have approached a great church from the west, through the outer court on that side of the monastic complex; so this was the public façade. It was not, however, the normal entrance front. A doorway in the end wall of a building was not a popular idea, and the main entry to a church was generally by a north door at the western end of the nave. However, western doorways for ceremonial occasions were quite usual; **Tewkesbury** (Glos) and **Malmesbury** (Wilts), for instance, both had one, set inside a single large arch. At **Lincoln** (Pl. 50) the late eleventh-century west front was later extended both outwards and upwards but has retained the original five recessed, arched openings. A more typical Norman west front had three portals, the central one higher than those at the sides. This arrangement can be appreciated in the ruins of St Botolph's Priory, **Colchester** (Essex, Pl. 51), though the north portal has gone. Much more elaborate west fronts can be seen at **Castle Acre** Priory (Norfolk, Pl. 52), with its richly arcaded composition, and at **Ely** Cathedral (Cambs, Pl. 55), whose central narthex tower and transepts are based on a Germanic type. Although the façade here is incomplete and has later additions, its great width, its central tower and twin turrets and its elaborate tiers of highly decorative blind arcading show that a formal west front on a grand scale was a well-established feature by the second half of the twelfth century.

Doors

The wooden doors of this period have been renewed by later generations, but examples of their iron fittings, such as the famous "sanctuary knocker" on the north door of Durham Cathedral (see p. 74) can still be seen. The stone archways of Norman doors have survived in large numbers. It was common for important doors, such as the south door of **Malmesbury** Abbey (Wilts, Pl. 53), to have a number of receding arches, each normally with its own separate columns and capitals (see Pls 51, 52, 91 and 92), forming a decorative recess set in the thickness of the wall and emphasizing the importance of the entrance. A doorway like this had the advantage that it provided a shallow porch for shelter. It was also economical to construct because it could be built one archway at a time, so that much less centering, or temporary wooden support, was needed

Pl. 51 *The ruined west front of the Norman church of St Botolph's Priory at Colchester, Essex, founded in the late eleventh century; Roman bricks were used in the rubble walls as well as for the arches of the doorways and blind arcading.*

Pl. 52 *The central door in the west front of the twelfth-century church of the Cluniac priory at Castle Acre, Norfolk, showing the richly ornamented entrance portal and four tiers of decorative blind arcading.*

than for a single very deep arch. The tympanum or flat space above a door between the straight lintel and the rounded arch was often richly carved, generally with a figure of Christ symbolic of the doorway to salvation. He appears for instance at **Rochester** (Kent) accompanied by the signs of the Evangelists and at **Ely** (Pl. 54) surrounded by angels.

Towers

A central position over the crossing, as at **Norwich** (Pl. 57), was the normal place for a prominent tower, except in Cistercian houses, where only plain squat ones were allowed. Sometimes larger churches had

western towers as well. At **Ely** (Pl. 55) there was only one, but usually there were two, as at **Durham** (Pl. 58), which left a central space for a west window. **Exeter** (Pl. 56) is unusual in having a pair of flanking towers, later incorporated into its north and south transepts. The placing of towers was to some extent determined by structural considerations, for the extra weight of a central tower above the crossing counteracted the inward pressure on its arches from the choir, nave and transepts, while the bulk of a western tower buttressed the west wall of the nave. One tower was needed to house a belfry; the main purpose in having three, as at **Southwell** (Notts), seems to have been simply to add to the grandeur

Pl. 53 *The ornate south doorway at Malmesbury Abbey, Wiltshire (c.1160–70), showing its eight recessed arches without capitals, which are richly carved with bands of continuous patterning and related Old and New Testament subjects; the sculptured lunette seen inside the porch is one of a pair, each showing six seated apostles with an angel flying overhead.*

Pl. 54 *A detail of the Prior's Door at Ely Cathedral (c.1135), which originally led into the Norman cloister, now vanished; the doorway is carved in relief with foliage scrolls and figures of men and animals, while the tympanum shows a seated Christ between two angels.*

of the architectural effect, and towers vary in height according to the importance of the building. No contemporary tower roof has survived, but most of these structures would probably have been topped with low wooden pyramidal spires. Norman towers, for instance at Norwich, can be recognized by their massive proportions and an elaborate use of blind arcading which tends to become increasingly complex towards the end of the twelfth century. Shallow buttresses and characteristic Norman ornament, such as zig-zag, are also found. The lantern towers of the early Norman period have vanished, because they collapsed under the pressure of the walls of the arms of the church against the arches of the crossing. The greater weight of the higher and more solid towers which have survived provided the extra downwards pressure to counteract this thrust, and they were structurally much more successful. This was, however, a period of experiment which led to many disasters, for instance at Ely, where the crossing tower crashed down on 22 February 1322, destroying part of the choir only minutes after the monks had left it.

The east end

The presbytery or east end of the church was for the exclusive use of the monks and clergy. It was partitioned off from the rest of the building by a rood screen (see below) across the nave; so the transepts and the central crossing belonged with it rather than forming part of the nave area. East ends of this period have nearly all been replaced or much altered. The eleventh century favoured a plan with an apse, or sometimes a whole row of apses parallel to each other, which provided space for extra chapels on either side of the main altar. A few polygonal versions were built of the French "chevet", an east end with a semicircular ambulatory or aisle running round behind the high altar with its stone reredos. Off this ambulatory opened a ring of apsidal chapels which acted as buttresses to the outer walls. Although archaeological evidence of this plan has been found elsewhere, **Norwich** (Pl. 57, Fig. 9) is one of the few Norman churches which has retained its apse and ambulatory in their original form. By the mid twelfth century the English preference for a square-ended chancel, thought to stem from the importance attached to altars being aligned to face exactly eastwards, had reasserted itself and we find several later Norman variants on this idea. In large churches like **St Albans** and **Winchester** there is a rectangular aisle leading round behind the high altar, but some of the smaller monastic churches have a short aisle at either side, terminating in an altar, or even no aisles at all, as at **Lindisfarne** (Holy Island, Northumberland) and **Easby** (N. Yorks). The early Cistercians preferred a modest presbytery, aisleless and square-ended, as has been discovered in excavations of the plans of their first churches at **Waverley** (Surrey, Pl. 59) and **Tintern** (Gwent). This suited their original commitment to simplicity but in time, as more of the monks became priests in order to cater for the demands of patrons, it had to be modified to accommodate further altars. These were increasingly needed as a growing number of donors gave money to monastic churches in exchange for regular Masses to care for the perpetual welfare of their souls. **Roche Abbey** (S. Yorks), for example, had two straight-ended chapels on each side of the chancel, and **Kirkstall Abbey** (W. Yorks) had three.

The Lady chapel

The most important of all subsidiary chapels was the one devoted to the Virgin Mary, often a separate lower building opening off the presbytery at the extreme east end of the building. This was a suitably

important position behind the high altar but it was probably chosen for practical reasons too, because like the earlier ring of apsidal chapels it buttressed the eastern wall of the presbytery and sometimes helped to support the weight of a heavy stone vault as well. Such chapels are not found in Cistercian houses, which were all dedicated to the Virgin and therefore had no need of a separate chapel devoted to her. Few Lady chapels escaped destruction at the time of the Reformation.

Shrines and crypts

It was believed that devotion to the cult of a saint would secure his or her intercession on a Christian's behalf, an idea encouraged by the clergy because of the lucrative pilgrimages and rich gifts which it brought to the church. The reliquaries of Saxon saints were reinstated

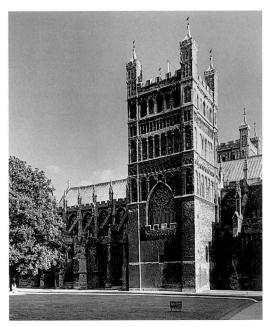

Pl. 55 *The late twelfth-century west tower of Ely Cathedral; its octagonal upper storey was added towards the end of the fourteenth century and replaced a stone spire of* C.1230.

Pl. 56 *The north and behind it the south tower of Exeter Cathedral, built on either side of the choir in the early twelfth century and incorporated into the transepts in* C.1285.

Pl. 57 *The twelfth-century tower above the crossing at Norwich Cathedral with corner spirelets and a recessed spire dating from the fifteenth century; note the surviving Norman apse and ambulatory with a clerestory added in* C.1362–9 *and flying buttresses supporting a late fifteenth-century vault.*

Pl. 58 *Durham Cathedral seen from the south-west across the River Wear, showing the twin towers of the Norman west front with its projecting Galilee chapel and the crossing tower rebuilt in the fifteenth century; the west window is fourteenth-century and the exterior appearance of the Galilee is the result of medieval and later alterations.*

Pl. 59 *The simple square-ended presbytery of the church at Waverley Abbey, Surrey, founded by the Cistercians in 1128, as it was rebuilt in the thirteenth century.*

Canterbury the tomb of the martyred St Thomas à Becket (d. 1170), which attracted huge crowds, was moved in 1184 into the crypt behind the high altar, below a new Trinity chapel built in the saint's honour where his shrine was set up in 1220.

Chantries

Often an individual would arrange to have his tomb placed in the church of a religious house he had helped to endow, and chantry chapels, where Masses were regularly said for the souls of such benefactors, accounted for much of the later proliferation of altars during the Middle Ages. They were not always confined to the east end of the church but were also placed in the nave and against the eastern walls of the transepts. Early transept chapels were apsidal, as at **Romsey** (Hants) and **Tewkesbury** (Glos), but a rectangular form was soon adopted, as at **Peterborough** and **Durham**.

The choir

Since the main purpose of the majority of monastic orders was the chanting of offices for considerable periods of time at regular intervals throughout the day, from the small hours of the morning until long after nightfall, the choir where the monks prayed was central to their existence. It was placed in the middle of the building beneath the crossing, generally occupying the first two bays of the nave and extending eastwards towards the high altar. On this side it was open, with a clear view of the presbytery at the east end of the church where the priests officiated. Until the eleventh century it was normal for a priest to celebrate Mass standing behind the altar, but by the twelfth century he would have stood in front of it facing eastwards and it began to be possible to place an ornamented screen immediately behind the high altar. To the west the choir of a great church was closed off from the nave by a pulpitum (a Latin word meaning scaffold or platform) or stone screen, and further screens separated it from the transepts and side aisles, so that it formed an enclosed and self-contained space within the main body of the church. Its position is still recalled by the arrangement of some of our present choirs, for example at **Norwich, Gloucester, St Albans** (Pl. 61) and **Winchester**. Their stalls also reflect the seating for the monks ranged round the sides of the choir, but very few choir furnishings have survived from this early period (see p. 71).

Since the choir was always entered from the west through a central door in the pulpitum, there was a second parallel screen further west, so

by the Normans in their new churches, but the shrines built to contain them and later holy relics have almost all vanished. They were often housed beneath the sanctuary, and the crypts which still exist, for example at **Worcester** and **Winchester** (Pl. 60) (both of the late eleventh century), show how separate entrances and exits were sometimes provided to ease the circulation of visiting pilgrims. An important shrine might be put at ground level in a place of honour between the high altar and the Lady chapel. A later example of this arrangement can still be seen at **St Albans**, where the reconstructed fourteenth-century shrine of the patron saint is in that position. At

Pl. 60 *Characteristic Norman drum piers with cushion capitals in the crypt beneath the presbytery at Winchester Cathedral, built in the late eleventh century to house the relics of St Swithun.*

Pl. 61 *The late eleventh-century choir and crossing of St Albans cathedral, looking towards the thirteenth-century presbytery with its painted wooden vault and reredos of 1484; the choir stalls in the foreground date from 1905.*

that the monks could not be seen from the nave as they came and went. This was the rood screen (see p. 196), which took its name from the Great Rood or crucifix, generally flanked by the figures of the Virgin and St John, which was placed above it. On the western face of the rood screen in a monastic church stood the main nave altar, with a door on either side which gave access to the rest of the church.

The nave

The nave (from Latin *navis*, ship) or main body of the church provided a separate and self-contained place of worship which sometimes served as a parish church for the people of the immediate neighbourhood. In the case of Cistercian monasteries, it was used by the lay brothers, but its main purpose seems to have been to provide space for processions rather than to accommodate a large congregation. Often the local population worshipped in another church nearby, and many monasteries, especially the Cistercian ones, built smaller chapels especially for their use. It has been suggested that a service for lay people in the nave would have been disturbed by the sound of chanting from the monks' choir and that this may explain the construction of a second church beside the monastic one, for instance at **Evesham** (Worcs), where there are two churches actually within the abbey precinct. It has also been conjectured that monasteries may have preferred to avoid the responsibility for parish duties. Many naves continued in use as parish churches after their choirs were destroyed at the time of the Dissolution; at **Bolton** (N. Yorks), for example, one can see very clearly that the present building is a truncated part of the original abbey church. Some Norman naves are immensely long, as at **Winchester** and **Ely** (Pl. 62), which both have twelve bays, and **Norwich** (Pl. 63), with fourteen. Where they were used by lay brothers they had stone screens enclosing the main body of the nave, and parts of these can still be seen at **Tintern** (Gwent) and **Strata Florida** (Dyfed). This arrangement left the side aisles simply as corridors which were essential for processions. The Benedictines had both east and west doorways between the church and the cloister, so that they could include three sides of it in their circuit. The Cistercians took a slightly different route and sometimes preferred to re-enter the church through a special porch covering the west door of the nave. These porches came to be known as Galilees (Pl. 64) because the abbot at the head of his procession of monks was seen as representing Christ leading his disciples into Galilee.

Norman naves have massive cylindrical columns, round arches and the incised or carved decoration characteristic of all buildings of this period. During the twelfth century we also find alternate circular and octagonal piers, for example at Christ Church Cathedral, **Oxford**. Two of the most impressive Norman arcades can be seen at **Norwich** (Pl. 63) and **Durham** (Pl. 65), where drum-piers alternate with columns made up of clusters of shafts. These are an early indication of the incipient Gothic style, and another innovation at Durham was that the transverse arches in the nave, which run across from side to side at two-bay intervals, are not round but slightly pointed. This is because it had been realized that the thrust of the

Pl. 62 *The early twelfth-century nave at Ely cathedral, looking towards the crossing and presbytery; the cambered wooden ceiling dates from the mid nineteenth century.*

Pl. 63 *The early twelfth-century nave at Norwich cathedral with lierne vault of c.1462–72; the spiral-grooved drum pier was originally one of four, two on either side of the sanctuary surrounding the nave altar to the west of the pulpitum.*

heavy rib vault would be carried downwards more effectively along a steeper curve. The Durham nave was completed as early as 1133, but the discovery of the structural value of the pointed arch looks ahead to the early Gothic of the thirteenth century. In vaulting the nave with stone, its builders were encountering new problems needing new solutions. Norman nave roofs were usually wooden and have not survived in their original form. **Peterborough** (Cambs) still has its very early thirteenth-century timber ceiling, much repainted, and therefore provides the most nearly complete remaining example of the effect of a characteristic Norman interior. Spaces with small spans, such as side aisles, were habitually roofed in stone, using tunnel or barrel vaults, but Durham had

the first rib vaults in Europe (c.1095–1100) in the choir aisles and its nave was vaulted by 1133. This was the earliest English cathedral where stone was used throughout and its rib vaults were widely imitated as pointed arches became progressively more common during the later twelfth century. From about 1170 onwards we find increasingly that corbels projecting from the walls are used to support the vaults of roofs, a device imported from France by the Cistercians which also tends towards a Gothic lightness.

Above the nave arcade all large churches had a triforium, which provided either a passageway or galleries above the side aisles, and then a clerestory or row of upper windows to provide light from above. There are therefore three storeys of arcading, ranging in complexity from the

Pl. 64 *The interior of the Galilee at Durham cathedral built in c.1170–80 and robustly decorated with Norman zig-zag ornament; the slender coupled columns with waterleaf capitals suggest the emerging Gothic.*

Pl. 65 *Incised drum piers alternating with clustered columns in the nave at Durham Cathedral, where the stone rib vault was completed as early as 1133.*

Pl. 66 *The austere Norman nave arcade of the early twelfth-century abbey church at Romsey, Hampshire, with a simple billet frieze at triforium level; the three bays on the right date from the thirteenth century.*

The ornamentation of the interior

The Cistercian order, with its commitment to absolute simplicity, kept its churches plain, free from painted or sculptured ornament and coloured glass. One can still get some idea of the Cistercians' calm austerity in the tranquil ruins of the early medieval buildings at **Valle Crucis** (Clwyd) or **Rievaulx** (N. Yorks). Their absence of ornament was a deliberate reaction against the opulence of contemporary Benedictine interiors and is not typical of the majority of Norman churches, which,

simple geometry found at **Binham** (Norfolk, Pl. 67) to the elaborate interplay of round arches of varying sizes at **Romsey** (Hants, Pl. 66). As church buildings grew progressively taller, the masons had to find further ways of reinforcing the lower walls; at **Durham**, for example, the wide vault in the nave is buttressed by transverse quarter-circles inside the triforium gallery which carry the weight of the clerestory on to the outer walls of the aisles.

Pl. 67 *The unornamented Norman nave, triforium and clerestory arcade of c.1170–80 at Binham Priory, Norfolk, now the parish church; the late medieval font in the foreground is carved with the Seven Sacraments and the Trinity.*

Pl. 68 *Detail from the Raising of Lazarus on a stone panel of* c.1125–50, *thought to be part of the twelfth-century choir screen, at Chichester Cathedral, West Sussex.*

like their Saxon predecessors, would have looked very different from the way we see them now. Apart from their architectural decoration, they would have had vivid wall-paintings (see p. 71) and rich furnishings. Twelfth-century stained glass (see p. 71) can still be seen at **Canterbury**, **Lincoln** and **York**. Carvings have also survived, for instance in the south choir aisle at **Chichester** (Pls 70 and 68), where there are two stone panels (*c.*1125–50) of German Romanesque inspiration, showing Christ at the House of Mary and the Raising of Lazarus. They were found behind the choir stalls, where they had been reused as building stones, and were almost certainly part of the twelfth-century choir

Pl. 70 *Detail from Christ in the House of Mary on a stone panel of c.1125–50, thought to be part of the twelfth-century choir screen, at Chichester Cathedral, West Sussex.*

Pl. 69 *A panel from the washing trough at Much Wenlock Priory, Shropshire, showing Christ walking on the water of the Sea of Galilee, watched by His disciples in their boat.*

screen. A relief of the Virgin and Child in **York** Minster and two screen panels depicting scenes from the life of Christ at **Durham** (both *c.*1155) show Byzantine influence. The newly founded Cluniac monasteries (see p. 47) brought a new French sophistication to figure sculpture, which is evident in the fragments of a lavabo or washing trough (*c.*1180) at **Much Wenlock** Priory (Shropshire, Pl. 69), while the series of life-sized figures of prophets and apostles (*c.*1180–85) from St Mary's Abbey, **York** (now in the Yorkshire Museum), show an increasing awareness of antique classical sculpture. **Lincoln** and **Winchester** both have handsome mid twelfth-century fonts, decorated with beasts, birds and human figures, which are made of black marble imported from Tournai in Belgium, where they were probably carved. There are marble effigies on the tombs of late Norman bishops and abbots at **Exeter**, **Peterborough** and **Salisbury**. A richly ornamented gilt candlestick made of copper alloy, with openwork decoration of beasts and human figures enmeshed in foliage, now in the Victoria and Albert Museum, London, was commissioned in *c.*1107–13 by the Benedictine abbey at Gloucester (now the cathedral), and shows the skill and sophistication which was possible in the finest metalwork at this period. For the Benedictine orders their church was the house of God and the centre of their community, where it was their duty to display the greatest possible architectural and artistic magnificence.

Parish churches

When the Normans set about replacing the Saxons' timber churches on their newly acquired estates, one may imagine that they were expressing their thanks to God for the good fortune of their successful conquest and perhaps trying to atone for the ruthlessness of their victory, but they were also asserting their authority over their new dependants. They built large numbers of simple stone churches with little ornament, so that it is often difficult to differentiate between late Saxon and early Norman work. Although the new rulers were French, they would have used native craftsmen and there was no sudden and dramatic change of style immediately after 1066. The strongest architectural influence was monastic, and the newly established religious houses also built churches for the laity on their lands. Innovations in design and sculptured ornament appear in parish churches in the late eleventh century and throughout the twelfth but on a much less ambitious scale than in monasteries, since these little buildings were meant only for a single priest to minister to a small congregation.

PLANS

Church plans were either rectangular, cruciform or occasionally circular. The rectangular version had an unaisled nave and a simple sanctuary, either square-ended or with an apse. This basic plan came to be extended from two to three compartments, when a square chancel, often the base of a tower, was introduced between the nave and the sanctuary, as at **Iffley** (Oxon) or **Stewkley** (Bucks, Pl. 76, Fig. 8). A more elaborate two-tier chancel survives at **Compton** (Surrey), where a timber-roofed upper gallery was built over a stone-vaulted sanctuary. Many early

Norman churches were enlarged in the second half of the twelfth century, when it was common to add an arcaded aisle to the nave, as can be seen at **Pittington** (Co. Durham). Cruciform churches such as **Melbourne** (Derbyshire) had a central crossing square, between the nave, sanctuary and transepts, which formed the base of the tower. Many, though not all, of the the few surviving twelfth-century round churches were built by the Knights Templar and Hospitaller (see p. 50) and some at least are believed to have been based on the church of

Pl. 71 *The round church of the Holy Sepulchre at Cambridge built c.1130 and heavily restored in 1841.*

Pl. 72 *The circular nave and ambulatory of the early twelfth-century church of the Holy Sepulchre at Northampton, used as a baptistry; the font and its cover date from the nineteenth century.*

Pl. 73 *The Norman crossing tower of the cruciform church of St Mary de Haura at New Shoreham, West Sussex, built c.1130; the upper stage was remodelled in the late twelfth century.*

Pl. 74 *The round west tower of the complete Norman church of St Margaret at Hales, Norfolk, with bell-openings dating from the fourteenth century.*

the Holy Sepulchre in Jerusalem. Apart from the Temple Church in the City of **London**, there are the ruins of others at **Ludlow** Castle (Shropshire) and at **Orphir** (Orkney), but the best-preserved are two Churches of the Holy Sepulchre, one at **Cambridge** (Pl. 71) and the other at **Northampton** (Pl. 72), where one can see the complete form, with a circular central nave surrounded by an arcaded ambulatory. This plan was not generally adopted and lies outside the mainstream of church development in Britain.

TOWERS

Towers on smaller churches were not common before the fifteenth century, though there are some Norman examples like the crossing towers on the cruciform village churches at **New Shoreham** (*c.*1130 and late twelfth-century, Pl. 73) and **Old Shoreham** (*c.*1140, both W. Sussex). The little church at **Kilpeck** (Herefordshire) retains a renewed version of a characteristic feature of the period, a small timber bellcote on the west gable. Some round towers are found, especially in East Anglia (see pp. 32–33), for instance at **Hales** (Norfolk, Pl. 74).

ARCHITECTURAL ORNAMENT

Small parish churches had no barrier between the nave and chancel, though there may have been an open screen or railing such as survives in the upper gallery at **Compton** (Surrey, see p. 66). In order to emphasize its importance as the entrance to the sanctuary, the chancel arch came to be richly ornamented with sculptured patterns, which might also, as at **Stewkley** (Bucks, Pl. 76) or **Tickencote** (Rutland, Pl. 75), appear on the ribs of the stone vault above the altar. Tickencote even has a projecting boss, carved with three heads, which is the keystone where the ribs intersect, but this was a very rare feature during the Norman period. The use of decorative sculpture increased throughout the twelfth century,

Pl. 75 *The crude but powerful twelfth-century chancel arch of the church of St Peter and St Paul at Tickencote, Rutland, with five carved bands of characteristic Norman decoration, including beak head, zig-zag, billet and crenellated ornament and both human and animal heads; the rectangular font dates from c.1200.*

Pl. 76 *The remarkably preserved Norman interior of St Michael's church at Stewkley, Buckinghamshire, built c.1150–80, showing its arches accentuated with double bands of zig-zag ornament.*

famous and remarkably complete church at Kilpeck, introduced a rich and lively form of sculpture, thought to have been inspired by a sculptor who had been with his patron on a pilgrimage through France to Santiago de Compostela in Spain. Carving also appears on fonts, which have survived in large numbers (see pp. 72–74). The original decorative ironwork can still be seen on some church doors (see p. 74). The earliest surviving wall-paintings (see p. 75) date from this period, and their strong colours must have done a lot to brighten the rather dark interiors of these buildings with their few small windows. Most examples of

Pl. 77 *Detail of the mid twelfth-century south doorway of the sumptuously ornamented Norman church of St Mary and St David at Kilpeck, Herefordshire, carved with birds, dragons, fantastic beakheads, a flying angel and a Tree of Life on the tympanum.*

to ornament entrance (usually south) doorways with their recessed arches (see pp. 52–53), arcades and windows. It is also found on the exterior walls of churches, on towers and on corbel tables, or projecting courses of masonry, supported by rows of carved stone heads running round the building below the eaves, as at **Kilpeck** (Hereford and Worcester, Pls 77 and 78). The capitals of columns, which in the eleventh century were usually of the "cushion" or "scalloped" type, begin to be ornately carved with people and animals as well as stylized patterns. Crude figure sculpture appears, for instance, on "tympana" or flat semi-circular spaces above doors (see p. 53). Viking influence is found, for instance at St Nicholas' Church, **Ipswich** (Suffolk), on a tympanum with a boar and on a relief showing St Michael fighting the Dragon (both *c.*1120). The carving of the Herefordshire school, best known for the

Pl. 78 *Humans and weird animals on the corbel table round the apse of the remarkably complete mid twelfth-century church of St Mary and St David at Kilpeck, Herefordshire.*

stained glass surviving from the twelfth century are in more important centres (see p. 75), and it is unlikely that a parish church would have had any as early as this.

CHURCH FURNISHINGS

Few Norman church furnishings survive; many were replaced during the medieval period, and others were destroyed at the Reformation (see p. 175).

Furnishings of the choir

Little remains of the special furnishings which were provided in the choirs of cathedrals and abbey churches, and those which survive date almost entirely from the medieval period (see pp. 178–183), when the eastern part of so many Norman churches was either enlarged or rebuilt. The monks' stalls were ranged round the sides of the choir; the abbot's and prior's seats were to the south and north of the entrance, and a lectern (see pp. 74–75) was set in the middle of the floor. Later lecterns in this position can be seen at **Norwich**, **Peterborough** and **Southwell**. No pulpitum (see p. 58) survives from this period, though Ely's (of the twelfth century) remained in place until the mid eighteenth century, and carved panels (see p. 65) from **Chichester** Cathedral's stone choir screen (*c.*1125–50, Pls 68 and 70) can still be seen in the south choir aisle. The oldest surviving choir stalls (see p. 178) date from the thirteenth century, and a single misericord of *c.*1200 at **Hemingbrough** (N. Yorks) is probably the earliest anywhere in England.

Altars

Altars can seldom be seen uncovered today; so even where early examples have survived they are unlikely to be recognizable. They were generally plain stone structures, their slabs incised with five crosses to represent the wounds of Christ and their bases providing a hollow space for the insertion of relics.

Sedilia

Rows of sedilia (from Latin *sedere*, to sit), consisting of three or more seats, were built into the walls of the chancels in larger churches (see Pl. 197). These were for the use of the priests who officiated at the Mass, and early examples have survived, for instance at **Earls Barton** (Northants) and St Mary de Castro, **Leicester**. There are generally three of them, recessed into the south wall of the chancel and "stepped" so that each seat is at a different height within its own canopied arch. The celebrant sat nearest to the altar, with the deacon and sub-deacon beside him in descending positions. Sedilia are found only in larger churches where several priests were involved and would not have been put into a simple parish church, where the Mass was celebrated by one priest on his own.

Piscinas

To the east of the sedilia was the piscina (literally pool or fishpond, from Latin *pisces*, fish) (see p. 176), a bowl with a drain which was used by the priest for washing his hands and rinsing out the communion vessels during the Mass. It consisted of a bowl supported on a stone pillar, like the surviving example at **South Leigh** (Oxon). The pillar might be very elaborately carved, with a base, patterned column and capital, as at **Tollerton** (Notts), where the shaft, the only part of the piscina to survive, was rescued from a nearby shrubbery in *c.*1900 and can now be seen in the chancel.

Stoups

Holy water blessed by the priest was provided for the congregation near the entrance to the church, in a stoup such as the surviving example at

Kilpeck (Herefordshire), which probably dates from the early twelfth century. People would dip their fingers into the water before crossing themselves as they came in.

Fonts

The Normans seem to have replaced the Saxons' fonts as thoroughly as they did their churches, and this may partly have been because both were generally made of wood. A wooden font was considered uncanonical,

Pl. 79 *The late Norman font in St Peter's Church at Southrop, Gloucestershire, ornately carved with armed figures of Virtues trampling on Vices, shown under an arcade beneath a wide band of acanthus leaf and beaded interlace pattern.*

Pl. 80 *The late Norman font in St Michael's church at Castle Frome, Herefordshire, with three huge crouching figures round the base and a bowl carved with the Baptism of Christ and the Signs of the Evangelists. St John stands beside a pool where Christ and two fishes share the rippling water, while the Hand of God the Father and the Dove of the Holy Ghost hover overhead; on the left is the Angel of St Matthew.*

because water could seep out of it, and although a lead lining could get round this problem, making new fonts in stone would obviously have been more satisfactory. It has been suggested that the twisting cable patterns so often found carved on Norman fonts may imply that they replaced earlier wooden ones held together with bands of rope. Alternatively it may be that this type of ornament appears so often because it had already become a popular decorative pattern in England during Saxon times. Eleventh- and twelfth-century fonts are large round or sometimes square tubs, the later ones generally mounted on either a single stand or a group of five or more cylindrical shafts or columns; unmounted versions are normally circular. Many of these fonts were plain, but large numbers survive which are carved with crude figures and animals, as at **Stone** (Bucks), bold patterns and schematic foliage, as at **Buckland in the Moor** (Devon), or intersecting arcading, as at **Portchester** (Hants). Surprisingly, zig-zag ornament is very rarely found. Arcades peopled with figures, as at **Southrop** (Glos, Pl. 79), are common, and these are also found on a number of lead fonts which have survived, for instance at **Wareham** (Dorset), **Dorchester** (Oxon) and **Walton-on-the-Hill** (Surrey). Some of the sculpture found on Norman

fonts is purely abstract decoration but most is narrative. Scenes from the Bible are popular subjects, as at **Hook Norton** (Oxon), where Adam and Eve appear with signs of the zodiac, and at Holy Trinity, **New Lenton** (Notts, Pl. 81), and **Castle Frome** (Herefordshire, Pl. 80), which both show graphic depictions of scenes from the life of Christ. Large numbers of Norman fonts remain in use throughout the country. They are particularly numerous in the parish churches of Devon and Cornwall, which were less prosperous counties during the Middle

Pl. 82 *The late twelfth- or early thirteenth-century cylindrical lead font in St Augustine's church at Brookland, Kent, decorated with small scenes of the Signs of the Zodiac and the Labours of the Months shown under two tiers of arcading.*

Pl. 81 *The rectangular mid twelfth-century narrative font from Lenton Priory, now in the nineteenth-century church of the Holy Trinity at New Lenton, Nottingham; tiers of cherubim and seraphim surround the central scene depicting the Baptism of Christ and the other sides show the Crucifixion, the Entombment and the Resurrection.*

Ages, while there are far fewer in East Anglia, where medieval church building flourished. Their survival gives a vivid indication of the amazing richness and variety of Norman sculpture, so little of which escaped later destruction or mutilation.

It is thought that all these stone fonts would originally have been painted. We know too that they had lids which could be locked. Water that had been blessed was left in a font for long periods and not only did it have to be kept clean but it also needed to be protected from people who might want to use it for superstitious purposes. Early font lids have not survived, but there are often signs of the iron staples which were used for attaching them.

Some of the earliest lead fonts, such as the superb, elaborately arcaded bowl at **Brookland** (Kent, Pl. 82) have been attributed to the Norman period but it is possible that although their decoration looks earlier, they may not have been made before the late twelfth or early thirteenth century when this material was especially popular.

Metalwork

The ironwork on entrance doors can occasionally be seen, for instance at **Staplehurst** (Kent, Pl. 83), where the south door (now brought inside) has a huge and elaborate C-shaped hinge and is ornamented with a variety of sea creatures arranged in an abstract pattern beneath a crescent moon. A few handsome ring handles have also survived, as at Adel, **Leeds** (W. Yorks), where a beast is shown devouring a man whose head protrudes from its mouth, and at **Durham** Cathedral, where the original "sanctuary knocker" from the north door (there replaced by a replica) is on display in the Treasury. These handles are often described as "sanctuary rings" in the belief that fugitives grasped them when seeking refuge in churches; but since the right of sanctuary existed in a church-yard as well as in the building itself, the name suggests an element of picturesque exaggeration.

Pl. 83 *The Norman ironwork on the south door of All Saints' church at Staplehurst, Kent, perhaps made as early as the eleventh century; the elaborate C-shaped hinge is decorated with a variety of sea creatures, a boat and a cross within a circle.*

Seating

Norman churches did not provide seating for the congregation, although ledges or benches were sometimes built along the walls or round the bases of piers for the use of the sick, aged or disabled and mothers with young babies. There must have been some moveable furniture and a wooden armchair (*c.* 1200), a rare and important example of Norman carpentry, still stands in the chancel at **Hereford**.

Pulpits and lecterns

Pulpits for preaching are known to have existed, and there were sloping stone lecterns, which stood in the chancel, for readings from the gospel. Two very early lecterns at **Norton** (originally from Evesham Abbey, where it was dug up in the churchyard in 1813) and **Crowle** (both in Worcs) date from *c.*1200, though Crowle's has been much altered by restoration. Each of these lecterns rests on the head of a seated or kneeling figure surrounded by foliage and takes the form of a supporting column with a wedge-shaped capital, the top of which is sloped to provide a reading desk. A third, slightly earlier lectern, with foliage issuing from three inverted masks, was excavated in the ruins of **Much Wenlock** Priory (Shropshire).

Chests

Wooden chests were used for parish records or in larger churches for plate or vestments. The simplest are made of hollowed-out tree trunks and may, like one at **Bishop's Cleeve** (Glos), which has twelfth-century locks, date from as early as the Norman period.

Tombs

Tombs consisted of flat slabs like the coffin lid of St Osmund (d.1099) in the retrochoir at **Salisbury**, which is made of black marble, probably from Tournai in France. Sometimes they have effigies carved in very low relief. One of these appears on the wall monument now in the south transept at **Norwich**, which is possibly the lid of the original tomb of the cathedral's founder Bishop Losinga (d.1119) and there is another in the Lady Chapel at **Exeter**, which may represent Bishop Iscanus (d.1184)

Wall paintings

One can still see rare examples of the paintings which covered the walls of churches at this period. Even in their faded state, they convey the contemporary artists' love of pattern and colour, but they were not merely decorative. Their purpose was to instruct an illiterate congregation pictorially, by telling stories from the Bible or the lives of the saints. A remarkably complete cycle of murals survives at **Kempley** (Glos), which is dominated by the figure of Christ seated on a rainbow on the ceiling of the chancel. At **Copford** (Essex) the apse of the chancel shows a mid twelfth-century Christ in Glory surrounded by angels, which has been much restored and repainted but gives a good general impression of the original medieval scheme. A most unusual Last Judgement scene of c.1200 can still be seen above the chancel arch at **Chaldon** (Surrey, Pl. 84). Hell with its devils is graphically depicted below and above it Purgatory, with the Archangel Michael weighing souls, while the whole composition is dramatically bisected by a vertical ladder swarming with naked figures scrambling up to receive judgement.

Stained glass

Windows provided a similar opportunity for instruction. The earliest surviving stained-glass windows in Britain date from the twelfth century, though the technique was known much earlier (see p. 24). An ambitious glazing programme was begun at **Canterbury** c.1178, and enough of it survives to give an idea of its scope. In the clerestory of the choir there were two tiers of tall figures of the forebears of Christ, boldly painted so as to show up clearly from ground level, while lower down in the choir and elsewhere, windows which could be seen closer to were filled with an overall design of small narrative panels set against a background of scrolling foliage. The subject matter was carefully worked out, and windows might tell the story of the life of a saint, by depicting its main incidents, or present a scheme consisting of "types", or Old Testament scenes, shown beside related "anti-types", or New Testament subjects which they were thought to have foreshadowed. The Fall of Man, for instance, showing Adam and Eve with the Tree of Knowledge which was their undoing, is paired with the Crucifixion, with Christ dying on the tree of the Cross; while the story of Jonah, who spent three days inside the whale before being restored to the world, is juxtaposed with the Entombment of Christ before His Resurrection. A similar type of grouping occurs, for example, in the east window of the Corona, the chapel at the eastern end of the cathedral, where the New Testament story from Good Friday to Pentecost is told by depicting each main event at the centre of a quatrefoil, surrounded by four related Old Testament scenes. The Crucifixion is shown together with the sacrifice of Isaac (comparable with God's sacrifice of His own son), the preparing of the Passover Lamb (whose blood saved the Israelites in Egypt, as Christ's blood was shed for man's salvation), Moses striking the rock (to produce water, symbol of Salvation) and his spies bringing back the grapes of Eshcol (suggesting wine, signifying Christ's blood in the Eucharist) from Canaan (the Promised Land). The idea was to emphasize the prophetic role of the Old Testament in God's preordained plan for Jesus's life on earth and His death for man's salvation.

The rich colours used in the glass included deep reds and blues but also yellow, green and purple. Tracery had not yet evolved and each window was a single opening without mullions. The glass was supported by an armature or criss-cross of iron bars, which were sometimes curved to follow the shape of the design, for instance where a straight line would have cut across a roundel. English and French stained glass were very close at this date. Throughout the Middle Ages all the coloured glass used in England was imported from France or Germany, and only some of the clear glass was made in Britain.

Pl. 84 *The graphic wall-painting of the Last Judgement (c.1200) above the chancel arch of the Church of St Peter and St Paul at Chaldon, Surrey. At the bottom is Hell with its devils, and above it is Purgatory, where the Archangel Michael is weighing souls; little naked figures are scrambling up the central ladder towards Christ in Judgement shown in a medallion at the top.*

SECULAR ARCHITECTURE

Castles

In the early years after the Conquest the speedy construction of castles was a military priority. A twelfth-century writer describes how William I brought a pre-fabricated fort with him and erected it at Hastings immediately after his victory. His earliest castles are known to us from contemporary records as well as from the evidence of excavations and a graphic account survives in the Bayeux Tapestry, which depicts the construction of Hastings Castle. It shows how in this type of "motte and bailey" castle the main keep was built on a substructure of wood or, occasionally, stone (which would be reduced in importance where an existing hillock or rocky outcrop on the site provided a natural base). Soil was heaped up so as to incorporate the foundations in a solid "motte" or earth mound, leaving a ditch all round it where the earth had been dug out. This was often filled with water to form a moat. Around and in front of it lay the bailey or courtyard, also surrounded by a protective earthwork. Sometimes there were two of these enclosures, an inner and an outer bailey. These defences were strengthened by timber stockades, and a wooden tower would be built on the motte with a hall on the first floor and the domestic offices beneath it. Further living accommodation would be provided in wooden huts outside the bailey.

About a hundred of these castles had been built by the time of the Domesday survey (1086), and mottes, many of which can still be seen, for example at **Oxford** or **Carisbrooke** (Isle of Wight), continued to be constructed until the mid twelfth century. Such forts could be put up quite quickly, and masonry was seldom used during William I's reign. It is found, however, at his White Tower, the central keep (without the turrets, which were added later) of the Tower of **London** (Pl. 85). Even in Saxon times, London was a very important and cosmopolitan trading centre and therefore a town where organized resistance must have been a serious threat. The Tower was built of stone imported from Caen, then plastered and whitewashed (hence its name). It was evidently intended to look intimidating, but it was not as large as the massive early keep at **Colchester** (Essex), which may possibly have been built in response to a threat of Danish invasion. It was also constructed of stone and brick, presumably because Roman materials were there for reusing, and it stands on top of the remains of a Romano-British temple which provided ready-made foundations. The Norman castle builders were glad to make use of any man-made or natural features which made their task easier, and this is one of the reasons why their castles are not uniform but vary according to the advantages of the site. Existing Roman or Saxon defences were often brought back into use in the interests of quick fortification. Stone tower keeps were being built in Normandy and elsewhere on the Continent well before the Conquest, and a few English examples date from the late eleventh century; but it was only later, when their supremacy was assured, that the Normans had leisure for building their more impressive stone castles, many of which were constructed by Henry II when he set about restoring law and order and establishing the Crown's essential control of land ownership (see p. 46).

Contemporary warfare was based on the idea of maintaining a secure stronghold from which to control the surrounding neighbourhood. This meant that the ability to withstand a siege was a crucial need in military architecture. The earliest stone keeps varied considerably in size, and larger ones like **Norwich** (Pl. 86) required structural innovation to produce floors and roofs which were too wide to be built, according to the methods of the time, with a single span. Often, as at **Rochester** (Kent), an internal wall was constructed across the building, so that the internal space was divided into two rooms at each level, thus reducing the length of the rafters required. Since the occupants of a castle might need to be self-sufficient for long periods, the ground floor provided plenty of storage space for provisions. It had no external door and could be reached only by a stairway from above. There was a ready supply of water from a well inside the building. Some keeps seem to have been in daily use as houses but in many cases there would have been more comfortable living quarters in the bailey and the keep would have been needed only in times of emergency. However, we know from surviving castles that some provided a reasonable degree of domestic comfort. The main rooms would have been plastered and furnished with hangings and some basic furniture. In the thickness of the walls there would have been some smaller private rooms and also "garderobes" (latrines which emptied down chutes).

A characteristic Norman keep like the one at **Castle Hedingham** (Essex, Pl. 87) was rectangular, tall in relation to its ground plan, between two and four storeys high and extremely solidly built. Its thick walls were reinforced at the corners and along their length with wide, shallow buttresses, and their footings were protected by a "battered" (outward-sloping) plinth. The windows, which were high up, were often double openings inside a single arch. The lower apertures were only narrow slits, more for defence or ventilation than for light. This was because the main rooms were on the second or third storey, with the entrance at the same level and approached by an external staircase. As time went

Pl. 85 *The central Norman hall keep of the Tower of London, built in the late eleventh century and known as the White Tower because it was originally whitewashed; in their present form the corner turrets date from the sixteenth, the battlements from the seventeenth and the windows from the eighteenth century.*

Pl. 86 *The massive hall keep of Norwich Castle built on an earlier Norman motte from c.1120 onwards and completely refaced in the nineteenth century.*

on this was enclosed in a forebuilding like the one surviving at Rochester, which provided an entrance lobby and landing and sometimes housed a chapel. This and other additional structures, such as corner towers and gatehouses, were generally rectangular in plan. However, it soon became apparent that square corners made a keep very vulnerable because they were so easily undermined. An enemy could tunnel beneath a corner, supporting his underground workings with wooden props. He would then set fire to these so that they collapsed, destroying the foundations of the building and bringing down the masonry above. Corners could also be broken up with crowbars by enemies trying to breach the walls. To overcome this weakness polygonal designs were tried, as at **Orford** (Suffolk), and circular plans were subsequently popular. The earliest of these, at **Conisbrough** (S. Yorks), was buttressed with rectangular towers, but these perpetuated the corner problem and they were omitted from later round keeps. Sometimes towers were built on a D-plan, with the straight edge along the wall they were defending and the curved side facing out towards the enemy. A circular shape was in itself very strong, and curved walls presented a tough surface which could more easily be kept within the defenders' field of vision.

Some castles, for example **Lincoln**, **Berkeley** (Glos), **Restormel** (Cornwall, Fig. 5) and **Totnes** (Devon), took the form of a shell keep, a stone substitute for the original wooden palisade which would have encircled the motte. This type was a circular building with its rooms arranged round an open central courtyard. The outer palisade round the bailey was also rebuilt in stone as a "curtain wall", with towers at regular intervals to command the view of the entire outer surface. By the end of the twelfth century strong outer fortifications were becoming progressively more important, and the occupants of a castle had much more room for manoeuvre inside a far larger defended area.

The word "dungeon" meaning "keep" is derived from the French *donjon*, and it was not until later that it came to be used to describe a subterranean prison. It is derived from the Latin word *dominium* ("lordship") and reflects the fact that these castles were the houses of noblemen. Inside they were not just fortresses but homes as well. One can get an idea of their domestic arrangements from the way the internal space was divided up into rooms, which included a great hall with a large stone fireplace, a "solar" or private chamber for the owner of the house and his wife, and a chapel. It is only where sufficient detail

Pl. 87 *The splendid Norman keep at Castle Hedingham, Essex, built on an earlier motte c.1140, showing its battered plinth and the remains of the forebuilding in front of the entrance.*

has survived, as at **Rochester** (Kent) or **Castle Hedingham** (Essex), that one can get an idea of the more sophisticated architecture of this period. Excavated fragments of window glass and traces of primitive lead plumbing both suggest a reasonable degree of comfort, as does the fact that garderobes became a standard amenity. Every castle had to have a deep well to ensure a reliable and protected water supply, and at Rochester the shaft of the well came right up through the cross-wall of the keep so that water could be drawn on each of its floors.

The difficulty was that arrangements for the comfort of the occupants inevitably interfered with the military strength of the building. Most floors were made of wood, which could easily catch fire, and staircases, fireplaces, chimneys, small private chambers and garderobes, all built in the thickness of the walls, served to reduce their strength. Windows provided openings which a besieging enemy might enlarge in order to begin the process of breaking through the walls, while entrance doors were particularly vulnerable. Even when they could be successfully defended, these keeps were unsatisfactory from a military point of view. They could not withstand a siege indefinitely, and a sufficiently determined enemy had only to bide his time until the people trapped inside were finally starved into submission.

Although Roman walls guarded by projecting towers had survived in England, for example at **Pevensey** (E. Sussex) and **Portchester** (Hants, Pl. 9), the new emphasis on outer fortifications in Norman castles of the twelfth century represented a scientific approach to the problems of defence, which led on to the idea of the castle with concentric lines of walls, rather than the single fortress tower. The introduction into England of strong curtain walls made life inside a castle much less restricted and provided proper security for all the extra buildings sited in the outer bailey. As the keep became less important defensively, it was possible to improve domestic comfort, while at the same time providing a bigger garrison for forays and one which could hold out against a siege long enough for the enemy to lose heart and give up. The larger defended area also meant that domestic animals could be kept so as to ensure a supply of dairy produce and fresh meat over a lengthy period of isolation. **Dover** Castle (Kent, c.1180) retained the square keep but also had a curtain wall with ten watchtowers, two gatehouses and two "barbicans" or outer works to protect its entrances. As gatehouses were heightened and enlarged, they became increasingly significant and keeps were progressively less important defensively. Indeed by the end of the twelfth century we find a new type of castle, as at **Framlingham** (Suffolk, c.1190, Fig. 5), which has high curtain walls with rectangular towers but no keep at all. Instead it had living accommodation in a building which resembled the sort of manor houses beginning to be built in the country-side at this period (see below). It used to be maintained that much innovation in the design of castles in Britain resulted from experience of Byzantine fortifications gained during English participation in the Crusades to the Holy Land during the late eleventh and twelfth centuries but it is now believed that foreign influence came mainly from France.

Royal residences

Fortified residences like the White Tower at the Tower of **London** (Pl. 85) and the great keep of **Windsor** Castle (Berks) can still be seen, but apart from the walls of Westminster Hall (see p. 233), nothing remains of the Normans' extensive royal palaces. They were built as aisled great halls which had the royal apartments at one end and the kitchen at the other. Ranged around them were further buildings providing the king's chapel, chambers for the various departments of government, which travelled with the court from place to place, and the domestic offices.

Houses

Manor houses

Just as the Normans' castles were homes as well, their manor houses were built for security as well as domestic comfort. Like contemporary wooden fortresses, the timber houses of this period have not survived, and, as with castles, we are left only with a few examples of those manor houses which were built in stone. Manors, which were the homes of the tenants of the big secular and religious landowners, began to be built in the countryside during the latter part of the twelfth century, when Henry II had restored political stability and defence was no longer the paramount consideration. These houses have much in common with the domestic buildings put up at the same time inside castle walls, for instance at **Framlingham** (see p. 81), where the earliest known cylindrical chimneys (*c*.1150–60) have been found. Some defensive features continued in use throughout the medieval period, particularly moats, which also had the practical advantage of providing water near the house and a ready supply of fish. Two well-preserved examples of the Norman manor house can be seen at **Hemingford Grey** (Cambs, Pl. 89) and **Boothby Pagnell** (Lincs, Pl. 88). From these and other less complete survivals we know that it was normal for the hall, which was the main room, to be on the first floor, with the entrance to the house at this level, approached by an outside staircase. Sometimes, as at Wensum lodge (formerly known

as the Music House) in **Norwich** (Norfolk), this was enclosed by a forebuilding. The ground floor or basement, with a stone vault or sometimes a wooden ceiling, had narrow slits for windows and provided space for storage and the domestic offices. The owner and his family lived upstairs. The roof of the house would have been made of timber and was probably thatched, though oval oak shingles laid in a kind of scale pattern were sometimes used. The hall was the all-purpose living and dining room. It had a fireplace halfway along its long wall and two-light windows, sometimes with built-in stone window seats. Glass was still a rare luxury, so there would have been wooden shutters rather than glazing. The lord had his own table for meals at the "upper", least draughty end of the hall, and behind it was a "solar" or private room for him and his family, separated by a partition from the main part of the hall, where the rest of the household lived, ate and slept (see pp. 84–86).

Towns

Older towns prospered under the Normans and new ones grew up around the castles they built throughout the country. The civilian population provided for the needs of the fortress and ensured that plenty of extra manpower was available when it was needed, while the presence of the castle offered protection and trade for the townspeople. Norman town walls can still be seen, for instance at **Pembroke** (Dyfed), where the town was built inside the extended outer fortifications of the castle. Monastic foundations also laid out new towns, for instance at **Bury St Edmunds** (Suffolk), where Abbot Baldwin's plan resulted in the building of nearly 350 houses by the time of the Domesday survey in 1086. As also at **Ludlow** (Shropshire), the original grid plan can still be recognized in the modern streets.

Norman public buildings have not survived and it seems unlikely that urban life was sufficiently developed to have resulted in ambitious architectural projects. The great halls of castles may have been used for civic gatherings. We know that guilds were in existence at this time but the earliest surviving guildhalls date from the medieval period.

Town houses

Town houses were planned like manors, though it seems likely that their ground floors may have been used for commercial purposes. We can still see surviving stone houses with their entrances at street level, which reflects the fact that law and order were well established in urban

Pl. 88 *The exceptionally well preserved late Norman manor house at Boothby Pagnell, Lincolnshire, built c.1200 as the chamber block of a larger domestic complex; the four-light window was inserted in the fifteenth century.*

life during this period. Few domestic buildings were made of stone
and it has been generally assumed that many of those which survive
were built by Jewish immigrants, who first arrived in England under
William I. They were highly successful moneylenders and the king
needed their help to raise money, both for military reasons and to
finance his ambitious building projects. He gave the Jews his protection
but also profited from the taxes he levied on their financial transactions.
Christians were prohibited by Canon Law from charging interest on
loans, and so ironically it was the Jews who financed the construction
of many of our great cathedrals and monasteries. Their success made
them rich but also very unpopular, and for both these reasons it
must have suited them to live in stone houses which provided a better
standard of comfort and much greater security. It was particularly
important for them to protect the documents relating to their financial
dealings from the ever-present risk of fire in towns built largely of
timber with wattle and daub. Surviving town houses of the Norman
period like the Jew's House in the Strait at **Lincoln** (Pl. 90) often bear
the names of individual Jews but there is no certainty that they were
their original owners; in the case of the late twelfth-century Norman
House, formerly known as Aaron's House on Steep Hill at **Lincoln**, it
has been established that this wealthy moneylender (d. 1186) lived in a
different part of the town.

The domestic interior

Since only castles and rich men's houses have survived, architectural
evidence about how people lived at this period is restricted to the
upper levels of society. In order to understand how these buildings
worked, one has to realize that they were not just the homes of
individuals and their families but accommodated large dependent
households as well. These naturally varied in size and grandeur according to the status of the owner, but they invariably included people
at all social levels from gentlemen, who might be administrators and
secretaries, to men-at-arms, household servants and the most menial
domestics. Apart from a very few gentlewomen or nurses employed in
attending the lady of the house and her children, these were all-male
communities; even the kitchen was entirely staffed by men. This was
a practical arrangement, since everyone had to live, eat and sleep in the
hall together. Moreover these cumbersome households were frequently
on the move and transporting whole families of women and children
as well would have been totally impracticable. Some of the gentlemen
employed in lordly households also had lands and estates of their own,

Pl. 89 *A small two-light Norman window with built-in stone seats in the late
twelfth-century manor house at Hemingford Grey, Cambridgeshire, showing
deep reveals splayed to admit as much light as possible; the wooden shutters
are modern replacements.*

which their wives could supervise in their absence, and local women
living in the neighbourhood of a castle or manor were probably
employed as outside staff for jobs like washing or sewing; but women
were not members of the entourage which travelled with the lord
from one house to another. William I's policy of giving each of his
followers a number of separate estates in different places (see p. 45)
meant that, in order to administer their lands and live off their own
produce, landowners had to travel from one estate to the next, taking

Pl. 90 *The late Norman town house known as the Jew's House, built* c.1170–80 *in the Strait at Lincoln.*

their households with them. Very few permanent servants were needed to look after their empty dwellings when they were not in use. The grandeur a lord displayed when he was on the move and the lavishness of his entertaining when in residence were to become increasingly important signs of his status and prestige throughout the Middle Ages.

Life in a Norman house revolved round the great hall, where everyone lived. No roofs of this early date survive, perhaps because they were generally covered with reeds or thatch and were highly combustible; so we must imagine looking up at a frame of beams and rafters supported on the stone walls below. In the great upper hall at **Orford** Castle (Suffolk, 1165–7) one can still see the projecting stone corbels which carried the steeply raking joists supporting its conical roof. The walls of a hall would have been whitewashed and from the mid twelfth century onwards they may have been decorated with mural paintings. When the lord was in residence they would have been furnished with woven hangings to warm the room, visually with cheerful colours and literally by keeping out draughts. The floor would have been strewn with rushes to absorb and cover the food and filth dropped by men and animals alike. It was known as the "marsh", and even when the rushes were changed frequently it must have stunk horribly. It is not surprising that the owner preferred to distance himself from the main area and eat his own meals at the "upper" and warmer end of the room, furthest from the doors, facing each other on opposite sides of the building, which are thought to have been left open to provide ventilation for the fire. These entrances were screened from the room by low partitions but must have let in bitterly cold draughts in winter. Glass was not yet used in domestic settings and the windows would either have been filled with horn, which was translucent enough to admit some light, or simply fitted with wooden shutters. The room was heated by a central hearth or, in the case of two-storey buildings, by a fireplace (see below) halfway along one of the long walls. Early twelfth-century chimneys have been found at **Castle Hedingham** (Essex), and those at **Framlingham** (Suffolk) date from c.1150–60. Fire-risk determined that cooking took place outside the main building in a separate wooden kitchen with huge fireplaces often big enough to roast several whole oxen at once. When the head of the household wanted greater privacy, he could retreat with his family to the solar or private room beyond the high table; this was screened off from the rest of the hall by a leather curtain or wooden partition and it also served as a bedroom. The rest of the household slept on the hall floor after the meal had been cleared away. The trestle tables and benches used for meals were easily dismantled and set aside when the

floor space was needed for other purposes. Apart from these very basic items, furnishings were not treated as fixtures but travelled with the household whenever it moved to another place. Much of the time Norman houses and castles would have stood empty while tapestries, hangings, gold and silver plate, jewels, the chapel vestments, bedding and even pots and pans were in use elsewhere. A chair was a piece of furniture reserved for the head of the household or a really important guest; most people sat on stools or benches. Expectations of comfort were low, though some basic amenities such as domestic water supplies and latrines were beginning to be provided, especially in castles and royal palaces.

Fireplaces

A typical Norman fireplace was set inside the thickness of the wall behind a round-headed arch decorated with zig-zag ornament. It had a short conical flue to direct the smoke out through vents in the outside wall, but these are unlikely to have been very effective except in ideal weather conditions. In castle keeps like Hedingham or Rochester, there were vents on either side of an external buttress behind the fireplace, so that the one on the windward side could be closed and the other, which remained open, would be screened by masonry. The main difficulty was that the smoke was not taken high enough before being directed outside and it must often have blown back into the room. To overcome this problem, fireplaces with a conical internal smoke hood began to be built towards the end of the Norman period, as at **Conisbrough** (S. Yorks), and this was to become the standard type of early medieval fireplace (see p. 246).

Ireland

RELIGIOUS ARCHITECTURE

The building traditions of the sixth-century founders of the Irish monasteries lasted for about six hundred years, producing small simple box-like churches, carved high crosses (see p. 41) and tall round towers (see p. 40). It was not until the mid twelfth century that Ireland was affected by Carolingian developments based on the basilica church. Romanesque architecture and decoration were introduced into Ireland by the Cistercians, who founded their first monastery at **Mellifont** (Co. Louth) in 1142. From then on we find Romanesque ornament even in the simplest churches, where it is mainly restricted by their architectural limitations to chancel arches and doorways as at **Killeshin** (Co. Laois, Pl. 91) and **Dysert O'Dea** (Co. Clare, Pl. 92). The rich variety that was possible in

Pl. 91 *Detail of the finely carved ornament on the Romanesque doorway of the twelfth-century church at Killeshin, County Laois.*

Pl. 92 *Geometric ornament and strange human masks on the Romanesque doorway of the twelfth-century church at Dysert O'Dea, County Clare.*

more sophisticated buildings is illustrated by the mid twelfth-century Cormac's Chapel at **Cashel** (Co. Tipperary), which has a typical Irish stone roof, supported internally by an upper arch (see p. 40), but also shows the strong influence of English Romanesque in both design and decoration. However, the exuberant late twelfth-century west doorway of the cathedral at **Clonfert** (Co. Galway), with its wild mixture of motifs including both human and animal heads, is a purely Irish manifestation.

By the time of its late arrival in Ireland, Norman architecture was already well into the transitional stage of its development (see p. 94). Christ Church Cathedral, **Dublin**, built in the late twelfth century, belongs more to the emerging Gothic style than to the Romanesque.

SECULAR ARCHITECTURE

When the Normans arrived in Ireland *c*.1170, they came as a missionary army with the ostensible purpose of bringing Christianity to a barbarous people. Henry II used the backing of the Pope as a pretext to invade the country, and he eventually succeeded in controlling about three quarters of it by establishing an "English land" ruled from Dublin. He made sure that the many Norman feudal lords who had taken land in Ireland were prepared to acknowledge him as overlord, even though they were not willing to be governed direct from England. Only the Gaelic kingdoms in the west retained their independence. The Normans began by building "motte and bailey" castles, and it was only at the end of the twelfth

Pl. 93 *St Magnus Cathedral, built at Kirkwall on Mainland, Orkney, in the twelfth century.*

Pl. 94 *Deeply cut dog-tooth ornament on the processional doorway leading from the cloister into the church at Dryburgh Abbey, Borders, where the well-preserved ruins date from the twelfth and thirteenth centuries.*

Pl. 95 *The great late twelfth- and early thirteenth-century church of Jedburgh Abbey in the Scottish Borders, founded by David I* c.1138.

century that they started to use stone for their fortifications (see p. 77). **Carrickfergus** Castle (Co. Antrim), begun between *c.*1180 and 1205, has a characteristically Norman four-storey rectangular keep and curtain walls with rectangular projecting towers.

The domestic architecture of this period has not survived.

Scotland

RELIGIOUS ARCHITECTURE

As part of his reorganization of the Scottish church on Anglo-Norman lines, David I (see below) founded abbeys and priories in the borders region, for example a house for Augustinians at **Jedburgh** (Pl. 95) and one for Premonstratensian canons at **Dryburgh** (Pl. 94). His successors continued with foundations like William the Lion's Cluniac **Arbroath** Abbey (Tayside, 1178), whose ruins can still be visited. One can also see the splendid nave of the great Benedictine church originally founded by Queen Margaret at **Dunfermline** (Fife Pl. 96), which was rebuilt in the mid twelfth century, but only the east gable of the cathedral at **St Andrews** (Fife), begun in 1160, remains to remind us that this great building with its nave of fourteen bays would have been one of the longest in Britain. Continental influence in Scotland at this period is emphasized by the fact that as far away as **Kirkwall** (Mainland, Orkney, Pl. 93), in the distant Orkney Islands, where the Norse tradition was still strong, Earl Rognvald built a cathedral which shows a definite familiarity with architecture in Europe. On the other hand, the parish churches built by landowners on their estates were generally small, with rectangular naves, square-ended chancels, small deeply splayed windows and little ornament. There is a remarkably complete example at **Birnie** (Grampian) and another at **Cruggleton** (Dumfries and Galloway, Pl. 97), which was restored from a ruin in *c.*1890, but none of the larger town churches which existed at this time has survived.

SECULAR ARCHITECTURE

At the time of the Norman conquest of England, Scotland was ruled by **Malcolm III** of the Canmore dynasty, which was to unite the country under its authority for two centuries. His wife **Margaret** was the sister of the Saxon king Edgar, and she introduced a civilized English way of life into eleventh-century Scotland. Her work was carried on by their

son **David I**, whose sister was the wife of the English king Henry I. By giving them generous grants of land, he and his successors encouraged Anglo-Norman barons to settle north of the border, and their castles were similar to those being built in England at the same time. At first they were of the "motte and bailey" type, but the stone castles which replaced these were built with curtain walls and lean-to buildings round an open courtyard. They may be compared with English shell keeps; the earliest extant example, **Castle Sween** (Strathclyde), dates from the late twelfth century.

Contemporary domestic architecture has not survived.

Wales

RELIGIOUS ARCHITECTURE

In church architecture we find both a native and an Anglo-Norman tradition. Early Christian design persisted in the independent areas of Wales, but with the use of a Celtic type of square-ended chancel rather than an apse. Small churches, as at **Llanrhwydrys** (Anglesey), were wide in relation to their length, with a simple nave and chancel, and they would not have had towers. Instead there would have been a bellcote of the sort still to be seen at **Kilpeck** (Hereford and Worcester), near the Welsh border. Larger churches, for example **Penmon** Priory (Anglesey), were cruciform, with square chancel and transepts, a short, aisled nave and a massive tower. This church is an example of a type built for a *clas* or community of canons, who worshipped in the chancel. Such churches were generally very plain but they sometimes borrowed simple Norman forms of decoration. The many monastic churches founded during the twelfth century derived from their parent institutions on the Continent and are therefore of foreign origin, but the architectural restraint of the Cistercians, as at **Valle Crucis** Abbey (Clwyd), was in harmony with the austerity of contemporary Welsh buildings. The first churches which the Normans built in the conquered areas of south Wales featured a continental apse, but they later reverted to a square-ended chancel. Cathedrals were built at **Llandaff** (Glamorgan, *c.*1120), though little work of this period survives either there or at **St David's** (Dyfed, Pl. 98), where the church (begun in 1180), with its richly decorated

Pl. 96 The fine mid twelfth-century nave arcade of Dunfermline Abbey, Fife, founded by Queen Margaret in the eleventh century.

Norman nave, can still be seen beside the extensive remains of the fourteenth-century bishop's palace.

SECULAR ARCHITECTURE

There are only fragmentary remains of the profusion of defensive works which existed throughout Wales at this time. In the late eleventh and twelfth centuries there was constant warfare between the independent Welsh princes and the Normans, who attacked their frontiers, anxious to extend their newly won territories in Britain and determined to overcome all local opposition. This led to a rash of castle building, both by the invaders along the western and southern borders and by the native Welsh in the mountainous, and therefore more easily defended, areas of mid and north Wales. At first these castles were of the "motte and bailey" type, but, as in England, many were later rebuilt in stone with towers or keeps, rectangular at first and later round or polygonal too, and curtain walls. The earliest native stone castles date mainly from the thirteenth century, but twelfth-century Norman castles can be seen, for instance at **Manorbier** and **Pembroke** (both in Dyfed).

Domestic buildings of this period have not survived.

Pl. 97 *The simple eleventh- century parish church at Cruggleton, Dumfries and Galloway, which was restored from a ruin c.1890.*

Recognizing Norman Buildings

Walls
Massively built with ashlar masonry (often vanished) over rubble core; some reused Roman brick; quoins of squarish stones to strengthen corners.

Buttresses
Tall straight strips, very shallow.

Columns
Round and solid, sometimes with incised zig-zag, spiral or trellis decoration, with cushion, scalloped or crudely carved capitals; also rectangular piers, sometimes with recessed circular corner shafts or attached half-columns; columns and piers used alternately in arcades.

Arches
Round-headed, perhaps with carved decoration, for example zig-zag; later, earliest pointed arches.

Vaults
Tunnel or groin type, later with very simple ribs.

Roofs
Timber over wide spans; stone vaults for narrow spaces or some aisled structures.

Doors
Round-headed; entrance doors often on first floor (castles and manors) or set inside recessed arches, especially in churches.

Windows
Small, round-headed in internally splayed openings; sometimes in pairs, perhaps inside a larger relieving arch; often high up.

Decoration
Stonework carved with rich variety of patterns, especially on arches, for example zig-zag, beakhead, billet; some lively animal and figure sculpture, sometimes on capitals and especially on tympana above doors; wall-surface decoration, especially intersecting blind arcading; earliest surviving wall-paintings and stained glass.

Interiors
Fireplaces in thickness of walls or with conical projecting hoods; built-in stone furniture: in houses window seats, garderobes; in churches, priests' and monks' stalls, sedilia, piscinas.

Pl. 98 *The transition from Norman to Gothic is apparent in the late twelfth-century nave of St David's Cathedral, Dyfed, where round headed arcades contrast with the pointed arches of the triforium; the intricate Irish oak ceiling dates from the early sixteenth century.*

TYPES OF BUILDINGS

Cathedrals and monastic churches

Cruciform plan with short transepts; ambulatory behind presbytery to east of choir (then an enclosed space beneath the crossing), sometimes crypt beneath; very long nave with massive arcades; arches of triforium and clerestory arranged as pairs, continuous rows or multiple openings within larger relieving arches; galleries over aisles concealing transverse arches buttressing upper walls of nave; timber main roofs (replacements), stone vaults in aisles; tower over crossing; Lady chapel to east of main altar; Galilee chapel at western entrance; chapels along eastern walls of transepts.

Monastic ruins

Remains showing: four main buildings (church, dormitory, refectory and stores) grouped round cloister; infirmary generally to the east, outer court to the west; chapter house with stone seating; wall with one or more gatehouses surrounding whole precinct; traces of water supply and sanitary arrangements.

Parish churches

Rectangular two- or three-cell plan, also cruciform or circular; tower over crossing or at west end; some round towers, especially in East Anglia; blind arcading, especially on walls of towers; sculptured capitals, tympana and corbel tables; later, ornate interiors with richly carved patterns, especially on chancel arches, nave arcades and ribs and bosses of vaults; many stone and some lead fonts.

Castles

Early: tall rectangular keeps, sometimes with forebuilding at entrance; later: circular and polygonal keeps; shell keeps; curtain walls with rectangular towers and gatehouses.

Houses

Rectangular living room hall on first floor above vaulted basement; solar at end farthest from door.

The transition from Norman to Gothic architecture

During the twelfth century new developments are much more noticeable in decoration than in structure. The most significant technical innovation was the gradual introduction of slightly pointed arches and slender clustered columns into buildings which were in every other respect typically Norman. Both these features are found in the early years of the century at Durham, where stone vaulting on an unprecedented scale demanded a considerable advance in building science, notably in the use of internal buttresses to counteract the outward thrust caused by the sheer weight of the roof (see p. 60–63). As we have seen, the transverse pointed arches of the vault were introduced for practical rather than aesthetic reasons, and their structural possibilities were increasingly appreciated towards the end of the twelfth century. Norman architecture depended on strength rather than accurate calculation. Its massive round columns, which were generally made of rubble and only faced with stone, relied on bulk for their solidity.

The height of a semicircular arch was rigidly determined by the spacing of its columns, and it could only be made higher if it was "stilted" by continuing the straight sides above the capitals of the columns which supported it. A pointed arch, on the other hand, could achieve added height without greater width, and being lighter it did not need such massive columns to carry it. It also had obvious aesthetic qualities and its combination of grace, lightness and strength made possible the soaring new effects of the thirteenth century.

The rebuilding of the choir of Canterbury Cathedral which was begun by a French master mason, William of Sens, after a fire in 1174, introduced the contemporary French Gothic style directly into England (see p. 126). From about 1180 onwards, we find a period of overlap, with pointed arches, for instance, combined with Romanesque decoration, as in the church of St Cross Hospital, **Winchester** (Hants), and this marks the transition from Norman to early Gothic architecture.

Pl. 99 *Juxtaposition of Norman and Gothic: a detail of the late Norman blind arcading in the ruined chancel of Bolton Priory at Bolton Abbey, North Yorkshire, beneath a frieze of trefoil ornament dating from the substantial rebuilding of the church which took place after 1325.*

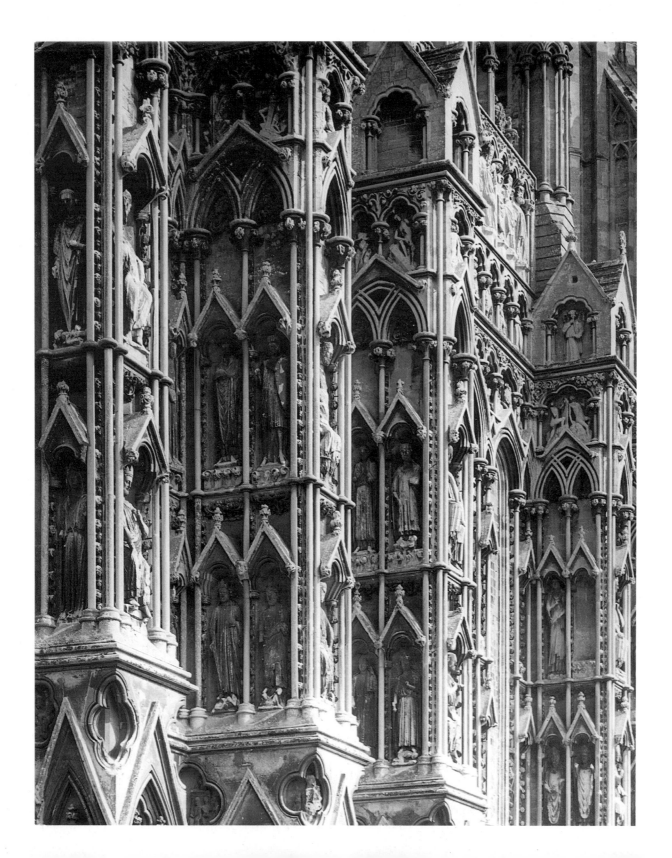

THE MEDIEVAL PERIOD

Introduction

The Gothic architecture of medieval Britain divides into three main but overlapping phases which correspond very roughly with the thirteenth, the first half of the fourteenth and the mid fourteenth to early sixteenth centuries and are generally known by their nineteenth-century descriptions as "Early English", "Decorated" and "Perpendicular". "Gothic" is a stylistic rather than a political label. The name was coined during the sixteenth century to suggest the work of barbarian Goths rather than the civilized orderliness of classical architecture. It has continued to be used as a convenient, though irrelevant, description of the pointed architecture of the Middle Ages. It refers to the style of all stone buildings, both secular and religious, but particularly to cathedrals and churches. Older traditions persisted in wooden building but there were also many medieval timber-framed houses which used a "cruck" construction (see p. 249) based on a crude form of pointed arch.

Early English

HISTORICAL BACKGROUND

The Early English period covers the reigns of four English kings of Angevin descent:

> Richard I ("the Lionheart") 1189–1199
> John 1199–1216
> Henry III 1216–1272
> Edward I 1272–1307

They were the descendants of Henry II, whose reign, as we have seen, coincided with the beginning of the transitional stage between Norman

Pl. 100 *Detail showing the upper part of the thirteenth-century west front of Wells Cathedral, Somerset, divided into five parts by six massive buttresses, which are decorated with two tiers of gabled blind arcading peopled with statues of saints, bishops and kings.*

and Gothic architecture. **Richard I** was primarily a soldier and spent most of his reign abroad, participating in the Third Crusade, after the capture of Jerusalem by the Mohammedans in 1187, and defending his Norman kingdom in France. His main activity when briefly at home was raising money to finance his military campaigns by the sale of offices in church and state and by granting charters to various towns, including London, which thus became increasingly self-governing. In his absence the country was ruled by the Justiciar and Archbishop of Canterbury Hubert Walter, who managed, in spite of the king's crippling taxation of his subjects, to maintain law and order, by giving the knights of the shires responsibility for helping to keep the King's Peace. As a result there was sufficient political stability for domestic and religious building to continue throughout the country. Richard's most impressive castle was Château Gaillard (1197) in France, on a rocky spur above the Seine to protect the river crossing at Les Andelys (Normandy), which was designed, in the light of the experience he had gained during the Third Crusade, so that the entire area beneath its walls could be defended by missiles thrown from inside. His knowledge of the most up-to-date ballistic machines and undermining methods enabled him to make use of the advances in military architecture which he had observed at the Siege of Acre and in Crusader castles, such as the Syrian fortress of Margat. As well as building new ones, he also modernized his existing castles, for instance carrying out a refortification of the Tower of **London** with a new outer wall and ditch.

His brother **John** lost Château Gaillard in 1203 and with it his Norman and Angevin lands, with the result that Britain subsequently became increasingly insular and less affected by architectural developments in France. Moreover the king quarrelled with Pope Innocent III over the choice of a new Archbishop of Canterbury in 1205. The Pope tried unsuccessfully to impose his authority by setting aside the king's candidate and imposing one of his own. John reacted by refusing him entry and seizing church property, and in retaliation the Pope issued an interdict of 1208 temporarily suspending religious worship in England. Britain's subsequent isolation from the church in Rome caused a further separation from the affairs of the continental mainland. John was also at loggerheads with his barons, who forced him to accept limitations on his power by signing their Magna Carta or Great Charter at Runnymede in 1215. It was only the king's death the following year that saved the country from civil war. Like his predecessor, John spent large sums of money on constructing or modernizing castles, besides being an enthusiastic builder of fortified manors and hunting lodges. A number of surviving thirteenth-century houses bear his name, and in a few cases these may have been authentic royal residences, since he is known to have been constantly on the move, for both legal and political reasons, as well as because of his passion for hunting. The king also issued licences to reliable subjects allowing them to "crenellate" or protect their houses with stone walls and battlements, usually surrounded by a moat.

Conflict between the king and his subjects continued during the reign of **Henry III**. Again the barons got the better of a weak and ineffectual ruler, and this time they were finally able to establish that the king was not outside the law. Their ascendancy was reflected in a proliferation of castles and fortified manors. Surviving examples include the great castle of **Caerphilly** (Gwent), built by the powerful Lord Gilbert de Clare (*c.* 1270), and **Little Wenham** Hall (Suffolk), begun at about the same time. It has been suggested that Henry threw himself into grandiose building schemes to compensate for his failure to achieve political power, but his patronage of the arts sprang from a real aesthetic interest and practical involvement. His religious and cultivated tastes and the fact that, because of his French wife, Eleanor of Provence, numerous foreigners were attached to his court, brought the English church back into close contact with the artistic life of Europe. The king's rebuilding of Westminster Abbey as a shrine for Edward the Confessor was in the French Gothic style, directly influenced by contemporary buildings commissioned by his brother-in-law Louis IX at Rheims, Royaumont, St-Denis and in Paris (the Sainte Chapelle). This created an architectural link between his English coronation church and the most important French royal churches of the time, thus associating the English monarchy with the idea of sacred kingship which still existed in France. The new Westminster Abbey was to have considerable influence in spreading a knowledge of French Gothic throughout the country, and the fact that Henry set up a "Royal Works", employing its own craftsmen, established the monarch as an important patron of architecture.

The strong and efficient rule of **Edward I** brought about a reform of administration and justice and encouraged commerce. His first Statute of Westminster (1275) consolidated his own financial position by giving the Crown a substantial regular income from a tax on the export of wool and leather. His Statute of Mortmain (1279) curbed the wealth of the religious foundations by controlling gifts of land into the "dead hand" of the church, which paid no revenues to the king. His second Statute of Westminster (1285) established the system of entail, whereby landowners could pass land from one eldest son to the next, thus keeping large estates intact instead of subdividing them at each generation. In 1290 Edward expelled the Jews, whose money-lending activities, condemned by the Church as sinful usury, had been so convenient and unpopular (see

p. 84), and made use of the services of merchant bankers instead. His reign also saw the subjugation of the independent areas of Wales, culminating in the death of Prince Llewellyn II in 1282, and consolidated by the construction of powerful and awe-inspiring castles and walled towns, especially along the north Welsh coast. He had hoped to bring about the peaceful union of England and Scotland by the marriage of his eldest son to Margaret, the "Maid of Norway", granddaughter and heir of the Scottish king Alexander III. This plan was foiled by her tragic death in 1290. Subsequent hostilities between the two countries were prolonged. Edward succeeded in removing the Scottish coronation stone of Scone to Westminster in 1296 but his victory was short-lived. An abortive uprising led by William Wallace in 1292 was followed in 1305 by the emergence of a new and successful Scottish national leader, Robert the Bruce. Edward died in 1307 still attempting the conquest of Scotland.

The court style of architecture which grew up during his reign was extremely influential, and it was the crosses he set up along the funeral route of his queen (whose body was brought to London from Harby in Nottinghamshire in 1290 for burial in Westminster Abbey) that introduced the ogee curve, which was to become such a popular motif of the Decorated style. Surviving crosses can be seen at three of the places where her cortege halted on its journey, **Geddington** (Pl. 102) and **Hardingstone** (Northants) and **Waltham Cross** (Herts, whose original statues have been on loan to the Victoria and Albert Museum, London, since 1985). The last stage of the journey was Charing Cross in London, where the cross, demolished in 1647, was subsequently replaced by an equestrian statue of Charles I.

THE EARLY ENGLISH STYLE

Early English buildings show Gothic in its first and simplest form. Structurally the new style represented a dramatic change from what had been possible before, comparable with the architectural revolution caused by the invention of the steel frame for modern buildings. It was also comparable with modern architecture in that it was a new way of building expressing the spirit of a new age which valued prodigious height and vast areas of glass for symbolic reasons. Suddenly, with the general adoption of the pointed arch, it became possible to build large

Pl. 101 *The west wall of the early thirteenth-century north transept at Lincoln Cathedral, showing the characteristic pointed arches, rib vaults, clustered columns and stiff-leaf capitals of the Early English style.*

Pl. 102 *The Eleanor Cross at Geddington, Northamptonshire, erected shortly after 1294 to mark one of the halts on the funeral route of Edward I's deceased queen; its design shows the transition between the Early English and Decorated styles.*

tall buildings with big windows to let in plenty of light. This was because the walls no longer needed to be massively solid in order to provide adequate support for the roof; so large areas could be filled with glass without weakening the structure. Round arches could be used only to vault a square space, because in order to reach the same height they had also to be of equal width, whereas since there was no problem in bringing pointed arches of different spans to the same height, these could also be used for rectangular areas. We have seen that during the transitional period round arches were used in conjunction with pointed, and the full potential of the pointed arch was not realized. The only way to build round arches of different spans but all equally tall was to make them spring, or begin to curve, from different heights. It was only when all the arches were pointed that they could all spring from the same level, whatever their span, and produce a rectangular vault. Once this was understood, buildings rose higher and higher, and to counteract the increased outward pressure caused by their height, their buttresses had to be taller and far stronger, weighted from above by heavy stones carved as decorative pinnacles. In contrast with the shallow pilasters used by the Normans, Gothic buttresses spread out widely at the base of the walls to carry the thrusts from above down into the ground.

It used to be taken for granted that the stability of a Gothic building depended on a well-balanced frame made up of columns, buttresses and the ribs of the vaulting, but it is now believed that the evolution of the Gothic style depended quite as much on aesthetic considerations as on structural necessity. During the Second World War there were cases of bomb damage where medieval vaults did not collapse even though their ribs had been partially destroyed, and the inference is that the main function of the ribs was decorative. However, the original builders certainly thought of them as adding strength, and during construction they served the invaluable purpose of making it possible to erect a vault one section at a time. This meant that much less scaffolding was needed and the amount of "centering", or temporary wooden support, could be greatly reduced because smaller sections could now be used over and over again as panels were filled in one at a time. The limited areas involved meant that lighter masonry could be used, and it was this greatly reduced weight, combined with the new understanding of buttressing, which gave the Gothic vault its stability. During the later phases of the Gothic style, the ribs were increasingly used as surface decoration, until all attempt at structural logic was finally abandoned with the introduction of the fan vault (see Pls 109, 112, 122 and 150, Fig. 11). Clustered columns became common, sometimes including shafts which run right up the wall surface (Pl. 101) to support the ribs of the vault, and arches are often deeply moulded. Simple pointed windows known as lancets are characteristic of the Early English period, and we see the development of window tracery (see Fig. 10), from openings cut through flat areas of stonework (plate tracery) to moulded bars dividing up the openings (bar tracery) as at Lincoln Cathedral (Pl. 104). In the early stages a pair or row of lancet windows would be enclosed by a single dripstone hood designed to prevent rainwater running down the outside of the glass. This would leave a blank space above the lancets which might be pierced by a trefoil (cloverleaf) or vesica (pointed oval) opening. In time the edges of all the openings were chamfered and the flat areas gradually reduced until only narrow bands of stone were left between the glass. The design of its window tracery is one of the clearest indications of the date of any Gothic building. Although sculptured ornament was not used as profusely as during the Romanesque period, it now became much finer, dog-tooth (Pl. 106) succeeding zig-zag as one of the most popular decorative patterns. "Stiff-leaf" or formal foliage carving is common at this period, especially on capitals (Pl. 101 and Fig. 4), and is an especially English feature of Gothic architecture. When figures appear among the leaves, they are often highly individual portraits.

Decorated

HISTORICAL BACKGROUND

The middle or Decorated period of Gothic architecture occupies the earlier part of the fourteenth century and coincides with the reigns of

Edward II 1307–1327
Edward III 1327–1377

Edward II, who lacked both competence and maturity, was ill-equipped to take on the constitutional and financial problems inherited from the reign of his father Edward I. It was not until about 1320 that he was sufficiently solvent to undertake serious building at Westminster, including continuing his father's work on St Stephen's Chapel. His greatest effect on the architecture of this highly productive period was indirect, through the influence of Westminster craftsmen who would have been engaged on royal projects but were forced to look for work elsewhere because of the king's inability to employ them. As an aesthete Edward was given to displays of personal magnificence and impressive architectural projects, but politically he was inept. His disastrous attempt to conquer Scotland ended in ignominious defeat by Robert the Bruce at Bannockburn (1314).

The general hatred of his ambitious and unpopular favourites made his royal authority resented, and the barons banded together once again to restrict the power of the Crown. It was with their support that Edward's queen, Isabella of France, eventually had him deposed and murdered.

His son **Edward III** then ruled for half a century. His reign saw continued hostilities against Scotland and the start of the Hundred Years' War (1337), which began partly in order to protect English territorial interests in France but also, more importantly, to maintain the country's vital trade with Flanders, where exported English wool was woven into cloth. Flemish weavers were also encouraged to settle in England to help establish a native cloth industry which was to bring great prosperity to the country by the fifteenth century. At home the Black Death (1348–9), which devastated both towns and countryside, led to legislation to control the increased wage demands of the surviving workers. Against this troubled background, Edward undertook building works to rival those of Henry III, with ambitious projects like the completion of St Stephen's Chapel, Westminster, and the reconstruction of Windsor Castle. One of the most important was his huge circular castle at **Queenborough** (Kent), designed for the defence of the Thames estuary, which was completed in 1375 but totally destroyed in the mid seventeenth century. The king was concerned equally with comfort and decoration, for instance at Westminster, where his bathroom had hot and cold running water and his splendid new interiors included the famous Star Chamber. At Queenborough he had one of the first English mechanical striking clocks.

THE DECORATED STYLE

The name "Decorated" is given to the second stage of the development of Gothic architecture in Britain because of the increased elaboration we find when the early experimental style gives way to more confident and complex effects. This is particularly evident in window tracery (Fig. 10), where sophisticated curves, especially the ogee or double S, take over from the more rigid geometry of the thirteenth century. Intersecting pointed arches are succeeded by more flowing "reticulated", or network, and "curvilinear" patterns. There is a tendency for arches and the surfaces of walls and gables to be richly covered with all-over patterns, such as diaper, and the formal ballflower ornament (Pl. 105) is very characteristic of the mouldings of this period. Sculptured decoration, such as the foliage ornament on the capitals in the chapter house at **Southwell** (Notts, Pl. 103), becomes highly naturalistic, and it may be deeply

encrusted, its three-dimensional effect heightened, for instance, by the use of the "nodding", or forward-curving, ogee arch (Pl. 138). The octagon emerges as a popular shape for columns, capitals and fonts. Buildings are planned for deliberate spatial effects, and tracery may even be substituted for solid walls, as in the cathedrals of **Bristol** (Pl. 149) and **Wells**, to produce lighter and more open interiors. The octagonal crossing at **Ely** (*c*.1320, Pl. 107 and 159) is the earliest design to introduce the idea of the diagonal vista. Vaults become more complicated and also more decorative, with the introduction of "liernes", or subsidiary ribs, which run between those expressing the main structure to produce star-shaped geometrical designs. The twenty-eight angels carved on the triangular spandrels of the Angel Choir at **Lincoln** Cathedral (Pl. 108) show sculptured decoration deliberately designed to fit the space it is intended to fill.

Perpendicular

HISTORICAL BACKGROUND

It seems ironical that the orderly Perpendicular style should have coincided with one of the most unsettled periods in English history. The kings who followed each other, often with very dubious rights of succession, were:

> Richard II 1377–1399
> Henry IV 1399–1413
> Henry V 1413–1422
> Henry VI 1422–1461
> (*restored briefly* 1470–1471)
> Edward IV 1461–1483
> Edward V (*one of the "Princes in the Tower"*) 1483
> Richard III 1483–1485
> Henry VII 1485–1509

Three of these monarchs came to the throne as minors, which resulted in bitter power struggles between their adult relatives, and the repeated lack of a clear line of descent led to constant fighting between rival claimants and their supporting factions. **Richard II**'s reign saw a considerable weakening of the power of the church, which was already unpopular for its immense wealth and undisguised worldliness and no longer commanded the reverence of the laity. The prestige of the papacy had suffered during its enforced residence at Avignon (the "Babylonian Captivity", 1309–78) and as a result of the "Great Schism" (1398–1415) during which separate French and Italian lines of popes denounced each other and excommunicated their rivals' followers. When the Oxford reformer John Wycliffe (1320–84) attacked the clergy for their worldly way of life and pursuit of temporal power, the bishops failed to find secular support in their efforts to silence him (1377–8). It was only his later heresy that alienated his powerful friends. He sent poor itinerant preachers, the "Lollards", to spread his heretical doctrines throughout the country, and he made the first English translation of the

Pl. 103 *Detail of the door to the late thirteenth-century chapter house at Southwell Minster with shafts of black Purbeck marble and superb three-dimensional carvings of highly naturalistic leaves.*

Pl. 104 *The thirteenth-century east front of Lincoln Cathedral, where the great eight-light east window with its geometric bar tracery dates from c.1275.*

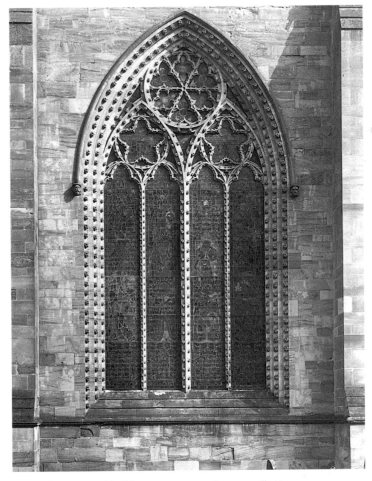

Pl. 105 *Formal ballflower ornament used to great effect in c.1310 on a window in the south aisle of the priory church of St Peter and St Paul at Leominster, Herefordshire.*

was not until 1396 that he made peace with France. After a minority dominated by the rule of his uncles, he took control in 1389. Richard was a lover of beauty and pleasure who had no taste for war or politics. He favoured elaborate ceremonial, which led to considerable grandeur and formality at court and produced his greatest contribution to our architecture, the reconstruction of Westminster Hall (1394–1401). During the last two years of his life, his murder of his uncle, the Duke of Gloucester, and despotic attacks on various members of the nobility

Pl. 106 *Lavish use of dog-tooth ornament on the ribs of the mid thirteenth-century Galilee porch at Lincoln Cathedral.*

Bible, which had previously been only in Latin, the language of scholarship, rather than in the native tongue for the common people. It was not just the authority of the church which was weakening. The old manorial system of dependent labour on the land was also breaking up and the late fourteenth century saw the "Peasants' Revolt" against serfdom (1381) and the pursuit of increased wages for free workmen. Although these aims were not immediately realized, by the fifteenth century England had a largely free peasantry.

Richard II was only ten years old at his accession. The first year of his reign saw renewed French attacks along the south-east coastline, and it

Pl. 107 *The Norman nave and north aisle of Ely Cathedral seen from the early fourteenth-century octagonal crossing, which has ogee-arched niches characteristic of the Decorated style.*

Pl. 108 *Seated angels designed to fit the triangular spaces in the spandrels of the mid to late thirteenth-century Angel Choir at Lincoln Cathedral.*

turned the country against him. He was deposed and afterwards murdered by his cousin **Henry IV**, whose tenuous claim to the throne succeeded only because he had popular and parliamentary support.

Henry had a practical and up-to-date attitude to warfare. He understood guns and their potential and used them to good effect in Britain and abroad. He had to deal with rebellions both at home and in Wales, where Owen Glendower led a successful nationalist uprising. The expense of quelling his opponents was very great and since the king depended on his ministers for the necessary funds, the growing influence of Parliament was an important political development during his reign. In executing the Archbishop of York for conspiracy, Henry showed his independent attitude towards the church, but, like all the other wealthy men in the country, he was ruthless in his persecution of the Lollards for their dangerous denunciation of riches.

This persecution was continued with even greater intensity by his son **Henry V**, whose opposition to heresy demonstrated his firm allegiance to the church. A pious and able soldier and administrator, he began his reign by putting right, as far as possible, the wrongs committed by his father when he seized the throne. He strengthened his political position by successful military campaigns in France and increased his territories there, especially as a result of his famous victory at Agincourt. His marriage to the daughter of Charles VI, who was persuaded to disinherit his own son, established his line as heirs to the French throne.

However, these gains did not long survive his premature death and the lengthy, ineffectual rule of his son, **Henry VI**, a mild, peace-loving and religious man but no statesman. Within thirty years England had lost all her French possessions except Calais. France had rallied, inspired by the heroism of Joan of Arc and helped by the support of the Duke of Burgundy, who had defected from the English side; England, demoralized by the breakdown of law and order at home, was not strong enough to resist. Henry was less than a year old when he succeeded to the throne, and in adult life he was subject to bouts of insanity; so power during much of his reign was wielded by his uncles and their friends. Rivalry between the Dukes of York and Somerset intensified after the king's deteriorating health made a protectorship necessary (1453–4), and the fighting which followed was the beginning of the Wars of the Roses, which plunged the country into thirty years of intermittent civil war. The weak king had proved unequal to controlling his nobles, who kept their own private armies of dependent gentry and yeomen to fight for them in exchange for protection from the law under the illegal system of "livery and maintenance", and now either sided with the royal family of Lancaster or took up the cause of the rival house of York. The king's

cousin Edward of York seized power and was crowned Edward IV at Westminster in 1461, though Henry was briefly restored to the throne by his mother and her allies in 1470–71. The political instability of his reign was not conducive to the building of palaces, but he is remembered for his major religious and educational foundations, Eton College near Windsor, and King's College, Cambridge.

Edward IV's was another troubled reign. His powerful cousin, the "Kingmaker" Earl of Warwick, who had supported his accession, became his bitter enemy and sided with Edward's brother Clarence in a bloody insurrection. After ten years of strife, culminating in the brief restoration and subsequent death of Henry VI in 1470–71, Edward's reign settled into a prosperity based on extra riches for the Crown from the forfeited estates of nobles convicted of treason, customs dues from the flourishing wool trade, and "benevolences" or forced loans extorted illegally from the rich as tokens of their goodwill towards the monarchy. These new sources of income gave the king the freedom of being independent of Parliament, though it was with government money that he attacked France in 1475. He concluded his invasion, greatly to his own financial advantage, by accepting a gift of 75,000 crowns and a large pension from Louis XI in exchange for returning home without fighting. He used this French windfall to finance two great architectural projects, **Eltham** Palace in Kent and the rebuilding of St George's Chapel, **Windsor** (Pl. 109). Thanks to his business acumen, the finances of the royal household were brought under control, so that he was the first king since Norman times who was not in debt when he died.

Edward's murder of his brother Clarence in 1478, only five years before his own death, foreshadowed the fate of his own son, the child king **Edward V**, who with his younger brother, Richard of York, is said to have met his end in the Tower of London in 1483. This has never been proved, and it will always remain uncertain how he died. The traditional story asserts that the "Princes in the Tower" were murdered by their uncle **Richard III**, who had seized the opportunity of his nephew's minority to usurp the throne. Having lost his only son in 1484 and his wife a year later, Richard then proposed to marry the sister of the boys he had so ruthlessly killed, his niece Elizabeth, daughter of Edward IV. This version of events may be suspect, since the generally accepted picture of Richard as the cruel hunch-backed villain, immortalized by Shakespeare, is based on later accounts by Tudor historians with an interest in denigrating his memory in order to bolster the very dubious right to the throne of

Pl. 109 *St George's Chapel, Windsor, begun in 1475 and completed by 1511, showing the fan-vaulted crossing and three-tiered choir stalls of 1478–85.*

Henry VII and his successors. Richard had considerable ability as a soldier and administrator and combined firm government with a determination to suppress intimidation and corruption, for instance by the abolition of benevolences (see p. 106). His short reign ended with his death at the Battle of Bosworth in 1485, after his defeat by the Earl of Richmond, who then seized the throne.

Richmond's accession as **Henry VII** and his marriage to Edward I's eldest daughter eventually brought an end to Yorkist supremacy, though attempts to overthrow him continued until the end of the century. Through his mother, the new king was a member of the House of Lancaster, but his father was a Welshman, Edmund Tudor, and Henry therefore became the first monarch of that name. Determined to suppress the power of the old nobility, he imposed large fines on those who controlled private armies under the corrupt system of "livery and maintenance" (see p. 106) and encouraged the rise of the middle class. His approach was soundly commercial and he found many ingenious ways of enriching the throne at the expense of his subjects. He also brought prosperity to the nation by promoting foreign trade, protecting England's shipping interests and supporting the native wool industry. He brought Irish legislation under English control and his eldest daughter married the Scottish king James I in 1502. By the end of his reign England was a rich and politically stable country, well-placed to exploit the new opportunities of the sixteenth century. Henry's memorial is the splendid new Lady chapel he began to build at Westminster Abbey in 1503, which was unfinished at his death. It was completed as his chantry by his successor Henry VIII and is known as Henry VII's Chapel (Pls 150 and 156).

THE PERPENDICULAR STYLE

The curvilinear tracery which evolved in Britain during the Decorated period did not, as in France, lead on to a "Flamboyant" style, where the tracery lights were filled with shapes like flickering flames. Instead it seems to have been influenced by the "Rayonnant" (radiating) style of French rose windows, with their thin bars and wide expanses of geometrical panels of tracery. The Perpendicular is a peculiarly English phenomenon which lies outside the general pattern of the development of European Gothic, and it continued to dominate our architecture long after the period which bears its name. Its formal geometry lays strong emphasis on the rectangle. Perpendicular or vertical mullions run the whole height of windows in assertively parallel lines. Grid pattern tracery first appeared in the rebuilding of St Stephen's Chapel, **Westminster**

(1292–1348), and before it was finished the fully fledged Perpendicular style emerged at **Gloucester** (Pl. 110), where the choir and south transept were rebuilt in the mid-fourteenth century to house the splendid tomb of Edward II (d. 1327). Here the tracery was used as a surface covering for the interior walls and provided the framework for huge windows like glass curtains. It was economical because it transformed much of the earlier Romanesque structure without involving total rebuilding, as is found subsequently elsewhere, for instance in the remodelling of the

Pl. 110 *The choir of Gloucester Cathedral rebuilt in the Perpendicular style in the mid fourteenth century, which still has its original choir stalls and medieval stained glass in the east window.*

Pl. 111 *The chapel of King's College, Cambridge, founded by Henry VI and built between 1446 and 1515; the decorative carving on the buttresses near the south door dates from the early sixteenth century.*

Norman nave at Winchester in the late fourteenth century. Taller windows were strengthened with stone cross-bars or transoms. The size of glazed areas increased dramatically at this period, and they became much squarer. Arches were either less acutely pointed or of the much flatter, "four-centred" type (see Fig. 1). Sometimes the "hoodmoulds" or dripstones above window arches (known as labels when they have square corners) were developed into rectangular heads, which also served the purpose of preventing the rain from running down the outside of doors or windows (see Pls 105 and 305). The characteristic patterns

of Perpendicular tracery, based on the motif of a panel with a cusped arch, were also used to decorate wall surfaces of every kind, even such small areas as battlements or the sides of buttresses, which now projected even further from the walls, sometimes in the form of double half-arches. The discovery of lead as a roof covering meant that roofs could be made almost flat rather than acutely pitched. As a result walls were made taller to compensate for the consequent loss of height, and supporting buttresses gained in importance. At first these were used diagonally at the corners of buildings, then in pairs one each side of the angle (see Fig. 3). The ever-increasing areas of glass in the walls of churches during the late medieval period made it necessary to articulate walls with a supporting buttress between each window all along every façade, for example at King's College Chapel, **Cambridge** (Pl. 111). The distinctive form of late medieval tracery was used to its greatest dramatic and decorative effect in the fan vaulting (see p. 141) which is such a recognizable feature of the Perpendicular style. It began in small spaces like tombs and porches. The earliest important scheme to survive is the cloisters at **Gloucester** (mid fourteenth-century, Pl. 122). It was not until the mid fifteenth century that fan vaulting was used for the stone roofs of large churches, like **Sherborne** Abbey (Dorset, c.1450, Pl. 112), though wide wooden vaults are known earlier, for instance in **Winchester** College chapel (Hants, c.1390).

Religious architecture

HISTORICAL INTRODUCTION

The church in the Middle Ages

The early Middle Ages was a period of major construction, which produced many of our finest cathedrals, such as Canterbury, Wells, Lincoln and Salisbury and great monastic churches, like Hexham Priory and Whitby Abbey. The Statute of Mortmain of 1279 (see p. 98), which restricted the power of the religious houses by depriving them of further grants of land, encouraged benefactions to non-monastic churches and augmented the importance of the secular clergy. The church had a monopoly on scholarship, and its doctrines were as yet undisputed. Revenues from its vast lands, unlimited gifts from rich donors and a huge income from pilgrims to shrines and holy relics all contributed to finance building on an unprecedented scale. The success of the monastic orders, which brought them immense wealth, meant that they were increasingly

Pl. 112 *The magnificent nave roof of c.1450 at Sherborne Abbey, Dorset, the earliest major example of fan vaulting.*

preoccupied with their lands and property. This naturally brought them into much closer contact with secular society and its corrupting influences. Inevitably they began to waver in their zeal for a life of simple, single-minded dedication, and even the reformed orders (see p. 50) accumulated riches and spent lavishly on new buildings. There was as yet no shortage of recruits to the established religious houses, and the new orders of friars (see below) expanded rapidly. Gradually during the fourteenth century the situation began to change, and by the late Middle Ages the authority of the church was increasingly challenged by a literate and critical laity with anti-clerical attitudes and a strong sense of national pride, which resented the dominance in English affairs of a foreign Pope. Dogmatic attitudes and corruption in the church both attracted public censure, and the obvious decline in the strict moral and physical observance of monastic ideals accelerated a decline in the numbers entering religious houses.

The early fifteenth century saw a final severing of ecclesiastical links with France, some of which went back to Norman times. Revenues paid by English monasteries to French mother-houses, even during periods when the two countries were at war, had long been a source of deep royal resentment. Those which had not become naturalized earlier were now either subordinated to English houses or suppressed and their income used to found educational establishments. Both Eton and Winchester were funded in this way.

Religious offices were in the king's gift and he used them to finance his secular government by granting appointments in the church to statesmen and civil servants. Since it was not possible for the same man to be both a leading churchman and an active courtier and politician, bishops who were also in important positions, as royal ministers, diplomats or top civil servants, habitually delegated the running of their dioceses to subordinates, such as suffragan or assistant bishops and vicars general. Church affairs had become inextricably involved with legal rights, vested interests and elaborate protocol, and these absentee bishops failed to control the many abuses which resulted from the lack of proper supervision. Their neglect of their duties attracted much criticism, though it sometimes had practical advantages. A bishop's visit, which involved his hosts in expensive hospitality and obligatory dues, could be a financial disaster for an impoverished area; in 1428 the archdeaconry of Richmond (N. Yorks) sent out a deputation to waylay their approaching bishop and implore him to accept a fee to stay away.

With the secularization of top religious appointments and the decline of monasticism, the impetus for the building of major churches slackened, and parish churches, whose naves were the responsibility of the

congregation rather than the incumbent (see below), attracted the bulk of patronage during the fifteenth century. Alterations continued to be made to existing great churches. Stone vaults frequently replaced wooden roofs, as at **Norwich**, where the timber ceiling of the chancel survived, out of sight above the late fifteenth-century rib vault, until 1955. Towers were frequently added, generally above the central crossing, as at **Durham** (Pl. 58) and **York**, or, if the piers were not strong enough to bear the extra weight, as free-standing structures like the great bell tower at **Magdalen College, Oxford** (Pl. 113). It was also fashionable to build new Lady chapels, for the cult of the Virgin Mary had a strong appeal for people

Pl. 113 *The free-standing bell tower at Magdalen College, Oxford, nearly 44 metres (144 feet) high, begun in 1492 and completed by c.1509, showing the upper stage with its paired three-light bell openings, decorative pierced parapet and eight tall pinnacles.*

who saw Christ as a terrible judge with power to condemn them to hellfire. It was believed that His mother could intercede for them to gain them His mercy for their sins; in an early fourteenth-century wall-painting of the Last Judgement at **Nassington** (Northants), the Virgin is actually depicted tipping St Michael's scales with her rosary. Lady chapels, and others, such as chantries and royal chapels dedicated to special uses, form an important category of late medieval buildings, while the remarkable number of smaller churches in parishes throughout the kingdom made a major contribution to the architecture of this period.

Developments in monasticism

The thirteenth century was a period of continuing expansion for the established monastic orders, though the number of religious houses did not multiply as fast as during the previous century. There are some surviving buildings, like **Abbey Dore** church (Herefordshire, Pl. 114) and **Lacock** Abbey (Wilts), which date entirely from the early Middle Ages, but much of the important work of this period took the form of rebuilding, for instance of the cloisters at **Norwich** (begun 1297), or additional structures, like the Chapel of the Nine Altars at **Fountains Abbey** and a new presbytery at **Rievaulx** (both in N. Yorks).

The monastic buildings

Although many of them were originally Norman foundations (see pp. 47–50), most of the early monastic sites in Britain underwent extensive later reconstruction, and the ruins we see now date mainly from the early medieval period. The gradual decline of the monasteries began c.1300; after this date they embarked on a long process of adapting and contracting their accommodation, and there was relatively little new building.

PLAN

The arrangement of the buildings which served the monastic churches was dictated by the rules of the different orders and by practical considerations. Although the layout was by no means standard, there is a recognizable pattern in their general disposition which was established in Norman times and continued to be adapted throughout the Middle Ages. An exception to this is the Carthusian plan, with its quite different arrangement of individual cells grouped round three sides of a cloister with the church on the fourth; a fourteenth-century example is still to be

Pl. 114 *The ambulatory of c.1200 in the late Norman monastic church at Abbey Dore, Herefordshire.*

seen at **Mount Grace** (N. Yorks). Most monasteries had communal living arrangements, and the four sides of their cloisters were formed by the church, the "dorter" or dormitory, the "frater" or refectory, and the "cellarer's range" or storehouse. The church was normally built on the highest ground, with the cloister on its south to get the sun. Where there were other factors to be considered, it is sometimes found on the north, for instance in towns like Chester, where noise or shortage of space had to be taken into account, or in places like Tintern, where the layout of the site was dictated by the position of the natural water supply. The

Pl. 115 *The surviving back wall of the west cloister walk at Fountains Abbey,*
North Yorkshire, built against the cellarer's range where the upper windows
lit the lay brothers' dormitory.

Pl. 116 *The thirteenth-century dorter block at Forde Abbey, Dorset, where the*
monks' dormitory with its narrow lancet windows was built above a
vaulted undercroft.

ideal stream flowed from west to east so that, without having to be diverted, it reached the kitchen first before flowing under the reredorter to flush out the monks' lavatories.

THE CLOISTERS

The name cloister means simply an enclosed space (Latin *claustrum*), but it has come to refer not just to the open ground in the middle of a monastic quadrangle but more particularly to the sheltered alleys which surround it (see Pls 115, 122, 126 and 128; Figs 7a and 7b). Some early cloisters were lean-to timber structures but from the twelfth century onwards their roofs were normally supported by open stone arcades resting on dwarf walls. At the back of the cloisters, there were stone benches along the walls for the monks to sit on, and wooden cubicles were built against the open arcades to provide studies where they could read or write. These are unlikely to have been in general use, at any rate in winter, before the introduction of glazing in the thirteenth century. There are signs at York that glass may have been held in place by wooden frames inside the stone arches, and at Salisbury one can still see grooves designed to take glazing in the stonework of the tracery. There are later stone cubicles in the south walk of the cloister at Gloucester, which was completed by 1412. However, the primary purpose of the cloister was to provide a covered walk for the monks and a means for them to get from one part of the buildings to another without having to go outside.

THE DORMITORY

The dorter, however, had direct access to the church (see Figs 7a and 7b). It was built at right angles to it, normally to the east, so that the monks who slept on the first floor, as at **Forde Abbey** (Dorset, Pl. 116), could come down a night staircase leading into the south transept, specially designed for use when attending the first services of the monastic day in the early hours of the morning. The survival of such stairs, for example at **Hexham** (Northumberland, early thirteenth-century, Pl. 118), gives a visible clue to the layout of vanished monastic buildings.

Beside the monks' dormitory was their reredorter or lavatory. Here there were rows of pierced seats, either along the walls or back to back, built directly above a channel of running water. A good supply of water and efficient drainage were a high priority in the planning of these sites, and the monks were pioneers in domestic hygiene. A "slype" or passageway running through the dorter building led to the "farmery" or infirmary that lay behind. This was where sick and old members of the community were cared for; beyond it, with perfect logic, lay the monks' cemetery.

Pl. 117 *The early thirteenth-century warming room, part of the surviving nunnery buildings at Lacock Abbey, Wiltshire; the bell-metal cauldron, made at Malines, Belgium, c.1500, was placed here in 1903.*

Pl. 118 *The early thirteenth-century night stairs in the south transept at Hexham Priory, Northumberland, which gave access from the church to the canons' dormitory.*

The ground floor of the dorter block housed the sacristy for the communion vessels and the "warming room" as at **Lacock** (Wilts, Pl. 117), where monks could retreat when they got too cold, to thaw out beside a blaze which burned continually during the winter months. At **Fountains Abbey** wood fires were lit in the two enormous fireplaces on the first day of November and kept in until Easter. A second staircase from the dormitory above, intended for use during the day, led to the side nearest the "chapter house", a large room or hall opening off the cloister which was used for the daily meetings of the community. This took its name from the fact that prayers and business were always accompanied by the reading of a chapter from the Rule of the order. A mid twelfth-century example still in use, as a chapel, can be seen at **Forde Abbey** (Dorset). The later development of more ambitious chapter houses, too high to fit into the space below the dormitory and polygonal so that they did not fit into a rectangular plan, led to these eventually becoming separate buildings (see p. 153). Sometimes one can still find the remains of the stone benches for the monks running round the walls, for example in the ruins of the twelfth-century chapter house of the Cluniac priory at **Castle Acre** (Norfolk) and at **Kirkstall Abbey** (W. Yorks, late twelfth- and early thirteenth-century, Pl. 119). At Fountains the central position at the east end, where the abbot had his chair, is marked by a break in the benching; and in front of the benches at **Byland** (N. Yorks) there is the socket for the lectern which stood in front of the abbot's seat. A chapter house might also be used to house the monastic library, and it was traditionally the burial place for the heads of religious houses.

THE REFECTORY

The frater was either on the ground floor or raised above an undercroft, much like any other medieval great hall (Pl. 120). It had a high table for the abbot and officers at one end and tables for the monks running down the room parallel with the long walls. Near the high table was the pulpit, forerunner of those still familiar in churches today. This was reached by a staircase in the thickness of the wall and it was used by one of the monks for reading aloud to the rest during meals. Examples survive in the monastic precincts at **Chester** Cathedral (*c.*1290) and at **Beaulieu** (Hants, *c.*1230), where the refectory of the thirteenth-century abbey later became the parish church. At the end of the room opposite the high table there was a buttery for serving the food, which could be handed in through a service hatch, an arrangement which can still be seen in the ruins of the thirteenth-century refectory at **Monk Bretton** Priory (S. Yorks). The kitchen was a separate room at the back, as was normal at

Pl. 119 *The late twelfth- to early thirteenth-century chapter house at Kirkstall Abbey, West Yorkshire, showing traces of the stone benches which ran along the walls.*

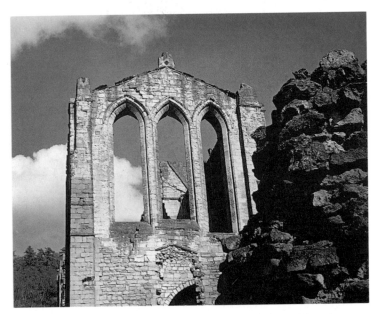

Pl. 120 *The imposing ruins of the high walls and large windows of the refectory at Fountains Abbey, North Yorkhire, built above an earlier substructure C.1225–40.*

this period, because of the risk of fire. A trough of water in the cloister beside the door to the refectory was the "lavatory" for the monks to wash their hands before meals. The deep stone ledge and trough which one can still see in the fourteenth-century cloisters at **Gloucester** (Pl. 122) originally supported a lead tank with spigots to dispense the water. At **Fountains** there were lead-lined basins under the surviving arcading next to the refectory door, and nearby, beside the day stair to the monks' dormitory, one can still see the arched recess on the outer wall of the warming room, which was the cupboard where their towels were kept.

THE STOREHOUSE

The cellarer was in charge of all aspects of catering for the whole monastery. His cellarer's range stored everything the community needed, whether home-produced or brought in from outside, as in the vast undercroft at **Fountains Abbey** (N. Yorks, Pl. 121). It lay on the western side of the cloister, between it and the outer court which separated the monastery from the outside world, so that provisions could be delivered and business conducted without disturbing the spiritual life of the inmates. This building also housed the monastic parlour (from French *parler*, to speak), where lay people could converse with the monks without entering the main buildings. Where there was no separate guest house, the upper floor was sometimes used for visitors. Later, when abbots and priors abandoned the original practice of sharing a dormitory with the rest of the monks, it might become the separate quarters of a head of house, though detached houses like secular manors were also built for this purpose, for instance at **Finchale** Priory (Co. Durham) in the thirteenth century. In a Cistercian monastery the cellarer's range provided accommodation for the lay brothers, with a refectory on the ground floor and a dormitory upstairs.

Pl. 121 *The vast vaulted undercroft of the cellarer's range at Fountains Abbey, North Yorkshire, which housed the lay brothers' refectory; the north end was originally partitioned for various purposes.*

THE OUTER PRECINCT

As their worldliness and wealth made the religious houses increasingly unpopular with the lay population, it became common for them to obtain licences for enclosure, so as to protect their entire precincts with encircling walls, as at **Norwich** (1276), **Lincoln** and **York** (1285), **Lichfield** (1299) and **Canterbury** (1309, Pl. 124). Although these were not military

Pl. 123 *The mid fourteenth-century Great Gate set in the precinct wall of the Benedictine abbey at Bury St Edmunds, Suffolk, begun after the monastery was sacked during riots in 1327.*

Pl. 122 *The monks' lavatory in the fan-vaulted north walk of the fourteenth-century cloisters at Gloucester Cathedral; lead tanks at the back of the deep stone shelf had spigots to dispense water into the shallow washing trough at the front.*

defences, they were strong enough to keep out civil disturbance, as at **Bury St Edmunds** (Suffolk, Pl. 123) after the riots of 1327 and at **Thornton Abbey** (Lincs) in 1382, shortly after the Peasants' Revolt (see p. 104). These enclosures established the separateness of the church's territory, which can still be felt wherever a cathedral close has survived up to the present day, for example at **Salisbury**.

The wall surrounding the monastic precinct had one or more gatehouses, each generally two or more storeys high. Two of the original four at **Bury St Edmunds** have survived, and two can still be seen at

Pl. 124 *Canterbury Cathedral seen from the east, showing part of the massive wall surrounding the medieval monastic precinct.*

Canterbury. The rooms inside them served various purposes and might, for instance, provide a chapel for local people or a prison for lay offenders, for whom the abbot, as feudal lord, was responsible. Near the gate would be the "almonry", where alms were distributed to the poor, and there might also be a school run by the monks. In or just outside the precinct there would be ponds to provide the fish which was a very important part of the monks' diet, and further off would be outlying farms or "granges" to supply the needs of the community.

MONASTIC BUILDINGS TODAY

Almost all the monastic buildings which have remained in use since the Middle Ages are churches, but they are few and often incomplete. When Henry VIII decided to sever all links with Rome after his

excommunication in 1533 (see pp. 308–309), he set about the dissolution of the monasteries, which were not national institutions but belonged to orders spread throughout Europe and still owed their allegiance to the Pope. By this time the riches and degenerate lifestyle of many of the religious houses had long been a source of resentment, and sweeping them away gave Henry a providential opportunity to be seen to be addressing this abuse, while at the same time consolidating his own position by taking over their enormous wealth and subsequently selling much of their extensive land to his supporters.

The swift suppression of about 800 monasteries in England and Wales led to destruction on a massive scale. Asset stripping was carried out with a ruthless disregard for the buildings' artistic importance. At **Roche Abbey** (S. Yorks), for instance, the choir stalls were chopped up to provide firewood for the furnace which melted down the lead removed from the roof. The churches were occasionally spared. Some were bought by local communities after the Dissolution and became parish churches. Those naves already used by lay people continued to serve their congregations as before, and some abbey churches were subsequently raised to cathedral status, as happened at Chester in 1541. The existing cathedrals retained their old function but with secular priests not bound by the rule of a monastic order. The monks' choirs were torn out of all abbey churches because they were no longer required, and most of the domestic quarters were either demolished or left to crumble away and be pillaged for building materials. Because of their isolated positions in wild and uninhabited areas, the Cistercian abbeys were less systematically destroyed. Fortunately enough good examples have survived in a ruined state to make it possible for us to reconstruct them in imagination. As well as churches, there are also monastic remains incorporated into numerous houses, many of which still bear the name of abbey or priory; and a few, such as **Anglesey** Abbey (Cambs), **Forde Abbey** (Dorset, Pl. 116), **Lacock** Abbey (Wilts, Pl. 117) and **Stoneleigh** Abbey (Warwicks), have preserved some parts of their medieval buildings almost intact.

In Ireland a late medieval flowering of monastic repair and building work was abruptly terminated by Henry VIII, when he declared himself "King of Ireland" in 1540 and closed down the monasteries so as to appropriate their lands. In spite of this, some religious houses continued covertly in use until they were finally destroyed a century later by Oliver Cromwell, who looted and burnt the remaining churches with ruthless thoroughness in 1649–50.

In Scotland, whose Reformation came later, destruction was less thorough and more gradual. The preaching of Calvin's disciple John Knox prompted mob violence against the abbeys, and when the

Parliament of 1560 rejected the authority of the Pope and abolished the Mass as the principal form of worship, it became official policy to "cleanse" monastic churches of all traces of their old patterns of worship. Where windows and roofs were stripped out, as at Perth in 1559, the damage became irretrievable but a number of churches and conventual buildings, such as those of **Arbroath** (Tayside) or **Melrose** (Borders), were adapted for new uses, and the royal palaces at both **Holyrood** (Edinburgh) and **Dunfermline** (Fife) grew out of religious houses.

WORLDLY PRESSURES

The designers of the monastic buildings of the twelfth and thirteenth centuries were well in advance of their times where comfort, and especially hygiene, were concerned. When life outside their walls was generally a great deal harsher, a life of comparative security with guaranteed, if spartan, meals and shelter must have exercised a strong attraction. The arrangement of buildings devised in Norman times (see p. 20) remained satisfactory while the orders maintained their original way of life. As they became richer during the thirteenth century, they were able to enlarge and beautify their churches. At **Westminster** Abbey, for example, the choir was rebuilt and a chapter house added (*c*.1245–50), and at **Binham** Priory (Norfolk, Pl. 125) a new west front (probably before 1244), with decorative blind arcading and a huge, dramatic window, was attached to the Norman church. By the early fourteenth century secular living standards had caught up and the domestic buildings of the early monks were beginning to seem unacceptably primitive. However, the religious houses no longer had adequate income or endowments to pay for the complete modernization which was needed. Instead they made piecemeal alterations or converted existing buildings to new uses, so as to provide greater comfort and privacy. This inevitably led to extra expense, not only for luxuries like glazed windows, panelling, beds and fires, but for the day-to-day cost of a more comfortable lifestyle. Monks now expected better food and more of it, pocket money and holidays with pay. They were also allowed more time for reading and meditation, which meant that more paid servants had to be employed to do the manual work. By the late Middle Ages, when their numbers steadily increased, the monks themselves accounted for only about one third of the monastic population.

Another growing expense for religious houses was the duty of hospitality, since the number of travellers who could demand board and lodging was constantly increasing and their contributions were often quite inadequate to meet costs. Some monasteries, especially those on popular pilgrimage routes, solved this problem by establishing inns for

Pl. 125 *The ruined thirteenth-century west front of the monastic church at Binham Priory, Norfolk, built before 1244; its bar tracery, perhaps the earliest in England, has been replaced with brick infill.*

the passing traffic (see pp. 272–274). Loss of monastic income was not just the result of a decline in popular support. Agricultural profits were greatly reduced after the Black Death (see p. 262), labour costs were much higher and the growing ambitions of heads of houses meant that they often appropriated the monastery's funds for their own personal use.

There were, however, ways for religious houses to make extra money. Nunneries, which still provided the favoured way of life for the spinster daughters of the nobility and gentry, were the only orders whose numbers did not fall. They were therefore in a position to raise substantial endowments in the form of dowries, presented by the families of the women who entered the convent. They increased this source of finance by accepting girls from the rising merchant class, who brought them large capital sums. They also made an income from running elementary schools for both boys and girls.

Any monastery with holy relics could expect handsome takings from pilgrims, and important shrines, such as that of St Thomas à Becket at Canterbury, were major moneyspinners. Another ruthless but effective way of securing extra revenues was the appropriation of churches, and this became increasingly common during the fourteenth century. A monastery would lay claim to a church solely in order to take over all its income from tithes and other dues, employing a low-paid vicar or curate to carry out the parish duties.

THE QUEST FOR COMFORT

Changes in education (see pp. 279–287) and living standards during the late medieval period are reflected in the alterations which the monasteries made to their buildings. As growing numbers of monks had had a university education, scholarship increased and the library became more important. It now had a special space to itself, rather than just a cupboard in the sacristy. To give the monks warm and private places for their studies, the old large apartments were divided up into single rooms with fireplaces, as on the ground floor of the cellarer's range at **Rievaulx** or in the dorter undercroft at **Byland** (both in N. Yorks). Dormitories and infirmaries were also divided by partitions into separate cubicles. The invention of tracery made it possible to put large windows into cloisters to protect their alleys from the weather without making them dark. This meant that they could also be used to provide more comfortable study cubicles (see p. 113) and extra rooms, as at **Canterbury**, where the south alley of the Great Cloister (Pl. 126), the place where the novices received instruction, was glazed in the late fifteenth century. At **Durham** there are traces of the cupboard for the novices' school books in the western alley, and at **Tintern** the bay which housed the abbot's seat and lectern marks the place where he read aloud to the monks before Compline, the last service of the monastic day.

Now that individuals had their own fires, the communal warming house lost its original function and either became a common room or was adapted for domestic or other purposes. When a meat diet became normal for all, and not just for the patients in the farmery (infirmary), a new meat kitchen large enough to cater for the whole community was often built next to the frater (refectory), as at **Jervaulx** (N. Yorks). Sometimes, as at **Lindisfarne** (Northumberland)

and **Muchelney** (Somerset, Pl. 127), the frater became the private great hall of the abbot or prior and everyone ate there. As time went on the domestic offices and stores frequently took over disused parts of monastic buildings, while a smaller establishment grew up which was centred on the living quarters of the head of house. There was an increasing tendency for him to enlarge his own establishment at the expense of the rest of the monastic complex. Extensive fifteenth-century rebuilding at the Great Hospital in Norwich, a charitable foundation dating from 1249, included a new cloister incorporating a Master's Lodging (Pl. 128) like a rich man's residence with a great hall, screens passage and service block. After the labour shortages caused by the Black Death brought an end to the system of having lay brothers in Cistercian houses, the abbot was able to extend his own lodgings into their dormitory. Some monasteries were even fragmented into several separate households, each with its own kitchen, as at **Ely** (Cambs), where there were four. The ultimate sign of the disintegration of the early plan came when the cloister, which had originally unified the whole complex, both architecturally and symbolically, fell into disuse, for instance at **Valle Crucis** (Clwyd), where the late medieval stairs to the abbot's quarters blocked off the eastern alley.

THE MENDICANT ORDERS

However, there were orders which did not succumb to worldly pressures. One was the Carthusian (see p. 50), which held uncompromisingly to its strict rule; others were the friars, whose outward-looking approach was in sharp contrast to the ideal of cloistered seclusion. These were mendicant orders (from Latin *mendicare*, to beg) who renounced all personal possessions and lived on the charity of the rest of the community. Instead of shutting themselves away from the world, they were dedicated to going out teaching and preaching among the people and setting them an example of the Christian life. The first to arrive in England, in 1224, were the Dominicans or black friars, founded in Italy by St Dominic. Three years later came the Franciscans or grey friars, followers of St Francis of Assisi, and later the Augustinian or Austin friars, the Carmelites or white friars, and others. Because of their missionary purpose they settled mainly in the towns in small, very simple buildings, often on restricted sites between existing buildings. By 1300 all four main orders were established in many of the more important towns, including London, Oxford, Cambridge, Canterbury and York. In time the friars too became corrupt and gradually lost credibility with the people. Few new friaries came into existence after the mid fourteenth century.

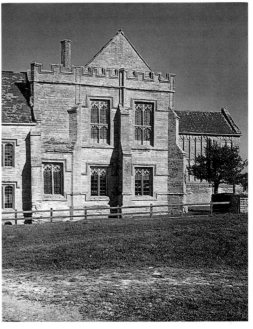

Pl. 126 *The Great Cloister at Canterbury Cathedral, rebuilt some time between 1390 and 1411 with decorative lierne vaults and 825 heraldic bosses.*

Pl. 127 *The early sixteenth-century Abbot's Lodging at Muchelney, Somerset, previously the refectory of the Benedictine abbey.*

FRIARIES

There are not many medieval friary buildings still to be seen and those which have survived are generally only fragmented remains. Friary churches do not seem to have continued in use as parish churches after the Dissolution of the Monasteries, as many abbey and priory churches did. This is presumably because they were smaller and more cheaply built than other monastic buildings and perhaps, too, because urban sites have always been more frequently redeveloped. Their names – Blackfriars, Greyfriars and Whitefriars – still record their presence in many towns. The friars were not able to make their houses conform to a standard pattern, because, being latecomers, they often had to fit their buildings into cramped sites near the city walls, making the best use they could of the limited space available. Their buildings were generally grouped round a cloister in the manner of the older orders, but they had to be more compact; so their cloister alleys were not built against the inner walls of the surrounding buildings but ran round inside the ground floor of the buildings themselves so as to form an internal corridor. This arrangement has survived at **Aylesford** (Kent), where the remaining west and south ranges of the mid-fifteenth-century cloister were incorporated into a house after the Reformation.

A friary church consisted of two independent but linked structures. The choir for the friars was a simple, unaisled building, though some were later enlarged to meet the demand for space for benefactors' tombs. The nave was a much bigger, aisled hall, designed to be almost as wide as it was long because a more or less square area was suited to the large congregations who came to hear and see the friars preaching their sermons. These two separate compartments were divided by a narrow covered cross-passageway, which might be the continuation of an entrance path or friary lane leading through into the cloister. This passage took the place of the crossing in a cruciform church and above it there might be a tower, like the rare fourteenth-century example, with an octagonal lantern and tall steeple, which survives at Greyfriars, **King's Lynn** (Norfolk). Sometimes, as at the Friary at **Little Walsingham** (also in Norfolk; founded in 1347), the church did not form one side of the cloister, as was normal, but was separated from it by a lane. The most complete surviving friary church is Blackfriars, **Norwich** (built 1440–70), now St Andrew's Hall. In spite of the collapse of its tower in 1712, extensive nineteenth-century restoration, and the inevitable effects of change of use, it retains much of its original form and appearance, especially in the chancel, which has been little altered.

The medieval builders

The medieval period was an age of faith, and much has been said about enthusiastic popular participation in raising the vast new cathedrals which went up throughout the country. That they were the products of genuine religious zeal is not in question, but, although they were

Pl. 128 *The mid fifteenth-century north walk of the cloisters of the Great Hospital incorporating the parish church of St Helen at Norwich; the building seen across the quadrangle was the Master's Lodging.*

Pl. 129 *The early Gothic choir of Canterbury Cathedral, rebuilt in 1175–9, looking towards the Trinity Chapel and Corona which were completed by 1184; the choir screens date from 1304–5 and the choir stalls are nineteenth-century.*

Pl. 130 *A pictorial boss of c.1400 in the Great Cloister at Canterbury records the death of St Thomas à Becket, who was murdered in the Cathedral in 1170.*

Pl. 131 *The early thirteenth-century nave of Wells Cathedral, showing the strong horizontal emphasis provided by the triforium arcades and the monumental scale of the strainer arches built c.1338–48 to strengthen the crossing tower.*

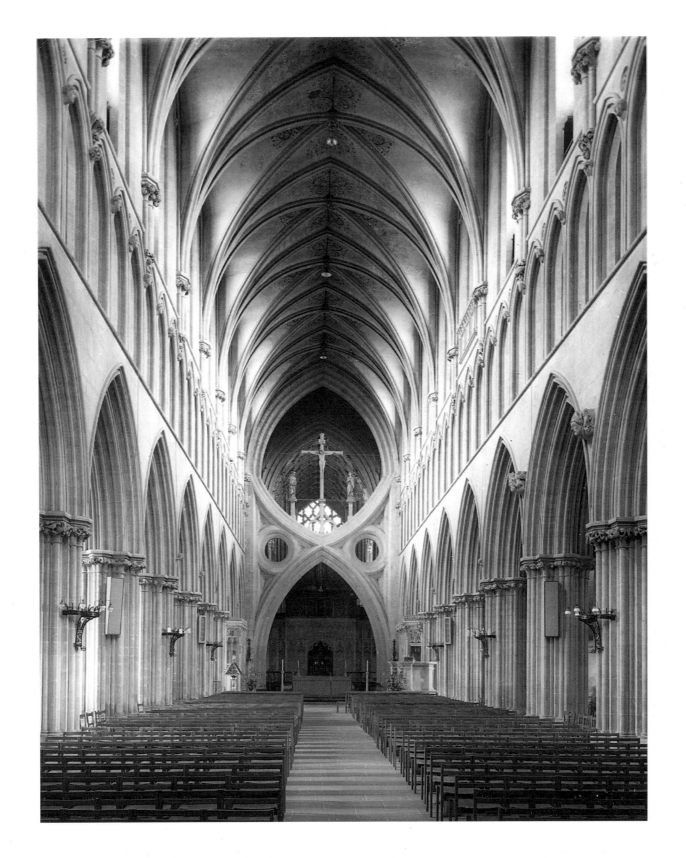

sometimes experimental, there was nothing amateur about their design or building technique. It is clear that this was fully appreciated by the patrons who commissioned them. They had a serious and informed interest in new ideas and developments, in Europe as well as at home, but they were not professional designers and evidently had great respect for the master builders who were actually responsible for the work. William Wynford, who designed numerous buildings for William of Wykeham, frequently dined with him at the high table at New College, Oxford, as did Henry Yevele, who collaborated with the royal carpenter Hugh Herland over the design of Westminster Hall.

Research has shown that such men were architects in all but name. Surviving records give details of many of them and throw light on their conditions of employment. They were engaged on much longer contracts and were far more highly paid than ordinary stonemasons, and because their services were in constant demand they could insist on very favourable terms. By the late thirteenth-century one man would be in charge of several new buildings at a time, not living on a site throughout construction but moving from one project to another to supervise work in progress. Although they undoubtedly had a practical knowledge of stonecraft, these master masons had also worked in the "tracing house"; contemporary drawings which have survived in France show that they provided plans, elevations, sections and details for the builders to work from. None of these has been found in England but in the chapter house vestibule at **York** and above the north porch at **Wells** there are surviving thirteenth-century "tracing floors" marked with complex webs of incised lines, where successive designers scratched full-scale details into a plaster surface. In the University Museum of Archaeology and Anthropology at **Cambridge** there is a chunk of stone, discovered in 1869 during the demolition of the early thirteenth-century chapel at St John's College, which has part of the design of the tracery of the medieval east window clearly scratched on to it.

The complex geometry of the buildings produced by the medieval designers bears witness to their ingenuity and sophistication. The masons on the job were also extremely skilled, and, unlike other craftsmen such as carpenters, plasterers or tilers, who could make a living anywhere, they had to go where the work was and could not expect to stay in the same place all the time. While joiners could prepare almost everything in their workshops and transport completed components to the site, stonemasons had to work mainly on the spot. Hence their strong sense of brotherhood, which lay behind the "masonic lodges" that grew up to protect their interests. Not only did they have to live away from home, sometimes as "impressed" or forced labour on royal building projects, but they also had to make common cause against unscrupulous employers and ward off the hostility of other local workers, in the areas where they were temporarily based.

French influence

Gothic architecture was well established in France, for instance at Chartres, before the end of the twelfth century. The new style first appeared at St-Denis, just outside Paris, in the large basilica church built in 1136–47 by the learned statesman Abbot Suger. Here one can still see his eastern ambulatory, chancel and crypt and his west front, with its pointed and rounded arches, blind arcades, gallery of statues and innovative central rose window. In Britain the Cistercian abbeys which had multiplied, especially in the north, had already introduced pointed arches and rib vaults, for example at **Fountains** (N. Yorks, perhaps as early as 1135–47), and **Kirkstall** (W. Yorks, completed 1175). Rib vaulting, which is often thought of as a French Gothic innovation, first appeared in Europe at Durham Cathedral c.1095 (see p. 61), and it seems likely that it spread from there via Normandy to Paris, where it was used with great skill at St-Denis.

In the south of England, the eastern arm of **Canterbury** Cathedral (Pl. 129), rebuilt after a fire in 1174, was extremely influential in introducing the French Gothic style into Britain. It was the work of a French master mason, William of Sens, and the stone for its construction was even imported from Caen in Normandy.

English characteristics

However, the design at Canterbury was required to take account of the earlier plan of the church and preserve as much as possible of the old choir, so that although it had a semicircular ambulatory, as opposed to the rectangular east end favoured in England, it retained English characteristics too. The main windows and lower arcading of the remodelled walls of the transepts, for example, have kept their Norman proportions even though they have mouldings and shafting in the new Gothic style. In 1179 William of Sens was so badly injured by a fall from the scaffolding that he returned to France, and his work was completed by William the Englishman, who built the crypt, the Trinity chapel and the circular vaulted and buttressed Corona, known as "Becket's Crown", which is its eastern culmination. The blend of up-to-date French Gothic and new features, such as the lavish use of shafts of black polished Purbeck marble, which was peculiar to England, produced a distinctive Anglo-Norman style which spread rapidly throughout the country. The

Pl. 132 *Blind tracery peopled with statues forms a sculpture screen covering the wide thirteenth-century façade of the west front of Wells Cathedral; the upper stages of the towers were added in the fourteenth and fifteenth centuries.*

architectural excitement of piers which rose higher without being thicker, tall pointed rather than lower round-headed arches, and a soaring rib vault instead of a flat wooden ceiling must have made a great impact on all who saw it, especially in view of the importance and prestige of Canterbury itself. Not only was it the great church of the archbishopric but it also attracted huge crowds of pilgrims to the immensely popular shrine of St Thomas à Becket (Pl. 130), murdered inside the cathedral in 1170 (see p. 46). His death in such a holy place, in defiance of the laws of sanctuary (see p. 74), had shocked the whole Christian world, and his cult was already well established by the time of his canonization in 1173. He was revered by all social classes, even kings, like Louis VII of France who came to pray for the saint's mediation in securing his son's recovery from illness in 1179.

Towards the end of the twelfth century, another version of native Gothic was developing in the west of England, where **Wells** Cathedral (Somerset, Pl. 131) clearly illustrates the horizontal emphasis which is a salient English characteristic. Whereas the French consistently accentuated the soaring height of the new pointed arches, the English used them in designs which stressed the enormous length of their great cathedrals and monastic churches. At Wells, the triforium arches form a solid band the full length of the nave (built 1190–1239), and the shafts supporting the vault do not rise from floor level, so as to connect the clustered columns of the nave with the space above it, but rest on corbels at clerestory level. The famous strainer arches, inserted in the fourteenth century in order to strengthen the crossing, add to the impression of length by letting the eye travel beyond them to the east window. The stress on the horizontal in English Gothic goes with a lively development of surface patterns. These are displayed to prominent effect on west fronts in the form of wide screens encrusted with sculpture, for instance at Wells (begun 1230, Pl. 132) or **Lichfield** (Staffs, begun 1280).

Three of the salient features of English medieval architecture can be most easily appreciated in cathedrals and monastic churches, because they were developed there on such a vast scale. These are tracery, composite columns, and rib vaulting, all very useful indicators for the dating of a Gothic building.

TRACERY

Tracery (see pp. 101–110) is not found only in windows and internal arcades; it also provided a standard type of decoration for wall surfaces both inside and outside a building. However, it is the windows that one is likely to notice first, since the builders of the greater medieval churches had ample opportunity to experiment with exceptionally large areas of glazing, as well as extensive screens of stone in their triforium arcades. Even simple lancets arranged in rows make a dramatic impression when they are used on a grand scale, as on the west front of **Ripon** Cathedral (Pl. 133) or in the "Five Sisters" window at **York** (Pl. 135), and glass gradually came to be used not just to fill large areas but for entire walls, as in the mid-thirteenth century chapter houses at **Westminster** Abbey (Pl. 137) and **Salisbury** and **Lincoln** cathedrals. The early development of plate tracery can be seen in the triforium of **Salisbury** Cathedral, although its windows are of the lancet type. It was easier to experiment with extensive screens of carved stone in internal arcades than in windows because no glazing was involved. Arches with trefoil heads often appeared in wall arcading by the early thirteenth century but

Pl. 133 *The lancet windows of the Early English style used to dramatic effect on the west front of Ripon Cathedral c.1220–50.*

Pl. 134 *Narrow lancets and plate tracery used in the north transept at Lincoln Cathedral, where the early thirteenth-century rose window is known as the "Dean's Eye".*

house there inspired many direct imitations, as at **Salisbury** and **Wells**.

Window design had to take into account the problems involved in supporting extremely heavy sheets of leaded-up glass. This meant that the area to be glazed had to be subdivided into quite small panels, using vertical stone mullions and transoms or crossbars, while the leads were secured by wires to a series of horizontal iron saddlebars which helped to distribute and support the weight. Oppor-tunities for decorative variety occurred mainly at the tops of the windows, where intersecting geometrical curves, found for instance in the early thirteenth-century chapter house at **Lincoln**, gave way to more flowing and undulating lines, as seen in the late fourteenth-century Lady chapel at **Ely** (Pl. 138), and finally to a grid pattern, for example in the late fifteenth-century St George's Chapel at **Windsor** (Pl. 139).

The Black Death took a heavy toll of stonemasons, perhaps because they were concentrated in the towns, where the plague spread most rapidly. After the mid fourteenth century, joinery seems to have developed more vigorously and may even have had an influence on stonework, which came increasingly to resemble wooden panelling, covering large areas with repetitive motifs. This may have been largely due to the need for mass-production methods at a time when labour was short and building was booming. In the case of church windows, tracery was now being designed not just for its own aesthetic effect but also as a supporting framework for lively, vigorous and colourful stained glass.

COMPOSITE COLUMNS

Composite piers and columns seem to have developed as a result of the wish to provide a clear visual connection between elaborately moulded triforium arcades and rib-vaulted roofs and the pillars which supported their weight at ground level. A single rectangular pier or cylindrical column would have sufficed to bear the loads involved, but several shafts of a vault rising from a single capital look very awkward, as can be seen in the choir at **Canterbury** (Pl. 129), where the early Gothic vault rests on Norman piers. Clusters of shafts, each of which could be seen to carry the weight of an individual moulding or rib, must have been adopted because they were aesthetically satisfying. A circular pillar with four shafts clustered evenly round it (see Pl. 193) became the commonest type of column during the Middle Ages, its design varying to suit changing styles. Keel mouldings (see Pl. 350) on the shafts, for instance, as at **Lichfield**, are characteristic of the thirteenth century, whereas octagonal capitals, as found at **Winchester** (Pl. 144), are a sign of fourteenth-century date. In greater churches clustered columns often became very elaborate indeed,

they were not generally used in windows for another fifty years. Another new window shape took the form of a triangle with convex sides, its tracery made up of a pattern of circles, as in the clerestory at **Lichfield** (Pl. 136). Traceried circular or "rose" windows were often used in the gable ends of transepts, as at **Lincoln** (*c.*1220, Pl. 134), and Old St Paul's (destroyed by the Fire of London in 1666) had an eastern rose window; but western rose windows are not found in cathedrals in England as they are in France. Henry III's reconstructed **Westminster** Abbey (mid thirteenth-century) was perhaps the first building in Britain where bar tracery appeared on a grand scale, and its use in the chapter

Pl. 135 *The "Five Sisters" window in the north transept of York Minster, composed of tall lancets filled with important mid thirteenth-century grisaille glass;*
the wooden rib vault of c.1400 was rebuilt in the twentieth century.

Pl. 136 *The geometrical tracery in the mid thirteenth-century nave of Lichfield Cathedral, where each clerestory*
window contains three trefoils within a curved triangle.

Pl. 137 *The huge mid thirteenth-century windows of the octagonal chapter house at Westminster Abbey, one of the earliest examples of bar tracery used on a grand scale; the seated figure of Christ in a quatrefoiled circle dates from the nineteenth century, when the central column and vault were also rebuilt.*

Pl. 138 *Tracery in the Decorated style used in the early fourteenth-century Lady chapel at Ely Cathedral, where extensive areas of glass fill the walls above the ogee-arched canopies of the stone seats lining the walls; the nodding or forward-curving arch shown here is used to accentuate the canopies between the windows.*

Pl. 139 *The assertive grid pattern of the Perpendicular tracery in the west window of St George's Chapel, Windsor, completed with its magnificent lierne vault in the early sixteenth century.*

Pl. 140 *The elegant column supporting the vault of the chapter house at Salisbury Cathedral, begun in 1279, showing the light bands of moulded stone which attach its eight slender shafts to the main pillar; the bar tracery in the windows follows the pattern introduced at Westminster Abbey thirty years earlier.*

Pl. 141 *The thirteenth-century nave of Salisbury Cathedral seen from the west end, showing the horizonal emphasis provided by the string courses and the extensive use of dark Purbeck marble shafts to articulate the arcades.*

the four shafts multiplying to eight at **Lincoln**, sixteen at **Exeter** (Pl. 142) and twenty-four at **Wells.** The earliest shafts, which were separate from their main pillar, were attached only by light bands of moulded stonework, for instance on the early thirteenth-century west front of **Peterborough** Cathedral and in the chapter house at **Salisbury** (*c.*1279–*c.*1300, Pl. 140). Black Purbeck marble, first introduced in the choir at Canterbury in the late twelfth century, often provided a colour contrast, as can be seen at **Salisbury** (Pl. 141) and **Lincoln.** This use of black or grey marble is a particularly English feature, seldom found in

French Gothic. During the mid-Gothic period the separate shafts of columns are attached together like a firm, rather square bundle (see Pl. 142), while by the late Middle Ages the individual members are no longer very prominent but form part of a single composite pier with convex as well as concave mouldings (see Pl. 174).

Pl. 142 *Detail of one of the clustered columns with sixteen shafts in the fourteenth-century nave of Exeter Cathedral with, above it, a carved corbel showing the figure of a tumbler upside down and below him a minstrel with a dog looking out between his feet.*

Pl. 143 *The clustered columns of the nave arcade at Canterbury Cathedral, built between 1391 and 1405, which appear to dissolve into a continuous wall of slender vertical shafts.*

Pl. 144 *The nave of Winchester Cathedral as remodelled in the second half of the fourteenth century, when earlier drum piers were cut back to produce composite columns, which have both vertical mouldings and shafts with bases raised above seating level.*

The pillars of an arcade were almost invariably as thick as the wall they had to support, but throughout the Middle Ages there were attempts to make them appear slimmer and lighter when viewed as a row from one end to the other, for instance in the nave at **Canterbury** (1391–1405, Pl. 143), where they dissolve into a continuous wall of slender vertical shafts. Even when it is effectively just part of one single composition, each

separate shaft has its own moulded base and moulded or carved capital. Many thirteenth-century bases have a trough-like groove round the top which is known as a "water hollow" because it could theoretically hold water, though obviously it never did. Deeply cut mouldings are characteristic of this period, whereas the popularity of the ogee curve in the later Middle Ages produced shallower and less subtle effects. Towards the end of the medieval period bases were sometimes raised to the level of the plinths used on other walls in the same building, perhaps so that they could be seen above the benches and pews which were beginning to be installed. These higher bases can be seen, for instance, at **Winchester** (Pl. 144), where the Norman nave was completely remodelled during the second half of the fourteenth century.

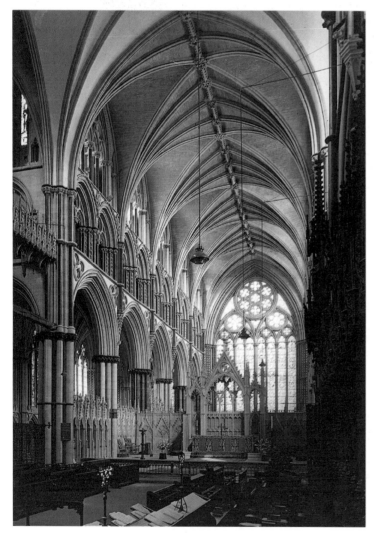

Pl. 145 *A longitudinal ridge rib combined with diagonal ribs and tiercerons in the mid thirteenth-century vault of the Angel Choir at Lincoln Cathedral, where the intersections are decorated with a series of magnificent carved bosses; the stone screen behind the altar is eighteenth-century.*

Pl. 146 *The decorative lierne vault in the nave of Tewkesbury Abbey, which replaced the Norman wooden roof c.1340.*

RIB VAULTS

Rib vaults had been constructed at **Durham** in the late eleventh century (see pp. 60–61), but their development belongs to the medieval period. At first there were transverse and diagonal ribs which followed the structural shape of the vault itself, dividing it into logical units so that it could be constructed one section at a time (see Fig. 11). Then a longitudinal ridge rib was introduced which ran the full length of the vault (Pls 61 and 145). "Tierceron" (from French *tiers*, third) or subsidiary ribs are first found at **Lincoln** in the "crazy" vault of St Hugh's Choir (*c.*1200), so called because of its odd, asymmetrical zig-zag effect, and they are used

to bold effect in the Angel Choir (Pl. 145) of 1256–80. A tierceron joined one of the main springing points of a vault to a point along the length of one of the ridge ribs (see Fig. 11). The inclusion of these extra ribs made a more decorative vault and one which could be built in smaller sections. Further subdivisions became possible, from the early fourteenth

Pl. 148 *One of a series of fourteenth-century bosses in the south cloister walk at Norwich Cathedral illustrating subjects from the Apocalypse described in the Revelation of St John the Divine; here the Angel sounds the Second Trumpet and a mountain of fire is cast into the sea, causing the water behind him to surge upwards and swamp the drowning people on the left, while those in the other boat are shown making gestures of despair.*

Pl. 147 *A boss in the late fourteenth- and early fifteenth-century cloisters at Canterbury Cathedral, showing a Green Man with leaves sprouting from his face.*

century onwards, with the introduction of "liernes" (from French *lier*, to tie) which are used, for example, in the nave vault at **Tewkesbury** (*c*.1340, Pl. 146). These do not touch any of the main springing points but run between one rib and another, giving yet greater opportunity for patterns like the stellar vault in the choir at **Ely** (1322–36), the highly influential prototype for this type of work.

BOSSES

By this time the long ridge ribs of the early Middle Ages were disappearing and instead of a single line of bosses (or carved projecting keystones) where the main ribs intersect, there are frequently bosses at the intersections of the subsidiary ribs as well. These are generally decorated with foliage, stylized during the thirteenth century and becoming more naturalistic from the fourteenth century onwards. They were frequently decorated with carvings of pagan origin, for instance at Christ Church Cathedral, **Oxford**, or in the cloisters at **Canterbury** (Pl. 147), where we find the Green Man, a man's face entwined with foliage growing from his head or even out of his mouth, which had its origins in the Celtic worship of the human head. This "Jack o' the Green" was an extremely popular subject in carved ornament of the fourteenth and fifteenth centuries and was evidently connected with May Day ceremonies associated with tree worship and fertility rites. Bosses also portray figures and an endless variety of biblical and apocryphal scenes, such as the Devil swallowing Judas Iscariot on a late fifteenth-century wooden boss, now displayed on the west wall of the nave of **Southwark** Cathedral, where it is clearly visible from ground level. In the cloisters at **Norwich** (late thirteenth – mid fifteenth-century) there is a superb series of nearly four hundred sculptured bosses, depicting scenes from the Apocalypse (Pl. 148), the life of the Virgin, the life of Christ and the life of St Thomas à Becket.

DECORATIVE ELABORATION

Ribs themselves became progressively more elaborately moulded and sometimes they were also made more decorative by the use of cusping (Pl. 151), as found in the early fourteenth-century choir at **Bristol**, an idea which seems to have originated at **Tewkesbury** and **Wells**. Another Bristol innovation was "flying" or detached ribs. These appear in the antechapel to the Berkeley Chapel and form the skeleton of a vault with no infilling of its cells, so that one sees straight through it to a flat stone ceiling above. This unusual arrangement can also be seen in the passage through the pulpitum at both **Lincoln** and **Southwell**. A further variation on the idea of ribs detached from a vault is found in the use of flying ribs

in the choir aisles at **Bristol** (Pl. 149). Here the spandrels beneath the bridging bars, which transfer the weight of the chancel roof on to the outer walls of the building, are not solid but filled with tracery, leaving a "mouchette" or curved dagger-shaped opening. An unique use of tracery is found at St Mary's Church, **Warwick** (late fourteenth-century), where flying ribs rising from the walls below a flattish tierceron vault create a subsidiary web of stone, with angles filled with cusped tracery or knobs where the ribs intersect.

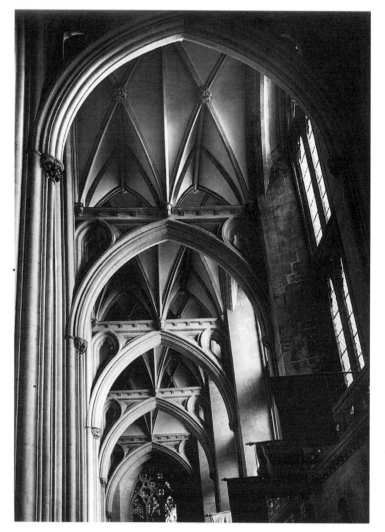

Pl. 149 *The early fourteenth-century choir aisle vaults at Bristol Cathedral, showing the use of bridging bars and spandrels with "mouchette" openings on either side.*

Fan vaulting

The medieval delight in pattern reached its peak with the invention of fan vaulting (Pls 109, 112, 122 and 150, Fig. 11), where huge cone shapes seem to rise up to support intermediate areas of flat ceiling, as in the south walk of the late fourteenth-century cloister at **Gloucester**. By the end of the fifteenth century this highly ornate technique, decorative rather than practical, had been elaborated to the point where it was possible to produce the spectacular encrusted vaults of King's College Chapel, **Cambridge** (Pl. 329), and Henry VII's Chapel at **Westminster** Abbey (Pl. 150). At King's there are central bosses at the intersection of the ridge ribs, but at Westminster these have been elongated into pendants, and further huge cone-shaped pendants are supported by the transverse ribs, which rise on each side to vanish above the ceiling and are in turn tied to the walls by subsidiary arches out of sight. It is clear from its extraordinary complexity that this amazing vault was designed purely for a deliberate dramatic effect.

Pl. 150 *The spectacular early sixteenth-century fan vault of King Henry VII's Chapel at Westminster Abbey with its ornate cone-shaped pendants.*

Pl. 151 *The late fourteenth-century Wykeham Chantry in the nave of Winchester Cathedral, showing its unglazed window openings, cusped lierne vault and on the left the upper tier of its sculptured reredos.*

NICHES

A niche with a canopy above it is one of the commonest features of medieval church architecture and was used in a variety of ways, from providing settings for figures of saints or holy men to framing piscinas, sedilia or the individual seats in choir stalls. Variations on the niche include recessed tombs and Easter sepulchres, while fonts often have elaborate canopies which imply a similar architectural enclosure. Figures in stained glass windows stand in serried ranks, each one depicted in its own niche beneath its separate canopy. The whole of a church building was seen as enclosing a space representing God's heavenly kingdom, and every niche inside it, however small, was a microcosm of Heaven, illustrating Christ's reassurance to his disciples (St John xiv:2) that "In my Father's house are many mansions".

Cathedrals and abbey churches

As during the Norman period there was little difference in design between cathedrals and the greater abbey and priory churches of the religious orders, since both were used in the same way, and some even combined both functions. In abbey or priory churches, however, one may occasionally notice monastic features which are missing in secular foundations. These are more often in the associated buildings than in the church itself, and the exceptionally well-preserved early thirteenth-century night stair which connected the church to the monks' dormitory at **Hexham** (Northumberland) is a rare survival. The proliferation of tombs and chapels in the naves of monastic churches, which did not have to provide space for lay congregations, have mostly been cleared away, though the Wykeham Chantry Chapel (1366–1404, Pl. 151) survives in the nave at **Winchester.** However, in the crowded press of royal tombs round the shrine of Edward the Confessor in Westminster Abbey one can still get some idea of the effect of the multiplication of chantries and chapels which took place throughout the medieval period. Much of the partitioning which this involved survived until comparatively recent times, for instance at **Ely,** where the rows of chapels along the eastern aisles of both north and south transepts, divided off from the main spaces by wooden screens, were not destroyed until the nineteenth century.

During the Middle Ages there were nine monastic cathedrals, including Canterbury and Ely, and nine secular, such as Lincoln, Salisbury and Wells. The monastic pattern was so well established that throughout the medieval period secular cathedrals continued to be built with a surrounding precinct or close, and some even had cloisters. **Salisbury** Cathedral has the largest in the country, though it consists merely of a covered walk without any doors leading off it, since there were no monastic buildings for it to serve.

Plan

The typical plan of a great church of the Middle Ages is best seen at **Salisbury** (Pls 152–155; Fig. 9), since an entirely new cathedral, begun in 1220 and consecrated in 1258, was built here to replace the Norman cathedral at Old Sarum nearby. Being on a completely new site, the plan did not have to take account of any earlier building, and because the church was all built at one time, we are able to appreciate that variations in architectural treatment were not due to separate phases of construction but were deliberately used to differentiate between one part of the building and another and to draw attention to its liturgical purpose. In the eastern limb of the building, for example, the arcade piers are varied so as to mark the change from the choir to the presbytery, whereas in the nave they are all the same. Salisbury shows very clearly that by the thirteenth century changes in use had affected the planning of larger medieval churches, especially of their eastern ends. There is now room for the whole of the choir inside a much longer eastern arm of the building; so the pulpitum has been moved into the eastern arch of the crossing, leaving the transepts open to the lay congregation in the nave. A second pair of shorter transepts has been built at the eastern end of the new choir, to accommodate more altars and perhaps also to reproduce the old arrangement of the choir beneath the crossing. There is further elongation of the plan in the presbytery. The high altar is now two bays west of the east wall, and the Lady chapel extends a further two bays beyond that. There is still a central tower over the crossing but a further pair of smaller towers has been added at the western end of the building, where they extend the façade to make it wider than the body of the nave behind it. The west front has three doorways, but, presumably because opening them would have made the building draughty, they were used only occasionally, for ceremonial purposes, and the main entrance was at the side of the building, through the two-storeyed north porch. To the south of the church are the cloister (completed c.1300) and chapter house (begun c.1279), and there is a later thirteenth-century sacristy and former muniment room leading out of the south-east transept. Apart from these additions the plan is an immensely long and deliberately symmetrical composition, almost equally divided into the priests' eastern part and the public nave and transepts. The openness we see today gives a false idea of the original arrangement, where the space inside the church was broken

Pl. 152 *The late thirteenth-century cloisters at Salisbury, looking towards the west end of the Cathedral; since this was not a monastic foundation, the only building opening off this covered walk is the early fourteenth-century chapter house.*

Pl. 153 *View from the north-east of the spacious Cathedral Close at Salisbury, which has surviving fourteenth-century walls and gates; clergy and choristers have been housed here since the thirteenth century.*

up into numerous separate compartments. The pulpitum closed off the choir, screens divided the nave from its aisles and each of the numerous altars throughout the church was enclosed within its own partitions.

A great deal of alteration and rebuilding took place during the early Middle Ages so as to adapt many of the existing Norman cathedrals and monastic churches to the new pattern dictated by the needs of increasing numbers of priests and the demands of benefactors. The congregation was not expected to participate or even to see or hear clearly, and since the services were in Latin, they would in any case have been incomprehensible to most ordinary people.

Exterior

The outside of a medieval church expresses the structure behind the internal elevations, and, with the progressive development of Gothic architecture, buttresses (see Fig. 3) come to play an increasingly important part. The development of Gothic vaults made it necessary to thicken the shallow pilasters of Norman times, so that they widened towards the

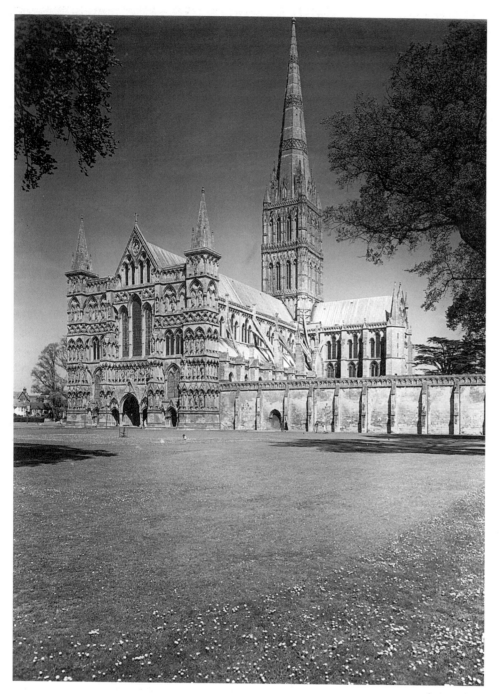

Pl. 154 *The unified design of Salisbury Cathedral seen from the south-west; built between 1220 and* C.1266, *it incorporated no earlier work, but the upper stage of the tower with its slender spire was not begun until* 1334.

Pl. 155 *The lofty nave of Salisbury Cathedral, roofed in* C.1266, *looking towards the crossing and presbytery; the simple rib vault adds to the impression of height while the assertive horizontal band of the triforium emphasises its great length.*

base in order to counteract the extra weight and thrust from above. Gothic buttresses often have several "set-offs" or outward slopes, where their thickness increases, and they were sometimes topped with little tiled half-gables. These were later superseded by pinnacles, which weighted the buttresses and could be carved to form very decorative features. As buildings and especially stone vaults rose higher, buttresses became more and more elaborate. Higher walls on wider buildings needed flying buttresses, which were arched to carry the thrust from an inner wall over an aisle and on to the buttresses supporting its outer wall. At **Westminster** Abbey the nave (fourteenth-century) has no fewer than three tiers of flyers rising from the outer piers to support the upper walls, while the full decorative potential of flying buttresses reached its climax with Henry VII's richly ornate chapel (begun 1503, Pl. 156). By the fifteenth century the medieval love of pattern on every available wall surface expressed itself in a lavish use of blind arcading and traceried panels, which may appear on any available flat area, however limited, for example on battlements and buttresses.

Pl. 156 *The richly decorated flying buttresses supporting the ornate fan vault above King Henry VII's Chapel at Westminster Abbey, begun in 1503.*

THE WEST FRONT

Only on the west or public front facing the outer world (see p. 52) was there an attempt to design an architectural set-piece which was more than just the back of the inside walls. Here there was a deliberate wish to make the building appear larger than it really was by constructing a broader screen of masonry across this end of the church. Impressive western façades wider than the nave and aisles behind them had already been built in Norman times, and they became common during the medieval period, when they were used to emphasize the size and grandeur of cathedrals and abbey churches. Where contemporary French west fronts combine large portals with elaborate sculpture and tall towers to accentuate their height, in England the emphasis is on width, with low doorways almost lost in the grandeur of the overall design and corner towers or turrets contributing more to breadth than altitude. The early thirteenth-century west front at **Wells,** which had its towers extended upwards in the late fourteenth and early fifteenth centuries, originally resembled a huge outdoor reredos peopled with nearly 400 statues in traceried niches, its small doorways tucked unobtrusively into the plinth. **Salisbury**'s effect (Pl. 154) is rather similar, though its central portal and tall west window cut more assertively across the horizontal arcading. The rows of niches provided by tier upon tier of blank arcading made this kind of western façade a perfect showcase for the sculptured figures of prophets, saints and kings. Another early

thirteenth-century western façade, at **Peterborough** (Pl. 157), features three vast portals the full height of the walls, with three gables above them, which, if one ignores the low central porch added in the fourteenth century, entirely dominate the composition. The proportions of the whole are not arbitrary but meticulously worked out. The elevation up to the level of the stringcourse above the arches is a rectangle twice as long as it is high (a double square), which is also found at **Wells** (Pl. 132). It has also been argued that the arches and buttressing towers relate to each other in complex mathematical proportions corresponding to classical musical consonances of mystical significance.

Recent conservation work has revealed substantial traces of paint on the west front at **Wells** (Pl. 100) These show that a west front of this kind was first whitewashed and lined out in red to indicate ashlar blocks, then its statues and their architectural settings were brightly coloured and richly gilded in a way which to modern eyes, accustomed to admiring worn and mellow stone, would probably seem thoroughly garish. Yet bright pigments were as much a part of the conspicuous display of these façades as their sculptured ornament and surface patterning.

DOORWAYS

Early Gothic doors, with their pointed arches, were wider and higher than Norman doorways, but they were still set inside deep recesses made up of stepped shafts (see pp. 52–53) and composite arches with carved

Pl. 157 *The three tall gabled portals which dominate the design of the early thirteenth-century west front of Peterborough Cathedral; the low central porch is a fourteenth-century addition.*

PORCHES

From the late thirteenth century onwards it became normal for every church to have a porch, which served many liturgical and legal purposes (see pp. 161–165), besides sheltering the entrance from the weather. Greater churches often had a two-storeyed porch; the upper room could be used as a courtroom, a school or an office for financial transactions. Late medieval monastic porches often developed into towers so as to emphasize the importance of the entrance and provide a useful space for secular business outside the monks' precinct. The splendid late fifteenth-century porch at **Cirencester** (Pl. 158) is a large three-storeyed building with a fan-vaulted ground floor, two-tier oriel windows, panelled stonework on its walls and buttresses and ornate openwork battlements. Its administrative function continued when it became the town hall after the Dissolution of the Monasteries (see p. 119), but it was handed back to the church in the eighteenth century.

TOWERS

As in Norman times, it was usual to have a central tower, whose presence often indicates rebuilding on an earlier plan, but during the medieval period it generally rose higher to provide more space for bells. The extra weight this placed on the crossing piers inevitably led to structural problems, especially when, as often happened, earlier towers were extended upwards. Their foundations were frequently inadequate for the purpose, and at **Wells**, for example, the addition of a tall belfry stage caused the whole tower to lean westwards almost immediately after completion. The bold strainer arches which were used to shore it up were designed for deliberate dramatic effect, and comparable screens to strengthen the crossing arches are a common feature of greater medieval churches elsewhere. At **Salisbury** scissor-shaped arches were used to reinforce the piers of the eastern transepts, while the arches of the central crossing were prevented from collapsing inwards by broad girders of pierced stonework of a type also used at **Canterbury**. The octagonal timber lantern which crowns the crossing at **Ely** (Pl. 159) replaced the collapsed Norman tower (see p. 55) and is another example of felicitous experiment, this time with the common medieval design problem of how to treat the transition when raising an octagon above a square crossing.

Salisbury Cathedral's magnificent mid fourteenth-century spire (Pl. 154) rises above its tall tower to a height of 404 feet (147m). It has remained standing for over 650 years and although its stonework had reached a state of advanced and alarming decay by the time major restoration was carried out in 1986–95, the original timber framework

decoration and deep grooves cut between their mouldings to give strong contrast between light and shade. During the later Middle Ages, when it became usual to have an entrance porch (see below), outer doorways needed less recession because they no longer had to supply protection from the weather. In Perpendicular Gothic buildings, a four-centred archway was often used for an entrance with only a square-cornered dripstone or label mould above it to protect it from rain running down the walls. There is still a surprising number of medieval doors in use. Some are quite plain, but many are ornamented with fine decorative metalwork or rich carving (see pp. 192–196).

Pl. 158 *The grand three-storeyed late fifteenth-century porch of the large parish church of St John the Baptist at Cirencester, Gloucestershire.*

restorations of the cathedral, though the central spire was rebuilt twice, first in the seventeenth and again in the eighteenth century. They serve to remind us of the many others which have vanished, for instance at **Lincoln**, whose central spire, said to have been 160m (524 feet) tall, came down in a gale in 1548, while those on its western towers survived until the early nineteenth century.

A pair of western towers or turrets was common in the Middle Ages, even where the central tower already housed a belfry. As in the earlier period (see pp. 53–55), the reason for this was partly practical but mainly aesthetic. Sometimes western towers were built on the continental pattern, as at **York** and **Beverley** (Pl. 160), where they are high and massive enough to form part of a tall and impressive composition. Elsewhere they were used to emphasize the width of a characteristically English screen façade, as at **Salisbury**, which has corner turrets, or **Wells**, whose broad squat towers are widened yet further by projecting angle buttresses. The decorative possibilities of towers were fully appreciated and their wall surfaces were frequently richly patterned with contemporary Gothic motifs.

Interior

THE EAST END

By the thirteenth century the choir was being moved into an elongated eastern limb (see p. 153); so the monks' and priests' part of the church was divided off at what we now call the chancel arch, which meant that the crossing and transepts no longer formed part of the east end. As during the Norman period, the elevations of the walls, like those in the nave and transepts, were divided horizontally into a main arcade, a triforium and a clerestory stage, and their development followed the same pattern (see p. 156). The positioning of subsidiary eastern transepts (see p. 142) varied. They might, as at **Salisbury**, divide the choir from the presbytery, an idea probably derived from Cluny. Alternatively they might be either side of the high altar, as at **York**, while at **Durham** they are at the end of the building, where they follow the arrangement at **Fountains Abbey** (N. Yorks) and are incorporated into the Chapel of the Nine Altars along its eastern wall. The retrochoir or space to the east of the main altar was either built to the full height of the building, as at **Ely** and **Beverley**, or, as at **Winchester** and **Salisbury**, took the form of a lower vaulted hall beyond the tall end wall with its big east window.

During the later Middle Ages the east end of a great church tended to be a large open architectural space, quite different from its Norman counterpart with ambulatory and projecting chapels, as at Norwich. An uncluttered view of the east wall was therefore possible and provided the perfect

inside the spire and the lattice of wrought-iron bars which strengthened the tower above the crossing vault were still in good condition. A medieval tower would generally have been finished with a pitched timber roof. This type of immensely tall spire was not very common in Britain but belongs to the Gothic tradition in France, with its emphasis on soaring height. It is often likened to a finger pointing upwards towards Heaven, but its builders probably saw it simply as a spectacular and daring architectural feat, intended to amaze and impress, emphasizing the building's importance and making it a landmark for miles around. Tall spires were extremely vulnerable, and few are still in existence. **Lichfield** is now unique in retaining three, which have survived numerous

Pl. 159 *The fourteenth-century octagonal timber lantern above the crossing at Ely, built to replace the Norman tower which collapsed in 1322; the choir stalls date from* c.1341–2 *but the screen is nineteenth-century.*

Pl. 160 *View from the south of Beverley Minster, East Riding of Yorkshire, begun* c.1230, *showing, on the left, the fifteenth-century west front with its prominent twin towers, one concealed by the other.*

setting for huge windows filled with colourful pictorial glass, for example at **Gloucester**. The floor on the other hand was not left clear but was crowded with chapels and furnishings, rather like the present retrochoir at **Winchester** (Pls 161 and 163). Subsidiary chapels with their own altars proliferated in response to the requirements of the growing number of monks who were becoming priests and needed altars where they could say Masses daily. The popularity of the cult of the Virgin Mary (see pp. 111–112) also led to the provision of numerous extra chapels dedicated to her.

The eastern end of the building, as the most sacred part of the church, accommodated ever-increasing numbers of tombs and shrines with holy relics (see pp. 151–153). It has even been suggested that ornate medieval east ends should in themselves be seen as vast scaled-up reliquaries, for their niches, figures, gables and pinnacles are all found in miniature on metalwork too. We can still appreciate some of their effect today at the Sainte Chapelle in Paris, a building which directly inspired the setting of Edward the Confessor's shrine at Westminster. With its casket form and brilliant stained glass it still resembles a huge and splendid jewelled box.

The presbytery

The reasons for the enlarged presbytery of the Middle Ages were not just religious but also soundly commercial. Benefactors and pilgrims represented two very lucrative sources of income, and a larger floor area was needed to exploit their potential. The extra space in the retro-choir behind the high altar provided more room between the piers of its arcades for the tombs of those who gave handsomely to the church, which took the form of life-sized recumbent effigies lying at table height on rectangular stone bases (see pp. 208–209). It also allowed for the free circulation of crowds of pilgrims to shrines (see pp. 151–153), like those of St Thomas at **Canterbury** and St Hugh at **Lincoln**. Few shrines escaped devastation at the Reformation, when an edict of 1541 ordered the demolition of "all Relics, Images, Table Monuments of Miracles and Shrines". St Etheldreda's at **Ely** was just one of hundreds which were savagely demolished. The Civil War in the seventeenth century brought a new wave of violent destruction, for instance at **Peterborough**, where every one of the cathedral's monuments was lost. Yet further tombs fell victim to subsequent rearrangement, for example in the late eighteenth century at **Salisbury**, where the architect James Wyatt's emptying and lengthening of the east end included removing what a contemporary writer described as "the monuments of an incredible number of illustrious personages" and resiting them between the pillars of the nave arcades, often putting the effigies back on the wrong bases.

Pl. 161 *The open central space in the crowded early thirteenth-century retrochoir of Winchester Cathedral, showing the feretory screen (C.1320) of the Shrine of St Swithun with the fifteenth-century Beaufort and Waynflete Chantries on either side; the floor tiles date from C.1235.*

The medieval reredos or decorated screen (see pp. 175–176) rising behind the high altar has seldom survived, because its numerous statues were a prime target for iconoclasm, but piscinas and sedilia (see pp. 176–178) were not generally destroyed, in spite of the fact that they were no longer required after the Reformation, when alterations in the liturgy made them redundant.

Chapels

There were numerous chapels placed between the piers of the aisles and transepts of great medieval churches. They were habitually enclosed by decorative screens of wood or stone (see p. 196) or ornate metal grilles and were sometimes, as at **Salisbury**, raised a step higher than the floor of the main church to give them extra importance.

The Lady chapel

By the late twelfth century the cult of the Virgin Mary had become so important that a solemn Mass to her was celebrated every day in all the more important churches in the country. The chapel devoted to her (see p. 56) maintained its importance throughout the Middle Ages and was built either to the east of the main altar, as at **Salisbury**, or beside the chancel, as at Worksop Priory (Pl. 162) and **Bristol** (Elder Lady Chapel, both thirteenth-century) and **Ely** (fourteenth-century). Most of these chapels were square-ended, though a few had polygonal apses, like those at **Lichfield** and **Wells** (both early fourteenth-century). Some Lady chapels are not as tall as the main eastern arm of the church; these may, as at **Salisbury**, belong architecturally with a lower retrochoir housing a shrine, like St Swithun's at **Winchester**. Others, for instance at **Bristol** and **Lichfield**, rise to the full height of the adjacent choir. The integration of the Lady chapel with the main building is especially sophisticated at **Wells**. Here it forms part of an elongated octagonal composition extending into and interlinking with the retrochoir, which is a lower structure.

Many Lady chapels are richly ornate and have fine rib vaults. One of the most spectacular, at **Ely**, has the widest Gothic vault in England – 14m (46 ft) – and is ornamented throughout with elaborate Decorated carving. When one imagines the sculpture which has been lost from its niches, the bright paint once on its stonework (traces of which are still visible) and the brilliant colours of its vanished stained glass, one gets some impression of the overwhelming richness of its original impact and the deep reverence felt by the medieval congregation for the mother of Christ.

Chantries

Chantry chapels (see p. 58) remained popular throughout the Middle Ages. The timber or stone screens which separated them from the rest of the church have often been lost, but one very recognizable type can still be seen. This is built as a tiny internal room enclosing a tomb, as at **Winchester** (Pl. 163) which has seven, of medieval dates and later. The walls of these tiny chapels have traceried openings like unglazed windows,

Pl. 162 *The exterior of the graceful Lady chapel added to the east end of the Norman church at Worksop Priory in the thirteenth century and originally intended to be vaulted.*

so that, as in the case of Prince Arthur's Chantry at **Worcester** (Pl. 164), the interior is visible from outside. These tombs are placed on an east–west axis between the pillars of an arcade, either in the eastern arm of the church or in the nave. Their tracery and pinnacled canopies provided opportunities for extravagantly carved decoration, like that on the chantry of Bishop Waynflete (d. 1486) at **Winchester**. The largest and most elaborate of all surviving medieval chantries, the Beauchamp Chapel (fifteenth-century, Pl. 165) in St Mary's Church, **Warwick**, was richly decorated, elaborately vaulted and superbly glazed to the glory of God and in honour of its earthly occupant, Richard Beauchamp, Earl of Warwick (d. 1439).

Shrines

Crypts (see p. 58) were much less common in the Middle Ages than in Norman times, though thirteenth-century examples exist, for instance under the early medieval extension to the eastern arm of **Rochester** Cathedral, where two bays of the Norman crypt can also be seen, and beneath the chapter house at **Wells**. A favourite place for a medieval shrine was in the presbytery, in a position of honour immediately behind

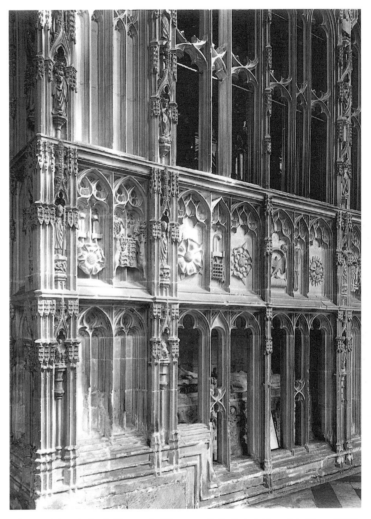

Pl. 164 *Prince Arthur's Chantry in Worcester Cathedral, dedicated to Henry VIII's elder brother who died in 1502, where his tomb chest occupies a tiny upper chapel with a richly carved and vaulted interior; the open substructure contains two much earlier monuments of c.1300 to Bishop Giffard and a female member of his family.*

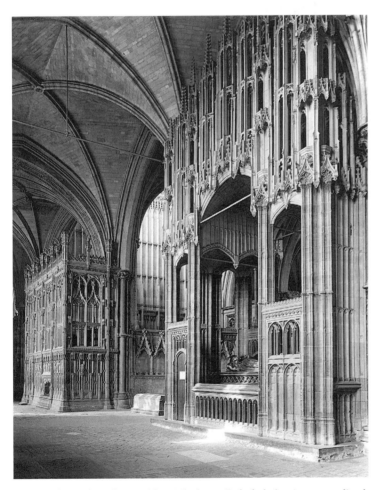

Pl. 163 *The south presbytery aisle at Winchester Cathedral, showing two medieval chantries of Cardinal Beaufort (on right, died 1447) and Bishop Fox (on left, died 1528).*

the high altar. In spite of their universal popularity during the Middle Ages, these shrines have almost entirely disappeared, though one can still see one very rare survival, the modest but complete shrine of St Wite at **Whitechurch Canonicorum** (Dorset, Pl. 166), like a small stone altar with three mandorla-shaped openings. From the scanty remaining evidence we know that a typical shrine took the form of a carved tomb-chest with an effigy of the saint lying on it. This was surmounted by a canopy which

Pl. 165 *The fifteenth-century Beauchamp Chapel at St Mary's church, Warwick,*
with in the foreground the splendid marble and copper-gilt tomb of Richard
Beauchamp, Earl of Warwick, who died in 1439.

The reason for raising relics to a considerable height above an elaborate substructure was that a shrine had to look impressive at ground level as well as being visible above the heads of crowds of pilgrims approaching close to it. It was also designed to be seen from the west end of the church, its upper part rising above the altar and the reredos behind it. The tall base which is all that has survived of the magnificent thirteenth-century shrine to Edward the Confessor can still be seen behind the high altar in **Westminster** Abbey, as also the reconstructed bases of St Alban's shrine at **St Albans** (early fourteenth-century) and St Werburgh's at **Chester** (*c.*1340).

One must picture these shrines festooned with the pilgrims' numerous offerings hung above them. These were images, made in gold, silver or often wax, in the form of miniature replicas of men, women and children who visited the shrine for help or alternatively of the parts of their bodies they hoped to have cured. So there would have been model hands, arms, legs and hearts, as well as candles specially made to the height of the sick person seeking to be restored to health.

It was customary to keep watch over medieval shrines day and night because of their extreme sanctity and also to guard against the theft of the relics, which were extremely valuable, since their possession guaranteed

Pl. 166 *The simple altar shrine, still allegedly containing the bones of St Wite,*
which survives in St Candida's Church at Whitechurch Canonicorum, Dorset;
diseased limbs or articles associated with their illnesses are thought to have
been put into the mandorla-shaped holes by pilgrims seeking to be healed.

supported the *feretrum* or shrine proper containing the actual relics. The late thirteenth-century shrine of St Thomas Cantelupe in the north transept at **Hereford** still has its six-bay tomb-chest carved with lively figures of knights under an arcade, and at Christ Church Cathedral, **Oxford,** St Frideswide's late thirteenth-century shrine, reconstructed in the late nineteenth century in the north choir aisle, also has a canopy of three bays with arches which were originally cusped and naturalistic foliage in the spandrels. The Yorkshire Museum at **York** has important fragments from the mid fourteenth-century shrine of St William of York.

substantial revenue from pilgrims. Two "watching lofts" for the priests or monks on duty by the shrine have survived from the fifteenth century, one at Christ Church Cathedral, **Oxford**, and the other at **St Albans**. These timber structures consist of an upper chamber with a row of window openings on the side facing the shrine. Like the shrine itself, each is raised on a base, the one at Oxford made of stone, like a tomb-chest with a canopy, and the one at St Albans wooden, its projecting upper part coved outwards like a rood loft supported on a screen.

The chapter house

The chapter house, originally a room in the dorter block of the monastic buildings (see p. 114), is generally found to the east of the cloisters (see pp. 112–113). Most of those which survive date from the medieval period, by which time it had often become a separate building. Many, like the one at **Hereford**, were rebuildings of Norman originals, and at **Worcester** a circular twelfth-century building was altered in the fourteenth century and made ten-sided. A polygonal plan with a central pier was usual during the Middle Ages, for instance at **Salisbury** and **Wells** (both octagonal) and **Lincoln** (ten-sided, Pl. 167), though rectangular chapter houses also existed, for example at **Canterbury**, **Durham** and **Gloucester**. Octagonal examples without a central pier can be seen at **Southwell** and **York**, but the large space needed to allow for seating all the members of a big chapter round the edge of the room meant that a roof unsupported in the middle was not usual. As early as the mid thirteenth century, the chapter house built at **Westminster** Abbey had upper walls consisting predominantly of glass. Intense brightness, especially where there is no longer any stained or painted glass in the huge windows, is a salient characteristic of these buildings today. Their architectural details, and especially the design of the stalls for the members of the chapter, display superb examples of Gothic carving of every period, such as the famous naturalistic leaves on the capitals at **Southwell** (late thirteenth-century) and the superb palmtree effect of the tierceron vault at **Wells** (fourteenth-century), where no fewer than thirty-two ribs rise from a central pier.

THE CHOIR

In the Middle Ages the choir was designed for the exclusive use of priests or monks; it was not intended for lay singers, the equivalent of our modern church choirs, who were originally accommodated in the rood loft above the pulpitum (see p. 156). Although an earlier choir was often enlarged or rebuilt in the early Middle Ages, so that it could be contained within the eastern limb of the church, its form remained the same as

Pl. 167 *The early to mid thirteenth-century chapter house at Lincoln Cathedral, showing the vault of twenty ribs rising from its central pier and the blind arcading on the lower walls behind the stalls for the members of the chapter.*

in the Norman period. The only difference was that instead of being screened on three sides and open towards the east, it was now closed off from the east end as well by a tall reredos, or perhaps a shrine behind the high altar. Round the sides of the choir were the monks' or secular priests' stalls, and at the west end the pulpitum ran across the eastern arch of the crossing to shut off the rest of the church. This arrangement survives in numerous cathedrals and larger churches today, though the pulpitum has generally been replaced by a screen. Some original choir furnishings

Pl. 168 *The splendid stone pulpitum in Exeter Cathedral, completed in 1324, which had an organ placed on it as early as the fourteenth century; there were originally solid partitions behind the altars at either side and the niches of the parapet contained stone images, replaced by the present painted scenes of biblical subjects in the early seventeenth century. The present organ case dates from 1665.*

Pl. 169 *The mid fifteenth-century pulpitum in York Minster with figures of the Kings of England standing in niches beneath tall crocketed canopies; the passage roof has lively carved bosses and the inner porch is fan vaulted.*

(see pp. 178–183) are still in use after nearly seven centuries, and the sophisticated form and elaborate decoration of the many surviving sets of stalls reflect the significance of the choir at the heart of a medieval church, and the wealth and importance of those who worshipped there.

The pulpitum

Salisbury's thirteenth-century stone pulpitum which divided the choir from the nave can still be seen in the north-east transept, where it was moved in the late eighteenth century, but it is unusual to find any screens, especially wooden ones, which are earlier than the fifteenth century (see pp. 196–201). Fourteenth-century pulpitums have survived, however, for instance at **Exeter** (Pl. 168), **Lincoln** and **Southwell**. These were substantial stone structures, with a passageway leading through the middle and a staircase inside leading up to the loft above. At **Lincoln** there is even a vaulted chamber within the screen and the passageway is also vaulted, with flying ribs and carved bosses, as at **Southwell**. Sometimes there would have been an altar on top of the pulpitum, perhaps with a rood above it, or this might have been the position for an organ. Sculptured decoration abounded, and in the niches on the west front of the pulpitum facing the nave at both **Canterbury** (*c*.1390–1411) and **York** (mid-fifteenth-century, Pl. 169) there are surviving rows of the standing figures of English kings from Ethelbert to Henry VI.

THE NAVE

The lengthening of the choir and presbytery from the thirteenth century onwards meant that the nave of a medieval cathedral or abbey church was not as long in relation to the eastern part of the building as it had been in Norman times. It continued to be divided into an enclosed central space with aisles on either side, and at **Salisbury** one can still see a continuous plinth running between the columns of the nave arcade, broken only by gaps which gave access for processions. During the course of the Middle Ages arcading became lighter and more elegant, with piers progressively slenderer and more widely spaced. Clustered columns (see pp. 129–138) became the norm, and the contrast between paler stone and dark Purbeck marble was sometimes used, as at **Salisbury** and **Chichester**, to accentuate the design. During the Early English period the arches are sharply pointed, as at **Lincoln**, but as the gaps between the columns grow wider with the introduction of the Decorated style, they become less acute, for example at **Exeter**, until as the Perpendicular develops they begin to flatten, as at **Canterbury**.

Like their Norman predecessors, early medieval churches were constructed in bays, but these separate compartments were progressively absorbed into an overall design. The development of increasingly complex vaults (see pp. 139–140) tended to unify the roof, as at **Exeter**, where a continuous web of tierceron ribs creates an effect like a forest of tall branching trees. The treatment of the triforium as a continuous arcade, for instance at **Wells**, was another unifying factor, as was the use of thin label mouldings above the arches of the nave arcade at **Canterbury** (1391–1405), which combine with the mullions of the clerestory windows to emphasize the effect of length by forming two parallel horizontal lines. These indicate the position of the former triforium, a feature which gradually dwindled in size and importance as the clerestory became higher and higher, with ever larger windows to admit a flood of light. During the thirteenth century the triforium was almost as high as the clerestory and much more elaborately decorated, as at **Salisbury**. A century later it had been reduced to a shallow decorative band, for instance at **Exeter**. In the late medieval period it had disappeared from most churches, leaving only a carved stringcourse as a reminder of its earlier presence. This no longer provided a broad horizontal band accentuated by strong effects of light and shade, and the whole emphasis in the design of the nave walls had shifted from length to height. By abandoning the triforium, a much larger proportion of the wall area could be given over to glazing, and the extra light from the clerestory windows drew the eye upwards. The late medieval nave was a very open, well-lit rectangular space. Seating for the congregation was not generally introduced until the fifteenth century (see pp. 183–186), and in all our greater churches it has invariably been replaced since then, often several times.

Ornamentation of the interior

It is still possible to get some idea of the richness of the interior of a great medieval church from the beauty and vigour of surviving sculptured ornament (see pp. 174–175) and church furnishings (see pp. 175–220) throughout the building. Their beauty would have been enhanced not only by colour (see p. 211), wall paintings (see pp. 211–215) and stained glass (see p. 215–217) but also by a profusion of precious artefacts. Woven and embroidered textiles provided vestments, altar frontals and tapestries; finely wrought metalwork included gold and silver communion vessels, often set with precious stones, and caskets or reliquaries decorated with gilt and enamels; ivory was carved to form a wide variety of objects from figures and plaques to crucifixes and croziers; there were exquisite illuminated manuscripts and ornate book covers of superb craftsmanship. Many of these valuable things were kept in a sacristy and brought out only for use. Surviving examples can still be seen in museums and cathedral treasuries, and the "Medieval Treasury" gallery at the Victoria and Albert Museum, **London**, houses an outstanding collection of these exquisite ecclesiastical works of art.

Parish churches

The process of building new stone churches throughout the country, which had begun under the Normans, continued into the thirteenth century, and throughout the Middle Ages more were continually being put up, often as more ambitious replacements for these simple early buildings. The grandeur of many mid to late medieval parish churches reflected regional wealth, as in the Cotswolds and East Anglia, where fortunes made in the wool trade were spent lavishly on architecture. London, with a population of about forty thousand people, had more than a hundred churches by the time of the Black Death.

The medieval church was more than just a place of worship. Maintaining the nave was the responsibility of the parishioners, who used it rather like a modern parish hall for all sorts of secular purposes, such as brewing the church ale and later consuming it amid dancing and jollity. The "church house" nearby, where the ale was stored, was the forerunner of the public house or inn that is still to be found beside many a medieval parish church.

With the economic recovery at the end of the fourteenth century, late medieval patrons built larger churches or extended existing ones. Typical additions included either one or more nave aisles, porches, vestries, side chapels and western towers. A cruciform church was often turned into a large rectangle when its transepts were absorbed into wide side aisles. Some churches were immensely broad, with four or even five parallel aisles, for example **Manchester** Cathedral (fifteenth-century, a parish church until 1847, Pl. 170), where there are double nave arcades and outer aisles which were originally occupied by chantry chapels. Since medieval towns were split up into a number of parishes, they tended to have several smaller churches rather than one very big one, and this explains the large number of medieval churches surviving in towns like **Norwich** and **York**.

Plan

A typical thirteenth-century parish church consisted of a nave with fairly narrow side aisles and a long chancel which was almost as wide. By the fourteenth century it was common to have at least one broader nave aisle,

Pl. 170 *The nave of the enormous parish church which is now Manchester Cathedral, rebuilt in the fifteenth century with double arcades on either side; the outer aisles were occupied by chantry chapels.*

an entrance porch and a small room leading off the chancel, which served as a sacristy. By the fifteenth century the continuing process of widening meant that the nave might eventually become almost as broad as it was long. Sometimes "squints" or oblique holes were cut through the arcade piers, as at **Backwell** (Somerset), to provide a view into the chancel from side chapels or aisles. It was now usual to have both a north and a south

Pl. 171 *The spacious nave of the church of the Holy Trinity at Blythburgh, Suffolk, built like a large aisled hall in the second half of the fifteenth century; the tie beams of the low-pitched roof have bosses in the form of angels with outspread wings.*

Pl. 172 *The church of St Peter and St Paul at Lavenham, Suffolk, largely rebuilt in the fifteenth and early sixteenth century with big windows and a high clerestory which floods the interior with light.*

porch and a western tower of solid masonry with deep buttresses and often a spiral staircase built into a turret in one corner. This massive addition helped to support the weight of the much longer west wall of an enlarged nave. The chancel frequently became wider too, with an arcade on one side opening into a guild or chantry chapel of equal size. Many later medieval churches, especially in towns, were built on the simple rectangular plan introduced by the friars (see p. 123) because it provided a large aisled hall, which was ideal for preaching to large congregations. Prosperous areas like East Anglia and the West Country adopted this form for parish churches on a grand scale, for instance at **Blythburgh** (Suffolk, Pl. 171) and **Yeovil** (Somerset). As with cathedrals and abbey churches, one must picture the original interior not as the open uncluttered space we generally see today but broken up by screens into numerous compartments (see p. 196).

Walls

The external walls of early medieval parish churches are articulated with buttresses and punctuated by their chancel and aisle windows. Sometimes there are quite small openings which light the clerestory. In areas like the south-east, which are not exposed to very rough weather, the walls of later medieval churches tended to rise higher as roofs became flatter (see p. 110), and because a low pitch does not exert as much thrust they needed considerably less buttressing. Their taller walls are taken up with large areas of glazing and flood the church with light at two levels, for example at **Lavenham** (Suffolk, Pl. 172). Clerestory windows are often placed in pairs, two above each aisle window.

Most medieval parish churches were built of rubble and covered with plaster to resemble ashlar (blocks of cut stone). Because of the nineteenth-century fashion for stripping off the plaster, the roughly textured core of the walls, which was never intended to be seen, is now often exposed to view. When, as sometimes happens, it has been pointed in cement, it produces a crazy-paving effect of deliberate irregularity which is the very opposite of the smooth finish of the medieval plaster. There were normally stone facings round the doors and windows, but it was unusual for an entire church to be finished in ashlar before the fourteenth century, when improved communications began to make it easier to bring stone from some distance. Late medieval masonry tends to be more even and more closely jointed than earlier work and one can sometimes see small incised shapes, such as circles, squares, triangles and diamonds, or signs, such as bent arrows, which are the "masons' marks" of the craftsmen responsible. These are not to be confused with

Pl. 173 *Ornamental stone-and-flint flushwork decorating the north porch of St Mary's church at Woodbridge, Suffolk, built* c.1455.

the crosses used to mark the place where the bishop anointed the church wall with oil at the consecration of the building.

A local facing material much favoured in East Anglia was flint (see pp. 32–33), which could be knapped or broken with a hammer to produce a smooth surface made up of even-sized pieces. It was often combined with stone in "flushwork", where shapes cut out of slabs of stone were filled with split or squared flints to produce elaborate and decorative patterns on the wall surface, as at **Mendlesham** and **Woodbridge** (Suffolk, Pl. 173), both churches dedicated to the Virgin, whose crown and monogram form part of the design.

Pl. 174 *The nave of the fifteenth-century church of the Holy Trinity at Torbryan, Devon, showing its plastered waggon roof, traceried screen painted with figures of saints and eighteenth-century box pews enclosing the original benches.*

Roofs

Some medieval churches were vaulted in stone, but, as during the Norman period, most churches had wooden pitched roofs, which were either thatched or tiled. Their carpentry was generally similar to the secular timber construction of the period (see pp. 249–255), but in Devon and Cornwall there was a different local tradition. Here a church roof generally took the form of a timber barrel vault, its curved timbers completely open to view, as at **Morwenstow** (Cornwall). Some, like the church at **Torbryan** (Devon, Pl. 174), have panels of plaster between the timbers, while others, as at **Chawleigh** (Devon), have been entirely covered up with wooden planks and plastered to form a vaulted ceiling, though this may have been a later development. It has been suggested that this type of roof construction evolved firstly because it spread the weight more evenly on walls which were made of cob, a mixture of mud and straw used in an area where lime was not readily available for masonry, and also because it was easily constructed with the boat-builders' tools of a predominantly fishing community. A typical aisled church, such as **Kilkhampton** (Cornwall), has a separate pitched roof above each of its three parallel barrel vaults, which often run uninterrupted the full length of the building, though at **Luppitt** (Devon), for example, there is a very unusual vaulted crossing. These roofs are decorated with carved bosses where the timbers intersect, and there may be extra enrichment, such as painted suns and stars, on a "celure" or cross-boarded area marking the bay above the rood screen, as at **Hatherleigh** (Devon). At **Cullompton** (Devon, Pl. 175) this celure runs the whole length of a late medieval waggon roof, resting on angel brackets and richly decorated with carved and painted ornament on its ribs and bosses.

An important development in the later Middle Ages was the use of shallow-pitched timber roofs, covered with lead, for the clerestoried churches of the fifteenth century (see p. 159). Because these roofs were almost flat, they could not have been made weatherproof with thatch, tiles or slates, and it was lead that made them feasible. This was not a new material, for lead-mining had been established in Britain since Roman times, particularly in the Mendips but also in many other parts of the country, including Derbyshire and the Lake District. Supplies were plentiful throughout the Middle Ages, and lead was regularly used in glazing (see pp. 215–217) and sometimes for fonts (see pp. 189–190). Used as a roofing material, in sheets weighing 7–8lb per square foot (24–27kg per square metre), it had the advantage of being lighter than either tiles or slates, and more durable, while no heavier, than thatch. It was also versatile and could be used on very steep pitches like spires, though its weight tended to make

it "creep" out of place. Because it was a very expensive material, lead roofs were not common in the early Middle Ages, and it was the affluence of the fifteenth-century patrons and religious houses which allowed it to be used for buildings in the new Perpendicular style like St Edmund's Church, **Southwold** (Suffolk, begun c.1430, Pl. 176). Their timber roof construction was not only structurally sophisticated but often very decorative as well. The bright colouring and rich carving of these roofs must have provided much of the interest of the otherwise rather uninventive church interiors of the fifteenth century, with their predictable variations on the theme of the panel motif. The "angel roofs" of East Anglia (see p. 255), adorned with the carved figures of flying angels on their hammer-beams, as at **March** (Cambs, Pl. 177) and **Mildenhall** (Suffolk), are one of the greatest glories of late medieval church architecture.

GARGOYLES

Externally such low-pitched roofs lacked presence, since they could hardly be seen at all from ground level. To provide a finish to the building, the designers of late medieval churches, such as **Winchcombe** (Glos, Pl. 178) and **Lavenham** (Suffolk), added a parapet, generally battlemented and often made of pierced stonework, with a gutter behind it. To solve the problem of getting the rainwater away from this gutter, they provided a series of gargoyles or spouts projecting through the parapet and extending far enough to throw the water clear of the footings of the wall below. Medieval stonemasons made these an opportunity for a rich variety of sculpture, turning purely utilitarian outlet pipes into humorous portraits, lively animal heads or grotesque gaping monsters. Many of the subjects are frankly pagan and stem from earlier religious beliefs, which the medieval church tolerated because it could not eradicate them. From the sixteenth century onwards, these gargoyles were sometimes supplied with downpipes, which were fixed to the wall immediately below them to catch the water from their spouts.

Porches

Porches were single- or sometimes, as at **Northleach** (Glos, Pl. 179), two-storey structures (see p. 146). Where there were two porches, the one at the south was most often used as the main entrance to the church. Inside the porch there were stone or wooden benches along the side walls, many of which survive today, and there might be a stoup for holy water and even an altar.

The porch played an important part in church life. Marriage contracts were made here and many ceremonies like baptisms, the churching of

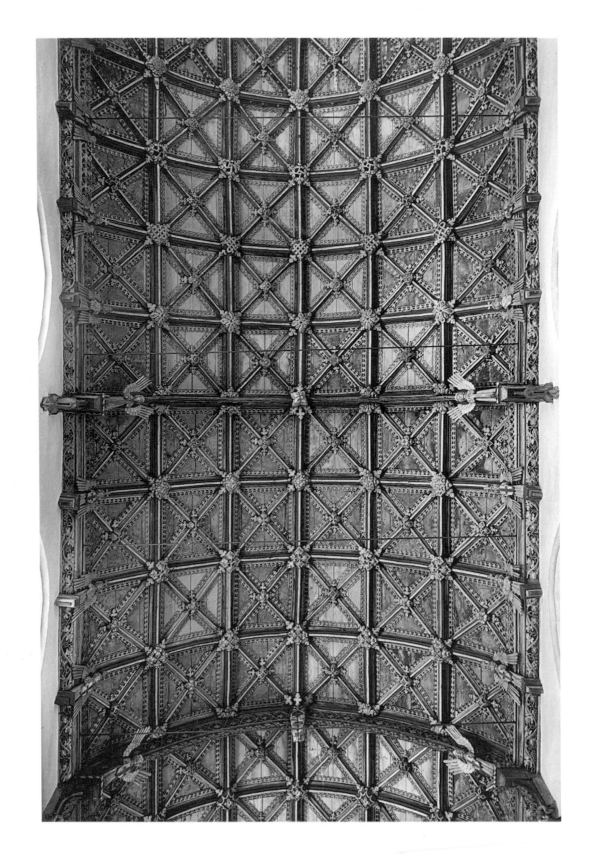

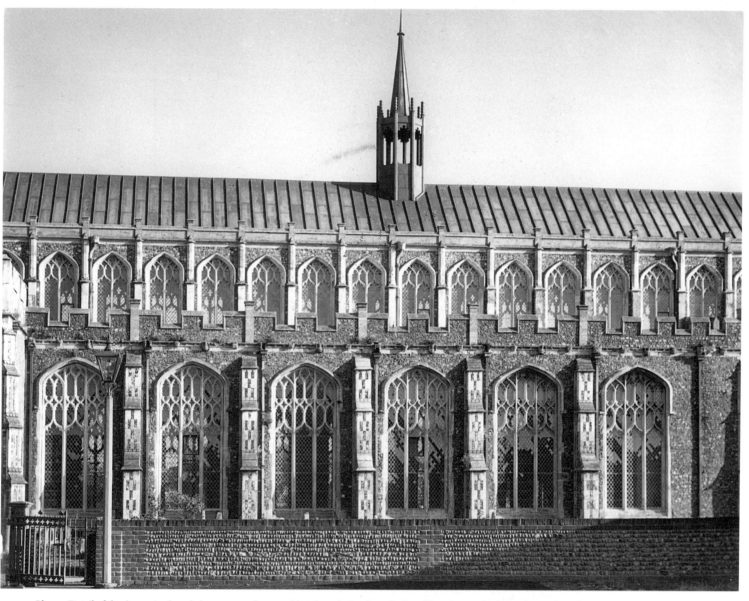

Pl. 175 *Detail of the decorative boarded waggon roof on angel brackets, dating from the late fifteenth or early sixteenth century, which runs the full length of the nave in St Andrew's church at Cullompton, Devon.*

Pl. 176 *The flint-faced mid fifteenth-century church of St Edmund at Southwold, Suffolk, with its high clerestory and low-pitched timber roof covered with lead; the little spirelet dates from 1867.*

Pl. 177 *The early sixteenth-century double hammerbeam roof of St Wendreda's church at March, Cambridgeshire, showing three tiers of angels with outspread wings decorating the corbels and the ends of the hammerbeams.*

Pl. 178 *One of a series of grotesque gargoyles or water spouts on St Peter's church at Winchcombe, Gloucestershire, built c.1465.*

women after childbirth and the absolution of penitents began at the church door. On Palm Sunday the congregation processed under a portable shrine held aloft in the porch, and at Easter the Paschal candle was lighted there so that the new fire of the Light of the World could be spread from the church to the homes of the parishioners, who brought their lanterns to be kindled by the symbolic flame. Porches might also be used as schoolrooms, courtrooms and even priests' living quarters. The upper rooms, when provided, were convenient for these purposes or might even be used as Lady chapels, as at **Mildenhall** (Suffolk) and **Fordham** (Cambs). Some of these chambers above porches still house the muniments or church records first deposited there in the Middle Ages, though most of these have now been removed to public record offices. Other porch rooms were used for safe storage of the arms used by the soldiers that each parish was required to be able to supply and equip for military service. Sundials were often scratched on to porch walls as at **Alfriston** (E. Sussex), with heavy markings showing the times of the Mass.

Lychgates

Many churches also have a lychgate (from the Old English *lic* – corpse) or roofed passageway at the entrance to the churchyard, built of timber or stone depending on the locality. It may have two gates side by side and the internal space is sometimes divided by a long flat central slab, where the corpse could be set down before a burial. This arrangement can be seen at **Atherington** (Devon), while the benches which were often fitted along the sides of a lychgate are found, for instance, at **Boughton Monchelsea** (Kent). Medieval lychgates have survived, for example at **Ashwell** (Herts, Pl. 180), **Bray** (Berks), **Beckenham** (London) and **Isleham** (Cambs) but many of the earliest of these covered gateways date from the Post-Reformation period, when the funeral service no longer began at the home of the deceased. The order for the Burial of the Dead in the prayer book of 1549 starts with "the priest meting the Corps at the Churche style" or gate, where it became desirable to provide a resting place for the body and shelter for the assembled mourners.

Towers

During the Middle Ages church towers lost the rather squat, solid appearance of Norman times and became taller, slimmer structures, which were technically better designed and therefore much more stable. They were also far more decorative, often crowned with ornate parapets and soaring pinnacles and adorned with elaborate wall surface patterns and traceried bell openings. Built to be seen for miles around, they were intended to impress, and adjacent parishes vied with each other in architectural splendour. The most spectacular towers occur in areas of the greatest prosperity, especially where the booming wool trade (see p. 101) brought enormous wealth to merchant benefactors.

Tall spires are found as early as the thirteenth century, notably in Lincolnshire and in Northamptonshire, where one sees a characteristic local type known as a "broach" spire. This developed from experiments with building an octagonal spire on a square tower and filling in the corners with "broaches" or pyramidal supports, as at **Raunds** (Northants, thirteenth-century) and **Ketton** and **Wardley** (Rutland, fourteenth-century, Pls 182 and 184). Broaches were still being used on the earliest of the "recessed" spires, which were set back behind battlements, as at **Deene** (Northants, thirteenth-century). These slender spires are the finest of all, and superb examples, sumptuously ornamented in the Decorated style, can still be seen, for example at **Higham Ferrers** (Pl. 181), **Kettering** and **Oundle** (Northants, Pl. 183). In the early Middle Ages every church had some sort of spire, though it may only have taken the form of a

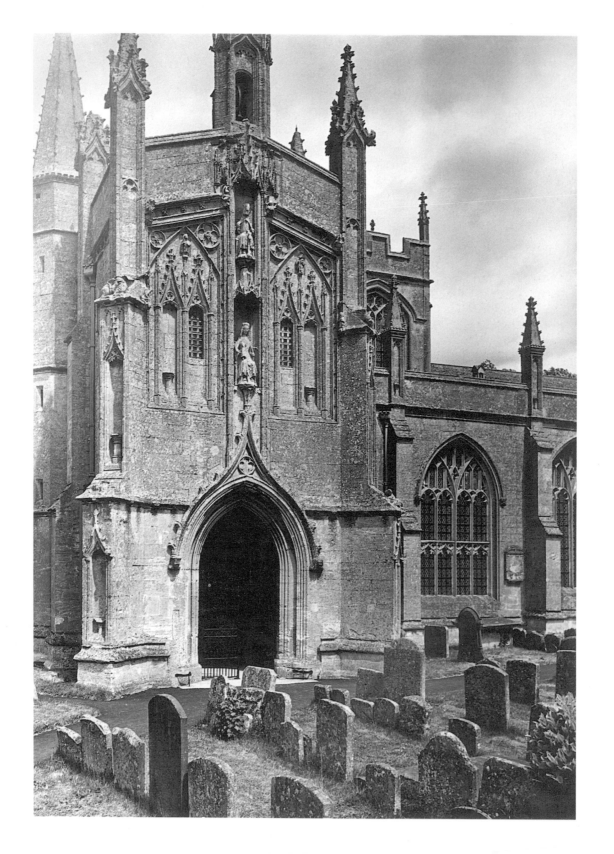

stage of the wooden framework has warped and twisted round on the one below to produce a precarious drunken lean. An alternative covering for spires was shingles or slices of split wood, shaped like tiles and fixed with wooden pins to laths or battens. Shingled spires still exist, for instance at **Burstow** or **Witley** (Surrey) and **Bosham** (W. Sussex, Pl. 186), but the wooden shingles have to be renewed every hundred years or so, and modern replacements are now made in Canadian cedarwood instead of the original English oak.

Pl. 179 *The two-storeyed south porch of the church of St Peter and St Paul at Northleach, Gloucestershire, built during the first half of the fifteenth century; the buttress and pinnacle on the far left conceal the chimney for the fireplace in the upper room.*

Pl. 180 *The fifteenth-century timber lychgate at Ashwell, Hertfordshire, with two parallel passageways under a single roof.*

pointed wooden roof. Most surviving medieval spires are built of stone, but many were constructed with a wooden framework covered with lead, as at **Long Sutton** (Lincs, early thirteenth-century), where the lead, which is laid in a herringbone pattern of strips so that the individual pieces are not too heavy to stay in place, forms an attractive texture which does not reflect too much light. The tallest surviving example of this type is the famous crooked spire at **Chesterfield** (Derbys, Pl. 185), where each

Pl. 181 *The spire of St Mary's church at Higham Ferrers, Northamptonshire, dating from c.1250–80; in the foreground is Archbishop Chichele's School of c.1422.*

Pl. 182 *The early fourteenth-century broach spire above the crossing of St Mary's church at Ketton, Rutland, with lucarnes which have tracery in the Decorated style.*

Pl. 183 *The fourteenth-century recessed spire with three tiers of lucarnes, which is set behind battlements on the tower of St Peter's church at Oundle, Northamptonshire.*

Wall arcading and bell openings on towers naturally followed contemporary developments in tracery design (see pp. 128–129), as did the "lucarnes" (from Old French *lucane*, dormer) or openings in the sides of spires, which were necessary to provide ventilation and reduce wind resistance. The towers of the great medieval cathedrals and abbey churches were a strong influence on the designs adopted by parish churches; Gloucester and Wells, for example, inspired a remarkable group of lofty West Country church towers. Somerset is justly famous for its large number of exceptionally tall examples, richly ornamented in their upper stages, either two or three, depending on the funds available. Up to the level of the nave roof they are fairly plain but above

that the entire wall surface is pierced by windows and bell openings and covered with blind arcading. This forms an all-over design, with "descending" or full-height mullions making a pattern of assertive and parallel vertical lines which increases the effect of height. Sometimes, as at **Evercreech** or St Cuthbert, **Wells**, the whole of the upper part of the tower is designed as one stage; elsewhere, for example at

Pl. 184 *The church of St Botolph at Wardley, Rutland, with a solid fourteenth-century tower and squat broach spire; the chancel was rebuilt in 1871.*

Pl. 185 *The twisted profile of the famous crooked spire of the church of St Mary and All Saints at Chesterfield, Derbyshire, seen rising high above the roofs of the modern town.*

Pl. 186 *The fifteenth-century shingled broach spire on the Saxon tower of Holy Trinity church at Bosham, West Sussex.*

Pl. 187 *The fifteenth-century recessed spire of the church of St John the Baptist at Thaxted, Essex, with flying buttresses rising from the pinnacles of the tower; it was reconstructed after being struck by lightning in 1814.*

Huish Episcopi (Pl. 188) or **Ile Abbots**, it is divided horizontally by a stringcourse. The vertical always predominates, however, and height is emphasized yet further by ornate pierced stone battlements and tall crocketed pinnacles, as at **Kingston** or **North Petherton**. The fenestration of these towers varies considerably, from two-light openings one above the other, as at **Chew Magna**, to much more complex combinations of three-light openings, for example at St Mary Magdalene, **Taunton**.

Buttresses also afford wide opportunities for variations in decorative effect. In Somerset they are generally set back from the angles of the tower, as they are at **Probus** (Cornwall, Pl. 189), which drew its inspiration from Somerset, but other areas favoured "diagonal" buttresses against the actual corners (see Fig. 3). Buttresses topped with shafts and pinnacles result in delightful and often intricate variety of design higher up, for instance at **Huish Episcopi** and **Ile Abbots**.

Another feature of these medieval towers may be a staircase turret, either at one corner or in the middle of one side (usually the south), and perhaps finished with its own little spire and pinnacles, as at **Ilminster**. Inside the church there may be a vaulted ceiling beneath the tower which combines further decoration with extra structural support.

During the later Middle Ages handsome towers and spires were built throughout the country but especially in the more prosperous areas like the Cotswolds, for instance the elaborately ornamental tower at **Chipping Campden** (Glos, Pl. 190), and East Anglia, where **Thaxted** (Pl. 187) has the only surviving Essex spire.

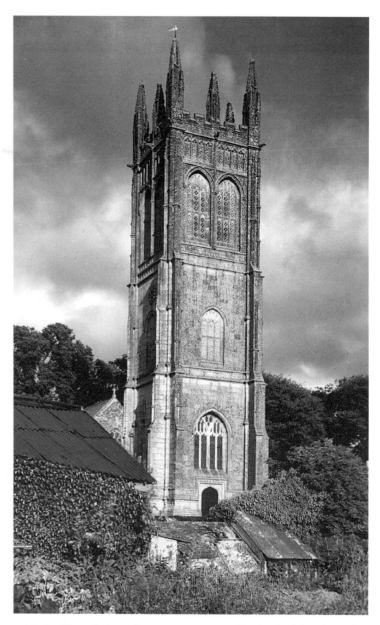

Pl. 189 *The early sixteenth-century west tower of the church of St Probus and St Grace at Probus, Cornwall, showing its set-back buttresses, bands of quatrefoiled ornament and the blind arcading below the battlements, which emphasizes its exceptional height.*

Pl. 188 *The tall, highly ornate fifteenth-century west tower of St Mary's church at Huish Episcopi, Somerset, showing its stages defined by bands of quatrefoil frieze and the three tiers of attached pinnacles on each of its set-back buttresses.*

Pl. 190 *The late fifteenth-century west tower of St James's church at Chipping Campden, Gloucestershire, with diagonal buttresses topped by pinnacles; the strong vertical emphasis of the full-height ogee-arched strip decoration is balanced by the bold horizontal stringcourses dividing the three main stages.*

Architectural ornament

In contrast to the richness of architectural ornament inside many of our cathedrals and abbey churches (see pp. 142–157), the interiors of early English parish churches are often very plain, with simple lancet windows and arcades with round or polygonal columns, though some are much more ambitious in their design. Windows may be arranged in groups behind internal arcades, as at **Cherry Hinton** (Cambs) (*c.*1230–50), and

there is frequently a group of three or more lancets, almost always an uneven number, producing the effect of a larger east window, as at **Uffington** (Oxon) (*c.*1250). Chancels may be vaulted, as at St Mary's, **Guildford** (Surrey), and composite columns, carved capitals and moulded arches begin to appear, as at **Whitechurch Canonicorum** (Dorset, thirteenth-century, Pl. 193) or in the north aisle (*c.*1235–40) at **Eaton Bray** (Bedfordshire), where the slightly earlier south aisle (*c.*1220) has octagonal piers. Compared with the exuberant carved decoration of Norman doorways and chancel arches, early thirteenth-century ornament seems modest and restrained, with dog-tooth neatly emphasizing arches and capitals sprouting stiffly controlled leaves. Later in the medieval period, increasingly elaborate use was made of carving to adorn every architectural feature and to ornament wall surfaces. The Decorated style (see pp. 101–103) brought sophisticated tracery

Pl. 191 *Encrusted ornament typical of the Decorated style in the Lady chapel at Ely Cathedral, where the face of a Green Man peers out through the luxuriant foliage growing from his brow and out of his mouth.*

Pl. 192 *A Wild Man wielding a cudgel carved on one of the spandrels of the fifteenth-century west doorway of St Mary's church at Cratfield, Suffolk, facing a dragon on the other side.*

with sinuous outlines, ogee arches, encrusted ornament (Pl. 191) and "ballflower" (Pl. 105) as a recurrent motif. The Perpendicular architecture which succeeded it covered every kind of surface, from walls and screens to fonts and bench ends, with variations on the theme of blind arcading, counteracting the rectilinear monotony in its structure with a wealth of surface decoration and reconciling curves and right angles by deliberately framing its flat four-centred arches with square-topped heads. The spandrels or corner spaces provided further opportunities for carved decoration, as on the west door at **Cratfield** (Suffolk, Pl. 192).

It must be remembered how much figure sculpture has been lost

Pl. 193 *The early thirteenth-century nave arcade of the church of St Candida at Whitechurch Canonicorum, Dorset, with clustered columns, moulded arches and capitals carved with foliage and geometrical patterns.*

from the decorative blind arcades which cover the fittings of medieval churches, from fonts to tombs, many of which were thickly peopled with angels, saints and holy men. Nonetheless medieval churches still contain numerous examples of their original wealth of applied and once colourful decoration, not only on their walls, roofs, arches, doorways and windows but extensively in their surviving furnishings as well.

Church furnishings

The destruction of churches and their contents which resulted from the Dissolution of the Monasteries in 1536–40 swept away almost all traces of early church furnishings. Cartloads of precious treasures were removed (twenty-six from the shrine of St Thomas à Becket at Canterbury alone), and sculptures which could not be taken away were subsequently defaced. After the devastation of the Reformation, the Puritan iconoclasm of the seventeenth century, the zeal of the nineteenth-century restorers and the general depredations of time have all taken their toll. In the more important buildings most of the fittings have inevitably been replaced many times since the Middle Ages, and rare and valuable items like plate or candlesticks are now locked away in cathedral treasuries or museums. Major survivals such as choir stalls (see pp. 178–183) can still be seen in some cathedrals and abbey churches, but the sheer variety in the furnishings which have somehow been preserved is best appreciated by visiting parish churches throughout the country, when unexpected discoveries are a source of endless interest.

Chancel furnishings

ALTARS

Medieval stone altars were universally thrown out at the Reformation (see pp. 308–309), when an injunction of 1550 ordered the replacement of all stone altars by communion tables. A few evidently escaped unnoticed, for example one in the small vestry on the north side of the chancel at **Northleach** (Glos), perhaps part of an earlier chapel which survived the fifteenth-century rebuilding of the church. In the same church the present high altar consists of the original stone mensa (from Latin *mensa*, table) supported on a modern wooden base; and in a number of church floors there are altar slabs (see p. 71) which have been reused as paving stones.

REREDOSES

Behind a medieval altar there was a reredos, which took the form of an ornamented screen or a decorated wall surface, but this has seldom

Pl. 194 The Crucified Christ with the Virgin and St John on the central panel of the early fourteenth-century retable in St Mary's church at Thornham Parva, Suffolk, which has four more saints on either side.

survived. The few we can still see, for example at **St Albans** and **Winchester**, were heavily restored in the nineteenth century. The monumental but battered example at **Christchurch** Priory (Dorset, *c*.1350, Pl. 195) gives a much better idea of how they originally looked. The mutilated state of this reredos, with its carved biblical scenes and sculptured figures, is a vivid reminder of the damage such furnishings suffered at the Reformation, as is the fact that the "Neville Screen" reredos at **Durham** has lost all of its 107 alabaster statues. Panels of sculptured alabaster, produced on a large scale at Nottingham, were

often used for a reredos; the fine fifteenth-century example which survives at **Yarnton** (Oxon) depicts four scenes from the life of Christ. A wooden reredos of *c*.1250, with traces of original gesso and painted decoration, which came from **Canterbury** Cathedral can now be seen in the south transept of the parish church at **Adisham** (Kent).

RETABLES

Instead of, or as well as, a reredos, there might be a retable or painted picture. This might be a diptych with two hinged panels so that it could be closed like a flat box when not in use. Much less common in Britain was the triptych, with a central panel and two hinged wings, like the Flemish one of *c*.1520 which survives in the south chancel aisle of the Church of St Cross, **Winchester**. Each of the wings was half the width of the middle panel, so that together they covered the central painting when the triptych was shut. One can still see some of these pictures showing scenes from the Bible and figures of saints. Famous examples include the Thornham retable (*c*.1330–40), painted with a Crucifixion and eight saints, at **Thornham Parva** (Suffolk, Pl. 194) and the Wilton Diptych in the National Gallery, **London**, which shows St Edmund, Edward the Confessor and John the Baptist behind the kneeling figure of King Richard II, who is adoring the Virgin and Child surrounded by angels.

PISCINAS

Set into the wall near the altar there was a niche containing a stone piscina (see pp. 71–72) or basin with a drain which was used by the priest to wash his hands and to rinse out the communion vessels. Since it was so often designed to match the adjacent sedilia (see below), the two may usefully be treated as part of the same architectural composition. A piscina was sited as close as possible to the altar it served, and in a medieval church it was often built into a projection from the eastern jamb of the south window of the chancel. These "angle piscinas" had two arches, one facing south and the other west, as can be seen at **Blyford** (Suffolk). Sometimes there was a stone shelf for the sacred vessels higher up in the niche above the drain, as at **East Hendred** (Oxon), and wooden shelves or the grooves which held them in place have also survived. From the late thirteenth century onwards there were double piscinas with one drain where the priest washed his hands and another for rinsing the chalice and paten, as at **Grosmont** (Gwent); three drains are also found, for instance at **Brecon** Cathedral (Powys). A double drain usually has two arches set inside a larger arch, but a type found in East Anglia, for instance in the chapel at Jesus College, **Cambridge** (Pl. 196), has a rectangular surround

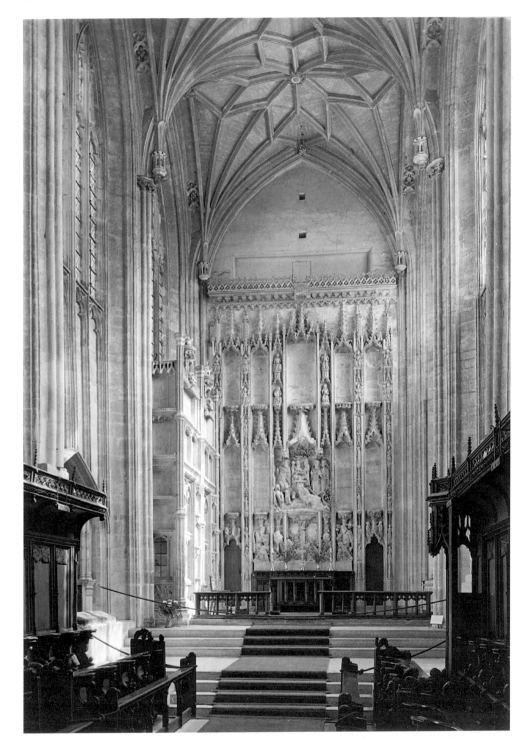

Pl. 195 *The monumental mid fourteenth-century reredos re-erected in the late medieval chancel of Christchurch Priory, Dorset, showing in the lower tier Daniel and Solomon flanking a recumbent Jesse and above him the Adoration of the Magi; the remaining statues are missing and the cresting along the top is early sixteenth-century; the choir stalls date from c.1525–30.*

Pl. 196 *The double piscina in the mid thirteenth-century chancel of the chapel at Jesus College, Cambridge, designed with intersecting arcading inside a rectangular frame.*

filled with intersecting arcading. Single piscinas became fashionable again during the fourteenth and fifteenth centuries, so the existence of only one drain does not necessarily imply an early date.

AUMBRIES

Aumbries or cupboards for the church plate were occasionally designed "en suite", as at **Longfield** (Kent), where the piscina and aumbry are linked. The only remaining sign of this type of cupboard is a recessed space, usually in the north wall of the chancel. Its function has been usurped by the modern safe.

EASTER SEPULCHRES

A recessed Easter sepulchre was another chancel fitting which could form part of the overall design of the piscina and sedilia. The setting up of a wooden model of Jesus's tomb in the Garden of Gethsemane was part of the Easter ritual of the medieval church, and the same idea is perpetuated in the model gardens which form part of the Easter decorations of our churches today. On Good Friday the sepulchre was placed on the north side of the chancel, and watchers kept constant candlelit vigil over the Host placed in the breast of the image of the buried Christ until it was time for it to be taken out in triumph on Easter Sunday morning. The crucifix from the high altar might also be placed in the sepulchre during this period. At the end of the Easter festival, the model was packed away again until the following year. These temporary wooden structures have not survived, since they were broken up after the Reformation, but there were others which took the form of a permanent stone niche, sometimes mounted on a base resembling a tomb-chest, in the north wall of the chancel. Examples of these are still in existence and they are easily recognized by the subject matter of their sculptured decoration. This may include, on the base, the sleeping figures of the Roman soldiers on watch, as at **Lincoln** Cathedral (*c*.1300), and, above, the risen Christ, for instance at **Patrington** (E. Riding of Yorks, fourteenth-century), where he is flanked by angels swinging censers, or at **Heckington** (Lincs, *c*.1330), which shows the figures of the three Marys and the angel, two figures on either side of the niche. At **Hawton** (Notts, 1330) there are both these scenes with above them a Resurrection scene showing the Apostles standing gazing upwards as Christ's feet disappear into Heaven. Heckington's sepulchre is designed as a massive decorative frame round a small triangular-headed niche, while Hawton's cavity is much larger and occupies the entire width behind its triple arched openings with their elaborate canopies. There are other rather similar highly decorative recesses without specific carved ornament, for example at **Swineshead** (Bedfordshire), which were probably Easter sepulchres, though they may have been intended as tombs; many simpler niches now housing later monuments or just left empty may once have been used for this purpose. At **East Bergholt** (Suffolk) there is a niche which was evidently a sepulchre because of the fifteenth-century painting of the Resurrection surviving on its back wall.

Like these purpose-built stone niches, the recessed or canopied tomb of the founder of a church was also habitually placed on the north wall, and its flat slab may often have been used as a convenient place for displaying a wooden sepulchre during Easter week.

CHANCEL SEATING

Sedilia

Sedilia (see p. 71) were built-in seats for the officiating clergy, generally stepped in descending heights to reflect the priestly hierarchy of their occupants. Their design reflects the stylistic developments of the various phases of Gothic during the medieval period. A set of sedilia with piscina at **Monyash** (Derbys) dating from *c*.1200 has segmental arches with dog-tooth ornament and shafts with stiffleaf capitals, while another at **Ilkeston** in the same county (*c*.1280) is designed with pointed arches, bar tracery and shafts with foliage capitals. The most elaborate, for instance those at **Cliffe** (Kent, Pl. 197) and **Heckington** (Lincs), are in the Decorated style and date from the early fourteenth century. Sedilia can have up to five seats, as in the wooden example at **Hexham** Priory (Northumberland).

CHOIR STALLS

Choir stalls were rows of built-in seating enclosing the choir on every side but the east. They are nearly always found in monastic or collegiate churches, though they are occasionally present in large parish churches, such as **Boston** (Lincs) and **Nantwich** (Cheshire), which have fine late fourteenth-century sets. Each of the seats in a medieval choir had a curved back with arm-rests. Stone examples still exist, for instance the return stalls on either side of the entrance through the pulpitum at **Southwell** (Notts) but by the medieval period choir stalls were almost invariably made of wood. Thirteenth-century survivals include parts of the choir seating at **Rochester** (*c*.1227), now in the back stalls, and at **Peterborough**

Pl. 197 *The elaborate vaulted sedilia and piscina in the Decorated style in St Helen's church at Cliffe, Kent, which was remodelled in the early fourteenth century.*

(*c.*1240), moved to the north transept. There is also a set of mid thirteenth-century misericords (see pp. 181–183) at **Exeter**, incorporated into replacement seating installed in the late nineteenth century. The early twentieth-century canopies over the stalls at Salisbury are quite incorrect for the mid thirteenth century, when stalls had no superstructure but would have been placed directly against a partition wall, built to enclose

Pl. 199 *Detail showing the arm-rests of the mid fourteenth-century choir stalls at Ely Cathedral, decorated with beasts and human faces.*

Pl. 198 *The fifteenth-century choir stalls in the church of the Holy Trinity at Balsham, Cambridgeshire, with arm-rests in the form of human and animal figures.*

the choir area and probably either frescoed or hung with tapestries. **Salisbury** has the earliest full set of choir stalls to survive (probably finished before 1245), and there is an almost complete set at **Winchester** (*c.*1308). Other fourteenth-century examples can be seen at **Chester**, **Gloucester**, **Hereford** and **Lincoln**. The number of seats varied widely, from nearly seventy, as at **Beverley** (E. Riding of Yorks) with sixty-eight and **Wells** (Somerset) with sixty-four, to twenty, as at **Abergavenny** (Gwent), or twenty-four at **Nantwich** (Cheshire).

The stalls were normally in two rows along the north and south sides of the choir; on the west they were placed against the eastern side of the pulpitum, with a gap in the middle for the passageway through the screen. The two seats on either side of this central aisle were reserved for the head of house and his deputy. The front row of stalls had a free-standing desk in front of it and a shelf built along its back to provide a desk for the row behind. The back row of seats was set higher than the one in front, so as to give its occupants a better view, and from the fourteenth century onwards the stalls had canopies above them, either one to a seat, as at **Lincoln**, or with each canopy covering two seats, as at **Winchester**. Sometimes the canopies form one continuous row, as at **Norwich**, or there may be a double row of canopies, one above the other, as at **Chester** and **Ripon**. Elaborately pinnacled canopies like those at **Ely** (*c.*1340, Pl. 159) were extremely popular throughout the later Middle Ages and continued to be made in the north of England until the Reformation. Those that can still be seen today have generally been very skilfully restored during the Victorian period. Practically none of their original coloured decoration has survived, but at **Carlisle** there are paintings of apostles and saints (*c.*1500) on the backs of the seats. Choir stalls were commonly enlivened with intricate carved decoration showing flowers, foliage and animals, and patterned with carved tracery, for instance on the panels of the desk along the front. Structural supports might be shown as columns or buttresses, while capitals and pinnacles provided further opportunities for a wealth of elaboration. Arm-rests could take the form of human figures as at **Ely** *c.*1340, Pl. 199) or animals as at **Balsham** (Cambs, fifteenth-century, Pl. 198), and the ends of the stalls, which were also decorated, were finished with figure and foliate "poppy-head" finials (see p. 183), as at **Chester**.

MISERICORDS

When they were not in use, the choir seats were tipped up to reveal shallow shelf-like projections supported by elaborately carved blocks of wood. These misericords (from Latin *misericordia*, mercy) provided the monks with something to lean against, which supported the base of the spine and helped ease the backache which must have resulted from long periods of standing. They have survived in delightful variety, and because their supporting brackets were normally tucked away out of sight, carpenters seem to have felt little inhibition about their choice of subject matter, which was more often secular than religious. The thirteenth-century misericords at **Salisbury** have simple foliate decoration, but from the fourteenth century onwards lively narrative becomes common. English misericords differ from continental ones in generally having "supporters" or subsidiary carvings descending from the edges

Pl. 200 *One of the carved misericords under the seats of the fourteenth-century choir stalls at Chichester Cathedral, showing a swimming mermaid with a mirror in her hand.*

Pl. 201 *One of the carved misericords under the seats of the fourteenth-century choir stalls at Chichester Cathedral, showing two lively musicians with mask-like faces on either side.*

of the seat. In this position an elaborate scene may be compressed into a purely schematic arrangement, as at **Lincoln** (*c.*1365–70), where a man is ploughing in a very tight corner. Sometimes supporters introduce extra subject matter into complex narrative scenes, as at **Ely** (*c.*1340), where two men playing at dice in the central carving are tempted to add to the vice of their gambling by yielding to a seductive woman on one side and a man with a tankard of ale on the other. Manuscript illustrations, from books like the much-copied *Biblia Pauperum* (Bible of the Poor), versions of which began to circulate *c.*1300, and the fourteenth-century *Speculum Humanae Salvationis* (Mirror of Man's Salvation), were one of the sources for subjects. A fifteenth-century misericord in **Ripon** Cathedral, for example, showing Samson carrying off the gates of Gaza, is taken directly from a woodcut in a blockbook version of the *Biblia Pauperum*, one of the first works to be produced in the Netherlands when the invention of printing made it possible for books to become widely known. The twelfth-century *Bestiary*, a book thought to have originated in a Greek work in fifth-century Alexandria, inspired numerous carvings of mythical and symbolic animals, such as the unicorn with its head in the virgin's lap, deliberately making itself vulnerable as Christ did when he entered the Virgin's womb, or the Pelican in her Piety, reviving her fledglings with her own blood just as Christ shed His blood to save mankind from sin (both at **Lincoln**). Symbolic meanings of this kind were well understood, as were the attributes of mythical creatures like the mermaid with

Pl. 203 *A king with his crown and sceptre, traditionally believed to be Richard III, on one of the carved misericords under the seats of the early sixteenth-century choir stalls at Christchurch Priory, Dorset.*

her mirror and comb, representing vanity and temptation to sin, and the wodehouse or wild man who was both animal tamer and satyr (both at **Ripon**, late fifteenth-century). Mermaids at **Chichester** (Pl. 200), fabulous beasts and legendary characters were all popular subjects and later misericords were also inspired by medieval romances, like *Tristan and Isolde* (**Chester**, late fourteenth-century). Religious subjects include saints, such as St George and the Dragon (**Lincoln**) and the life of St Werburgh (**Chester**), and biblical scenes, such as the series including the temptation of Eve, Moses descending from Mount Sinai, and the judgement of Solomon (**Worcester**, 1379). There are portraits of great men such as bishops or kings, like Richard III (**Christchurch**, *c.*1330, Pl. 203) and heraldic devices like the Prince of Wales's feathers (**Ludlow**, 1447). Many carvings are taken from everyday life, showing domestic animals, such as a sow with her litter (also **Worcester**), scenes from home life, like a family brawl (**Lincoln**, *c.*1365–70), a man wheeling his scolding wife in a wheelbarrow (**Beverley**, 1520), music making (**Chichester**, 1330, Pl. 201) hunting, hawking and other sports, such as bearbaiting (**Manchester**, *c.*1508), farming activities, like ploughing (**Lincoln**), or shoeing a horse (**Ely**, Pl. 202), and the Labours of the Months, where a man sitting by his fireside represents January (**Ludlow**, 1447). Often there is a strong streak of wry

Pl. 202 *Three men shoeing a horse on one of the narrative misericords under the seats of the fourteenth-century choir stalls at Ely Cathedral.*

humour in the many scenes of retribution which occur, for instance where a hare roasts a huntsman on a spit (**Manchester**) or a fox is being hanged by geese (**Beverley**). There is also a didactic element, with illustrations of proverbs, like the knight tumbling from his horse who represents the Fall of Pride (**Lincoln**). The sheer variety and infectious zest of these carvings give us vivid glimpses of the reality of everyday life in medieval Britain.

Chancel seating was a major feature of cathedrals and abbey churches, but unless it was a collegiate church with a body of priests to be accommodated, a medieval parish church did not need any seats in this position, apart from the sedilia (see p. 178). What we now call choir stalls were not used for lay singers, who generally occupied the rood loft. Many sets of stalls now in parish churches are not original fittings but were brought in from monastic churches after the Reformation or are of much later, often nineteenth-century, date. Surviving examples of medieval stalls range from the simple stone seats still to be seen along parts of the north and south walls of the chancel at **Chipstead** (Surrey) to wooden stalls with elaborately carved fronts at **Noseley** (Leics) or lively misericords at **Boston** (Lincs). Canopies are seldom found in smaller churches, however, even in East Anglia, where carved stalls are particularly common, for instance in Suffolk at **Lavenham, Southwold** and **Sudbury** (St Gregory) and in Norfolk at **East Harling, King's Lynn** (St Margaret) and **Salle**.

CHAIRS

Bishops' thrones have occasionally survived, for instance at **St David's** (Dyfed), **Hereford** and **Durham** (all fourteenth-century). The earliest wooden example is the Coronation Chair at **Westminster** Abbey, made in 1300–1301 to accommodate the Stone of Scone, brought there from Scotland by Edward I (see p. 98). The grandest is at **Exeter** (early fourteenth-century) and has a canopy designed with nodding ogee arches and lofty pinnacles. **Durham**'s throne is unique in being set up on a platform above the tomb of Bishop Hatfield (d. 1381), who commissioned it. **Lincoln**'s early fourteenth-century episcopal stone chair decorated with carved quatrefoils has lost its arms, which were made in the form of crouching lions, and has been moved out of the choir into the chapter house.

CONGREGATIONAL SEATING

Early nave seating consisted only of stone benches for the elderly or infirm. Surviving examples include the deep ledge running almost all round the nave at **Patrington** (E. Riding of Yorks) and the seats around

each pillar at **Sutton Bonnington** (Notts). There are also a few surviving wooden benches, for example at **Dunsfold** (Surrey), which are thought to date from as early as the beginning of the fourteenth century, but before the late medieval period most of the worshippers stood when they were not kneeling. It was during the fifteenth century that the provision of congregational seating became general. This took the form of benches, plain except for their ends, which were often elaborately carved on the side facing the aisle. Their decoration frequently has a liveliness comparable with the carving on misericords, and it may be that their survival during the Reformation was due to their rather earthy depiction even of religious subject matter, for example the robust Seven Deadly Sins at **Blythburgh** (Suffolk).

Bench ends were normally rectangular in the west of the country, for example at **Launcells** (Cornwall, Pl. 204), where there is a complete set, but elsewhere they tended to be finished with carved finials, typically in the form of a *fleur de lys*. These are known as "poppyheads" (from the French *poupée*, doll) because they often take the form of little figures, as at **Cley-next-the-Sea** (Norfolk, Pl. 205) or **Blythburgh** (Suffolk, where a whole series can still be seen). Their name has nothing to do with poppies, although flowers and seed-heads sometimes appear in this position, for instance at **Fressingfield** (Suffolk, Pl. 206). East Anglian benches like those at **Ufford** (Suffolk, Pl. 207) can be very ornate and may even have carving on their backs and baseplates as well.

The earliest benches had no backrests. These did not become general before the late fifteenth century, and early examples are found mainly in the Midlands, for instance on the roughly made seats at **Gaddesby** (Leics, thirteenth-century) and the simple panelled set at **Finedon** (Northants, fourteenth-century). **Winchester** Cathedral still has some wooden benches dating from the fifteenth century, and East Anglia has many excellent examples from this period, for instance at **Blythburgh** and at St Mary, **South Walsham** (Norfolk). A rich variety of vigorous carving is also found on bench ends in the West Country made during the sixteenth century, for example at **Launcells** (Cornwall, Pl. 204) and **Bishop's Lydeard** (Somerset). Carving was concentrated on the areas where it would be most noticeable and therefore produce the greatest decorative effect. Pews in side aisles were generally simpler and more economical versions, backless but often with poppyhead ends.

Attempts by parishioners to claim their own seats were deplored by the Bishop of Exeter as early as 1287, but the oldest surviving churchwardens' accounts make it clear that by the fifteenth century pews reserved for individuals or families had become commonplace. The word "pew" probably derives from the Middle English *puwe* or balcony, which suggests an

Pl. 204 *Rectangular bench ends in the late medieval church of St Andrew and St Swithin at Launcells, Cornwall, carved with symbols representing Christ's Passion; the Royal Arms are those of Charles II and other furnishings date from the Gothic Revival of the late eighteenth and nineteenth centuries.*

Pl. 205 *A poppyhead with a human face on one of the fifteenth-century bench ends in St Margaret's church at Cley-next-the-Sea, Norfolk.*

Pl. 206 *Detail of the complete surviving set of fine fifteenth-century traceried bench ends in the church of St Peter and St Paul at Fressingfield, Suffolk, showing sinuous foliage poppyheads and a winged griffin.*

Pl. 207 *The traceried late medieval bench ends in St Mary's church at Ufford, Suffolk, surmounted by poppyheads between figures of animals.*

PULPITS

The fixed pulpit had been a standard fitting in monastic refectories since Norman times (see p. 114), but it was introduced into churches only towards the end of the medieval period. Moveable versions, which could be used anywhere in the church, had existed earlier but it is thought that priests also addressed their congregations from the rood loft above the pulpitum (see p. 156), which would explain why the new kind of enclosed preaching platform shared the same name as the screen between nave and choir. The earliest surviving pulpits date from the

Pl. 208 *Late medieval box pews with traceried panels and poppyheads in St Mary's church at Croscombe, Somerset; the screen and pulpit date from 1616.*

enclosed space. Seats with high backs and sides like those at **Croscombe** (Somerset, Pl. 208) must have done a lot to counter the effect of draughts in unheated churches, and there are contemporary references to doors with locks and even soft furnishings. A lord's box pew provided with cushions, carpets and curtains is described in John Russell's *Boke of Nature* as early as 1450, though at this date such exclusive luxury can have been only for the wealthiest.

late fourteenth century. Stone examples are especially common in the Cotswolds and the West Country, where this material was readily available, but about two thirds of those still in existence are wooden and they are distributed throughout the country.

A medieval pulpit was shaped like a polygonal tub resting on a much narrower shaft and was approached by a short flight of steps at the back which was sometimes attached to a pillar behind it. The more sophisticated fifteenth-century pulpits, for example at **Northleach** (Glos, Pl. 209)

Pl. 210 *The wooden early fifteenth-century pulpit in St James's church at Castle Acre, Norfolk, showing its panels painted with the figures of the four Latin Fathers of the Church which may have come from an earlier screen; the staircase on the left led up to the rood loft.*

Pl. 209 *The fifteenth-century octagonal stone pupit in the church of St Peter and St Paul at Northleach, Gloucestershire, with traceried sides and a slender stem.*

(stone) or **Burnham Norton** (Norfolk) (wood), have bases with the slenderness and elegant curves of the stems of wineglasses. Some of these timber stems were replaced in the nineteenth century by stronger stone bases. The pulpit itself was hexagonal or octagonal, its sides consisting of traceried panels which were originally painted and gilded. Some of this painting can still be seen, including figures in the panels, like those of the

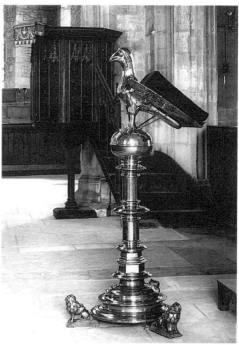

Pl. 211 *The fourteenth-century wooden lectern in St Mary's church at Ottery St Mary, Devon, in the form of a gilded eagle with outspread wings.*

Pl. 212 *The late fifteenth-century brass eagle lectern in St Peter's church at Oundle, Northamptonshire, on a moulded stand with lions round the base.*

Fathers of the Church, Sts Ambrose, Augustine, Gregory and Jerome, at **Castle Acre** (Norfolk, Pl. 210). Carved figures are sometimes found in the south-west, for instance at **Trull** (Somerset, early sixteenth-century). Only one example survives of the tester, or sounding-board, suspended above the head of the priest, which was a feature of the late medieval period. This is the tiered and pinnacled canopy still in position above the much restored late medieval pulpit at **Edlesborough** (Bucks). Another remarkable survival is the tall half-cylindrical pulpit, thought to date from *c.*1498, which still stands in the choir at **Winchester** Cathedral.

LECTERNS

The oldest wooden lecterns date from the early fourteenth century. A fine example, made like a sloping desk with only one bookrest, can be seen at **Bury** (Cambs). It is elaborately carved with oak leaves, acorns and foliage with a Green Man (see p. 140), while on the back, facing the congregation, there is a decorative arcade of ogee-topped arches. Only a little later is the outstanding mid fourteenth-century example at **Detling** (Kent), carved with pierced roundels of tracery, flowers and leaves and peopled with small animals and grotesque faces. This was designed to take four books and stands on an elaborate octagonal traceried column with a heavy buttressed base. There are also medieval brass versions of this desk type of lectern, notably in St George's Chapel, **Windsor**, and at **Eton** College (both in Berks). Similarly the earliest eagle lecterns are wooden, while later examples are made of brass. The fine wooden eagle from **Exeter** Cathedral (now in St Thomas's church in the same city) dates from *c.*1320, and there are other fourteenth-century examples at **Ottery St Mary** (Devon, Pl. 211) (still gilded) and **Leighton Buzzard** (Beds).

Medieval brass eagles seem to have been made in East Anglia, possibly at **King's Lynn**, where fifteenth-century examples survive in both the town's great churches, St Nicholas's and St Margaret's, or at **Norwich**, although the brass lectern in the cathedral (*c.* 1450), in the form of a pelican rather than an eagle, is said to be of Flemish manufacture. Whether or not it was a foreign fashion that first introduced the brass eagle lecterns, they were evidently produced in England in considerable numbers and are not only found extensively in East Anglia, for example at **Cavendish** and **Woolpit** (Suffolk), but also as far afield as **Oundle** (Northants, Pl. 212), **Chipping Camden** (Glos) and **Yeovil** (Somerset). Sometimes there is a double eagle, as at St Margaret, **King's Lynn**, **Redenhall** (Norfolk) or **Clare** (Suffolk). It has been suggested that this kind of double lectern may have been intended for groups of singers using

both sides at the same time. Other lecterns doubled as almsboxes as at **Isleham** (Cambs), with a hole for offerings in the eagle's beak and a stopper in its tail where the coins could be removed.

STOUPS

These containers for holy water (see p. 72) are normally found on the right-hand side, either in the porch or just inside the door, as one enters a church. They vary in shape from a block of stone with a hollowed-out top, as at **Wooton Courteney** (Somerset) and **Clayworth** (Notts), to a basin set on a column, as at **Harlton** (Cambs), or inside a niche in the wall, as at **Bozeat** (Northants) and **Frostenden** (Suffolk). Sometimes all that has survived is the niche, like the one with a trefoil head at **St Ive** (Cornwall). They are often so plain that they are difficult to date but where there is carved decoration, it reflects contemporary architectural fashion, for instance in the use of ballflower ornament at **Eastdean** (E. Sussex) or heraldic shields at **St Endellion** (Cornwall).

FONTS

The large number of Norman fonts (see pp. 72–74) still in use today shows how often the font, symbolically associated with the sacrament of baptism, escaped replacement when an earlier church was rebuilt during the Middle Ages. However, new churches must have created a steady demand for up-to-date versions. Medieval fonts of all periods have survived in considerable numbers and there is a clear pattern of development in their design. Presumably as part of the general tendency towards greater comfort, it became normal for a font to be mounted on a base so as to bring it to a more convenient height. During the thirteenth and fourteenth centuries we find groups of squat pillars supporting bowls which are either circular, as at **Leighton Linslade** (Beds) and **Chollerton** (Northumberland, Pl. 34), or polygonal, as at **Stow** (Lincs, Pl. 30). A round or square font had five of these supports, a thick central column surrounded by four slimmer ones, while an octagonal bowl required nine, one in the middle and another at each of the eight angles. Polygonal shapes of all kinds were used for fonts; up to twelve sides are known, for instance at **Patrington** (E. Riding of Yorks), but the octagon (Pls 214–218) became increasingly popular until by the late Middle Ages it was the standard type. Late twelfth- and early thirteenth-century lead fonts are found in considerable numbers and include a group of six in Gloucestershire all made from the same pattern: one of these can been be seen at **Frampton-on-Severn** and another from the ruined Norman church at Lancaut is now in the Lady chapel at Gloucester Cathedral. The lead was probably cast flat, then rolled into a cylinder and soldered in place. These fonts show six seated figures beneath an arcade of twelve round-headed arches with scroll-work and other elaborate patterning. Stylistically they belong to the Norman period (see p. 74)

Thirteenth-century fonts can be divided by material into two main categories. The most popular type used Purbeck or some other similar kind of shell marble, which was not suitable for sculpture in depth but lent itself to simple decoration, consisting mainly of mouldings, as at **Ashbourne** (Derbys), and a highly polished finish which showed up the beauty of the material. It has been suggested that the shallow arcades which often appear on the sides of the bowls may originally have been peopled with painted figures, but this is merely conjecture. Fonts made of

Pl. 213 *The thirteenth-century font in St Mary's church at Eaton Bray, Bedfordshire, with a circular bowl supported on five squat columns and carved with vigorous stiff-leaf ornament, contemporary with the splendid nave arcades built c.1220–40.*

Pl. 214 *The fourteenth-century font in the church of St Lawrence at North Hinksey, Oxfordshire, with a different tracery pattern on each of its eight sides.*

the shafts on the base of the font to be attached to the central column, as at Ashbourne, a development which led on to the solid bases of the later medieval period.

By the fourteenth century marble fonts were no longer so fashionable, perhaps because in time the material was seen to lose its glossy finish or possibly because of a wish for greater scope in decorative carving. Circular and square bowls become rare and we no longer find detached shafts used on pedestals. There are some deep tub-shaped fonts of this period which

Pl. 215 *The ornate late medieval font dated 1544 in the grand Norman church of All Saints at Walsoken, Norfolk, with the Seven Sacraments and the Crucifixion on the eight sides of the bowl and saints in the panels round the stem.*

freestone, on the other hand, are generally more ornate because this type of stone was finely-grained and homogenous enough to be cut freely in all directions. It could therefore be carved in much greater detail and gave far more scope for variety and invention. Some stone fonts, like the unusual example at **Barnack** (Cambs), with scrolling foliage on a cylindrical bowl and broad arcaded base, look back to the exuberance of the Romanesque period, while others, like the one at **Eaton Bray** (Beds, Pl. 213), with its stiffleaf decoration, echo types of ornament used in contemporary architecture. Towards the end of the thirteenth century it became common for

Pl. 216 *The fifteenth-century font in St Mary's church at Stoke-by-Nayland, Suffolk, raised on steps with three built-in seats; the bowl, which is carved with the signs of the Evangelists, is supported by angels.*

have no bases, for example at **Burford** (Oxon) and **Poynings** (W. Sussex), but a form with a polygonal bowl and pedestal, providing flat rectangular surfaces suitable for elaborate sculptured decoration, was the type most widely adopted. The sides of these fonts were frequently carved to resemble niches, which could be highly ornate. The triangular-headed niches on the font at **Patrington** (E. Riding of Yorks) have cusped tracery, crockets and finials, while at **Fishlake** (S. Yorks) we find elaborately foliated nodding ogee arches. All kinds of tracery appear on fonts; sometimes, as at **North Hinksey** (Oxon, Pl. 214), **Offley** (Herts) and **Brailes** (Warwicks), a series of miniature window designs provides the only decoration, a different type appearing on each face. During the later fourteenth century, other architectural features are reproduced in scaled-down form to ornament fonts, for example buttresses around the pedestal, as at **Hull** (E. Riding of Yorks) and **Hitchin** (Herts), or battlements along the top of the bowl, as at **Rattlesden** (Suffolk).

By the fifteenth century the standard shape for a font was an octagonal bowl supported by a solid octagonal shaft and sometimes set up on a stepped platform, as at **Cratfield** (Suffolk), to give the congregation a better view of the baptism. This shape provided two sets of eight rectangular panels, one on the bowl and another on the base. These panels, which were given architectural frames, provided suitable spaces for a series of carvings of didactic subjects, similar to those found painted on contemporary screens or in stained-glass windows. Surviving traces of paint suggest that fonts were also rich in colour. This period saw the revival of figure sculpture; biblical scenes, angels, saints and holy men were all common subjects. The Seven Sacraments and the Crucifixion provided a favourite sequence for filling a set of eight panels, for example at **Cratfield** (Suffolk) and **Walsoken** (Norfolk, Pl. 215), as did the four symbols of the Evangelists, the angel of St Matthew, the lion of St Mark, the ox of St Luke and the eagle of St John, alternating with figures, as at **Stoke-by-Nayland** (Suffolk, Pl. 216) or angels, as at **Caistor St Edmund** (Norfolk). The symbol of the Trinity and the instruments of Christ's Passion are other subjects which are often found on fonts, as at **Fakenham** (Norfolk). Lions are extremely popular and appear not only round the pedestal, as at **East Dereham** (Norfolk), but sometimes, for example at **Wingfield** (Suffolk), on the bowl as well. More unusual animal subjects include the small creatures crawling round the base of the stem of the font at **Snape** (Suffolk). East Anglia, which was a prosperous area in the later Middle Ages, is particularly rich in elaborately carved fonts of this type, which also make use of more formal ornament, such as quatrefoils, shields and Tudor roses. By contrast Cornwall, which was not in contact with the mainstream development of Gothic architecture,

continued to produce fonts which, as at **Boconnoc** and **St Neot**, appear in some respects to be much older than they are, because earlier forms and ornament remained in favour in this area long after they had been superseded elsewhere.

Font covers

Fonts were always kept covered and locked when not in use (see p. 74). Medieval font covers were almost always designed to be taken off when the font was in use, but a very few exceptional examples were permanently fixed in position. The simplest removable type was held in place by an iron bar fastened to staples leaded into the sides of the bowl of the font. This kind of cover was just a flat lid, which may originally have been painted. One can often see the marks where the staples which secured it were subsequently wrenched out of the stonework.

During the later Middle Ages, when carpentry was becoming much more sophisticated, font covers took the form of increasingly elaborate openwork spires, like the spectacular pinnacled example, nearly twenty feet (6m) high, which is now in **Worlingworth** Church (Suffolk) but is said to have come from the abbey of Bury St Edmunds. Another impressive cover, at **Salle** (Norfolk), still has the pulley which was required to lift up its considerable weight; the beam which supported the pulley can still be seen at **North Walsham** and **Sheringham** (both also Norfolk). Sometimes, as at **Ufford** (Suffolk, Pl. 217), only the lower part of the cover was raised, so that it slid telescopically over the upper part when the font was in use and was held in position by counterweights.

Permanently fixed covers were a later development; three have survived from this period, and the only other example of the kind, in **Durham** Cathedral, was made in 1663. These structures were free-standing, with open sides, and were large enough for the priest and the sponsors for the christening to stand round the font inside them. An ornate stone version at St Mary, **Luton**, dates from as early as *c.*1330, but the elaborate wooden examples with canopied superstructures at St Peter Mancroft, **Norwich**, and **Trunch** (Norfolk, Pl. 218) belong to the end of the fifteenth century.

DOORS

Early medieval doors, both single and double, have quite often survived, complete with their original ironwork. Iron was expensive and would have been used extensively only in wealthier buildings, but where funds were available, the craftsmen who made these doors developed the basic necessity for holding planks of wood together into a positive art form. In

Pl. 217 *The magnificent fifteenth-century font cover in St Mary's church at Ufford, Suffolk, with three tall tiers of intricately carved canopies and a Pelican in her Piety at the top; when it is raised the lower section slides upwards to cover the upper part; the octagonal font with its bowl supported by sculptured heads is carved with shields and roses and dates from the same period, as does the fine timber roof.*

Pl. 218 *The splendid fixed cover of c.1500 above the contemporary octagonal font in St Botolph's church at Trunch, Norfolk, which is richly decorated with carved foliage and flowers and crowned with an ornate vaulted canopy.*

Pl. 219 *The south door of St Mary's Church at Eaton Bray, Bedfordshire, covered with ornate scrolling ironwork dating from the mid thirteenth century.*

the Middle Ages most of the iron used in Britain came from the Sussex Weald or the Forest of Dean and was produced by smelting the ore with charcoal, which has a much lower sulphur content than the coal or coke used in modern times. As a result medieval iron was very durable, for although at first it corroded it then formed a protective black coating which prevented it from rusting; so where it has survived it is still in remarkably good condition. Probably the best-known example can be seen at **Windsor** Castle, where the doors to Henry III's chapel (now the Albert Memorial Chapel) bear the name of the thirteenth-century craftsman, "Gilebertus", who made them. A similar pattern of scrolling iron tendrils covers the entire surface of the south doors at **Eaton Bray** (Pl. 219)

and **Turvey** (both in Bedfordshire), where the hinges are absorbed into the overall design. At **Uffington** (Oxon) there are C-shaped hinges reminiscent of those found on Norman doors, for instance those at **Staplehurst** (Kent) and **Old Woking** (Surrey); and as at Staplehurst there are sometimes designs including strange creatures, for example dragons' heads at **Faringdon** (Oxon, thirteenth-century) and prancing leopards at **Dartmouth** (S. Devon), where the fourteenth-century south door is

Pl. 220 *The fifteenth-century external door in the fourteenth-century south porch of St Dunstan's church at Cranbrook, Kent, showing the vertical timbers on the outer surface secured by large nails to horizontal ledges on the inside.*

Pl. 221 *The intricately carved fifteenth-century south door of St Mary's church at Stoke-by-Nayland, Suffolk, with narrow panels of tracery and the small figures of a Jesse Tree.*

for example, at St Gregory, **Norwich** (now in the south chapel), where it takes the form of a lion's mask with a man's head in its jaws. This subject has been seen either as a victim being swallowed up, representing a warning that the jaws of Hell await anyone violating the laws of sanctuary, or as a man emerging safely from a beast's mouth, symbolizing the power of the church to save Christians from earthly or spiritual danger. These are both Christian interpretations of a pagan motif, which was found all over Europe in pre-Christian Celtic iconography and was absorbed into the repertoire of Romanesque and Gothic church builders. Animals often feature as decoration on handles, for instance lions' heads at **St Osyth** Priory (Essex, Pl. 222), **Boston** (Lincs) and All Saints, Pavement, **York**, lizards at Boston, salamanders at **Withersfield** (Suffolk) and winged dragons at **Iwade** (Kent). Sometimes the design of the metalwork surrounding the handle is expanded, as at **Tunstead** (Norfolk), where it measures about 1.22m (4 feet) and takes the form of a huge foliated cross, a motif which also dominated the overall design of the south door at **Haddiscoe** (Norfolk).

As the charcoal burners devastated the forests for fuel during the later Middle Ages, restrictions on ironworks had to be introduced, and by the sixteenth century the industry was legally prevented from expanding. This and the development of increasing skills in carpentry must have encouraged a new fashion for carved wooden doors of great sophistication, and they have survived in large numbers from the fifteenth century onwards. The characteristic tendency of the Perpendicular style to use tracery patterns for covering every flat surface with blank arcading lent itself perfectly to the decoration of doors. During the Middle Ages it was common to make external doors with a double layer of wood as at **Cranbrook** (Kent, Pl. 220) the vertical boards on the outside secured by nails to the horizontal "ledges" of the inner surface, producing a considerable thickness. This allowed for carving in high relief and the ornamentation of these doors mirrors the stylistic development of the period, with the decorative features of window design reproduced in miniature in wood. There is reticulated tracery on the door at **Brent Eleigh** (Suffolk) and **Brent Pelham** (Herts), ballflower ornament appears at **Gedney** (Lincs) and "mouchettes" (curved dagger-shaped tracery motifs) are found at **Higham** (Kent). Sometimes the blank arcading is peopled with figures, like the crucified Christ and symbolic birds at **Finchingfield** (Essex) or the ancestors of Christ in the Tree of Jesse on the south door at **Stoke-by-Nayland** (Suffolk, Pl. 221). The saints in the Perpendicular tracery border of the door at **Harpley** (Norfolk) also feature on its wicket, one of the relatively few of these doors within doors to have survived from medieval times. A secular

deceptively dated 1631, presumably the year when it was restored after the addition of a new porch. A more formal design based on intersecting circles covers the south door at **Skipwith** (N. Yorks).

Compared with such spectacular ironwork, medieval doorhandles are easily overlooked, but even when they are very simple and unobtrusive, as at **Adderbury** (Oxon), they display the same high quality of workmanship. The earlier type of ring handle showing an animal devouring its victim, like the late Norman example at Adel, **Leeds** (W. Yorks), persists,

Pl. 222 *A doorhandle in the form of a lion's mask in the late fifteenth-century gatehouse of St Osyth Priory, Essex.*

symbol is found on the plain north door at **Littlebury** (Essex), where a pair of carved shears makes it clear that it was the wool trade that financed the building.

Individual donors are rarely commemorated, but on the former south door of the redundant church at **Sco Ruston** (Norfolk), now in the care of the Norfolk Museums Service, the patron had his own name and his wife's recorded, and two donors are named at **Worsborough** (W. Yorks). Carved inscriptions of this kind are not very common, but at **Gedney** (Lincs) there are three – on the outside a Latin prayer that the peace of Christ

may bless the church and its congregation, on the wicket simply "*In hope*", and on the inside lock a practical injunction to mind your step: "*Johannes Pette auyseth beware before*".

SCREENS

Screens played a prominent part in every medieval church, where the interior was not the open space we see today but a series of different compartments. The most important division was between the nave and the sanctuary, where the screen protected the sanctity of the east end. It had doors which were kept locked whenever the nave was in use for secular purposes. The locks were fitted on the eastern side and the priest who locked up would leave the church through the south door of the chancel. Since this dividing screen formed the base for the rood or Crucifixion group (see p. 60), most of them were systematically destroyed when roods were torn down at the Reformation (see p. 175).

We can get some idea of the appearance of a complete rood screen in rare cases where its silhouette can still be seen against a solid background. At **Wenhaston** (Suffolk), where the boarded tympanum which filled the upper part of the chancel arch has survived, one can make out the white shape of the Crucifixion group surrounded by a painted scene of the Last Judgement. Another indication of the former presence of a rood screen is at the fifteenth-century Church of St Peter Mancroft in **Norwich**, where the pulley and boss for the lenten veil which covered the rood during Lent are still in position.

However, medieval chancel screens, not all of which carried a rood, have occasionally survived. A very early wooden example at **Kirkstead** (Lincs, *c.*1230–40, Pl. 223) has simple lancet openings above and plain panelling below. The original stone choir screen (*c.*1235–50) at **Salisbury** Cathedral (see p. 142) was moved from the eastern arch of the crossing in the late eighteenth century and can now be seen in the south-east transept. Fourteenth-century wooden screens imitating stone usually have trefoiled arches with turned shafts instead of the mullions found in later work. The great majority of surviving screens are in the Perpendicular style of the late Middle Ages. Some were not rood screens but "parcloses" or partitions to shut off side aisles as at **East Harling** (Norfolk, Pl. 224 and **Dennington** (Suffolk, Pl. 225).

Screens were also used to enclose chantries and other subsidiary chapels. Surviving examples include the Decorated style Percy Screen in stone and Purbeck marble which supported the shrine of St John of **Beverley** and numerous openwork screens enclosing chantry chapels at **Canterbury**, **Tewkesbury**, **Wells** and **Winchester**. During the later Middle

Pl. 223 *The wooden screen, with polygonal shafts between open arches, in St Leonard's church at Kirkstead, Lincolnshire, built c.1230–40 as a chapel belonging to Kirkstead Abbey; the screen is believed to be contemporary with the church and may therefore be one of the earliest wooden screens in existence.*

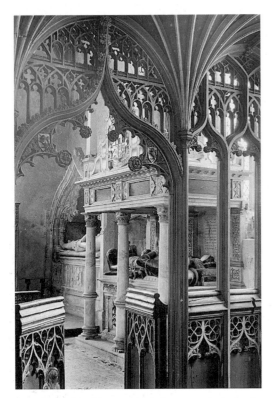

Pl. 224 *The fifteenth-century parclose screen enclosing the chapel in the south aisle of the church of St Peter and St Paul at East Harling, Norfolk, showing its Perpendicular tracery and coved loft; the monuments date from c.1435 and 1604.*

Pl. 225 *The fifteenth-century parclose screen enclosing the monument to Lord Bardolph (died 1441) in the south nave aisle of St Mary's church at Dennington, Suffolk, showing its intricate tracery and tall loft with cresting along the top.*

Pl. 226 *The fine fifteenth-century East Anglian screen in St Helen's church at Ranworth, Norfolk, showing some of its twenty-six painted panels, its delicately cusped arches, the ribbed and painted coving of its rood loft and the spaces for nave altars on either side of the entrance to the chancel; the wooden eagle lectern dates from the nineteenth century.*

Ages wooden screens became very common and some early medieval stone screens, for example at **Tintinhull** (Somerset) and **Yatton** (Avon), were replaced by timber versions coved at the top to support the wide rood lofts which were coming into fashion.

There are noticeable local variations in the types of screen which have survived. In East Anglia tall open screens, generally running across the nave only, have the finely carved detail and high-quality painting which is found, for instance, at **Ranworth** and **Attleborough** (both in Norfolk,

Pl. 227 *Detail of the splendid early sixteenth-century screen which runs across the full width of the nave and aisles in St Mary's church, Attleborough, Norfolk, showing its ribbed coving and loft parapet painted with the arms of the twenty-four late medieval English bishoprics; the figures in the wall painting, possibly associated with the vanished rood, include Moses and David with angels holding the instruments of Christ's Passion.*

the Midlands screens are sometimes found with all the carved detail on the western side and the east-facing back left undecorated. In the south-west of England one finds long low screens, often stretching across the entire width of a church where the nave aisles continue eastwards into the chancel, for instance at **Dunster** (Somerset). West Country screens, as at **Kenton** (Devon, Pl. 229), are heavily constructed, consisting of a dado made up of solid panels, frequently decorated with paintings

Pl. 228 *The mid fourteenth-century stone screen which fills the chancel arch of the church of St Mary the Virgin at Stebbing, Essex; the three figures of the rood originally stood on the horizontal transom across the central arch.*

Pls 226 and 227) and **Southwold** (Suffolk). There may be two tiers of tracery, as at **Castle Hedingham** (Essex). In some cases where the screen is not fitted with doors to close the central opening, it is thought that there was a further barrier to the west preventing access to the chancel from the nave. Stone screens like traceried windows filling up the entire chancel arch occur in Essex at **Stebbing** (Pl. 228) and **Great Bardfield**. In

of saints, and above it openings like traceried windows, each divided by mullions into four vertical lights; along the top runs a richly carved beam. Typical Welsh screens, like the one at **Llananno** (Powys), have low dados and rectangular-headed tracery in the "window" openings. They appear to have had less painted decoration than is found in other regions, but they are rich in an abundance of exuberant carving.

Rood lofts

These lofts are found mainly in Wales and the West Country, for example at **Berry Pomeroy** (Devon), and perhaps owe their survival to the fact that removing them would have done irreparable damage to the screens which carry them. Narrower rood lofts were supported by the top of the screen and a parallel beam about 60cm (two feet) in front of it. The space

Pl. 229 *The handsome late fifteenth- or early sixteenth-century screen running the full width of the nave in All Saints' Church at Kenton, Devon, showing its painted panels, traceried openings, fan coving and much-renewed cornice; the restored rood loft dates from 1899 and 1935–6.*

between was boarded in to form a gallery with panelled sides, as in the case of the early sixteenth-century loft at **Flamborough** (E. Riding of Yorks). Alternatively a loft was made between two parallel screens, for instance at **Edington** (Wilts, heavily restored). Wider lofts with parapets supported by coving are found in Wales (see p. 305), where they have sometimes survived unchanged in remote churches like **Patrisio** or **Patrishow** (Powys, c.1500, Pl. 230). Generally all that is left to indicate the former presence of a rood loft is the narrow staircase (see Pl. 210) which gave access to it. These can frequently be seen disappearing into the side wall of the nave at ground level and emerging above at the level of the top of the former screen, as at **Horning** (Norfolk) or **Deddington** (Oxon).

CHESTS

The chest was a very common piece of furniture in medieval times and was used for numerous storage purposes. A church chest (Pl. 231) would have housed books and documents, plate or vestments, or might be used for collecting alms, in which case it had a slot in its lid. Three locks were generally provided, not just for strength but also to guard against fraud, for it ensured that the vicar and two churchwardens, each holding his own separate key, all had to be present at the same time before the chest could be opened. The locks might form part of a pattern of ornate ironwork frequently used to provide reinforcement for these wooden chests, which were generally decorated in some way, often with paint or carving. External carving has largely vanished, but painting is still sometimes found on the inside, for instance under the lid of the late thirteenth-century chest in **Newport** Church (Essex) where there are five scenes, a Crucifixion flanked by saints; the Richard of Bury chest (c.1340) in the Burrell Collection, **Glasgow**, has four heraldic shields with supporters executed in tempera in remarkably bright red, yellow, blue and white on a green background.

Cope chests

Chests in the shape of a semicircle or a quadrant were specially made to take copes, for these valuable circular vestments needed to be stored either flat or folded in half or in quarters. Such chests now survive only in cathedrals. Semicircular examples can still be seen at **Gloucester** and **Salisbury** and quadrant-shaped versions at **Wells** and **York**.

Almsboxes

There are only a very few medieval poor boxes still in existence today. A fifteenth-century box at St George's Chapel, **Windsor**, marked with the letter H and thought to have been intended for offerings at the tomb of King Henry VI, is made of iron, but other surviving examples are wooden. They range from a simple chest made of a hollowed-out tree trunk at **Keddington** (Suffolk) to much more elaborate versions, such as the box with three locks mounted on a solid oak pedestal at **Smarden** (Kent) or the tall pillar with traceried panels at **Blythburgh** (Suffolk).

Pl. 230 *Detail of the superbly carved rood loft of c.1500 in the church of St Ishow at Partrishow or Patrisio, Powys.*

Pl. 231 *A fourteenth-century chest with scrolling ironwork in All Saints' church at Icklingham All Saints, Suffolk, with, in the background, a row of reed hassocks resting on a plain wooden storage box of indeterminate date.*

Pl. 232 *The late fourteenth-century tomb of Richard Fitzalan and his wife in Chichester Cathedral, West Sussex; the hands of the two separate figures were joined during restoration in 1844.*

MONUMENTS

Thirteenth-century monuments were generally made of English shell limestones which more or less resembled marble, but these were gradually displaced by local freestones, and from the fourteenth century onwards there was a fashion for alabaster. This had the great advantage that it was softer than other stones and could be carved easily to show very fine detail.

Effigies were popular as memorials throughout the Middle Ages. The subjects were generally knights or churchmen, though a knight such as Richard Fitzalan at **Chichester** (W. Sussex, late fourteenth-century, Pl. 232) might be accompanied by his wife and a few prominent women had tombs of their own. The figures were almost always full-length rather than half-length or busts. The faces register no emotion, and personal likenesses do not normally appear to have been attempted. An identical set of features would appear on more than one tomb, for example at **Winchester**, where Archbishop Courtenay (1396) exactly resembles William of Wykeham (1404). Fashionable dress, ecclesiastical vestments and up-to-date armour were faithfully reproduced, however, and individuals were identified by inscriptions and heraldic devices.

Late twelfth-century figures, like Bishop Bartolomeus Iscanus (1184) of **Exeter**, were carved in low relief out of the slabs in which they were set, but during the thirteenth century separate sculptured forms emerged, with effigies like that of King John (*c.*1230) in **Worcester** Cathedral, which was carved out of dark Purbeck marble, a popular material during the thirteenth and fourteenth centuries. From the late thirteenth century onwards we find figures which are quite separate from the chests they lie on and are even made in a different material; for example, the gilded bronze effigies of Henry III and Queen Eleanor (Pl. 233), wife of Edward I (both 1291), at **Westminster** Abbey and the alabaster figure of Edward II (*c.*1330, Pl. 234) in **Gloucester** Cathedral all rest on Purbeck marble tomb-chests. While the figures of the deceased are almost always shown lying down, some early postures, like that of Bishop Roger (1139) at **Salisbury**, are clearly copied from standing positions. A kneeling figure appears as early as *c.* 1380 in **Tewkesbury** Abbey, where Edward Despenser (Pl. 236) is shown on the roof of his chantry praying under a canopy. A woman is usually made to appear youthful and slender, dressed in loose draperies, her feet resting on a pet dog and her hands either folded in prayer or perhaps holding a heraldic shield or a heart. In contrast Philippa of Hainault (1369, Pl. 235), wife of Edward III, is shown in **Westminster** Abbey in the realistic manner traditional in France, as a portly matron in close-fitting fashionable clothes. Until the fifteenth century, when

Pl. 233 *A gilded bronze effigy of 1291 in Westminster Abbey, showing Queen Eleanor, wife of Edward I, resting on a Purbeck marble tomb-chest.*

skeletons and shrouds were sometimes introduced, as on the tomb of Bishop Fleming (1431) at **Lincoln**, the subject was always depicted alive.

The posture used for military effigies varies throughout the medieval period. Early thirteenth-century figures are stretched straight out, like William Longespée (1226, Pl. 237) at **Salisbury**, who lies with his head on a pillow and a shield on his left arm. His son (1250), also at **Salisbury**, is shown with his legs crossed, a very popular contemporary fashion which lasted until the mid fourteenth century. Movement and great vitality are found in the figure of a knight (*c.*1280, Pl. 239) at **Dorchester** (Oxon), but

Pl. 234 *Detail of the alabaster figure of Edward II (c.1330) on a Purbeck marble tomb-chest in Gloucester Cathedral.*

Pl. 235 *Philippa of Hainault, wife of Edward III, who died in 1369, realistically portrayed in fashionable clothes on her marble tomb-chest in Westminster Abbey.*

Pl. 236 *The life-sized figure of Edward Despenser kneeling in prayer on the roof of his chantry, the Trinity Chapel in Tewkesbury Abbey, Gloucestershire, which was built soon after his death in 1375.*

serenity became popular during the later Middle Ages, with the general adoption of a peaceful pose with the hands placed together in prayer, which is found for instance on the alabaster figure of Alice, Duchess of Suffolk (*c.*1480), at **Ewelme** (Oxon).

The tomb-chest supporting the effigy became an increasingly important part of the design of any important memorial from the late thirteenth century onwards. These bases were decorated with carved

Pl. 238 *Detail of the splendid tomb chest (*C.1450*) of Richard Beauchamp, Earl of Warwick, in the Beauchamp Chapel at St Mary's church, Warwick, showing the gilded copper figures of monks, ladies and angel weepers.*

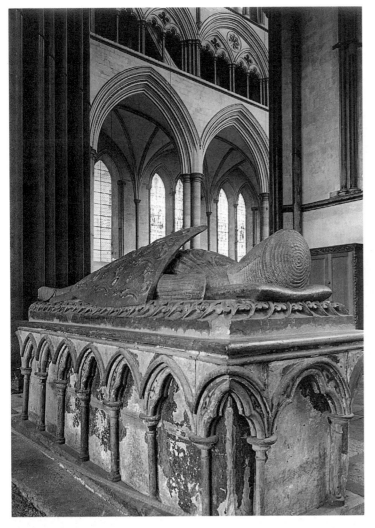

Pl. 237 *The rigid effigy of William Longspée the Elder, who died in 1226, shown lying on a wooden tomb-chest in Salisbury Cathedral, clad in mail with his shield on his arm.*

ornament and heraldic devices, as well as with figure sculpture, such as rows of mourning relatives, a fashion derived from France. These appear on a group of ambitious monuments made by the court workshops of Edward I, including the tombs of Archbishop Peckham (d. 1292) at **Canterbury**, Edmund Crouchback, Earl of Lancaster (d. 1296), at **Westminster** Abbey and Bishop de Luda (d. 1299) at **Ely**. Angel weepers were an English variant on these mourners and they became increasingly popular from the mid-fourteenth century onwards, for instance on the tomb of Richard Beauchamp, Earl of Warwick (d. 1439, Pls 165 and 238), in the Beauchamp Chapel at St Mary's Church, **Warwick**.

Brasses

A less costly alternative to the three-dimensional form of memorial was a flat effigy engraved on brass and set in a slab of stone. These began to appear towards the end of the thirteenth century, at first representing knights such as Sir Robert de Septvans (d. 1306) at **Chartham** (Kent, Pl. 240) but in smaller and inferior later versions recording civilians as

Pl. 239 *Movement and great vitality in the recumbent figure (c.1280) of a knight drawing his sword at Dorchester Abbey, Oxfordshire.*

Pl. 240 *A very early life-sized brass memorial in St Mary's church at Chartham, Kent, commemorating Sir Robert de Septvans who died in 1306.*

standing under tripartite canopies, with their young sons set on pedestals at their feet. The Flemish method of producing this type of memorial did not involve cutting but used a complete rectangular sheet of brass engraved all over its surface. Imported brasses of this kind are common, especially in eastern areas of England, for example at St Margaret, **King's Lynn** (Norfolk), where two of the largest known record Adam de Walsokne (d. 1349) and Robert Braunche (d. 1364), both depicted with

Pl. 241 *Sir John de la Pole and his wife, shown almost life-sized beneath a tripartite arch, on a fine brass of c.1380 in the church of the Holy Trinity at Chrishall, Essex.*

well. The English tradition used pieces of brass engraved and cut out into the necessary shapes, which were then let into the stone flush with its surface as at **Chrishall** (Essex, Pl. 241). An exceptionally large group at **Cobham** (Kent) includes two very fine brasses to Sir Reginald Braybrok (d. 1405) and Sir Nicholas Hawberk (d. 1407), which show their tall figures their wives and beneath rich canopies. Brasses provide a fascinating source of information on medieval armour and costume, which are shown in realistic detail. It seems likely that certain design conventions introduced on brasses, such as separate kneeling rows of the sons and daughters of the deceased, seen in profile facing each other, or a husband and wife shown impassively holding hands, may well have influenced sculptured tombs where the same features occur.

INTERIOR DECORATION

Colour

The walls of important churches would normally have been plastered and whitewashed, then painted with red lines to imitate blocks of masonry. Even wooden ceilings, such as the cusped lierne vault in the chapel at **Winchester** College (Hants, late fourteenth-century), might be painted to resemble stone. Architectural features such as capitals, bosses, canopies, monuments or statues would have been brightly coloured and many flat areas filled with decorative patterns or scenes depicting events from the Bible or the lives of the saints. Traces of original pigment can still be seen on much surviving sculpture, such as the thirteenth-century wooden Virgin and Child in the Victoria and Albert Museum, **London**. Contemporary English figures made in wood and still brightly painted exist in some numbers in Scandinavia, evidently as a result of a flourishing export trade at that time, for example St Michael and the Dragon in the Trondheim University Museum or a Crucifixion figure in the Historical Museum of the University of Bergen. The early thirteenth-century painted ceiling of the nave at **Peterborough** Cathedral (Cambs) preserves the original colouring in its lozenge patterns and figures of saints and kings.

Wall paintings

A few extant wall paintings, such as the Deposition in the Chapel of the Holy Sepulchre at **Winchester** (c.1230), the five thirteenth-century Crucifixion scenes on the piers at **St Albans** (Pl. 242), or the mid fourteenth-century Last Judgement and Apocalypse in the chapter house at **Westminster** Abbey, give a faint echo of the richly painted pictorial and patterned decoration which must have been common on the walls of all our great churches during the Middle Ages but has rarely survived. However, a surprising number of parish churches, such as **Attleborough** (Norfolk, Pl. 226), retain some traces of their didactic paintings and a few comprehensive schemes can still be seen (see p. 213). Modern restoration is greatly increasing our understanding and appreciation of these

Pl. 242 *A thirteenth-century Crucifixion and Virgin and Child, originally above an altar set against one of the nave piers in St Albans Cathedral, Hertfordshire, where an exceptional amount of medieval wall painting has survived.*

paintings, very few of which are now in a recognizable state. Most of them are not true frescoes, where the pigment is applied to wet plaster and bonds securely with it, but were painted in *tempera* (powdered colour mixed with lime-water, egg or skimmed milk) on to plaster which had already dried; they were therefore liable to fade or flake off. These paintings were generally done in earth colours, like ochre, brick red and shades of brown and grey, which were common and therefore cheap. Bright colours such as blue, made from *lapis lazuli*, and green, from

Pl. 243 *The much repainted early sixteenth-century Last Judgement above the chancel arch of the church of St Thomas of Canterbury at Salisbury, Wiltshire; on the left the righteous dead are rising from their graves, on the right the wicked are being driven into the jaws of Hell and at the top is Christ, seated on a rainbow between the Virgin and St John.*

Pl. 244 *The fourteenth-century wall painting of the Crucifixion, painted at the east end of the south aisle in Dorchester Abbey, Oxfordshire.*

malachite, were extremely expensive and were only used for rich patrons in important buildings, such as **Canterbury** and **Durham** cathedrals.

Where they can still be seen at all, medieval wall paintings convey only ghostly reflections of their original brilliance and vigour, but a better idea of their strong impact comes across in the church of St Thomas of Canterbury at **Salisbury** (Pl. 243) where the entire wall surrounding the chancel arch is covered with a complete, because extensively repainted, early sixteenth-century Last Judgement. Their impact can be appreciated too, to a certain extent, in some High Victorian churches like **Studley Royal** (N. Yorks) by William Burges (1871–8), where, although the style of the decorations is so different, one finds the overwhelming effect of an entire, richly painted interior with every surface used as a vehicle for pattern and ornament. At **Garton-on-the-Wolds** (E. Yorks) there is another complete scheme, by Clayton and Bell (1873–6), which integrates medievalizing wall paintings with stained glass in the style and glowing colours of the thirteenth century, producing an artistically and iconographically unified effect.

Cleaning and restoration at **Chalgrove** (Oxon) in 1988 made this church one of the best and most complete surviving medieval parish churches fully decorated with wall paintings. Another recent restoration took place in the small Norman church at **Little Tey** (Essex), where the ghostly but identifiable remains of two schemes of the thirteenth and fourteenth centuries were discovered, one on top of the other. The medieval church of St Teilo at Llandeilo Tal-y-Bont (Glamorgan) has been rebuilt at the Welsh Folk Museum at **St Fagans** near Cardiff, and restoration of its almost complete cycle of wall paintings has recreated the blaze of colour and proliferation of pattern in the original interior.

Much of the decoration of medieval church interiors took the form of geometrical or floral patterns or overall effects like simulated masonry (see above). Pictorial subjects, where they are found, reflect the use of the different parts of the church. The pictures on the walls of the nave might provide instruction, for instance by depicting scenes from the life of Christ, like the fourteenth-century Crucifixion at **Dorchester** Abbey (Oxon, Pl. 244). They might also issue dire warnings to those who erred, with paintings which were reminders of the dreadful death awaiting unrepentant sinners, enjoin good behaviour, for example by showing the devil knocking together the heads of two gossiping women, or offer support, for instance by inviting prayer to St Christopher, patron saint of travellers. He habitually appeared opposite the main door so that people could feel the comfort of his presence as they came in and ask for his protection on their journeys before they went out. There are examples of all these subjects at **Peakirk** (Cambs), where the greater part of a comprehensive fourteenth-century scheme can still be seen.

Christ in Majesty was shown in the chancel, where He was present in the Sacrament, and the Doom or Last Judgement was frequently painted above the chancel arch, the division between the laymen's and the priests' parts of the building, which symbolized the transition between the church on earth and salvation in Heaven. There are remarkable examples of chancel paintings, some from as early as the twelfth century, at **Copford** (Essex) and **Kempley** (Glos) (see p. 75), and a moving thirteenth-century Virgin and Child at **Great Canfield** (Essex, Pl. 246). Dooms that have survived range from the pre-medieval period, for instance at **Hardham** (W. Sussex, c.1120–40) and **Clayton** (W. Sussex, c.1140), to the early sixteenth century, as at **Wenhaston** (Suffolk, c.1520, Pl. 245). Here a Last Judgement painted on wooden boards, which originally hung above the chancel arch, was found in 1892 under a coat of whitewash.

The west wall, which presented another large and very visible space suitable for a balanced composition, was also used for this subject, for example at **Chaldon** (Surrey, c.1200), with its central Purgatorial Ladder

Pl. 245 *Detail of the early sixteenth-century Last Judgement in St Peter's church at Wenhaston, Suffolk, showing a devil dragging the damned into the jaws of Hell; the painting was originally behind the rood, which stood in front of the unpainted area on the left.*

Pl. 246 *The thirteenth-century wall painting of the Virgin and Child behind the altar in the chancel of St Mary's church at Great Canfield, Essex.*

(Pl. 84), and at **Trotton** (W. Sussex, *c.*1380), where the Seven Deadly Sins on one side are matched by the Seven Acts of Mercy on the other.

During the fourteenth century there was a tendency for very popular subjects to be included in churches for their own sake, rather than as part of a particular programme. There was a considerable vogue for apocryphal legends of the life of the Virgin, as at **Chalgrove** (Oxon), and moral lessons like the Three Living and the Three Dead (a Flemish story of three young and vigorous kings warned by three corpses of the inevitability of death), which can be seen at **Widford** (Oxon).

It was natural that wall paintings in refectories should emphasize Christ's Sacrifice of His Body and Blood, represented in the Eucharist by bread and wine. These large rooms also gave plenty of space for the celebration of patronage. A splendid thirteenth-century scheme in the Refectory at **Horsham St Faith** Priory (Norfolk) was made up of a boldly painted Crucifixion and a series of narrative pictures showing the donors' pilgrimage and their subsequent building of the monastery dedicated to the saint who delivered them from brigands.

During the later Middle Ages glass assumed an increasingly important decorative and didactic role, as ever larger windows provided greater scope for the glaziers. The wall-paintings which have survived from this period, such as the grey and brown scenes in the Lady Chapel at **Winchester** Cathedral depicting the Miracles of the Virgin, lack the richness and vitality of earlier examples, but brilliant colour and graphic detail were supplied by windows planned on an ambitious scale.

STAINED GLASS

Medieval stained-glass windows hardly ever survive in their entirety, but remnants can often be seen in churches throughout the country, either in fragments, such as the fifteenth-century glass at **Bagendon** (Glos, Pl. 248), or in panels, such as the nearly complete fourteenth-century Resurrection at **Wrangle** (Lincs, Pl. 247). The sheer size of the cathedrals and great monastic churches meant that they provided the greatest scope for windows containing elaborate programmes of pictorial instruction. Much of the late twelfth-century glazing of the eastern end of **Canterbury** Cathedral has survived in the building, so that it is possible to imagine the effect of the original scheme (see p. 75), with its juxtapositions of Old and New Testament subjects. Early thirteenth-century windows, like the great round "Dean's Eye" in the north transept at **Lincoln** Cathedral, have the strong, deep tones of contemporary French glass, since they were made with coloured "pot metal" imported from the same sources (see p. 75). Windows made with the indigenous plain glass were often given variety

Pl. 247 *The almost complete fourteenth-century Resurrection which survives in the east window of the church of St Mary and St Nicholas at Wrangle, Lincolnshire.*

by the addition of "grisaille" patterns or black foliage outlines painted on the surface. The rather sombre effect was sometimes relieved with small quantities of coloured glass, as in the mid thirteenth-century Seven Sisters window at **York** Minster. Around the beginning of the fourteenth century it was discovered that a yellow colour known as "silver stain" could be fired directly on to clear glass to add features like hair, a halo, a crown or patterns on drapery. This meant that much greater detail could be introduced without the need for cutting and leading separate pieces of glass, and it increased the use of clear and lighter coloured glass, for instance at **Great Malvern** Priory (Worcestershire, Pl. 249), which has the most complete fifteenth-century glazing scheme to have survived.

Its forty windows originally included subjects such as seventy-two scenes from the Old Testament, numerous episodes from the life of Christ, eleven Joys of Mary or illustrations from the Magnificat, and figures of angels, saints, bishops and martyrs. The richly pictorial effect is brighter than earlier work, because the tones of late medieval glass were generally paler and let in more light.

The round-headed openings of the Norman period had provided an uninterrupted window area which could accommodate large figures or arrangements of medallions set against a patterned background. The development, from the thirteenth century onwards, of tracery (see pp. 128–129) with close-set mullions meant that glaziers were faced with the problem of filling tall thin areas with vertical strips of glazing too narrow to be treated in the earlier ways. In order to produce an overall effect using these awkward spaces, they designed windows with horizontal rows of

Pl. 248 *A surviving fragment of fifteenth-century stained glass in the chancel of St Margaret's church at Bagendon, Gloucestershire, showing the Virgin Mary with her hands outstretched.*

Pl. 249 *Detail showing the heads of two women, possibly donors, in one of the stained-glass windows in the north choir aisle of Malvern Priory at Great Malvern, Worcestershire, which has the most complete fifteenth-century glazing scheme to have survived.*

smaller figures, as in the Pilgrims Window at **York** Minster, often standing under tall and elaborate architectural canopies introduced to occupy extra height. In Jesse windows, popular throughout the Middle Ages, the entire glazed area was taken up with the branches of a spreading tree springing from the recumbent form of Christ's ancestor Jesse and peopled with the figures of his descendants. Surviving panels from thirteenth-century Jesse windows can be seen at **Canterbury**, **Salisbury** and **York**, but the total effect is best understood by looking at the remarkably complete (though restored) composition in the east window of the parish church at **Margaretting** (Essex, fifteenth-century).

The figures or coats of arms of benefactors who paid for stained-glass windows appear from the thirteenth century onwards, for instance at **York** Minster, where Richard Tunnoc, a goldsmith and bellfounder, is actually depicted presenting his window to St William of York (*c.*1325). Such donors were given increasing prominence towards the end of the medieval period, with lifelike portraits of kneeling figures such as Sir Thomas Clopton and his wife at **Long Melford** (Suffolk, late fifteenth-century). Patterned borders began to be used, for instance in the chapter house at **York** (*c.*1285–90), and these provided scope for an unlimited range of decorative effects, based, for instance, on architectural elements, as at Merton College, **Oxford** (1309–12), or plant forms, as at **Tewkesbury** (Glos, 1340–44).

The broader windows of the Perpendicular style lent themselves to tiers of rectangular narrative scenes, as in the early fifteenth-century Apocalypse Window at **York** Minster. Subjects such as the Seven Sacraments were also well suited to this treatment, and they include much interesting background shedding light on the social history of the period, for example in the details of costume and furnishings of the domestic interior seen in a window at All Saints' Church, North Street, **York** (early fifteenth-century), which illustrates the Seven Corporal Acts of Mercy.

The famous early sixteenth-century glass at **Fairford** (Glos, Pl. 250) is an unique example of a complete medieval glazing scheme. Its twenty-eight large windows, which miraculously survived both the Reformation and the Puritan iconoclasm of the seventeenth century, provide a visual representation of the entire Catholic Faith in episodes from both the Old and the New Testament, drawing extensively on a well-known blockbook, the *Biblia Pauperum* (see p. 182), printed in the Netherlands in 1460–65. This superb glass in a pictorial Netherlandish style is thought to have been the work of both English and foreign craftsmen, probably associated with the Fleming Barnard Flower, King's Glazier to Henry VII.

TILES

Floor tiles

Floor tiles can be seen quite frequently, for instance at **Byland Abbey** (N. Yorks) and **Winchester** Cathedral (both thirteenth-century), **Ely** (fourteenth-century) and **Gloucester** (fifteenth-century). Although isolated earlier examples have survived, it was only in the thirteenth century that they began to be used regularly, when the technique for making inlaid patterns was brought to Britain, probably from France. Medieval tiles were not painted but derived their colours – brown, yellow, green and black – from various different combinations of the clays and lead glazes used in their manufacture. Patterns were produced either by fitting together tiles of different shapes to form a geometrical mosaic pavement, as in the south transept of the church at **Byland Abbey** (thirteenth-century), or by the use of impressed designs filled with clay of a contrasting colour, as in the chapter house at **Westminster** Abbey (mid thirteenth-century, Pl. 251 and 252). Here foliage designs and a rose window motif are combined with shields and figure subjects, including St Edward and the Pilgrim. The floor of Prior Crauden's Chapel (*c*.1325) in the precincts at **Ely** combines the two techniques, for while the tiles have a mosaic layout they are also decorated with impressed geometrical, animal and foliage patterns, and in the centre is a scene showing the Temptation in the Garden of Eden. However, in this case the impressions are not filled, so there is no colour contrast to emphasize the design.

Relief tiles of this kind were made in East Anglia during the second half of the fourteenth century, some with raised and others with sunk patterns. Inlaid tiles were much the most popular type, however, and were made all over the country, especially in Wessex in the thirteenth century, in the Midlands during the fourteenth and in the Severn valley round Gloucester and Malvern in the fifteenth. By using a contrasting slip to fill in the impression left by a stamped design, manufacturers could produce a wide range of decorative motifs, including birds, animals, foliage and geometrical patterns, in various shades of brown and yellow, the colours obtained by applying a clear glaze to red earthenware and white firing-clay. Green was not used for inlaid tiles, because the green glaze of the period was too opaque for a contrasting colour to show through it, but plain green tiles are sometimes found together with patterned ones. In the Chilterns during the fourteenth century, a process was evolved whereby the slip was printed on to the tiles in a single operation, and this method was subsequently adopted in other areas. Polychrome medieval tiles can still be seen in quantity. In greater churches, they are found, for example, in the retrochoir at **Winchester**

Pl. 250 *The early sixteenth-century stained glass depicting the Last Judgement in the west window of St Mary's church at Fairford, Gloucestershire, where the entire original glazing scheme has survived in twenty-eight windows dating from c.1500–20.*

Pl. 251 *Heraldic tiles of c.1253–7 in the paving on the floor of the chapter house at Westminster Abbey.*

Cathedral and in front of the high altar at **Gloucester** Cathedral and at **Great Malvern** Priory. There are also a few parish churches which have areas of intact paving, for instance the entire sanctuary at **Brook** (Kent) and the north transept at **Acton Burnell** (Shropshire).

During the early Middle Ages tiles were found in royal palaces and rich ecclesiastical buildings; by the fourteenth century they were evidently in general use. In parish churches they would have been confined to the sanctuary, though wealthier foundations could afford to have them elsewhere too. They also had other more sophisticated types of pavement like the early thirteenth-century "opus Alexandrinum" mosaic floor of the Trinity Chapel at **Canterbury** Cathedral, where coloured marbles are arranged in geometrical patterns. In the Presbytery (dated 1268) and the Feretory (or Chapel of Edward the Confessor) at **Westminster** Abbey there is "Cosmati work", made by craftsmen brought from Rome using red and green porphyry and white and gold glass mosaic.

Pl. 252 *Detail of the paving on the floor of the chapter house at Westminster Abbey, showing tiles of c.1253–7 with a repeated tracery motif like the original design of the rose window in the north transept.*

Wall tiles

About twelve hundred fifteenth-century wall tiles, with ninety different inlaid patterns, in shades of brown ranging from pinkish to lavender, can be seen at **Great Malvern** Priory (Hereford and Worcester), where they were removed from the walls behind the high altar and reset in the chancel screen. These are a very rare survival, though they are known to have existed elsewhere. In the outstanding collection of medieval tiles at the British Museum, **London**, there is a fourteenth-century pictorial tile with inlaid slip and *sgraffito,* or scratched-on, decoration. This is part of a frieze showing apocryphal scenes from the life of Christ which is thought to have come from Tring (Herts).

Secular architecture

CASTLES

The Middle Ages were the great period of castle building in Britain, when increasingly ingenious defences were devised to match a growing sophistication in methods of attack. Designers now concentrated on trying to prevent an enemy from getting too close to the castle walls. For this reason outer defences gained in importance and water fortifications were a normal feature of the strongest castles. At the same time the domestic arrangements in a castle had to be much more complex, so as to provide its occupants with the greater convenience and privacy which were now expected. The Normans had already discovered (see p. 81) that providing for domestic comfort inevitably reduced security and the larger windows needed for better-lit rooms made it impossible to combine strong fortifications with pleasant living accommodation.

The solution was to surround the residential part of the castle with separate defences designed to withstand up-to-date methods of siege warfare. Besides ladders, siege towers, battering rams and undermining, a bombarding enemy could now make use of a whole range of immensely powerful weapons. The "ballista" or giant cross-bow shot huge iron darts, while the "mangonel" or catapult and the "trebuchet" or sling could hurl huge stones or other weighty missiles. Edward I had large numbers of these vast contraptions, which had individual names like nineteenth-century steam engines. There was also "Greek Fire", a Byzantine discovery containing no gunpowder (which was not used for firearms until the early fourteenth century) that released on the enemy a combustible material so highly inflammable that it was almost impossible to put out.

Faced with such formidable weapons, it was useless to rely entirely on archers to keep an enemy at a distance, though longbows, which the English tended to prefer, and crossbows, whose range was gradually increased to almost four hundred yards (365m), continued to be used throughout the medieval period. Battlements gave some protection to defenders manning the tops of castle walls, while wooden fighting platforms, jutting out just below parapet level, made it possible to attack an enemy from above with heavy objects dropped through holes in its floor. The vestiges of one of these temporary projections can still be seen high up on the walls of **Hermitage** Castle (Scottish Borders, fourteenth-century, Pl. 253), and at **Craigmillar** (Lothian, fifteenth-century) there is a well-preserved example of the permanent machicolations which later took their place. These were projecting stone parapets, supported on corbels built out from the walls, which provided holes in the floor for dropping missiles and sheltered standing room.

As castles became more sophisticated during the thirteenth century, their numbers gradually dwindled, until castle building became something that only the richest could afford. This process had begun in the late twelfth century under Henry II (see p. 46). Besides dispossessing the barons of their independent castles, he had used such advanced military technology in the design of his royal strongholds that he greatly increased the standard needed for an effective fortress, with the result that very few of his subjects could afford to compete.

In times of peace many castles were neglected and quickly deteriorated, when the wet got in and caused crumbling of masonry and dry rot in the timbers. Noblemen who could not aspire to castles built fortified manor houses (see pp. 233–240), which were proof against casual attack but no serious challenge to royal authority. A house could, in any case, fulfil the same social function as a castle by providing the economic centre of a district. The local population supplied the occupants with goods and services, and the lord, with his large extended household, was both patron and employer. Apart from its defensive role, a castle was effectively a country house surrounded by its estate, and the peasants would cultivate the land either up to its walls or to the edge of the moat. The knowledge that in the event of a siege the surrounding area would be devastated and the trade of the entire neighbourhood disrupted must have been a powerful incentive to avoid provocation.

As with the twentieth-century arms race, increasing the stakes tended to reduce the incidence of conflict but also increased the horrors when it occurred. New castles were built to be as nearly impregnable as possible, so that only the hardiest would attempt to besiege them. The late twelfth-century circular keep at **Conisbrough** (S. Yorks), with its massive

rectangular buttresses, had introduced the idea of curved wall surfaces. Thirteenth-century curtain walls were designed with projecting round towers which could command every inch of their outer surface and counter any possible form of attack. Those along the outer walls of the bailey at Conisbrough were built of solid masonry, but by c.1220–40, as at **White Castle, Skenfrith** and **Grosmont** (all in Gwent), they were made hollow, so that they could have useful rooms inside them or provide a series of fighting platforms along the curtain. By the mid thirteenth century, towers with a D-shaped plan, curved on the outside and straight inside, were introduced, for example at **Pevensey** (E. Sussex) c.1250, to provide more useful living space without loss of strength. Access to the towers might be at ground level from the courtyard or on the first floor by way of an external staircase, but their upper floors could be reached only from the top of the curtain. This meant that an enemy who got over the top of the wall could not capture the entire castle simply by getting into one of its towers from above. Massive wooden doors along the wall-walk ensured that, in turn, each of the towers could resist attack independently and every one had to be taken separately.

The entrance gates in curtain walls were defended with special care by gatehouses like those at **Pevensey, Criccieth** (Gwynedd) and **White Castle** (Gwent) There might be two, as at **Beaumaris** (Gwynedd), although one was more usual. Each gate was flanked by tall D-plan towers commanding a drawbridge, which was either counterpoised or hinged. Early drawbridges were not raised and lowered like later examples but worked like a see-saw, controlled by weights at the end nearest the gateway. The two ends of its pivot were fixed into the sides of the flanking towers, where the holes to take them can still sometimes be seen. At **Conway** (Gwynedd) the roller of the replica drawbridge occupies the original pivot holes. The bridge would be kept in a vertical position when not in use, but when it was lowered, so that people could cross, it would be fastened down with bolts to prevent the weights swinging it back up again. Later drawbridges took the form of flaps which could be raised to prevent anyone crossing the moat while at the same time providing a protective covering for the entrance gate. The inner end had hinges at ground level and the outer was controlled by chains or ropes from the upper storey of the gatehouse, as at **Beaumaris**, where the chain holes can still be seen high up on the outer arch of the "Gate next the Sea". On the inner side of the drawbridge was the portcullis, a wooden grille reinforced with metal which could be lowered on chains through a slot in the floor above the entrance archway, so as to close it off and prevent access. These slots can still be seen, for instance at **Caernarvon** (Gwynedd), where the King's Gate bears the traces of no fewer than six

portcullises, as well as five doors. Where there was not enough space for a portcullis with its winching mechanism, which was often the case in Scottish castles, the alternative was a *yett* or strong iron gate immediately behind the wooden entrance door. Good surviving examples can be seen at **Blackness** Castle (Central Region) and **Greenknowe** Tower (Borders). Because the door swung open inwards, it was impossible for it to be opened while the yett was in place. Even if the gate was burned, the defenders still had this metal barrier between them and the enemy and could shoot at their attackers through its bars.

The walls of the guard chambers on either side of the entrance to a castle were provided with arrow-loops or slits for aiming at invaders and inside the entrance archway the gate was again defended, as at **Pevensey** (E. Sussex) by *meurtrières* (murder holes) in the vault above it, which may also be found in projections on the outer face of the gatehouse. Through these holes, stones could be dropped or scalding liquids poured on to the assailants' heads, though molten lead and boiling oil are now thought to be figments of the imaginations of past military historians. It seems most unlikely that such expensive commodities would have been used so unnecessarily.

The Edwardian castles

The most spectacular of all British castles were those built in Wales during the late thirteenth century by Edward I whose master builder was James of St George, a Frenchman from Savoy. Unlike so many contemporary castles they were not adaptations of earlier fortresses but expertly designed new buildings, incorporating the most up-to-date developments in military architecture. They were all sited either on the coast or on tidal rivers, so as to take advantage of Edward's supremacy at sea. Their garrisons could take in supplies which arrived by water without having to go outside their own defences, and in 1294 only thirty-seven men were able to hold **Harlech** (Gwynedd, Pl. 254) against the entire Welsh army. The wet moats of these castles gave them a tremendous advantage, since they precluded any attempt at undermining the outer walls. At **Caernarvon** and **Conway** (both Gwynedd) the defended area included a walled town, planned as part of the whole scheme and still surviving almost intact, but the greatest innovation

Pl. 253 *Hermitage Castle, a grim fourteenth-century stronghold in the Scottish Borders, with holes in the masonry showing the position of the wooden fighting platforms which projected from the upper walls below the parapet.*

of all was the concentric castle which was used whenever the site permitted. **Beaumaris** on Anglesey (Gwynedd, Fig. 5) is an absolutely regular example of this type with its double ring of walls and towers and its massive gatehouses. The inner curtain of a concentric castle was protected by a much lower outer wall with towers at intervals along its length. This was kept low so that the defenders inside the castle could fire at the enemy over the heads of their own soldiers in the outer turrets. External fortifications were generally open at the back so that if the enemy took them he would not gain any shelter but could be attacked by arrows or missiles from within the castle proper.

Castle-building had now reached its peak with buildings which were both architectural masterpieces and virtually impregnable fortresses. They were also palaces which provided considerable luxury, for military and domestic architecture were not entirely separate and the same master mason would be used for both. Royal apartments, such as the great hall in the north gatehouse at Beaumaris would have been splendid rooms and **Caernarvon** (Gwynedd), grandest of all the Welsh castles, had suites both for the king and queen and for their eldest son, the first heir to the English throne to be called the Prince of Wales. Apart from magnificent interiors, any castle where the king and queen took up residence would have had a carefully laid out garden. The royal accounts mention a fishpond at **Rhuddlan** (Clwyd) and a lawn at Conway, while at Caernarvon a swans' nest was built for the royal birds, which probably lived on the water surrounding all these residences. Caernarvon differs from the other castles in having polygonal rather than circular towers and walls patterned with bands of coloured stone. This reflects the fact that these features appeared on the walls of Constantinople; Edward made deliberate reference to the great Byzantine city in this design. He chose the site of the old capital of the kings of Gwynedd for the centre of his new government of Wales and made sure that, even though the building was only half-finished at the time, his first child should be truly a Prince of Wales by being born in temporary quarters in the viceregal castle.

His Welsh castles cost Edward prodigious sums of money and took armies of workmen many years to build. Some were never entirely finished. At Beaumaris, for example, the towers and northern gatehouse were left incomplete; in spite of a total bill of £14,400, money ran short and work came to a premature halt. Towards the end of his reign the king's funds were low and he needed all his available resources for his Scottish campaigns, which had to be given priority. There is no castle in Scotland which can be compared with the splendid Welsh fortresses, for Edward was prevented by his inability to pay his workmen from carrying out ambitious schemes there.

Pl. 254 *Harlech Castle in Gwynedd, one of the eight formidable fortresses built by Edward I in the late thirteenth century for the subjugation of Wales.*

Later medieval castles

The political life of late thirteenth- and fourteenth-century England was dominated by wars, which took the nobility away from their own estates to fight in Wales or Scotland or France. Their houses were no longer in the main field of conflict and therefore tended to be less heavily fortified. Many of them were not really castles at all but merely defended dwellings, like **Stokesay Castle** (Shropshire, Pls 255 and 265), which was built as a manor house rather than a fortress in spite of the fact that its owner had been granted a licence to crenellate (see p. 237) in 1290.

By the fifteenth century warfare tended to centre on the towns, where more of the population was now concentrated, and castles in the countryside were fortified as much for show as for defence. The tendency to provide more and better domestic amenities eroded the military strength of these buildings. More and bigger doors and windows weakened their walls, and the increasing use of wood, for lining rooms with wainscotting, made them more vulnerable to fire. Their plans also became more complex. Extra staircases were provided so that private chambers could be reached directly without passing through other rooms. As early as 1254 outside steps were built to provide a new entrance to the chapel at **Rochester** (Kent), where the only access had been through Henry III's bedroom. Garderobes became more numerous and were sometimes housed in a separate tower serving all levels of the main block, as at **Ludlow** (Shropshire), where there is a double privy on each of the four floors. More often a single privy served an adjacent chamber and in order to get it as far away from the room as possible, it was approached along a dog-legged passage in the thickness of the wall, whose right-angled corner was designed to reduce the inevitable problem of smell.

Developments of this sort are indicative of a more stable political climate, but the changing social pattern of the time led to a fresh threat to security, which gave rise to a new development in castle building. The gradual decline of the old feudal arrangement, whereby a lord exacted military service from his dependants, gave way to a "bastard feudalism" involving the use of "mercenary" or hired soldiers. This was known as the system of "livery and maintenance" (see p. 106) and had the disadvantage that nobles lived in constant fear of the revolt of their paid followers, who might desert at any time for higher rewards elsewhere. By the late fourteenth century such private armies were very numerous and had led to the building of a new type of castle, designed to provide the owner and his retainers with entirely separate quarters. The lord with his family generally lived in the gatehouse, where he could be certain of controlling the castle and commanding its entrance in the event of a mutiny by his garrison. **Harlech** Castle (Gwynedd), begun by Edward I as early as 1283, has a gatehouse built as a separate stronghold, which was imitated by the builder of **Dunstanburgh** (Northumberland), begun in 1314. The exceptionally well-preserved rectangular castle at **Maxstoke** (Warwicks), begun about thirty years later, had residential accommodation which could be shut off from the guards' quarters, and there was direct access to the battlements for the owner in case of need. At **Bodiam** (E. Sussex, Pl. 256), begun in 1385, there is a house inside the fortifications of the curtain wall, which was divided into two entirely separate parts, one for the lord and the other for his garrison. Like Bolton Castle (c.1379) at **Castle Bolton** (N. Yorks), Bodiam represents the most complete balance of military, domestic and architectural considerations to be found in English castle building. It is not a picturesque amalgam of the work of various periods but has four ranges of living quarters with four corner towers, symmetrically arranged round a square courtyard in a complete and formal composition. Constructed to defend the coastline against a possible French invasion, it incorporates in its gatehouse a new feature, the provision of gunports for firing cannon. These recall the earlier arrow-loops (see p. 223) but have circular openings for the barrels of the guns at their lower ends and viewing slots above them, so that they look rather like upside-down keyholes.

Although firearms had first been introduced in about 1326, it was not until the early fifteenth century that they came to have a decisive effect on siege warfare. In 1405 Henry IV used cannon to subjugate the Earl of Northumberland's powerful castles at **Berwick**, **Alnwick** and **Warkworth**, but his successors failed to follow the French and Spanish example and grasp the opportunity to establish a royal monopoly on the casting of cannon and the manufacture of gunpowder. A strong monarchy with absolute control of firearms might have prevented the Wars of the Roses by making resistance useless. The neglect of many of the royal castles under the Lancastrian kings, and especially

Pl. 255 *Stokesay Castle in Shropshire, a fortified manor house built c.1270–80 to incorporate the early or mid thirteenth-century tower seen in the foreground; the windows of its projecting upper storey date from the seventeenth century, as does the half-timbered gatehouse seen on the left.*

Pl. 256 *The late fourteenth-century moated castle at Bodiam, East Sussex, which was thoroughly restored in 1919; the living accommodation inside consisted of two unconnected residences, one for the lord and the other for his retainers.*

Pl. 257 *Raglan Castle in Gwent, showing on the right the gatehouse of the palatial mid fifteenth-century residential accommodation and on the left the moat encircling the earlier Yellow Tower built in the 1430s.*

Pl. 258 *The impressive brick keep of Tattershall Castle in Lincolnshire begun in 1434–5, showing the machicolations projecting from its upper walls and the domestic chimneys emerging from the structure on the roof; on the right is part of the moat surrounding the inner bailey.*

Henry VI, allowed the greater part of the country to be controlled by private strongholds, and it was not until Henry VII had restored the royal finances at the very end of the fifteenth century that the sovereign was in a position to make political use of the technological advances in warfare.

After the mid fifteenth century, castles lost their importance as lordly residences. The Wars of the Roses largely destroyed the old nobility, and their successors under the Tudors brought in a new way of life. It was they who built the earliest of our great country houses in an age when fortification was no longer a serious consideration in domestic architecture. The forerunners of these great mansions were the fortified manors of the later Middle Ages (see pp. 233–240).

TOWER HOUSES

A late medieval lord's own separately defensible quarters sometimes took the form of a great tower or keep within the castle precincts. At **Warwick** two were built in the late fourteenth century, each six storeys high. They provided three floors of domestic apartments, with the private garrison housed above them and, in the case of Caesar's Tower, a dungeon or prison below the storage rooms in the basement. At **Raglan** (Gwent,

Pl. 260 *The decorative brick lierne vaulting in the third floor lobby of the fifteenth-century keep at Tattershall Castle, Lincolnshire.*

Pl. 259 *Detail of the brickwork inside the south-west turret opening off the audience chamber on the second floor of the fifteenth-century keep at Tattershall Castle, Lincolnshire.*

Pl. 257) the mid fifteenth-century Yellow Tower of Gwent even had a separate moat and drawbridge, making it effectively an independent castle within the larger fortress. Some of these towers were made of brick. An impressive example is the huge keep at **Tattershall** (Lincs, Pl. 258–260), built by the immensely wealthy Ralph Cromwell, Treasurer to Henry VI, in the second quarter of the fifteenth century, a period when the full potential of brick architecture was beginning to be exploited. Its three entrances, large windows with rich tracery, and wooden floors all suggest that although there was evidently some defensive purpose, it was mainly intended to be a grand residence which would testify to a rich man's wealth and power. Keeps had been unfashionable for British castles since the thirteenth century but they had continued to be built in France. This may have provided the idea for Tattershall, which in turn inspired others, such as the surviving brick tower at **Farnham** (Surrey), built by Cromwell's executor, William Waynflete, Bishop of Winchester, in 1470–5. At about the same time Waynflete also built the handsome brick gatehouse at **Esher** Place (Surrey) not far away, a purely domestic and decorative building which looks ahead to the extravagant display at **Layer Marney** Towers (Essex, Pl. 351) half a century later.

Other contemporary tower houses were genuine strongholds. These were built in the north of England, where the threat from the Scottish border, which became a serious problem during the fourteenth century, led to the construction of impressive new castles as well as the refortification of existing ones. Instead of building the concentric castles which were the pattern in the south by this time (see p. 223), the border lords continued the traditional idea of a keep, but adapted it for use as a tower house. **Belsay** Castle (Northumberland), with its "bartizans" or corner turrets, is characteristic of this type. A different and much larger sort of tower had a much more elaborate ground plan enclosed within four high walls. The huge and powerful castle at **Warkworth** (also Northumberland) combines accommodation for a large garrison with a private residence on a palatial scale. This is a version of a French "collapsed courtyard" design, where the space enclosed by the four walls and corner towers is so restricted that it forms a well rather than a courtyard and may be compared with **Nunney** (Somerset) and **Old Wardour** (Wilts). At Warkworth a central lantern and interior windows were skilfully contrived to allow light to penetrate into the inner rooms.

From the fourteenth century onwards the areas immediately north and south of the border were organized into three "marches", or areas, controlled by wardens or sheriffs, whose duty it was to keep the peace by administering the Border Laws. They relied on a network of beacons and signal stations, with a tower or castle every two or three miles. This system was controlled from large castles which, like **Hermitage** in Liddesdale (Borders, mid fourteenth-century, Pl. 253), were important as prisons as well as for defence. The chilling aspect of the ruins of this cliff-like tower still evoke the horror of the threat of incarceration in such a grim fortress.

Smaller subsidiary "pele towers" were far more numerous. Their name derives from the fact that the original towers were built with palisades made up of "piles" or wooden pales. Although it was not common to build them of masonry until the sixteenth century, there

are some much earlier stone examples like the fourteenth-century tower later incorporated into **Gilling** Castle (N. Yorks) or the one at **Sizergh** (Cumbria), which dates from the fifteenth century. Many, like the Vicar's Pele at **Corbridge** (Northumberland, mid fourteenth-century or earlier), were built by the clergy, who shared the desire to protect themselves and their property from marauders. Another type of small fortified house was the "bastel" (from the French *bastille*, a small fortress). These were long narrow stone keeps, which had external steps to an upstairs entrance and space for keeping cattle in a vaulted basement.

Scottish tower houses

As in northern England, the tower house was adopted in Scotland as a response to the absolute necessity for an owner to be able to provide effective and inexpensive protection for himself and his family during the turbulent years of the later Middle Ages. This type of fortress-cum-residence first appeared in Scotland during the late fourteenth century, when there was a perpetual state of conflict between the native population and the English invaders. It was based on the Norman keep and was an extremely solid rectangular building, with massively thick walls, two or three barrel-vaulted storeys and a low-pitched roof of thick stone slabs. The basement was used for service and storage purposes, and access to the entrance on the first floor was by an external staircase or a ladder which could be drawn up in times of danger. The domestic house occupied the middle floors. At the top there were temporary quarters for a garrison when it was needed, with access to projecting wooden hoardings, whose presence can still be recognized by holes left in the masonry. These provided a fighting platform for attacking an enemy outside the walls (see p. 221).

The basic rectangular plan found at **Threave** (Dumfries and Galloway, *c*.1370), one of the earliest tower houses, led on to numerous dwellings which were much more complex internally but always inward-looking, and therefore easily defensible, within massive outside walls. As more space was needed, a wing built at right angles to the main block produced an L-shaped house, such as **Neidpath** Castle near Peebles (Borders, late fourteenth-century, Pl. 261). This later led on to a Z-plan, with towers at diagonally opposite corners, which became fashionable by the late sixteenth century, for example at **Claypotts** Castle near Dundee (Tayside, 1569–88, late fifteenth-century, Pl. 262). Additions might take the form of further buildings within the "barmkin", or kine barrier, which served as a cattle compound during a siege. These stoutly walled enclosures came to produce a courtyard arrangement, for instance at **Craigmillar**

Pl. 261 *Neidpath Castle near Peebles in the Scottish Borders, an L-plan tower house begun in the late fourteenth century.*

Pl. 262 *Claypotts Castle near Dundee, Tayside, built between 1569 and 1588 on a Z-plan with towers at diagonally opposite corners.*

(Lothian, late fifteenth-century), where the original strong tower, like the large late fourteenth-century tower at **Cawdor** (Highland), remains the centrepiece among much later addition.

As the Scottish monarchy re-established its authority from the time of James I (1406–1437) onwards, security became a less pressing consideration and the desire for convenience began to prevail, for example in the substitution of ground floor for upstairs entrances. In the fifteenth century the pursuit of comfort led to more sophisticated planning, as at **Balvaird** (Tayside), which had a convenient ground-floor kitchen and privies cunningly designed so that rainwater from the roof flushed out the chutes and all the soil could be emptied by lifting a single stone slab at ground level. Scotland's defensive towers were beginning to turn into the comfortable homes which many of them still are today.

ROYAL RESIDENCES

The Angevin kings owned numerous small manor houses or hunting lodges which were mainly built of timber and have therefore vanished. King John had nearly thirty and in spite of being forced by his barons to give up some which he had wrested from their owners, he passed more than twenty on to Henry III. Henry was a knowledgeable aesthete and an enthusiastic builder, who spent a tenth of his income on architecture. He carried out major work, for instance to his town palaces at Windsor and Westminster and to his country seats at Clarendon, Woodstock and Guildford, but the only one of his buildings to survive (though much restored in the nineteenth century) is the great hall of **Winchester Castle** (1222–35).

As well as undertaking new projects, he greatly increased the standard of comfort in his various houses, as well as decorating them with lavish furniture, hangings, tiles and wall paintings. A reconstruction, based on nineteenth-century copies, records the vanished murals in the king's bedchamber at the Palace of **Westminster**, painted at the time of his marriage in 1236–7, with additions later in the fourteenth century. Their subjects included Old Testament scenes, a Jesse tree, virtues and vices, the four Evangelists, a map of the world, birds and beasts, a calendar, St Edward with the pilgrim, the coronation of Edward the Confessor and soldier guardians on either side of the bed. The extensive scheme of this Painted Chamber shows the amazing richness of decoration which must be imagined in a royal palace during the medieval period. Henry had fifty private chapels for himself and his wife, eight of which he built new. The rest were refurbished and adorned with wall paintings,

Pl. 263 The massive timber roof of Westminster Hall in London built by Edward III at the end of the fourteenth century; this is one of the earliest and finest of all surviving examples of hammerbeam construction on a grand scale.

sculpture, metalwork and stained glass. Royal patronage was never to reach such heights again. Edward I provided comfortable royal apartments in his Welsh castles (see p. 223), and he modernized his other residences, for instance by carrying out improvements to the plumbing at Westminster, where he also began building a magnificent new chapel dedicated to St Stephen. This was continued by his son and completed by his grandson; it became the House of Commons in 1548 and was largely destroyed during the nineteenth century but the Lower Chapel or crypt has survived.

Nothing remains of the other major royal works of this period, such as Edward II's favourite country residence at King's Langley (Herts) or Edward III's palaces at Sheen and Eltham (both near London). By Edward II's time **Westminster** had developed into two separate palaces, one for the monarch and his family and another to house the national administration. Both he and his son made extensive additions there, but they have not survived. Edward III made many alterations at **Windsor** in connection with his foundation of the knightly Order of the Garter (*c.*1347–8) and the priestly College of St George. He spent over £50,000 altering the lower ward and reconstructing the upper ward with new royal lodgings, built under the supervision of William of Wykeham, founder of Winchester College, and a gatehouse of 1359, now misleadingly known as the "Norman Gate". Although much of his work has vanished beneath later reconstruction, one can still see the undercroft of his State Apartments and his cloisters next to St George's Chapel. Richard II had a particular interest in Westminster because of his personal devotion to the memory of Edward the Confessor. His remodelling of Westminster Hall (begun in 1394, Pl. 263) was the work of the mason Henry Yevele and the carpenter Hugh Herland. With its massive timber roof weighing

six hundred and sixty tons, it is one of the earliest and finest surviving examples of hammerbeam construction on a grand scale. The hall is impressive not only for the technical skill of its carpentry but also for the stone frieze, with corbels which support the roof timbers, and the carved tracery which fills the spandrels. In his grief at the death of his queen, Anne of Bohemia, in 1384, Richard ordered the destruction of his favourite palace at Sheen. It was rebuilt in the newly fashionable red brick (see pp. 229–230) by Henry V, in celebration of his French victories, with a quadrangle over 60m (200ft) long and a hall and chapel on a huge scale. The whole unfinished complex of buildings was destroyed by fire in 1499 and rebuilt for a second time in the early sixteenth century by Henry VII, who renamed it Richmond Palace.

Against a troubled political background, the fifteenth-century kings continued to improve their existing palaces. Henry IV, for instance, carried out additions at Eltham, while Henry VI's architectural energies were devoted to his collegiate buildings at **Eton** and **Cambridge** (see pp. 282–283 and 287). Edward IV's magnificent Great Hall at **Eltham** Palace (*c.*1475–80) survives in south-east London, though much restored, with its fine hammerbeam roof and large windows, which were originally filled with a rich display of Yorkist heraldic glass. He also rebuilt St George's Chapel at **Windsor** Castle (begun in 1475, Pl. 109), one of the greatest surviving monuments of the period. Its roof was unfinished at the time of his death, and it was Henry VII, the first of the Tudors, who completed the building with its magnificent continuous stone vault.

HOUSES

Too few thirteenth-century houses survive sufficiently unaltered for them to be a recognizable type, but about a hundred still exist, at least in part. The evidence suggests that ground- and first-floor halls were more or less equally popular, and for the first time stone halls were not invariably raised above vaulted basements but began to be built at ground-floor level too, when it seemed safe to do so. Bigger halls, like the one which survives at **Oakham** Castle (Rutland, *c.*1190, Pl. 264), were often aisled so as to allow a wide roof span. Efforts were now made, as at the Old Deanery, **Salisbury** (Wilts, 1258–74), and **Stokesay** (Shropshire, *c.*1285–1305, Pl. 265), to find ways of avoiding the use of posts or columns, which obstructed the floor area, by developing more sophisticated forms of roof construction. The layout and use of a great hall, still the main living room of the household, continued as before, and the most noticeable difference lay in the design of doors, with pointed rather

Pl. 264 *Oakham Castle at Oakham in Rutland built as an aisled great hall c.1190; the central doorway has been moved from its original position at the service end of the building and the dormers seen in the south aisle roof are nineteenth-century.*

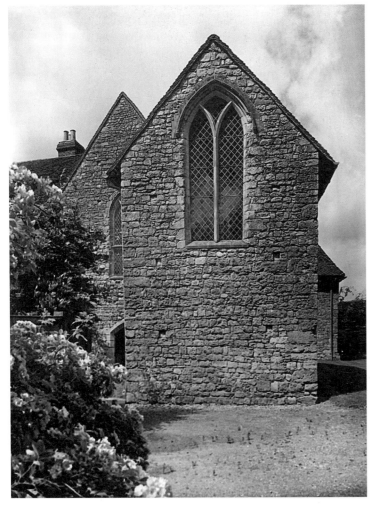

Pl. 265 *The Great Hall of Stokesay Castle in Shropshire, a fortified manor house built* c.*1270–80, showing its high cruck roof and the medieval staircase at the north end. On the right is the entrance doorway, which was at the opposite end of the room from the surviving open hearth; the door up the steps on the left gave access to living accommodation in the north tower and the passage below the stairs led to the kitchen and buttery.*

Pl. 266 *Old Soar Manor at Plaxtol, Kent, the complete solar end of a stone house built* c.*1290, showing the solar itself on the left with the chapel in front of it to the right; the Y-tracery in the east window is not original.*

Pl. 267 *The interior of the solar at Old Soar Manor at Plaxtol, Kent, built* c.*1290, showing its crown post roof, a window with built-in stone seats and, in the corner, the staircase leading down to the undercroft.*

than round arches, and windows, either in the form of lancets or perhaps with simple plate tracery. Some windows would now have had glass, but this was a rare luxury and was often used only in the top part of

a window, with a wooden shutter over the lower part of the opening.

More complicated house plans began to evolve from the earlier basic rectangle. It became common for a two-storey block to be built at one end of the hall, in order to provide a solar above stores or workrooms, as at **Old Soar** Manor, Plaxtol (Kent, c.1290, Pls 266 and 267). Here the hall itself has vanished but one can still see the spiral stair which led up from it to the solar, where there are two projections housing a garderobe and a chapel. These show that, like castles, manor houses of this date were designed to cater for people who expected a more convenient and

comfortable way of life. An L-shaped house plan was also emerging, for instance at **Little Wenham** Hall (Suffolk, *c.*1270–80, Pl. 268), which has a tower attached to the main building. Towers like these became a feature

of the domestic architecture of this period, when private owners were granted licences to crenellate or fortify their houses (see p. 98).

It has recently been suggested that Little Wenham Hall may originally have been a larger house with a timber great hall at its south-west corner and that what we see now may be only the private chamber block for the lord and his family. This surviving structure is unusual in being one of the first buildings in Britain since Roman times to have been built of

Pl. 268 *Little Wenham Hall, Suffolk, built in brick* C.1270–80, *which may have been the chamber block of a larger house with a timber great hall. The tower has a chapel on the first floor with a chamber above it; for defensive reasons the windows at ground level are small and narrow.*

Pl. 269 *Detail of the projecting oriel lighting both storeys of Grevel's House at Chipping Campden, Gloucestershire, showing the decorative blank arcading between the two windows and the gargoyles at the top.*

Pl. 270 *Grevel's House in the High Street at Chipping Campden, Gloucestershire, built for a rich merchant* C.1400, *with a wide arched entrance doorway and a tall oriel window.*

Pl. 271 *St Clair's Hall near St Osyth, Essex, a half-timbered H-plan house where the central block is a rare surviving example of an aisled hall; the cross-wings were much altered in the sixteenth century and the bay window on the left dates from the Georgian period.*

Pl. 272 *The late fourteenth-century moated manor at Lower Brockhampton, Herefordshire, combining both square and close studded timber framing, and in the foreground its picturesque fifteenth-century gatehouse.*

brick. The Anglo-Saxons and Normans had made extensive use of reused Roman bricks but those used here were contemporary, perhaps imported from Germany or the Low Countries, where brick was by now an established building material. On the evidence of archaeological discoveries, brick-making is now thought to have been revived in Britain much earlier, though it was not common before the fifteenth century. It was later to become very popular in East Anglia and other parts of England where stone was not available locally. At first it was simply referred to as "tile" and did not have a separate name. The word "brick" was introduced

Pl. 273 *The mid fourteenth-century domestic chapel on the first floor of Woodlands Manor at Mere, Wiltshire, which was originally reached by an outside staircase; the window on the right dates from the fifteenth century and the room was converted to domestic use c.1570.*

during the late Middle Ages from France, which provided the inspiration for buildings such as **Herstmonceux** Castle (E. Sussex, 1441), whose owners had served in the French wars.

Relatively few medieval stone houses have survived, even in areas where local stone was readily available. The best and most complete fourteenth-century example is **Penshurst** Place (Kent), where the Great Hall built *c.*1341 retains its traceried windows, timber roof, tiled floor with central hearth and even vestiges of contemporary wall-paintings. Doors in the south-west corner lead up to the solar and down into the undercroft beneath it, while behind the sixteenth-century screen at the other end of the room there are the three openings traditionally found in medieval halls, two doors leading into the pantry and buttery with between them a central archway, giving access along a passageway to an external kitchen. This arrangement also survives at **Clevedon** Court (Somerset), an early fourteenth-century house which retains its original two-storeyed porch, by now a normal feature, and a chapel with square-headed windows filled with ogee reticulated tracery. Another characteristic amenity in fifteenth-century houses is an oriel or bay window above ground level, as at Grevel's House (*c.*1400) in the High Street at **Chipping Campden** (Glos, Pls 269 and 270). Such windows were frequently included in the design of new houses or added to older ones in order to light the owner's high table (see pp. 244–245) at the "upper" end of the hall. A stone oriel (*c.*1480) can be seen at **Gainsborough** Old Hall (Lincs), where it was inserted into the existing (mid fifteenth-century) timber-framed hall.

One of the earliest surviving timber-framed houses, **Fyfield** Hall (Essex), dates from the very end of the thirteenth century. In its original form it was a very simple rectangular aisled hall of two bays. Houses such as St Clair's Hall at **St Osyth** (Essex, Pl. 271), based on this method of construction (see pp. 248–260), survive in significant numbers from the fourteenth century onwards; their plan, consisting of a high central hall with two-storey living quarters at one end and the domestic offices at the other, provided the standard pattern which was followed for three hundred years. Most of these are privately owned but the late fourteenth-century moated manor house, with a picturesque fifteenth-century gatehouse, which is set in a beautiful wooded valley at **Lower Brockhampton** (Herefordshire, Pl. 272) is a National Trust property and open to visitors.

Lodgings

During the late Middle Ages the size of an important man's household was continually increasing, as it became necessary for him to court popularity by generous hospitality and to impress with the number of his retainers and the splendour of his lifestyle. A weak monarchy meant that rich noblemen, competing with each other for power and influence, felt obliged to live on an ever grander scale. To house their huge retinues and also their guests, they needed lodgings which ranged from single rooms to suites of half a dozen rooms, depending on the importance of the occupants. A few examples of these buildings can still be seen, for instance at **Dartington** (Devon), where there is a two-storey range (*c.*1388–1400), with outside staircases to the upper floor. As the need for accommodation increased, lodgings would form four sides of a quadrangle, like the Retainers' Court at **Cotehele** (Cornwall, late fifteenth-century), or proliferate into a whole series of courtyards, as at **Hampton Court** Palace (Greater London) in the sixteenth century.

The medieval buildings of academic foundations also had lodgings for monks and scholars, and surviving examples include Mob Quad, Merton College, **Oxford** (early fourteenth-century), and Chamber Court, **Winchester** College (Hants, late fourteenth-century). They provided both communal bedrooms and living space divided up for individual study. Three original wooden examples of these cubicles, dating from the late fifteenth century, survive at Magdalene College, **Cambridge**, and similar partitions, replaced many times over the years, are still in use at Winchester College.

Domestic chapels

Every medieval noblemen had at least one chapel for attendance at Mass, which was an important part of his daily routine. In the Norman period this would have been a barrel-vaulted chamber built into the keep of a castle. It was usually on either the first or the second floor, with easy access from the lord's own apartment, or in the forebuilding (see pp. 77–81) which enclosed the entrance stairs. During the thirteenth and fourteenth centuries it generally remained in an upstairs position as at Woodlands Manor, **Mere** (Wilts, mid fourteenth-century, Pl. 273), but sometimes occupied two storeys, as at **Broughton** Castle (Oxon, *c.*1300) and **Warkworth** Castle (Northumberland, late fourteenth-century). By the fifteenth century the chapel was normally on the ground floor, and at its west end there was often a gallery, for the lord and his family, which communicated with the adjoining great chamber. This arrangement is reflected in the position of the Chapel Drawing Room at **Compton Wynyates** (Warwicks), where the family could look down through open mullions on services in the original chapel (built 1515–20). There is also a two-storeyed west end at Jesus Chapel, **East Hendred** (Oxon), with its adjoining priest's house. A chapel may occasionally be

Pl. 274 *The handsome mid fourteenth-century Abbot's Kitchen at Glastonbury, Somerset, a square structure with a fireplace built across each of its four corners to produce an octagonal interior; the openings in the sides of the two-tiered lantern on the roof were designed to let out the smoke.*

found in a tower, as at **Stanton Harcourt** (Oxon, *c.*1460–71), or above a porch, as at **Congresbury** Vicarage (Somerset, *c.*1470).

Kitchens

Cooking in an early medieval hall took place over the central hearth, but separate kitchens, like the surviving monastic kitchen at **Chichester** (W. Sussex), began to be introduced during the thirteenth century, and they were common throughout the later Middle Ages. Most of them were built of wood, perhaps plastered, and have not survived but domestic stone kitchens can still be seen, for instance at **Haddon Hall** (Derbyshire, early fourteenth-century) and **Raby Castle** (Durham, c.1378). Six still exist in **Oxford** colleges alone, for example at Magdalen (thirteenth-century), New College (fourteenth-century) and Corpus (fifteenth-century). The handsome octagonal Abbot's Kitchen at **Glastonbury** (Somerset, mid-fourteenth-century, Pl. 274) had four large fireplaces, one in each corner, and served a household of three hundred people. It was vaulted in stone, like the comparable monastic kitchen at **Durham** (1366–71), to provide the perfect fireproof roof. Timber roofs were also widely used, as at **Stanton Harcourt** (Oxon, c.1460–83), which like Glastonbury is basically a rectangular building with a spectacular octagonal pyramid roof. Brick, which had obvious advantages, was used for the construction of the kitchen at **Gainsborough** Old Hall (Lincs), which is unusual in having six small subsidiary rooms for the cook and other kitchen servants, built one above the other, two each in three of its four corners. It also has two brick ovens, often found in a separate bakehouse at this period, as well as two huge open fireplaces, each big enough to roast a whole ox.

During the Middle Ages most food was cooked on open fires, and it was crucial to provide adequate ventilation, especially in kitchens catering for large numbers, in order to disperse the smell and fumes from huge pieces of meat roasting on spits, which were slowly rotated by a system of weights and pulleys. This explains the considerable height of big medieval kitchens, like the one at **Glastonbury**, where the two-tiered pyramid roof has openings all round the sides of both of its lanterns to let out the smoke. Even so the heat for those working inside this kind of kitchen must have been overpowering. The Glastonbury kitchen can still be seen as a free-standing building, but many originally separate kitchens were subsequently incorporated into later work, for example at **Haddon Hall** (Derbyshire). During the later Middle Ages, when kitchens were generally rectangular, they tended to be roofed like any other building. A square or oblong shape was easily integrated into the rest of the domestic complex, as at the ruined mid fifteenth-century **South Wingfield** Manor (Derbyshire).

From the fourteenth century onwards, kitchen fireplaces began to be set in arched openings in the thickness of the walls, where it was possible to provide flues to carry away the smoke (see pp. 246–248). These were so much cleaner and safer that from then on the kitchen could be built as part of the main house, rather than a separate outbuilding though this was not common before the sixteenth century.

The domestic interior

The plan of a surviving medieval house and the number and arrangement of the rooms can still give quite a good idea of how it was originally used. By the end of the period every house of any size would have had a hall, a chamber and a parlour, as well as a kitchen, a chapel and lodgings for retainers and guests. By the thirteenth century standards of comfort for the nobility and gentry were beginning to improve considerably.

Pl. 275 *The remarkably well-preserved fourteenth-century wall paintings in the Great Chamber on the first floor of Longthorpe Tower near Peterborough, Cambridgeshire, showing the north wall depicting the Seven Ages of Man and the Birth of Christ.*

Pl. 276 *Detail of the Wheel of the Senses on the east wall of the Great Chamber at Longthorpe Tower, Cambridgeshire, showing a kingly figure, with his hand on one of the spokes, standing between a spider's web (symbolising touch) on the left and a boar (symbolising hearing), whose nose can be seen on the right.*

Skilled craftsmen were now available to make rooms warmer and brighter, with plastered walls, wainscotting and hangings. Plaster and wood both provided insulation and could be decorated with colourful pigments. It had long been thought that whitewash was good for stone surfaces, and it was normal practice to paint plaster too, marking it out into masonry blocks with lines of reddish ochre and decorating it with motifs such as formal flowers or stiff leaves.

Wall paintings depicted biblical scenes and the lives of the saints but also secular subjects like the Seven Ages of Man or the Five Senses. A valuable survival is the complete scheme in a painted chamber at **Longthorpe Tower** (Cambs, *c.*1300, Pls 275 and 276), discovered under layers of whitewash and distemper in 1945, whose themes contrast the dangers of worldliness with the rewards of the spiritual life. Even the vault of this small room was originally painted, showing how every surface of a medieval interior seems to have been covered with decoration. Another outstanding example of wall painting in a domestic setting was discovered in 1953 in the main first-floor room of the Byward Tower of the **Tower of London**. Here the late fourteenth-century figures of St John the Baptist, the Virgin and St Michael originally flanked a Crucifixion, which was destroyed to make way for a fireplace in Tudor times. A contemporary Annunciation was uncovered at **Fiddleford** Manor (Dorset) in 1990. It shows the Angel Gabriel and the Virgin Mary (the latter largely destroyed by earlier plaster repairs) on either side of the window in the north wall of the solar. A cottage at **Piccotts End** (Herts, Pl. 277) has well-preserved paintings, again of religious subjects, on what was originally the wall behind the dais of a fifteenth-century hall. At **Belsay** Castle (Northumberland) there are the remains of painted mural decorations, thought to date from the early fifteenth century, which may be intended to imitate tapestries. These show shields hanging from trees against a floral background and above them sailing ships. The Gatehouse at **Berry Pomeroy** (Devon) has a fifteenth-century Flemish-inspired Adoration of the Magi in the room which was its domestic chapel.

It was not only plaster which was decorated. Panelled walls were also painted, as at Cross Farm, **Westhay** (Somerset), where a bold pattern of crude foliage covers simple stud and plank panelling. Wainscotting became gradually more sophisticated, until the late fifteenth century saw a vogue for "linenfold" panelling as found at **Compton Wynyates** (Warwickshire, early sixteenth-century, Pl. 278), with rows of moulded ribs carved to resemble panels of cloth arranged in vertical unpressed pleats. Doors and windows both provided opportunities for sculptured decoration, for instance of hoodmoulds. During the Perpendicular phase of Gothic, these became rectangular labels, which left triangular corner spaces which could be used for heraldic or other ornament.

It is important to remember the sheer wealth of decoration involved, since it was crucial to the effect of medieval interiors as they became progressively more sophisticated. One can still see enough to imagine the richness of their carved decoration in wood or stone, but, except in small quantities of surviving stained glass, the colour which was so important has almost entirely vanished. Some idea of it can still be gained from contemporary textiles. These would have been a major source of colour and interior display. Wall hangings were either painted cloths or tapestries, known as "arras work" after the French town which was famous for their manufacture. Both were in use from the fourteenth century onwards, initially at the upper end of the hall to provide both draught-proofing and a decorative setting for the high table. Tapestry, being more expensive, was found in wealthier households. It was regularly

transported from one residence to another (see p. 86) and installed on rows of wooden pegs. By the fifteenth century it was normal for any important house to have tapestry on the walls of both the hall and the great chamber. Much of it was imported from France and Flanders, but it is known that tapestry was being made in London by the early fourteenth century, whereas carpet manufacture was not established in England until the 1560s.

In Norman times a typical house had consisted of a great hall with the solar at one end and the domestic offices at the other. By the thirteenth century the lord's table at the upper end of the hall began to be raised on

Pl. 277 *Detail of the religious wall paintings of c.1500, originally behind the dais of a great hall, which have survived in what is now a cottage at Piccott's End, Hertfordshire; on the left is the Virgin Mary with her dying Son on her lap and on the right Christ in Majesty.*

Pl. 278 *The early sixteenth-century great hall at Compton Wynyates in Warwickshire, showing the screens passage carved with linenfold panelling and above it an open gallery; the hall roof which is not original to the house was probably installed in the mid eighteenth century.*

a dais. This was partly to emphasize its importance but also, more practically, to raise it above the rush-strewn floor, standing on a platform of boards which was easier to keep clean. Floors paved with tiles (see pp. 219–220), hitherto used only in royal residences or wealthy ecclesiastical buildings, were introduced from the fourteenth century onwards. Improvements of this kind mark the beginning of a tendency to make the hall progressively more comfortable. By now it was usual to have a mural fireplace (see below), rather than the much smokier central hearth, and screens began to be installed at the lower end of the room to shut out the draughts. At first these were moveable, like the rare free-standing example (*c.*1500) which survives at **Rufford Old Hall** (Lancs), but by the early fifteenth century they were generally permanent structures running the full width of the room, as at Milton Abbey, **Milton Abbas** (Dorset, Pl. 279), and had doors in them, which could be shut whenever the outside doors had to be kept open. This was often necessary in order to make the fire draw satisfactorily, and it became normal in the later Middle Ages to build a porch to shelter the entrance.

Sometimes there was a gallery above the screen at the lower end of the hall, which might also give access to the upstairs rooms over the pantry and buttery, as at **Ockwells** (Berks, *c.*1465), where the gallery was also used for musicians. The introduction of tall windows made halls much lighter, especially where there was an oriel (see p. 240) at the upper end. By the late fifteenth century, windows were sometimes placed high up, as at **Old Wardour** Castle (Wilts) and **Sudeley** Castle (Glos), so as to leave room for tapestries to be hung on the walls below them. Glass, which was still treated as moveable furniture, was increasingly used in wealthy households, and colourful heraldic windows, like the set of eighteen armorial shields surviving at Ockwells (fifteenth-century), were especially popular.

By the fourteenth century, noblemen were beginning to abandon the communal life of the hall, preferring, except on formal occasions, to live, eat and sleep in a separate room, which was generally upstairs behind the high table. In cases where the owner had previously had a chamber above the service rooms at the other end of the hall, this would in future be used for guests or other important members of the household. Having his personal domain in an upper room reinforced a lord's exalted position, and the fact that he no longer had to walk the full length of the room to reach his private quarters set him apart at a time when formality was increasing. In the houses of the rich and powerful, who vied with each other in conspicuous display, the serving of meals followed such ponderous procedures that food must frequently have been cold by the time it was eaten. It was brought in a solemn procession of richly dressed

Pl. 279 *The fifteenth-century Abbot's Hall of Milton Abbey at Milton Abbas, Dorset, dated 1498, showing the panelled screen with its cusped and crocketed arches and the dense timberwork of the heavy hammerbeam roof.*

retainers along the passageway from the outer kitchen, which ran between the buttery and pantry, and emerged through the middle of the three doors at the lower end of the hall. It then passed through the screen, to fanfares of trumpets from the gallery above, was paraded along the hall with ostentatious formality, and finally carried up a staircase, such as the mid fourteenth-century spiral staircase built in the oriel at Penshurst, and into the great chamber. Here elaborate preparations had been made for its reception. Tables were set up for each meal and taken down afterwards, while other trestles supported "cupboards" for displaying gold and silver plate. There was a carefully established method for laying the table and folding the cloth, and complex rituals attended the serving of the food and drink, each attendant nobleman or servant having his own very specific duties. Elaborate protocol produced a ceremonial atmosphere which must have stifled conviviality. The hall, with its noise and jollity, was left to the retainers and suffered a gradual decline in importance, until by the nineteenth century it was remembered only in the living and dining room for the domestic staff or "servants' hall".

The great chamber, being an upstairs room, could have a high and ornamental roof, as at Alston Court, **Nayland** (Suffolk, *c.*1472), or **Cothay** Manor (Somerset, *c.*1480), which looked impressive but must have made it difficult to heat in cold weather. Just as **Caister** Castle (Norfolk, built 1432–5) had a ground-floor winter hall and another on the first floor for the summer, in the fifteenth century the cellar or undercroft below a great chamber was sometimes made into a snug low-ceilinged chamber. At **Haddon Hall** an eight-light window was inserted *c.*1500 "to light the parlure", now the dining room. A parlour had a monastic origin (see p. 116) as a place for conversation, and until Tudor times it might also be used as a bedroom. The presence of a bed, even in the grandest of living rooms, was quite normal in the late Middle Ages, though it is unlikely that the bed in the great chamber of a royal or aristocratic house was actually used for sleeping. The name "bedchamber" does not appear until the mid sixteenth century, when it became usual to have separate rooms for different purposes.

Furniture was still sparse during the Middle Ages, and it was habitually carried from one house to another (see p. 86), but one can still occasionally recognize built-in fittings, such as corbels with sculptured decoration which provided brackets for standing lamps (see below) or, as in a rare survival at Norrington Manor near, **Alvediston** (Wilts, *c.*1377), had metal spikes to take candles. "Lavers", or washbasins, with a hole to drain away the water, were provided in most chambers by the late Middle Ages. They were also placed at the entrance to the hall for washing hands before and after meals, essential when forks were not yet in general use and fingers, as well as spoons and knives, were used for eating. Lavers could be designed for deliberate decorative effect, as at **Little Wenham** Hall, where there is an early fifteenth-century example set in an ogee-arched alcove beneath battlements and blank arcading, built into the south wall of the thirteenth-century hall. Bath tubs were in use at this period but were not permanent fixtures. Other common domestic fittings included latrines, which had seats which were generally pierced wooden planks but were sometimes made of stone, like the surviving early fourteenth-century example at **Longthorpe Tower** (Cambs). These little rooms always had a window or some other form of ventilation, such as

the two small quatrefoil openings in the wall of the garderobe in the manor house at **Yardley Hastings** (Northants, *c.*1320–40). It is interesting to note that it was already fashionable to use euphemisms comparable with our word "toilet" to describe these "privies" or private chambers, also referred to as "garderobes". This was a French word meaning not a cupboard but an important room with a fireplace, used for storing clothing and valuables and carrying out work of various kinds; it would normally have had a privy opening off it.

Fireplaces

There are surviving medieval fireplaces built of both brick and stone. Wooden houses would have had plastered timber smoke canopies, invariably replaced by later generations because of the fire risk. During the thirteenth century a typical stone fireplace projected from the wall surface. It had a tall hood like a flattened cone, which acted as a flue, and sometimes extended upwards to guide the smoke directly out through the roof. The hood rested on a lintel, corbelled out from the supporting jamb shafts, as at **Conisbrough** Castle (S. Yorks, *c.*1190), or sometimes from the surface of the wall, as at **Boothby Pagnell** (Lincs, *c.*1200). It was often constructed with "joggled" or zig-zag joints to prevent the stones slipping out of place. This type persisted into the fourteenth century and sometimes had brackets for standing lamps built into the angles where the fireplace meets the wall, as at the Prior's House, **Ely** (Cambs, *c.*1325). Projecting hoods disappeared after about 1350, when it became normal to build a fireplace in the thickness of the wall and construct a separate flue in an external chimney stack. A "shouldered" or wide, shallow, rectangular hood, which rises vertically above the lintel, is still found in the fifteenth century, for instance at Red Lion House, **Burford** (Oxon), but from the second half of the fourteenth century onwards, fireplaces were generally set into the wall beneath an arch or flat lintel as in the Abbot's Parlour at **Muchelney** (Somerset, *c.*1509–14, Pl. 280) They derived from a type that originated with the Normans, for instance at **Castle Hedingham** (see p. 86), which relied on primitive flues leading to vents in the outer surface of the wall, so that the smoke must often have blown back into the room. A variant occasionally found in thirteenth-century buildings, for example at **Stokesay** (Shropshire), made good use of space by putting the fireplace inside a thick wall but got rid of the smoke much more effectively by guiding it upwards inside a chimney stack so that it emerged above the roof. Chimneys, which were introduced in the mid twelfth century, were made of plaster, wicker and wood as well as more durable materials. Medieval stone and brick

Pl. 280 *The fireplace of c.1509–14 in the Abbot's Parlour at Muchelney Abbey, Somerset, decorated with four bold quatrefoils on the lintel and two large lions above the overmantel.*

Pl. 281 *The thirteenth-century chimney of the Checker at Abingdon Abbey, Oxfordshire, topped with vents in the form of small gables pierced with stepped lancets.*

examples, mainly of the fourteenth and fifteenth centuries, survive in great variety. They are either cylindrical, rectangular or octagonal and may be topped with ornamental vents like those on the thirteenth-century chimney of the Checker (or Chequer) at **Abingdon** Abbey (Oxon, Pl. 281).

Late Gothic fireplaces became increasingly ornate, especially when quatrefoil ornament for decorating flat lintels became popular in the second half of the fifteenth century. Four-centred arches were often used, as at the Archbishop's Palace, **Southwell** (Notts, mid fifteenth-century), where there is a fireplace surmounted by blind arcading and a battlemented cornice. Lintels were also used to display coats of arms, as on Bishop Courtnay's fireplace in **Exeter** Palace (Devon, *c*.1486). This elaborate design, topped with a highly decorated ogee arch and rosebush finials, shows that by the late Middle Ages the fireplace had become not just a standard amenity but a focus for architectural ornament.

TIMBER-FRAMED BUILDINGS

Preparation

All medieval wooden buildings, both houses and barns, were constructed with a basic prefabricated frame. This was made up of a whole kit of carefully shaped parts, systematically marked with variants on roman numerals, so that each joint could be identified and its components would fit together perfectly. The preliminary carpentry often took place at a distance, and it is recorded, for instance, that all the timbers for the huge frame of Westminster Hall were prepared at Farnham in Surrey before being transported to the site for assembly.

Wood was used in many different ways. A whole tree might be shaped with an axe or adze to produce a solid square beam or sawn or split in half to make two rectangular timbers. If it was "slabbed" it yielded four thick planks. Smaller trunks were halved for rafters. Larger branches were suitable for brackets. Provided that the structural surfaces were the right size, the other sides of the timber might be left rough, sometimes even with the bark still attached. Much of the skill of the medieval carpenter lay in making good use of the timber available to him, in spite of its irregularities. There was an art, for instance, in using curved pieces where they would have a deliberate aesthetic impact, for instance by producing the effect of an arch spanning the building. Joists and rafters were always laid flat instead of on their sides, which would theoretically

have been stronger, presumably because in that position they provided a smooth upper surface suitable for attaching floorboards or roof battens. Wood was always used as economically as possible and pieces too small for structural timbers were split up for use as poles, staves, laths or pegs. Often whole walls or sections of a building would be put together on the ground and the resulting frame raised into position in one piece. However, much of the construction would have been done one piece at a time, in a systematic order determined by the method of jointing.

Joints

The strength of a timber frame depended on its joints. Though these were numerous and often extremely complex, they were basically of three kinds. Mortice and tenon joints joined two timbers at right angles. The end of one timber was cut to a narrow tongue so that it could be slotted into a matching groove in the other and secured with oak pegs. It was these joints which held the frame firmly together and ensured that it remained stiff, even if unseasoned timber shrank or warped after construction. Scarf joints used many variations of the "tongue and groove" method to join one straight length of timber to another, and they are found near the main structural uprights of a building. Lap joints are much less common and occur where one beam is let into a groove cut into another, so as to attach them firmly together where they intersect. These are most often to be found securing tie-beams, which run across the building to join the main uprights of the frame at the level of the "wall-plate" or beam running along the top of the wall.

Construction

Earlier timber houses had been based on posts set into the ground, but wood in contact with the earth is bound to get damp and rot below ground level. During the Middle Ages this problem was obviated by using a "sill plate" or horizontal beam along the foot of the walls. During building operations it might be raised on temporary blocks to keep it off the ground; then after the structure had been completed, a stone or brick plinth could be inserted underneath and precisely fitted to take account of any irregularities in the frame. Frames were of two kinds, those built with crucks and those based on a box shape, and they were erected by different methods. So although there are some buildings which combine the two types, in general terms there were two distinct methods of medieval timber-framed construction.

Crucks

Cruck buildings (Pls 282–284) were based on A-shaped cross-frames made of pairs of curved timbers joined both at the apex and again, lower down, by a tie-beam or collar. These crucks were assembled on the ground and then raised, one at a time, into a vertical position. The purlins or roof timbers running the length of the building were then dropped into their prepared sockets so that the entire structure was held rigid. Some buildings used only "base crucks", which supported the tie-beam but did not rise above it. These had a separate roof structure,

Pl. 282 *The original A-shaped cruck frame still visible on the gable end of a much altered cottage at Didbrook, Gloucestershire, which may date from the fifteenth century.*

as can be seen at **West Bromwich** Manor (West Midlands, *c.*1300; now a public house). The inward curve of the crucks meant that, like hammerbeams (see p. 255), base crucks offered an alternative to an aisled construction for larger buildings.

Crucks are used for houses and barns of all sizes and are found throughout the "highland" areas of the country, the parts to the north and west of a line drawn roughly from the Humber to the Isle of Wight. They are not found in the "lowland" east and south-east. It is generally believed that they developed from a primitive hut construction, but the technical sophistication of early medieval crucks suggests that the idea may have originated in rich men's buildings and been copied later by humbler imitators. The curved shape of the timbers is not apparent from outside, unless they have been left exposed. This is because of the addition of vertical posts, running up from ground level to the "cruck spurs" below the wall-plate, to produce a rectangular structure.

Box frames

Box frame buildings are characteristic of the "lowland" areas (see above), though they are also found elsewhere, especially during the post-medieval period. This type of frame was usually put together one piece at a time, beginning with the vertical timbers. These would be held temporarily in position, until they were fixed upright when the wall-plates were lowered on to them. The side walls would then be joined to each other by tie-beams, so that the frame became firmly braced, and then the roof would be added. Sometimes the corners between uprights and tie-beams would be reinforced with "knee braces".

Roofs

Medieval roofs are most easily appreciated in the high open spaces of great halls, churches and barns, though many still survive hidden above the ceilings of houses and other two-storied buildings. Their carpentry, in both timber and stone buildings, is too complex a subject to examine in detail here but one needs to understand the basic method of construction (Fig. 6). A roof was supported by a series of trusses or cross-frames, one for each section or bay of the building, whose dimensions were largely determined by the size and length of the timbers available. It rested on beams running along the tops of the side walls and the tie-beams which joined these wall-plates formed the bases of the triangular trusses which supported the roof. These triangles were completed by the rafters. Sometimes there were principal rafters as well as the common rafters

Pl. 283 *Interior of a cruck barn at Esthwaite, Cumbria, showing the curved timbers joined both at the apex and by a tie-beam or collar lower down.*

Pl. 284 *Some of the numerous fourteenth- and fifteenth-century timber-framed houses which survive at Weobley in Herefordshire, showing both cruck and box-frame construction.*

which bore the weight of the roof covering. These carried purlins, or longitudinal beams, running from end to end of the building. Often they were "trenched" with square notches, so that the rafters could be slotted into them, and the junction of rafter and purlin might be stiffened by the addition of a "windbrace". The purlins in turn bore the weight of the common rafters.

As a result of continuing experiment throughout the Middle Ages, there is wide variety in methods of construction, which evolved mainly on a regional basis. Different types are often found in combination with each other and neat categorization is not possible, but because they are immediately recognizable, certain prominent structural details of roof trusses have given their names to different types of roof. A "crown post" construction as at Tiptofts, **Wimbish** (Essex, *c*.1350, Pl. 285) and Great

Pl. 285 *Detail of the crown post roof of the mid fourteenth-century aisled hall of Tiptofts at Wimbish, Essex, where the upper floor seen here was a later insertion.*

Pl. 286 *The roof of the late fifteenth-century hall at Great Dixter in Sussex, showing tie beams with curved braces supporting the crown posts, which carry the weight of the longitudinal crown plate attached to the underside of the collar beams at the apex.*

Pl. 287 *Curved timbers used for the arched braces of the tie beams in the Long Gallery at Abingdon Abbey, Oxfordshire; this was a cloister walk giving access to various rooms and the windows were never glazed.*

Pl. 288 *The handsome carved double-hammerbeam roof above the Great Hall of Gifford's Hall near Stoke-by-Nayland, Suffolk, which dates from the early sixteenth century.*

Dixter, **Northiam** (E. Sussex, *c.*1470, Pl. 286) needed only one set of rafters, because it had a central "crown plate" or longitudinal beam instead of side purlins. This rested on a "crown post" (Fig. 6a), standing on the tie-beam and held in place by a pair of diagonal braces attached to the underside of the "collar", a short horizontal beam, which rested on the crown plate and joined the rafters below the apex of the roof. Early crown posts were square or chamfered but later examples might take the form of a column with a carved capital and base. They are found throughout the period, from the thirteenth century, as at **Old Soar** (Kent), to the early sixteenth, as at **Cotehele** (Cornwall).

A "king post" (Fig. 6b) differs from a "crown post" because instead of carrying the weight of the collar beams below the apex of the roof, it supports the ridge beam itself. In the type of roof which bears its name, there is at least one truss with a "king post" between the tie-beam and the roof-ridge, and it may be reinforced by a pair of diagonal timbers rising from its base to the side purlins. The lower joint of the king post is held in tension so that instead of pressing down on the tie-beam and causing it to sag, it pulls it upwards towards the roof-ridge. This was therefore an efficient type of roof for a wide span. In medieval times it seems to have been restricted to the north of England, especially Yorkshire, where it can still be seen, for example, at Shibden Hall, **Halifax**, and in the magnificent later tithe barn (*c.*1640) at **East Riddlesden** Hall, Keighley.

A rather different type of roof structure, which seems to be derived from aisled buildings, uses what are known as "queen posts" (Fig. 6c). These are found in pairs, standing on the tie-beam and supporting side purlins which carry a collar beam below the apex of the roof; "queen struts" (Fig. 6d) are similar but support the two ends of the collar itself. "Queen post" roofs are to be found especially in Suffolk, where there are fine examples in parish churches, for instance at **Mildenhall** and **Lakenheath** (fifteenth-century).

Another legacy of aisled buildings is the "hammerbeam roof" (Fig. 6e), which arose from the wish to do away with posts obstructing the floor area. The weight of the roof was carried on squat upright "hammerposts" standing on short projecting supports or "hammerbeams" cantilevered in from the sides of the building and braced by curved timbers against the walls below. A double hammerbeam construction, such as can be seen in the late medieval churches at **Woolpit** (Suffolk) and **March** (Cambs, Pl. 177), made it possible to build even wider buildings, with roofs which, like the fine early sixteenth-century example above the Great Hall at Gifford's Hall, **Stoke-by-Nayland** (Suffolk, Pl. 288), were both technical triumphs and decorative masterpieces.

Roofs of great halls

The size of the great hall of a medieval house, rising the full height of the building, made it necessary to have an open truss about halfway along its length. Unlike the end trusses, which were incorporated into the walls, this had to be designed so that it did not break up the effect of space in the centre of the room. Curved timbers were used to brace the tie-beam and produce the effect of an arch as at **Abingdon** Abbey (Oxon, *c.*1500, Pl. 287), which rose as high as the particular type of construction would permit.

The first bay at the service end of the room might have a full-height "spere-truss", another transverse timber frame, which indicates the position of a screen. Its function was to support speres or spurs, which were short partitions projecting on either side, leaving a wide central opening opposite the middle passageway from the kitchen into the hall, as at **Rufford Old Hall** (Lancs, *c.*1480).

Although there had been mural fireplaces in more important buildings since Norman times, halls with central fireplaces continued to be built throughout the medieval period. These needed ventilation in the form of a smoke outlet in the roof. Nearly all these louvres (from French *l'ouvert*, opening) have vanished with the later replacement of medieval roofs, but a timber smoke turret made for the great hall at **Gainsborough** Old Hall (Lincs) *c.*1460 has been preserved and is on show inside the house. Thirteenth- and fourteenth-century pottery ventilators in the form of human heads, with holes for eyes and mouths, have been found in excavations; the Fitzwilliam Museum, **Cambridge**, has two examples, one in the form of a nobleman in a coronet, the other depicting a mail-clad knight. Roof tiles were in use at least by the early thirteenth century, and these louvres were part of a growing fashion for decorative ridge tiles and finials.

Medieval houses were thatched with plants of all kinds. Wheat and rye straw, broad beans, gorse, broom, bracken and weeds have all been identified in the few fourteenth- and fifteenth-century roofs, found mainly in Devon, which still retain their original thatch under later layers. It was common practice to cover worn roofs rather than stripping them and some of the oldest surviving roofs are as much as eight feet (2.4m) thick. As time went on, thatch began to give way to less combustible roof coverings in better houses. The price of wooden shingles rose sharply in the fourteenth century, and both stone slates and pottery tiles, which had begun to appear in the late thirteenth century, became cheaper. There was a brisk trade in slates from Dorset, Devon and Cornwall, but Welsh slates were not yet exported beyond Chester. Lead became especially popular in the fifteenth century for covering the low-pitched roofs of buildings in the Perpendicular style.

Doors and windows

While the frames for the walls of timber-framed buildings were being assembled, doors and windows could be jointed directly into the relevant openings. At first doors did not have surrounds but made use of the timber of the frame itself. An external door always opened inwards, flat against the wall without a rebate. The door itself was either made of vertical planks, held together by heavy "ledges" or cross-bars at the back,

Pl. 290 *Detail of a fine timber-framed house of c.1500 in Myddelton Place at Saffron Walden, Essex, showing the jettied upper storey and a small oriel window with moulded mullions and a corbelled sill.*

Pl. 289 *The carved doorway of De Vere House at Lavenham, Suffolk, an ornate timber-framed building of the fifteenth century; the herring-bone brick infilling dates from modern restoration.*

or it was composed of a double layer of uprights, with the boards on one side covering the joins on the other. Such doors were often reinforced with iron studs and might have carved decoration. They were hung on either vertical wooden pins or strong leather straps attached to the door jambs, and they could be secured from within by an iron drawbar which slotted into the frame on either side. Doors gradually became more ornate (Pl. 289), with refinements like carved door heads appearing during the later Middle Ages.

Early windows for lighting high great halls were tall and narrow but in

Pl. 291 *Detail showing the medieval timber coving below the renewed oriel window of a fifteenth-century house in Main Street at Newport, Essex, known as Monk's Barn; the carving depicts the Virgin and Child between two angel musicians.*

two-storey houses they were generally long and low, made simply with upright mullions in the form of square bars set diagonally up to 8 inches (20cm) apart. The openings were not glazed but had shutters to keep out the weather, either hinged or, more often, sliding vertically or horizontally. One can sometimes see marks where lattices with diamond panes were wired to the window bars, before fixed glazing became general in the late sixteenth century. Some wooden windows emulate the mouldings and carving found on contemporary stone mullions. Like doors, windows became more ornate towards the end of the medieval period, when "oriels" or projecting bays were also introduced (Pls 290 and 291).

Pl. 292 *Jettied upper storeys in the medieval Shambles at York, where surviving timber-framed buildings date from the fourteenth to the seventeenth century.*

Walls

Once the timber frame of a building had been completed, it remained to fill in the walls. The carpentry used for this purpose varied according to the region; three main types emerge. On the western side of the country (Pls 272 and 284), from Cheshire to Hampshire, we find panels which are more or less square, sometimes with decorative timbers at the corners, and short straight angle braces slope upwards from post to wall-plate. Plain square panels were cheaper than those which used more wood and they are often found throughout the country on the less important walls of houses, with showier timbering at the front. In the eastern parts of the country, and especially in East Anglia (Pls 271 and 290), panels which are generally tall and narrow fill the spaces between timbers set close together ("close studding") and braces run downwards from post to sill. In the north the timber sill below the posts was omitted, and, although stone slabs, tiles and slate have occasionally been found as infill, the walls between the timbers were most commonly made of wattle and daub. For square panels, pointed staves were pushed into holes at the top and then fed into a slot along the bottom until they were vertical. Withies were then used to weave a basketwork filling, which was daubed with a mixture of clay, dung and horsehair, and finally plastered. Tall narrow panels might be filled with laths, woven from top to bottom round short horizontal staves, or small straight laths might simply be let into grooves on either side of the panel to provide a base for the daub. In the case of barns, where ventilation was required, a solid wall was not suitable, and panels made like woven hurdles have been found.

Jetties

Two-storeyed buildings, especially on restricted sites in towns, were often built with "jettied", overhanging or "oversailing" upper storeys (Pl. 302). It has been suggested that jetties actually strengthened upper floors, since the weight of the walls above, which rested on the ends of the joists, counteracted the tendency for them to sag in the middle, especially under the weight of a heavy piece of furniture in the centre of a room. Merchants like the builder of Paycocke's at **Coggeshall** (Essex, *c.*1500, Pls 293 and 303) evidently relished the opportunity they provided for carved ornament. Jetties were not confined to two-storey buildings; two overhangs are sometimes found, one above the other, as on the Guildhall and other neighbouring houses at **Thaxted** (Essex, fifteenth-century, Pl. 308). Double overhangs on houses like Southfields, built for a rich

Pl. 293 *Detail of the jettied upper story of Paycocke's (c.1500) in West Street at Coggeshall, Essex, showing its moulded and carved bressumer or horizontal beam and richly decorated door.*

Pl. 294 *Moulded ornament on the carved dragon post of a late fifteenth-century building by the churchyard gate at Clavering, Essex, probably built as almshouses.*

clothier at **Dedham** (Essex) in the fifteenth century, show that, although they may have been primarily intended to maximize floor area on cramped urban sites like the Shambles in **York** (Pl. 292), they were also used for conspicuous architectural effect in situations where land shortage was not a problem. Surviving structures with jetties on all sides, like the Guildhall at Thaxted and the Town Hall at **Fordwich** (Kent, early sixteenth-century), also suggest that they were felt to give added importance to public buildings.

The practical advantages of these overhangs were that they provided a greater floor area upstairs than on the ground floor, without the extra expense of a larger basic frame, and that they incidentally sheltered the lower part of the building and kept the footings dry. Up to about 2ft (60cm) of overhang could be achieved by cantilevering the joists of the upper floor, so that they were strong enough to bear the weight of walls at their outer ends. The joists always had to run outwards; so in order to carry a jetty round two sides of a building, an angle timber or "dragon beam" was needed at the corner. The "dragon post" or bracket below it would often provide an excuse for elaborately carved decoration as at **Clavering** (Essex, late fifteenth-century, Pl. 294). In more sophisticated buildings one may see coved plasterwork below the overhang, or there may be evidence that projecting ground-floor windows were jointed into the underside of the jetty.

"Wealden" houses

The jetty is the most prominent feature of "Wealden" houses, which were common in the fifteenth century and still found in the sixteenth. This type gets its name from the central weald of eastern Sussex and western Kent, but it is found throughout the prosperous agricultural areas of the "lowland" east and south-east, and sometimes also in towns in the "highland" areas of the north and west. Its open hall and jettied upper rooms at one or both ends are all covered by a single hipped roof as at Pattenden near **Goudhurst** (Kent, begun *c.*1470, Pl. 295), so that its central section appears to be recessed. An early fifteenth-century example from Chiddingstone (Kent) has been re-erected at the Weald and Downland Open Air Museum at **Singleton** (W. Sussex).

Decoration

There is no doubt that many of the timbers used in medieval framed structures made deliberate decorative patterns and were intended to be seen, but modern "restoration" all too frequently exposes a great many

which would originally have been covered up by a protective and insulating layer of plaster. In buildings of this type, there was a tendency for the panels to shrink, leaving gaps between the timbers and the plaster infill, and houses would have been limewashed at regular intervals to fill in any chinks which appeared. White was the natural colour of the chalk or limestone used to produce this basic whitewash, which had been used since Saxon times to protect porous wall surfaces from the weather. The familiar black-and-white colour scheme, dark timbers contrasting with a light wall surface, seems to have originated during the nineteenth century. Most beams would originally have been left unpainted, so that they weathered to a natural greyish-brown. Earth colours such as ochre or rusty red might be added to limewash to tint it or used to pick out the timbers, as they were to outline blocks of masonry or pick out patterns on plaster. These were the readily accessible, and therefore cheaper, "common" colours, used to produce soft yellowy creams and the light terracotta which was the true "Suffolk pink". Unlike modern paints, they weathered and mellowed with age. Pretty uniform pastel pinks, blues, mauves and apple greens did not appear until modern times.

Late medieval elaboration

By the fifteenth century there were many wealthy men who wanted the appearance of their houses to reflect their status. Close-studding was a sign of success because it used a lot of timber and was evidently expensive. Carved window or door heads, projecting windows and elaborate jetties all provided excuses for ostentatious displays, which blossomed into a profusion of opulent pattern and ornament in the timber-framed buildings of the Tudor period.

FARM BUILDINGS

Agriculture in the Middle Ages

The Normans' feudal system of agriculture continued unchanged during the early Middle Ages. All land was controlled by the king and under him by the nobility, the clergy and the monastic foundations. The peasants cultivated strips of land allocated to them on the three communal fields attached to their lord's manor, but they could not have their own holdings.

By the fifteenth century all that had changed, and the farm, in our modern sense, had come into being. Many factors, both social and

Pl. 295 *Pattenden near Goudhurst, Kent, a Wealden house built* c.1470 *with a full-height hall flanked by wings with jettied upper storeys, all covered by a single hipped roof; the upper floor of the central block dates from the sixteenth century.*

economic, combined to destroy the manorial system. The Normans had introduced the principle of primogeniture, whereby an estate was inherited intact by the eldest son rather than being repeatedly subdivided, so that landowners would remain rich enough to supply the monarch with a fighting force when he needed it (see p. 45). This meant that younger sons had to make their lives elsewhere, frequently in the church or as soldiers, on the Continent as well as at home. It brought them into contact with a wider world and broke down established social barriers. The nobility found itself mixing with the rising merchant middle class of the prosperous towns, and this led to marriages between old families and new money. On the land there was a continual expansion of sheep farming, initiated by the Cistercian monasteries and spreading with their growing popularity and ever-increasing land-ownership. Wool was profitable and needed much less labour than arable farming, a major consideration after the Black Death had almost halved the population in the mid fourteenth century. The conversion of great tracts of arable land into sheep runs coincided with a deterioration in the climate, when large areas of water-logged land were lost to cultivation. By 1340 the population had almost doubled since the Norman Conquest and the threat of famine loomed. During the second half of the century it was not land but labour which was in short supply. The peasants who had survived the plague were no longer captive workers but could sell their services to the highest bidder. Tied labour and barter were replaced by money, which was increasingly used as payment for both work and produce. Soaring wages and the difficulty of getting or keeping a workforce encouraged many lords to let holdings of land in exchange for rent. Enterprising individuals fortunate enough to survive in stricken communities annexed parts of the communal fields and fenced them round for their own use. The lord's manorial land remained the largest single unit, but the increasing number of smaller holdings, on which yeomen built modest hall houses like **Purton Green** Farmhouse (half a mile north of Stansfield, Suffolk, late thirteenth-century) and Sanders, a longhouse at **Lettaford** (Devon, *c.*1500), set the pattern for the farms of the future.

Barns

The few medieval farm buildings left are almost all barns, belonging mainly to the great ecclesiastical landowners who could afford to build really solidly and needed huge spaces to store corn and other crops. They were made either of wood, like the early thirteenth-century barley barn (Pl. 296) at **Cressing Temple,** a settlement of the Knights Templar (later

Pl. 296 *The huge timber-framed barley barn at Cressing Temple in Essex, built by the Knights Templar c.1200–20; the brick plinth is a later insertion.*

Pl. 297 *The interior of the massive thirteenth-century monastic stone barn at Great Coxwell, Oxfordshire, showing the timber structure supporting the heavy roof with its stone slates.*

taken over by the Hospitallers), and the fifteenth-century Prior's Hall barn at **Widdington** (both in Essex), or of stone, as at **Glastonbury** (Somerset, *c.*1500) and at **Great Coxwell** (Oxon, thirteenth-century, Pl. 297), where one can visit a massive barn which was part of a manor belonging to the Cistercian abbey of Beaulieu (Hants). These huge structures, generally built on an aisled plan for greater width, are usually referred to as "tithe barns", though this is not necessarily correct. They were not all used for the collection of tithes, which were payments to an overlord in the form of a tenth part of the crops and other produce of those who held land under him. Often these buildings were simply large warehouses for storing the produce of considerable estates.

The systematic stacking of the various crops, so that each would be accessible when it was needed, was a matter for skilled organization, and many such barns had a room for an overseer built over the porch of one of the entrances, as at **Bredon** (Worcs). The building had to be well ventilated to keep the grain dry and prevent it from going mouldy. Slits or small apertures were built into the walls of stone barns, though these should not be confused with the nesting holes sometimes supplied for pigeons, for example at Great Coxwell, which has a pigeon loft incorporated into its eastern gable. Woven panels have been found in timber buildings but wooden construction must have allowed some circulation

Pl. 298 *The surviving part of the monumental monastic stone barn built* c.1400 *at Abbotsbury, Dorset, showing on the right a projecting porch marking the position of one of its two threshing floors; the second was at the far end of the barn, which is a roofless ruin.*

Pl. 299 *The thatched stone barn at Place Farm, Tisbury, Wiltshire, about 60 metres (200 feet) long, built by the nunnery of Shaftesbury in the fifteenth century and said to be the largest barn in England.*

Pl. 300 *Detail of the interior of the medieval dovecot at Sibthorpe, Nottinghamshire, which dates from the thirteenth or fourteenth century, showing the roof structure above the 1260 nesting holes arranged in 28 tiers.*

of air in any case, especially when wattle or weatherboarding were used.

The floor plan of a barn was generally cruciform, with the arms or transepts formed by two porches, one on each side of the building as at Place Farm, **Tisbury** (Wilts, fifteenth-century, Pl. 299). This was because the entrance had to be tall enough for laden waggons to drive in and because the extra width provided by the porches increased the size of the threshing floor inside, as well as protecting it from driving rain when the doors were open. The threshing area was generally more or less in the centre of the floor and placed between two doors, because a through draught helped with winnowing (separating the grain from the chaff.). Where the doors were both equally high, waggons could drive in at one side and out at the other, but sometimes the second entrance was much smaller and intended only to let in light and provide much-needed fresh air for labourers threshing with flails, a dusty and unhealthy job which frequently affected the lungs. Some barns had more than one threshing floor. The monumental examples at **Bradford-on-Avon** (Wilts, fourteenth-century) and **Abbotsbury** (Dorset, c.1400, Pl. 298) had two each, while the late medieval one at **Harmondsworth** (Greater London) had three, but a greater floor area did not necessarily go with a larger number of threshing floors.

With the introduction of steam-threshing in 1786, it was no longer necessary to store unthreshed corn, and the Tithe Act of 1836 commuted all remaining tithes into money payments. The *raison d'être* of these huge barns disappeared. Some were put to new uses, but vast numbers were neglected and either fell to pieces or were demolished. Only a small number survive today, and of these there are very few which, like William of Wykeham's tithe barn at **Upper Heyford** (Oxon), are still used for agricultural purposes.

Dovecots

During the Middle Ages there were no root crops that could be used to feed cattle, most of which were slaughtered in the autumn to provide salted meat for the winter months. Pigeons were an important source of fresh meat to vary the diet at this time of year, and, besides the pigeon lofts built into barn walls (see above), separate free-standing dovecots were often provided for them. Early examples, which, as with barns, are generally those belonging to religious houses, are circular buildings, like the one at **Dunster** Priory (Somerset), where the potence or revolving ladder used for catching young birds and cleaning out the nesting boxes is still in position inside the building. At **Sibthorpe** (Notts, Pls 300 and 301) the dovecot, which formed part of a group of buildings belonging to

Pl. 301 *The thirteenth- or fourteenth-century circular dovecot, which belonged to the collegiate church at Sibthorpe, Nottinghamshire, showing the projecting stringcourse designed to prevent rats from climbing up the walls.*

the collegiate church, has a projecting stringcourse running round the outside, a feature designed to prevent rats from climbing up the walls. Later medieval stone dovecots, such as the tall gabled structure at **Bruton** Abbey (Somerset, possibly sixteenth-century), are generally rectangular. A cruck-built example at **Hill Croome** (Worcs) may perhaps have been built during the fifteenth century but timber-framed dovecots date mainly from the late sixteenth century onwards.

Pl. 302 *Close-studded timber-framing at Lavenham in Suffolk, where numerous medieval houses have survived; those on the right still have their protective and insulating plaster covering structural beams which were not intended to be seen.*

URBAN ARCHITECTURE

Towns

The expansion of commerce brought wealth to the towns and with it political power and independence. Burgesses and landowners began to build more permanently, and rich merchants, who needed security for their goods and valuables, fortified their cities with strong, high walls such as can still be seen at **Southampton** (Hants) or **Caernarvon** (Gwynedd). At intervals they built towers, generally D-shaped and open at the back, to provide fighting platforms which commanded a view of the whole curtain. Older town walls were rebuilt using up-to-date improvements

Pl. 304 *The octagonal stone Market Cross at Chichester, West Sussex, built in 1501; the lantern partly visible at the top was altered in 1746.*

Pl. 303 *Paycocke's in West Street at Coggeshall, Essex, built for a rich merchant c.1500, showing its opulent use of close studding and carved decoration.*

in design, as at **Oxford** (1226–40), where a section with projecting bastions can still be seen in the garden at New College.

The stone cellars of thirteenth-century merchants' houses have been found in a number of towns, like **Chester**, where No. 48 Bridge Street also has some stonework above ground. Although some of these cellars must have belonged to stone houses, they seem often to have been the basements of timber-framed houses which have subsequently been rebuilt. Most town houses were built of wood throughout the Middle

Ages, but from the late thirteenth or early fourteenth century onwards it was common for them to have stone footings. Certain rules had to be laid down for the public good, and as early as Henry II's reign there had been regulations about party walls and drainage. Fire risk was an ever-present anxiety and the fourteenth-century London Ordinances prohibited the use of wood for chimneys (which included smoke vents), decreeing that in future they must be built of non-inflammable materials like stone, tiles or plaster.

Houses were generally built at right angles to the highway, with only a gable end on to the street frontage. This was often jettied so as to produce extra space upstairs, and some streets had jetties on both sides which very nearly met overhead and blocked out almost all the light from the ground-floor rooms. In the Shambles at **York** (Pl. 292) one can still see upper floors so close together that it would be possible to shake hands across the street. At **Chester** there is a late thirteenth-century arrangement unique in Britain which is known as "the Rows". This is a raised pedestrian walkway built at first-floor level over vaulted stone cellars and protected from the weather by a projecting upper storey.

The evident determination to make maximum use of space suggests that medieval towns were extremely cramped, but this does not seem to have been the case, since there was plenty of room for gardens and sometimes even farms inside the walls. It may simply reflect the absence of planning, which allowed these towns to evolve with irregular street patterns determined by land-ownership and commercial considerations. Except in a few military settlements, like **Caernarvon** (Gwynedd) or **Winchelsea** (E. Sussex), which used a grid plan, medieval towns are characterized by a picturesquely haphazard layout which can still be recognized in the old centres of numerous towns today, even when none of the original buildings has survived.

The growth in population meant that towns became divided up into a number of different parishes, each with its own church, and this too can be traced on the plans of modern towns, such as **Norwich**, which still has its medieval street pattern and no fewer than thirty-five medieval churches, though many are no longer in use and three are ruins. **King's Lynn** (also in Norfolk, Pl. 309) still has a remarkable number of medieval buildings, several churches, two guildhalls, merchants' houses, warehouses and the traces, both in masonry and in street names, of numerous friaries (see p. 123), a sure sign of the importance of any town in the later Middle Ages. Smaller towns where medieval timber-framed buildings have survived in unusual numbers are **Weobley** (Herefordshire, Pl. 284) and **Lavenham** (Suffolk, Pl. 302), where the market square is still dominated by its late fifteenth-century guildhall.

Pl. 305 *The impressive entrance front of late fifteenth-century Angel and Royal Inn at Grantham in Lincolnshire, originally the property of the Knights Templar; the windows are now sashed but above them are the original dripmoulds.*

A medieval town would not have had a geometrically laid out square at its centre, but there would always have been an open space, perhaps outside the gates of a castle or monastery, which provided a meeting place for the inhabitants and enough room for the market, as at **Bury St Edmunds** (Suffolk), where Angel Hill outside the great gateway of the abbey was used for centuries for the Bury Fair. This space might be near the site of a Saxon

Pl. 306 *Detail showing an angel holding a crown on the carved corbel supporting the oriel window above the entrance arch of the late fifteenth-century Angel and Royal Inn at Grantham, Lincolnshire.*

Pl. 307 *The George Inn at Glastonbury, Somerset, built like a monastic gatehouse in the early sixteenth century to provide board and lodging for pilgrims to the abbey.*

cross erected as a meeting place for the faithful (see p. 18), and just as those crosses preceded churches, the market crosses of medieval times anticipated later covered markets. At first these were simple wooden shelters with platforms for displaying merchandise for barter or sale, but later they came to be rebuilt in more elaborate form, either in stone, as at **Chichester** (W. Sussex, 1501, Pl. 304), or in wood, as at **Wymondham** (Norfolk, 1617).

Larger town houses

The increasing prosperity of the later Middle Ages is reflected in the longer street frontages of the houses of rich merchants, whose ground

floors were generally let out as shops. These double-fronted houses had a way through to the back, where there would be a wing at right angles to the main building or even a whole range of buildings surrounding a courtyard. Archaeological evidence shows that the quays at **Southampton** were lined with handsome stone merchants' houses from the late twelfth century onwards. The booming wool trade brought particular affluence to the West Riding of Yorkshire, the Cotswolds and East Anglia, where there are magnificent surviving fifteenth-century houses, such as Shibden Hall, **Halifax** (W. Yorks), Grevel's House, **Chipping Campden** (Glos, Pls 269 and 270), and Paycocke's, **Coggeshall** (Essex, Pls 293 and 303).

Inns

By the fifteenth century we find the earliest inns, often built by the monasteries. In the late Middle Ages the duty of religious houses to offer

Pl. 308 The fifteenth-century timber-framed Guildhall at Thaxted in Essex, built with two upper storeys, jettied on three sides, above an open arched ground floor.

Pl. 309 The chequered flint and stone Guildhall at King's Lynn, Norfolk, built for the Guild of Holy Trinity in 1421.

Pl. 310 *The Hospital of St Cross at Winchester in Hampshire, founded in 1136, showing the cruciform church completed in the thirteenth century with a clerestory added in 1334–5. The almshouses on the left date from c.1445; the accommodation was divided into sets of four three-roomed lodgings, each sharing one of the tall octagonal chimney stacks.*

hospitality to huge numbers of pilgrims or to noblemen with their entire retinues had become a crippling financial burden, and the regular income to be expected from catering for them commercially made large new buildings a good investment. Architecturally, inns were of two distinct kinds. The first type was built round a courtyard like a rich man's town house, which is still known in France as an *hôtel*. These were generally timber-framed buildings, like the New Inn, **Gloucester**, and the George, **Dorchester** (Oxon). The other type resembled a contemporary monastic gatehouse and was a rectangular stone building of two or three storeys incorporating a gateway, like the Angel and Royal, **Grantham** (Lincs, Pl. 305 and 306), and the George, **Glastonbury** (Somerset, Pl. 307).

Town halls

The members of the merchant guild of a medieval town represented all its traders and drew up strict rules to protect and regulate all business conducted there. During the fourteenth century the various craftsmen were also organized into separate guilds, according to their occupations. All those following the same trade became concentrated in the same ward or district of the town, with the result that their representatives increasingly dominated local politics. Every town had its own "guildhall" but few of these early town halls have survived. Some were built in stone on the pattern of great halls of the time, but unlike domestic buildings they generally had the entrance at one end, as in a large church. The City of **London**'s Guildhall (completed 1422) still exists, though in much altered form, with its original porch and the eastern part of its crypt. Another impressive stone guildhall, at **York** (1447–8), was extensively damaged during the Second World War but has been restored. Chequered flint and stone guildhalls survive in Norfolk at **King's Lynn** (1421, Pl. 309) and **Norwich** (begun 1407–13 and completed 1535). More modest timber-framed versions also survive, like those at **Thaxted** (Essex, Pl. 308), above an open ground floor, and **Hadleigh** (Suffolk), originally with almshouses underneath. Both were built in the fifteenth century, with two jetties or overhanging upper storeys.

Almshouses

Special housing for the old and needy had existed since Norman times. The Hospital of St Cross at **Winchester** (Hants, Pl. 310) was founded in 1136, and its chapel, begun in the twelfth century and completed in the thirteenth, belongs to the period of stylistic transition when Norman was giving way to Gothic. The present almshouses were built

in the mid fifteenth century, and the two-storeyed west range contains lodgings (see pp. 240–241) for the brethren or old men resident there. Each unit consists of four three-roomed flats, with living room, bedroom and scullery, two flats downstairs and two above, sharing a central staircase. The overall plan resembles a monastery with all the rooms opening off the courtyard, except for the fact that the accommodation is not communal but takes the form of individual living quarters more like academic lodgings of the period. Almshouses where old people

Pl. 311 *Interior of the chapel opening off the living accommodation of St John's Almshouses at Sherborne in Dorset, built in 1437–48.*

could live in small sets of rooms grouped round a courtyard and eat in a communal dining hall became the pattern for the late Middle Ages and beyond, and they are coming back into favour in the late twentieth century. After four hundred years St Cross is still serving its original purpose. The earliest of the three sets of almshouses in the churchyard of St Helen's, **Abingdon** (Oxon, Pl. 312), dating from 1446, also survives, though with much later alteration, as do St John's Almshouses at

Pl. 313 A late medieval terrace at Melbourn in Cambridgeshire, consisting of a row of small cottages under a single roof; the shutters, which were hinged to the sills could be raised to cover the windows at night.

Sherborne (Dorset, 1437–48, Pl. 311), which are still in use and originally had a dormitory on two storeys to provide separate accommodation for the twelve poor men and four poor women who lived there.

Hospitals

The earliest hospitals, as opposed to the infirmaries belonging to monastic houses, also date back to Norman times. St Mary's, **Chichester** (W. Sussex), was founded by secular canons *c.*1158, and its present building (*c.*1290–1300) has flint and timber-framed walls and a huge roof 42ft (13m) high, with eaves only 7ft (2m) from the ground. It was built like a large aisled church, the "nave" accommodating the patients and the "chancel" being the chapel, so that both physical and spiritual succour were close at hand. This hospital is unique for being still lived in, since the interior was converted in the seventeenth century into almshouses, which are still in use. St Mary's Almshouses, **Glastonbury** (Somerset, fourteenth-century), were built on a similar plan under a single roof. The two parallel rows of houses which survive, with a chapel at the far end, were originally all part of the same building. The dwellings ran along the two sides of a "nave" which was the communal hall, while the chapel was in the

Pl. 312 Christ's Hospital or the Long Alley Almshouses in the churchyard of St Helen's at Abingdon, Oxfordshire, built in 1446 and altered in the seventeenth century; the lantern on the roof was added in 1707.

position of the "chancel". The mid thirteenth-century Great Hospital at Norwich was built to incorporate the parish church of St Helen which lay between the separate men's and women's wards at either end. The only surviving part of the Savoy Hospital, **London**, is its chapel (1508). This was originally at the centre of a large cruciform building, like a church with transepts, so it was easily accessible from all four arms or wards.

Terraces

Terraced housing has survived at **Wells** (Somerset), where Vicars Close, built in the mid fourteenth century to house vicars (from Latin *vicarius*, deputy) acting for absent prebendaries of the cathedral, has been fully restored. It consists of a street 456ft (138m) long, with two identical terraces facing each other and front gardens added *c.*1410–20. The chapel at one end and the hall at the other both date from the fifteenth century. A terrace of six two-storeyed "Wealden" houses with jettied solars can be seen at Spon Street, **Coventry** (West Midlands, late fourteenth-century), while a row of cottages, Nos. 34–50 Church Street, **Tewkesbury** (Glos), gives another indication that terraced housing was already being built in towns by the early fifteenth century. There is evidence that these were originally twenty-nine tenements built by the monks as a speculative development just outside the abbey precincts and rented out to artisans. A comparable later medieval terrace survives at **Melbourn** (Cambs, Pl. 313) where there is a row of small cottages dating from the sixteenth century.

Shops

Each of these little houses may have had a shop at the front, with a hall or living room behind it, and was small enough to fit under the single-span roof which stretched the whole length of the building. During restoration at Tewkesbury, it was possible to reconstruct the arrangement whereby the shutters over the shop windows could be lowered during trading hours to provide a wide shelf or counter. It was normal for shops to form part of dwelling houses, and business would also be conducted in the ground floors or undercrofts of merchants' town houses.

Public lavatories

There were public lavatories in London as early as the twelfth century, and a row of twelve late thirteenth-century privies, probably for the use of Edward I's administrative staff, can still be seen in the town wall at **Conway** (Gwynedd).

Bridges

A number of fourteenth- and fifteenth-century stone bridges survive, as at **St Ives** (Cambs) and **Yeolmbridge** (Cornwall). They can be recognized by their narrow roadways, not more than seven or eight feet (2–2.5m) overall, their very slightly pointed arches and their "cutwaters" or piers projecting on the upstream side. These are sharply chamfered to direct the current smoothly through the openings and reduce the pressure on joints which were made with lime-mortar and were liable to wear away with the force of the water. The curious fourteenth-century Triangular Bridge originally spanning three streams at **Crowland** (Lincs, Pl. 315) has three arches meeting at the middle, where it is thought there may have been a great cross. **Chester**'s Dee Bridge had a tower (demolished in 1593) and there was often a shrine or chapel halfway across a bridge, where money was collected to pay for the cost of its upkeep. These have survived only at **Bradford-on-Avon** (Wilts, Pl. 314), **Rotherham** (S. Yorks), **St Ives** (Cambs) and most impressively at **Wakefield** (W. Yorks), where the bridge has nine arches and the chapel is in a full-blown version of the Decorated style, complete with flowing tracery and crocketed pinnacles.

Most bridges would have been much simpler structures, with wooden parapets which were narrower than stone ones and saved on masonry. All that survives of these is a basic humped structure often known as a "packhorse bridge", in reference to the fact that there was practically no wheeled traffic during the Middle Ages and almost all journeys were made on foot or with animals. Examples of these survive in mountainous areas like the Lake District (Cumbria), where they are still used by farmers and fellwalkers.

Town walls

Traces of medieval fortifications with wall-walks and entrance gatehouses can be seen in many towns, especially those like **Norwich** (Pl. 316) and **Hull**, where the wool and cloth trades brought prosperity. At both **York** (Pl. 317) and **Chester** one can still make a circuit of the wall-walks and enter the city by a medieval gateway. Apart from these surviving gateways or "bars", such as Monk Bar at **York**, there are many which have been rebuilt. Numerous others, though demolished, are recorded in street names like Castlegate, Fossgate, Micklegate or Northgate.

Pl. 314 *The thirteenth-century Town Bridge at Bradford-on-Avon in Wiltshire, showing the tiny chapel halfway across; the bridge was much altered in the seventeenth century, when the chapel, later used as a lockup for the temporary detention of malefactors, was given its domed roof.*

Pl. 315 *The fourteenth-century Triangular Bridge, which originally spanned three streams at Crowland in Lincolnshire, showing the junction of its three arches where there may once have been a great cross; the seated figure, who is probably Christ, may have come from the gable on the west front of Croyland Abbey.*

Pl. 316 *The medieval city walls at Norwich in Norfolk which were begun in 1294, showing, on the left, the Black Tower on Carrow Hill built in c.1334.*

Pl. 317 *The walkway along the top of the city walls at York, which date from c.1250 and are the longest in England; much of the stonework was renovated in the nineteenth and twentieth centuries.*

Educational establishments

Schools

During the Middle Ages the sons of noblemen were taught either at home or in the great households of both secular and religious magnates, where they learned to read and write, acquired courtly manners and were

Pl. 319 *The medieval Chamber Court at Winchester College, completed by 1404; the doorway in the corner leads to the staircase up to the Hall, seen on the left, which was built above the original school room.*

Pl. 318 *View through the vaulted archway of the fourteenth-century Inner Gate at Winchester College looking into Chamber Court, which has chambers or school rooms opening off it.*

trained in both sporting skills and the arts of war. These households also provided a means to social advancement for boys from humbler backgrounds. Geoffrey Chaucer in the fourteenth century and Sir Thomas More in the late fifteenth both began successful careers in public life as children in noble service. Until the fourteenth century, schools were the preserve of the church, which needed to train its clergy in both canon and civil law, but from then onwards, the law, administration and

Pl. 320 *The medieval buildings of Sherborne School at Sherborne in Dorset, originally part of the monastic precinct of Sherborne Abbey; in front of the Norman abbey church with its Perpendicular crossing tower lie the fifteenth-century Abbot's Lodging and, on the right, the Norman and medieval Abbot's Hall built above a vaulted undercroft.*

Pl. 321 *Mob Quad at Merton College, the earliest college quadrangle at Oxford, which was built in the fourteenth century; behind it lies the thirteenth-century chapel with its tower of 1448–51.*

Pl. 322 *The interior of Merton College Chapel, Oxford, showing a detail of one of the many-shafted piers of the crossing, which dates from c.1330–35.*

Pl. 323 *The interior of the antechapel in the chapel of All Soul's College, Oxford, consecrated in 1442; the main chapel lies beyond the screen on the left, which dates from 1664 but was remodelled in 1716.*

trade were viable alternatives to a career in the church. Monastic and cathedral schools sometimes taught boys as well as young men, but a system of education from childhood to university came into being only in the fifteenth century. An important pioneer was William of Wykeham, founder of New College, Oxford (see below), who established **Winchester** College (Hants, Pls 318 and 319) in 1382. This school for seventy "poor and needy scholars" and up to ten commoners or paying pupils was

purpose-built and not part of an existing complex. It was planned on monastic lines with lodgings for the scholars (see p. 241) ranged round an inner courtyard. Its gatehouses, Outer and Chamber Courts, hall, chapel and cloister, all completed by 1404, can still be seen. Winchester was the model for Henry VI's **Eton** College (Berks), founded in 1440. Its fifteenth-century chapel, hall and cloisters have survived, but the original school building, a detached brick range containing the present Long

Chamber and Lower School, was altered in the seventeenth century. The monastic school at **Sherborne** (Dorset, Pl. 320), refounded in the sixteenth century by Edward VI, still uses the medieval abbey buildings dating from the thirteenth to the fifteenth century.

The fifteenth century saw the large-scale endowment of schools by bishops and churchmen and also by guilds and merchants. The new and independent middle class of self-made businessmen played an important part in ensuring that by the late Middle Ages there was a well-established system of academic secondary education. Practical skills were not taught in schools but were passed on by craftsmen to their

apprentices, who learned over a specified period, normally seven years, of working on the job. The first grammar schools, established during this period, were designed to give a thorough grounding in Latin, the essential language which all educated people had to master, as well as subjects like logic, mathematics and astronomy. The Inns of Court, law schools modelled on the colleges at Oxford and Cambridge (see below), were established in **London** during the fourteenth century. Almost all their present buildings date from later periods, but at Lincoln's Inn one can still see the red brick east court (1490–1520) and gatehouse with its original oak doors (1518), which are now known as the "Old Building".

Universities

Oxford University must have come into existence some time during the Norman period, since it was already renowned for its learning in the twelfth century, and it is known that some of its scholars migrated to Cambridge in 1209. Its first statute is recorded in 1253, at a time when a growing need for able administrators demanded a broader form of education than that provided by the monastic schools; but the first colleges were not built until the end of the thirteenth century. At first the students lived together in halls, which were often small, only loosely organized and lacking in any comfort. Until 1379, when William of Wykeham founded his New College to house both graduates and under-graduates together, colleges were only for scholars who had already taken their degrees. The earliest seems to have been Merton College (1262, Pls 321 and 322), named after its founder Walter de Merton, Chancellor of England under Henry III. Two halls of thirteenth-century origin are still in use, as is the chapel (c.1290), the choir of an unfinished church, which has well-preserved fourteenth-century stained glass. It lies on the west side of the Front Quad, the first college quadrangle, begun in 1304 but not completed until the building of the library in 1371–8. Oxford's next surviving buildings are at New College, which was built according to a carefully worked-out plan in c.1379–86. It had a gatehouse containing the warden's lodgings, so that he could command the entrance of the building like a contemporary nobleman in his castle, a quadrangle with a hall, library and chapel and next to it a cloister. Much of this can still be seen today and, even where the buildings have been refaced, one can often make out the pattern of the original windows, single lights denoting study cubicles and wider two- or three-light openings the larger shared bedrooms. The chapel takes the form of a cruciform church, minus its nave, whose transepts act as an antechapel to the choir. It may well have been copying the unfinished chapel at Merton, which was intended to

Pl. 324 *The fifteenth-century chapel and beyond it the bell tower of 1492–1509 at Magdalen College, Oxford, seen from the north cloister walk of the Great Quadrangle, which dates from 1475–90.*

Pl. 325 *Looking through the early sixteenth-century
entrance gateway in Tom Tower at Christ Church,
Oxford, towards the thirteenth-century upper stage of
the crossing tower of the Norman cathedral on the far
side of Tom Quad.*

Pl. 326 *The Divinity School at Oxford begun c.1420,
showing its superb stone vault, decorated with heraldic
and pictorial bosses and small statuettes, which was
completed in c.1490; although resembling a fan vault
with prominent bosses, this is in fact a lierne vault with
its weight pressing on the arches, the outer walls and
the buttresses which support them.*

Canterbury College in 1363. Its name survives in the Canterbury Quadrangle of the college, which grew up around the Augustinian priory founded by Henry I (1122), and its chapel is now the cathedral. Older foundations were also extending their accommodation with buildings, like the warden's lodgings at Merton and the library range of the front quadrangle at Balliol. The first of the separate university buildings funded by various benefactors was the Divinity School (Pl. 326), begun *c.*1420 but not completed, with its superb stone lierne vault, until *c.*1490.

Peterhouse, the first college at **Cambridge**, was founded in 1280 by the Bishop of Ely, specifically on the pattern of Merton, Oxford, but little

Pl. 327 *The fourteenth-century Old Court at Corpus Christi College, Cambridge, which was founded in 1352; the buildings originally had only two storeys and the buttresses and attic rooms date from the sixteenth century.*

have a nave and aisles, but the date of the New College cloisters makes it clear that the idea of building a nave was abandoned early on. The truncated form of the existing building set the pattern for many later college chapels, like those at All Souls and Magdalen.

The building of colleges continued throughout the fifteenth century with Lincoln (1427), All Souls (1438, Pl. 323) and Magdalen (1474–1510, Pl. 324), as well as others which now form part of colleges subsequently renamed, for instance Christ Church (Pl. 325), originally founded as

Pl. 328 *The noble Great Gate at Trinity College, Cambridge, built at the end of the fifteenth century with corner turrets added in 1528–9; the statue of Henry VIII in the niche above the entrance dates from 1615.*

Pl. 329 *The splendid interior of King's College Chapel, Cambridge, founded by Henry VI in 1441, showing its magnificent fan vault of 1512–15; the trumpeting angels stand above the organ, which dates from the seventeenth century.*

Pl. 330 *The three-storeyed early sixteenth-century gatehouse of St John's College, Cambridge, showing the repainted heraldic carvings of creatures with goats' heads, antelopes' bodies and elephants' tails which decorate the wall above the entrance arch; the figure of St John dates from 1662.*

remains of its hall, the university's only surviving thirteenth-century building. By 1475 there were twelve colleges at Cambridge, though the medieval buildings were not put up inside the little town but around it. Each college had its various buildings centred on a great hall and was sited

near a parish church which served as a chapel. From the beginning Oxford had the advantage of being able to use the good-quality oolite limestone of the Cotswolds. Cambridge was less fortunate, and as early as the mid fourteenth century was abandoning the unsatisfactory local "clunch" or chalk limestone in favour of brick, sometimes of the whitish clay common in the area. Magdalene (then Buckingham) College (begun 1428) had all its walls faced in brick, as did Queens' (1440) and Jesus (1497). Medieval Oxford has impressive quadrangles, which are hardly found in contemporary Cambridge, though the irregular rectangle of Old Court at Corpus Christi College (founded in 1352, Pl. 327) was completed by 1377. Cambridge, on the other hand, has a much larger number of noble gatehouses, for instance at Trinity (c.1430 and c.1490, Pl. 328), Queens' (c.1450), Jesus (1497) and St John's (founded in 1511, Pl. 330). Apart from King's, where Henry VI's magnificent chapel (Pls 111 and 329) was the only completed part of a scheme directly imitating New College at Oxford, Cambridge colleges did not follow a formal layout but resembled late medieval manor houses, with a great hall opposite the entrance gateway, as at Pembroke, where the present nineteenth-century hall replaced a fourteenth-century predecessor.

Ireland

RELIGIOUS ARCHITECTURE

The Norman invasion of Ireland in the late twelfth century had taken place with papal backing for its ostensibly Christian missionary purpose (see p. 87), and it was followed by an extensive programme of religious building. Cathedrals in the early Gothic style were erected, for instance at **Dublin** and **Kilkenny**. The monastic orders, especially the Cistercians, continued to establish houses, generally in or close to the Anglo-Norman towns, though some were also built in the west, which kept the invaders at bay and still retained a Romanesque building tradition well into the thirteenth century, as at **Ballintober** (Co. Mayo, Pl. 331). Some surviving ruins are the Augustinian **Athassel** Priory (Co. Tipperary, pre-1205), the Cistercian **Dunbrody** Abbey (Co. Wexford, 1210 onwards, Pl. 332), and the Dominican Friary of **Kilmallock** (Co. Limerick, 1291); at **Inistioge** (Co. Kilkenny, Pl. 333) some of the remaining parts of the adjoining Augustinian priory are incorporated in the parish church of 1824. A few fragments of early medieval cloisters still exist but the earliest surviving examples date from the fifteenth century, for example at **Jerpoint** (Co. Kilkenny, c.1400), where the richly carved decoration is unusual for

Pl. 331 *The interior of the cruciform thirteenth-century church of Ballintober (or Ballintubber) Abbey in County Mayo, showing carved capitals and ribbed vaulting in the chancel which belong to the transition between Romanesque and Gothic architecture.*

including figure sculpture of both humans and animals. Later fifteenth-century cloisters can be seen, for instance at the Cistercian **Holycross** Abbey (Co. Tipperary) and in the Dominican abbey at **Sligo** and the Franciscan **Muckross** Friary (Co. Kerry, Pl. 334). The ruins of the late twelfth-century Cistercian church of **Grey Abbey** (Co. Down) belong to the earliest period of Gothic in Ireland. This was an aisleless cruciform building, with two chapels in each transept and a tower above the crossing. The cathedral at **Cashel** (Co. Tipperary) has a similar plan and was the work of three successive Irish bishops between 1224 and

1289. Churches founded by the native Irish tended to be simpler than those built with Norman patronage because they had less money to spend. The mid thirteenth-century St Brendan's, **Ardfert** (Co. Kerry), for example, is a simple rectangular structure with a south aisle. Parish churches were smaller and plainer than their English counterparts, and the few large ones were mainly built in the Norman towns like **New Ross** (Co. Wexford), where William the Marshal, Earl of Pembroke, founded St Mary's Church c.1210–20. Such churches were generally cruciform in plan and had fine, tall lancet windows, especially in the choir. Towers began to be built during the fourteenth century, when the characteristically Irish arrangement of "stepped battlements" (see p. 291) probably originated, and they became common during the fifteenth and early sixteenth centuries. They were generally in a position just east of centre, above the crossing in cruciform churches. Towers were also added to many existing buildings, such as **Dunbrody** Abbey (Co. Wexford) and **Athassel** Priory (Co. Tipperary).

The devastating consequences of the Black Death meant that there was very little church building during the late fourteenth century, but a gradual economic recovery took place and considerable numbers of small churches were built, especially in the western part of the country, during the fifteenth and sixteenth centuries. These were generally unadorned rectangular buildings, like **Kileen Cowpark** (Co. Limerick), sometimes with fortified towers, as at **Templecross** (Co. Westmeath), whose western tower includes a priest's room on the first floor. In the eastern area of English influence they were sometimes more elaborate, like the mid fifteenth-century manorial churches at **Dunsany** and **Killeen** (both in Co. Meath) in the Pale (see p. 293). Each of these has a nave and a chancel that is only slightly shorter, two western turrets and, at the east end, a south turret roughly balanced by a three-storey tower containing the sacristy and above it living quarters for a priest. No cathedrals were built during the later Middle Ages, though chapels were added at Limerick and a new chancel arch at **Clonfert** (Co. Galway). Relatively few medieval churches have survived, often only as roofless ruins. The ruthless suppression of the Catholic church during the eighteenth century meant that maintenance lapsed and many buildings deteriorated beyond repair.

The most important late medieval architecture was monastic, for the religious houses had grown extremely wealthy. Smaller numbers of monks, living in greater comfort but without the assistance of lay brethren (see p. 50), relied not on their own labour but on the rents they received from mills, fisheries and land let to farmers. This sub-stantial income financed additions like belfries and cloisters to the

Pl. 332 *The ruins of Dunbrody Abbey in County Wexford, begun in 1210, showing the austere cruciform church, which is one of the longest Cistercian churches in Ireland; the tower with its characteristic Irish stepped battlements was added in the fifteenth century.*

Pl. 333 *The ruins of the medieval buildings of the Augustinian priory at Inistioge in County Kilkenny, showing the roofless church and tower with stepped battlements; the tower now forms part of a Church of Ireland church of 1824, which lies beyond it.*

existing buildings of the older monastic orders, especially the Cistercians, for instance at **Holycross** Abbey (Co. Tipperary). There was also a remarkable expansion in the numbers of new houses built by the friars, especially the Franciscans, who had about seventy-five during the fifteenth century. This was made possible by their enormous popularity, which brought rich gifts of property and money. The inevitable conflict between this new-found wealth and the original simplicity of their calling (see p. 121) led in the second half of the fifteenth century to the founding of many Irish "Observantine" houses, which adopted a Rule of Strict Observance.

Since the friars were mendicant orders and dedicated to a life of poverty, none of their buildings was richly ornamented. New friaries built in the fifteenth century were generally on rural sites in the south and west of the country, perhaps near a small town or castle. They have very recognizable tall thin towers, often with a stringcourse or band of stone marking each floor level, and characteristically Irish stepped battlements (Pl. 332 and 333). Among the best-preserved of their surviving ruins are the small tertiary (Third Order) or minor house at **Rosserk** (Co. Mayo, pre-1441) and the large complex of late fifteenth-century buildings at **Ross Errilly** (Co. Galway).

SECULAR ARCHITECTURE

The territorial expansion of the Norman families who arrived in Ireland at the end of the twelfth century led to considerable architectural activity. Most of the castles built at this period are closely comparable with their English counterparts, for instance **Trim** (Co. Meath), which has a square keep with projecting towers, curtain walls which have D-plan turrets and two fortified gatehouses. It also had a moat, probably added in the mid thirteenth century. There was a round keep at **Dundrum** (Co. Down) and a polygonal one at **Athlone** (Co. Westmeath), while castles with no keeps at all survive, for example at **Ballintober** (Co. Roscommon) and **Liscarroll** (Co. Cork). A specifically Norman-Irish kind of castle, a rectangular keep with round corner towers, as at **Kilkenny** (Pl. 335), but no courtyard, can still be seen, for instance at **Carlow** (Co. Carlow), **Ferns** (Co. Wexford) and **Lea** (Co. Laois) and the picturesquely sited **Dunluce** (Co. Antrim, Pl. 336), though it is easier to imagine the original appearance at **Enniscorthy** (Co. Wexford), where a more complete version, rebuilt in the seventeenth century, now houses a museum. Another Irish form of castle, found, for example, at **Kindelestown** (Co. Wicklow) and **Rathumney** (Co. Wexford), was built as a long hall with rooms above it.

The Normans' conquest of Ireland had been much less determined and thorough than their subjugation of Wales and Scotland, and during the medieval period the English kings were generally far too preoccupied with political problems at home and on the Continent to find either time or money for consolidating earlier gains. The "English Land" controlled by Dublin (see p. 87) got gradually smaller with the expansion of the "liberties" or free lands controlled by the barons of Anglo-Norman extraction. These noblemen were theoretically subservient to the English monarchy, but in practice they guarded their own privileges and

Pl. 334 *The fifteenth-century cloisters of the Franciscan Muckross Friary at Killarney in County Kerry, which appears to have been built in stages, since each of its four arcades is differently designed.*

increasingly intermarried with the native Irish, speaking the Gaelic language and adopting local customs. In order to bind the most powerful among them to the English interest and gain their vital support, three great earldoms of Desmond, Ormond and Kildare were created *c.*1330. At the same time the independent Gaelic kingdoms also increased their territory and set up standing armies of professional soldiers of Gaelic-Norse stock, imported from the north of Scotland and the Isles.

After the Scottish victory over the English at Bannockburn in 1314 (see p. 101) confirmed Robert I's authority in Scotland, his brother Edward Bruce, who had the backing of the Ulster chiftains, made an attempt to become king of the whole of Ireland. His invasion, launched in 1315 and ending with his death three years later, inspired widespread uprisings against the Anglo-Norman rulers and devastated whole towns and settlements. In 1348–9 the Black Death decimated the English colony, and about two thirds of the country reverted to Gaelic rule. Richard II made two expeditions to Ireland without achieving any lasting victory, first in 1394 and again in 1399, when Bolingbroke (the future Henry IV) seized the opportunity of his absence to usurp his throne.

By the beginning of the fifteenth century the English controlled only a small strip of land around Dublin, about thirty miles long and twenty wide, which was known as the "Pale" (meaning literally a wooden stake for fencing, and by extension a boundary) and gave rise to the expression "beyond the pale". There were only brief periods when governors were sent out from England, and the barons took advantage of England's involvement in domestic and political troubles (see pp. 106–108) to establish a successful movement for home rule. Although its leaders were officially acting as English viceroys, in practice the country was governed by the Home Rule party until the reign of Henry VII. During the Wars of the Roses some of its leaders openly supported the House of Lancaster, amongst them the Earls of Kildare, who were the effective rulers of late fifteenth-century Ireland.

The combination of baronial rule and Gaelic resurgence brought stability to large areas of the country during the later Middle Ages, and, apart from minor feuds and battles, Ireland enjoyed considerable periods of peace, when architecture was able to flourish. The ordinary domestic buildings of the towns and countryside have not survived, but one can still see tall, narrow late medieval keeps, such as **Dungory** Castle (Co. Galway), which are comparable with Scottish tower houses

Pl. 335 Kilkenny Castle, built in 1204, where the original rectangular keep and round corner towers have survived despite much alteration and reconstruction in the seventeenth and nineteenth centuries.

(see p. 230–232). This type of house was surrounded by or built into a "bawn" or walled enclosure with one or more rectangular (or occasionally cylindrical) defensive towers. Its floors were supported on massive stone beams or, especially in the case of the family living room on the top storey, had stone vaults with pointed arches. As in Scotland, these defended houses continued to be built well after the medieval period. Some large castles were also built during the fifteenth century, for example the keep at **Blarney** (Co. Cork), **Bunratty** (Co. Clare), with its four angle-towers, and **Newcastle West** (Co. Limerick), which has two separate great halls.

Scotland

RELIGIOUS ARCHITECTURE

As a result of the administrative reform of the church by David I in the twelfth century (see p. 90), the thirteenth was a great period of church building in Scotland, which produced new cathedrals at **Glasgow** (Strathclyde, Pl. 337 and 338), **Dunblane** (Central Region) and **Elgin** (Grampian, Pl. 339 and 340). Monastic building also continued, especially in the fertile areas of the south and east, as a consequence of David I's close contact with the leaders of the Cistercian order, which had led to the first Cistercian monastery being established at **Melrose** (Borders) in 1136, only seven years after the earliest English foundation. Thirteenth-century parish churches, such as the roofless ruin of St Magridin's Church at **Abdie** (Fife), were long rectangular unaisled buildings with a timber screen separating the nave from a chancel lit by simple lancet windows. This arrangement can still be seen in the ruins of the old parish church of Cawdor at **Barevan** (Highland), and it continued to be followed until late in the sixteenth century.

The alliance with France in the fourteenth century brought Scotland closer to the mainstream of European Gothic, then in its "flamboyant" stage (see p. 108), with the result that the characteristically English Perpendicular style did not develop here. During the fifteenth century, the more important towns grew richer and competed with each other in building expensive new churches, like those which survive at **Edinburgh** (Lothian: St Giles'), **Haddington** (Lothian: St Mary's, Pl. 341) and **Stirling** (Central Region: Holy Rude). Their characteristic plan had an aisled nave and choir, both of equal width, five and three bays long respectively, a west tower, small transepts and a polygonal apsidal presbytery.

In the late Middle Ages baronial patrons turned their attention away

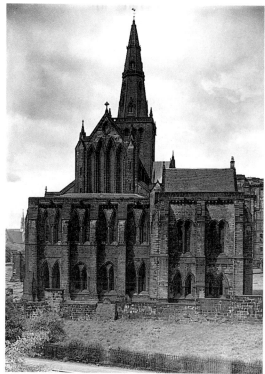

Pl. 336 *Dunluce Castle, built c.1300 on a rocky promontory in County Antrim, with later additions including a sixteenth-century gatehouse and early seventeenth-century living quarters, part of which collapsed into the sea in 1639.*

Pl. 337 *The interior of the thirteenth-century nave of Glasgow Cathedral, showing the shafted piers of the south arcade and the triforium and clerestory linked by an upper tier of enclosing arches; the open timber roof dates from the early twentieth century.*

Pl. 338 *Glasgow Cathedral as rebuilt in the mid to late t hirteenth century, showing the east window of the presbytery rising above the east wall of the ambulatory; the chapter house on the right and the central steeple were both reconstructed in the fifteenth century.*

Pl. 339 *The ruined thirteenth-century presbytery of Elgin Cathedral in Grampian, seen from the south transept where the tombs date from the later Middle Ages; the building gradually fell into decay after the See was dissolved in 1560.*

Pl. 340 *The powerful geometry of the eastern façade of Elgin Cathedral in Grampian, built near the end of the thirteenth century, showing two rows of lancets running the full width of the presbytery and a large rose window in the gable.*

Pl. 341 *Looking across the choir in the ruined east end of St Mary's church at Haddington, Lothian, seen before it was re-roofed and restored in 1971–3; the memorial to William Seton, Provost of Haddington, was erected in 1682.*

Pl. 342 *The chapel of King's College, Aberdeen, built c.1500, which still retains its original carved screen and double row of choir stalls; the crown on the tower was rebuilt in 1633.*

Pl. 343 *St Matthew's Chapel at Roslin in Lothian, the surviving aisled choir and ambulatory of a collegiate church built in the mid fifteenth century and decorated both inside and out with amazing richness; this view shows the south side with its highly ornamented tracery and buttresses topped by pinnacles encrusted with fantastic carving.*

from the foundation of monastic and parish churches and began instead to set up collegiate churches for secular clergy (see p. 110), such as the surviving King's College Chapel, **Aberdeen** (Grampian, Pl. 342), which was built for James IV and completed in 1505. Priority was given to building the choir and sometimes, as at **Roslin** (Lothian, Pl. 343), the nave remained unfinished. Some of these churches were built on a small rectangular plan, but a typical collegiate church was cruciform, with unaisled choir and transepts. The east end might be either square, as at **Crichton**, or polygonal, as at **Dalkeith** (both in Lothian).

SECULAR ARCHITECTURE

Scotland in the thirteenth century was an independent, well-run and prosperous country. The royal family was thoroughly Anglo-Norman in its attitudes and way of life, and the Scottish kings all held English lands and titles. It was now that rich noblemen began to replace the earlier "motte and bailey" castles with stone fortresses which, like contemporary English castles, incorporated European advances in design. **Dirleton** Castle (Lothian, Pl. 344), for example, was rebuilt with massive ashlar-faced walls and circular towers inspired by the Château de Coucy in France, while **Caerlaverock** (Dumfries and Galloway, Pl. 345) had an innovative triangular plan, round towers and extensive water defences. In the late twelfth and thirteenth centuries, the Scots also built large rectangular versions of the earlier "castles of enclosure" (see p. 90), with four ranges of buildings round a courtyard. Unfortunately these have not survived, although **Kincardine** Castle (Grampian) was demolished only in the seventeenth century. In the West Highlands and islands more modest hall houses, with their halls and well-protected entrances on the first floor, were comparable with contemporary English fortified manors.

Although the English kings had tried repeatedly to claim overlordship, the Scots successfully resisted this until the death of Alexander III in 1286 left the kingdom without a male heir. His grand-daughter was to have been married to the heir to the English throne, thus uniting the two kingdoms, but she died on the journey from Norway (see p. 98). In order to prevent civil war among the followers of thirteen rival claimants to the throne, a group of Scottish nobles asked the English king, Edward I, to decide the succession. His insistence on exacting homage from his chosen candidate, John Balliol, led to an alliance between Scotland and France and a struggle for independence which lasted until 1328, when Edward III acknowledged King Robert I and renounced all English claim to the Scottish throne. Robert's successors, the Stuarts, ruled Scotland for

nearly three hundred years, but the monarchy was constantly threatened by powerful barons and weakened by the fact that so many of the Stuart kings succeeded as minors. The later Middle Ages saw endless murder, intrigue and fighting, especially along the borders, where all houses had to be fortified against attack. Scottish tower houses (see pp. 230–232) were built in large numbers from the late fourteenth century onwards.

Pl. 344 *Looking out towards the Lammermuir Hills from the south-west tower of Dirleton Castle in Lothian, built in the thirteenth century and enlarged in the later Middle Ages; the depth of the window embrasure shows the massive thickness of its ashlar-faced walls.*

Pl. 345 *Caerlaverock Castle (c.1270) in Dumfries and Galloway, built on a triangular plan and surrounded by a wide moat; in the foreground are the thirteenth- and fourteenth-century south-west tower and part of the curtain walls and beyond lies the gatehouse with, to its right, the early seventeenth-century east range of residential accommodation.*

Pl. 346 *The ruined west front of the monastic church at Tintern Abbey in Gwent, rebuilt between 1269 and c.1310, showing the contrast between its simple thirteenth-century Cistercian architecture and the decorative early fourteenth-century tracery seen in the great west window and the blind arcading surrounding the ceremonial doorway.*

Wales

RELIGIOUS ARCHITECTURE

In Wales, as in England, the Gothic style is seen emerging well before the end of the Norman period, for example at **Llandaff** Cathedral (Glamorgan), where the nave was rebuilt in the late twelfth century

Pl. 348 *The early fourteenth-century west door of Tintern Abbey, Gwent, showing the fragmentary remains of the intricate carved decoration which originally filled the blind tracery in the upper part of the arch.*

Pl. 347 *The twin west towers of the ruined late twelfth- and early thirteenth-century church at Llanthony Priory, Gwent, founded in the Black Mountains in 1103; the use of both round and slightly pointed arches is characteristic of the transition between Norman and Gothic architecture.*

with graceful pointed arches. Work began in 1170, but the west front (c.1220) is a truly thirteenth-century composition, with tall pointed lancet windows. These also feature prominently at **Brecon** (Powys), where a row of five fills the entire east wall of the choir of the Benedictine church which is now the cathedral. The twin west towers of the twelfth-century Augustinian priory church at **Llanthony** (Gwent, Pl. 347) date from the early thirteenth century and also belong to this transitional period of architecture. **Tintern** Abbey (Gwent, Pls 48, 346 and 348) and **Strata Florida** (Dyfed), two of the most famous surviving Welsh monasteries, were both rebuilt during the thirteenth century by Welsh patrons. They combine the basic simplicity of the Cistercian order with native embellishments; for instance, the great west door at Strata Florida has six bands of roll mouldings and Celtic scroll ornament. The abbey church at Tintern, completed in *c*.1310, is a much more compact building than the great twelfth-century monastic churches and combines a shorter nave and presbytery with three-bay transepts. Its vast and elaborate east and west windows are superb examples of fourteenth-century tracery, for by this time the early Cistercian insistence on architectural simplicity (see p. 50) had been considerably relaxed. Medieval work at **St David's** Cathedral (Dyfed) included the thirteenth-century rebuilding of the choir with an enlarged presbytery to accommodate the shrine of St David; an amazing fourteenth-century stone pulpitum 15ft (4.5m) in depth; a handsome canopied bishop's throne of *c*.1500; and an early sixteenth-century chantry chapel of the Holy Trinity (Pl. 349).

Parish churches, however, were generally built in a restrained form of Gothic with a minimum of decoration. Many, like **Rudbaxton** (Dyfed), still had a simple nave and chancel, but some were wider, with nave arcades like that which survives at St Mary's, **Haverfordwest** (Dyfed, Pl. 350). Cruciform plans also continue, for instance at **Llanbadarn Fawr** (Dyfed), which has a squat crossing tower. During the thirteenth century towers became common; apart from housing the bells, they would have been useful as lookouts or, like the strongly fortified tower of **Brecon** Cathedral (Powys), as places to retreat to in case of an attack. Sometimes, as at **Llandaff** (Glamorgan), the tower was built as a separate structure uphill from the church itself, either to command a wider view or so that the sound of the bells would carry further. Along the south coast, towers often had very distinctive pitched or "saddleback" roofs, as at **Uzmaston** (Powys) or **Rhossili** (Glamorgan), while along the border with England and in eastern mid Wales, for instance at the ruined church of **Newtown** (Powys), they were crowned with wooden lantern belfries, which had originated in a separate timber construction supported on posts standing on the nave floor. Wood was generally used for church roofs, and "waggon roofs" (see p. 161) were a common type, particularly in the eastern areas, where wood was in good supply. These were constructed by using framed trusses and attaching shaped braces underneath the tie-beams and rafters to produce a framework which could be panelled in wood or plaster to make a curved ceiling. Stone roofs are not common, though slightly pointed barrel vaults are found in the Pembrokeshire area of Dyfed, and the craftsmanship of the small but beautiful chapter

Pl. 349 *The early sixteenth-century chantry chapel of the Holy Trinity immediately behind the presbytery in St David's Cathedral, Dyfed, showing the Perpendicular stone screening which separates it from the south choir aisle.*

house at **Valle Crucis** near Llangollen (Clwyd) is a reminder that there must have been comparable work in other larger medieval churches which has vanished.

The nationalist uprising led by Owen Glendower in the early years of the fifteenth century (see p. 106) was the result of hatred of foreign domination, exacerbated by agricultural depression and poverty. It was not just a popular movement but had the enthusiastic support of Welsh scholars, clergymen and monks, for one of its aims was to establish a separate Welsh national church and two independent Welsh universities. The many churches destroyed or damaged during the bitter conflict between patriots and the English remained in ruins for half a century. Rebuilding took place from the mid fifteenth century onwards, and churches were often enlarged by doubling or adding a wide side aisle to the nave, perhaps with a separate chancel and altar dedicated to St Mary at a time of popular enthusiasm for the cult of the Virgin (see p. 150).

There are many outstanding Perpendicular churches in Wales dating from the late medieval period. One of a famous group of six built in Clwyd by Margaret Beaufort, Lady Stanley, is St Giles, **Wrexham** (Clwyd,

Pl. 350 *Detail showing the composite columns with keel-moulded shafts and the foliage, animals and grotesque heads carved on the vigorous thirteenth-century capitals in St Mary's church at Haverfordwest, Dyfed, built c.1240; the nave roof and clerestory seen on the left date from the late fifteenth century.*

c.1465), which has five-light aisle windows, a well-lit clerestory below a flat wooden ceiling, an octagonal choir and a five-stage tower decorated with statues in ogee-arched niches and topped by ornate pinnacles and octagonal turrets. Sometimes a church was attached by a stone passage to the shrine of a local saint, built on the site of a much earlier foundation, as at **Clynnog Fawr** (Gwynedd), where St Beuno, second in importance only to St David, was revered by pilgrims bound for Bardsey Island.

There is one interior feature of medieval churches which has survived far more often in Wales than in the rest of Britain because much of the country was remote enough to escape the iconoclasm of the Reformation. This is the rood screen (see pp. 201–203), intricately carved in a variety of very local styles, its loft often wider in Wales than elsewhere, presumably to accommodate the larger choirs of an exceptionally musical nation.

SECULAR ARCHITECTURE

One can still see the remains of about a dozen of the numerous castles dating from the thirteenth century which are of native origin. They were built in those areas of north and mid Wales still ruled by the Welsh princes, which the Normans had not been able to subdue. Some of these castles, like **Criccieth** and **Dolwyddelan** (both in Gwynedd), were repaired by Edward I when he surrounded the newly conquered independent Welsh kingdom with vast fortresses, reaching all round the coast from **Flint** (Clwyd) to **Aberystwyth** (Dyfed) (see p. 223). Other castles, such as **Caerphilly** (Mid Glamorgan, begun in 1271), were built by the Norman barons who had settled in South Wales or the Marches in the twelfth century and were constantly under threat of attack by the native Welsh. The bishops also felt the need to protect themselves, for they too were foreign overlords, and their palaces, such as **St David's** and **Lamphey** (both thirteenth- and fourteenth-century and in Dyfed), combine practical defence with architectural magnificence and sophistication, in such details as the use of an arcaded parapet faced with chequerwork patterns in stone. The late thirteenth-century Bishop's Palace at **Llandaff** (Glamorgan), with its walls, towers and tall gatehouse, has much in common with Caerphilly Castle and may have been built by the same masons.

Towns did not exist in Wales before the thirteenth century, but during the Middle Ages many grew up around the castles built by the Norman colonists and were enclosed by defensive fortifications attached to their curtain walls. It suited the English overlords to have a source of manpower immediately available for defence, and the towndwellers were rewarded with valuable privileges like the right to hold fairs and markets. After central sites had been chosen for the church and the market, individual plots were allocated to the burgesses. The streets would then be laid out, not to a standard plan but according to the demands and limitations of the site. Many of these medieval layouts can still be seen and some, like **Cowbridge** (Glamorgan) or **Pembroke** (Dyfed), still have their town walls. The towns attached to Edward I's castles along the north coast were modelled on the "bastides" of southwest France and are built in a regular grid pattern still to be seen, for instance, at **Flint** (Clwyd) and **Caernarvon** (Gwynedd).

Late medieval timber-framed buildings are the earliest which have survived, though the plans of earlier houses are probably reflected in later vernacular buildings, some of the earliest of which can be seen reconstructed at the Welsh Folk Museum, **St Fagans** (Glamorgan). The "bwthyn" or single-storey one- or two-roomed cottage developed into the "ty-hir" or longhouse (see p. 36), with humans living at one end and animals at the other, the two parts divided by a cross-passage with doors into each. Cruck-built hall houses (see p. 249) were also common, and, as elsewhere, both these and longhouses gradually developed into two-storey buildings. Wood and clay were more commonly used building materials than stone, and a wooden frame may sometimes be found within stone outer walls.

There are still a few medieval stone houses in Normanized areas such as the Pembrokeshire peninsula (Dyfed), for instance at **Tenby**, where one can see the early fifteenth-century "Plantagenet House" and next door to it the "Tudor Merchant's House" (owned by the National Trust), which dates from the end of the same century. Defensive tower houses were also built, for example at **Talgarth** (Powys), with the main rooms on the second or third floors; but they are much less common than in Scotland, where they are found mainly from the mid fourteenth century onwards (see p. 230), or in Ireland during the fifteenth and sixteenth centuries. The very few which still exist in Wales are mainly in the south. There are larger fortified manor houses dating from the late Middle Ages, for instance at **Tretower** (Powys), where an L-shaped fifteenth-century house with a walled courtyard and strong gatehouse replaced the nearby Norman castle.

Recognizing Medieval Buildings

Walls

Taller and thinner than in Norman buildings with increasingly larger areas of window in relation to wall; on houses: timber framing with square panels, close studding and sometimes carved beams; jettied upper stories.

Buttresses

Taller and larger, projecting further at the base, decorated with carved pinnacles to provide extra weight; later, flying buttresses.

Columns

Proportions taller and slimmer; octagonal, clustered and moulded columns introduced. Capitals with still-leaf and later naturalistic foliage ornament or moulded decoration.

Arches

Pointed: early tall and narrow, later wider sometimes ogee-shaped; finally four-centred or rectangular with square-cornered dripstone or label; popular ornament: early dogtooth, later ballflower.

Vaults

Built with ribbed construction: ribs first simple intersecting, then becoming more complex and decorative with tiercerons and subsidiary liernes; increasingly elaborate bosses at intersections; later: fan-vaulting.

Roofs

Early thatched or tiled, steeply pitched; later lead-covered, with shallow pitch behind parapet; timber roof construction, including king-post and hammerbeam (sometimes with angels); stone vaults.

Doors

Made of vertical planks with horizontal ledges or with double thickness of wood reinforced with metal studs and decorated with ornamental ironwork or carving, e.g. tracery and blank arcading; set in pointed, Decorated-style or four-centred arches with sculptured ornament.

Windows

Wooden: long and low with diagonally-set mullions, unglazed with hinged or sliding shutters; sometimes with carved mouldings; stone: with vertical stone mullions and glazing secured to horizontal iron saddle bars; tracery progressively lighter and more elaborate.

Decoration

Early English: sculptured ornament becoming finer with dog-tooth patterning and stiff-leaf foliage very popular. Decorated: ogee and S-curves in reticulated and curvilinear tracery; diaper and ball-flower patterning; encrusted ornament and naturalistic carving including foliage; the octagon emerges as a popular shape. Perpendicular: grid-pattern tracery, based on motif of panel with cusped arch, used for wall surface decoration as well as in windows and later extended to fan vaulting; extensive use of niches with canopies; decorative blind arcades peopled with figure sculpture.

Interiors

Great halls with galleries, oriel windows and screens; private rooms such as Great Chamber, parlour, chapel; mural fireplaces, lavers, garde-robes, wall paintings, painted or carved panelling, handsome timber roofs. In churches: wide variety of surviving furnishings and fittings including seating (sedilia, choir stalls, benches with carved ends), piscinas, fonts, pulpits, lecterns, screens, chantries, chests, monuments and brasses, wall paintings, tiles and stained glass.

Types of buildings

Cathedrals and monastic churches

Extended cruciform plan with greatly enlarged choir and presbytery and sometimes a second pair of eastern transepts; Lady chapel east of high altar; pulpitum in eastern arch of crossing; tower above crossing and often two more, one on either side of wide, formal west front with grand portals and elaborate sculpture; stone rib vaults throughout, supported by massive (sometimes flying) buttresses; clerestory progressively higher with larger windows while triforium dwindles.

Monastic precincts

Church, dormitory, refectory and storehouse built round cloister follow-ing Norman plan; surviving buildings mainly thirteenth-century with later medieval alterations and additions; chapter house now a separate building, often circular or polygonal; later: partitions in monks' quarters providing greater privacy; extra kitchens; separate residential buildings for head of house.

Parish churches

Early narrow nave and chancel later widening with the addition of broader aisles and chapels; later churches tall, wide and well-lit, built like aisled halls with large windows and high, low-pitched roofs needing less buttressing; handsome timber roofs, sometimes ornamented with carving; north and south porches; towers and spires becoming slimmer and more decorative.

Castles

Curtain walls with projecting round or D-shaped towers; outer curtain walls and water defences; massive gatehouses; concentric castles; gatehouse strongholds; residential keeps with garrisons built inside castles; tower houses and pele towers.

Houses

Stone or timber-framed houses centred on Great Hall either at ground floor level or on first floor above vaulted basement; service rooms at one end, private family rooms at the other; larger halls aisled; kitchen, a separate building with massive fireplaces and high roof, later incorporated into main house; evolution of more complex house plans with addition of two-storeyed wing or tower; ranges of lodgings with external staircases attached to great houses for accomodation of retainers and guests.

Rural buildings

BARNS

Massive aisled structures in timber or stone with tall waggon entrances; doors placed in pairs opposite each other.

DOVECOTS

Generally circular, the internal walls fitted with nesting boxes reached from a revolving ladder.

Urban buildings

INNS

Either timber-framed built round a courtyard or in the form of an enlarged stone gatehouse.

GUILDHALLS

Timber-framed above an open ground floor or stone above a vaulted crypt.

ALMSHOUSES

Small sets of rooms built round courtyard with communal chapel.

Also in towns

Sections of original walls and gates of medieval towns which have sometimes preserved their grid street plan. Occasional survival of terraced housing, which may include shops. Medieval bridges, a very few with surviving chapels.

Schools and university colleges

Buildings grouped round quadrangle with living accommodation like monastic lodgings, hall, chapel and cloister; handsome gatehouses.

The close of the Middle Ages

THE RENAISSANCE

The Renaissance (Rebirth) of learning which began in Italy in the mid fourteenth century stemmed from the study of the ancient classical world, which had been neglected since the sack of Rome by the Goths in the early fifth century. Greek manuscripts preserved in Constantinople helped to revive this lost culture, which inspired a new and questioning approach to every kind of human activity, from scholarship and education to art, architecture, exploration and science. Its habit of intellectual enquiry and delight in the beauty of the natural world was in direct opposition to the authoritarianism of the medieval church, with its emphasis on obedience and belief in original sin, and it had a profound effect on religious thought.

Renaissance ideas spread rapidly throughout Europe and reached Britain towards the end of the fifteenth century. Henry VII's mother, Margaret Beaufort, was a patroness of the new learning and founder of two Cambridge colleges. English intellectuals were in contact with the foremost scholars in other countries. Thomas Linacre, physician to both Henry VII (1485–1509) and Henry VIII (1509–47), had studied in Italy with the Medici princes who had made Florence the pre-eminent centre for Greek scholarship from the mid fifteenth century onwards. The Dutch scholar Erasmus had many English friends, including John Colet of Oxford University and the ill-fated Sir Thomas More.

THE REFORMATION

While Renaissance ideas challenged the church intellectually, the Reformation confronted it morally and spiritually. By the end of the fifteenth century its blatant abuse of power and privilege caused an accelerating reaction against its worldliness and corruption. Pressure for action arose in many quarters. In Florence the friar Savonarola denounced the Pope, in Holland and England Erasmus and More advocated peaceful reform from within, and in Germany Martin Luther struck at the scandalous sale of indulgences, whereby sins could be cancelled for cash. His defiance of the Catholic church led ultimately to the setting up of an alternative "Lutheran" Protestant church, which was later followed by another, founded in Geneva by the Frenchman John Calvin. Britain did not join this break-away movement. Protestantism was refuted by Henry VIII in a "Golden Book" which earned him the title *Fidei Defensor* (Defender of the Faith) from Pope Leo X in 1521. His rift with Rome arose when he divorced his queen, Catherine of Aragon, in the hope that a new wife, Anne Boleyn, whom he married in 1533, would produce the male heir he needed to secure the succession. Pope Clement VII refused to annul the earlier marriage and Henry was

Pl. 351 *Layer Marney Towers in Essex, the surviving gatehouse of c.1520 for a grand Tudor mansion which its owner did not live to erect; this building typifies the confident architecture of the powerful secular society which began to emerge in the early sixteenth century.*

subsequently excommunicated. It was only because of his failure to obtain a divorce within the Catholic church that in 1534 he took the decision to evade its jurisdiction by establishing an independent Church of England with himself as its head.

THE RISE OF THE SECULAR STATE

The Tudor monarchy of the sixteenth century presided over a period of transition between the medieval world dominated by the church and the increasingly secular society that took its place. In England the change from the Roman Catholic faith to a Protestant Church of England coincided with the introduction of humanist ideas originating in Renaissance Italy and widely disseminated by the introduction of printed books in the late fifteenth century. Christian dogma was undermined by a new culture inspired by the study of the classical past, and both influences are apparent in Tudor architecture, which retains the Perpendicular Gothic of the late Middle Ages but combines it with early experiments in the use of classical form and decoration.

A shift in the types of buildings constructed at this time is also indicative of new values in contemporary society. Whereas previously a rich and powerful church had ensured that ecclesiastical building dominated the scene, Henry VIII's Dissolution of the Monasteries (see p. 119) and the rise of a prosperous merchant class meant that for the first time the laity began to rival the clerics in undertaking new projects. The story of Britain's architecture up to the end of the Middle Ages is dominated by churches, cathedrals and monastic foundations; from then onwards it is mainly concerned with houses and public buildings.

Pl. 352 *Detail of a carved beam supporting the ceiling of the Great Hall in the Prior's Lodging at Clare Priory in Suffolk, where the cellarer's range was converted into the prior's residence in the early sixteenth century; the devil is shown seizing a cleric at a church door.*

GAZETTEER OF SITES IN BRITAIN AND IRELAND

compiled in collaboration with Emily Cole

In general the buildings and monuments listed in the gazetteer fall within the date bracket 600–1500 but especially in areas where the medieval tradition persisted longer, they also spill over into the sixteenth century (and very occasionally beyond that). This applies particularly to Ireland and because the destruction and decay of ecclesiastical architecture there has left so few churches intact, even modest remains are included as significant survivals. There are also entries (see p. 437) for the small number of much earlier sites which are mentioned in the text.

ABBREVIATIONS USED IN GAZETTEER

CADW — Welsh Historic Monuments
Crown Building, Cathays Park, Cardiff, CF1 3NQ

CCT — Churches Conservation Trust (for care of redundant churches of the Church of England)
89 Fleet Street, London EC4Y 1DH

Dúchas — Heritage Service of the Office of Public Works (OPW), Republic of Ireland
51 St Stephen's Green, Dublin 2

EH — English Heritage
PO Box 9019, London SW1E 5ZS

EHS — Environment and Heritage Service, Department of the Environment of Northern Ireland (DOENI)
5–33 Hill Street, Belfast, BT1 1NB

HHA — Historic Houses Association (private owners who open their houses)
Heritage House, PO Box 21, Baldock, Hertfordshire, SG7 5SH

HS — Historic Scotland
Longmore House, Salisbury Place, Edinburgh, EH9 1SH

LT — Landmark Trust (historic buildings to rent for holidays)
Shottesbrooke, Maidenhead, Berkshire, SL6 3SW

MNH — Manx National Heritage
The Manx Museum and National Trust, Douglas, Isle of Man

NT — National Trust
PO Box 39, Bromley, Kent, BR1 3XL

NTS — National Trust for Scotland
5 Charlotte Square, Edinburgh, EH2 4DU

OCT — Open Churches Trust (for opening of churches)
22 Tower Street, London WC2H 9NS

SCS — Scotland's Churches Scheme (for opening of churches)
Dunedin, Holehouse Road, Eaglesham, Glasgow, G76 0JF

OPENING TIMES

Opening arrangements are liable to change and readers are strongly advised to get up-to-date information before visiting. This can be obtained either from local Tourist Information Offices or by consulting a current guide to properties open to the public, such as *Hudson's Historic Houses and Gardens, including Historic Sites of Interest,* which is published annually and covers the whole of Britain and Ireland. Organisations responsible for large numbers of historic buildings, like English Heritage and the National Trust, publish updated handbooks every year and membership gives access to an unlimited number of their properties. The Landmark Trust also publishes an annual handbook giving details of its historic buildings, which are not open to the public but can be rented for holidays.

Any property marked CADW (Welsh Historic Monuments), EH (English Heritage), EHS (Environment and Heritage Service, Northern Ireland), HS (Historic Scotland), Dúchas (Heritage Service, Republic of Ireland), NT (National Trust) or NTS (National Trust for Scotland) will have regular times when it is open to the public. There are some privately or publicly owned properties, including museums, which have nationally advertised opening arrangements and these are marked with an asterisk (*). There are many more which advertise locally or may open only occasionally. Details of these can be obtained from the nearest Tourist Information Office.

RELIGIOUS BUILDINGS

Cathedrals and their associated buildings can generally be visited daily.

Churches are normally open except during services, provided they are not among the increasing number which for security reasons are now sadly kept locked. Some have a notice in the porch to tell visitors where the key is kept but this cannot be relied on and anyone wishing to see a particular church is advised to contact the vicar or priest-in-charge to arrange an appointment in advance. Details are given in *Crockford's Clerical Directory*, which is a biennial publication, and further information may be found in the annual *Diocesan Directory* for the relevant diocese. Churches in popular tourist centres are the most likely to be kept open every day, often with a team of invigilators. In some dioceses there are Guided Church Tours taking participants round a succession of churches in a given area and there is also a growing number of locally-organized "Church Trails" which can be followed independently. These suggest round trips taking in a number of churches, following directions in an accompanying information pack which gives practical details including a map and provides a well-illustrated card for each church, describing both the building and its contents and drawing attention to points of special interest. There is no central source of information about any of these arrangements but details may be found at Tourist Information Offices, Visitor Centres and Cathedral or other local bookshops, as well as in churches. In case of difficulty readers are advised to contact Diocesan Offices, which are listed in *Crockford's Clerical Directory*, or the National Churches Tourism Group, The Arthur Rank Centre, Stoneleigh Park, Warwickshire, CV8 2LZ.

By helping to fund the cost of invigilation, the Open Churches Trust (OCT) promotes the opening of locked churches of all periods and denominations which are of major architectural importance. Members receive regional brochures giving descriptions of churches which have joined the scheme and details of opening and service times. Churches marked SCS have joined Scotland's Churches Scheme, whose annual publication *Churches to Visit in Scotland* gives details of abbeys, churches and places of worship of all periods with opening arrangements and times of services. Redundant Church of England churches marked CCT are no longer in use and are in the care of the Churches Conservation Trust. It publishes a series of leaflets covering England by region, which give a description of each church and details of arrangements for access.

SECULAR BUILDINGS

Houses belonging to the National Trust, the National Trust for Scotland and other conservation bodies have regular opening times from spring to autumn. Privately-owned houses marked HHA (Historic Houses Association) are also open to the public but sometimes on a less regular basis and with more restricted hours. The gazetteer also includes a number of privately-owned houses marked * which are regularly open. Where this asterisk does not appear, it should be assumed that the house in question cannot be visited but it is always worth asking about occasional opening days at the nearest Tourist Information Office. Gardens which allow access are mentioned where they provide an opportunity to see the exterior of a house not open to the public. Houses in towns or villages can usually be seen from the street. Finally a few privately-owned houses of outstanding architectural importance are listed, in spite of the fact that they are not accessible to the public. It may in some cases be possible for those with a serious architectural interest to arrange a visit by writing well in advance.

Please respect the privacy of their owners and do not arrive unannounced.

AGRICULTURAL BUILDINGS

Farm buildings still in agricultural use are not accessible to the public, though many can be seen from the outside from a public road or path, but others which are preserved for their architectural importance, mainly barns, have advertised opening times.

PUBLIC BUILDINGS

Municipal buildings, such as guildhalls, which are still in use often allow limited access. **Castles** are generally open to the public, administered mainly by the national bodies responsible for historic sites or by local authorities. **Monuments** such as crosses or holy wells can usually be seen from a public road or path. All buildings which are listed as **museums** have regular opening hours. **Schools and colleges** normally allow access to the public at certain times. **Hotels and inns** can be visited during normal opening hours.

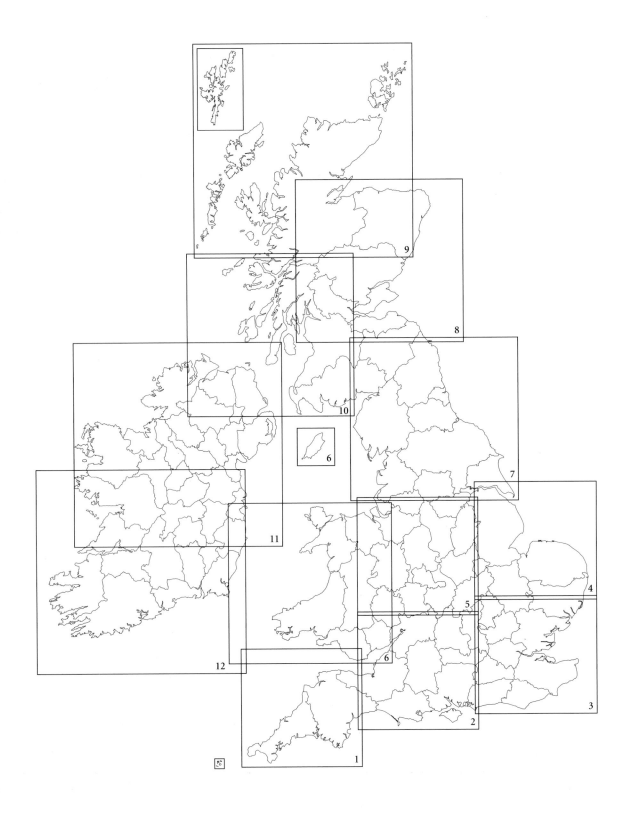

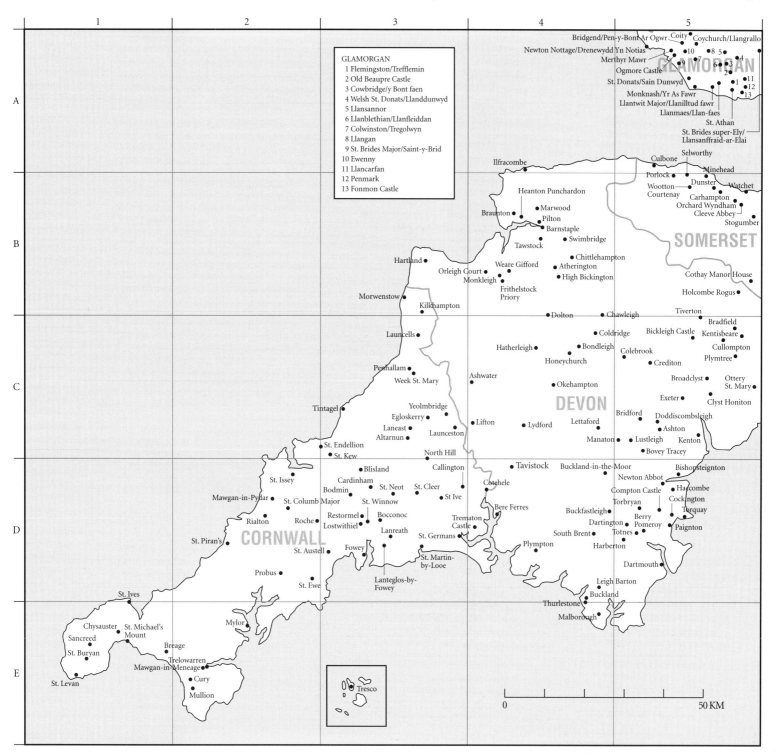

GLAMORGAN
1 Flemingston/Trefflemin
2 Old Beaupre Castle
3 Cowbridge/y Bont faen
4 Welsh St. Donats/Llanddunwyd
5 Llansannor
6 Llanblethian/Llanfleiddan
7 Colwinston/Tregolwyn
8 Llangan
9 St. Brides Major/Saint-y-Brid
10 Ewenny
11 Llancarfan
12 Penmark
13 Fonmon Castle

GLAMORGAN

Bridgend/Pen-y-Bont Ar Ogwr · Coity · Coychurch/Llangrallo
Newton Nottage/Drenewydd Yn Notias
10 · 8 · 5
Merthyr Mawr · 9 · 4
Ogmore Castle · 6 · 3 · 11
St. Donats/Sain Dunwyd · 2 · 1 · 12
Monknash/Yr As Fawr · 13
Llantwit Major/Llanilltud fawr
Llanmaes/Llan-faes
St. Athan
St. Brides super-Ely/
Llansanffraid-ar-Elai

SOMERSET

Ilfracombe · Culbone · Selworthy
Porlock · Minehead
Wootton · Dunster · Watchet
Courtenay · Carhampton
Heanton Punchardon · Orchard Wyndham
Braunton · Marwood · Cleeve Abbey
Pilton · Stogumber
Barnstaple
Tawstock · Swimbridge
Chittlehampton
Hartland · Weare Gifford · Atherington · Cothay Manor House
Orleigh Court · High Bickington
Monkleigh · Holcombe Rogus
Morwenstow · Frithelstock Priory
Kilkhampton
Dolton · Chawleigh · Tiverton
Launcells · Coldridge · Bradfield
Bickleigh Castle · Kentisbeare
Hatherleigh · Bondleigh · Cullompton
Penhallam · Colebrook
Honeychurch · Crediton · Plymtree
Week St. Mary · Okehampton · Broadclyst · Ottery
Ashwater · St. Mary
Exeter · Clyst Honiton
Tintagel · Yeolmbridge · Lifton · Bridford · Doddiscombsleigh
Egloskerry · Lydford · Lettaford · Ashton
Laneast · Launceston · Manaton · Lustleigh · Kenton
Altarnun · North Hill · Bovey Tracey
St. Endellion
St. Kew

DEVON

Tavistock · Buckland-in-the-Moor · Bishopsteignton
Blisland · Callington · Newton Abbot
St. Issey · Cardinham · St. Neot · St. Cleer · Cotehele · Compton Castle · Haccombe
Bodmin · Torbryan · Cockington
Mawgan-in-Pydar · St. Winnow · St. Ive · Bere Ferres · Buckfastleigh · Torquay
St. Columb Major · Bocconoc · Berry · Paignton
Rialton · Roche · Restormel · Lanreath · Trematon · Dartington · Pomeroy
Lostwithiel · Castle · South Brent · Totnes
St. Piran's · St. Germans · Plympton · Harberton
Fowey · St. Martin- · Dartmouth
St. Austell · by-Looe
Probus · Lanteglos-by- · Leigh Barton
St. Ewe · Fowey · Buckland
Thurlestone
St. Ives · Malborough
Chysauster · St. Michael's
Sancreed · Mount · Mylor
St. Buryan · Breage
Trelowarren
Mawgan-in-Meneage
St. Levan · Cury
Mullion

CORNWALL

Tresco

0 —————————————— 50 KM

MAP 1

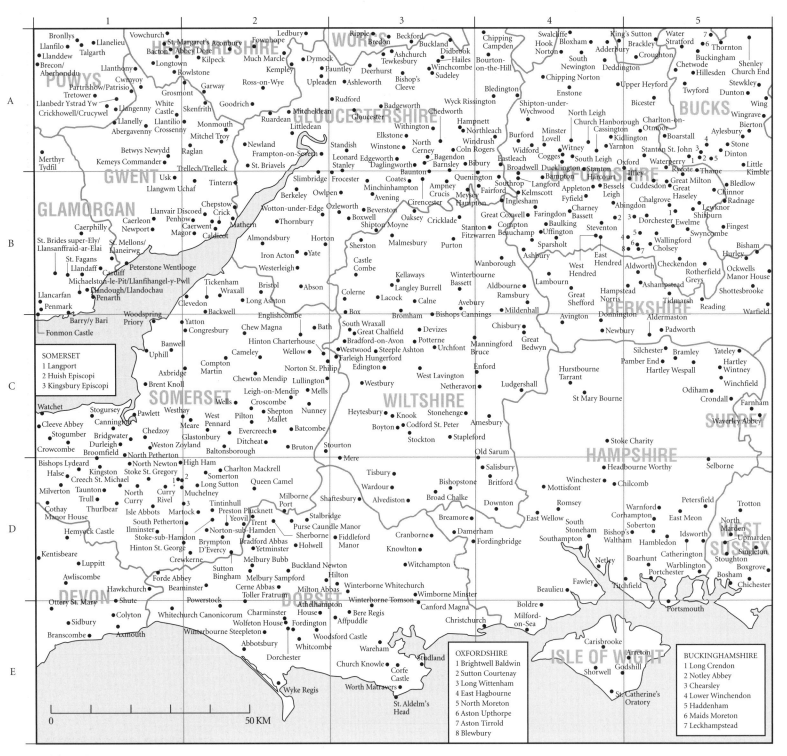

MAP 2

MAP 3

RUTLAND
1 Empingham
2 Tickencote
3 Great Casterton
4 Little Casterton
5 Wing
6 Seaton
7 Lyddington
8 Stoke Dry
9 Uppingham
10 Edith Weston
11 North Luffenham
12 South Luffenham
13 Barrowden
14 Preston

CAMBRIDGE
1 Hinchingbrooke
2 Brampton
3 Godmanchester
4 Leighton Bromswold
5 Castor
6 Chesterton
7 Alwalton
8 Orton Longueville

NORTHAMPTONSHIRE
1 Easton-on-the-Hill
2 Duddington
3 Wakerley

0   50 KM

MAP 4

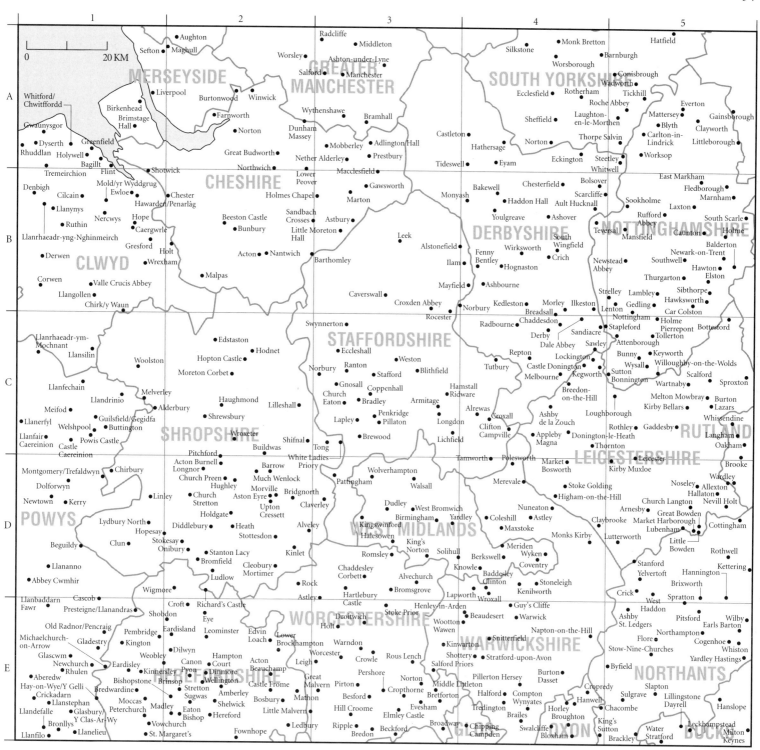

0 ___ 20 KM

MERSEYSIDE

GREATER MANCHESTER

SOUTH YORKSHIRE

Aughton
Sefton · Maghull
Radcliffe · Middleton
Silkstone · Monk Bretton
Hatfield
Worsley · Barnburgh
Worsborough
Ashton-under-Lyne
Salford · Ecclesfield · Conisbrough
Burtonwood · Winwick · GREATER MANCHESTER · Wadworth
Whitford/Chwitffordd
Liverpool · Farnworth · Wythenshawe · Rotherham · Tickill · Everton
Birkenhead · Bramhall · Roche Abbey · Mattersey · Gainsborough
Brimstage Hall · Norton · Dunham Massey · Sheffield · Laughton-en-le-Morthen · Blyth · Clayworth
Gwaunysgor · Great Budworth · Mobberley · Adlington Hall · Castleton · Thorpe Salvin · Carlton-in-Lindrick · Littleborough
Dyserth · Greenfield · Nether Alderley · Prestbury · Hathersage · Norton · Eckington · Steetley · Worksop
Rhuddlan · Holywell · Northwich · Macclesfield · Tideswell · Eyam · Whitwell
Bagillt · Flint · Shotwick
Tremeirchion · Lower Peover · Bakewell · Chesterfield · Bolsover · East Markham · Fledborough
CHESHIRE · Gawsworth · Monyash · Haddon Hall · Scarcliffe · Marnham
Denbigh · Mold/yr Wyddgrug · Holmes Chapel · Ault Hucknall · Sookholme · Laxton
Cilcain · Ewloe · Chester · Marton · Youlgreave · Ashover · Rufford Abbey · South Scarle
Llanynys · Hawarden/Penarlâg · Beeston Castle · Sandbach Crosses · Astbury · Leek · Alstonefield · South Wingfield · Teversal · Caunton · Balderton
Nercwys · Hope · Bunbury · Little Moreton Hall · Fenny Bentley · Wirksworth · Mansfield · Newark-on-Trent
Llanrhaeadr-yng-Nghinmeirch · Caergwrle · Acton · Nantwich · Barthomley · Ilam · Hognaston · Crich · Newstead Abbey · Southwell · Hawton
Ruthin · Gresford · Holt · Mayfield · Ashbourne · Kedleston · Morley · Strelley · Thurgarton · Elston
Derwen · Wrexham · Norbury · Breadsall · Ilkeston · Lambley · Sibthorpe
CLWYD · Caverswall · Croxden Abbey · Radbourne · Chaddesden · Lenton · Gedling · Hawksworth
Corwen · Valle Crucis Abbey · Rocester · Derby · Sandiacre · Nottingham · Car Colston
Llangollen · Malpas · Swynnerton · Dale Abbey · Stapleford · Holme Pierrepont · Bottesford
Chirk/y Waun · Sawley · Attenborough · Tollerton
STAFFORDSHIRE · Edstaston · Repton · Lockington · Bunny · Keyworth
Llanrhaeadr-ym-Mochnant · Woolston · Hodnet · Eccleshall · Weston · Castle Donington · Wysall · Willoughby-on-the-Wolds
Llansilin · Hopton Castle · Norbury · Ranton · Stafford · Blithfield · Tutbury · Melbourne · Kegworth · Sutton Bonnington · Scalford · Sproxton
Llanfechain · Moreton Corbet · Gnosall · Hamstall Ridware · Breedon-on-the-Hill · Melton Mowbray · Burton Lazars
Meifod · Llandrinio · Melverley · Church Eaton · Bradley · Coppenhall · Armitage · Ashby de la Zouch · Loughborough · Kirby Bellars · Whissendine
Llanerfyl · Haughmond · Lilleshall · Lapley · Penkridge · Alrewas · Longdon · Croxall · Appleby Magna · Donington-le-Heath · Rothley · Gaddesby
Welshpool · Guilsfield/Gegidfa · Shrewsbury · Pillaton · Clifton Campville · Thornton · **RUTLAND**
Llanfair Caereinion · Buttington · Wroxeter · Shifnal · Brewood · Lichfield · Tamworth · Polesworth · Market Bosworth · Donington-le-Heath · Oakham
Castle Caereinion · Powis Castle · **SHROPSHIRE** · Buildwas · Tong · White Ladies Priory · Leicester · Brooke
Pitchford · Barrow · Wolverhampton · Merevale · Kirby Muxloe · Noseley · Wardley
Montgomery/Trefaldwyn · Chirbury · Acton Burnell · Longnor · Much Wenlock · Patshull · Walsall · Market · Allexton · Hallaton · Nevill Holt
Dolforwyn · Church Preen · Hughley · Morville · Bridgnorth · Nuneaton · Stoke Golding · Bosworth · Arnesby · Church Langton
Newtown · Kerry · Linley · Church Stretton · Aston Eyre · Claverley · Dudley · West Bromwich · Higham-on-the-Hill · Claybrooke · Great Bowden
POWYS · Lydbury North · Diddlebury · Heath · Upton Cressett · Alveley · Birmingham · Yardley · Coleshill · Astley · Market Harborough · Lubenham · Cottingham
Hopesay · Stottesdon · Kingswinford · Halesowen · King's Norton · Solihull · Berkswell · Meriden · Monks Kirby · Lutterworth · Little Bowden · Rothwell
Beguildy · Clun · Onibury · Stanton Lacy · Kinlet · Romsley · Wyken · Coventry · Stanford
Llananno · Stokesay · Bromfield · Cleobury Mortimer · Chaddesley Corbett · Alvechurch · Knowle · Baddesley Clinton · Yelvertoft · Kettering
Abbey Cwmhir · Ludlow · Rock · Astley · Hartlebury Castle · Bromsgrove · Kenilworth · Stoneleigh · Crick · West Haddon
Wigmore · Cascob · Croft · Richard's Castle · Droitwich · Henley-in-Arden · Guy's Cliffe · Ashby St. Ledgers · Brixworth · Hannington
WORCESTERSHIRE · Stoke Prior · Beaudesert · Warwick · Pitsford · Wilby
Llanbadarn Fawr · Presteigne/Llanandras · Shobdon · Eye · Holt · Wootton Wawen · Napton-on-the-Hill · Northampton · Earls Barton
Old Radnor/Pencraig · Pembridge · Eardisland · Leominster · Edvin Loach · Lower Brockhampton · Warndon · Worcester · Snitterfield · Flore · Cogenhoe · Whiston
Michaelchurch-on-Arrow · Gladestry · Kington · Dilwyn · Acton Beauchamp · Leigh · Crowle · Kinwarton · Shottery · Stratford-upon-Avon · Byfield · Stow-Nine-Churches · Yardley Hastings
Glascwm · Newchurch · Weobley · Canon Pyon · Hampton Court · Salford Priors · Pillerton Hersey · Burton Dasset · **NORTHANTS**
Aberedw · Rhulen · Eardisley · Kinnersley · Dinmore · Castle Frome · Pershore · Norton · Pirton · Middle Littleton · Halford · Compton Wynyates · Cropredy · Slapton
Hay-on-Wye/Y Gelli · Bishopstone · Brinsop · Wellington · Amberley · Bosbury · Cropthorne · Bretforton · Tredington · Hanwell · Sulgrave · Lillingstone Dayrell · Hanslope
Crickadarn · Bredwardine · Stretton Sugwas · Shelwick · Great Malvern · Besford · Evesham · Braies · Horley · Broughton · Chacombe
Llanstephan · Moccas · Madley · Eaton Bishop · Hill Croome · Elmley Castle · Tredington · Swalcliffe · King's Sutton · Water Stratford
Llandefalle · Glasbury/Y Clas-Ar-Wy · Peterchurch · Little Malvern · Ripple · Broadway · Chipping Campden · Bloxham · Brackley · Leckhampstead · Milton Keynes
Bronllys · Vowchurch · Hereford · Little Malvern · Beckford · Bredon
Llanfilo · Llanelieu · St. Margaret's · Fownhope · Ledbury · Mathon
HEREFORDSHIRE

DERBYSHIRE

NOTTINGHAMSHIRE

LEICESTERSHIRE

WEST MIDLANDS

WARWICKSHIRE

OXON

BUCKS

GLOUCESTERSHIRE

MAP 5

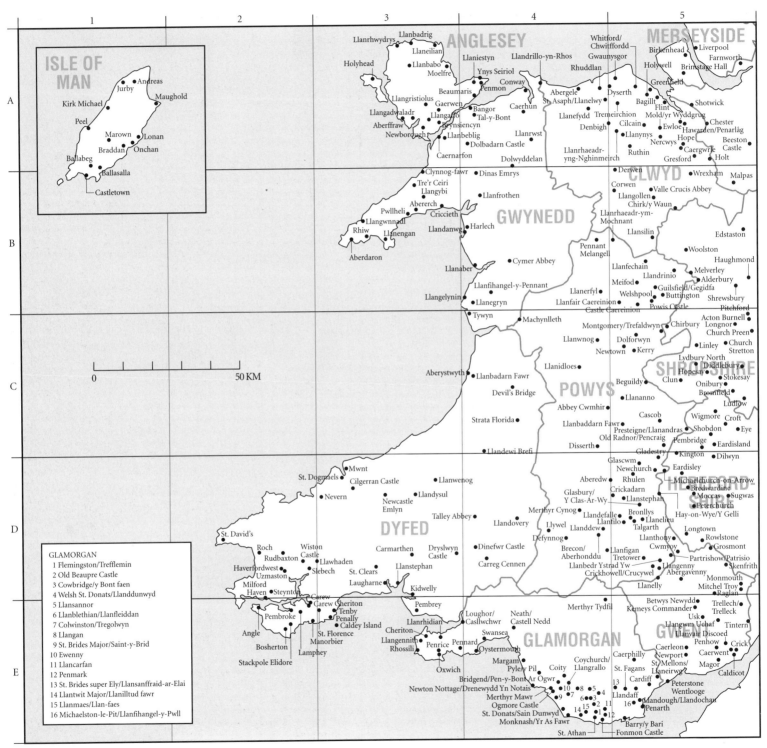

ISLE OF MAN

Andreas
Jurby
Maughold
Kirk Michael
Peel
Marown Lonan
Braddan Onchan
Ballabeg
Ballasalla
Castletown

ANGLESEY

Llanrhwydrys Llanbadrig
Llaneilian
Holyhead Llanbabo
Moelfre Llaniestyn
Ynys Seiriol
Llangristiolus Conway
Beaumaris Penmon
Gaerwen
Llangadwaladr Bangor Caerhun
Aberffraw Llangafo Tal-y-Bont
Newborough Brynsiencyn
Llanbeblig
Caernarfon Llanrwst

Clynnog-fawr Dinas Emrys
Tre'r Ceiri
Llangybi Llanfrothen
Abererch
Pwllheli Criccieth
Rhiw Llandanwg
Llangwnnadl Llanengan Harlech

Aberdaron

Llanaber

Llanfihangel-y-Pennant
Cymer Abbey
Llangelynin Llanegryn
Tywyn Machynlleth

Whitford/
Chwitffordd Greenfield
Llandrillo-yn-Rhos Holywell
Gwaunysgor
Rhuddlan
Abergele Dyserth
St. Asaph/Llanelwy Bagillt
Tremeirchion Flint
Llanefydd Cilcain Mold/yr Wyddgrug
Denbigh Llannynys
Nercwys
Ruthin Gresford
Llanrhaeadr-
yng-Nghinmeirch
Derwen
Corwen
Valle Crucis Abbey
Llangollen
Chirk/y Waun
Llanrhaeadr-ym-
Mochnant
Llansilin
Pennant
Melangell
Llanfechain
Meifod Llandrinio
Welshpool Guilsfield/Gegidfa
Llanfyllin Buttington
Llanfair Caereinion Powis Castle
Castle Caereinion
Montgomery/Trefaldwyn Chirbury
Llanwnog Dolforwyn
Newtown Kerry
Llanidloes
Aberystwyth Llanbadarn Fawr
Devil's Bridge
Strata Florida
Llanbaddarn Fawr
Llandewi Brefi

MERSEYSIDE

Birkenhead Liverpool
Farnworth
Holywell Brimstage Hall
Shotwick
Hawarden/Penarlâg Chester
Hope
Caergwrle Beeston Castle
Holt
Wrexham Malpas
Edstaston
Woolston Haughmond
Melverley
Alderbury
Shrewsbury
Pitchford
Acton Burnell
Longnor
Church Preen
Linley Church Stretton
Lydbury North
Diddlebury
Hopesay Stokesay
Clun Onibury
Bromfield
Ludlow
Wigmore Croft
Presteigne/Llanandras Shobdon Eye
Old Radnor/Pencraig Pembridge Eardisland
Disserth
Gladestry Kington Dilwyn
Glascwm Eardisley
Newchurch
Aberedw Rhulen Michaelchurch-on-Arrow
Crickadarn Bredwardine
Glasbury/ Llanstephan Moccas Sugwas
Y Clas-Ar-Wy Peterchurch
Merthyr Cynog Bronllys Hay-on-Wye/Y Gelli
Llandefalle Llanelieu
Llandovery Llanfilo Talgarth
Llywel Llanddew Longtown
Defynnog Llanthony Rowlstone
Brecon/ Llanfigan Cwmyoy Grosmont
Aberhonddu Tretower Partrishow/Patrisio
Llanbedr Ystrad Yw Llangenny Skenfrith
Crickhowell/Crucywel Abergavenny
Llanelly Monmouth
Mitchel Troy
Raglan
Betwys Newydd
Kemeys Commander Trellech/
Trelleck
Usk
Llangwm Uchaf
Llanvair Discoed Tintern
Penhow Crick
Caerleon
St. Mellons/ Newport Caerwent
Llaneirwg Magor
Caerphilly Caldicot
St. Fagans
13 Cardiff
Llandaff
Mandough/Llandochau
16 Penarth
Barry/y Bari

GWYNEDD

POWYS

SHROPSHIRE

HEREFORD-
SHIRE

DYFED

St. Dogmaels Mwnt
Cilgerran Castle
Nevern Llandysul Llanwenog
Newcastle
Emlyn Talley Abbey
St. David's Llandovery
Roch Carmarthen Dryslwyn
Rudbaxton Castle Dinefwr Castle
Wiston Carreg Cennen
Castle
Haverfordwest Llawhaden
Uzmaston St. Clears Llanstephan
Milford Slebech
Haven Steynton Laugharne Kidwelly
Carew Cheriton
Pembroke Tenby
Angle Penally
Caldey Island
Bosherton St. Florence
Manorbier
Lamphey
Stackpole Elidore

GLAMORGAN

1 Flemingston/Trefflemin
2 Old Beaupre Castle
3 Cowbridge/y Bont faen
4 Welsh St. Donats/Llanddunwyd
5 Llansannor
6 Llanblethian/Llanfleiddan
7 Colwinston/Tregolwyn
8 Llangan
9 St. Brides Major/Saint-y-Brid
10 Ewenny
11 Llancarfan
12 Penmark
13 St. Brides super Ely/Llansanffraid-ar-Elai
14 Llantwit Major/Llanilltud fawr
15 Llanmaes/Llan-faes
16 Michaelston-le-Pit/Llanfihangel-y-Pwll

Loughor/
Casllwchwr
Llanrhidian Neath/
Castell Nedd
Llangennith Swansea
Rhossili Penrice Pennard
Oystermouth
Oxwich Margam
Pyle/y Pil
Bridgend/Pen-y-Bont Ar Ogwr
Newton Nottage/Drenewydd Yn Notais
Merthyr Mawr
Ogmore Castle
St. Donats/Sain Dunwyd
Monknash/Yr As Fawr
St. Athan

Merthyr Tydfil

GLAMORGAN

Coychurch/
Llangrallo
Coity
10
8 5
9 6 4
7 3
14 15 2 11
12
Fonmon Castle

CLWYD

50 KM
0

MAP 6

1 2 3 4 5

Lanark

Neidpath • Peebles
Stobo

Crosshall
Smailholm

Twizel
Etal
Ford

Holy Island

Bamburgh

A

Melrose
Dryburgh
Abbey

Kelso
Linton
Cessford

Kirknewton

Chillingham

Preston
Tower

BORDERS

Jedburgh
Ferniehirst

Old Bewick

Rock

Dunstanburgh Castle

Newark Castle

Hulne Priory
Alnwick

Auchencass

Edlingham

Warkworth

Lochwood Tower

Hermitage

Whitton

Brinkburn

NORTHUMBERLAND

Elsdon

Mitford

DUMFRIES &
GALLOWAY

Spedlins Castle

Hartburn

Bothal
Morpeth

Woodhorn

B

Lochmaben

Kirkwhelpington
Thockrington

Bolam

Belsay

Whalton

Dumfries • Torthorwald
Kirkconnell House
Comlongon Castle
New • Ruthwell
Abbey
Caerlaverock

Merkland Smithy

Bewcastle

Chipchase Castle
Haughton Castle

Ryal

Ponteland

Seaton Delaval

Askerton Castle

Chollerton
Hadrian's Wall

Aydon Castle

Newcastle-
upon-Tyne

Tynemouth

Lanercost
Naworth Castle
Denton

Haydon
Bridge

Warden

Newburn
Gateshead

Jarrow

TYNE & WEAR

West Boldon

Bowness-on-Solway

Haltwhistle
Langley Castle
Newbiggin

Hexham

Corbridge

Hylton Castle
Monkwearmouth

Newton Arlosh
Warwick
Carlisle Wetheral

Blanchland

Chester-le-Street

Houghton-le-Spring

Abbey Town
Dalston

Cross
Canonbury
Aspatria
Boltongate
Dearham Torpenhow
Bridekirk

Kirkoswald

Chester-le-Street
Great Lumley
Lanchester
Finchale Priory
Durham

Seaham

C

Seaham

Greystoke
Penrith
Yanwath Brougham
Dacre Clifton

Long
Marton

Brancepeth

Pittington

Kelloe

Hartlepool

St. Bees
Egremont
Calder
Gosforth
Irton

Askham Hall
Bolton
Morland

Shap
Ormside

Bishop
Auckland

Escomb

Sedgefield
South Church

Hart

Billingham
Norton

CUMBRIA

Appleby-in-
Westmoreland
Brough

Romaldkirk
Barnard Castle
Egglestone Abbey

Raby Castle
Staindrop

Heighington

Haughton-le-Skerne

Gainford

Hawkshead
Bowness-on-Windermere

Bowes
Mortham

Darlington

Guisborough

Whitby

Kendal
Sizergh

Grinton

Croft-
on-Tees

Sockburn

Easby

D

Aske Hall

Richmond

Mount Grace Priory

Hauxwell
Hornby

Brompton-in-Allertonshire

Lastingham

Hackness

Millom

Preston
Patrick

Sedbergh

Castle Bolton
Nappa Hall

Middleham
Jervaulx Abbey

Bedale
Northallerton

Rievaulx
Abbey

Kirkdale

Middleton

Scarborough

Dalton-in-Furness
Barrow-in-Furness

Cartmel
Heversham

Kirkby Lonsdale

Middleham
Jervaulx Abbey

Middleham

Helmsley
Byland Abbey

Pickering

Seamer

Aldingham

Tunstall

Masham
West Tanfield

Coxwold

Appleton-le-
Street

Rillington

Filey

Heysham

Warton

Hornby

Lancaster

Studley Royal
Topcliffe
Fountains Abbey
Sawley
Markenfield Hall

Thirsk

Ripon

Newburgh
Priory

Malton
North Grimston
Kirkham Priory
Foston

Wintringham
Weaverthorpe

Flamborough

Aldborough
Alne

Wharram-
le-Street

Great
Driffield

Bridlington
Burton Agnes
Lowthorpe

Cockerham

Bolton Abbey

Kirk Hammerton
Nun Monkton

Cowlam
Garton-
on-the-
Wolds

Barmston

Skelton

Bossall

Kirkburn

Skipsea

Skipton

Ripley
Knaresborough

Collingham

Bilton
Ainsty
Bishopthorpe

York

North Frodingham

Kirkland

Sawley

Spofforth
Ilkley

Healaugh

Nunburnholme

Watton Abbey

Hornsea

Clitheroe

Otley
Harewood

WEST Adel
Bardsey

Stillingfleet
Cawood

Sutton-upon-Derwent

Beverley

E

Samlesbury

Whalley

Riddlesden

Skipwith
Aughton

Goodmanham
Newbald

Skirlaugh
Swine

Burnley

Bradford
Halifax

Kirkstall
Kippax

Sherburn-in-Elmet
Steeton Hall

Monk
Fryston

Riccall
Selby

Wressle

Cottingham

Hull

Hedon
Halsham

YORKSHIRE
Ledsham

Hemingbrough
Birkin

Howden

Eastrington

Patrington

Rufford
Turton

Dewsbury
Thornhill

Wakefield

Drax
Snaith

Barton-upon-Number

Welwick
Easington

LANCASHIRE

Almondbury

Sandal Magna
Darrington

Fishlake

Winteringham

Halsall
Ormskirk
Aughton

Bolton
Radcliffe
Middleton

Rochdale

Campsall

Hatfield

Bonby
Thornton
Curtis

Thornton Abbey

Grimsby

Monk Bretton

LINCOLNSHIRE

Broughton

0   50 KM

MAP 7

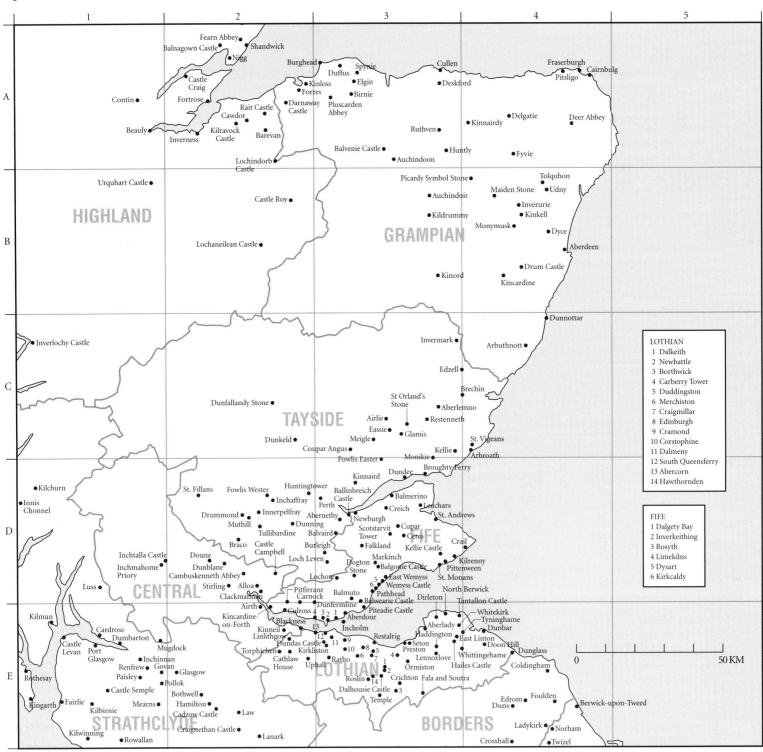

1   2   3   4   5

Fearn Abbey
Balnagown Castle ● Shandwick
Nigg
Burghead   Spynie   Cullen   Fraserburgh
Duffus   Elgin   Cairnbulg
Castle   Kinloss   Pitsligo
Craig   Forres   Birnie   Deer Abbey
A   Contin   Fortrose   Darnaway   Deskford
Rait Castle   Castle
Cawdor   Pluscarden   Delgatie
Abbey   Kinnairdy
Beauly   Kilravock   Barevan   Ruthven   Deer Abbey
Inverness   Castle   Balvenie Castle   Huntly
Lochindorb   Auchindoun   Fyvie
Castle

Urquhart Castle ●   Picardy Symbol Stone ●   Tolquhon
Maiden Stone   Udny
HIGHLAND   Castle Roy   Auchindoir   Inverurie
Monymusk   Kinkell
B   Lochaneilean Castle ●   Kildrummy   Dyce
Aberdeen
Drum Castle
Kinord   Kincardine

Dunnottar
Inverlochy Castle ●   Invermark   Arbuthnott
Edzell
C
Brechin
Dunfallandy Stone ●   St Orland's
TAYSIDE   Stone   Aberlemno
Airlie   Restenneth
Eassie   Glamis
Dunkeld   Meigle   St. Vigeans
Coupar Angus   Monikie   Arbroath
Fowlis Easter   Kellie

Kinnaird   Dundee
St. Fillans   Huntingtower   Broughty Ferry
Kilchurn ●   Fowlis Wester   Ballinbreich
Innis   Inchaffray   Castle   Balmerino
Channel   Perth   Creich   Leuchars
Drummond   Innerpelfray   Abernethy   St. Andrews
D   Muthill   Dunning   Newburgh
Tullibardine   Balvaird   Scotstarvit   Cupar
Braco   Castle   Tower   Ceres
Inchtalla Castle ●   Doune   Campbell Burleigh   Falkland   Kellie Castle   Crail
Inchmahome   Dunblane   Loch Leven   Markinch   Kilrenny
Priory   Cambuskenneth Abbey   Dogton   Balgonie Castle   Pittenweem
Luss   Stirling   Alloa   Lochore Stone   St. Monans
CENTRAL   Clackmannan   Pitfirrane Balmuto East Wemyss North Berwick
Kilmun   Airth   Carnock Dunfermline Pathhead Wemyss Castle
Cardross   Kincardine-   Blackness Aberdour Balwearie Castle Dirleton Tantallon Castle
Dumbarton   on-Forth   Piteadie Castle   Whitekirk
Castle   Port   Kinneil Incholm   Tyninghame
Levan   Glasgow   Mugdock   Linlithgow   Restalrig Aberlady   Dunbar
Inchinnan   Dundas Castle   Haddington East Linton
Renfrew   Govan   Torphichen   Kirkliston   Seton   Lennoxlove Doon Hill
Paisley   Glasgow   Cathlaw   Ratho Preston Whittingehame Dunglass
E   Rothesay Castle Semple Pollok   House Uphall   Ormiston   Hailes Castle   Coldingham
Kingarth   Fairlie   Mearns   LOTHIAN Crichton Fala and Soutra
Kilbirnie   Hamilton   Roslin   Temple   Edrom   Foulden
Bothwell   Cadzow Castle Law   Dalhousie Castle   Duns   Berwick-upon-Tweed
Kilwinning STRATHCLYDE Craignethan Castle   Temple
Rowallan   Lanark   BORDERS   Ladykirk   Norham
Crosshall   Twizel

LOTHIAN
1 Dalkeith
2 Newbattle
3 Borthwick
4 Carberry Tower
5 Duddingston
6 Merchiston
7 Craigmillar
8 Edinburgh
9 Cramond
10 Corstophine
11 Dalmeny
12 South Queensferry
13 Abercorn
14 Hawthornden

FIFE
1 Dalgety Bay
2 Inverkeithing
3 Rosyth
4 Limekilns
5 Dysart
6 Kirkcaldy

0   50 KM

MAP 8

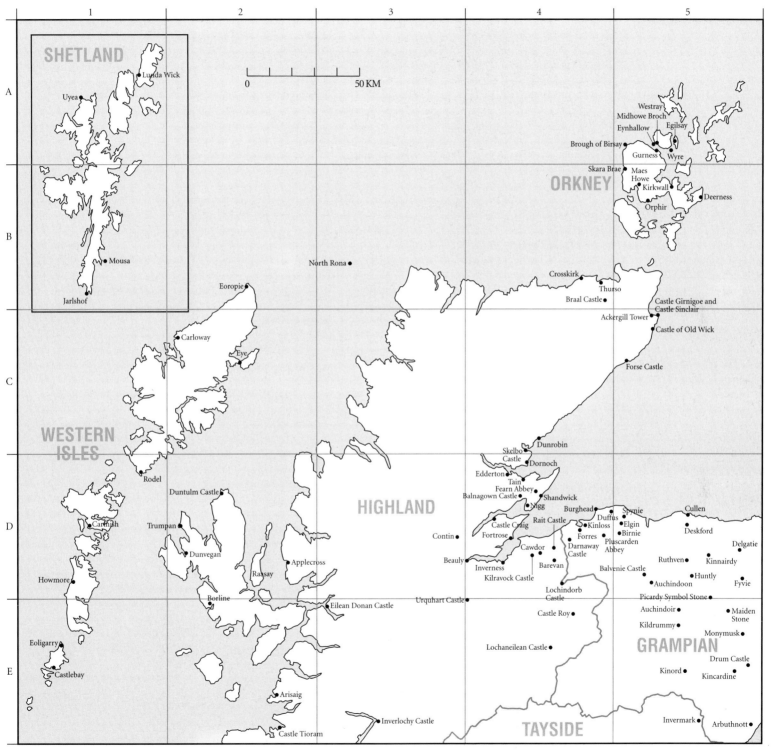

1 2 3 4 5

SHETLAND

• Lunda Wick

• Uyea

A

• Mousa

B

• Jarlshof

WESTERN ISLES

• Eoropie

• Carloway

• Eye

C

• Rodel

• Duntulm Castle

• Carnish

• Trumpan

• Dunvegan

• Raasay

• Applecross

• Howmore

• Borline

• Eilean Donan Castle

• Eoligarry

• Castlebay

• Arisaig

E

• Inverlochy Castle

• Castle Tioram

ORKNEY

Westray
Midhowe Broch
Eynhallow   • Egilsay
Brough of Birsay •   •
Gurness   • Wyre
Skara Brae •   Maes
Howe
• Kirkwall   • Deerness
• Orphir

• Crosskirk
• Thurso
Braal Castle •   Castle Girnigoe and
Castle Sinclair
Ackergill Tower •   • Castle of Old Wick

• Forse Castle

Skelbo   • Dunrobin
Castle   • Dornoch
Edderton •
Tain
Fearn Abbey •
Balnagown Castle •   • Shandwick
• Nigg   Burghead •   • Spynie   • Cullen
Castle Craig •   Rait Castle   Duffus •
HIGHLAND   Fortrose •   Kinloss • • Elgin   • Deskford
• Contin   • Forres • Birnie
Cawdor •   Darnaway   Pluscarden   • Delgatie
• Beauly   Castle   Abbey
• Inverness   • Barevan   Balvenie Castle •   • Ruthven   • Kinnairdy
Kilravock Castle •   • Auchindoon   • Huntly   • Fyvie
Lochindorb
Urquhart Castle •   Castle   Picardy Symbol Stone •
• Castle Roy   Auchindoir •   • Maiden
Kildrummy •   Stone
Lochaneilean Castle •   • Monymusk
GRAMPIAN
• Drum Castle
Kinord •   • Kincardine

TAYSIDE   • Invermark   • Arbuthnott

0 ———————— 50 KM

• North Rona

MAP 9

1 2 3 4 5

HIGHLAND

TAYSIDE

Mingary Castle

Breachacha

A

Lochaline Ardtornish
Pennygown   Lismore   Castle Stalker
Inchkenneth   Duart   Ardchattan
Iona   Lochbuie   Dunstaffnage   Kilchurn   St. Fillans   Fowlis Wester

Innis Chonnel   Innerpelfray
Drummond
Muthill
Eileach-An-Naoimh   Tullibardine

Inchtalla Castle   Doune
B   Kilmartin Glen   Inchmahome   Dunblane
Priory   Cambuskenneth Abbey
Luss   Stirling   Alloa
Oronsay   Clachan of   Clackmannan
Glendaruel   Kilmun   Airth
Keills   Cardross
Castle Sween   Dumbarton
Eilean   Kilmory Knap Chapel   Castle   Mugdock
Mor   Kames   Levan   Port   Inchinnan
Kilberry   Glasgow   Renfrew   Govan
Castle   Rothesay   Paisley   Glasgow
Skipness   Castle Semple   Pollok
Kingarth   Fairlie   Bothwell
C   Kildalton Cross   Mearns   Hamilton
Kilbirnie   Cadzow Castle   Law
Killean   Lochranza   Kilwinning   Craignethan Castle
Rowallan   Lanark
Brodick   Dean
Saddell   Lamlash   Dundonald   STRATHCLYDE
Douglas
Campbeltown   Mauchline

Ayr

Dunure
Maybole   Sanquhar
Culdaff   Crossraguel
Carndonagh   Abbey   Morton Castle
D   DONEGAL   Greencastle   Bonamargy Friary   Loch Doon Castle   Thornhill
Moville
Buncrana   Portstewart   Dunluce
Fahan   Castle   Churchfield   DUMFRIES &
Inch Island   Magilligan   Armoy   GALLOWAY
Macosquin   Turraloskin   Cushendall
Greenan   Drenagh   Red Bay
Londonderry   Corsewall Castle   Garlies Castle   Hills Tower
Boveragh   Doonbought   Castle Stewart   Barholm
LONDONDERRY   Castle   Lochnaw Castle   Castle   Rusco   Threave
Mullaboy   Dungiven   Stranraer   Tower   Castle
Raphoe   Feeny   Maghera   ANTRIM   Glenluce   Old Place of   Carsluith   Buittle   Orchardton
Newtown Stewart   Ballynascreen   Church Island   Kirkmadrine   Mochrum   Cardoness   Tower
E   Chapel   Crugleton
Dunmulian   Churchtown   Carrickfergus   Finian   Whithorn   Dundrennan
Antrim   Monreith   Isle of Whithorn
TYRONE   Arboe   Crumlin   St. Ninian's Cave
Holywood

0   50 KM

MAP 10

MAP 11

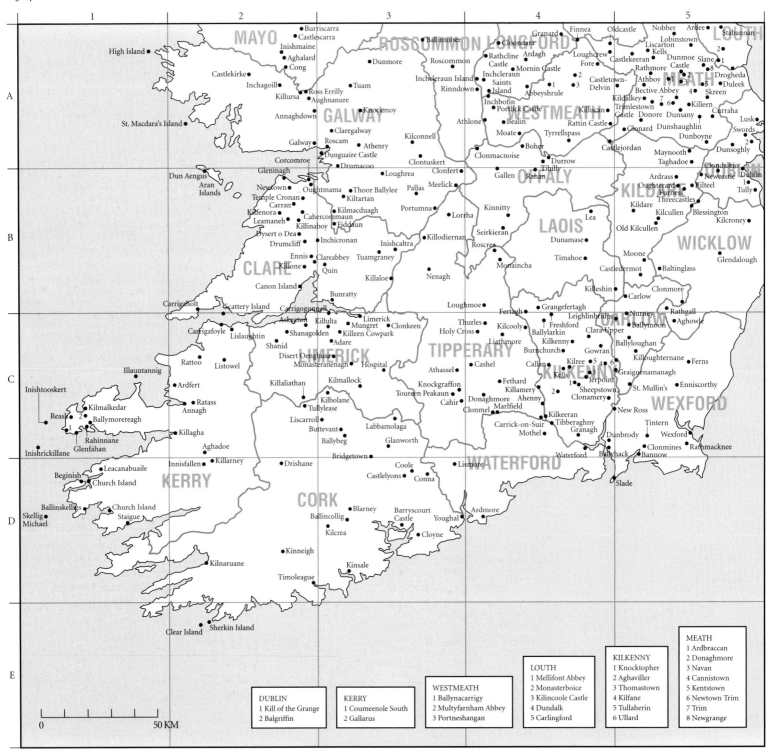

MAP 12

ABBEY CWMHIR, POWYS, 6,4C
Cwmhir Abbey Ruins of Cistercian abbey founded 1143 and refounded 1176

ABBEY DORE, HEREFS, 2,1A
Church of St Mary Surviving chancel, crossing and transepts of late 12th- to early 13th-C abbey, now parish church; tower added 1600s

ABBEYLARAGH,
CO. LONGFORD, 11,3D
See Granard

ABBEYSHRULE (6.5 km./4 m. NE of Ballymahon), CO. LONGFORD, 11,3D
Abbey [Dúchas] Remains of Cistercian abbey founded c.1200 on east bank of River Inny include 12th- to 13th-C church and altered tower; carved shaft of High Cross in graveyard nearby

ABBEY TOWN, CUMBRIA, 7,1B
Church of St Mary Surviving part of nave, minus aisles, of 12th-C Holme Cultram Abbey with subsequent medieval and later work; early 16th-C west porch

ABBOTSBURY, DORSET, 2,2E
Abbotsbury Abbey [EH] Ruins of surviving buildings of Benedictine monastery founded 11th C
Church of St Nicholas Former abbey church built mainly 14th and 15th C
St Catherine's Chapel [EH] 15th-C chapel on hill beside church
Abbey Barn One of largest surviving tithe barns in Britain, built c.1400

ABBOTS LANGLEY, HERTS, 3,1B
Church of St Lawrence Norman and medieval church with 12th-C nave arcades, 14th-C south chancel chapel and 15th-C nave roof

ABDIE, FIFE
Old Parish Church of St Magridin Roofless shell of 13th-C church with 17th-C additions and 19th-C restoration

ABERCORN, LOTHIAN, 8,3E
Parish Church Church of 12th-C origin with much 16th- to 19th-C remodelling retains original south door with tympanum; medieval sculptural fragments include parts of 8th-C crosses, hogback tombstones, and 13th-C coffin lids

ABERDARON, GWYNEDD, 6,3B
Church of St Hywyn Sited near crossing for pilgrims to Bardsey Island (Ynys Enlli), Norman church enlarged 14th and 16th C has surviving 12th-C north arcade and west door

ABERDEEN, GRAMPIAN, 8,4B
Church of St Nicholas [SCS], Upper Kirkgate Church of 12th-C origin largely rebuilt 18th and 19th C retains vaulted 15th-C crypt (St Mary's Chapel) founded 1420, partially restored 1898; rare medieval brass, good effigies and monuments
Church of St John, Crown Terrace Church contains good early 16th-C font (originally at Kinkell) with depiction of Five Wounds of Christ
Bridge of Dee Bridge of seven arches built 1520–7 and widened 1842
King's College, High Street, Old Aberdeen Handsome college founded 1495, part of Aberdeen University since 1860, retains fine chapel built 1500–5 with tower and elaborate crown steeple (reworked after 1633); richly carved screen and canopied stalls with misericords (amongst finest medieval woodwork in Scotland); good pulpit of 1540, previously at cathedral
St Machar's Cathedral [Transepts – HS] [SCS], Old Aberdeen. Surviving nave of 14th- and 15th-C cathedral which now serves as parish church; imposing twin-towered west front with spires added c.1522; ruined transepts; rich heraldic oak ceiling of c.1520 (restored); good late medieval effigies and tombs
Brig O' Balgownie or **Auld Brig O' Don** (1.5 km. /¾ m. N of cathedral). Fine late 13th- to early 14th-C bridge restored 1607 crosses pool of River Don (oldest medieval bridge in Scotland)

ABERDOUR, FIFE, 8,3E
Aberdour Castle [HS] 14th-C tower with 16th- and 17th-C additions;
Church of St Fillan Hawkcraig Road; Simple church built c.1140 with south aisle of c.1500, early 16th-C south porch and transeptal north aisle added 1608

ABEREDW, POWYS, 6,5D
Church of St Cewydd 14th-C church reworked 1500s with large north porch and simple west tower; 15th-C screen

ABERERCH, GWYNEDD, 6,3B
Church of St Cawdaf Double-naved medieval church with arched door supported on large corbels; medieval cross slab in chancel floor; 16th-C stalls
Pennarth Fawr [CADW] (2 km / 1¼ m. E) 15th-C hall-house altered 17th C

ABERFFRAW (ANGLESEY), GWYNEDD, 6,3A
Church of St Beuno 12th-C church enlarged 16th C has reset late Norman arch roughly carved with chevrons and animal heads
Church of St Cwyfan, Llangwyfan (on island in bay); Mainly 14th-C church with blocked-up arcade of demolished 16th-C north aisle
Church of St Mary Tal-y-llyn (4km. / 2½m. N)Tiny 12th- to 14th-C church with 16th-C chancel and 17th-C south chapel

ABERGAVENNY, GWENT, 6,5D
Church of St Mary Large mainly 14th-C cruciform church of Benedictine priory, founded before 1090, has Norman font, huge wooden figure of recumbent Jesse, medieval tomb effigies, and 15th-C carved choir stalls with misericords
Castle Remains of Norman and medieval castle include 12th-C curtain wall and 13th- to 14th-C west towers and gatehouse

ABERGELE, CLWYD, 6,4A
Church of St Michael Spacious late medieval double-naved church restored 19th C has west tower heightened 1861; two early 14th-C crosses near south door and altered rood screen

ABERLADY, LOTHIAN, 8,3E
Parish Church Main Street [SCS] Church recast 1886 retains 15th- or 16th-C west tower; 8th-C cross
Carmelite Friary (W. of Luffness House) Fragment of late 13th-C church of Carmelite friary with contemporary effigy of knight

ABERLEMNO, TAYSIDE, 8,3C
Sculptured Stones [HS] Four carved Pictish stones of 6th to 9th C, three at roadside and one in churchyard with Celtic cross in high relief, entwined beasts and battle scene

ABERNETHY (10 km. / 6 m. SE of Perth), TAYSIDE, 8,3D
Abernethy Round Tower [HS] Fine Round Tower of Irish type, one of only two surviving in Scotland (see Brechin), with 9th-C lower part and upper storeys added 11th or 12th C; sculptured Pictish stone at foot

ABERYSTWYTH, DYFED, 6,4C
Aberystwyth Castle [CADW] Surviving ruins of castle built 1277–89 by Edward I on concentric diamond-shaped plan with inner and outer wards, each retaining double-towered gatehouses

ABINGDON, OXON, 2,4B
Abingdon Abbey Fragmentary remains of abbey founded 7th C include 13th-C Checker (or Chequer – perhaps exchequer or treasury) and stone and timber-framed Long Gallery of c.1500
Church of St Helen Medieval church remodelled 15th and 16th C with surviving 13th-C steeple; exquisite late 14th-C panelled and painted ceiling in north aisle depicting Tree of Jesse
Abingdon Bridge 15th-C bridge much rebuilt 1927
Christ Church, Northcourt Road Former tithe barn of Abingdon Abbey, attributed to 1200s, with late medieval timber roof; converted to church 1961
Christ's Hospital or **Long Alley Almshouses**, St Helen's churchyard. Almshouses built 1446 and reworked 17th and 18th C retain 15th-C face to river

ABSON, GLOS, 2,2B
Church of St James Church of Norman origin with medieval rebuilding and work of c.1600 retains north and south door-ways of 1100s, 13th-C east window, and fine 15th-C west tower with rich battle-ments; good late medieval font

ACKERGILL TOWER (4 km./ 2½ m. NW of Wick), HIGHLAND, 9,5C
Ackergill Tower Late 15th-C rectangular tower house with alterations and additions of 1851

ACLE, NORFOLK, 4,5D
Church of St Edmund Norman church with medieval and 19th-C rebuilding retains 11th-C round tower with 13th-C octagonal upper storey; 15th-C font and screen

ACONBURY, HEREFS, 5,2A
Church of St John the Baptist Small 13th-C priory church with later timber bell-turret and porch

ACTON, CHESHIRE, 5,2B
Church of St Mary 13th- and 14th-C church with top of tower rebuilt 1700s; Norman sculptured stones in south aisle; handsome canopied tomb with alabaster effigy of knight (d.1399)

ACTON, SUFFOLK, 3,3A
Church of All Saints Church built c.1300 with upper part of tower rebuilt in early 20th C; exceptionally fine early brass (1302) with full-size figure of knight in armour

ACTON BEAUCHAMP, HEREFS, 5, 2E
Church of St Giles Norman church rebuilt 19th C retains original south doorway and west tower; 9th-C Saxon carved stone used as lintel above tower door

ACTON BURNELL, SHROPS, 5, 2D
Church of St Mary 13th-C church with original font and medieval tiles in north transept
Acton Burnell Castle [EH] Ruins of late 13th-C fortified manor house

ADARE, CO. LIMERICK, 12, 3C
Adare Castle [Dúchas] Ruins of handsome 13th-C tower keep fronting onto River Maigue with ramparts and two great halls
Church of St Nicholas of Myra [Dúchas] Chapel north of castle built between 13th and 16th C
White Monastery (or White Church) [Dúchas] Fine mainly 15th-C church of Trinitarian monastery founded c.1230, partly rebuilt 19th C for parish worship and still in use
Augustinian and Franciscan Friaries [Dúchas] Remains of 14th-C Augustinian friary by river with 15th-C additions including well-preserved cloisters; church (now Church of Ireland Parish Church) restored 1807 to former beauty and monastic refectory re-roofed 1814 to serve as school house; Franciscan friary founded 1464 and restored 1800s (now surrounded by golf course)

ADDERBURY, OXON, 2, 4A
Church of St Mary the Virgin 13th-C cruciform church enlarged 14th C with addition of west tower and spire and much lively carved ornament; early 15th-C chancel and screen

ADDLETHORPE, LINCS, 4, 2B
Church of St Nicholas 15th-C church retains fine carved screens, pew-ends and roof with figures of angels; chancel demolished 1706

ADEL (Outer Leeds), W. YORKS, 7, 3E
Church of St John the Baptist Remarkably complete Norman church of c.1160 with fine sculptured south doorway, corbel table and chancel arch; bronze ring door-handle showing monster swallowing man

ADISHAM, KENT, 3, 4D
Church of the Holy Innocents Cruciform church of Norman origin enlarged 13th to 14th C has 12th-C tower arches, crossing tower and 13th-C north doorway; Norman font and good 13th-C tiles

ADLINGTON, CHESHIRE, 5, 3A
Adlington Hall (visits by prior arrangement only) Great hall dated 1505 survives in 16th- and 18th-C mansion

AFFLECK CASTLE, TAYSIDE, 8, 3C
See Monikie

AFFPUDDLE, DORSET, 2, 3E
Church of St Lawrence 13th-C church with 15th-C aisle and west tower

AGHADOE, CO. KERRY, 12, 2C
Church and Round Tower [Dúchas] Ruined church on site of 7th-C monastery has western part finished 1158 with good doorway (incorrectly reassembled) and 13th-C eastern addition; stump of altered Round Tower survives nearby
Parkavonear Castle [Dúchas] 13th-C round castle set in enclosure with wall and moat

AGHAGOWER, CO. MAYO, 11, 1C
Church and Round Tower [Dúchas] Monastic site houses Round Tower (possibly 12th-C) with modern entrance and 15th-C church incorporating earlier work

AGHALARD (1.5 km. / 1 m. NNW of Cong), CO. MAYO, 11, 1D
Castle [Dúchas] Ruined 15th-C tower house in polygonal bawn

AGHALURCHER, CO. FERMANAGH, 11, 3C
See Lisnaskea

AGHAVILLER, CO. KILKENNY, 12, 4C
Church and Round Tower [Dúchas] Stump of Round Tower, sole survivor of early monastery; nearby former church tower built 12th or 13th C and fortified c.1600

AGHOWLE, CO. WICKLOW, 12, 5C
Church and Cross [Dúchas] Site of early monastery houses ruins of long early 12th-C church with massive flat-headed west doorway; early cross slab, gravestones and cross

AHENNY (or Kilclispeen), CO. TIPPERARY, 12, 4C
High Crosses [Dúchas] Two splendid High Crosses (possibly 8th-C, among earliest in Ireland) with important sculptured ornament

AIRLIE, TAYSIDE, 8, 3C
Church Church built mainly 1781 contains (in east vestibule) medieval stone aumbry with depiction of Five Wounds of Christ

AIRTH (6.5 km. / 4 m. N of Falkirk), CENTRAL, 8, 2E
Airth Castle (now hotel) 14th-C keep (now known as Wallace's Tower) extended 1500s and much altered 19th C
Church Overgrown remains of church with 12th-C work, south transeptal chapel built 1450–87, laird's aisle dated 1593, and chancel added 1647

ALCONBURY, CAMBS, 4, 1E
St Peter and St Paul Late 13th-C church retains fine steeple with broach spire and chancel with blank arcading; additions of c.1330 and 15th C
Bridge 15th-C bridge of four arches

ALDBOROUGH, N. YORKS, 7, 3D
Church of St Andrew Medieval church rebuilt 19th C has nave and aisles of c.1360 and 15th-C west tower, clerestory and chancel
Village Cross Shaft of late medieval cross

ALDBOURNE, WILTS, 2, 4B
Church of St Michael Norman church with extensive medieval additions including 15th-C roof and west tower

ALDBURY, HERTS, 3, 1B
Church of St John the Baptist Church of 13th-C origin has 14th-C nave arcades and tower arch, low nave and chancel, and tall west tower; Pendley Chapel with fine 15th-C screen and monument of c.1452
The Old Manor House Late medieval house with exposed timber-framing and later additions

ALDEBURGH, SUFFOLK, 3, 5A
Church of St Peter and St Paul Surviving 14th-C tower of church rebuilt mainly 16th C

ALDENHAM, HERTS, 3, 1B
Church of St John the Baptist Medieval church built 13th to 15th C has west tower with thin timber spire, clerestoried nave, chancel restored 1800s and 1900s, and chancel chapels; 14th-C coffer, 15th-C roofs, and fine monuments

ALDERBURY, SHROPS, 5, 1C
Church of St Michael Spacious medieval church has north tower built c.1300, handsome Loton Chapel of c.1320–30, and good nave roof; chancel added 1845
Alderbury Castle Ruins of medieval castle with walls and tower

Alderbury Priory Remains of church of Augustinian priory founded c.1225 survive incorporated in farmhouse

ALDERFORD, NORFOLK, 4, 4D
Church of St John the Baptist Early 14th-C church with small tower and porch added 1374; elaborately carved Seven Sacraments font

ALDERMASTON, BERKS, 2, 5C
Church of St Mary Church of Norman origin reworked early 13th-C with chancel and south transept; fine Norman head, timber roof to chancel, medieval wall painting, and excellent monument to Sir G. Forster and wife (d.1526, made probably c.1530)

ALDINGHAM, CUMBRIA, 7, 1D
Church of St Cuthbert Norman church with nave arcade of c.1190 and chancel rebuilt c.1300

ALDWINCLE, NORTHANTS, 4, 1E
Church of St Peter Norman church with 13th and 14th-C additions; surviving early 14th-C stained glass in south windows
Church of All Saints (CCT) 13th-C church extensively rebuilt 1400s

ALDWORTH, BERKS, 2, 5B
Church of St Mary 14th-C church, heavily restored 19th C, contains eight contemporary monuments to de la Beche family with huge stone effigies beneath carved canopies

ALFORD, LINCS, 4, 2B
Church of St Wilfred 14th-C church with later medieval additions, enlarged and restored 1800s

ALFRISTON, E. SUSSEX, 3, 2E
Church of St Andrew Cruciform 14th-C church with Easter Sepulchre and unusual piscina and sedilia; fragments of medieval stained glass
Alfriston Clergy House [NT] 14th-C half-timbered hall-house of "Wealden" type

ALLEXTON, LEICS, 5, 5D
Church of St Peter Church of late Norman origin enlarged 14th C retains north arcade of c.1160 (reconstructed 1862 during extensive restoration) and chancel arch responds of c.1180

ALLOA, CENTRAL, 8, 2D
Alloa Tower [NTS] Handsome tower house built 1497 and remodelled early 1700s has parapet walk, original vaulting on second floor, and fine medieval timber roof to solar on upper level

ALMONDBURY, W. YORKS, 7, 3E
Church of All Hallows 14th-C church much altered 1400s with handsome three-tiered font cover and fragments of 15th-C stained glass in north chapel; early 16th-C ceiling with good bosses

ALMONDSBURY, GLOS, 2, 2B
Church of St Mary the Virgin Church of Norman origin with 13th-C central tower and fine broach spire; extensive 19th-C restoration included rebuilding of nave in 1834

ALNE, N. YORKS, 7, 4D
Church of St Mary Norman church with ornate carved south doorway, 14th-C chapel, and 15th-C nave arcade; good font

ALNWICK, NORTHUMBERLAND, 7, 3A
Church of St Michael Church rebuilt late 15th C with traces of Norman and earlier medieval work
Alnwick Castle [HHA] Mid 12th-C Norman shell keep incorporated into imposing 14th-C castle (extensively restored, altered and enlarged 18th and 19th C)

ALREWAS, STAFFS, 5, 4C
Church of All Saints Two reset Norman doorways in medieval church with 13th-C chancel and 14th-C west tower; roofs heightened 16th-C

ALSTONEFIELD, STAFFS, 5, 3B
Church of St Peter Norman church with carved chancel arch; alterations and additions of 13th, 14th and 15th C

ALTARNUN, CORNWALL, 1, 3C
Church of St Nonna Large 15th-C church with tall tower; splendid Norman font, full-width traceried rood screen and fine set of seventy-nine 16th-C carved bench ends

ALVECHURCH, WORCS, 5, 3D
Church of St Laurence Norman church with 13th-C chancel and later medieval rebuilding, much altered by 19th-C restoration

ALVEDISTON, WILTS, 2, 3D
Norrington Manor (1.5 km / 1 m. NW) Surviving great hall and porch of late 14th-C manor house with 17th-C additions

ALVELEY, SHROPS, 5 2,D
Church of St Mary Church rebuilt 13th, 14th and 15th C retains late Norman tower heightened late 1700s; exterior renewed 19th C

ALWALTON, CAMBS, 4, 1D
Church of St Andrew Mainly 12th- and 13th-C church with north arcade of c.1170, west tower, transepts and some 15th-C work

AMBERLEY, HEREFS, 5, 2E
Chapel Early 14th-C chapel with bellcote
Amberley Court Well-preserved 14th-C hall-house with important timberwork to hall and solar and buttery wings

AMBERLEY, W. SUSSEX, 3, 1E
Church of St Michael Norman church with 13th-C additions including tower
Amberley Castle Ruins of late Norman and 13th-C manor house fortified 14th C as palace of Bishops of Chichester

AMERSHAM, BUCKS, 3, 1B
Church of St Mary Medieval church of 13th, 14th and 15th C; thorough 19th-C restoration included refacing exterior

AMESBURY, WILTS, 2, 4C
Church of St Mary and St Melor Norman cruciform church largely rebuilt 13th C with later medieval additions

AMPNEY CRUCIS, GLOS, 2, 3B
Church of the Holy Rood Saxon, Norman and medieval church with 15th-C west tower and bellcote; remains of early 14th-C wall painting; important churchyard cross of c.1415

AMPTHILL, BEDS, 3, 1A
Church of St Andrew 14th-C church with 15th-C tower and nave roof

AMPTON, SUFFOLK, 4, 3E
Church of St Peter [OCT] Medieval church much restored 19th C with chantry chapel of c.1479; several late 15th-C brasses

ANDREAS, ISLE OF MAN, 6, 1A
Crosses Church contains Celtic and Norse crosses with excellent, well-preserved carved work (including scenes from Norse mythology) and runic inscriptions

ANGLE, DYFED, 6, 2E
Church of St Mary and Chapel of St Anthony Tiny fishermen's chapel (founded 1447), built above crypt with outside steps, survives in graveyard of medieval church
Angle Tower Small machicolated medieval tower

ANGLESEY ABBEY, CAMBS, 4, 2E
See Lode

ANNAGH, CO. KERRY, 12, 2C
Church [Dúchas] Late medieval parish church contains (on interior wall by south doorway) 13th-C carving of armed horseman

ANNAGHDOWN, CO. GALWAY, 12, 2A
Churches and Priory [Dúchas] Remains of ecclesiastical buildings of 11th to 15th C include fortified priory of 12th C and later with fragments of well carved chancel arch built into wall in south-west corner and simple 15th-C cathedral with north doorway of c.1200 and fine east window
Castle; 15th-C tower of castle survives by lake to south-east of priory

ANSTEY, HERTS, 3, 2A
Church of St George Late Norman cruciform church with 13th-, 14th- and 15th-C additions; crude Norman font; 15th- or 16th-C carved misericords; late medieval lychgate

ANTRIM, CO. ANTRIM, 11, 5B
Round Tower [EHS] Almost complete Round Tower of early Christian monastery (built probably 10th or 11th C)
Antrim Castle (gardens open*) Motte and bailey survives near ruins of 17th and 19th-C house burnt down 1922

APPLEBY-IN-WESTMORLAND, CUMBRIA, 7, 2C
Church of St Lawrence 14th- and 15th-C church with later additions
Church of St Michael, Bongate Medieval church with Saxon hogback tombstone used as lintel over north doorway
Appleby Castle * Castle with extensive post-medieval reworking retains fine Norman keep with dramatic view from top, 12th-C curtain walls and defensive earthworks

APPLEBY, LINCS
Church of St Bartholomew Medieval church extensively rebuilt 19th C retains late 13th- or early 14th-C arcades and 15th-C chancel arch

APPLEBY MAGNA, LEICS, 5, 4C
Church of St Michael Large mainly 14th-C church extensively restored c. 1830

APPLECROSS, HIGHLAND, 9, 2D
Applecross Church Church built 1817 contains carved fragments of cross slabs with more complete, 8th-C example by gate
Applecross Chapel Overgrown remains of charming 15th-C chapel survive near church

APPLEDORE, KENT, 3, 4D
Church of St Peter and St Paul 13th-C church once belonging to St Martin's Priory, Dover, much reworked after 1380, retains original west tower (doorway inserted 1510) and north transept chapel with unusual sanctuary; timber chancel arch and 15th-C windows in south aisle; good screens (north and south probably c.1380)
Horne's Place Chapel [EH] (2.5 km. / 1 ½m. N) (by arrangement only) Handsome 14th-C chapel (licensed 1366), formerly attached to manor house

APPLETON, OXON, 2, 4B
Church of St Lawrence Norman church with later medieval west tower
Appleton Manor Surviving part of Norman manor house built late 12th C with impressive entrance doorway

APPLETON-LE-STREET, N. YORKS, 7, 4D
Church of All Saints Late Saxon church tower altered and heightened 11th and 12th C; chancel and aisles of 13th to 14th C

ARAN ISLANDS (ie. Inishmore, Inishmaan and Inisheer) (accessible by boat from Galway), CO. GALWAY, 11, 1E
Pagan and Early Christian Fortified and Monastic Sites [Dúchas] Numerous fascinating monuments, mostly undatable, scattered over all three islands include forts, churches, Round Tower and 12th-C crosses,

ARBOE, CO. TYRONE, 11, 4B
High Cross and Abbey [EHS] Fine large cross of probably early 10th C with carved biblical scenes marks area of monastery founded possibly 6th C; featureless remains of small abbey in field north of graveyard

ARBROATH, TAYSIDE, 8, 4C
Arbroath Abbey [HS] Extensive remains of large late 12th- and 13th-C Tironensian abbey church (founded 1178) with impressive twin-towered west front, sacristy and treasury block added 1400s, and parts of conventual buildings including precinct wall, gatehouse, and 15th- to 16th-C Abbot's House housing museum

ARBUTHNOTT (4 km. / 2 ½ m. from Inverbervie), GRAMPIAN, 8, 4C
St Ternan's Church [SCS] Medieval church consecrated 1242 and much restored 1889–90 retains good early 13th-C

chancel, and tower and Lady Chapel (now Arbuthnott family aisle) added late 1400s; Priest's Room with squint to chapel survives above Arbuthnott Aisle; 13th-C military effigy of Hugh Arbuthnott

ARDAGH, CO. LONGFORD, 11,3D
St Mel's Cathedral Remains of small 8th-C cathedral church built with large blocks of masonry

ARDBRACCAN, CO. MEATH, 11,4D
Church Tower Surviving 15th- or 16th-C church tower with post-medieval upper levels

ARDCHATTAN (on N. shore of Loch Etive 10 km. / 6 m. NE of Oban) STRATHCLYDE, 10,4A
Ardchattan Priory [HS] Ruins of Valliscaulian priory founded 1230–1 include transepts and other fragments of church; parts of conventual buildings incorporated in house to south (still occupied)

ARDEE, CO. LOUTH, 11,4D
Church of St Mary Mainly early 19th-C Protestant church incorporates parts of medieval predecessor; primitive font
St Leger's Castle Late medieval fortified town house (largest to survive in Ireland) later converted to courthouse and gaol
Hatch Castle Tower house built 15th or 16th C and reworked 1800s survives on main street
Chantry College Ruins of southern part of chantry college established before 1487
Tower House off Jervis Street Late medieval tower house now forming part of farmyard
Kildemock 'Jumping Church' (2 km. / 1 ¼ m. SSE, Millockstown) Ruins of medieval church with west gable curiously situated within foundations
Smarmore Castle (4 km. / 2 ½ m. SSW) Tower house built c.1320 with adjoining 18th-C blocks and early 19th-C alterations

ARDFERT, CO. KERRY, 12,2C
St Brendan's Cathedral and Churches [Dúchas] Interesting group of buildings on site of early monastery with cathedral (12th to 17th C) incorporating fine 12th-C west doorway and blank arcading; late 13th- to early 14th-C effigies of bishops; 12th-C nave of Temple Na Hoe and simple 15th-C Temple Na Griffin
Friary [Dúchas] Church of Franciscan friary founded c.1253 with late 13th-C nave and chancel; 14th-C effigy of bishop; tower and cloisters added 15th C

ARDGLASS, CO. DOWN, 11,5C
Castles or Merchants' Houses [Jordan's Castle – EHS] Formerly important village has remains of five 14th- to 16th-C tower houses; Cowd Castle, Margaret's Castle, King's Castle, Horn Castle (incorporated in 1790 Ardglass Castle) and Jordan's Castle (restored after 1911)

ARDKEEN (6.5 km. / 4 m.N of Portaferry) CO. DOWN, 11,5C
Ardkeen Castle, Castle Hill Remains of motte and bailey castle built c.1180
Church of St Mary Altered medieval manorial church with good lancet windows on north side

ARDMORE, CO. WATERFORD, 12,4D
Round Tower and Church of St Declan (or Cathedral) [Dúchas] Site of early monastery houses remains of impressive Round Tower (one of best-preserved in Ireland), good late 12th-C church with remarkable arcading in west wall containing figure sculpture, and small St Declan's Oratory to east (partly modern, said to contain Saint's grave)

ARDNAREE, CO. SLIGO, 11,2C
Ballina Friary [Dúchas] Remains of church of Augustinian friary founded c.1375 or 1427 with finely carved west doorway

ARDRASS, CO. KILDARE, 11,4E
St Patrick's Chapel Small stone oratory built probably 15th C (restored 1888) with rare surviving medieval stone roof

ARDTOLE (1.5 km./ 1 m. NE of Ardglass), CO. DOWN, 11,5C
Ardtole Church [EHS] Ruined parish church built mainly 15th C on impressive elevated site

ARDTORNISH, HIGHLAND, 10,3A
Ardtornish Castle Fortified 14th-C hall-house of Lords of Isles

ARISAIG, HIGHLAND, 9,2E
St Maelrubha's Church Ruined 16th-C church in graveyard of 19th-C St Mary's contains good 15th-C graveslabs

ARKESDEN, ESSEX, 3,2A
Church of St Mary 13th-C church with mid 19th-C restoration including rebuilt west tower

ARLINGTON, E. SUSSEX, 3,2E
Church of St Pancras Saxon and Norman church with 14th-C additions; traces of wall paintings in nave

ARMAGH, CO. ARMAGH, 11,4C
Armagh Friary [EHS] Remains of 13th-C church of once important Franciscan friary (founded 1263–4, ruined by 1600)
Protestant Cathedral of St Patrick Cathedral built 1261–8 on site of earlier hill fort with 14th-, 15th- and 17th-C work and extensive rebuilding of 1834–7; shaft and broken head of finely carved High Cross in north aisle; collection of medieval and earlier sculpture in north transept; remains of stone cross in churchyard (possibly 11th-C)

ARMITAGE, STAFFS, 5,3C
Church of St John Church built 1844–7 with west tower of 1632 retains fine Norman font with carved figures

ARMOY, CO. ANTRIM, 11,5A
Round Tower Stump of Round Tower (all that remains of early monastery) survives near Protestant church

ARNESBY, LEICS, 5,5D
Church of St Peter Norman church enlarged 14th to 15th C and restored 1866–7 retains early 12th-C arcades, west tower of c.1300 and chancel built c.1330; 14th-C double piscina and sedilia

ARRETON, ISLE OF WIGHT
Church of St George Norman church with traces of Saxon work, early 13th-C aisles, and later medieval additions including 14th-C buttressed tower

ARRINGTON, CAMBS, 3,2A
Church of St Nicholas Modest church with sumptuous chancel added late 1200s; rich double piscina and blocked priest's doorway

ARUNDEL, W. SUSSEX, 3,1E
Church of St Nicholas Late 14th-C church divided into two parts, parish church and Fitzalan Chapel for private use of Dukes of Norfolk (accessible only through castle grounds); chapel contains contemporary wall-painting and remarkable number of fine brasses and sculptured monuments to 15th-C and later members of Norfolk family
Arundel Castle * Large Norman castle with motte and barbican transformed by major 19th-C rebuilding

ASHAMPSTEAD, BERKS, 2,5B
Church of St Clement Church with early 13th-C nave and chancel and good timber roofs retains important wall paintings of c.1230–40

ASHBOURNE, DERBYS, 5,4B
Church of St Oswald Medieval church of Saxon origin built 13th, 14th and 15th C; Boothby Chapel with 14th- to 15th-C monuments

ASHBURY, OXON, 2,4B
Church of St Mary Church of Norman origin has 13th-C transepts with later windows, west tower built late 1200s, 15th-C arcades and two-storeyed north porch
Manor House Late medieval manor house with work of 1697

ASHBY DE LA ZOUCH, LEICS, 5,4C
Church of St Helen Late 15th-C church with additions of 1878–80
Ashby de la Zouch Castle [EH] Norman castle with later medieval additions substantially enlarged and remodelled 15th C

ASHBY ST LEDGERS NORTHANTS, 5,5E
Church of St Leodegarius Medieval church with 14th-C west tower, four-bay arcades, and nave of c.1470–90; rood screen and good set of wall paintings of c.1500 depicting Passion of Christ

ASHCHURCH, GLOS, 2,3A
Church of St Nicholas Norman church with narrow nave, short chancel rebuilt 1200s, late 13th-C north aisle, and west tower built late 1300s; fine 15th-C rood screen and roofs

ASHLEWORH, GLOS, 2,3A
Church of St Andrew and St Bartholomew Norman church of c.1100 with 13th-C chancel and later medieval additions
Ashleworth Tithe Barn [NT] Huge monastic barn built late 15th C
Ashleworth Court (open by appointment only) L-shaped house of c.1460 with hall and solar
Ashleworth Manor (open by appointment only) Late medieval timber-framed house on E plan

ASHOVER, DERBYS, 5,4B
Church of All Saints Medieval church with late 13th-C south doorway, 14th-C north arcade and early 15th-C west tower; important lead font of c.1200, rood screen and monuments of early 16th C

ASHTON, DEVON, 1,5C
Church of St John the Baptist Large 15th-C church with contemporary painted rood and parclose screens, wall painting and stained glass

ASHTON-UNDER-LYNE,
GREATER MANCHESTER, 5, 3A
Church of St Michael and All Angels
[OCT] Spacious church built early 15th to
early 16th C and extensively remodelled
19th C retains fine set of original stained
glass

ASHWATER, DEVON, 1, 4C
Church of St Peter Medieval church with
wide nave and west tower contains
excellent 15th-C tomb chest with
recumbent effigy of member of
Carminow family

ASHWELL, HERTS, 3, 2A
Church of St Mary 14th-C church with
handsome four-stage west tower
completed 15th C with octagonal lantern
and slender spire; medieval graffiti on
north tower wall includes references to
Black Death and scratched drawing of
Old St Paul's Cathedral; 15th-C timber
lychgate

ASKEATON, CO. LIMERICK, 12, 2C
Castle [Dúchas] Remains of castle on
island in River Deel consists of rocky
upper ward with 15th-C tower and lower
ward with splendid Great Hall or
Banqueting House built 1440–59; Friary
(or Rock Abbey) [Dúchas]; remains of
Franciscan friary founded probably 1389
include church (mainly 1420–40) with
good sedilia, niches and carved windows,
and very well preserved cloister (carving
of St Francis in north-east corner)

ASKE HALL, N. YORKS, 7, 3C
Aske Hall * Mansion house with extensive
additions of 18th to 20th C retains 15th-C
pele tower behind east wing of mansion
dating from 18th to 20th C

ASKERTON CASTLE (1.5 km. / 1 m.
NE of Kirkcambeck), CUMBRIA, 7, 2B
Askerton Castle Medieval castle with later
additions retains 15th-C south range with
towers added c.1500–10; original timber
roof to hall

ASKHAM, CUMBRIA, 7, 2C
Askham Hall Late 14th-C manor house
with 16th- and 17th-C work retains original tower wing remodelled c.1685–90

ASPATRIA, CUMBRIA, 7, 1C
Church of St Kentigern Church rebuilt
19th C retains Norman arch reused as
vestry doorway; fragments of Anglo-
Danish sculpture in churchyard; carved
hogback coffin

ASTBURY, CHESHIRE, 5, 3B
Church of St Mary 14th-C church
substantially rebuilt 15th C; ornate
roofs with bosses and pendants; screens,
stained glass and wall painting of c.1500

ASTLEY, WARWS, 5, 4D
Church of St Mary the Virgin Cruciform
collegiate church of 14th C rescued from
decay 17th C and restored as parish
church; important set of stalls of
c.1400 with painted backs and carved
misericords; 15th-C brass and alabaster
monuments

ASTLEY, WORCS, 5, 3D
Church of St Peter Norman church of
c.1160 with corbel frieze and buttresses
like engaged columns; later medieval
and 19th-C additions

ASTON, W. MIDLANDS
See Birmingham

ASTON EYRE, SHROPS, 5, 2D
Church Small Norman church with
splendid carved tympanum above
south door showing Christ entering
Jerusalem riding on an ass

ASTON TIRROLD, OXON, 2, 5B
Church of St Michael Medieval church of
Saxon origin with 11th-C south doorway

ASTON UPTHORPE, OXON, 2, 5B
Church of All Saints Small Norman
church with 19th-C chancel and bell turret

ATHASSEL, CO. TIPPERARY, 12, 3C
St Edmund's Priory [Dúchas] Extensive
remains of largest medieval priory in
Ireland (Augustinian, founded late 1100s)
include 13th-C cruciform church with
good doorway of c.1260 in screen between
nave and choir and tower rebuilt after fire
of 1447, remnants of altered 13th-C buildings and cloister and, outside immediate
complex, walls and gatehouse

ATHBOY, CO. MEATH, 11, 4D
Church of St James Large 15th-C tower
of medieval church survives attached
to 18th-C hall and 19th-C church; late
medieval tomb chest by tower with
effigies of knight and lady; early 16th-C
carved panels
Causetown Castle (2.5 km. / 1 ½ m. SW)
Ruins of 15th- or early 16th-C tower house

ATHELHAMPTON, DORSET, 2, 2E
Athelhampton House [HHA] Handsome
manor house of c.1500 retains original
hall with fine timber roof, oriel window
and early 16th-C screen; late medieval
dovecot

ATHENRY, CO. GALWAY, 11, 2D
Friary of St Peter and St Paul [Dúchas]
Ruined church of Dominican friary
founded 1241 with early 14th-C additions
and rebuilding of after 1423; fine collection
of 13th- to 15th-C tomb niches
Athenry Castle [Dúchas] Remains of
castle with early 13th-C town or curtain
walling enclosing well preserved three
storeyed keep
Town Extensive sections of town walls
built after 1312 and fragment of 15th-C
market cross

ATHERINGTON, DEVON, 1, 4B
Church of St Mary Late medieval church
with wagon roofs, carved bench ends
and screens (including surviving 16th-C
rood loft gallery); 13th-, 14th- and 15th-C
monuments in chancel; lychgate with
coffin slab

ATHLONE, CO. WESTMEATH, 11, 3D
Athlone Castle [Dúchas] Massive castle
begun early 13th C (much reconstructed
c.1800–27) by River Shannon to guard
gateway to Connaught retains curtain
walls, bastions and unusual polygonal
keep

ATHLUMNEY CASTLE,
CO. MEATH, 11, 4D
See Navan

ATTENBOROUGH, NOTTS, 5, 5C
Church of St Mary Magdalene Medieval
church with rebuilding of 1869 has 13th-C
arcades with capitals reworked 1300s, and
late 14th-C steeple to west tower

ATTLEBOROUGH, NORFOLK, 4, 4D
Church of St Mary Norman church
largely rebuilt 14th C with early 15th-C
two-storeyed porch; magnificent late
15th- or early 16th-C carved and painted
rood screen across nave and aisles; wall
paintings

AUCHENCASS (2 km. / 1 ¼ m. NW
of Beattock), DUMFRIES AND
GALLOWAY, 7, 1A
Auchencass Ruins of castle of enclosure
built late 1200s

AUCHINDOIR (nr Lumsden,
5 km. / 3 m. N of Kildrummy)
GRAMPIAN, 8, 3B
St Mary's Kirk [HS] Well-preserved
remains of fine 13th-C parish church with
rich doorway of c.1200 and excellent early
14th-C sacrament house

AUCHINDOON (4 km. / 2 ½ m. SE
of Dufftown), GRAMPIAN, 8, 3A
Auchindoon Castle [HS] (not accessible
to public) Ruins of imposing L-plan tower
house built probably 15th C with ranges of
buildings in courtyard

AUCKLAND CASTLE
CO. DURHAM, 7, 3C
See Bishop Auckland

AUDLEY'S CASTLE,
CASTLEWARD, CO. DOWN, 11, 5C
Audley's Castle [EHS] Well-preserved
15th-C tower house with two projecting
turrets; fireplaces, window seats, spiral
stair and reconstructed wooden floor and
barrel vault to first floor room

AUGHNANURE, CO. GALWAY, 11, 2D
Aughnanure Castle [Dúchas] Remains of
once fine castle built c.1500 on rocky
site near Lough Corrib include six-
storeyed tower house and two bawns,
the outer enclosing ruined 16th-C
banqueting hall

AUGHTON, E. RIDING OF
YORKS, 7, 4E
Church of All Saints Norman church with
fine carved chancel arch, south doorway
and font

AUGHTON, E. RIDING OF
YORKS, 7, 1E
Church of St Michael Church of Norman
origin with medieval, mid 16th- and
19th-C work retains original south
doorway, 14th-C north tower, and fine
roofs to nave and north aisle; remains
of 9th- to 10th-C cross head

AULT HUCKNALL, DERBYS, 5, 4B
Church of St John the Baptist [OCT]
Early Norman embattled church restored
1885–8 with 11th-C nave and north aisle,
tympanum on west front, crossing tower
with 15th-C upper levels, and 14th-C
south arcade

AVEBURY, WILTS, 2, 3B
Church of St James Church of Saxon
origin restored 19th C has original circular
clerestory windows, 12th-C south
doorway, late 13th-C chancel rebuilt
1879, and 15th-C west tower; fine carved
Norman font and late medieval rood
screen

AVELEY, ESSEX, 3, 2C
Church of St Michael 12th-, 13th- and
14th-C church with square Norman font
and important brass of c.1370

AVENING, GLOS, 2,3B
Church of the Holy Cross Early Norman cruciform church with later Norman and medieval additions; sculptured panels of c.1160 beside north doorway

AVINGTON, BERKS, 2,4C
Church of St Mark and St Luke Small, remarkably complete Norman church with original carved south doorway, windows, chancel arch and font

AVONCROFT MUSEUM OF
 BUILDINGS, WORCS, 5,3D
See Bromsgrove

AWLISCOMBE, DEVON, 2,1D
Church of St Michael Medieval church remodelled early 1500s retains fine early 16th-C stone screen with battlements

AXBRIDGE, SOMERSET, 2,2C
Church of St John the Baptist Late 14th to early 15th-C church with tall crossing tower; fine 17th-C plaster ceiling in nave

AXMOUTH, DEVON, 2,1E
Church of St Michael Norman and medieval church restored 19th C retains fine carved 12th-C doorway

AYDON CASTLE,
 NORTHUMBERLAND, 7,3B
Aydon Castle [EH] Well-preserved fortified manor house of late 13th and 14th C with 17th-C work retains hall and solar ranges

AYLESBURY, BUCKS, 2,5A
Church of St Mary Large cruciform church of 13th, 14th and 15th C much restored 1800s; sophisticated late 12th-C font; rare 15th-C vestment press
King's Head Hotel Market Square; Altered 15th-C building with big windows and good timberwork

AYLESFORD, KENT, 3,3D
Church of St Peter Mainly medieval church restored 19th C retains Norman west tower with 15th-C upper stage and rood loft stair turret; brass of c.1426
The Friars Remains of two Carmelite houses founded 1242 with 16th-C additions include part of medieval cloister walks and Prior's Hall with 15th-C doorway
Bridge 14th-C bridge crossing River Medway

AYLESTONE, LEICS, 5,5D
See Leicester

AYR, STRATHCLYDE, 10,4D
Auld Brig (town centre) and
Brig o'Doon (Alloway) Medieval bridges over Rivers Ayr and Doon
St John's Tower Handsome 15th-C tower much altered 1778 and restored 1913–14, all that survives of late 12th-C Church of St John
Loudoun Hall, Boat Vennel Well-restored late medieval merchant's house

BABRAHAM, CAMBS, 3,2A
Church of St Peter 13th-C church with later medieval nave, reroofed 18th C; plain oak benches and traceried pulpit

BACKWELL, SOMERSET, 2,2B
Church of St Andrew 13th-C church with 14th-C and later additions including unusual tall west tower

BACONSTHORPE, NORFOLK, 4,4C
Church of St Mary Medieval church much restored 19th C has 13th-C chancel with piscina of c.1260–80; 15th-C Easter Sepulchre
Baconsthorpe Castle [EH] Remains of moated castle built c.1450–1486 with wall, towers and gatehouses

BACTON, HEREFS, 2,1A
Church of St Faith 13th-C church with late 16th-C tower; late medieval carved stalls

BACTON, NORFOLK, 4,5C
Church of St Andrew Mainly 15th-C church with west tower and 14th-C font
Broomholm Priory; Ruins of priory founded 1113 with parts of late Norman and 13th-C transepts

BACTON, SUFFOLK, 4,4E
Church of St Mary Mid to late medieval church with restored double hammer-beam roof and flint and stonework decorating clerestory; faded Doom painting above chancel arch

BADDESLEY CLINTON, WARWS, 5,4D
Baddesley Clinton Hall [NT], Rising Lane Well-preserved moated manor house with handsome north side built 1400s and 16th- to 18th-C alterations

BADGEWORTH, GLOS, 2,3A
Church of the Holy Trinity Mainly 14th-C church with liberal use of ballflower ornament on door and windows; fragments of medieval stained glass

BADINGHAM, SUFFOLK, 4,5E
Church of St John the Baptist Norman and medieval church with fine hammer-beam roof; Seven Sacraments font

BAG ENDERBY, LINCS, 4,2B
Church of St Margaret 14th-C church with contemporary font and 15th-C tower; some surviving medieval stained glass

BAGENDON, GLOS, 2,3A
Church of St Margaret 12th-C church with medieval additions has Norman font and stone coffin lids and fragments of 15th-C stained glass

BAGILLT, CLWYD, 6,5A
Basingwerk Castle Foundations of Norman and medieval castle revealed by excavations 1954–7

BAINTON, E. RIDING OF
 YORKS, 7,4E
Church of St Andrew Mid 14th-C church with reticulated tracery throughout and numerous carved gargoyles and headstops on hoodmoulds; Norman font; 14th-C monument and 15th-C brass

BAKEWELL, DERBYS, 5,4B
Church of All Saints; Norman church with additions of 13th, 14th and 15th C; sculptured Saxon and Norman fragments; early 14th-C font, and 15th-C screen; numerous medieval memorials include headstones and coffin slabs and unusual and important Foljambe wall-monument carved 1385; well-preserved stump of carved Saxon cross in churchyard

BALDERTON, NOTTS, 5,5B
Church of St Giles Church of Norman origin retains good 12th-C doorway to north porch with original figure in niche above; 13th-C steeple with late 14th- or early 15th-C spire; medieval font, screen, bench ends and fragments of stained glass

BALDOCK, HERTS, 3,2A
Church of St Mary Embattled church built mainly early 14th C has big west tower with octagonal lantern, two-storeyed south porch, south chapel, and spacious interior with six-bay nave arcades; good full-width 15th-C screens and brasses

BALDONGAN, CO. DUBLIN, 11,5D
Church [Dúchas] Remains of nave and chancel church built possibly early 1400s with imposing later west tower

BALGONIE CASTLE (1 km. / 1½ m. W of Milton of Balgonie), FIFE, 8,3D
Balgonie Castle * Remains of imposing late medieval castle with 14th-C chapel, early 15th-C gatehouse, rectangular north-west tower, north range of 1496

remodelled c.1640, and 17th- and 18th-C additions

BALGRIFFIN, CO. DUBLIN, 11,5D
Church of St Doulagh Impressive and unusual church with much medieval and 19th-C work retains stone-roofed 12th-C eastern end to chancel

BALLA, CO. MAYO, 11,2C
Round Tower [Dúchas] Stump of Round Tower on site of early monastery

BALLABEG, ISLE OF MAN, 6,1A
The Friary Chapel, Friary Farm (S of Arbory Parish Church) Original chapel of Franciscan friary founded 1367 has survived preserved as farm building since dissolution of 1540

BALLASALLA, ISLE OF MAN, 6,1A
Rushen Abbey * Mainly 13th- to 15th-C remains of important Cistercian abbey established 1134 include tower of church, infirmary and chapter house
The Monk's Bridge 14th-C bridge across River Silverburn (Island's only surviving medieval example) probably built by monks of nearby abbey

BALLEEGHAM ABBEY (3 km. / 2 m. NNE of Manorcunningham)
 CO. DONEGAL, 11,3B
Balleegham Abbey Remains of large and imposing Franciscan church founded late 1400s on shore of Lough Swilly with well-preserved east window

BALLINA FRIARY
 CO. SLIGO, 11,2C
See Ardnaree

BALLINAMANTAIN CASTLE
 CO. GALWAY, 11,2E
See Kiltartan

BALLINBREICH CASTLE (4. km. 2½ m. E of Newburgh), FIFE, 8,3D
Ballinbreich Castle Remains of 14th-C castle with 15th- and late 16th-C additions include original curtain walling and rectangular south-west tower

BALLINCOLLIG, CO. CORK
Ballincollig Castle Ruins of 14th-C castle with tall tower and large fortified enclosure

BALLINDOON, CO. SLIGO, 11,2C
Friary [Dúchas] Unusual church of Dominican friary founded 1507 on shores of Lough Arrow retains remarkable central tower which also acted as rood screen

BALLINSKELLIGS, CO. KERRY, 12, 1D
Monastery [Dúchas] Sea-eroded remains of two 15th-C churches together with cloister garth of Augustinian monastery founded 12th or 13th C from Skellig Michael

BALLINTOBER (or Toberbride), CO. ROSCOMMON, 11, 2D
Ballintober Castle [Dúchas] Remains of large square moated castle built c.1300 (in use until 19th C) with twin towered gatehouse, polygonal corner towers and open courtyard

BALLINTUBBER (or Ballintober), CO. MAYO, 11, 1D
Abbey [Dúchas] Remains of small Augustinian abbey founded 1216, restored and reconstructed 19th and 20th C, include church with well-preserved capitals, carved lancet windows, rib-vaulting to chancel, and 15th-C west doorway; fragments of domestic buildings (mainly 15th-C) with fine 13th-C doorway to chapter house

BALLUG CASTLE, CO. LOUTH, 11, 5C
See Grange

BALLYBEG, CO. CORK, 12, 3C
Abbey [Dúchas] Remains of Augustinian priory founded 1229 or 1237 include 13th-C church with good west windows and 15th-C west and central towers; unusual, well preserved dovecot to east-south-east

BALLYBOGGAN ABBEY, CO. MEATH, 11, 4D
See Clonard

BALLYGARTH, CO. MEATH, 11, 4D
See Julianstown

BALLYGAWLEY, CO. TYRONE, 11, 4B
Church of St Kiernan (4.5 km. / 2¾ m. W) Remains of medieval church possibly connected to monastery founded 1489; carved cross head

BALLYHACK, CO. WEXFORD, 12, 4C
Ballyhack Castle [Dúchas] Remains of five-storeyed castle built 15th or 16th C by Waterford estuary, site of earlier preceptory of Knights Templar

BALLYLAHAN, CO. MAYO, 11, 2C
Castle [Dúchas] Ruined 13th-C castle with curtain wall and twin-towered gatehouse (c.1260)

BALLYLARKIN, CO. KILKENNY, 12, 4C
Church [Dúchas]; Small 13th-C church with fortified appearance; fine carved stonework includes corbels and 14th-C triple sedilia

BALLYLOUGHAN, CO. CARLOW, 12, 5C
Ballyloughan Castle [Dúchas] Fragmentary remains of castle built probably 13th C include entrance gate with large flanking towers

BALLYMOON, CO. CARLOW, 12, 5C
Ballymoon Castle [Dúchas] Castle built probably 1290–1310 has curtain walls with three towers and gatehouse on fourth side

BALLYMOREREAGH (Dingle Peninsula, 5.5 km. / 3½ m. WNW of Dingle), CO. KERRY, 12, 1C
Teampull Geal (White Church) [Dúchas] Remains of incomplete early stone oratory (similar to that at Gallarus) with flat-headed doorway

BALLYMOTE, CO. SLIGO, 11, 2C
Castle [Dúchas] Overgrown remains of remarkable square castle built c.1300 with round corner towers and twin-towered gatehouse

BALLYNACARRIGY, CO. WESTMEATH, 11, 3D
Tristernagh Abbey (4 km. / 2½ m. NE) Surviving parts of Augustinian abbey founded c.1200 and incorporated into house c.1783
Templecross Church (3.5 km. / 2¼ m. NE) Remains of chapel built late 1400s include two-storeyed tower with roofless priest's room

BALLYNASCREEN (6.5 km. / 4 m. SW of Draperstown), CO. LONDONDERRY, 11, 4B
Church Remains of medieval church on ancient site known as Columcille's Shrine (Scrin Cholaim Chille)

BALLYSADARE, CO. SLIGO, 11, 2C
Church [Dúchas] Picturesque site of monastery founded 7th C houses remains of medieval church (Teampall Mor Feichin) with good 12th-C doorway; ruined church nearby (to W) with 15th-C tower marks site of priory

BALLYSAGGART FRIARY, CO. DONEGAL, 11, 2B
See St John's Point

BALLYWILLAN, CO. LONDONDERRY, 11, 4B
See Portstewart

BALMERINO (7.5 km. / 4½ m. SW of Newport on Tay), FIFE, 8, 3D
Balmerino Abbey Remains of Cistercian abbey founded c.1227 with church, cloister, sacristy, tunnel vaulted parlour and well preserved chapter house
Balmerino Farm Farm with early 18th-C house incorporates 15th-C abbot's barn in north range

BALMUTO (1 km. / ½m. S of Auchtertool), FIFE, 8, 3D
Balmuto Late medieval house with 17th and 18th-C additions and reconstruction of 1974-84 retains tower house built c.1400 and 16th-C west and south ranges

BALNAGOWN CASTLE (1 km. / ½ m. N of Milton of Kildary) HIGHLAND, 9, 4D
Balnagown Castle 15th-C tower house with 16th to 19th-C reconstruction and enlargements

BALSHAM, CAMBS, 3, 3A
Church of the Holy Trinity Mainly 14th-C church with 13th-C tower and later medieval additions; rood screen and carved stalls with misericords; 15th-C brasses

BALTINGLASS, CO. WICKLOW, 12, 5B
Baltinglass Abbey [Dúchas] Impressive remains of Cistercian abbey of Vallis Salutis founded c.1148 include church (complete by 1170 or 1180) with good nave piers and capitals, fine carved work (eg. processional doorway to cloister), later medieval crossing tower (housing medieval fragments and tiles) and 19th-C alterations; reconstructed fragments of original cloister (found during 1931 excavation)

BALTONSBOROUGH, SOMERSET, 2, 2C
Parish House [LT] Church house built c.1500; ground floor still used as parish meeting room

BALVAIRD (1.5 km. / 1 m. S of Glen Farg), TAYSIDE, 8, 3D
Balvaird Castle [HS] (limited opening) Handsome, very well-preserved tower house built late 15th or early 16th C with good internal fittings including water basin and richly carved aumbry in hall (latter possibly brought from elsewhere); gatehouse range added later 1500s

BALVENIE CASTLE (1 km. / ½ m. N of Dufftown), GRAMPIAN, 8, 3A
Balvenie Castle [HS] Ruins of 13th-C castle much rebuilt as fortress during 15th and 16th C
Mortlach Church (St Moluag's) (1 km. / ½ m. S) Mainly 12th-C church with 13th-C lancets to chancel and north aisle added 19th C survives on early Christian site; Battle Stone (Pictish symbol stone) in churchyard

BALWEARIE CASTLE (2.5 km. / 1½ m. SW of Kirkcaldy), FIFE, 8, 3D
Balwearie Castle Remains of rectangular tower house licensed 1484

BAMBURGH, NORTHUMBERLAND, 7, 3A
Church of St Aidan Late 12th- to early 13th-C church with remarkable crypt beneath fine chancel added c.1230; some later medieval additions
Bamburgh Castle [HHA] Imposing castle begun mid 12th C with later rebuilding retains original keep and ruins of Norman chapel; fine views from ramparts take in Holy Island

BAMPTON, OXON, 2, 4B
Church of St Mary Spacious late Norman church remodelled 13th to early 14th C and restored 1867–9 has crossing tower with spire of c.1270, transepts and lancet windows; 13th-C sedilia and piscina, and rich 15th-C Easter Sepulchre

BANAGHER, CO. LONDONDERRY, 11, 4B
See Feeny

BANGOR, GWYNEDD, 6, 4A
Cathedral Cruciform Norman cathedral, mainly rebuilt 13th to 15th C and restored 19th C, with fine nave arcades and central tower; west tower added 1532; medieval "Eva Stone" (gravestone) superbly carved in low relief c.1380; 14th-C tiles; late medieval font and "Mostyn Christ" (large wooden Calvary figure)

BANNOW (8 km. / 5 m. SSW of Wellington Bridge), CO. WEXFORD, 12, 5C
Church of St Mary Remains of simple 13th-C church with 14th-C east window and later porches; excellent late 13th-C double head-slab; traces of small chapel nearby

BANWELL, SOMERSET, 2, 1C
Church of St Andrew Mainly 15th-C church with impressive tall west tower, pierced parapets and fine wagon roof; Norman font; late medieval pulpit,

benches, fragments of stained glass and brasses; fine rood screen of 1522

BARDFIELD SALING, ESSEX, 3,3B
Church of St Peter and St Paul 14th-C church shortened 19th C with round west tower and late 14th-C screen

BARDSEY, W. YORKS, 7,3E
Church of All Hallows Church of Saxon origin has original west tower with late medieval top, Norman arcades, aisles widened 15th C, and early 14th-C chancel

BARDWELL, SUFFOLK, 4,4E
Church of St Peter and St Paul 15th-C church with handsome west tower and tall porch ornamented with flushwork; fine hammerbeam roof with some original colouring; panels from traceried screen; 15th-C stained glass

BAREVAN, HIGHLAND, 9,4D
Church of St Aibind Remains of early 13th-C church abandoned after 1619; good double piscina and grave slabs on floor

BARFRESTON, KENT, 3,4D
Church of St Nicholas Small Norman church with some 19th-C rebuilding retains superb carving of c.1180; ornate late 12th-C south doorway with tympanum, priest's doorway and rich chancel arch; traces of wall paintings

BARHAM, CAMBS, 4,1E
Church of St Giles Late Norman church with 13th-C chancel; bellcote added 19th C

BARHOLM CASTLE (1.5 km. / 1m. SE of Kirkdale), DUMFRIES AND GALLOWAY, 10,5E
Barholm Castle Roofless four-storeyed tower house of mainly early 16th C with post medieval alterations

BARMSTON, E. RIDING OF YORKS, 7,5D
Church of All Saints Mainly 15th-C church with fine Norman font; part of hogback tombstone and fragments of medieval stained glass

BARNACK, CAMBS, 4,1D
Church of St John the Baptist Early 11th-C church rebuilt 12th to 14th C except for characteristic late Saxon tower; outstanding sculpted figure of seated Christ (c.1020) and ornate 13th-C font

BARNARD CASTLE, CO. DURHAM, 7,3C
Barnard Castle [EH] Substantial ruins of medieval castle built near River Tees

include 12th-C tower and 14th-C great hall
Church of St Mary [OCT] Late Norman and medieval church with rebuilt north-west tower dating from restoration of 1873–4; 14th-C tomb effigy

BARNBURGH, S. YORKS, 5,4A
Church of St Peter Church of Norman origin much rebuilt 15th C retains original west tower with late medieval top, arcade of c.1200, and 14th-C chancel; fragments of late Norman cross shaft and fine early 14th-C oaken effigy of knight

BARNSLEY, GLOS, 2,3A
Church of St Mary Church of Norman origin much rebuilt c.1500 and restored 1843–7 has 12th-C north doorway, parts of original corbel table, 13th-C chancel arch with Norman piers, and 15th-C west tower with top added c.1600; fine 14th-C roof and aumbry in chancel

BARNSTAPLE, DEVON, 1,4B
Church of St Peter and St Paul Late 12th-to early 13th-C church with broach spire of 1388–9
St Anne's Chapel (in churchyard, now museum) 14th-C chantry chapel (subsequently grammar school) above earlier undercroft

BARRINGTON, CAMBS, 3,2A
Church of All Saints 13th-C church with later medieval and 19th-C alterations has imposing west tower, 14th-C clerestory and nave roof, and 15th-C porches and north chapel; well-preserved late medieval rood stairs and part of wall painting

BARROW, SHROPS, 5,2D
Church of St Giles Church of Saxon origin has original chancel, early Norman nave, and west doorway with tympanum (now tower arch); south porch built 1705 and 19th-C north transept

BARROW-IN-FURNESS, CUMBRIA, 7,1D
Furness Abbey [EH] (2.5 km. / 1½ m. N) Fine, well-preserved remains of Cistercian abbey founded 1123 with medieval additions include church, chapter house and cloister of c.1230–40, and infirmary built c.1300
Bow Bridge [EH] Late medieval stone bridge across Mill Beck leading to Furness Abbey
Piel Castle [EH] Piel Island (accessible by boat from Roa Island) Substantial ruins of 14th-C castle on Piel Island

BARROWDEN, RUTLAND, 4,1D
Church of St Peter 13th-C church with later medieval additions including west tower with spire; late 12th-C ironwork on south door
Bridge Medieval bridge with five arches; upper part rebuilt 1793

BARRY / Y BARRI, S.GLAMORGAN, 6,5E
St Baruch's Chapel, Friars Road, Barry Island Ruins of Norman pilgrimage chapel
Castle, Park Road Ruined early 14th-C gatehouse and hall of medieval castle
Dovecot Cadoxton Court Fine circular dovecot built 13th C

BARRYSCOURT CASTLE (nr Carrigtohill), CO. CORK
Barryscourt Castle [Dúchas] Imposing 15th-C tower house and bawn wall with alterations and additions of 16th C

BARSHAM, SUFFOLK, 9,5E
Church of the Holy Trinity Norman and later church with round tower and unique stone and flintwork trellis decoration (of indeterminate date) covering exterior east wall and incorporating east window; Norman (disused) and late medieval fonts

BARTHOMLEY, CHESHIRE, 5,2B
Church of St Bertoline Late medieval church with fine 15th-C nave roof, four-bay arcades, west tower, south (Crewe) chapel, and chancel built 1925 retains reset Norman doorway; good late 14th-C effigy of knight, and parclose screen

BARTLOW, CAMBS, 3,3A
Church of St Mary Small church of Norman origin has 12th-C round tower and late medieval north porch and north and south doorways; several good 15th-C wall paintings

BARTON-LE-CLAY, BEDS, 3,1A
Church of St Nicholas Medieval church retains 13th-C arcades and chancel with sedilia, piscina and Easter Sepulchre; imposing 15th-C west tower; carved bosses to roof and good early 16th-C painting of St Nicholas

BARTON TURF, NORFOLK, 4,5D
Church of St Michael and All Angels 14th-and 15th-C church with flint and stone flushwork on tower; 15th-C screens with painted panels

BARTON-UPON-HUMBER, LINCS, 7,5E
Church of St Peter [EH] 13th-, 14th- and 15th-C church has western end originally a small 10th-C Saxon church with Norman bell-stage added to tower
Church of St Mary Major mid to late 12th-C Norman church with later medieval additions

BASINGWERK ABBEY, CLWYD, 6,5A
See Greenfield

BASINGWERK CASTLE, CLWYD, 6,5A
See Bagillt

BASSINGBOURN, CAMBS, 3,1A
Church St Peter and St Paul Medieval church with west tower reworked 1879 retains excellent chancel of c.1340–50 with big east window, good roof, and sedilia and double piscina; rood screen and aumbry

BATCOMBE, SOMERSET, 2,2C
Church of St Mary 14th- to 15th-C church with 16th-C west tower and 17th-C south porch; two octagonal late medieval fonts

BATH, AVON, 2,2C
Bath Abbey Rebuilt church of Saxon and Norman foundation, begun 1499 but not completed until 17th C; superb early 16th-C fan-vaulting, extended to nave 19th C; elaborately carved west front with fine west door of 1617
Church of St Mary Magdalen, Holloway Former chapel of hospital built 1495 and enlarged 1823–4
Church of St Thomas à Becket, Church Street, Widcombe; Parish church built late 15th C with west tower; chancel reworked 1746 and 1861 retains original east window
Sally Lunn's House, 3 Old Liliput Alley Medieval town house much reworked 1600s
Town Walls Fragments of much restored medieval walls survive in Upper Boro' Walls

BATTLE, E. SUSSEX, 3,3E
Church of St Mary Norman church of early and late 12th C with later medieval additions; Norman font with late medieval cover
Battle Abbey [EH] Remains of abbey founded by William I with 13th-C dormitory and 14th-C gatehouse
Pilgrim's Rest Handsome 15th-C timber-framed hall-house

BAULKING, OXON, 2, 4B
Church of St Nicholas Small 13th-C church with unusual stone chancel screen

BAUNTON, GLOS, 2, 3B
Church of St Mary Magdalene Simple towerless Norman church retains original chancel arch, 15th-C south porch, and north vestry added 1800s; good 14th-C wall painting of St Christopher

BAYHAM, E. SUSSEX, 3, 3D
Bayham Old Abbey [EH] Imposing ruins of church and monastic buildings of Premonstratensian abbey founded c.1200 survive in 18th-C landscape setting

BEALIN, CO. WESTMEATH, 11, 3D
Bealin Cross [Dúchas], Twyford (1 km. / ½ m. E of Moydrum Castle ruins) Early 9th-C High Cross with Celtic interlace carving

BEAMINSTER, DORSET, 2, 2D
Church of St Mary Late medieval church with impressive west tower of c.1500 and north chapel of 1505; 19th-C additions; 12th- or 13th-C font

BEAUDESERT (Henley-in-Arden) WARWS, 5, 4E
Church of St Nicholas Norman church with ornate chancel arch and later medieval west tower

BEAULIEU, CO. LOUTH, 11, 4D
Church Small church retains unusual cadaver monument with skeletal effigy of woman (probably mid 15th-C, one of earliest of its kind in Ireland), and late medieval tomb slabs against wall of two-storeyed tower

BEAULIEU, HANTS, 2, 4D
Church of St James Former monastic refectory, best preserved of remaining buildings of 13th-C Cistercian Beaulieu Abbey; surviving mural staircase leading to ornate conical bracket which supported pulpit
Palace House * 14th-C abbey gatehouse incorporated into now mainly 19th-C ancestral home of Dukes of Montagu

BEAULY (Inverness), HIGHLAND, 9, 3D
Beauly Priory [HS] Roofless cruciform church of Valliscaulian monastery founded c.1230 and restored 1900–1 retains chancel completed before 1287, early 14th-C transepts, and west end of nave reconstructed after 1537; two good 15th-C monuments

BEAUMARIS (ANGLESEY), GWYNEDD, 6, 4A
Beaumaris Castle [CADW] The most ambitious and technically sophisticated of all Edward I's castles begun 1295 and left incomplete thirty-five years later; built on a symmetrical plan it has inner ward with six towers and two gatehouses, outer ward with octagonal curtain wall, and encircling moat
Church of St Mary and St Nicholas Early 14th-C church enlarged with new chancel c.1500 and north clerestory of c.1600; medieval monuments, stalls and misericords; in south porch, 13th-C coffin and fine carved coverstone, traditionally believed to be gravestone of Siwan, wife of Lywelwyn ap Iorwerth (d.1237)
Medieval Hall House Tudor Rose (shop), 32 Castle Street 15th-C house with south wing extended and upper floor inserted in hall during 17th C; fine timber roof

BECCLES, SUFFOLK, 4, 5E
Church of St Michael 14th-C church much renewed 15th C has fine two-storeyed south porch, north-west stair turret, and tall 16th-C free-standing tower

BECKENHAM, GREATER LONDON, 3, 2C
Lychgate Late medieval timber lychgate at entrance to St George's churchyard

BECKFORD, WORCS, 5, 3E
Church of St John the Baptist Norman church rebuilt 1200s has fine original north and south doorways with tympana, 13th-C chancel and central tower; late medieval font

BECTIVE ABBEY, CO. MEATH, 11, 4D
Bective Abbey [Dúchas] Well-preserved remains of important Cistercian abbey founded 12th C, rebuilt 1400s, and converted to mansion after 1537 include late 13th-C chapter house, two impressive 15th-C cloister arcades, and imposing south-west tower

BEDALE, N. YORKS, 7, 3D
Church of St Gregory Medieval church has early 13th-C north arcade, south arcade of c.1300, tall 14th-C west tower with later medieval upper levels, and south chapel dated 1556; rib-vaulted crypt beneath chancel contains Saxon fragments; wall paintings and good 14th-C effigies

BEDDINGTON GREATER LONDON, 2, 3C
Church of St Mary the Virgin, Church Road 14th to 15th-C church of 11th-C origin with extensive 19th-C restoration; 13th-C font; chancel stalls with misericords and late medieval brasses

BEDFORD, BEDS, 3, 1A
Church of St Peter de Merton Early medieval church retains Saxon chancel (original nave), crossing tower with Norman bell stage (original west tower), and 19th-C arcades; fine 12th-C south doorway moved from St Peter Dunstable; 15th-C font
Church of St Paul St Paul's Square 14th- and 15th-C church with extensive 19th-C alterations and additions; 14th-C font, pulpit made from stone canopy of early 16th-C reredos, and chancel stalls with misericords
Church of St John the Baptist, St John's Street. Church, probably original chapel of medieval Hospital of St John, has 14th-C chancel, 15th-C west tower, and work of 1869–70
Church of St Mary, St Mary's Square Church of Norman origin with 19th-C additions retains original crossing tower with later medieval top, transepts built later 11th C, and 14th-C chancel

BEELEIGH ABBEY (2 km. / 1¼ m. W of Maldon), ESSEX, 3, 3B
Beeleigh Abbey Remains of Premonstratensian abbey founded c.1180 and incorporated into 16th-C house include rich 13th-C chapter house and dormitory undercroft

BEESTON, CHESHIRE, 5, 2B
Beeston Castle [EH] Remains of castle built c.1220 on high isolated rock include 13th-C inner gatehouse and two towers; remarkable well; stunning views over surrounding countryside

BEESTON, NORFOLK, 4, 3D
Church of St Mary Mainly 14th-C church with clerestory added c.1500 and hammerbeam roof with carved figures; rood screen with defaced painting; benches with poppyheads

BEGINISH (1.5 km. / 1 m. NW of Valentia Island, accessible by boat), CO. KERRY, 12, 1D
Stone Houses [Dúchas] Two stone houses dated by excavation to 1100–1200 survive on east part of island

BEGUILDY, POWYS, 6, 5C
Bryndraenog Late medieval timber house has impressive open hall of c.1480 with cruck trusses, and second hall with gallery of 1636

BELGRAVE, LEICS, 5, 5D
See Leicester

BELSAY, NORTHUMBERLAND, 7, 3B
Belsay Castle [EH] (in grounds of Belsay Hall) 14th-C castle and roofless ruin of two-storeyed 17th-C manor house (attached to medieval building 1614)

BENGEO (Hertford), HERTS, 3, 2B
Church of St Leonard Well-preserved Norman church with 18th- and 19th-C additions has original nave, north and south doorways, and chancel with apse

BENINGTON, HERTS, 3, 2B
Church of St Peter Church of late 13th to early 14th C with north chancel chapel of 1320–30 and 15th-C west tower; fine sedilia, piscina and effigies

BERDEN, ESSEX, 3, 2A
Church of St Nicholas Norman church with original nave, 13th-C transepts, chancel built c.1260–70 with fine internal window surrounds, and 15th-C west tower

BERE FERRERS, DEVON, 1, 4D
Church of St Andrew Church of 12th to 14th C with west tower, three piscinas and late 15th-C south porch; 14th-C east window retains some original glass; recess with figures of c.1340

BERE REGIS, DORSET, 2, 3E
Church of St John the Baptist Norman church with medieval additions including north and south chapels, flint and stone chequerwork tower, and splendid carved timber roof; Norman font and 16th-C traceried bench ends

BERKELEY, GLOS, 2, 2B
Church of St Mary [OCT] 12th-C church with additions of 13th C (including wall paintings), 14th (including Easter Sepulchre) and 15th C (including Berkeley Chapel with alabaster tomb)
Berkeley Castle [HHA] Impressive 12th-C castle remodelled 1340–50 with domestic interiors of the 15th and 16th C and later

BERKHAMSTED, HERTS, 3, 1B
Church of St Peter Large cruciform Norman church with later medieval additions and much 19th- and 20th-C restoration; medieval brasses

Berkhamsted Castle [EH] Extensive but fragmentary remains of large early Norman motte and bailey castle

BERKSWELL, W. MIDLANDS, 5,4D
Church of St John the Baptist Norman church with fine late 12th-C nave arcade, chancel and vaulted crypt with enigmatic octagonal extension

BERRY POMEROY, DEVON, 1,5D
Church of St Mary Medieval church restored 19th C retains full-width screen with original coving, cornice and cresting
Berry Pomeroy Castle [EH] Remains of late medieval castle set in romantic woods above deep ravine and river include gatehouse, stretches of curtain wall, and tower

BERWICK-UPON-TWEED
NORTHUMBERLAND, 8,4E
Berwick-upon-Tweed Castle [EH] Fragmentary remains of Norman and later castle
Town Walls [EH] Late 13th- to early 14th-C town walls, mainly incorporated into 16th-C ramparts

BESFORD, WORCS, 5,3E
Church of St Peter 14th-C timber-framed church restored 1800s with new chancel; 15th-C timber south porch and parts of original rood screen

BESSELS LEIGH, OXON, 2,4B
Church of St Lawrence Norman and medieval church with twin bellcote restored 1632; Norman pillar piscina

BETCHWORTH, SURREY, 3,1D
Church of St Michael Mid 13th-C church with some surviving late Saxon and Norman work (confused by two 19th-C restorations)

BETWYS NEWYDD, GWENT, 6,5E
Church Small medieval church with remarkable late 15th-C rood screen, reaching right up to roof and richly decorated with carved grape vine; Norman font

BEVERLEY, E. RIDING OF
YORKS, 7,5E
Minster Magnificent cathedral-sized 13th-C church with 14th-C nave and west front; Percy Tomb of 1300s in choir
Church of St Mary Splendid cruciform church of mainly 14th and 15th C with central tower rebuilt 1520–30; choir stalls with twenty-eight misericords of 1425–50; painted chancel ceiling of 1445

Dominican Friary, Friars Lane (now Youth Hostel) Remnants of 14th- and 15th-C buildings of friary founded c.1240
North Bar Two-storeyed brick gateway rebuilt 1409–10

BEVERSTON, GLOS, 2,3B
Church of St Mary Small Norman church with south arcade c.1200 and 14th-C chancel; 15th-C rood screen restored 1800s; mutilated Saxon sculpture of Resurrection on south face of tower

BEWCASTLE, CUMBRIA, 7,2B
Bewcastle Cross Tall surviving shaft of famous Northumbrian cross ornamented with superb relief sculpture (c.700) stands in graveyard of Church of St Cuthbert

BIBURY, GLOS, 2,3A
Church of St Mary Large Saxon church with Norman and medieval additions; late Norman font and 13th-C glass

BICESTER, OXON, 2,5A
Church of St Eadburg Norman and 13th-C church with later medieval additions; 13th-C font, and 15th-C screen in north chapel

BICKER, LINCS, 4,2C
Church of St Swithin Norman cruciform church with medieval additions retains two fine 12th-C bays to nave and clerestory, 13th-C chancel and 14th-C crossing; 13th-C sedilia

BICKLEIGH, DEVON, 1,5C
Bickleigh Castle [HHA] Remains of late medieval fortified manor house reworked 20th C with 15th-C gatehouse, and original south range of courtyard (now separately owned Old Court House)
Chapel Thatched Norman chapel has nave with 15th-C windows, and chancel with late medieval wagon roof
Old Court House Building originally part of castle retains medieval hall with good roof

BIERTON, BUCKS, 2,5A
Church of St James Early 14th-C church with crossing tower and tall arcades; some 14th- to 15th-C tiles and good late medieval nave roof

BIGBY, LINCS,
Church of All Saints 13th-C church retains west tower with corbel table; arcade piers with square seats; sculptured Virgin of c.1300; nine-sided medieval font

BILLINGHAM, CO. DURHAM, 7,4C
Church of St Cuthbert Saxon church with fine west tower built c.1000 and nave widened with aisles late 12th and early 13th C; chancel rebuilt 1847 and 1939; fragment of 8th-C cross shaft built into north tower wall

BILTON AINSTY, N. YORKS, 7,4E
Church of St Helen Well-preserved late Norman church retains chancel corbel table, fine west front, and 15th-C chancel chapels; fragments of Saxon crosses and late medieval lectern

BINHAM, NORFOLK, 4,4C
Binham Priory [EH] Norman priory church of 12th C (now parish church) with splendid west front of c.1230; late medieval Seven Sacraments font; ruins of monastic quarters
Binham Wayside Cross [EH] 15th-C cross on village green, marking site of annual fair

BIRKENHEAD, MERSEYSIDE, 5,1A
Birkenhead Priory Remains of Benedictine priory founded 12th C by River Mersey include original rib-vaulted chapter house (now chapel), parts of 13th-C church, guest hall in west range of cloister, and 14th-C refectory undercroft

BIRKIN, N. YORKS, 7,4E
Church of St Mary Complete Norman church with original corbel tables and sculptured ornament on south door, windows and chancel arch; south aisle added c.1330; fragments of 14th-C stained glass; unusual 14th-C monument

BIRMINGHAM,
W. MIDLANDS, 5,3D
Crown Inn, High Street, Deritend. Late medieval timber-framed house with overhanging upper floor and later alterations
Church of St Peter and St Paul, Aston (3 km. /2 m.N of city centre) Medieval church entirely rebuilt 1879–90 retains 15th-C west tower and good 14th to 15th-C monuments
Church of St Nicholas, King's Norton (8 km. / 5 m. SW of city centre) Church of Norman origin restored 1800s has arcades of late 13th and early 14th C, and 15th-C west tower with octagonal spire
Old Grammar School, King's Norton Medieval priest's house has early 15th-C half-timbered upper level and brick and stone ground floor, evidently under built in late 16th C
Saracen's Head Inn, King's Norton Late 15th-C building altered 19th C

Church of St Laurence, Northfield (9 km. / 5 ½ m. SW of city centre) Church of Norman origin retains fine 13th-C chancel, tower with late medieval upper levels, and 14th-C south arcade; late 15th-C roofs and timber trusses
Weoley Castle (museum) (6.5 km. / 4 m. SW of city centre) Excavations of moated sandstone castle built 1264 and fragments of earlier 13th-C wooden buildings which preceded it

BIRNIE (4 km. /2 ½ m. S of Elgin),
GRAMPIAN, 8,3A
Birnie Kirk (St Brandon's) Small well-preserved Norman church of c.1120–50 (altered 1734 and 1891) has original chancel arch and north and south doorways; 12th-C font; early Pictish stone in churchyard

BISHAM, BERKS, 2,5B
Bisham Abbey (open by appointment only) Remains of 13th-C preceptory of Templars (Augustinian priory after 1337 and abbey from 1537) with 14th- and 15th-C additions, converted for domestic use 16th C
Church of All Saints Mainly 19th-C church retains west tower of c.1170–80

BISHOP AUCKLAND
CO. DURHAM, 7,3C
Auckland Castle (Bishop's Palace) *
Medieval palace of Bishops of Durham remodelled 17th and 18th C contains fine great hall of c.1190 (now chapel)

BISHOPS CANNINGS, WILTS, 2,3C
Church of St Mary the Virgin Large cruciform 13th-C church of Norman origin with central tower topped by 15th-C spire

BISHOP'S CLEEVE, GLOS, 2,3A
Church of St Michael and All Angels Fine late Norman cruciform church retains handsome west front and south porch; rebuilt chancel (14th-C) and central tower (1700)
Rectory Parsonage built by Bishop of Worcester c.1250 and altered in 17th C retains original H-plan with hall (now divided) and solar and buttery wings; dovecot and tithe barn nearby

BISHOP'S COURT, DEVON, 1,5C
See Clyst Honiton

BISHOP'S LYDEARD
SOMERSET, 2,1D
Church of St Mary Medieval church with 19th-C additions has tall sumptuous west

tower, four-bay arcades, and low chancel; rood screen and rich early 16th-C benches

BISHOPS STORTFORD, HERTS, 3, 2B
Church of St Michael 15th-C church remodelled 17th and 19th C has spacious nave with six-bay arcades and original roof; 15th-C screen, chancel stalls and misericords
The Black Lion; Medieval timber-framed building with overhanging upper levels occupies prominent corner site

BISHOPSTEIGNTON, DEVON, 1, 5D
Church of St John the Baptist Norman church with west tower added 1815 retains fine original west doorway and tympanum in south wall; Norman font
Bishop's Palace (1 km. / ½ m. NE) Surviving walls of summer palace built 1332

BISHOPSTONE, E. SUSSEX, 3, 2E
Church of St Andrew Saxon church with medieval and 19th-C work retains 8th-C south porticus, Norman west tower, north aisle, chancel, and altar spaces; fine 12th-C carved coffin lid

BISHOPSTONE, HEREFS, 5, 2E
Church of St Lawrence Church of Norman origin restored 1842 has late 13th-C transepts, timber south porch added 14th C and 19th-C bell turret

BISHOPSTONE, WILTS, 2, 3D
Church of St John the Baptist Large cruciform medieval church of Norman origin with richly carved 14th-C ornament and later medieval embattled tower

BISHOPS WALTHAM, HANTS, 2, 5D
Church of St Peter Norman church with 15th-C and later alterations restored 19th C
Bishops Waltham Palace [EH] Norman Bishop's Palace extensively rebuilt 15th C retains 14th-C east range
Town Plan Mainly 17th- and 18th-C houses line parallel and cross streets reflecting medieval grid plan

BISHOPTHORPE, N. YORKS, 7, 4E
Archbishop's Palace Palace with extensive post-medieval rebuilding and front of 1763-9 retains fine 13th-C chapel with lancet windows

BLACKMORE, ESSEX, 3, 3B
Church of St Lawrence Church of former Augustinian priory founded c.1155–60 converted to parochial use 16th C retains splendid timber tower of c.1480 with internal posts

BLACKNESS (6.5 km. / 4 m. N of Linlithgow), CENTRAL, 8, 2E
Blackness Castle [HS] Important castle built 1440s on promontory by Firth of Forth, massively strengthed as artillery fortress during 16th C and restored 1920s, retains original mainmast tower

BLACKROCK, CO. LOUTH, 11, 4C
Heynestown Castle Remains of three-storyed tower house built probably 1500s
Dunmahon Castle (3 km. / 2 m. W) Ruins of square late medieval tower house with vaulted basement and octagonal angle towers
Haggardstown Church (1.5 km. / 1m. W) Ruinous late 15th- or early 16th-C church

BLAKENEY, NORFOLK, 4, 4C
Church of St Nicholas 13th-C church rebuilt 1434 and much restored 19th C; 15th-C west tower and another slender polygonal one at north-east corner (possibly beacon for shipping)
Blakeney Guildhall [EH] Surviving basement storey of building built 1300s, possibly as merchant's house

BLANCHLAND, NORTHUMBERLAND, 7, 3C
Church of St Mary the Virgin 18th-C L-plan church incorporates remains of 13th-C monastic church of Blanchland Abbey (converted to house after 1539 dissolution)
Village The Square, originally part of outer court of abbey, surrounded by surviving medieval monastic buildings including Lord Crewe Arms inn and 15th-C gatehouse

BLARNEY, CO. CORK, 12, 3D
Blarney Castle [Dúchas] Imposing L-shaped, five-storeyed tower-keep of castle built c.1446 on rock over Croomaun with famous Blarney Stone or Stone of Eloquence on parapet

BLEDINGTON, GLOS
Church of St Leonard Norman church enlarged during medieval period has south aisle arcade of c.1300 and fine 15th-C roofs and clerestory with some original stained glass; 12th-C font, 13th-C wall painting, 15th-C bench ends

BLEDLOW, BUCKS, 2, 5B
Church of the Holy Trinity Late Norman and 13th-C church with 14th-C south porch and door; Norman font and fragmentary medieval wall paintings

BLESSINGTON, CO. WICKLOW. 12, 5B
St Mark's Cross [Dúchas] Churchyard contains tall granite cross (formerly known as St Baoithin's Cross) removed from early monastic site (now submerged) at Burgage

BLETCHINGLEY, SURREY, 3, 2D
Church of St Mary the Virgin [OCT] Norman church with 13th- and 15th-C additions, restored 1870; late medieval brasses

BLEWBURY, OXON, 2, 5B
Church of St Michael Cruciform church of Norman origin rebuilt 14th and 15th C retains chancel and crossing work of c.1170–90; some medieval tiles, 15th-C brasses and fine door to rood loft

BLISLAND, CORNWALL, 1, 3D
Church of St Proteus and St Hyacinth Norman church with medieval additions; wagon roofs; Norman and 15th-C fonts

BLITHFIELD, STAFFS, 5, 3C
Church of St Leonard Medieval church built 13th to 14th C retains traceried bench ends with poppyheads

BLOXHAM, OXON, 2, 4A
Church of St Mary Large and impressive medieval church of Norman origin rebuilt 13th, 14th and 15th C; early 14th-C tower with octagon at base of spire; fragments of 14th-C stained glass and 15th-C wall paintings

BLUNDESTON, SUFFOLK, 4, 5D
Church of St Mary Norman church with nave rebuilt 14th C and chancel of 1851; round Norman west tower; medieval dado of rood screen and bench ends

BLUNHAM, BEDS, 3, 1A
Church of St James and St Edmund Good medieval church with Norman tower arch, 13th-C chancel, 15th-C arcades, and work of 1583; beautifully carved, though headless, alabaster effigy of Virgin (14th-C); impressive late medieval stone screen between chancel and south chapel

BLUNTISHAM, CAMBS, 4, 2E
Church of St Mary Medieval church has rare surviving 14th-C polygonal apse, tower with recessed spire, and 15th-C four-bay arcades; good stone corbels to nave roof

BLYBOROUGH, LINCS, 4, 1B
Church of St Alkmund Church much rebuilt 1877–8 retains 13th-C north arcade

and chancel arch; 18th-C west tower reuses medieval gargoyles; fragments of 10th- or 11th-C grave cover, and 15th-C tomb effigy

BLYFORD, SUFFOLK, 4, 5E
Church of All Saints Norman and medieval church has angle piscina with pointed trefoiled arch

BLYTH, NOTTS, 5, 5A
Priory Church of St Mary and St Martin Impressive west part of nave of severe Norman priory church built c.1100 and vaulted c.1400; east wall thought to incorporate part of original pulpitum; medieval south aisle and wooden screens

BLYTHBURGH, SUFFOLK, 4, 5E
Church of the Holy Trinity Big impressive church of mid to late 15th C with tall west tower; original north and south doors and lectern; carved stalls and unusual bench ends with figures in place of poppyheads; font with commemorative inscription of 1449

BOA ISLAND (accessible by boat) CO. FERMANAGH, 11, 3B
Figures [Dúchas] Caldragh graveyard on island in Lower Lough Erne contains two remarkable early Christian or earlier stones with carved figures resembling those at nearby White Island

BOARHUNT, HANTS
Church of St Nicholas Small almost complete Saxon church of c.1060 with 13th-C windows and 19th-C bell turret

BOARSTALL, BUCKS, 2, 5A
Boarstall Tower [NT] Medieval gatehouse with flanking turrets, only surviving part of large 14th-C moated house demolished 18th C

BOBBING, KENT, 3, 3C
Church of St Bartholomew Medieval church restored 1863 has 14th-C north aisle, south porch, west tower and low chancel; good roofs, tracery, brasses, and triple sedilia of c.1300 retaining carved west respond of c.1190

BOCONNOC, CORNWALL, 1, 3D
Church Medieval church mainly rebuilt 19th C has 15th-C font with carved tracery decoration, made in 13th-C shape long out of date

BODIAM, E. SUSSEX, 3, 3D
Bodiam Castle [NT] Splendid square late 14th-C castle with round angle towers and complete moat, thoroughly restored 1919

BODMIN, CORNWALL, 1,3D
Church of St Petroc Norman church mainly rebuilt 1469–72; 12th-C font and ivory Bodmin Casket

BODSEY HOUSE, (2.5 km./1½ m. N of Ramsey), CAMBS, 4,2E
Bodsey House Abbot's residence and chapel of 13th and 14th C with 16th-C alterations

BOHER (8 km./5 m. W of Clara), CO. OFFALY, 11,3D
Church Catholic church contains rare and exquisite roof-shaped shrine or reliquary made 1100s to house bones of St Manchan of nearby Lemanaghan; bronze figures added at later date

BOHO, CO. FERMANAGH, 11,3C
Boho High Cross Carved base and shaft of 9th- or 10th-C cross survives close to parish church
Aghanaglack Cross (2.5 km./1½ m. SW of Boho Crossroads) Base and shaft of medieval High Cross

BOLAM, NORTHUMBERLAND, 7,3B
Church of St Andrew Norman church with 13th-C additions retains late Saxon west tower; damaged 14th-C tomb effigy of knight

BOLDRE, HANTS, 2,4E
Church of St John Late Norman and 13th-C church; tower heightened in brick 1697

BOLINGBROKE CASTLE LINCS, 4,2B
See Old Bolingbroke

BOLSOVER, DERBYS, 5,4B
Church of St Mary Medieval church damaged by fire 1897 and 1960 retains carved tympanum to Norman south chancel door, 13th-C west tower, and fine late 13th-C relief carving of Nativity

BOLTON, CUMBRIA, 7,2C
Church of All Saints Norman church with 17th-C bell turret retains original north doorway with crude but vivid relief carving of two jousting knights above; chancel has late 12th-C lancets

BOLTON, GREATER MANCHESTER, 7,2E
Church of St Mary, Deane Mainly early 16th-C church with 14th-, 15th- and 19th-C work has west tower and good interior
Smithills Hall Museum, Smithills Dean Road * Medieval house (built 1300s) reworked 16th, 17th and 19th C retains early 15th-C great hall with screens passage and fine roof

BOLTON ABBEY, N. YORKS, 7,3D
Bolton Priory * Picturesque ruins of monastic buildings of 12th-C priory in delightful landscape setting; west part of 12th- and 13th-C church remains in use as parish church with east wall replacing vanished pulpitum

BOLTON CASTLE, N. YORKS, 7,3D
See Castle Bolton

BOLTONGATE, CUMBRIA, 7,1C
Church of All Saints 15th- and early 16th-C church has bellcote over west gable, north porch, vestry, transeptal chapels, and nave with fine stone tunnel vault

BONAMARGY FRIARY (1 km./ ½ m. E of Ballycastle), CO. ANTRIM, 11,5A
Bonamargy Friary [EHS] Remains of Franciscan friary probably founded c.1500 (in use until mid 1600s)

BONBY, LINCS, 4,1A
Church of St Andrew Norman and medieval church with 18th-C brick additions retains 12th-C nave and 13th-C chancel arch

BONDLEIGH, DEVON, 1,4C
Church of St James Norman church with much late medieval rebuilding retains 12th-C south doorway with tympanum, and fine carved capitals in wall at east of aisle; good Norman font, and effigy of priest in tomb recess

BONGATE, CUMBRIA, 7,2C
See Appleby

BOOTHBY PAGNELL, LINCS, 4,1C
Church of St Andrew Norman and medieval church heavily restored 19th C
Manor House (in grounds of Boothby Pagnell Hall) (visit by appointment only) Major survival of late Norman manor house with hall and solar above vaulted ground floor

BORLINE (Glen Eynort, Skye) HIGHLANDS (Inner Hebrides), 9,2E
Borline Churches and Cross-Shaft Ruins of two churches in burial ground with part of cross-shaft and several good carved slabs

BORTHWICK, LOTHIAN, 8,3E
Church of St Kentigern Church built mainly 1862–4 retains medieval east end with Norman apse, and sacristy converted to burial aisle c.1606; fine tomb of c.1450 in south chapel

Borthwick Castle Well-preserved castle built c.1430 and restored 1892–1914 on picturesque site with curtain walls and massive fortified tower house containing splendid medieval hall

BOSBURY, HEREFS, 5,2E
Church of the Holy Trinity Church of c.1200 with splendid late 15th- to early 16th-C Morton Chapel; original font

BOSHAM, W. SUSSEX
Church of the Holy Trinity Saxon church enlarged 12th, 13th and 14th C; top stage of tower added 1400s

BOSHERSTON, DYFED, 6,2E
Church of St Michael 13th-C church, with passage-squint between south chapel and chancel, has re-assembled 14th-C preaching cross in churchyard
St Govan's Chapel [CADW] At foot of long flight of steep steps, a tiny primitive 15th-C chapel, wedged between two cliffs at St Govan's Head; medieval holy well further down cliff

BOSSALL, N. YORKS, 7,4D
Church of St Botolph Cruciform church built c.1200 with later medieval alterations; ornate south doorway; odd shaped font (possibly Norman)

BOSTON, LINCS, 4,2C
Church of St Botolph One of Britain's largest parish churches built between c.1310 and c.1390 with famous lofty tower (Boston Stump) begun c.1425–30 and completed c.1510–20; fine set of medieval stalls with carved misericords under 19th-C canopies; medieval monuments and brasses
Shodfriars Hall, South Street Handsome timber-framed guildhall built probably 15th-C and extensively restored 1874
Hussey Tower, Skirbeck Road. Surviving solar wing of brick tower house built c.1450–60

BOTHAL, NORTHUMBERLAND, 7,3B
Church of St Andrew 13th- and 14th-C church with substantial remains of medieval stained glass in heads of aisle windows; 14th- or 15th-C font and cross slab monuments

BOTHWELL (5 km./3 m. NW of Hamilton), STRATHCLYDE, 10,5C
Church of St Bride [SCS] Collegiate church founded 1398 (still in use) has original choir with stone roof and 14th-C sacristy; nave and tower added 1833; sedilia and graveslab of Walter de Moravia, builder of Castle

Bothwell Castle [HS] Remains of magnificent castle probably begun c.1270 near River Clyde, much reworked 14th and 15th C, include massive original keep and fragments of chapel with aumbry and piscina

BOTTESFORD, LEICS, 5,5C
Church of St Mary Large 13th- and 14th-C church with magnificent tower and spire; chancel contains important medieval tombs and brasses from Croxton Abbey and Belvoir Priory as well as Rutland family monuments of 16th and 17th C

BOTTESFORD, LINCS
Church of St Peter's Chains Mainly 13th-C cruciform church restored 19th C has stone altars in transepts and unusual brass sanctuary bell; head of 13th-C cross in churchyard

BOTTISHAM, CAMBS, 3,2A
Church of the Holy Trinity 13th and early 14th-C church with tall west tower and west porch or galilee; medieval stone rood screen with 19th-C dado and two 14th-C wooden parclose screens

BOUGHTON MONCHELSEA KENT, 3,3D
Lychgate Medieval timber lychgate with crown-post roof and benches along sides survives at entrance to St Peter's churchyard

BOURN, CAMBS, 3,2A
Church of St Helen and St Mary Cruciform Norman church has 12th-C nave and fine mid 13th-C west tower with later battlements and crooked lead spire; 19th-C work including chancel arch; handsome hammerbeam roof to chancel, rood screen, and medieval benches and choir stalls (restored)

BOURNE, LINCS, 4,1D
Church of St Peter and St Paul Norman priory church with later medieval additions retains 12th-C nave arcades and 13th-C west front with twin towers (one incomplete)

BOURTON-ON-THE-HILL, GLOS, 2,4A
Church of St Lawrence Norman church with later medieval work including 14th-C chancel and 15th-C clerestory, north porch and font

BOVEVAGH, CO. LONDONDERRY, 11,4B
Old Church (0.5 km./¼ m. N of New Bridge) [EHS] Remains of 13th- or 14th-C church on impressive elevated site with

church-shaped mortuary house (possibly 12th-C) at south-west corner

BOVEY TRACEY, DEVON, 1,5C
Church of St Peter, St Paul and St Thomas of Canterbury Medieval church with 19th-C additions has fine rood screen, parclose screens and stone pulpit of c.1427

BOWES, CO. DURHAM, 7,3C
Bowes Castle [EH] Imposing late Norman tower keep on site of Roman fort

BOWHILL, DEVON, 1,5C
See Exeter

BOWNESS-ON-SOLWAY CUMBRIA, 7,1B
Church of St Michael Late Norman church with work of 1891 retains original north and south doorways and fine font with carved bowl

BOWNESS-ON-WINDERMERE CUMBRIA, 7,2D
Church of St Martin Church consecrated 1483 and restored 1870 retains fine late 15th-C east window possibly from Furness or Cartmel

BOX, WILTS, 2,3B
Church of St Thomas of Canterbury Mainly 14th-C church has central tower, north-east vestry, work of 1713, and south aisle added 1840
Chapel Plaster Simple hospice and chapel built 15th C has west porch, nave, north transept, and chancel

BOXFORD, SUFFOLK, 3,4A
Church of St Mary 14th-C church with original vaulted timber north porch and west tower, and 15th-C additions including nave aisles, chancel chapels and impressive stone-faced south porch

BOXGROVE, W. SUSSEX, 3,1E
Boxgrove Priory [EH] Ruins of Norman priory founded c.1117 with chapter house, guest house, and church of St Mary and St Blaise (dating mainly from c.1220) with 14th-C porch room and sacristy and 16th-C chantry

BOXWELL, GLOS, 2,3B
Church of St Mary 13th-C church with unusual stone bellcote, south porch with stoup, and fine nave arcade; piscina and credence shelf in chancel

BOYLE, CO. ROSCOMMON, 11,2C
Boyle Abbey [Dúchas] Impressive and well-preserved remains of Cistercian abbey founded 1148 and transferred to Boyle 1161 include fine late 12th to early 13th-C church (consecrated 1218) with barrel-vaulted chancel, transepts, crossing tower (heightened 15th C), and nave retaining carved capitals to arcades; domestic buildings added mainly 16th or 17th C although part of original east range survives; fine 13th-C slab with crozier and gloved hand

BOYTON, WILTS, 2,3C
Church of St Mary Medieval church retains 13th-C chancel, south chapel with two-bay arcade and fine west window of c.1280, 14th-C north chapel, transept and north porch tower; sedilia and piscina

BOZEAT, NORTHANTS, 4,1E
Church of St Mary Norman and medieval church with tower rebuilt 1880–3; 14th-C stoup, benches and screen with tracery above painted dado panels

BRAAL CASTLE (1 km. / ½ m. E of Halkirk), HIGHLANDS, 9,4B
Braal Castle Remains of medieval castle close to mansion of 1856 include small 14th-C tower

BRABOURNE, KENT, 3,4D
Church of St Mary Church rebuilt late 12th C has fine priest's doorway, tall nave and chancel, and 13th-C south aisle; good medieval stained glass and monuments include heart shrine of c.1300
Brabourne Mint Medieval hall-house with overhanging upper storey

BRACKLEY, NORTHANTS, 5,5E
Church of St Peter Church of Norman origin with medieval rebuilding retains original south doorway, 13th-C west tower, and early 14th-C chancel chapel; seated figures of 1200s in niches flanking west window
Chapel of St James (Magdalen College School) Chapel of former hospital founded c.1150 and refounded 1423 retains late Norman west doorway and much early 14th-C work; extensive restoration of 1869–70

BRADDAN, ISLE OF MAN, 6,1A
Crosses Good Celtic and Norse crosses with carved work including interlacing stylised dragon figures survive in old parish church

BRADFIELD, DEVON, 1,5C
Bradfield Hall Large medieval mansion house rebuilt 17th to 19th C with early 16th-C hammerbeam roof in hall

BRADFORD, W. YORKS, 7,3E
Cathedral (former Church of St Peter) Large 15th-C parish church with tower of 1493–1508, raised to cathedral status in 1919; superb late medieval font cover with tall spire, buttresses and tracery
Bolling Hall, Bowling Green Road 17th- and 18th-C house, now museum, incorporates medieval tower and other traces of early 15th-C fortified house

BRADFORD ABBAS, DORSET, 2,2D
Church of St Mary the Virgin 15th-C church retains ornate west tower with fine canopied niches (two still with figures); surviving furnishings include stone screen, octagonal font and bench-ends with linenfold panelling

BRADFORD-ON-AVON, WILTS, 2,3C
Church of St Lawrence Almost complete Saxon church rebuilt 10th C on early 8th-C foundations; relief sculpture of two floating angels (part of vanished rood group) on east wall of nave
Church of the Holy Trinity Norman church much rebuilt during medieval period
Tithe Barn [EH] Magnificent early 14th-C monastic granary
Town Bridge 13th-C bridge with chapel half way across, rebuilt 1600s

BRADLEY, STAFFS, 5,3C
Church of St Mary and All Saints Mainly late 13th- and early 14th-C church with tower completed 15th C; Norman font; fragments of medieval stained glass

BRADLEY MANOR, DEVON, 1,5D
See Newton Abbot

BRADLEY OLD HALL GATEHOUSE, LANCS
See Burtonwood

BRADWELL ABBEY, BUCKS, 3,1A
See Milton Keynes

BRADWELL-JUXTA-COGGESHALL, ESSEX, 3,3B
Church of the Holy Trinity Simple church with Norman north and south doorways and 14th-C timber south porch; fine wall paintings of c.1320 and 15th-C screen

BRADWELL-ON-SEA, ESSEX, 3,4B
Church of St Peter-on-the-Wall (3 km. / 2 m. NE) (accessible by footpath only) Remarkably complete nave of small early Saxon church built c.654 of stone with reused Roman bricks

BRAILES, WARWS, 5,4E
Church of St George Large 13th-C church with later medieval additions including imposing 15th-C west tower; 14th-C sedilia with stone arms to seats and font carved with tracery designs

BRAMBER, W. SUSSEX, 3,1E
St Mary's [HHA] Handsome timber-framed house built 1470, former residential quarters of Wardens of Bridge (monks from Sele Priory at Beeding)
Bramber Castle [EH] Ruins and earthworks of Norman castle with keep which also served as gatehouse

BRAMFIELD, SUFFOLK, 4,5E
Church of St Mary Norman round tower near but not attached to mainly 14th-C church with fine painted screen of c.1500

BRAMHALL, GREATER MANCHESTER, 5,3A
Bramhall Hall * House with much 16th-, 17th- and 19th-C work retains timber-framed 15th-C south wing (formerly solar wing) with excellent roof; some early 16th-C stained glass in chapel east window

BRAMLEY, HANTS, 2,5C
Church of St James Much-restored Norman church with many later additions including 17th-C brick west tower; 13th- and 15th-C wall paintings in nave and chancel; fragments of stained glass include 14th-C figures

BRAMPTON, CAMBS, 4,2E
Church of St Mary Mainly late medieval church retains late 13th-C chancel with original piscina and 14th-C west tower; good roofs to nave and aisles and fine misericords to stalls

BRANCEPETH, CO. DURHAM, 7,3C
Church of St Brandon (in castle grounds) Large mainly 13th to 14th-C church with tower begun late 1100s and chancel rebuilt 15th C; rich 15th-C clerestory and nave roof; sumptuous 17th-C furnishings; Brancepeth Castle Impressive castle of enclosure mostly built 1818–21 retains fragments of medieval work

BRANDSBUTT SYMBOL STONE, GRAMPIAN, 8,4B
See Inverurie

BRANSCOMBE, DEVON, 2,1E
Church of St Winfred Norman church with medieval additions retains original central tower and nave, 13th-C transepts and early 14th-C chancel

BRANT BROUGHTON, LINCS, 4, 1C
Church of St Helen Late 13th- and 14th-C church with west tower and tall spire, thoroughly restored late 19th C; 14th-C Trinity sculpture under tower

BRAUNTON, DEVON, 1, 4B
Church of St Brannoc Mainly 13th-C church with Norman south tower and later medieval additions including wagon roof to nave

BRAY, BERKS, 3, 1C
Church of St Michael Large much-restored 14th-C church has two medieval brasses and 15th-C timber lychgate

BREACHACHA (8 km. / 5 m. SW of Arinagour on island of Coll) **STRATHCLYDE, 10, 2A**
Breachacha Castle Curtain-walled 14th-C castle with later additions and restoration of 1965

BREADSALL, DERBYS, 5, 4B
Church of All Saints Medieval church reworked 1915 retains Norman south doorway and four-stage 13th-C tower with fine spire of early 1300s; wooden Pietà of late 14th C

BREAGE, CORNWALL, 1, 1E
Church of St Breaca 15th-C granite church restored 19th C with transepts, south porch, west tower, and fine wall paintings of late 1400s; good Saxon cross head in churchyard

BREAMORE, HANTS, 2, 3D
Church of St Mary Cruciform Saxon church of c.1010 with later Norman and medieval rebuilding; mutilated Saxon sculpture of crucifixion group above south door

BRECHIN, TAYSIDE, 8, 4C
Brechin Cathedral [Round Tower – HS] [SCS] Tall Round Tower of late 10th or early 11th C with richly carved doorway survives attached to 13th-, 14th- and 15th-C cathedral restored 1900–2; 12th-C font and collection of Pictish sculptures
Maison Dieu Chapel [HS] Fragment of south wall of late medieval chapel with good carved work to windows and doors, all that survives of hospital founded 1260s

BRECON / ABERHONDDU POWYS, 6, 4D
Cathedral Surviving 13th- and 14th-C church of Benedictine priory reworked 19th and 20th C retains fine chancel of 1201–8 with flanking chapels, transepts,

crossing tower with early 16th-C upper stage, and good early 14th-C north arcade; carved Norman font of c.1130–50 and 15th-C Golden Rood
Conventual Buildings 14th- and 15th-C buildings restored 17th, 19th and 20th C set within battlemented curtain wall include four-storey tower of canonry and prior's lodging
Christ College Surviving buildings of Dominican friary enlarged as public school 1850s include chapel of c.1240 and early 1300s (part of original friary church), and 14th-C refectory
Church of St Mary Chapel of ease to Benedictine priory reworked 13th to 15th C and 1800s has good arcades, aisles, south porch, and west tower of c.1510–20 with octagonal stair turret
Castle Remains of 12th- and 13th-C buildings of motte and bailey castle
Brecknock Museum, Glamorgan Street Well preserved Neuadd Siarman pillar cross of 10th C in former shire hall built 1839–43
Maen-du Holy Well (1.5 km. / 1 m. NW, on SE slope of Pen-y-Crug Iron Age hillfort) Reconstructed primitive early Christian stone hut

BREDE, E. SUSSEX, 3, 3E
Church of St George Late medieval church of Norman origin
Brede Place 15th-C stone manor house with chapel, altered 16th C with brick additions

BREDON, WORCS, 2, 3A
Church of St Giles Large late Norman church with later medieval additions including 13th-C south chapel and chancel rebuilt c.1300–10; central tower with recessed spire; medieval Easter Sepulchre, monuments, stained glass and heraldic tiles
Bredon Barn [NT] Stone-built 14th-C barn

BREDWARDINE, HEREFS, 5, 1E
Church of St Andrew Early Norman church enlarged c.1300 with 18th-C tower; Norman font and medieval monuments

BREEDON-ON-THE-HILL, LEICS, 5, 4C
Church of St Mary and St Hardulph 13th-C church on hilltop site of Saxon monastery; exceptional collection of late 8th-C carved friezes and sculptured panels mounted on interior walls

BRENT ELEIGH, SUFFOLK, 3, 3A
Church of St Mary Mainly 14th-C church with later west tower and 17th- and 18th-C furnishings; early 14th-C traceried south door and medieval wall paintings

BRENT KNOLL, SOMERSET, 2, 1C
Church of St Michael Church of Norman origin much rebuilt early 15th C has original south doorway, early 14th-C south porch and south transept, and fine roofs; benches with unusual carving

BRENT PELHAM, HERTS, 3, 2A
Church of St Mary Mid 14th-C church with 15th-C west tower retains early 14th-C south door carved with tracery

BRETFORTON, WORCS, 5, 3E
Church of St Leonard Medieval church has good late 12th- to early 13th-C arcades with carved capitals, late 13th-C chancel with lancets, transepts, and 15th-C tower and additions
The Fleece Inn [NT] Medieval half-timbered farmhouse, used as inn after 1848

BREWOOD, STAFFS, 5, 3C
Church of St Mary and St Chad 13th-C church with long chancel, enlarged and altered early 16th and again 19th C

BRIDEKIRK, CUMBRIA, 7, 1C
Church of St Bride Cruciform church built 1868–70 incorporates two Norman doorways and mid 12th-C font with splendid carvings

BRIDFORD, DEVON, 1, 5C
Church of St Thomas-à-Becket Medieval church retains fine rood screen of between 1508 and 1550 with lavish painted ornament and similar parclose screen, both with well preserved colour revealed 1974–81

BRIDGEND / PEN-Y-BONT AR OGWR, M. GLAMORGAN, 6, 4E
Newcastle [CADW] Remains of late 12th-C castle include curtain walling, south tower, and well preserved portal

BRIDGETOWN, CO. CORK, 12, 3C
Priory [Dúchas] Overgrown remains of church and domestic buildings (particularly good refectory) of Augustinian priory founded early 1200s

BRIDGNORTH, SHROPS, 5, 2D
Bridgnorth Castle Remains of medieval castle on River Severn with leaning Norman keep and part of curtain wall

BRIDGWATER, SOMERSET, 2, 1C
Church of St Mary Medieval church of 13th-C origin with fine 14th-C work including tall, elegant spire and 15th-C nave roof; 19th-C clerestory and other additions

BRIDLINGTON, E. RIDING OF YORKS, 7, 5D
Priory Church of St Mary Surviving aisled nave of Norman priory church rebuilt 13th and completed 15th C with rebuilt west end; upper stages of south-west tower added 1800s
The Bayle (now museum*) Late 14th-C priory gatehouse with 17th-C brick additions;

BRIGHTON, E. SUSSEX, 3, 2E
Church of St Nicholas 14th-C church extensively restored 1853 retains original tower and fine carved font of c.1160–70 See also: Portslade

BRIGHTWELL BALDWIN, OXON, 2, 5B
Church of St Bartholomew 14th-C church with 15th-C west tower; medieval stained glass and brasses

BRIGSTOCK, NORTHANTS, 4, 1E
Church of St Andrew Saxon church with medieval additions has original west tower with rounded turret and 14th-C spire, north aisle of c.1190, and 14th-C south arcade; 13th-C sedilia and 15th-C screen
Manor House Medieval manor house rebuilt 17th C, 1890 and 20th C retains single storeyed hall

BRIMSTAGE, MERSEYSIDE, 5, 1A
Brimstage Hall Remains of medieval tower house built after 1398 survive attached to farmhouse and include fine rib-vaulted room on ground floor

BRINKBURN, NORTHUMBERLAND, 7, 3B
Brinkburn Priory [EH] Restored late 12th-C church of Norman priory in beautiful riverside setting

BRINSOP, HEREFS, 5, 2E
Church of St George Small 14th-C church containing superb Norman sculpture of c.1150–60 including carved arches and tympanum with St George

BRISTOL, SOMERSET, 2, 2B
Cathedral Norman abbey church elevated to cathedral status 1542 retains 12th-C chapter house, Elder Lady Chapel

of c.1210–20, early 14th-C chancel, eastern Lady Chapel built 1298 to c.1330, and 14th-C Berkeley and Newton Chapels; transepts, crossing and central tower added c.1470–1515; nave and west towers completed 1868–88; numerous medieval monuments; rare late 15th-C brass chandelier in Berkeley Chapel

Cathedral Precinct Remains of monastic buildings altered 1800s include rib-vaulted chapter house of c.1150–70 with vestibule and sumptuous wall decoration, Norman Great Gateway with upper parts of c.1500, and south range with early 16th-C arcade to refectory

Church of St James Church associated with St James's Priory (founded 1129) retains Norman arcades, west front with wheel window, and 19th-C additions

Church of St John Baptist, Tower Lane Church above St John's Gate with tall 14th-C nave, chancel of after c.1475, and rib-vaulted crypt below

Lord Mayor's Chapel (Church of St Mark), College Green 13th-C chapel of Hospital of St Mark (founded 1220) bought by Bristol Corporation 1541; much late medieval and 19th-C alteration; timber roof, stained glass and numerous monuments of 13th to 15th C and later

Church of All Saints, Corn Street Norman and 15th-C church with 18th-C tower and chancel rebuilt 1850

Church of St Mary Redcliffe, Redcliffe Hill. Large and magnificent church of early 13th to 15th C with spectacular hexagonal north porch of c.1325 richly ornamented with delicately carved foliage; chancel with Lady Chapel and fine stone vaulting; 15th-C monuments and brasses

Church of St Nicholas, High Street Church built 1763–9 replacing medieval predecessor retains crypt or Lower Church of c.1330–50 with rib-vaulted roof and generously carved bosses

Church of St Philip and St Jacob Mainly 15th-C church partly rebuilt late 18th or early 19th C with good north chapel and nave roof

Church of St Stephen Big church built mid 1400s retains handsome slender south-west tower with crown

Temple Church [EH] Victoria Street Surviving tower and walls of 15th-C church on site of 12th-C oval church of Knights Templar

City Walls Scanty remains of medieval city walling

Foster's Almshouses, Colston Street 19th-C almshouses incorporate medieval Chapel of Three Kings of Cologne founded 1504

St Bartholomew's Hospital, Christmas Street. Medieval archway of hospital founded before 1207

Quaker Friars Remains of medieval house of Blackfriars with late 13th-C dormitory and fine roof to upper room in south range

Church of St Mary, Henbury (Outer Bristol) Norman church with good south doorway and six-bay arcade of c.1200

Church of Holy Trinity, Westbury-on-Trym (Outer Bristol) Medieval church with fine early 13th-C arcades and 15th-C polygonal chancel

Westbury College Gatehouse [NT], College Road, Westbury-on-Trym (by prior arrangement) Imposing 15th-C gate-tower of college of priests (founded 13th C)

BRITFORD, WILTS, 2,4D
Church of St Peter Cruciform Saxon and later church has unique carvings of 8th to 9th C and tomb effigy of c.1300.

BRIXWORTH, NORTHANTS, 5,5D
Church of All Saints Impressive early Saxon monastic church of c.675, built in stone with Roman brick arches; apse (rebuilt 10th C) with traces of ambulatory; later Saxon tower above original west porch, and rare outer crypt; Saxon sculpture and reliquary of c.1300

BROAD CHALKE, WILTS, 2,3D
Church of All Saints Medieval church has late 13th-C chancel, north transept with wagon roof, west front of c.1360–70, crossing tower with 15th-C top, and two-storeyed south porch

BROADCLYST, DEVON, 1,5C
Church of St John the Baptist 15th-C church retaining some 14th-C work; tower completed 16th C; roof and ribbed plaster vault dated 1832–3
Marker's Cottage [NT] Late medieval cob house with surviving painted decoration on cross-passage screen

BROADSTAIRS, KENT, 3,5C
Church of St Peter Spacious Norman church much restored 19th C retains long nave with five-bay arcades, north chapel with early 13th-C arcades, aisles widened 1300s, and west tower; 15th-C screen to chapel

BROADWATER (Worthing), W. SUSSEX, 3,1E
Church of St Mary Late Norman church built in stages throughout 12th C; chancel (heavily restored 19th C) contains fine brass of 1432 to John Mapilton

BROADWAY, WORCS, 5,3E
Church of St Eadburga Norman church rebuilt 13th and 14th C has interior dating back to 1200 and crossing tower with rib vault
Abbot's Grange 14th-C grange of Abbots of Evesham with 16th and 20th C additions retains hall, solar, and projecting chapel with fine east window

BROADWELL, OXON, 2,4B
Church of St Peter and St Paul Spacious late Norman church with remodellings of 13th C, 15th C and 1873 retains north and south doorways of c.1190, transepts built c.1250, and west tower with 13th-C octagonal spire; font of c.1200

BROCHEL CASTLE, HIGHLAND, 9,2D
See Raasay

BRODICK (Isle of Arran), STRATHCLYDE, 10,4C
Brodick Castle [NTS] (2.5 km. / 1 ½ m. N) Site of Viking fort houses medieval castle with 13th-C work and enlargements of 1652 and 1844

BROMFIELD, SHROPS, 5,2D
Church of St Mary Church of Benedictine priory founded 1155 with medieval and 19th-C work retains 12th-C east end and north-west tower built mainly c.1300
Priory Gatehouse [LT] Surviving 14th-C gatehouse of priory with later timber-framed upper storey

BROMHAM, BEDS, 3,1A
Church of St Owen Mainly late medieval church in grounds of Hall has north arcade of c.1300, 14th-C chancel, and 19th-C work; fine brass to Thomas Wideville and two wives (d.1435)
Bromham Hall House retains reset 14th-C doorway and good king-post roof
Bridge and Causeway Medieval bridge and causeway with rebuildings of late 15th C and 1813

BROMHAM, WILTS, 2,3B
Church of St Nicholas Norman church with good later medieval work including ornate Baynton Chapel of 1492 with pinnacles and painted ceiling; important monuments to Tocotes, Beauchamp and Baynton families

BROMPTON-IN-ALLERTONSHIRE, N. YORKS, 7,3D
Church of St Thomas Extensively restored late Norman church with important group of well-preserved Anglo-Danish hog-backed tombstones

BROMSGROVE, WORCS, 5,3D
Church of St John the Baptist Large red sandstone church of Norman origin rebuilt 13th, 14th and 19th C has west tower with tall spire, and good arch between chancel and north chapel; fine alabaster monuments include that to Sir Humphrey Stafford (d.1450)
Avoncroft Museum of Buildings* Rescued and restored historic buildings of all periods, including magnificent 14th-C roof of Guesten Hall of Worcester Cathedral

BRONLLYS, POWYS, 6,5D
Bronllys Castle [CADW] Round tower built early or mid 13th C on tall motte

BROOK, KENT, 3,4D
Church of St Mary Well-preserved early Norman church with monumental west tower containing upper chapel; 12th- to 14th-C wall paintings and fine tiles in sanctuary

BROOKE, RUTLAND, 5,5C
Church of St Peter Church of Norman origin remodelled 13th C and with work of c.1579 retains mid 12th-C north arcade, Norman doorway and 13th-C west tower; Norman font and late 12th-C ironwork on north door

BROOKLAND, KENT, 3,4D
Church of St Augustine Unrestored medieval church rebuilt c.1790 with mid 13th-C chancel and 14th-C timber porch; remarkable detached timber belfry of late 12th to 13th C with 15th-C work; fine lead font of c.1200 and 14th-C wall painting

BROOMFIELD, SOMERSET, 2,1C
Church of All Saints Medieval church retains west tower, early 14th-C chancel, early 16th-C north aisle, and wagon roofs with carved angles; good set of benches

BROOMHOLM PRIORY, NORFOLK, 4,5C
See Bacton

BROUGH, CUMBRIA, 7,2C
Brough Castle [EH] Norman castle with 13th- and 14th-C additions restored 17th C

BROUGH OF BIRSAY (on tidal island 30 km. / 20 m. NW of Kirkwall), ORKNEY, 9, 5A
Church of St Peter [HS] Remains of early 12th-C Norse church set in rectangular enclosure on small island; cast of late 7th-C Pictish stone and early medieval gravestone to south
Settlement [HS] Surviving foundations of Norse village set outside of church enclosure

BROUGHAM, CUMBRIA, 7, 2C
Brougham Castle [EH] Ruins of late 13th- to early 14th-C castle restored 1600s on banks of River Eamont

BROUGHTON, BUCKS, 3, 1A
Church of St Lawrence Church retains early 14th-C nave and chancel and later medieval west tower; fine, though restored, 14th- to 15th-C wall paintings include Pietà of c.1400

BROUGHTON, LINCS, 4, 1A
Church of St Mary Saxo-Norman church remodelled 12th to 15th and 19th C retains 11th-C west tower with late medieval upper levels, 13th-C chancel and 14th-C arcades; fine 14th-C effigies and brasses

BROUGHTON, OXON
Church of St Mary Church built c.1300 with later medieval alterations and 19th-C restoration retains good west tower with broach spire; Norman font, rare 14th-C stone screen, medieval wall paintings, and fine monuments
Broughton Castle [HHA] Well preserved fortified manor house begun c.1300 and remodelled and enlarged 16th C retains moat, gatehouse, great hall, and solar wing; unaltered chapel with 14th-C glass and tiles

BROUGHTY CASTLE, TAYSIDE, 8, 3D
See Broughty Ferry

BROUGHTY FERRY, TAYSIDE, 8, 3D
Broughty Castle [HS / Dundee Museums] Fine tower house built mainly early 16th C but dating from 1400s has 19th-C alterations; castle houses museum of whaling and fishery
Claypotts Castle [HS] Remarkably complete 16th-C Z-plan tower house

BROXBOURNE, HERTS, 3, 2B
Church of St Augustine Large 15th- and 16th-C church restored 1856–7 with west tower, rich west door, two-storeyed vestry, and chapels; good brasses and original roof to nave

BRUTON, SOMERSET, 2, 2C
Church of St Mary Medieval church with 14th-C crypt, north porch tower, 15th-C nave and fine west tower; chancel rebuilt 1743
Abbey Wall Surviving fragments of wall of Augustinian priory founded 1142
Abbey Court House Building of mid 1400s with timber-framed upper level
Dovecot Tall, four-gabled dovecot belonging to abbey, perhaps 16th-C

BRYMPTON D'EVERCY, SOMERSET, 2, 2C
Church of St Andrew Church has 14th-C transepts, chancel of c.1400, mid 15th-C north chancel chapel, and unusual western bellcote; font of early 1300s, stone rood screen, and good monuments
Brympton D'Evercy House House built c.1520 with later additions and alterations
Chantry House Oblong chantry house of 15th C

BRYNSIENCYN (ANGLESEY), GWYNEDD, 6, 3A
Llanidan Old Church (St Nidan's) Remaining 14th- to 15th-C ruins of fine double-naved medieval church largely demolished 1844 include nave arcade, window and door

BUCKDEN, CAMBS, 4, 2E
Church of St Mary Mainly 15th-C church has embattled aisles and clerestory, and rich south porch; 13th-C sedilia and piscina, monuments to bishops, and medieval stained glass
Buckden Palace Remains of palace of Bishops of Lincoln built before mid 13th C includes late 15th-C Great Tower, inner gatehouse, outer gateway and walling
Lion Hotel Timber-framed building of c.1500; entrance lounge has moulded beams and boss with Agnus Dei

BUCKFASTLEIGH, DEVON, 1, 4D
Buckfast Abbey * Important Cistercian monastery rebuilt on original plan as Benedictine house after 1882 with 20th-C additions retains 12th-C gateway, recently restored early 14th-C guest hall (in Outer Court), Abbot's Tower, and altered medieval gatehouse;
Church of Holy Trinity 13th-C church restored 1844–5 with original west tower, transepts, and 15th-C nave arcades; Norman font; ruins of 13th- to 14th-C chapel in churchyard

BUCKINGHAM, BUCKS, 2, 5A
Chantry Chapel [NT] Market Hill (interior visit by written appointment only); Oblong chapel built 1475, later converted to Latin School and restored 1875, retains Norman south doorway

BUCKLAND, DEVON, 1, 4D
Buckland Abbey [NT] 16th-C house converted from Cistercian abbey (founded 1278) incorporates nave, chancel and central tower of original church; large early 15th-C abbey barn

BUCKLAND, GLOS, 2, 3A
Church of St Michael Interesting medieval church built 13th to 15th C with 16th-C work; rood steps and aumbry survive; 14th-C table tomb in churchyard
Rectory Well-preserved stone parsonage house built between 1466 and 1483 with 17th- and 19th-C work retains fine hall with timber roof and some original stained glass

BUCKLAND IN THE MOOR, DEVON, 1, 4D
Church of St Peter Small medieval church with traceried and coved screen and wagon roofs in chancel, nave and south porch; boldly carved Norman font

BUCKLAND NEWTON, DORSET, 2, 2D
Church of the Holy Rood Medieval church with early 13th-C chancel, and 15th-C west tower and south porch retains unusual Norman sculpture above south doorway; early 16th-C benches

BUCKMINSTER, LEICS, 4, 1D
Church of St John the Baptist Medieval church remodelled 15th C and 1883–4 has late 13th-C tower and early 14th-C nave arcades; 13th-C double piscina and triple sedilia in chancel and 15th-C font

BUCKWORTH, CAMBS, 4, 1E
Church of All Saints Church of Norman origin much rebuilt 1200s has late 13th-C three-bay south arcade, fine west tower with broach spire, chancel built c.1300 with priest's doorway, and good late medieval nave roof

BUILDWAS, SHROPS, 5, 2C
Buildwas Abbey [EH] Picturesque remains of 12th-C abbey include chapter house, infirmary, monk's parlour, dormitory and church with central tower and transepts

BUITTLE, DUMFRIES AND GALLOWAY, 10, 5E
Old Parish Church Roofless remains of church built 12th and 13th C and altered 16th to 18th C with plain nave and more elaborate chancel

BUNBURY, CHESHIRE, 5, 2B
Church of St Boniface Church built 14th and 15th C with post-medieval alterations has west tower, wide chancel, treasury, and 19th-C clerestory; stone reredos, alabaster monument to Sir Hugh Calveley (d.1394), and important screen dated 1527 to south-east chapel

BUNCRANA, CO. DONEGAL, 11, 3A
O'Doherty's Castle [Dúchas] Three-storeyed keep by River Crana with first two levels built after 1333 and upper floor added 1602

BUNCTON, W. SUSSEX, 3, 1E
Church of All Saints Well-preserved Norman church with 14th-C piscina; 19th-C bellcote

BUNGAY, SUFFOLK, 4, 5E
Church of St Mary Church of former Benedictine nunnery founded c.1160 much altered 14th and 15th C retains splendid south-west tower begun c.1470, and two-storeyed north porch
Church of the Holy Trinity Modest church with medieval additions and 20th-C chancel retains 11th-C round tower and Norman north window in nave
Castle Remains of large Norman keep with rare 12th-C mining gallery in foundations

BUNNY, NOTTS, 5, 5C
Church of St Mary Mainly 14th-C church has west tower with crocketed spire, long chancel reroofed 1718, and sedilia and piscina

BUNRATTY, CO. CLARE, 12, 3B
Bunratty Castle [Dúchas] Well-preserved and restored castle built c.1450–67 on site of 13th-C predecessor has large banqueting hall on first floor (modern wooden roof) with handsome apartments above; fine collection of 14th- to 17th-C furniture and fittings

BURES, SUFFOLK, 3, 3A
Church of St Mary Handsome church built mainly 1300s to 1400s retaining tower of late 13th to early 14th C has attractive north porch, and ornate south (Waldegrave) chapel founded 1514; 14th-C wooden effigy of knight, 15th-C armorial

font, and late medieval founder's tomb in chancel

BURFORD, OXON, 2,4A
Church of St John the Baptist Norman church remodelled 15th C retains central tower of *c*.1160 with upper stage and spire added *c*.1450, 14th-C chapel with crypt, and ornate three-storeyed south porch; good medieval screens
Bridge; 14th to 15th-C bridge of four arches crosses River Windrush
Medieval Buildings Medieval buildings include: 14th-C Hill House; 15th-C London House; Great Almshouses founded 1457; Highway Hotel of *c*.1500

BURGHEAD, GRAMPIAN, 8,3A
Burghead Well [HS] King Street. Rock-cut well, supposedly early Christian baptistry

BURGH-NEXT-AYLSHAM, NORFOLK, 4,4D
Church of St Mary Medieval church has chancel of *c*.1220–30 with fine blank arcading, north chapel, 15th-C west tower, and 19th-C nave; 15th-C octagonal font

BURLEIGH, TAYSIDE, 8,3D
Burleigh Castle [HS] Remains of medieval castle include late 15th-C keep with upper hall and vaulted cellar, and round gate tower of 1582

BURLEY ON THE HILL, RUTLAND, 4,1D
Church of the Holy Cross Medieval and 19th-C church connected via corridor to late 17th-C Burley House has Norman north arcade, late 13th-C south arcade, and west tower built 1300s; fine 15th-C font

BURNCHURCH, CO. KILKENNY, 12,4C
Castle [Dúchas] Well-preserved six-storeyed 15th- or 16th-C castle (occupied until 1817) with sole surviving turret of bawn wall

BURNHAM, BUCKS, 3,1C
Church of St Peter Medieval church with 13th-C arcades and north transept; upper part of south transept tower added 1891
Burnham Abbey Extensive remains of Augustinian house founded 1266 and altered 16th C, now part of Anglican nunnery, include cloister east range with chapter house and 13th-C sacristy, infirmary, and precinct wall
Huntercombe Manor Medieval house with 17th- and 19th-C remodellings retains 14th-C work to interior

BURNHAM DEEPDALE, NORFOLK, 4,3C
Church of St Mary Church with Saxon round tower, north doorway of *c*.1190 and 14th-C north arcade; fine Norman font carved with labours of months

BURNHAM NORTON, NORFOLK, 4,3C
Church of St Margaret Church of Saxon origin with Norman round tower, arcades of *c*.1180, round-headed windows, and 13th- to 14th-C work; Norman font, rood screen of 1458, and fine paintings on wooden pulpit of *c*.1475
Friary Surviving 14th-C gatehouse of Carmelite friary founded 1241 with fine flushwork panelling

BURNLEY, LANCS, 7,2E
Townley Hall Art Gallery and Museum * Three ranges of courtyard house totally reworked 17th C, 1725–30 and 1817; original chapel from demolished east range (transferred to north-west corner *c*.1700) retains finely carved frieze of *c*.1500 and other woodwork

BURPHAM, W. SUSSEX, 3,1E
Church of St Mary Church built mainly 1160–1220 with 19th-C additions retains Norman north doorway, north transept, rich vaulted chancel, and tower of *c*.1400; 12th-C piscina and double aumbry

BURRISCARRA, CO. MAYO, 11,2D
Churches [Dúchas] Remains of mainly 15th-C church belonging to abbey founded 1298 and 14th-C parish church in graveyard nearby

BURRISHOOLE (3 km. / 2 m. NW of Newport), CO. MAYO, 11,1C
Friary [Dúchas] Ruins of Dominican friary founded 1486 by inlet of sea include church with well preserved windows and east wall of cloister

BURRY HOLMS, GLAMORGAN, 6,3E
See Llangennith

BURSTOW, SURREY, 3,2D
Church of St Bartholomew Church of Norman origin much rebuilt 15th to 16th C has unusual timber west tower with weatherboarding below and shingles above; late medieval font and piscina

BURTON, W. SUSSEX, 3,1E
Church Simple, unrestored church repaired 17th C retains Norman nave and chancel; good 15th-C rood screen with beam; stone effigy and wall painting

BURTON AGNES, E. RIDING OF YORKS, 7,5D
Church of St Martin Norman church has fine mid 12th-C north arcade, 13th-C south arcade, chancel rebuilt 1730 and 1800s, late medieval clerestory, and west tower; Norman font and fine monuments
Manor House [EH] Rare surviving Norman house built *c*.1170–80 and encased in brick in 18th C retains fine undercroft and hall with 15th-C roof

BURTON DASSETT, WARWS, 5,4E
Church of All Saints Norman church with later medieval additions retains 13th-C arcades, long chancel of *c*.1300, transepts, and 15th-C south aisle; medieval tiles

BURTON LAZARS, LEICS, 5,5C
Church of St James Medieval church has 13th-C bellcote with saddleback roof and spire, and four bay arcades; north doorway of *c*.1300 and 15th-C clerestory roof

BURTONWOOD, CHESHIRE, 5,2A
Bradley Old Hall Gatehouse Remains of gatehouse dating from *c*.1460–5

BURWELL, CAMBS, 4,3E
Church of St Mary Handsome church built mainly 15th C with large windows, spacious interior, ornate chancel, and good north porch retains Norman work to west tower; wheel window above chancel arch and fine tracery

BURY, CAMBS, 4,2E
Church of the Holy Cross Spacious church of Norman origin has 12th-C chancel arch, west portal with tympanum, north arcade of *c*.1230, good 13th-C west tower with lancets, and 15th-C south side; fine early 14th-C wooden lectern with stone of 1200s as base; late medieval screen and benches

BURY ST EDMUNDS, SUFFOLK, 4,3E
Abbey [EH] Remains of important Benedictine monastery include parts of abbey church, domestic buildings, precinct walls, Norman Gate of *c*.1120–48, and Great Gate built *c*.1330–40
Church of St Mary Handsome 15th-C church incorporating remains of older building has rich south façade, large west window, eastern rood stair turrets, and spacious interior with splendid carved timber roof
Moyse's Hall Museum *, Cornhill 12th-C domestic building, probably connected

with abbey, now housing local history museum
Town Surviving Norman and medieval town plan
Guildhall Former guildhall built probably late 15th C with wings reworked 1807 retains original king-post roof over whole length of building

BUSHMEAD, BEDS, 3,1A
Bushmead Priory [EH] Fragments of Augustinian priory founded *c*.1195 include refectory range and kitchen fireplace

BUTLEY PRIORY, SUFFOLK, 3,5A
Gatehouse Surviving early 14th-C gatehouse of former Augustinian priory founded 1171 boasts unusually early flushwork and heraldic decoration

BUTTEVANT, CO. CORK, 12,3C
Friary [Dúchas] Ruined 13th-C church of Franciscan Friary of St Thomas à Becket founded 1251 has long nave and choir, south transept, good carved details, and 15th-C work; crypt and sub-crypt beneath chancel; two early Barry tombs in nave

BUTTINGTON, POWYS, 6,5B
Church of All Saints Simple medieval church with weatherboarded bell turret, good 15th-C roof, rood beam, and porch dated 1686; fine capital of *c*.1220 (now font)

BYFIELD, NORTHANTS, 5,5E
Church of the Holy Cross Mainly 13th-C church retains rich west portal, west tower with 15th-C upper level, and tall chancel with fine windows

BYLAND ABBEY, N. YORKS, 7,4D
Byland Abbey [EH] Extensive ruins of important late 12th-C Cistercian monastery include cloister, kitchen and refectory; large, impressive church has outstanding capitals and medieval floor tiles

BYWELL, NORTHUMBERLAND, 7,3B
Church of St Andrew [CCT] Church with 19th-C additions retains fine late Saxon west tower; fragment of Saxon cross shaft and set of medieval cross slabs
Church of St Peter Church of Saxon origin with 19th-C work has chancel remodelled early 1200s and plain 14th-C west tower; medieval cross slabs
Village Cross 13th-C cross shaft with 18th-C finial
Bywell Castle Substantial remains of early 15th-C gatehouse tower

CADNEY, LINCS, 4, 1A
Church of All Saints Mainly 13th-C
church retains Norman south arcade;
fittings date from restoration of 1912–14

CADZOW CASTLE (2.5 km. / 1½ m. SE
of Hamilton), STRATHCLYDE, 10, 5C
Cadzow Castle [HS] (in grounds of
Chatelherault Country Park, view exterior
only) Ruins of castle begun 1500 and
finished c.1550

CAERGWRLE, CLWYD, 6, 5A
Hope Castle Ruins and earthworks of
mainly 13th-C castle survive on hilltop site

CAERHUN, GWYNEDD, 6, 4A
Church of St Mary 13th-C church with
15th- and 16th-C additions survives
in corner of ruins of Roman fort

CAERLAVEROCK, DUMFRIES
AND GALLOWAY, 7, 1B
Caerlaverock Castle [HS] Triangular
castle of 13th to 17th C with two south
towers and impressive double-fronted
gatehouse; west range built c.1500

CAERNARVON / CAERNARFON,
GWYNEDD, 6, 3A
Caernarvon Castle [CADW] Magnificent
stone castle with polygonal towers and
colour-banded masonry inspired by
Constantinople, begun 1283 for
Edward I on rocky site and left not
fully completed in 1327; domestic and
official accommodation mainly in towers
surrounding upper and lower wards;
King's Gate protected by drawbridge,
five gates and six portcullises
Church of St Mary Early 14th-C church,
partly rebuilt 1811
Town [Bath Tower – LT] Contemporary
walled town with eight towers and two
gates retains Edward I's grid street plan
Bridge Medieval bridge survives below
street outside East Gate

CAERPHILLY, GLAMORGAN, 6, 5E
Caerphilly Castle [CADW] Impressive
castle (largest in Wales) built c.1268–71
with ingenious and spectacular water
defences and famous leaning tower;
double concentric walls with four
gatehouses, and original great hall
remodelled 1320s
Court House (now public house)
Medieval courthouse much reworked
18th C

CAHERCOMMAUN, CO. CLARE, 12, 2B
Fort [Dúchas] Ambitious stone fort with
three concentric walls set on imposing
cliff edge

CAHIR, CO. TIPPERARY, 12, 3C
Cahir Castle [Dúchas], Castle Street
Remains of impressive, substantial castle
(among largest of period in Ireland) built
14th or 15th C on rock-island in River
Suir include towered curtain wall, three-
storeyed keep, and great hall reworked
1842 as church
Cahir Abbey (1 km. / ½ m. N) Remains
of choir and tower of Augustinian priory
founded c.1220

CAIRNBULG (4 km. / 2½ m. SE of
Fraserburgh), GRAMPIAN, 8, 4A
Cairnbulg Castle Medieval castle with
large 14th-C keep and 15th- and 16th-C
alterations and additions

CAISTER, NORFOLK, 4, 5D
Caister Castle Substantial remains of
rectangular brick castle built 1432–43
with moat include solar tower and
walls of great hall
Church of the Holy Trinity Medieval
church with early 13th-C nave and 15th-C
arcade; large font, and 14th-C sedilia and
piscina

CAISTOR, LINCS, 4, 1A
St Peter and St Paul Medieval church
retains 11th-C quoins to 12th-C tower, and
13th-C arcades; chancel and nave roof
restored 19th C; two fine 14th-C effigies

CAISTOR ST EDMUND,
NORFOLK
Church of St Edmund Medieval church
with chancel of c.1300 and west tower with
brick and flint battlements has richly
carved early 15th-C font and wall paintings

CALDER, CUMBRIA, 7, 1C
Calder Abbey Remains of Cistercian
abbey founded 1134 include church, 13th-C
chapter house, dormitory and 14th-C
gatehouse

CALDEY ISLAND (accessible by boat
from Tenby harbour), DYFED, 6, 3E
Old Priory Remains of Norman and
medieval Benedictine priory, now used
by modern Cistercian abbey; medieval
monastic buildings surrounding cloister,
the most complete group surviving in
Wales, include compact 13th-C church,
gatehouse, guest accommodation,
refectory, dormitory and Prior's
Tower

CALDICOT, GWENT, 6, 5E
Church of St Mary Fine medieval church
with central tower and richly decorated
south porch
Castle * Norman castle with

well-preserved early 13th-C keep, curtain
wall and towers of c.1250 and great gatehouse and Woodstock Tower of 1384–9

CALEDON, CO. TYRONE, 11, 4C
Cross (0.5 km. / ¼ m. NE of Caledon
House) Head and shaft of early Christian
High Cross survive at Lady Jane's Well
(removed from site of early monastery
at Glenarb in 1872)

CALLAN, CO. KILKENNY, 12, 4C
Friary [Dúchas] Remaining church of
friary founded 1462 for Augustinian
Observants (built 1467–70) has good
doorway and fine rich sedilia in choir
Church of St Mary [Dúchas] Interesting
medieval church built c.1460 retaining
square west tower of c.1250 has roofless
aisled nave and chancel restored for
Protestant use; fine sculptured details
(eg. head of lady above north door),
large font, and fragments of good 15th-
to 17th-C monuments

CALLINGTON, CORNWALL, 1, 3D
Church of St Mary Church consecrated
1438 with outer north aisle added 1882
retains three-storeyed west tower and
clerestory; good Norman font and early
16th-C monument to Sir Robert
Willoughby de Broke; late medieval
churchyard cross
Dupath Well [EH] (1.5 km. / 1 m. E) Near
complete well house built over holy well
of c.1500

CALNE, WILTS, 2, 3B
Church of St Mary Handsome church of
mainly 15th C retains nave arcades built
c.1160–70, 14th-C north chapel, and
vaulted north porch of c.1470; much
17th-and 19th-C work including north
tower added after 1638

CAMBRIDGE, CAMBS, 3, 2A
St Bene't's Church, St Bene't's Street
Saxon tower and tower arch (c.1040) of
church with nave and aisles rebuilt c.1300
'School of Pythagoras' (now part of St
John's College) Stone-built hall of late
12th C, with 13th- and 14th-C alterations,
probably built as private house
Round Church of the Holy Sepulchre,
Bridge Street. One of Britain's few
surviving Norman round churches
(c.1130), restored 19th C
Church of St Mary Magdalene,
Newmarket Road. Mid 12th-C church,
originally chapel of leper hospital
Timber-framed houses Medieval timber-
framed houses survive in Northampton
Street and Magdalene Street

University buildings Medieval buildings
include: **Peterhouse** – 13th-C hall (too
much altered to be recognizable); **Divinity
School** (north range of Cobble Court in
Old Schools building, King's Parade, late
14th-C); **Jesus College** – 12th to 13th-C
Benedictine nunnery buildings incorporated into College including the chapel
(the surviving part of the former nunnery
church) with double piscina and double
sedilia in the 13th-C chancel and some
carved bench ends of c.1500; gatehouse
1497; **Corpus Christi College** – Old Court
(14th-C); **Magdalene College** – First
Court (begun c.1430) and much restored
15th-C chapel; **Queens' College** – Front
Court and Great Gatehouse (mid 15th-C);
St John's College – First Court and
gatehouse (begun 1511); **Trinity College** –
"King Edward's Tower" (rebuilt gatehouse
of 1426–33) and Great Gate of c.1490 with
corner turrets added 1528–9
King's College Chapel *, off King's Parade
Famous late medieval chapel of King's
College founded 1441 by Henry VI with
magnificent fan vault and stained glass of
early 16th-C; fine brass lectern c.1515;
screen and stalls date from c.1530–5
St Mary the Great, King's Parade.
Impressive late 15th-C church has
splendid interior and fine nave roof
with large bosses, completed in 1508;
W tower 1593–1608
Medieval Churches Other medieval
churches include: **St Botolph**
(Trumpington Street); **St Edward**
(St Edward's Passage); **St Mary the
Less** (Trumpington Street); **St Michael**
(Trinity Street); **Holy Trinity**
(Market Street)

CAMBUSKENNETH ABBEY, (1.5 km. /
1 m. E of Stirling), CENTRAL, 10, 5B
Cambuskenneth Abbey [HS] (view
exterior only) Ruins of Augustinian
abbey founded c.1140 by River Forth
below Stirling Castle with fine, near
complete freestanding bell-tower
(mainly late 13th-C) and fragments
and foundations of church and
domestic buildings

CAMELEY, SOMERSET, 2, 2C
Church of St James Medieval church
retains Norman arch separating chancel
from nave and Norman font; unrestored
interior of 18th and 19th-C

CAMPBELTOWN,
STRATHCLYDE, 10, 3D
Campbeltown Cross NE end of Main
Street; 14th-C cross with finely carved

figures and motifs, removed 17th C from Kilkivan

CAMPSALL, S. YORKS, 7, 4E
Church of St Mary Magdalene Spacious Norman church with medieval reworking has fine original west tower, transepts, good 14th-C south doorway, and 15th-C embellishments; tall rood screen
Vicarage Medieval manor house built 15th C

CANFORD MAGNA, DORSET, 2, 3E
Church Saxon church retains original nave (now chancel) and Norman nave and north tower; west end of 1876–8
Canford Manor 19th-C mansion converted to school 1923 retains medieval John of Gaunt's kitchen with original fireplaces and louvred chimneys

CANNINGTON, SOMERSET, 2, 1C
Church of St Mary Spacious medieval church with rich late 14th-C west tower and early 16th-C body
Gurney Manor [LT] Late medieval house built around courtyard with later remodelling and additions has well-preserved original work including oratory and pentice

CANNISTOWN, CO. MEATH, 11, 4D
Church of St Brigid [Dúchas] Well-preserved remains of church built 12th C on ancient site and reworked late 15th or early 16th C; fine original chancel arch with carved imposts

CANON ISLAND (accessible only by boat), CO. CLARE, 12, 2B
Abbey [Dúchas] Remains of buildings of Augustinian abbey founded late 12th C include long early 13th-C church with south tower and chapels added 1400s and 15th-C domestic buildings

CANON PYON, HEREFS, 5, 2E
Church of St Lawrence 13th and 14th-C church with tower and fine interior; carved misericords and indents of c.1400

CANTERBURY, KENT, 3, 4D
Cathedral * Great Cathedral church of Archbishop of Canterbury retains crypt of after 1096 with finely carved capitals, splendid choir, Trinity Chapel and Corona of 1175–84, soaring nave rebuilt 1378–c.1405, south-west tower of 1424–34, and slender central tower ("Bell Harry") built c.1490–1503; remains of 7th-C Reculver church in crypt; important medieval stained glass, wall paintings and monuments

Monastic Buildings Extensive surviving buildings of large Norman monastery of Christ Church rebuilt 14th C include early 12th-C infirmary, large Court Gate, octagonal Lavatory Tower built before c.1160 to infirmary cloister, oblong chapter house (1304), early 14th-C pentice, and great cloister walks (1390–1411)
Archbishop's Palace Mansion built 1897–9 incorporates medieval work
Christ Church Gate Lavish gate begun 1517 and finished 1520–1
St Augustine's Abbey [EH] Remains of abbey founded 598 and partially incorporated in 19th-C college include walling of 7th-C church of St Pancras, Abbot Wulfric's rotunda of c.1050, crypt of church begun 1070, Great Gateway built 1300–9, and Cemetery Gate of before 1391
Conduit House [EH], King's Park Monastic waterworks which supplied St Augustine's Abbey
Blackfriars Blackfriars Street. Surviving 13th-C frater (refectory) and guest hall of Dominican friary
Greyfriars, Stour Street. Remains of friary with small 13th-C building on River Stour
Church of St Martin, St Martin's Hill Mainly early Saxon church of 7th C with 15th-C west tower and vestry added 1845 retains spacious nave and long chancel; fine mid 12th-C stone font
Medieval Churches Medieval churches include: St Alphege (Palace St); St Dunstan; Holy Cross (Westgate); St Margaret; St Mildred (Church Lane); St Peter; St Stephen, Hackington; medieval towers survive from churches of St George and St Mary Magdalene
City Walls Surviving stretches of Roman walling rebuilt 14th and 15th C
Westgate Imposing gate built c.1375–80 on bank of River Stour
Castle Norman keep built c.1100
Poor Priests' Hospital, Stour Street Hospital rebuilt 1373 by River Stour (converted to museum 1982) retains 14th-C hall and chapel
Eastbridge Hospital, All Saints Lane Hospital founded before 1180 with 12th-C aisled hall and 14th-C street front
St John's Hospital, Northgate. Hospital founded late 11th C retains part of late 12th-C chapel and hall amongst 19th-C almshouses
Medieval Buildings Late medieval buildings include Lenley's (Burgate) and Queen Elizabeth's Guest Chamber (reworked 17th C)

CAPEL-LE-FERNE, KENT, 3, 4D
Church of St Mary [CCT] Church of Norman origin with west tower, stone south porch and good 14th-C stone screen to chancel

CAPPAGH, CO. TYRONE, 11, 4B
See Dunmullan

CARBERRY TOWER (3.5 km. / 2 ¼ m. SE of Musselburgh), LOTHIAN, 8, 3E
Carberry Tower Early 16th-C tower incorporated into north-west of U-shaped house built late 16th to 19th C retains crenellated parapet and cornice with gargoyles and winged heads

CAR COLSTON, NOTTS, 5, 5B
Church of St Mary Medieval church has 13th-C west tower with 15th-C upper levels, fine mid 14th-C chancel, and arcades; 14th-C sedilia and piscina

CARDIFF, S. GLAMORGAN, 6, 5E
Church of St John the Baptist, St John's Street Medieval church much restored 19th C retains chancel south arcade of c.1300, handsome west tower with openwork crown of c.1490, 15th-C arcades, and outer aisles added 1889–91
Cardiff Castle* Remains of castle with twelve-sided keep of c.1140 and gate tower of c.1300 on tall motte, early 13th-C Black Tower (now museum), and early 15th-C western apartments extensively remodelled 18th and 19th C

CARDINHAM, CORNWALL, 1, 3D
Church of St Meubred Church of 13th-C origin with three stage west tower and wagon roofs in porch and aisles
Cross 9th- or 10th-C cross in churchyard carved with knotwork, plaitwork and interlace decoration

CARDONESS, DUMFRIES AND GALLOWAY, 10, 5E
Cardoness Castle [HS] Well-preserved late 15th-C tower house of four stages has remains of pit prison, lobby, hall and some original fireplaces

CARDROSS, STRATHCLYDE, 8, 1E
Church of St Mahew 14th and 15th-C church, originally chapel-of-ease to Rosneath, with later alterations and restoration of 1955; short chancel probably built before 1467 contains fine sacrament house

CAREW, DYFED, 6, 2E
Carew Castle * Splendid ruined 13th- and 14th-C castle built around courtyard with curtain walls and towers has early 14th-C

Great Hall, late 15th-C gatehouse and grand residential north wing built 16th-C
Carew Cross [CADW] (at roadside near castle) Early Christian wheel-head cross of c.1033–35, richly carved with knotwork and fret patterns

CAREW CHERITON, DYFED, 6, 2E
Church of St Mary Large 14th- to 15th-C cruciform church with west tower has medieval monuments and, in sanctuary, tiles of c.1500, said to have come from Carew Castle; detached building in churchyard believed to be medieval mortuary chapel

CARHAMPTON, SOMERSET, 1, 5B
Church of St John the Baptist Medieval church remodelled 19th C has long south aisle, mainly 15th-C exterior, and fine painted rood screen

CARINISH (North Uist), WESTERN ISLES (Outer Hebrides), 9, 1D
Church of the Holy Trinity (Teampull Na Trionaid) Scanty remains of church built c.1200 with adjoining 16th-C rectangular building (probably chapel)

CARISBROOKE, ISLE OF WIGHT, 2, 4E
Church of St Mary Norman church with medieval additions retains 12th-C south arcade, north and south doorways, chancel arch of c.1200 and 15th-C five-storey west tower; fine monument to Lady Wadham of c.1520
Carisbrooke Castle [EH] Substantial remains of Norman and medieval castle rebuilt 16th, 19th and 20th C with 12th-C curtain wall, garderobe, and shell keep; Great Hall of late 1100s, 13th-C chapel and grand gatehouse with round towers added c.1335–6

CARLINGFORD, CO. LOUTH, 11, 5C
King John's Castle [Dúchas] Substantial, imposing remains of castle built c.1210 to defend coastal pass with late medieval and 19th- to 20th-C alterations
Dominican Abbey Ruins of large friars' church, all that survives of abbey founded 1305, with belfry and fortified tower
Tholsel Original town gate much reworked 1800s
Town Plan Town retains medieval street layout and boundaries;

CARLISLE, CUMBRIA, 7, 2B
Cathedral * 12th-C monastic church (founded 1122) largely rebuilt 13th and 19th C; medieval stained galss

Carlisle Castle [EH] Norman castle with 12th-C keep and curtain wall and extensive medieval additions remodelled or rebuilt 16th and 19th C

CARLOW, CO. CARLOW, 12, 5B
Carlow Castle [Dúchas] Fragmentary remains of once fine Norman castle built early 13th C and much demolished after 1814

CARLTON-IN-LINDRICK
    NOTTS, 5, 5A
Church of St John the Evangelist Church built 11th to 13th C retains important 11th-C west tower reworked 1417–43; Norman north chancel windows and 12th-C north arcade; early Norman font

CARMARTHEN, DYFED, 6, 3D
Carmarthen Castle Fragmentary remains of Norman and medieval castle include 13th-C curtain wall and towers and 14th-C gatehouse and south-west tower
Church of St Peter Large double-naved medieval church of Norman origin, much restored 19th C, contains splendid tomb of c.1525

CARNDONAGH,
    CO. DONEGAL, 11, 4A
Cross and Slabs [Dúchas] (1 km. / ½ m. W) Site of monastery founded 6th C with group of three early stone monuments including High Cross (perhaps 8th-C) decorated with interlace carving
Donagh Parish Church Church built 1769 retains 15th-C doorway and medieval lintel with Celtic cross and other sculpture

CARNOCK, FIFE, 8, 2E
Former Parish Church Ruined rectangular church built before 1250, remodelled 1600s, and abandoned 1840

CARRAN, CO. CLARE, 12, 2B
Church [Dúchas] Medieval parish church with fortified west end retains fine 15th-C south doorway and east window

CARREG CENNEN, DYFED, 6, 4D
Carreg Cennen Castle [CADW] Ruins of stone castle built c.1283–1321 as English outpost on spectacular rocky hill-top, site of earlier Welsh stronghold; surviving remains of inner ward with hall, gatehouse, towers and vaulted passage leading to cave on cliff-edge below outer ward; outer ward incorporating barbican with gates and moveable bridges

CARRICK CHURCH
    CO. FERMANAGH, 11, 3C
See Derrygonnelly

CARRICKFERGUS,
    CO. ANTRIM, 11, 5B
Carrickfergus Castle [EHS] Impressive and important medieval castle set by Belfast Lough has polygonal inner ward begun c.1178 with keep, middle ward of 1217–1222, and gatehouse and outer ward probably added 1226–42
Church of St Nicholas Church begun 1185 and much rebuilt 1614 for Protestant use has late 12th-C arcades at west end and 14th to 15th-C chancel

CARRICKKILDAVNET,
    CO. MAYO, 11, 1C
Castle [Dúchas] Small castle built 15th C by inlet of sea with traces of original bawn

CARRICK-ON-SUIR
    CO. TIPPERARY, 12, 4C
Castle [Dúchas] Remains of castle built c.1450 by River Suir with impressive mansion added 1568 to north side

CARRIGAFOYLE (3 km. / 2 m. NNW of Ballylongford) CO. KERRY, 12, 2C
Carrigafoyle Castle [Dúchas] Castle built 15th or 16th C in picturesque position by sea retains fine five-storeyed tower and parts of inner bawn

CARRIGAHOLT, CO. CLARE, 12, 2B
Tower House [Dúchas] Tall tower house built late 15th C by Shannon Estuary with well preserved bawn and 17th-C work

CARRIGOGUNNELL,
    CO. LIMERICK, 12, 3B
Castle [Dúchas] Fragmentary remains of castle set on imposing volcanic rock overlooking Shannon Estuary with large keep, 15th-C enclosing wall and 16th-C house

CARROWMORE CROSSES
    CO. DONEGAL, 11, 4A
See Culdaff

CARSLUITH (5.5 km. 3 ½ m. S of Creetown) DUMFRIES AND GALLOWAY, 10, 5E
Carsluith Castle [HS] Picturesque ruins of tower house built early 16th C, extensively remodelled after 1560, with flanking 18th-C ranges of outhouses

CARSWELL MEDIEVAL HOUSE,
    DYFED, 6, 3E
See St Florence

CARTMEL, CUMBRIA, 7, 1D
Cartmel Priory Complete Augustinain priory church built c.1190–1220
Cartmel Priory Gatehouse [NT] Surviving 14th-C gatehouse which served as grammar school 1624–1790

CASCOB, POWYS, 6, 5C
Church of St Michael Medieval church built into mound has early 14th-C west tower with timber-framed bell stage and earlier nave; 15th-C roofs and screen

CASHEL, CO. TIPPERARY, 12, 4C
Rock of Cashel (St Patrick's Rock) [Dúchas] Spectacular rocky outcrop houses remains of important cluster of buildings consisting of: splendid, richly ornamented Cormac's Chapel or Cathedral built 1127–34 with tympana to good north and south doors, vaulted interior with blind arcading on side walls, grand chancel arch, Ireland's earliest surviving wall paintings (12th-C), and fine 12th-C tomb chest; well preserved 12th-C Round Tower; large ruined 13th-C Cathedral with 14th-C central tower, early 15th-C residential west tower or castle, and fragments of excellent tombs; 15th-C Hall of Vicars Choral adjoining main gateway with weathered St Patrick's Cross nearby (c.1150)
St Dominick's Abbey [Dúchas], Moor Lane. Remains of fine church of Dominican friary founded 1243 with south wing added c.1270 and rebuilding of c.1480
Hore Abbey [Dúchas], off Mount Judkin Road. Ruined buildings of Cistercian abbey founded 1272 with mainly 13th-C cruciform church (tower and screens added 1400s) and domestic buildings including cloister and good chapter house
Quirke's Castle, Main Street. 15th-C tower
Medieval Effigies Fine collection of medieval tomb effigies survives built into churchyard wall of Protestant cathedral and Church of St John the Baptist

CASSINGTON, OXON, 2, 4A
Church of St Peter Norman church with 14th- and 19th-C remodelling retains carved corbel table and original central tower with upper levels of c.1318; Norman font

CASTELL-Y-BERE,
    GWYNEDD, 6, 4B
See Llanfihangel-y-Pennant

CASTLE ACRE, NORFOLK, 4, 3D
Church of St James Large 15th-C church with west tower retains some 13th-C work; some original painting on tall late medieval font cover, stalls, pulpit and rood screen; benches carved with animals and poppyheads
Castle Acre Priory [EH] Substantial remains of priory founded 1090 include massive west front of church built c.1140–50, cloister walks and infirmary; early 16th-C prior's house and gatehouse
Castle Acre Castle [EH] Extensive earthworks of 11th-C castle with circular shell keep and 13th-C Bailey Gate providing entrance to village (on site of outer bailey)

CASTLEBAY / BAGH A
    CHAISTEIL (Barra), WESTERN
    ISLES (Outer Hebrides), 9, 1E
Tower, Dun Mhic Leoid (2 km. / 1 ¼ m. NW) Fragmentary remains of late medieval tower on islet in Loch Tangusdale
Kisimul Castle Ruins of late medieval castle on island site abandoned mid 18th C and consolidated 20th C include plain 15th-C tower house, curtain walling, north tower heightened c.1500, and hall enlarged 17th C

CASTLE BOLTON, N. YORKS, 7, 3D
Bolton Castle * Imposing 14th-C castle with enclosed courtyard and impressive corner towers

CASTLE CAEEREINION,
    POWYS, 6, 5B
Ty Mawr Aisled hall built possibly c.1400, converted to house 17th C, retains fine timber work

CASTLE CAMPBELL, (1 km. / ½ m. N of Dollar), CENTRAL, 8, 2D
Castle Campbell [HS / NTS] Remains of castle (formerly known as Castle Gloom) begun after 1481 on prominent site in wooded Dollar Glen (NTS) include good 15th-C north-east tower with adjoining 16th- and 17th-C ranges

CASTLECARRA, CO. MAYO, 11, 1D
Castle [Dúchas] Ruined tower and fortified bawn of castle built between 1238 and 1300 (extensively reworked 15th C) by Lough Carra

CASTLE COMBE, WILTS, 2, 3B
Church of St Andrew 15th-C church with work of 13th to 14th C retains unusual chancel arch; 14th-C font and tomb chest; extensive restoration of 1850–1

Castle Remains of motte and bailey castle built c.1140

CASTLE CRAIG, HIGHLAND, 9,4D
Castle Craig Well-preserved remains of early 16th-C tower house by Cromarty Firth

CASTLEDERMOT,
CO. KILDARE, 12,5B
Round Tower and Crosses [Dúchas], Church Lane. Site of monastery houses Round Tower built 919 with medieval upper part and two excellent 9th to 10th-C High Crosses with carved biblical scenes; good early Christian and medieval grave-slabs and reconstructed 12th-C west doorway of vanished church survive in churchyard
Friary [Dúchas], Abbey Street. Remains of Franciscan friary founded 1302 with fine 13th-C church enlarged 1300s and domestic residence to south (possibly 15th-C)
St John's or The Pigeon Tower [Dúchas] Possibly 15th-C tower, sole survivor of St John the Baptist's Hospital founded 13th C
Town Walls Fragments of walls built c.1295, best seen between Barrack and Main Streets

CASTLE DONINGTON, LEICS, 5,4C
Church of St Edward King and Martyr Embattled medieval church retains 13th-C nave arcades and chancel, 14th-C tower, and 15th-C clerestory; 14th- to 16th-C monuments

CASTLE FROME, HEREFS, 5,2E
Church of St Michael Small early Norman church with 19th-C timber-framed bell-turret and south porch contains famous great 12th-C sculptured font

CASTLE GIRNIGOE AND
CASTLE SINCLAIR (4.5 km. / 2 ¾ m. N of Wick), HIGHLAND, 9,5C
Castle Girnigoe and Castle Sinclair Remains of two adjacent tower houses built 15th to 17th C set on impressive promontory site

CASTLE HEDINGHAM,
ESSEX, 3,3A
Church of St Nicholas Norman church with complete 12th-C interior below medieval clerestory and double hammerbeam roof; 16th-C brick tower
Castle Hedingham Castle [HHA] Massive keep of major Norman castle built c.1140 on earlier motte; interior retains windows and fireplaces with carved zig-zag decoration

CASTLEJORDAN, CO. MEATH, 12,4A
Castlejordan Remains of castle founded early 1200s by River Boyne with late medieval tower house rebuilt 16th C
Castlejordan Bridge Medieval bridge with much later alteration
Newcastle (6 km. / 3 ¾ m. NW); Remains of four-storeyed tower house built probably 1400s

CASTLEKEERAN, CO. MEATH, 11,4D
High Crosses, Keim Churchyard (10 km. / 6 m. NE of Crossakiel) Three High Crosses of 8th to 10th C (possibly boundary crosses of early monastery); base of fourth in tributary of River Blackwater

CASTLEKIRKE (on island in Lough Corrib, accessible by boat),
CO. GALWAY, 12,2A
Castle [Dúchas] Remains of rectangular castle built c.1235 with corner turrets

CASTLE LEVAN (2.5 km. / 1 ½ m. SW of Gourock), STRATHCLYDE, 8,1E
Castle Levan Imposing 14th-C keep with adjoining 16th-C tower set by edge of ravine

CASTLELYONS, CO. CORK, 12,3D
Friary [Dúchas] Mainly 15th-C remains of church and domestic buildings of Dominican friary founded 1307; central tower of church has well preserved spiral staircase

CASTLE OF MOY,
STRATHCLYDE, 10,3A
See Lochbuie

CASTLE OF OLD WICK,
(2 km. / 1 ¼ m.SE of Wick),
HIGHLANDS, 9,5C
Castle of Old Wick [HS] Remains of early Norse stronghold on spectacular cliff top site

CASTLE RISING, NORFOLK, 4,3D
Church of St Lawrence Late Norman church with central tower altered 13th and 19th C
Cross Tall 15th-C cross on Green to west of church
Castle Rising Castle [EH] Grand and very well-preserved mid 12th-C castle with large hall keep surrounded by massive earth ramparts; Norman gatehouse and late medieval bridge across moat

CASTLE ROY (1.5km. / 1 m. N of Nethybridge), HIGHLAND, 9,4E
Castle Roy Remains of early 13th-C castle of enclosure

CASTLE RUSHEN,
ISLE OF MAN
See Castletown

CASTLE SEMPLE, (6.5 km. / 4 m. W of Howood), STRATHCLYDE, 8,1E
Castle Semple Collegiate Church [HS] Well-preserved remains of simple, aisleless collegiate church founded 1504 with small west tower and three sided apse; fine early 16th-C tomb of John, Lord Semple

CASTLESKREEN (5 km. / 3 m. S of Downpatrick), CO. DOWN, 11,5C
Castleskreen Motte (close to similar, earlier Castleskreen) with remains of medieval tower house

CASTLE STALKER (13 km. / 8 m. N of Connel, on island at mouth of Loch Laich), STRATHCLYDE, 10,4A
Castle Stalker* Restored remains of tower house built c.1500 on islet

CASTLE STEWART (2 km. / 1 ¼ m. N of Challoch), DUMFRIES AND GALLOWAY, 10,4E
Castle Stewart Ruins of tower house built c.1500

CASTLE SWEEN (on east shore of Loch Sween),
STRATHCLYDE, 10,3B
Castle Sween [HS] Substantial ruins of castle built late 12th C on ridge near Loch Sween (one of oldest standing castles in Scotland) with further fortifications added 13th C

CASTLE TIORAM (on island at head of Loch Moidart)
HIGHLAND, 9,2E
Castle Tioram Ruins of imposing 13th-C castle with wall walk, internal courtyard, and 14th-C keep

CASTLETON, DERBYS, 5,4A
Church of St Edmund 13th-C church with fine Norman archway and 15th-C west tower; heavily restored c.1837
Peveril Castle [EH], Market Place Norman castle built 11th and 12th C with additions of 1200s

CASTLETOWN, ISLE OF MAN, 6,1B
Castle Rushen [MNH] Well-preserved remains of impressive limestone castle built mainly 13th and 14th C (among most complete in Britain) include keep, curtain wall and outer gatehouse; round tower and Derby House added 1500s
St Mary's Chapel and Old Grammar School [MNH] Chapel built early 13th C used as school in post-medieval times

CASTLETOWN-DELVIN,
CO. WESTMEATH, 11,4D
Delvin Castle [Dúchas] Remains of castle built 13th C or later include south wall with two imposing round towers
Gillistown Castle (1.5 km. / 1 m. SW) Surviving lower parts of late medieval tower house
Martinstown Castle (2.5 km. / 1 ½ m. S) Large and imposing tower house built 15th-C retains unusual stair arrangement

CASTLEWELLAN, CO. DOWN, 11,5C
Drumadonnell Cross [EHS] (by arrangement only) Granite cross with tall base and ringed head re-erected 1970s in stone store in Castlewellan Forest Park

CASTOR, CAMBS, 4,1D
Church of St Kyneburga Norman church rebuilt 13th to 14th C retains splendid arcaded tower of c.1120; 9th-C sculptured stone and cross; good 14th-C wall paintings

CATHERINGTON, HANTS, 2,5D
Church of All Saints Largely original late 12th-C church restored 1883 with south-west tower, spacious north chapel and 14th-C wooden roof to nave; fine wall paintings of c.1350

CATHLAW HOUSE (1.5 km. / 1 m. E of Torphichen), LOTHIAN, 8,2E
Cathlaw House Early 18th-C house incorporates fine late medieval architectural fragments on front (possibly from south part of St Giles', Edinburgh)

CATWORTH, CAMBS, 4,1E
Church of St Leonard Late 14th-C church with west tower retains 13th-C south doorway and double piscina in chancel

CAUNTON, NOTTS, 5,5B
Church of St Andrew Church of Norman origin rebuilt 13th to 15th C and restored c.1869 retains original south arcade; 13th-C font

CAUSETOWN CASTLE
CO. MEATH, 11,4D
See Athboy

CAVENDISH, SUFFOLK, 3,3A
Church of St Mary Mainly 14th-C church with embattled west tower, stair turret, priest's doorway and piscina

CAVERSWALL, STAFFS, 5,3B
Church of St Peter 12th-C church rebuilt 17th C with 13th-C arcades and low 15th-C west tower

Caverswall Castle House of *c.*1615 incorporates large 13th-C castle with four angle towers

CAWDOR, HIGHLAND, 9,4D
Cawdor Castle [HHA] Splendid castle licensed 1454 retains fine 15th-C tower amidst 17th to 19th-C outer ranges, and original wall of enclosure

CAWOOD, N. YORKS, 7,4E
Cawood Castle (Gatehouse) [LT] Fine 15th-C gatehouse with part of domestic wing, all that survives of former castle of Archbishops of York, has oriel windows and vaulted archway
Church of All Saints Church of Norman origin retains 12th-C west doorway, 13th-C chancel, 15th-C north chapel and good west tower

CAWSTON, NORFOLK, 4,4D
Church of St Agnes Fine medieval church has early 14th-C south transept and chancel with priest's doorway; early 15th-C work includes high west tower and remarkable hammerbeam roof to nave; early 16th-C screen

CAYTHORPE, LINCS, 4,1C
Church of St Vincent Mainly 14th-C church with 19th-C additions has crossing tower and two-naved interior; fine tracery of *c.*1290–1300

CERES, FIFE, 8,3D
Parish Church Church built 1805–6 contains fine 15th-C effigy of knight

CERNE ABBAS, DORSET, 2,2D
Church of St Mary 13th-C church rebuilt 15th to 16th C retains original chancel with late 14th-C wall paintings; fine stone screen and early 16th-C statue on west tower
Cerne Abbey Fragments of monastery refounded 987 include vaulted porch to abbot's hall, guest house and barn
Abbey Street Range of medieval timber-framed houses with jettied upper floors
Tithe Barn Mid 14th-C barn retains two wagon porches

CESSFORD (11 km. / 7m. S of Kelso), BORDERS, 7,2A
Cessford Castle Ruins of massive late medieval castle

CHACOMBE, NORTHANTS, 5,4E
Church of St Peter and St Paul Mainly 14th-C church much restored 19th C with original arcades, south porch and west tower; Norman font
The Priory 16th- and 18th-C house

incorporates medieval chapel with late 13th-C doorway and window (possibly from Augustinian priory founded mid 12th C)

CHADDESDEN (nr Derby), DERBYS, 5,4C
Church of St Mary [OCT] College or chantry church built *c.*1357 with 15th-C tower and chancel restored 1857–8; carved rood screen, stall ends and font; piscinas and sedilia in chancel and both side aisles

CHADDESLEY CORBETT, WORCS, 5,3D
Church of St Cassian Church of Norman origin with original north aisle arcade and doorway, 14th-C chancel and 18th-C west tower; fine carved font of *c.*1160–70 and medieval monuments

CHALDON, SURREY, 3,2D
Church of St Peter and St Paul Small flint-built church of late 12th to early 13th C with later medieval work and south-west tower of 1843; important wall painting of *c.*1200 depicts Purgatorial Ladder

CHALFONT ST GILES, BUCKS, 3,1A
Chiltern Open Air Museum * Museum exhibits cruck barn of *c.*1500 and has plans to display further medieval buildings currently in store
Church of St Giles Church with 19th-C exterior retains 13th-C chancel and late medieval west tower; 13th-C font and wall paintings of *c.*1330 in early 14th-C south aisle

CHALGRAVE, BEDS, 3,1A
Church of All Saints Church consecrated 1219 with important 13th and 14th-C work; wall paintings of *c.*1310 and 14th-C piscina
Castle Remains of 12th-C motte and bailey castle

CHALGROVE, OXON, 2,5B
Church of St Mary Norman church with 14th- and 15th-C rebuilding has original arcades, 14th-C chancel, sedilia and piscina; well preserved series of wall paintings of mid 1300s

CHAPEL FINIAN (in remote position near coast road 4.5 km./ 2 ¾ km. W of Elrig and 8 km. / 5 m. NW of Port William), DUMFRIES AND GALLOWAY, 10,4E
Chapel Finian [HS] Remains of rectangular chapel and well in oval walled enclosure, thought to date from 10th or 11th C

CHARLTON MACKRELL, SOMERSET, 2,2D
Lytes Cary Manor [NT] Manor house with 18th-C additions and 20th-C work retains 14th-C chapel and 15th-C hall

CHARLTON-ON-OTMOOR, OXON, 2,5A
Church of St Mary 13th-C church extensively remodelled 14th C with 15th-C clerestory; fine carved rood screen and loft of early 16th C; fragment of 13th-C cross in churchyard

CHARLWOOD, SURREY, 3,2D
Church of St Nicholas Church of Norman origin rebuilt 13th C and enlarged 15th C has crossing tower, 14th-C wall paintings and lavish screen of *c.*1480

CHARMINSTER, DORSET, 2,2E
Church of St Mary Church of Norman origin with 12th-C five-bay arcades, chancel arch and four small original windows incorporated in late medieval clerestory; handsome early 16th-C west tower, chancel of *c.*1838 and other 19th-C additions

CHARNEY BASSETT, OXON, 2,4B
Church of St Peter Norman church rebuilt 15th and 17th C retains richly carved south doorway of 11th C with tympanum; 15th-C wooden pulpit
Manor House House rebuilt 19th C incorporates late 13th-C solar wing with original fireplace and roof

CHARTHAM, KENT, 3,4D
Church of St Mary Late 13th-C cruciform church has transepts, timber roofs and fine chancel of *c.*1294 with original windows; large 15th-C west tower; good brass of *c.*1306

CHAWLEIGH, DEVON, 1,4B
Church of St James Mainly late medieval church with south aisle, south porch, west tower, and ceiled wagon roofs; rood screen reworked 1910

CHEAM, GREATER LONDON, 3,2C
Lumley Chapel Flint chancel of medieval parish church survives in churchyard of St Dunstan's; good brasses
Whitehall, 1 Malden Road (now museum) * Timber-framed building of *c.*1500 with 16th to 17th-C additions and 18th-C weatherboarding; well of *c.*1400 in rear garden

CHEARSLEY, BUCKS, 2,5A
Church of St Nicholas Mainly 13th-C church with 15th-C west tower; Norman font and late medieval brasses

CHECKENDON, OXON, 2,5B
Church of St Peter and St Paul Norman church with medieval additions retains original south doorway, and chancel and sanctuary arches; apsidal east end and 15th-C west tower; early 13th-C wall paintings and good brasses

CHEDWORTH, GLOS, 2,3A
Church of St Andrew Late Norman church rebuilt 13th to 15th C retains original west tower and arcade with 13th-C south porch and lavish 15th-C south façade; north aisle added 1883; Norman font and late medieval stone pulpit

CHEDZOY, SOMERSET, 2,1C
Church of St Mary Medieval church with 13th-C aisle arcades and chancel, and 15th-C clerestory and west tower; good chancel roof

CHELMSCOTE MANOR (1.5 km./ 1 m. E of Soulbury), BUCKS, 3,1A
Chelmscote Manor Large manor house reworked 20th C retains well preserved 14th-C chapel to south

CHELMSFORD, ESSEX, 3,3B
Cathedral of St Mary New Street * Late medieval church (cathedral after 1914) with restoration and additions of 19th C and 1920s retains fine 15th-C south porch with flushwork decoration; imposing west tower with lantern of 1749

CHELSEA, LONDON
See London

CHEPSTOW, GWENT, 2,2B
Church of St Mary Church of Benedictine priory founded 11th C, partially rebuilt 19th C, retains Norman nave and west doorway; west tower added 1706; 12th and 15th-C fonts
Castle [CADW] Huge Norman and 13th-C castle on long narrow ridge between town and River Wye with stone keep of 1067–1071, 12th and 13th-C upper, middle and lower baileys, and further additions including Martens Tower of *c.*1270–1300
Port Wall South of castle, well-preserved stretch of town wall built 1272–8
Town Gate, High Street. Late medieval archway with battlemented upper room

CHERITON, GLAMORGAN, 6,3E
Church of St Cattwg Handsome and well-preserved early 13th-C church has central tower, original wagon roof to nave, and good south doorway; additions of 1874–5

CHERRY HINTON, CAMBS, 3,2A
Church of St Andrew Early and late medieval church retains excellent chancel of *c*.1230–50 with tall coupled lancet windows, lavish interior and restored roof of *c*.1500; rood screen with 19th-C additions

CHESTER, CHESHIRE, 6,5A
Cathedral * Norman abbey church (founded 1092), raised to cathedral status 1541, with extensive medieval and 16th-C alterations and additions; 13th-C chapter house and Lady Chapel; sanctuary, choir and crossing rebuilt late 13th- to early 14th-C; remarkably complete monastic buildings include late 13th- to early 14th-C refectory with stairs leading to reading pulpit
Church of St John Splendid Norman nave and crossing with 13th-C clerestory survives inside church remodelled 19th C
Chester Castle [EH] Medieval castle rebuilt 1788–1822 retains AgricolaTower of original inner bailey with late 12th or early 13th-C chapel and some 14th-C work
City walls Two-mile (3 km) circuit of massive medieval walls with towers and gates, built to incorporate Roman foundations
The Rows, in streets around the Cross Unique rows of shops on two levels with colonnaded upper walkways above half-sunken crypts, the earliest in Watergate dating from 13th C
Dee Bridge Late 14th-C bridge widened 1826, originally with tower and probably drawbridge at south end

CHESTERFIELD, DERBYS, 5,4B
Church of St Mary and All Saints Mainly 14th-C church rebuilt 18th and 19th C with crossing tower, chancel chapels and good nave of *c*.1350–75; distinctive warped spire
Peacock Inn Inn with timber-framed core of *c*.1500

CHESTER-LE-STREET, CO. DURHAM, 7,3B
Church of St Mary and St Cuthbert [OCT] Church of 11th-C origin rebuilt 13th to 15th C on site of Roman fort has west tower with octagonal upper storey and well preserved anchorage; fragments of Saxon sculpture, 13th-C sedilia and piscina, and good 13th- to 15th-C monuments

CHESTERTON, CAMBS, 4,1D
Church of St Michael 13th- and 14th-C church rebuilt *c*.1730 retains original west tower, south doorway and arcades; 15th-C

painting of Doom and benches with poppyheads
Chesterton Tower Mid 14th-C tower restored 1949, now dwelling

CHETWODE, BUCKS, 2,5A
Church of St Mary and St Nicholas Surviving remains of Augustinian priory church founded 1245 and converted to parish church *c*.1480; original chancel with fine lancet windows and 15th-C west tower; stained glass of *c*.1250 and 14th C

CHEVELEY, CAMBS, 4,3E
Church of St Mary and the Holy Ghost of Heaven Handsome cruciform church has 14th-C crossing tower with octagonal upper part, transepts, 14th-C nave, and later medieval south porch; good rood screen (possibly 14th-C)

CHEW MAGNA, SOMERSET, 2,2C
Church of St Andrew Large church of 12th- and 13th-C origin much rebuilt 1400s with fine early 16th-C west tower; Norman font, good monument of *c*.1450, and rood screen
Church House House built *c*.1510 has original doorway and timber roof
Bridge Good late 15th-C bridge of three arches crosses the River Tone

CHEWTON MENDIP, SOMERSET, 2,2C
Church of St Mary Magdalen Norman church with much medieval rebuilding has original north doorway, mid 13th-C chancel and south chancel aisle, and tall west tower completed mid 16th C; 14th-C monument

CHEYLESMORE, W. MIDLANDS, 5,4D
See Coventry

CHICHELEY, BUCKS, 3,1A
Church of St Laurence Mainly 15th-C church with central tower; early 14th-C north arcade and chancel of 1708

CHICHESTER, W.SUSSEX, 2,5D
Cathedral * Impressive cathedral built *c*.1091 to 1108 and remodelled 12th and 13th C retains original eight-bay nave with west towers, transepts with east chapels, chancel with fine retrochoir, 13th-C St Richard's Porch, and Lady Chapel of *c*.1300; crossing tower reconstructed 1861–6; well preserved figural panels of *c*.1125–50 (thought to have come from 12th-C choir screen) and 15th-C Arundel Screen re-erected 1960; detached bell tower added *c*.1375–1430

Cathedral Precinct Extensive remains of monastic buildings include Bishop's Palace (remodelled 1725–7) with fine 13th-C chapel, kitchen with timber roof, and early 14th-C gatehouse, 13th-C House of Royal Chaplains in south walk of cloister built *c*.1400, and 15th-C vicar's close reworked 18th to 19th C
Churches of All Saints in the Pallant and **St Andrew Oxmarket** Small unaisled 13th-C churches
Greyfriars, Priory Park. Surviving chancel of priory church completed by 1282 with 15th-C wagon roof
Church of St Mary Wyke Road. Plain 11th-C church reworked 1800s with original chancel arch and 13th-C lancets
St Mary's Hospital Unusual medieval hospital buildings of *c*.1290–1300 with timber-framed aisled hall retaining chapel, and ward divided into flats *c*.1680; splendid screen of *c*.1290 and good misericords
Market Cross Elaborate octagonal cross built 1501 has pinnacles, openwork crown, lantern altered 1746, and good vaulted interior with central pier
Former Church of St Olave, North Street Church of Norman origin much restored and now used as commercial premises retains 13th-C chancel

CHICKNEY, ESSEX, 3,3B
Church of St Mary [CCT] Saxon church with original nave and 13th-C chancel; 14th-C font

CHILCOMB, HANTS, 2,4D
Church of St Andrew Well-preserved Norman church with original chancel arch and pillar piscina

CHILDWALL, LANCS
See Liverpool

CHILHAM, KENT, 3,4D
Church of St Mary Medieval flint church with chancel and aisles added 1863 has two-storeyed south porch, transepts, 15th-C arcades and early 16th-C west tower
Castle Remains of octagonal keep of Norman castle built 1171–4 with curtain walls and forebuilding incorporating 11th-C stone hall
The Street Some good medieval timber-framed houses with jettied upper storeys

CHILLINGHAM NORTHUMBERLAND, 7,3A
Church of St Peter 12th-C church with medieval additions, bellcote of 1753, and 19th and 20th-C restorations; fine Grey monument of *c*.1450

Chillingham Castle [HHA] Monumental castle licensed 1344 with 16th-, early 17th- and 19th-C remodelling has angle towers and stone ranges; Great Hall and former chapel survive
Hepburn Bastle Roofless 15th-C strong house with vaulted lower floor

CHILTERN OPEN AIR MUSEUM, BUCKS, 3,1B
See Chalfont St Giles

CHINNOR, OXON, 2,5B
Church of St Andrew 13th-C church much remodelled 14th C with original nave arcades, chancel of early 1300s, and 15th-C nave clerestory; early 14th-C rood screen and good set of medieval brasses and stained glass

CHIPCHASE CASTLE, NORTHUMBERLAND, 7,2B
Chipchase Castle * (open June, by arrangement at other times) Large mid 14th-C tower attached to mansion built 1621 and 18th C retains circular bartizans, guardroom and portcullis chamber

CHIPPING CAMPDEN, GLOS, 2,4A
Church of St James Mainly 15th-C 'wool' church remodelled 19th and 20th C retains part of Norman chancel, 14th-C south porch and tall nave arcades of *c*.1488; 15th-C triple sedilia, altar hangings and cope
Grevel's House High Street; Late 14th-C house with fine two-storeyed gabled bay window
Woolstapler's Hall Late 14th-C Hall contains room with good oak roof and oriel window

CHIPPING NORTON, OXON, 2,4A
Church of St Mary Church of Norman origin with extensive medieval rebuilding has 13th-C chancel, north chapel, haxagonal south porch, and impressive spacious nave reworked *c*.1485

CHIPPING ONGAR, ESSEX, 3,2B
Church of St Martin of Tours Well-preserved Norman church with 15th-C belfry and south aisle added 1884

CHIPSTEAD, SURREY, 5,1D
Church of St Margaret Large 13th-C church with 17th-C tower and some 19th-C rebuilding has reset 12th-C north door and stone seats along chancel walls

CHIRBURY, SHROPS, 6,5C
Church of St Michael Spacious church of former Augustinian priory retains original

late 12th- or early 13th-C nave and aisle, and west tower begun *c.*1300; early 16th-C nave roof and chancel of 1733

CHIRK / Y WAUN, CLWYD, 6, 5B
Chirk Castle [NT] Castle begun after 1282 on courtyard plan with 15th-C chapel restored *c.*1894, early 17th-C north range, and east range added 1667–*c.*1678; well preserved towers and curtain walling

CHISBURY, WILTS, 2, 4C
Chapel of St Martin [EH] Thatched 13th-C chapel with simple rectangular plan

CHITTLEHAMPTON, DEVON, 1, 4B
Church of St Hieritha or Urith Ambitious medieval church with interior much restored 1871–4 and other 19th-C work retains fine four-stage west tower, transepts, and lavish 15th-C south porch; original timber ceilings to transepts and 15th-C ironwork to south door

CHOBHAM, SURREY, 3, 1C
Church of St Laurence Church of 11th-C origin with 19th-C additions retains four-bay south arcade built *c.*1170, late 12th-C south chapel, 15th-C tower, and timber west porch; 13th-C chest

CHOLLERTON, NORTHUMBERLAND, 7, 3B
Church of St Giles Church with 18th-C exterior retains 12th-C south arcade built with four reused Roman columns and 14th-C north arcade with octagonal piers; inverted Roman altar converted to font

CHOLSEY, OXON, 2, 5B
Church of St Mary Cruciform church of Norman origin with 12th-C windows and south doorway and additions of 13th and 19th C

CHRISHALL, ESSEX, 3, 2A
Church of the Holy Trinity Church of 13th-C origin much rebuilt 15th C retains west tower; fine brass of *c.*1380 to De La Poles

CHRISTCHURCH, DORSET, 2, 4E
Christchurch Castle and Norman House [EH] Well preserved motte, two walls of keep and ruined hall of of 12th-C castle; Constable's house built *c.*1160
Christchurch Priory Major Norman priory church with 15th-C tower; choir rebuilt 15th C has reredos carved with Tree of Jesse (*c.*1350) and full set of misericords (13th- and 16th-C)

CHURCH EATON, STAFFS, 5, 3C
Church of St Editha Church of Norman origin with medieval additions has late 12th- to early 13th-C west tower and north arcade of 1200s; good Norman font

CHURCHFIELD (3 km. / 2 m. SE of Ballycastle), CO. ANTRIM, 11, 5A
Culfeightrin Old Church Scanty remains of medieval church with good 15th-C window; two pillar stones in graveyard

CHURCH HANBOROUGH, OXON, 2, 4A
Church of St Peter and St Paul Church of early 12th-C origin with reworking of 13th C and *c.*1400 has original north and south doorways with tympana, and 15th-C west tower; late medieval font and screens

CHURCH ISLAND (3 km. / 2 m. SE of Bellaghy) CO. LONDONDERRY, 11, 4B
Church Remains of medieval monastic church with tower and spire added 1788; nearby font and bullaun stone

CHURCH ISLAND (in Valentia Harbour, off Beginish Island), CO. KERRY, 12, 1D
Monastic Site [Dúchas] Small island, site of early monastic settlement, houses long stone-built oratory, circular stone hut, square house and later enclosing wall

CHURCH ISLAND / INIS MOR (accessible by boat), CO. SLIGO, 11, 2C
Church [Dúchas] Remains of medieval church mark site of monastery founded 6th C on island in Lough Gill

CHURCH ISLAND / INIS UASAL (island in Lough Currane), CO. KERRY, 12, 1D
Church of St Finian [Dúchas] Remains of small 12th-C church on monastic island site with traces of oblong houses to west and nearby St Finian's Cell; cross-slabs and pillar-stones in graveyard

CHURCH KNOWLE, DORSET, 2, 3E
Church of St Peter Church built mainly late 1200s with transepts, west tower reworked 1741, and north aisle added 1833–41
Barnston Manor (1.5 km. / 1 m. WSW) Well preserved late 13th-C manor house remodelled mid 1500s

CHURCH LANGTON, LEICS, 5, 5D
Church of St Peter Church of 13th-C origin retains chancel built *c.*1330, two early 14th-C tomb recesses, and tall interior with 15th-C arcades and clerestory

CHURCH PREEN, SHROPS, 5, 2D
Church of St John the Baptist Simple 13th-C church formerly belonging to small monastic house (cell of Wenlock) with fine east lancets, south chapel added *c.*1920–5, and adjoining remains of 19th-C manor house

CHURCH STRETTON, SHROPS, 6, 5C
Church of St Lawrence Norman and 13th-C cruciform church with later remodelling has original nave and crossing tower built 1200s with 15th-C upper stages; good nave roof

CHURCHTOWN (6.5 km. / 4 m. SW of Randalstown), CO. ANTRIM, 11, 4B
Cranfield Church [EHS] Remains of small medieval church (possibly 13th-C) on shore of Lough Neagh; holy well survives to east

CILCAIN, CLWYD, 6, 5A
Church of St Mary Medieval double-naved church with restoration and additions of 1888–9 retains fine late 15th- or early 16th-C timber roof to south nave (re-used from elsewhere); fragments of 14th-C sepulchral slabs

CILGERRAN CASTLE, DYFED, 6, 3D
Cilgerran Castle [NT / CADW] Mainly 13th-C ruins of powerful 12th- to 14th-C castle overlooking wooded Teifi gorge with two massive round towers and curtain walls surrounding inner and outer wards

CIRENCESTER, GLOS, 2, 3B
Church of St John the Baptist Spacious church of Norman origin with medieval and 19th- to 20th-C additions has early 15th-C tower, Lady Chapel of *c.*1450, and remarkable three-storeyed south porch begun *c.*1490; tall nave of 1516–30; fine 15th-C stone pulpit and good brasses and screens
The Old Grammar School, Park Lane Medieval school with original hall and 17th- and 19th-C work
Cross, Gosditch Street. Medieval cross on 15th-C base
Weavers Hall or **St Thomas's Hospital** Stone hall founded early 1400s
St John's Hospital, Spitalgate. Late 12th-C hospital founded by Henry I retains original hall arcade
St Laurence's Almshouses Gloucester Road. Building founded 13th C as leper hospital and converted to almshouses

*c.*1336 with 19th-C additions
Saxon Arch Norman gatehouse of *c.*1180 rebuilt 1800s

CLACHAN OF GLENDARUEL (13 km. / 8 m. N of Colintraive), STRATHCLYDE, 10, 4B
Kilmodan Sculptured Stones [HS] Series of carved tomb slabs survive in churchyard

CLACKMANNAN, CENTRAL, 8, 2D
Clackmannan Tower [HS] (view exterior only) 14th-C keep with 15th-C enlargement and additions survives on summit of hill known as "King's Seat"; fine 16th-C fireplace to hall

CLAPHAM, BEDS, 3, 1A
St Thomas of Canterbury Medieval church of 12th C and earlier retains impressive west tower and 13th-C arcades; additions of 1861–3

CLARA UPPER, CO. KILKENNY, 12, 4C
Clara Castle [Dúchas] Small and unusually well-preserved 15th-C tower house retains original oak floor beams, murder hole, and fine fireplace on third floor

CLARE, SUFFOLK, 3, 3A
Church of St Peter and St Paul Spacious medieval church remodelled 15th to 16th C retains west tower built 1200s, 14th-C arcade piers, vaulted south porch and two rood stair turrets; good carved tracery on north and south doors
Clare Priory Remains of early 14th-C church and domestic buildings of priory founded 1248 and altered 16th C
Castle Surviving remains of 13th-C shell keep on mound
The Ancient House [LT], High Street Timber-framed former priest's house dated 1473 with later pargetting
Chapel Cottage (Wentford Chapel), Chilton Road Late 12th-C chapel with later alterations

CLAREABBEY, CO. CLARE, 12, 2B
Abbey [Dúchas] Remains of mainly 15th-C buildings of Augustinian abbey founded 1189; church with well preserved east window and tower of *c.*1461 retains some late 12th-C work

CLAREGALWAY, CO. GALWAY, 12, 3A
Friary [Dúchas] Ruins of fine Franciscan friary founded 1290 include church with 15th-C tower and north transept; triple sedilia of *c.*1300 in chancel

Castle Tower of 15th-C castle dominates crossing over Claregalway River

CLARE ISLAND (accessible by boat), CO. MAYO, 11, 1C
Church of St Bridget (or Clare Abbey) [Dúchas] Small ruined church of Cistercian cell of Knockmoy Abbey (established 1220) with work of mainly c.1500; good medieval wall paintings in chancel
Castle Three-storeyed castle built 15th or 16th C by harbour, much reworked 1831 as coastguard station

CLAVERING, ESSEX, 3, 2A
Church of St Mary and St Clement 15th-C church retains screen, benches and some stained glass; font of c.1200; early 13th-C marble effigy of knight
House (by churchyard gate) Late 15th-C building with long overhang, probably built as almshouses

CLAVERLEY, SHROPS, 5, 3D
Church of All Saints Spacious church founded 11th C has Norman north aisle and lower parts of tower, 13th-C south aisle, chancel rebuilt 14th C, and much late medieval work; important wall paintings of c.1200.
Vicarage 15th-C vicarage with work of 16th or 17th C

CLAYBROOKE, LEICS, 5, 4D
Church of St Peter Mainly early 14th-C church reworked 17th and 19th C has wide, ornate chancel of c.1340 and 15th-C nave arcade and roof

CLAYPOLE, LINCS, 4, 1C
Church of St Peter Mainly 14th-C church remodelled 15th C has late 13th-C lower section to west tower and Lady Chapel of c.1275 incorporated into 14th-C south transept; fine carved capitals to arcades of 1300s; fragments of medieval cross in churchyard

CLAYPOTTS CASTLE, TAYSIDE
See Broughty Ferry

CLAYTON, W. SUSSEX, 3, 2E
Church of St John the Baptist Modest Norman church with much 19th-C work in chancel retains fine 11th-C chancel arch and important, well preserved wall paintings of c.1140

CLAYWORTH, NOTTS, 5, 5A
Church of St Peter Church of Saxon origin with 15th-C rebuilding and restoration of 1874–5 has original

tower with late medieval upper level, and 13th-C chancel arch; stone parclose screen

CLEAR ISLAND (accessible only by boat), CO. CORK, 12, 2E
Church (Teampall Chiarain) [Dúchas] Simple church built c.1200 on monastic site; early cross-pillar to south

CLEEVE ABBEY, SOMERSET, 2, 1C
Cleeve Abbey [EH] Well-preserved remains of 13th-C buildings of Cistercian abbey founded 1198; refectory rebuilt early 16th C has splendid wagon roof

CLEOBURY MORTIMER, SHROPS, 5, 2D
Church of St Mary Church of Norman origin with west tower built 1100s to 1200s, fine 13th-C chancel arch, south porch, north chapel, and 14th-C roofs

CLEVEDON, SOMERSET, 2, 2B
Church of St Andrew Late Norman church with reworking of c.1200 and 15th C retains original crossing tower with later upper stages
Clevedon Court [NT] Early 14th-C manor house with additions of c.1575 and late 19th C has Norman tower and fine chapel over porch (c.1320–30)

CLEY-NEXT-THE-SEA, NORFOLK, 4, 4C
Church of St Margaret Unusual church of 14th, 15th and 19th C has fine clerestory with circular windows, ruinous transepts, and two-storeyed south porch; good medieval brasses

CLIFFE, KENT, 3, 3C
Church of St Helen Mainly 13th-C church reworked 14th C and restored 19th C has nave arcades of c.1200, transepts, and good chancel with 14th-C sedilia and piscina; tower screen of c.1370 and medieval wall painting

CLIFTON, BEDS, 3, 1A
Church of All Saints Church with 14th-C nave and chancel, good 15th-C north arcade and west tower, and north aisle added 1862; 13th-C font and fine early 16th-C alabaster tomb chest with effigies

CLIFTON, CUMBRIA, 7, 2C
Clifton Hall [EH] Surviving pele tower of manor house built c.1500

CLIFTON, NOTTS, 5, 5B
See Nottingham

CLIFTON CAMPVILLE, STAFFS, 5, 4C
Church of St Andrew Church built mainly c.1300–50 with fine tower retains 13th-C chancel, south chapel, and north-east annexe with upper garderobe; good screens and early 14th-C stalls

CLIFTON REYNES, BUCKS, 3, 1A
Church of St Mary Church of Norman origin much rebuilt 13th and 14th C and embellished 15th C retains 12th-C west tower; good oak monuments of c.1300 and 14th-C octagonal font

CLIMPING, W. SUSSEX, 3, 1E
Church of St Mary Well-preserved church built c.1220 with transepts, south aisle, and lancet windows retains late Norman west doorway and lower parts of tower; 13th-C piscina, aumbry and chest

CLIPSHAM, RUTLAND, 4, 1D
Church of St Mary Norman church with medieval additions has original north arcade, south arcade of c.1200, and unusual 13th- to 14th-C steeple; Norman font

CLITHEROE, LANCS, 7, 2E
Clitheroe Castle Remains of small Norman keep and bailey walls

CLOGHER, CO. TYRONE, 11, 4C
St Macartin's Cathedral Cathedral church built 1744 and rebuilt 1818 on early site contains fine slab cross (probably mid 7th-C), early Christian sundial and part of lintel (probably from 8th or 9th-C church) in porch

CLOGHERHEAD, CO. LOUTH, 11, 4D
Clogherhead Church Ruins of late medieval church on coastland site
Parsonstown Church (4 km. / 2 ½ m. NW) Substantial remains of church built c.1528
Glaspistol Castle (1 km. / ½ m. S) Well-preserved tower house of late 15th or early 16th C retains large upper chamber with murder hole, part of chimneypiece, and mural passage

CLONAMERY, CO. KILKENNY, 12, 4C
Church [Dúchas] Medieval church built on early site has west end with flat-headed doorway and Maltese Cross in relief above, and chancel added 12th C; small 15th- or 16th-C outbuilding (possibly sacristy)

CLONARD, CO. MEATH, 11, 4D
Church of St Finian Church built 1810 retains good font of c.1500 with carved panels
Ballyboggan Abbey (4 km. / 2 ½ m. S) Remains of important abbey in picturesque setting with unusually large church

CLONDALKIN, CO. DUBLIN, 11, 4E
Monastic Site [Dúchas] Site of monastery founded 7th C houses tall Round Tower with original conical cap, two granite crosses and font (in churchyard), and fragments of medieval church; small 16th-C tower (known as Tully's Castle) at east of town

CLONES, CO. MONAGHAN, 11, 4C
Monastic Remains [Dúchas] Abbey Street; Round Tower on site of early Irish monastery founded 6th C and carved house-shaped shrine (probably 12th-C) in nearby graveyard; fine earlier High Cross (perhaps 10th-C) now stands in Diamond at town centre; fragment of 12th-C church

CLONFEACLE, CO. TYRONE, 11, 4C
Clonfeacle Cross St Patrick's Churchyard Small possibly incomplete medieval cross on site of early monastery

CLONFERT, CO. GALWAY, 12, 3B
Cathedral [Dúchas] Handsome cathedral built 12th C on early monastic site retains exquisite and important west doorway in six orders with pointed hood above enclosing arcading and triangles with carved human heads; early 13th-C chancel has fine east windows; chancel arch, west tower, sacristy and inner order of west doorway added 1400s; good 15th-C font

CLONKEEN, CO. LIMERICK, 12, 3C
Church [Dúchas] Small ruined 12th-C church, sole survivor of early monastery, retains fine doorway with zig-zag carving; 15th-C eastern part

CLONMACNOISE, CO. OFFALY, 12, 4A
Monastic Site [Dúchas] Extensive remains (8th- to 15th-C) of early Irish monastery founded 548–9 with tall 10th-C Round Tower, cathedral (1080–c.1100 and later), several smaller churches (including fine Temple Ri of c.1200 and Temple Finghin incorporating Round Tower), splendidly carved 10th-C Cross of the Scriptures, and series of good gravestones; paved causeway leads east to 12th-C Nun's Church; fragments of castle built c.1212

CLONMEL, CO. TIPPERARY, 12, 4C
Church of St Mary and Town Walls
[Dúchas], Mary Street Church built
mainly 1857 incorporates interesting
15th-C chancel arch, lower part of tower,
east window and other work; churchyard
partly bounded by fragments of late
medieval town walls with towers

CLONMINES, CO. WEXFORD, 12, 5C
Churches and Castles [Dúchas] Remains
of once flourishing medieval town at head
of Bannow Bay (ruined by 1684) include
four castles and three churches (one built
c.1400 for Augustinian abbey)

CLONMORE, CO. CARLOW, 12, 5B
Castle and High Crosses [Dúchas] Late
13th-C castle with corner towers and
turrets and remains of buildings on
eastern side of courtyard; one plain High
Cross and fragments of another survive in
village graveyard (site of early monastery)

CLONTUSKERT, CO. GALWAY, 12, 3A
Clontuskert Abbey [Dúchas]; Remains of
Augustinian abbey include 13th-C church
almost totally rebuilt 1400s and reworked
again 1637; fine west door erected 1471
with good figure sculpture; fragments
of 14th or 15th-C rood screen

CLOONDARA,
          CO. LONGFORD, 11, 3D
Cloondara Church Remains of 13th-C
church with later medieval residence
incorporated at west end

CLOUGH, CO. DOWN, 11, 5C
Clough Castle [EHS] Anglo-Norman
motte and bailey castle with late 13th-C
stone keep (later remodelled as tower
house and restored 1981–2)

CLOYNE, CO. CORK, 12, 3D
Cathedral of St Colman [Dúchas]
Cruciform cathedral started c.1250 on
site of monastery founded 6th C has
projecting sacristy to north of choir
and extensive post-medieval alterations;
foundations of Fire House (early church
or oratory) survive in north-east of
churchyard
Round Tower [Dúchas] Tall, altered
Round Tower with battlemented top
added mid 1700s

CLUN, SHROPS, 6, 5C
Church of St George Norman church
with remodelling of 1877 retains late
12th-C arcades, clerestory, distinctive
west tower with pyramidal roof, and
north porch; fine roofs with carved angels

Bridge Picturesque medieval bridge of five
arches crosses River Clun
Clun Castle [EH] Impressive ruins and
earthworks of border castle with tall
Norman keep and 13th-C towers

CLYNNOG FAWR, GWYNEDD, 6, 3B
Church of St Beuno Large embattled late
15th- to early 16th-C church with fine
hammerbeam roof, which once housed
an important shrine on pilgrimage route
to Bardsey, connected by vaulted
passageway to south-west Chapel of
St Beuno; in churchyard, rare 10th- to
12th-C free-standing pillar carved
with sundial
St Beuno's Well (west of church)
Rectangular pool flanked by stone
benches inside walled enclosure

CLYST HONITON, DEVON, 1, 5C
Bishop's Court Mansion built c.1800 and
19th C incorporating remains of medieval
house of Bishops of Exeter; large barn
(probably early 14th-C) with good roof
survives to south-east; stables built
possibly early 1500s

COATES, GLOS, 2, 3B
Church of St Matthew Church of Norman
origin restored 18th and 19th C retains
late 12th-C south arcade to nave, 13th-C
priest's doorway, projecting north chantry
chapel built 1300s, baptistery, and fine
15th-C west tower

COBHAM, KENT, 3, 3C
Church of St Mary Magdalene Medieval
church has mid 13th-C chancel with lancet
windows, late 13th-C nave, and 14th-C
west tower; chancel arch of 1860; fine late
14th-C sculpture, piscina, sedilia and
extensive collection of brasses
College College founded 1362 and converted to almshouses 1598 retains 14th-C
work including hall with timber roof
Tudor Yeoman's House [NT],
Sole Street. 15th-C timber house

COCHWILLAN OLD HALL
          GWYNEDD, 6, 4A
See Tal-y-Bont

COCKAYNE HATLEY, BEDS, 3, 2A
Church of St John the Baptist Church
with 13th-C north arcade, 14th-C south
arcade, and four-stage 15th-C tower
retains fine medieval stained glass from
Yorkshire in east window of north aisle

COCKERHAM, LANCS, 7, 2D
Cockersand Abbey Remains of abbey
founded 1190 with fine octagonal chapter
house built c.1230

COCKERSAND ABBEY, LANCS, 7, 2D
See Cockerham

COCKINGTON (Torbay), **DEVON**, 1, 5D
Church of St George and St Mary Good
late medieval red sandstone church with
battlemented west tower, nave, aisles, and
projecting chancel; 15th-C font

CODFORD ST PETER, WILTS, 2, 3C
Church of St Peter Medieval church
rebuilt 1864 retains fragments of Norman
work in north and south walls, 13th-C
chancel, and 15th-C west tower; finely
carved 9th-C cross shaft and Norman font

COGENHOE, NORTHANTS, 5, 5E
Church of St Peter Church of Norman
origin has late 12th-C north and south
doorways, 13th-C piers to arcades, and
chancel with lancet windows and blank
arcading; vestry added 1869

COGGES, OXON, 2, 4A
Church of St Mary Church of Norman
origin with 14th-C enlargement retains
12th-C south aisle and doorway, 13th-C
porch, and rich mid 14th-C north chapel;
west tower with octagonal upper stage
Vicarage 13th-C building of Benedictine
priory incorporated in vicarage with 16th-
and 19th-C additions
Cogges Manor Farm Museum * L-shaped
manor house dating from 13th C with
rooms furnished to depict life in late 1800s

COGGESHALL, ESSEX, 3, 3B
Grange Barn [NT] Europe's oldest
surviving timber-framed barn, built for
12th-C Cistercian abbey
Paycocke's [NT], West Street; Richly
carved timber-framed merchant's house
of c.1500

COITY, GLAMORGAN, 6, 4E
Church of St Mary Spacious cruciform
church built early 1300s with early 16th-C
crossing tower; fine tracery, piscinas, triple
sedilia, and 15th-C wagon roof to nave;
rare timber Easter Sepulchre of c.1500
Coity Castle [CADW] Remains of
impressive medieval castle include keep
of 1180s enlarged 14th and 16th C, 14th-C
curtain walling, gatehouses, domestic
range, and good 15th-C garderobe tower

COLCHESTER, ESSEX, 3, 4B
Town Walls Several stretches of Roman
town walls with impressive Balkerne Gate
(2nd-C, altered 4th C and later) on
Balkerne Hill
Church of the Holy Trinity, Trinity Street
Saxon tower survives at west end of late
19th-C church

Colchester Castle Museum *, 14 Ryegate
Road. Norman castle built c.1085 with
largest keep in Europe (now museum),
built on site of former Roman temple
St Botolph's Priory [EH], off St Botolph's
Street. Impressive ruins of large
Augustinian priory church begun c.1090
St John's Abbey Gate [EH], St John's
Green. Medieval gatehouse of 15th-C
Benedictine abbey
Medieval Churches Churches with
medieval work include: St James the Great
(East Hill); St Martin (West Stockwell
Street); St Mary-at-the-Walls (Balkerne
Hill); St Nicholas (High Street);
St Peter (North Hill)

COLDINGHAM, BORDERS, 8, 4E
Coldingham Priory Surviving choir
of late 12th-C church belonging to
Benedictine priory (restored 19th C and
now used for parish worship) retains fine
blank arcading with carved capitals to
north and east walls; fragments of south
transept and claustral buildings

COLDRIDGE, DEVON, 1, 4C
Church of St Matthew Church of 12th-C
origin rebuilt 15th to 16th C has west
tower, north-east stair turret and ceiled
wagon roofs in aisles; good early
16th-C fittings include parclose screen
and pulpit
Lower Chilverton Late 15th-C farmhouse
remodelled 16th to 18th C retains original
screens, roof and thatch

COLEBROOKE, DEVON, 1, 5C
Church of St Andrew Mainly late
medieval church with good Copplestone
(north-east) Chapel built probably c.1460
retains early 14th-C chancel and south
transept

COLERNE, WILTS, 2, 3B
Church of St John the Baptist Church of
Norman origin restored 1875 has arcades
of c.1200–10, contemporary north chapel
with tomb recess of c.1300, and tall west
tower; fragments of fine 9th-C cross

COLESHILL, WARWS, 5, 4D
Church of St Peter and St Paul [OCT]
Spacious medieval church much restored
1859 has tall tower begun c.1385 and 14th to
15th-C arcades; fine late Norman font with
lively carving and two early 14th-C effigies
of knights

COLLINGHAM, W. YORKS, 7, 3E
Church of St Oswald Church of Saxon
origin reworked 19th C has north arcade

of *c.*1200 and 15th-C west tower; Saxon fragments include fine Apostles' Cross of *c.*800 and part of carved late 9th-C cross

COLN ROGERS, GLOS, 2, 3A
Church of St Andrew Saxon church with original nave and chancel arch, early 12th-C south doorway, 16th-C west tower and south porch; medieval oak chest and 15th-C stone pulpit
Priest's House House of 14th-C origin situated near church

COLP CHURCH, CO. LOUTH, 11, 4D
See Drogheda

COLWINSTON / TREGOLWYN
GLAMORGAN, 6, 4E
Church of St Michael and All Angels
Church of Norman origin with 14th to early 16th-C additions retains 12th-C chancel arch flanked by 14th-C image niches retaining original colouring; late medieval cross in churchyard

COLYTON, DEVON, 2, 1E
Church of St Andrew Church of Norman origin restored 18th to 20th C with 15th-C nave, west window and crossing tower; fragments of finely carved 10th-C cross

COMLONGON CASTLE (1 km. / ½ m. W of Clarencefield),
DUMFRIES AND GALLOWAY, 7, 1B
Comlongon Castle Imposing tower house built *c.*1450 adjacent to mansion of *c.*1890 retains fine hall with fireplace and timber ceiling

COMPTON, DEVON, 1, 5D
Compton Castle [NT] Impressive medieval castle retains hall of *c.*1340 (reconstructed 1955), chapel, parlour and solar of *c.*1450, and much work of *c.*1520 including curtain wall and fine show front with towers

COMPTON, SURREY, 3, 1D
Church of St Nicholas Important, well preserved 11th-C church remodelled 12th C retains original tower with later spire, remarkable two-storeyed sanctuary of *c.*1160 with rare late 12th-C guard rail, and nave and aisles rebuilt 1180; early Norman font

COMPTON BEAUCHAMP,
OXON, 2, 4B
Church of St Swithun Modest 13th-C chalk-built church with original west tower and chancel; good early 14th-C glass in north transept and chancel east windows

COMPTON MARTIN,
SOMERSET, 2, 2C
Church of St Michael Good Norman church has original aisle arcades, clerestory, and rib-vaulted chancel; 15th-C west tower and south chancel chapel; Norman font and monument of *c.*1290

COMPTON WYNYATES,
WARWS, 5, 4E
Compton Wynyates Splendid early 16th-C brick-built manor house with two timber-framed gables

CONG, CO. MAYO, 11, 1D
Cong Abbey [Dúchas] Augustinian abbey founded 12th C on site of early monastery between Lakes Conn and Corrib has chancel of church with fine north door (*c.*1200, assembled 1860), part of east range of conventual buildings with three excellent doorways of *c.*1200 (among best in Ireland), and fragment of contemporary cloister (some capitals carved 19th C during reconstruction)

CONGRESBURY, SOMERSET, 2, 2C
Church of St Andrew 13th-C church remodelled 1400s has original arcades and chancel arch, and 15th-C tower and south porch; timber rood screen
Vicarage Vicarage built *c.*1470 with attached block of *c.*1824

CONINGTON, CAMBS, 4, 1E
Church of All Saints Handsome church built *c.*1500 reworked 17th and 19th C has four-stage west tower with tall pinnacles, embattled nave and aisles, and clerestory; late Norman font, effigy of Franciscan tertiary of *c.*1300, and good sedilia in chancel

CONISBROUGH, S. YORKS, 5, 5A
Conisbrough Castle [EH] Important Norman castle in dominant position with tall round keep buttressed by massive towers (*c.*1180, oldest circular keep in England) and walls and towers of inner bailey (*c.*1200)
Church of St Peter Norman church dating mainly from *c.*1175

CONNA, CO. CORK, 12, 3D
Conna Castle [Dúchas] Tower house of *c.*1500 (partially restored 19th C) on dramatic rock over River Bride

CONTIN, HIGHLAND, 9, 3D
Church of St Maelrubha Church built mainly 1730s and heightened 1832 incorporates parts of medieval predecessor including good sacrament house of

*c.*1490 under gallery stair and two late medieval grave slabs

CONWALL OLD CHURCH,
(3 km. / 2 m. WSW of Letterkenny)
CO. DONEGAL, 11, 3B
Conwall Old Church [Dúchas] Ruins of medieval church on site of early Christian monastery with several good slabs and pillar stones to south

CONWAY / CONWY,
GWYNEDD, 6, 4A
Conway Castle [CADW] Splendid castle on promontory site built 1283–7 by Edward I with royal apartments in inner ward and outer ward housing permanent staff and garrison
Town walls Remarkable survival of almost contemporary town walls with twenty-one towers and three gates, which acted as outer defences for castle
Church of St Mary Much restored 14th-C church retains 15th-C screen and choir stalls
Church Gyffin (on south edge of town) 13th-C church with early 16th- and 19th-C additions retains 15th-C chancel roof painted with saints and symbols of Evangelists
Aberconwy House [NT], Castle Street 14th-C merchant's house with oversailing upper storey

COOLE, CO. CORK, 12, 3D
Churches [Dúchas] Remains of two early churches in grounds of Coole Abbey; larger building (in use until 18th C) retains 13th-C south-west porch

COOLEY CHURCHYARD
CO. DONEGAL, 11, 4A
See Moville

COOLING, KENT, 3, 3C
Church of St James Well-preserved mainly 14th-C church retains chancel with lower walling of *c.*1260, and south vestry adorned with cockle shells; 13th-C font, fine sedilia and double piscina
Castle Remains of castle licensed 1381 with outer and inner wards include well preserved outer gateway with large flanking towers, angle turrets and garderobe

COPFORD, ESSEX, 3, 7B
Church of St Mary the Virgin Well-preserved Norman church retains original nave, chancel and apse; remarkable rich wall paintings of *c.*1140–50 and font of *c.*1200

COPPENHALL, STAFFS, 5, 3C
Church of St Lawrence Small well-preserved 13th-C church with 19th-C bell turret

CORBRIDGE,
NORTHUMBERLAND, 7, 3B
Church of St Andrew Saxon church with extensive 13th-C additions and early 20th-C work retains original west tower and Norman south doorway; piscinas and medieval cross slabs
Vicar's Pele Mid 14th-C tower house in churchyard restored 1910 has bartizans and tunnel-vaulted lower floor
Low Hall 13th- or early 14th-C house reworked 16th C, *c.*1675 and *c.*1890 retains hall and solar with 15th-C tower

CORBY, NORTHANTS, 4, 1E
Church of St John the Baptist Medieval church retains south arcade of *c.*1200, south porch of *c.*1300 with unusual rib vault, and 14th-C west tower; 13th-C font and 15th-C tomb chest in churchyard

CORCOMROE, CO. CLARE, 12, 2B
Corcomroe Abbey [Dúchas] Surviving church of 12th-C Cistercian abbey named "St Mary of the Fertile Rock" after picturesque location; choir with vaulted roof, excellent capitals and 13th-C effigy of bishop, fine carving to transept chapels, and 15th-C wall screen in nave

CORFE CASTLE, DORSET, 2, 3E
Corfe Castle [NT] Ruins of Norman castle with 13th-C defences

CORHAMPTON, HANTS, 2, 5D
Church Saxon church with 19th-C work retains fine chancel arch; Saxon sundial near porch, Norman font and 13th-C wall paintings

CORICKMORE ABBEY,
CO. TYRONE, 11, 3B
See Newtown Stewart

CORSEWALL CASTLE (1.5 km. / 1 m. SE of Corsewall Point) DUMFRIES AND GALLOWAY, 10, 4E
Corsewall Castle Ruins of 15th-C tower house

CORSTORPHINE (Edinburgh),
LOTHIAN, 8, 3E
Old Parish Church, Kirk Loan [SCS] Church with late 14th- to early 15th-C nave and south chapel, chancel and west tower added after 1444, and extensive post-medieval reworking; fine tombs

include those of founders Sir Adam
Forrester (d.1405) and Sir John Forrester

CORWEN, CLWYD, 6, 5D
Church of St Mael and St Sulien Early
medieval church much altered 19th C
retains Norman font and 15th-C effigy;
12th-C cross in churchyard
Church of All Saints, Llangar [CADW]
(1.5 km. / 1 m. SW) Small medieval church
with restored 14th to 15th-C and later wall
paintings; 17th and 18th-C furnishings
Plas Uchaf [LT] (2.5 km. / 1 ½ m. W)
Restored hall-house built c.1400

**COSMESTON MEDIEVAL
VILLAGE, GLAMORGAN, 6, 5E**
See Penarth

COTEHELE, CORNWALL, 1, 4D
Cotehele [NT] Handsome medieval stone
manor house enlarged and remodelled
15th and 16th C

COTHAY, SOMERSET, 2, 1D
Manor House * Modest late 15th-C manor
house with 17th-C work has good east
front and some original wall paintings

COTTESMORE, RUTLAND, 4, 1D
Church of St Nicholas Church of Norman
origin enlarged 13th and 14th C has
original south doorway, 13th-C chancel
and west tower, and 14th-C clerestory;
font with carved base of c.1200 and
14th- or 15th-C bowl

COTTINGHAM,
   E. RIDING OF YORKS, 4, 1A
Church of St Mary Large medieval church
with 14th-C nave, chancel of late 1300s,
and tall 15th-C crossing tower reworked
18th C

COTTINGHAM, NORTHANTS, 5, 5D
Church of St Mary Magdalene Church
of Norman origin has mid 13th-C north
arcade with unusual capitals, fine tower
begun late 1200s, and chancel and south
arcade of c.1300

COTTON, SUFFOLK, 4, 4E
Church of St Andrew 14th-C church
retains fine west tower, south doorway
inside porch, and 15th-C double hammerbeam roof; good piscina and sedilia

**COULSDON, GREATER
   LONDON, 3, 2D**
Church of St John the Evangelist Mainly
13th-C church with mid 20th-C south
extension retains original blind arcading
in chancel, 15th-C arcades and west tower
with late spire; fine 13th-C sedilia and
piscina

COUMEENOLE SOUTH (Dingle
Peninsula), CO. KERRY, 12, 1C
Beehive Huts [Dúchas] Remains of
several good beehive huts include four
on summit of hill

COUPAR ANGUS, TAYSIDE, 8, 3C
Coupar Angus Abbey Impressive
gatehouse, all that survives of once
wealthy Cistercian abbey founded 1160s
by Malcolm IV; many carved stones
around modern church

COVEHITHE, SUFFOLK, 4, 5E
Church of St Andrew and Ruins [CCT]
Remains of medieval church with 14th-C
west tower, nave arcade, and projecting
15th-C chancel; octagonal font

COVENTRY, W. MIDLANDS, 5, 4D
Cathedral Church of St Michael *
Medieval church bombed 1940 and rebuilt
1951–62 by Sir Basil Spence retains late
13th-C south porch and tall steeple begun
1371; remains of fine chancel begun c.1430
with polygonal apse
Church of the Holy Trinity Large church
of 13th-C origin rebuilt c.1360 to c.1535–40
and later retains long chancel with
chapels, high crossing tower, and 15th-C
nave roof; late medieval stone pulpit,
and stalls with carved misericords
Church of St John the Baptist 14th-C
church much rebuilt 1400s has transepts
and crossing tower with 19th-C bartizans
The Whitefriars Remains of east range
of cloister of friary founded 1342 and
converted as house 16th C
Greyfriars, Warwick Lane. Surviving
octagonal steeple built c.1350 for house of
Greyfriars
Bablake School and Bod's Hospital, Hill
Street. Buildings around courtyard with
school (east) range of c.1500 and hospital
(north) range founded 1506; much 19th-C
rebuilding
Hospital of St John, Hales Street. Hospital
founded 12th C with post-medieval
remodelling retains 14th-C chapel,
north-west tower, and spacious interior
with 15th-C stalls
St Mary's Hall, Bayley Lane. Guildhall
built 1340–2 with enlargement of c.1400
and later alterations has original timber
framed kitchen, Caesar's Tower of 1390s,
and hall on vaulted undercroft with bay
window and minstrels' gallery; 15th-C
guild chair, statues and stained glass
in hall
City Walls and Gates Fragments of
walls licensed 1328 with two out of
original twelve gates surviving (ie.

Cook Street Gate and Swanswell Gate)
Charterhouse, Cheylesmore (Outer
Coventry) Remains of Charterhouse
founded 1381

**COWBRIDGE / Y BONT-FAEN
   GLAMORGAN, 1, 5A**
Church of the Holy Cross Late 13th-C
church with 19th- and 20th-C work
retains original tower with octagonal
upper stage, 15th-C south aisle and
north chancel chapel
Town Walls Remains of 13th-C walling
with surviving south gate of c.1300

COWDEN, KENT, 3, 2D
Church of St Mary Magdalene Church
with late medieval and 19th-C additions
has good shingled west steeple supported
by six huge posts within late 13th-C part
of nave
Hole Cottage [LT] Attractive timber-
framed cottage, cross-wing of former late
medieval hall-house (demolished 1833),
survives in picturesque setting

**COWLAM, E. RIDING OF
   YORKS, 7, 5D**
Church of St Mary Church built 1852
retains finely carved Norman font

COXWOLD, N. YORKS, 7, 4D
Church of St Michael Mainly 15th-C
church retains striking octagonal west
tower with openwork battlements and
chancel rebuilt 1774; original 15th-C
figures in tracery heads of most north
and south windows

**COYCHURCH / LLANGRALLO
   GLAMORGAN, 6, 4E**
Church of St Crallo Fine cruciform
church built mid to late 13th C and
reconstructed 1888 has good west front
and spacious interior with narrow nave
and 15th-C wagon roof; remains of two
10th- or early 11th-C crosses in aisles;
steps and shaft of cross in churchyard

CRAIGMILLAR (Edinburgh),
   LOTHIAN, 8, 3E
Craigmillar Castle [HS] Dramatic ruins
of castle built 15th to 17th C include
imposing tower house of late 1400s,
rectangular curtain wall with towers, and
courtyard buildings

CRAIGNETHAN CASTLE
   (7.5 km. / 4 ½ m. WNW of Lanark),
   STRATHCLYDE, 8, 2E
Craignethan Castle [HS] Well-preserved
and restored ruins of fine castle begun
1530s on attractive promontory site

incorporating imposing late 15th-C keep;
defensive caponier (gunners' hut)
discovered in dry moat during 1963
excavation

CRAIL, FIFE, 8, 4D
Church of St Mary (Parish Church)
Marketgate [SCS] Large church of
Norman origin dedicated 1243 with early
16th-, late 18th- and 19th-C rebuildings
retains early 13th-C west tower; Pictish
cross slab inside south entrance

CRAMOND (Edinburgh),
   LOTHIAN, 8, 3E
Cramond Tower Late medieval tower
house converted for domestic use 1979
Cramond Kirk Cramond Glebe Road
[SCS]; Cruciform church built mainly
1656 with later alterations retains
15th-C tower

CRANBORNE, DORSET, 2, 3D
Church of St Mary and St Bartholomew
Church of Norman origin, once attached
to priory founded 980, with original north
doorway and arcade of c.1300; 15th-C west
tower and east end of 1875; 13th-C font and
14th-C wall paintings

CRANBROOK, KENT, 3, 3D
Church of St Dunstan Medieval church of
13th-C origin has 14th-C south porch with
15th-C door; splendid bosses of c.1300 in
chancel; early 16th-C stained glass

CRANFIELD, CO. ANTRIM, 11, 4B
See Churchtown

CRATFIELD, SUFFOLK, 4, 5E
Church of St Mary 14th-C church
reworked 15th C has five bay arcades,
clerestory, west tower, and good chancel
roof; fine 15th-C font carved with Seven
Sacraments

CREAKE ABBEY, NORFOLK, 4, 3C
Creake Abbey [EH] Mainly late 13th-C
remains of Augustinian abbey founded
1206

CREDITON, DEVON, 1, 5C
Church of the Holy Cross Early 12th-C
cruciform church rebuilt 13th, 15th and
19th C with long chancel, crossing tower
and Lady Chapel; Norman font and
carved oak chest of c.1500

**CREECH ST MICHAEL
   SOMERSET, 2, 1D**
Church of St Michael 13th-C church
rebuilt 1400s has original nave, chancel
and south doorway; north tower with
upper levels added 1400s, and good
wagon roofs

CREEVELEA (1 km. / ½ m. W of Dromahaire), CO. LEITRIM, 11, 2C
Friary [Dúchas] Well-preserved remains of Franciscan friary founded 1508 (last pre-Reformation friary founded in Ireland) include church with good west doorway, altered tower, cloister and domestic buildings; fine carvings of St Francis on pillar on north side of cloister

CREICH, FIFE, 8, 3D
St Demhan's Cross (5 km. / 3 m. E of Bonar Bridge) Tall carved stone of 9th or 10th C survives in field east of graveyard **Church of St Devenic** Ruined medieval church with 14th-C south doorway and two tomb recesses in north wall; part of early 16th-C chapel and later work

CRESSING TEMPLE, ESSEX, 3, 3B
Barley Barn and Wheat Barn * Two noble 13th-C timber-framed barns belonging to earliest English settlement of Knights Templar

CREWKERNE, SOMERSET, 2, 2D
Church of St Bartholomew Late 15th and early 16th-C rebuilding of 13th-C church with crossing tower, tall clerestory, large windows, and west front with polygonal turrets; lavish panelled ceiling to north transept

CRICCIETH, GWYNEDD, 6, 3B
Criccieth Castle [CADW] Ruins and surviving high towers of small 13th-C native Welsh castle, repaired and altered 14th C

CRICH, DERBYS, 5, 4B
Church of St Michael Church with Norman work, chancel of c.1320–50, and late medieval west tower; rare built-in stone bible rest in chancel north wall

CRICHTON (2.5 km. / 1 ½ m. E of Gorebridge), LOTHIAN, 8, 3E
Church of St Mary and St Kentigern (Crichton Collegiate Church) [SCS] Impressive surviving chancel of collegiate church built 15th to early 16th C has transepts, square tower, and good interior with tunnel-vaults; triple sedilia and sacrament house
Crichton Castle [HS] Medieval castle on courtyard plan has late 14th-C keep with upper hall, 15th-C ranges, and rich late 16th-C additions

CRICK, GWENT, 6, 5E
Runston Chapel [CADW] (to NW of Runston deserted medieval village) Small roofless 12th-C church of St Keyna

CRICK, NORTHANTS, 5, 5D
Church of St Margaret Well-preserved 14th-C church retains west tower with broach spire, and sedilia and piscina in chancel; good Norman font

CRICKADARN, POWYS, 6, 5D
Church of St Mary Medieval church with later restorations has 14th-C nave and chancel, priest's doorway, good 15th-C south porch, and embattled tower added 1500s

CRICKHOWELL / CRUCYWEL POWYS, 6, 5D
Church of St Edmund Church built early 14th C and reworked 19th C has crossing tower, transepts, and fine chancel with priest's doorway; sepulchral recesses in chancel with two 14th-C effigies
Castle Ruins of medieval shell keep and towers on 11th-C motte

CRICKLADE, WILTS, 2, 3B
Church of St Sampson Church of Saxon origin retains original lesene above late Norman and late 13th-C south arcade, and imposing crossing tower built early 1550s; tomb chest, and complete High Cross in churchyard
Church of St Mary Norman church restored 19th and 20th C has original chancel arch, 13th-C west tower with late medieval top, north chapel, and 15th-C arcades; 13th-C font; complete 14th-C cross in churchyard

CROFT, HEREFS, 6, 5C
Church of St Michael Church of c.1300 with 17th-C additions retains medieval tiles and fine tomb chest to Sir Richard Croft (d. 1509) and wife
Croft Castle [NT] Late 14th- to early 15th-C castle with east side and interiors of 1750–60 retains original outer wall with round corner towers

CROFT, LINCS, 4, 2C
Church of All Saints Mainly 14th-C church with 16th to 17th and 19th-C work has original arcades and tower and chancel arches; good late 13th or early 14th-C brass and medieval lectern

CROFT-ON-TEES, CO. DURHAM, 7, 3C
Church of St Peter Church of Norman origin has 13th-C south arcade, 14th-C north arcade, long chancel, and low west tower; part of fine Saxon cross shaft, sedilia, piscina, and 15th-C screen
Bridge 15th-C bridge crosses River Tees

CROMER, NORFOLK, 4, 4C
Church of St Peter and St Paul Mainly 15th-C church with tall west tower and aisle windows, good west porch and doorway, and spacious interior; chancel rebuilt 1887–9

CRONDALL, HANTS, 2, 5C
Church of All Saints Norman and early 13th-C church with rib-vaulted chancel and 17th-C tower; fine 14th-C brass

CROOKSTON CASTLE STRATHCLYDE, 10, 5C
See Pollok

CROPREDY, OXON, 5, 4E
Church of St Mary Spacious medieval church has 13th-C south doorway, 14th-C arcades, vestry with priest's room above, and 15th-C west tower; rare lectern of 1400s

CROPTHORNE, WORCS, 5, 3E
Church of St Michael Norman church remodelled 13th and 15th C retains original west tower, four-bay arcades, and chancel arch; carved cross head of c.825–50 and 14th-C tomb recess

CROSCOMBE, SOMERSET, 2, 2C
Church of St Mary 13th-C church remodelled 15th and early 16th C retains south chancel chapel finished by 1459, two-storeyed treasury and clergy vestry of c.1507–12; octagonal font; box pews
The Old Hall [LT] Late medieval building, formerly great hall of manor house built c.1420, used as Baptist chapel for 250 years
Old Manor House Early 16th-C manor house retains hall oriel with stone ceiling

CROSS CANONBY, CUMBRIA, 7, 1C
Church of St John the Evangelist Church of Norman origin reworked 13th and 14th C with original chancel arch; part of 10th-C cross shaft and square 13th-C font

CROSSHALL (1 km. / ½ m. N of Eccles), BORDERS, 7, 4A
Crosshall Cross Tall medieval cross with good carved work on all four sides

CROSSKIRK (10 km. / 6 m. W of Thurso), HIGHLANDS, 9, 4B
St Mary's Chapel [HS] Small ruined dry-stone chapel probably built 12th C

CROSSRAGUEL ABBEY (3 km. / 2 m. SW of Maybole), STRATHCLYDE, 10, 4D
Crossraguel Abbey [HS] Extensive 13th- to 16th-C remains of Cluniac abbey founded 1244 include church with polygonal apse to choir (rebuilt 1400s), and cloister with sacristy, fine 15th-C groin-vaulted chapter house and treasury; dovecot, abbot's house and impressive mid 16th-C gatehouse

CROUGHTON, NORTHANTS, 2, 5A
Church of All Saints Church of Norman origin with late 12th-C west tower and north arcade, 13th-C south arcade, and clerestory of c.1300; good set of early 13th-C wall paintings discovered c.1921

CROWCOMBE, SOMERSET, 2, 1C
Church of the Holy Ghost Medieval church has 14th-C west tower, rich early 16th-C south aisle, and two-storeyed south porch; good octagonal carved font

CROWFIELD, SUFFOLK, 3, 4A
Church of All Saints Medieval church with fine, tall timber-framed chancel and 19th-C bell turret

CROWLAND, LINCS, 4, 2D
Croyland Abbey (Church of Our Lady, St Bartholomew and St Guthlac) Impressive fragment of church of abbey founded 716, now part ruin, part parish church; building dates from 12th C but was remodelled c.1281 with west tower added 1460–69
Triangular Bridge Late 14th-C bridge has three arches (originally spanning separate streams) joined in centre at angle of 120°

CROWLE, WORCS, 5, 3E
Church of St John the Baptist Medieval church largely rebuilt 19th C has 14th-C timber porch and important stone lectern of c.1200

CROXALL, STAFFS, 5, 4C
Church of St John the Baptist Medieval church retains chancel of c.1200 and 13th-C west tower with 15th-C upper level; good monuments

CROXDEN, STAFFS, 5, 3B
Croxden Abbey [EH] Ruins of church and monastic buildings of Cistercian abbey founded 1176 with imposing west wall of nave

CROYDON, GREATER
LONDON, 3, 2C
Archbishop's Palace, Old Palace Yard *
Medieval buildings of Archbishop's
palace situated around courtyards include
Great Hall built *c*.1381–96 (remodelled
c.1443–52), Great Parlour of *c*.1397–1414,
and brick chapel added *c*.1460–80

CROYLAND ABBEY, LINCS, 4, 2D
See Crowland

CRUGGLETON, DUMFRIES AND
GALLOWAY, 10, 5E
Church Small early 12th-C church much
restored and rebuilt *c*.1890

CRUICETOWN, CO. MEATH, 11, 4D
See Nobber

CRUMLIN / CAMLIN,
CO. ANTRIM, 11, 5B
Crumlin Church (1.5 km. / 1 m. ENE)
Remains of medieval church retaining
eight remarkable sedilia at east end

CUBBIE ROO'S CASTLE,
ORKNEY, 9, 5A
See Wyre

CUDDESDON, OXON, 2, 5B
Church of All Saints Cruciform church
built *c*.1180 with medieval and 19th-C
work has lavish crossing arches, late
13th-C aisles and arcades, good
14th-C west porch, and central
tower with stair-turret

CULBONE, SOMERSET, 1, 5A
Church of St Culbone Plain Norman
church (one of smallest medieval
churches in England) with south porch
and spire projecting through nave roof;
14th-C rood screen

CULDAFF, CO. DONEGAL, 11, 4A
St Buadan's Cross Tall green slate shaft
of 8th-C or later cross with finely carved
biblical scenes
Carrowmore Crosses [Dúchas]
(4 km. / 2 ½ m. SSW) Three medieval
crosses survive on site of monastery

CULFEIGHTRIN, CO. ANTRIM, 11, 5A
See Churchfield

CULLEN, GRAMPIAN, 9, 5D
Cullen Collegiate Church Well-preserved
church founded 1543 (still in use) with
13th-C nave, south transept of 1536, and
18th-C north transept; medieval grave slab
of John Duff; chancel contains excellent
sacrament house and effigy of Alexander
Ogilvie of Deskford (d.1554)

CULLOMPTON, DEVON, 1, 5C
Church of St Andrew Late medieval
church enlarged 16th C with fine wagon
roof and unique carved Golgotha
(originally situated above surviving
rood screen)

CULROSS, FIFE, 8, 2E
Culross Abbey, King Street [HS] [SCS]
Choir of church of Cistercian monastery
founded *c*.1215 and much restored 1905–6
(parish church since 1633) has splendid
west tower of *c*.1500 (former central
tower) incorporating original rood
screen and pulpitum, and post medieval
additions; south walling of nave and
retrochoir survive; remains of abbey
buildings include 13th-C walling, frater
with vaulted room beneath, and east
range with monk's dorter and
chapter house
St Mungo's Chapel [NTS] Remains of
church built *c*.1500 and excavated 1926
with south wall reconstructed 20th C
West Kirk Ruins of medieval church with
17th-C additions; grave slabs incised with
swords survive as doorway lintels with
others set in walls

CUPAR, FIFE, 8, 3D
**Old Parish and St Michael of Tarvit
Church, Kirkgate** Surviving north-west
tower heightened 1620 and north
aisle converted to sessions house
18th C of church built 1415 and
demolished 1785

CURRAHA, CO. MEATH, 11, 4D
Church Parish church contains finely
carved 15th-C font (now heavily
whitewashed) moved *c*.1904 from
Crickstown

CURRY RIVEL, SOMERSET, 2, 1D
Church of St Andrew 13th-C church
rebuilt 15th C retains six original tomb
recesses, effigies and piscina in north
chancel chapel; tall 15th-C west tower
rebuilt 1860; good parclose screens

CURY, CORNWALL, 1, 2E
Church of St Gunwalloe Church of
Norman origin with much 14th- and
15th-C work retains 12th-C south
doorway with tympanum, and
good font

CUSHENDALL, CO. ANTRIM, 11, 5A
Layd Church [EHS] (1.5 km. / 1 m.NE)
Ruins of medieval parish church (in use
until 1790) with later reworking; marks of
wicker centering survive under
vault of west tower

CWMHIR ABBEY, POWYS, 6, 4C
See Abbey Cwmhir

CWMYOY, GWENT, 6, 5D
Church of St Martin Small medieval
church with dramatically leaning
tower, heavily buttressed to counteract
effects of subsidence; Norman south
doorway and font

CYMER ABBEY, GWYNEDD, 6, 4B
Cymer Abbey [CADW] Ruins of small
Cistercian abbey founded 1199 with early
13th-C church and west tower of *c*.1350

DACRE, CUMBRIA, 7, 2C
Church of St Andrew Norman church has
original tower arch, west tower rebuilt
1810, late 12th-C chancel, and early 13th-C
arcades; fragments of two Saxon cross
shafts
Dacre Castle Well-preserved early 14th-C
pele tower with angle turrets, battlements,
and windows of *c*.1700

DAGLINGWORTH, GLOS, 2, 3A
Church of Holy Rood Church of Saxon
origin extensively rebuilt 1845–50 retains
original south doorway, 15th-C west tower
and south porch; fine Saxon sundial and
sculpture of *c*.1050

DALE ABBEY, DERBYS, 5, 4C
Abbey Surviving late 13th-C east window
of Premonstratensian abbey founded
c.1200
Church of All Saints [OCT] Small church
of Norman origin reworked 15th C has
aisle built *c*.1300; good late 13th-C wall-
paintings and timber roof

DALGETY BAY, FIFE, 8, 3E
Church of St Bridget [HS] (1.5 km. / 1m.
to NE) Ruins of church consecrated 1244
overlooking Firth of Forth with extensive
late 16th and early 17th-C additions

DALHOUSIE CASTLE (3.5 km. /
2 ¼ m. SSW of Dalkeith),
LOTHIAN, 8, 3E
Dalhousie Castle Castle replanned as
hotel 1972 retains curtain wall and tower
of *c*.1450 with extensive post-medieval
additions

DALKEITH, LOTHIAN, 8, 3E
**Church of St Nicholas (St Nicholas
Buccleuch Parish Church)**, High Street
[SCS] Late medieval church much
reworked 1851–4 retains fine roofless
chancel of *c*.1500 with three sided apse
(abandoned since 1590), sacristy (now
Buccleuch vault), and original nave

arcades; monument to Sir James Douglas,
First Earl of Morton (d. *c*.1498) and his
wife Joanna, daughter of James I

DALKEY ISLAND (off shore of
Dalkey, accessible only by boat),
CO. DUBLIN, 11, 5E
Church of St Begnet [Dúchas] Small early
Christian church with antae, flat-headed
west doorway, later bellcote, and east end
altered 19th C

DALMENY, LOTHIAN, 8, 3E
Church of St Cuthbert, Main Street [SCS]
Important mid 12th-C church, best
preserved of its period in country, with
nave, chancel and apse descending in
height and width; sumptuous south
door with intersecting arcading above,
and rich corbel table to chancel and
apse; carved stone coffin by south door
(possibly that of builder of church)

DALSTON, CUMBRIA, 7, 1B
Dalston Hall Manor house with 17th-C
work and main façade of 1899 retains pele
tower built *c*.1500 on garden front

DALTON-IN-FURNESS,
CUMBRIA, 7, 1D
Dalton Castle [NT] 14th-C tower in
Market Place

DAMERHAM, HANTS
Church of St George 12th- and 13th-C
church with later medieval and 17th-C
additions has good wagon roofs and a
Norman typanum in south porch

DARDISTOWN CASTLE,
CO. MEATH, 11, 4D
See Julianstown

DARLINGTON, CO. DURHAM, 7, 3D
Church of St Cuthbert Church begun
c.1192 and restored 19th C has crossing
tower, transepts and imposing west
front; fine 13th-C font cover, early
14th-C sedilia and piscina, and
15th-C Easter Sepulchre

DARNAWAY CASTLE, (6.5 km. / 4 m.
SW of Forres), GRAMPIAN, 8, 2A
Darnaway Castle (open as part of tour of
Darnaway Estate) Classical mansion built
19th C and 1902 incorporates 14th-C
Randolph's Hall at rear retaining
marvellous hammerbeam roof dated
to 1387 with finely carved work (one
of two medieval great halls in Scotland
with original roofs, the other being at
Edinburgh Castle)

DARRINGTON, W. YORKS, 7, 4E
Church of St Luke and All Saints Norman church with medieval rebuilding has original west tower with 15th-C top, early 13th-C arcades, chancel with 14th-C priest's doorway, and rood stair turret; good effigies of 1300s, 15th-C bench ends and chancel stalls

DARTINGTON, DEVON, 1, 5D
Dartington Hall (gardens only open *) Late 14th-C courtyard house (one of few rare survivals of medieval domestic architecture on grand scale) rebuilt 16th to 19th C and restored 1926–38; magnificent great hall, east and west ranges, hall porch and wide hall fireplace

DARTMOUTH, DEVON, 1, 5D
Church of St Saviour Late medieval church preserves south door with lively 15th-C ironwork
Dartmouth Castle [EH] Late 15th-C castle at entrance to Dart estuary
Kingswear Castle [LT] Tower finished 1502 on opposite shore from Dartmouth Castle, converted 19th-C as summer residence
Cove Fort [EH] Small artillery fort of 1509–10

DAVINGTON PRIORY, KENT, 3, 4C
See Faversham

DAVY'S ISLAND (in Castle Archdale Bay, 14 km. / 9m. N of Devenish), CO. FERMANAGH, 11, 3B
Church Remains of medieval church on early island site once belonging to Augustinians of Lisgoole

DEAN, BEDS, 4, 1E
Church of All Saints Mainly 14th-C church with west tower and 15th-C clerestory; elaborately carved gargoyles, nave roof with angels, and unusual screens

DEAN, (1.5 km. / 1 m. NE of Kilmarnock) STRATHCLYDE, 10, 4C
Dean Castle Well-preserved 15th-C tower house with 17th-C additions and early 20th-C restorations set in attractive grounds (country park); castle houses collection including arms and armour, tapestry, and musical instruments

DEARHAM, CUMBRIA, 7, 1C
Church of St Mungo Norman church retains south doorway of c.1170–90, west tower with later upper stages, and north aisle added 1882; finely carved font of

c.1170 and fragments of Anglo-Danish sculpture

DEBENHAM, SUFFOLK, 3, 4A
Church of St Mary Church of Saxo-Norman origin retains 11th-C tower with 14th-C top, 13th-C chancel, west porch and galilee built 1300s, and fine four-bay arcade

DEDDINGTON, OXON, 2, 4A
Church of St Peter and St Paul Mainly 13th-C church with 14th-C remodelling and 17th-C additions has early 13th-C nave and chancel, wide aisles, and north and south chapels; fine 13th-C sedilia and piscina, and 15th-C screen
Leadenporch House, New Street Hall-house of c.1325 remodelled 17th and 19th C
Deddington Castle [EH] Remains of 12th-C castle and earthworks

DEDHAM, ESSEX, 3, 4A
Church of St Mary Large late 15th-C church has handsome flint-faced tower completed c.1520 above passageway with richly carved vault
Southfields Wealthy clothier's substantial timber-framed house, offices and warehouse built around courtyard c.1500,

DEENE, NORTHANTS, 4, 1D
Church of St Peter Restored and rebuilt church retains 13th-C tower with carved west doorway and recessed broach spire

DEEPING ST JAMES, LINCS, 4, 1D
Church of St James Spacious former priory church founded 1139 with much medieval rebuilding retains fine late 12th-C south arcade with wall passage above; west tower added c.1717
Village Cross 15th-C cross converted to lock-up 1819

DEER ABBEY, (16 km. / 10 m. W of Peterhead), GRAMPIAN, 8, 4A
Deer Abbey [HS] Fragmentary and much reconstructed remains of Cistercian abbey founded 1219 on or near site of 7th-C monastery include abbot's house and infirmary

DEERHURST, GLOS, 2, 3A
Church of St Mary Important priory church built c.804 and 10th C retains tall, original nave, tower added 900s, and arcades of c.1200; superb carving on sanctuary arch, 8th- and 10th-C sculpture, late 9th-C font and 14th- to 15th-C stained glass
Odda's Chapel [EH] Well-preserved Saxon chapel (dedicated 1056 and

discovered 1885) forms west end of farmhouse
The Priory House Mainly 14th-C priory house of former 9th-C monastery

DEERNESS, ORKNEY, 9, 5B
Chapel and Settlement, Brough of Deerness Almost inaccessible remains of early medieval chapel and houses

DEFYNNOG, POWYS, 6, 4D
Church of St Cynog Church of Celtic origin has body of c.1500 with south porch and west tower; early 11th-C font with Runic writing, and early stoup

DELGATIE, GRAMPIAN, 8, 4A
Delgatie Castle * (3 km. / 2 m. E) Well-preserved medieval tower house (still occupied) rebuilt on L-plan c.1570 with groin-vaulted solar; wings added 1769 and 19th-C work

DELVIN CASTLE, CO. WESTMEATH, 11, 4D
See Castletown-Delvin

DENBIGH, CLWYD, 6, 5A
Denbigh Castle [CADW] Remains of medieval castle include 13th-C walling, curtain towers, and triple-towered Great Gatehouse of late 1200s or early 14th-C; defensive mantlet and sallyport
Town Walls [CADW] Extensive remains of town walls begun 1282 with walls, polygonal Goblin Tower, Countess Tower, and late 13th- or early 14th-C Burgess Gate
Chapel of St Hilary Surviving west wall and 14th- or early 15th-C tower of chapel built c.1300 (mainly demolished 1923)
Friary *, Abbey Road. Remains of church of Carmelite friary established late 13th C
Church of St Marcella Llanfarchell (Whitchurch) (Outer Denbigh). Medieval church remodelled late 15th or early 16th C with double nave; west tower and good timber roofs

DENNINGTON, SUFFOLK, 4, 4E
Church of St Mary 14th- and 15th-C church retains five-bay arcades, west tower, two-storeyed sacristy, and rich Bardolph Chapel with tomb chest of mid 1400s; rich variety of furnishings include 14th-C stained glass, lavish well-preserved parclose screens, font with cover, good set of benches, and rare pyx canopy dating from c.1500 (suspended above altar)

DENNY PRIORY, CAMBS, 4, 2E
Denny Priory * Remains of cell of Ely founded 1160, used by Templars during

13th C and converted for nuns of order of St Clare c.1342–50, include fragments of Norman church (incorporated in 18th-C house) and mid 14th-C refectory

DENSTON, SUFFOLK, 3, 3A
Church of St Nicholas [OCT] 15th-C church with rare surviving original rood beam

DENTON, CUMBRIA, 7, 2B
Church of St Cuthbert, Nether Denton Church built 1868–70 contains finely carved Norman figure of king set against cross
Church, Upper Denton Church with Norman chancel arch and north window retains earlier work

DERBY, DERBYS, 5, 4C
Cathedral Church of All Saints Church (cathedral after 1927) mainly rebuilt 1723–5 with east extension of 1967–72 retains handsome, richly decorated early 16th-C west tower of three tall storeys
Bridge Chapel of St Mary, Bridge Gate [OCT] Bridge chapel of 14th-C origin with much later alteration
Church of St Peter Medieval church extensively restored and rebuilt during 19th and 20th C

DERRY (2.5 km. / 1½ m. NE of Portaferry), CO. DOWN, 11, 5C
Churches [EHS] Remains of two small medieval churches, that to south possibly 10th- or 11th-C

DERRYBRUSK, CO. FERMANAGH, 11, 3C
See Derryvullan

DERRYGONNELLY, CO. FERMANAGH, 11, 3C
Carrick Church (3 km. / 2m. NW) Modest church built late 1400s on remote site by Carrick Lough

DERRYVULLAN (2.5 km. / 1½ m. W of Lisbellaw), CO. FERMANAGH, 11, 3C
Derrybrusk Old Church (2 km. / 1¼ m. S of Tamlaght Bridge) Small medieval church with late 16th-C restoration and east window

DERSINGHAM, NORFOLK, 4, 3C
Church of St Nicholas Large, mainly 15th-C church retains 14th-C chancel and arcades; good screen and splendid early 16th-C carved chest

DERWEN, CLWYD, 6, 5B
Church of St Mary Simple late medieval church restored 1857 with bellcote of 1688;

well-preserved rood screen and loft of late 15th or early 16th C; fine churchyard cross of 1400s [CADW]

DESKFORD (6.5 km. / 4 m. S of Cullen), GRAMPIAN, 8, 3A
Deskford Church (St John's) [HS] Ruins of small late medieval church with finely carved sacrament house of 1551 (preserved under sheet of glass)

DETLING, KENT, 3, 3D
Church of St Martin Early Norman church with 13th- and 15th-C work retains fine mid 14th-C carved lectern

DEVENISH ISLAND, (3 km. / 2 m. below Enniskillen in lower Lough Erne), CO. FERMANAGH, 11, 3C
Monastic Site [Dúchas] Site of important early monastery retains splendid five-storeyed Round Tower built probably 12th C, remains of small oratory (St Molaise's House) built probably late 1100s, ruined 12th-C St Molaise's Church (or Teampul Mor) with fine stone coffin in north-west corner, medieval St Mary's Abbey including remains of fine large church built 1449 with surviving crossing tower and ornate late 15th-C High Cross in cemetery

DEVIL'S BRIDGE, DYFED, 6, 4C
Devil's Bridge Lowest of three bridges, one above another spanning Mynach gorge, said to have been built by Abbey of Strata Florida during 12th C

DEVIZES, WILTS, 2, 3C
Church of St John Impressive Norman church with west front built 1861–2 retains original crossing tower, rib-vaulted chancel with blind arcading of c.1125–35, late 14th-C arcades, and lavish 15th-C south (Beauchamp) chapel
Church of St Mary Norman church rebuilt 15th C with tall west tower, clerestory, and two-storeyed south porch; fine original rib-vaulted chancel

DEWSBURY, W. YORKS, 7, 3E
Church of All Saints Medieval church with restoration and additions of c.1785 and 1884–5 retains 13th-C north arcade; fragments of important Saxon crosses and 13th-C coved coffin lid

DIDBROOK, GLOS, 2, 3A
Church of St George Church rebuilt 1475 with unusual tower rising from inside nave; 14th-C font

Cottages Two cruck-built cottages, perhaps as early as 15th-C

DIDDLEBURY, SHROPS, 5, 2D
Church of St Peter Late Saxon church with medieval and 19th-C additions has original nave with north doorway, west tower, and Norman chancel

DILWYN, HEREFS, 5, 2E
Church of St Mary Church largely built c.1300 retains Norman west tower reworked c.1250; good chancel, arcades, 14th-C south porch, and monuments

DINAS EMRYS, GWYNEDD, 6, 4B
Dinas Emrys Castle Ruins of 12th-C keep on site of Iron Age hill fort

DINEFWR CASTLE, DYFED, 6, 4D
Dinefwr Castle [CADW / NT] Norman keep and inner bailey of medieval castle, important centre of Welsh political power during 12th to 13th C; 14th-C alterations and late medieval curtain wall; castle converted to picturesque ruin in 18th C as part of landscape park surrounding Newton House

DINMORE, HEREFS, 5, 2E
Dinmore Manor * House built on remote site formerly belonging to preceptory of Knights of St John of Jerusalem (founded 1189) has reset early 14th-C doorways to east wing; work of c.1700 and west range added 1929–36; detached 14th-C chapel with west tower and 12th-C north doorway

DINTON, BUCKS, 2, 5A
Church of St Peter and St Paul Church with extensive late medieval remodelling retains fine, rich Norman south doorway with carved Tree of Life and lions in tympanum above; 13th-C chancel and south arcade
Dinton Hall House with complex building history (16th to 19th-C additions) retains late medieval range to west

DIRLETON, LOTHIAN, 8, 3E
Dirleton Castle [HS / NTS] (gardens also open) Castle of enclosure built 13th C on rocky outcrop with extensive 14th- to 16th-C additions retains original group of towers to south-west; seven-sided Lord's Chamber in Donjon Tower; later medieval east range with tunnel-vaulted chapel to north; fine 16th-C 'beehive' dovecot

DISERT OENGHUSA, CARRIGEEN, CO. LIMERICK, 12, 3C
Church and Round Tower [Dúchas] Round Tower and 15th- to 16th-C church mark site of early monastery

DISERTH, CLWYD
See Dyserth

DISSERTH, POWYS, 6, 4C
Church of St Cewydd Unrestored medieval church retains west tower of c.1400, mid 15th-C chancel and nave, and 16th- to 17th-C work; good 15th-C roofs and rood beam

DITCHEAT, SOMERSET, 2, 2C
Church of St Mary Magdalene Medieval church with spacious late 13th-C chancel enlarged late 1400s, and crossing tower built c.1300 and 15th C; wall painting of c.1500

DODDISCOMBSLEIGH, DEVON, 1, 5C
Church of St Michael Medieval church rebuilt 19th C has five original late 15th-C stained-glass windows

DOE CASTLE, (3 km. / 2 m. NE of Creeslough), CO. DONEGAL, 11, 3A
Doe Castle [Dúchas] Beautifully set castle built earlier 16th C on shores of Sheephaven Bay consists of four-storeyed tower enclosed by tall bawn (modernised c.1800, occupied until c.1900)

DOGTON STONE (2.5 km. 1½ m. ENE of Cardenden), FIFE, 8, 3D
Dogton Stone [HS], Dogton Farmhouse Weathered, carved cross slab dating from 10th C

DOLBADARN CASTLE GWYNEDD, 6, 4A
Dolbadarn Castle [CADW] Dramatically sited ruins of castle guarding Llanberis Pass built by Llywelyn the Great c.1216–40, with substantial round tower keep and unmortared curtain wall, and towers surviving only as footings

DOLFORWYN, POWYS, 6, 5C
Dolforwyn Castle [CADW] Remains of castle built 1273 with walled enclosure and round tower

DOLTON, DEVON, 1, 4C
Church of St Edmund Medieval church much reworked 1800s contains unusual font made from blocks of carved Saxon cross shaft

DOLWYDDELAN, GWYNEDD, 6, 4A
Dolwyddelan Castle [CADW] Spectacularly sited castle commanding Ledr Valley in Snowdonia, built by Llywelyn the Great c.1210–40, with curtain wall and massive rectangular keep heightened late 15th and heavily restored 19th C

DONAGHMORE, CO. DOWN, 11, 3C
Cross Carved 9th- to 10th-C High Cross set up 1891 on roof of large souterrain beneath Church of Ireland churchyard (site of 5th- to 6th-C monastery)

DONAGHMORE, CO. MEATH, 11, 40
Round Tower [Dúchas] Well-preserved tower built probably 1100s retains doorway with good relief carving of Crucifixion above
Dunmoe Castle [Dúchas] (1.5 km. / 1 m. E) Surviving south wall and corner towers of large four-storeyed medieval castle (built probably 15th C) on dramatic elevated site

DONAGHMORE, CO. TIPPERARY, 12, 4C
Church of St Farannan [Dúchas] Site of early monastery houses remains of small 12th-C church (partly restored 16th C) with original, finely carved west doorway and chancel arch with well-preserved capitals

DONAGHMORE, CO. TYRONE, 11, 4B
High Cross [EHS] Splendid early 9th- or early 10th-C sandstone cross with carved biblical scenes (re-erected 18th C) marks site of early Christian monastery

DONAGHMOYNE CO. MONAGHAN, 11, 3C
Manaan Castle [Dúchas] Remains of motte and bailey castle built c.1193 on hilltop site and encased in stone 1244

DONEGAL, CO. DONEGAL, 11, 3B
Franciscan Friary [Dúchas] Fragmentary remains of friary founded 1474 near River Esk and complete by 1488 include east and north sides of small and unusual cloister
Donegal Castle [Dúchas] Massive tower keep of 1505, altered early 17th C with addition of splendid fortified manor house wing
Magherabeg Abbey (1.5 km. / 1 m. SSW) Scanty remains of Franciscan tertiary friary built 1400s
St Ernans (3 km. / 2 m. SW) Picturesque island retreat with 10th-C or earlier relief carving from Donegal Abbey in rockery before early 19th-C cottage

DONINGTON-LE-HEATH,
LEICS, 5,4C
Donington-le-Heath Manor House,
Manor Road (now museum)* Moated
manor house of c.1280 remodelled 17th C
retains upper hall with original doorway,
roof and window

DONNINGTON, BERKS, 2,4C
Donnington Castle [EH] Substantial
remains of castle licensed 1386 with
corner towers and three-storeyed
gatehouse

DONORE, CO. MEATH
Donore Castle [Dúchas] Square, well-
preserved tower house built 1400s by
River Boyne

DOONBOUGHT CASTLE (1.5 km./
1 m. SSE of Clough),
CO. ANTRIM, 11,5B
Doonbought Castle Remains of medieval
castle on site of prehistoric fort

DOON HILL (3 km. / 2m. S of
Dunbar), LOTHIAN, 8,4E
Halls Remains of two timber halls (one
6th-C, the other 7th-C) revealed by
excavations

DORCHESTER, DORSET, 2,2E
Church of St Peter Mainly 15th-C church
with tall west tower has Norman south
doorway and 19th-C vestry; fine late
14th-C effigies of knights in south chapel.
See also Fordington

DORCHESTER, OXON, 2,5B
Abbey of St Peter and St Paul 12th-C
abbey church with 13th-, 14th- and
17th-C rebuilding retains original
north wall of nave and splendid choir
extended c.1340; fine lead font of c.1170,
stained glass of c.1290–1320, Jesse
window of c.1340, and medieval
monuments; 14th-C wall painting
of Crucifixion
Old School House 14th- or 15th-C
building, possibly abbey guest house,
converted to school c.1654
George Inn Timber-framed inn of c.1500
with jettied upper storey

DORNEY, BUCKS, 3,1C
Dorney Court* Manor house of c.1500
extensively altered 19th and 20th C has
original hall with fine roof and some
original fireplaces

DORNOCH, HIGHLAND, 9,4D
Cathedral [SCS] Cruciform cathedral
church begun after c.1223 with 15th- to
18th-C rebuilding and extensive

restoration of 1835–7 has lancet windows,
transepts and crossing tower; effigy
of c.1245
Dornoch Castle, The Square (now hotel)
Surviving south range of bishop's palace
built c.1500 with remodellings of 19th
and 20th C retains original five-storeyed
tower at north-west

DOUGLAS, STRATHCLYDE, 10,5C
St Bride's Church [HS], Main Street
Remains of late 14th-C parish church with
fragments of nave and roofed choir
housing three canopied medieval
monuments to Douglas family; heart
caskets on floor; south aisle rebuilt
19th C as burial vault

DOUNE, CENTRAL, 8,2D
Doune Castle [HS] Well-preserved and
restored remains of splendid, large castle
built late 14th C and reworked 19th C on
triangular site enclosed by moat and
rivers; fine gatehouse tower and range
containing Retainer's Hall with octagonal
hearth, and Lord's (or Duke's) Hall with
chamber above retaining oratory, piscina
and sacrament house

DOVER, KENT, 3,5D
Church of St Mary Cannon Street
Church of Norman origin much enlarged
1843–4 has early 12th-C five-stage west
tower and original nave arcades
Castle [EH] Massive cliff-top castle begun
1066 on Saxon site and rebuilt c.1168–85
with 13th-, 18th- and 19th-C work;
impressive square tower keep with
angle turrets, original curtain walling,
and gates and towers including fine
Constable's Tower of 1220s
Church of St Mary-in-Castro (within
Castle Precinct). Saxon church of c.1000
remodelled c.1190 and much restored
1860–2 retains original tower arches
and blocked south doorway, vaulted
chancel, and low central tower; tower
at western end was originally a
Roman lighthouse
Maison Dieu Biggin Street. Early 14th-C
former aisle of Maison Dieu (founded
c.1221 to care for poor and sick and
provide accommodation for pilgrims)
with tower and large windows survives
incorporated into eastern part of
Town Hall
St Edmund's Chapel Small chapel
consecrated 1253
Dover College Effingham Crescent
School founded 1868 incorporates
well-preserved buildings of 12th-C
St Martin's Priory including impressive

refectory with wall paintings, late
12th-C guest hall (now chapel), and
14th-C gatehouse
Knights Templar Church [EH] (on
Western Heights above town)
Foundations of small circular 12th-C
church

DOWNPATRICK, CO. DOWN, 11,5C
Cathedral of the Holy Trinity Cathedral
built 1790–1826 using east end of
Benedictine predecessor (begun 1184,
re-edified 1400s) retains fragments of
good medieval work; two pieces of
pre-Norman crosses set into east wall
of chapter room; 9th to 10th-C High
Cross re-erected 1897 to east of building

DOWNTON, WILTS, 2,4D
Church of St Lawrence Large Norman
church with medieval and 19th-C
remodelling retains original nave,
13th-C transepts altered 1300s, chancel
with priest's door, and crossing tower
reworked 17th C; 13th-C font

DRAX, N. YORKS, 7,4E
Church of St Peter and St Paul Norman
church with original west tower, north
arcade, chancel and south arcade dated
1230, 14th-C north chapel and lavish
15th-C clerestory; fine series of carved
figures above nave arcade

DRENAGH,
CO. LONDONDERRY, 7,4A
Church of St Cainnech, Drumachose
(1 km. / ½ m. SE of Drenagh House)
Remains of 13th-C church abandoned 1749

DRISHANE, CO. CORK, 12,2D
Castle [Dúchas] Tower house built 1450
with additions of c.1643 and later top

DROGHEDA, CO. LOUTH, 11,4D
Abbey and Hospital of St Mary D'Urso
Remains of church of abbey founded
c.1206 as hospital for poor survive in
unusual position straddling Abbey Lane
Magdalene Tower [Dúchas] Handsome
early 14th-C tower, all that survives
of church of Dominican friary
founded 1224
St Laurence's Gate [Dúchas] Fine
13th-C building with 14th- and 15th-C
enlargement, formerly part of medieval
defences, retains portcullis gate flanked
by monumental circular towers
Butter Gate [Dúchas] Remains of
medieval gate-tower with attached
fragment of town wall
Colp Church (3.5 km. / 2 ¼ m. ESE)
Church with imposing tower occupying

ancient site contains 10th-C High Cross
in porch

DROITWICH, WORCS, 5,3E
Church of St Andrew Medieval church
retains early 13th-C north tower and
chancel arch, early 14th-C south chapel,
arcades, 15th-C north chapel and good
roof to chancel; north aisle added c.1910
St Peter's Church Church of Norman
origin with later additions has original
chancel and arch, south transept built
early 1200s, and 14th-C north transept;
late medieval west tower and
timber-framed clerestory

DROMIN CHURCH,
CO. LOUTH, 11,4D
See Stabannan

DROMISKIN, CO. LOUTH, 11,4D
Church of St Ronan [Dúchas] Ruins of
late medieval church on site of 6th-C
monastery; fragment of large Celtic cross
re-erected as gravestone 1918; remains of
Round Tower built probably late 800s
with alterations of 1880
Milltown Castle (2 km. / 1 ¼ m. NW)
Tower house built 13th or 15th C with
round corner towers and later alterations
survives in farmyard

DROMORE, CO. DOWN, 11,5C
Dromore Cross [EHS] at edge of
cathedral graveyard; Cross from early
monastery (restored and re-erected 1887)
with finely carved panels to shaft
Cathedral Cathedral on site of monastery
contains early gravestone ("St Colman's
Pillow")

DRUMACOO, CO. GALWAY, 12,5A
Church of St Surney [Dúchas] Church
built mainly early 13th C with fine south
door incorporates earlier building with
flat-headed doorway to south-west;
north wing added c.1830

DRUMADONNELL CROSS
CO. DOWN, 11,5C
See Castlewellan

DRUMBO, CO. DOWN, 7,5B
Round Tower Stump of early Christian
Round Tower in Presbyterian churchyard
marks site of early monastery founded
by St Mo-Chumma

DRUM CASTLE (5 km. / 3 m. W of
Peterculter), GRAMPIAN, 8,4B
Drum Castle [NTS] Massive late 13th-C
tower house (known as Tower of Drum,
one of oldest such buildings in Scotland)
with attached mansion built 1619 and
additions of 1875

DRUMCLIFF, CO. CLARE, 12, 2B
Round Tower and Church [Dúchas]
Remains of Round Tower and ruined
15th-C church on monastic site

DRUMCLIFFE, CO. SLIGO, 11, 2C
High Cross and Round Tower [Dúchas]
Sculptured cross (perhaps c.1000) and
stump of Round Tower on site of
monastery founded c.575, now graveyard
of church where poet W. B. Yeats is buried

DRUMENA (4 km. / 2 ½ m. SW of
    Castlewellan), CO. DOWN, 11, 5C
Drumena Cashel and Souterrain [EHS]
Early Christain oval cashel (partially
rebuilt after 1925–6 excavation) and
souterrain

DRUMHALLAGH,
    CO. DONEGAL, 11, 3A
Cross Slab (5 km. / 3m.N of Rathmullen)
Small and handsome carved cross slab
(probably 8th-C)

DRUMLANE, CO. CAVAN, 11, 3C
Round Tower and Church [Dúchas]
Graveyard houses early Round Tower
with carvings of birds on north face and
medieval church (possibly late 13th-C,
altered 15th and 17th C) with fine
stonework

DRUMMOND, TAYSIDE, 8, 2D
Drummond Castle (gardens open only)
Handsome castle on rocky outcrop
consists of large 15th-C keep (upper
levels remodelled), 17th-C gatehouse
range, and 19th-C mansion

DRYBURGH ABBEY, (8 km. / 5 m. SE
    of Melrose), BORDERS, 7, 2A
Dryburgh Abbey [HS] Enchanting site
by River Tweed houses remains of
Premonstratensian abbey founded 1150
with ruined church (burial place of
Sir Walter Scott) and unusually well-
preserved 12th and 13th-C monastic
buildings including vaulted sacristy
(later chapel), slype, fine chapter
house with painted decoration,
and refectory; dormitory altered
16th C as fortified commendator's
house

DRYSLWYN CASTLE,
    DYFED, 6, 3D
Dryslwyn Castle [CADW] Remaining
ruins of 13th-C native Welsh castle with
round keep, two halls and polygonal
curtain wall, set on rocky outcrop in
Towy valley beside site of township
probably occupied from 13th to 15th C

DUART (5 km. / 3 m. S of Craignure),
    STRATHCLYDE, 10, 3A
Duart Castle Imposing castle dating from
c.1250 with massive tower house added
14th C, later ranges, and restoration
of 1912

DUBLIN, CO. DUBLIN, 11, 4E
Christ Church Cathedral * Imposing
cathedral begun c.1173 by Augustinian
canons and extensively restored, refaced
and rebuilt 1871–8 by G. E Street retains
well preserved groin-vaulted 12th-C crypt
(unusual in extending beneath entire
church), late 12th- to early 13th-C
transepts, and aisled nave of c.1212
lengthened to west after 1234; fine
medieval fragments in crypt; monuments
include late 13th-C demi-figure called
"Strongbow's Son" and effigy of
"Strongbow" (c.1340); remains of
priory's 13th-C chapter house to south
Church of St Audoen [Dúchas],
Cornmarket, High Street. Church
founded by Anglo-Normans and restored
19th C has west doorway of c.1190 or
c.1200, 13th-C nave with 15th-C windows,
and tower of mainly 1670; 14th-C chancel,
nave south aisle (widened 1431 as St Ann's
Chapel) and Chapel of the Blessed Virgin
or Portlester Chapel (c.1455) all survive
as roofless ruins; west porch contains
Portlester Cenotaph with effigies (late
15th-C) and other medieval sculpture
St Mary's Abbey [Dúchas], Meetinghouse
Lane, off Capel Street. Rib-vaulted
chapter house and slype (c.1190 or c.1200),
sole surviving remains of important
Benedictine abbey founded 1139
(Cistercian after 1147)
Cathedral of St Patrick, Patrick Street
Mainly 13th- to 14th-C cruciform
cathedral church (largest in Ireland) much
restored 1864–9 has Lady Chapel built 1270
(reworked 1845–50) and imposing north-
west tower of 1362 (spire added 1749–50);
good effigy of Archbishop Fulk de
Saundford (1271) in well-preserved choir,
fine figure of St Patrick, and excellent
monument to Archbishop Tregury
(1471 or later)
Church of St Werburgh *, Werburgh
Street. Church built 1715–19 and restored
1759–68 houses splendid Purcell double
tomb of 1500–20 in entrance hall with
effigies and niched figures of apostles
and saints
Dublin Castle [State Apartments –
Dúchas, Castle under management of
OPW] Castle built 13th C and almost
totally remodelled 1730–1800, former

official residence of Lords Deputy and
Lords Lieutenant (also used as law
courts, seat of parliaments, prison, etc.),
has medieval work visible on south side
including Record Tower and parts of wall;
two corner towers on north side can be
seen below ground after 1980s excavation

DUCKLINGTON, OXON, 2, 4A
Church of St Bartholomew 12th-C church
with 14th-C rebuilding retains original
three bay south arcade, 13th-C chancel,
and fine north aisle reworked c.1340 as
chantry chapel; Norman font and rich
founder's tomb

DUDDINGSTON (Edinburgh),
    LOTHIAN, 8, 3E
Duddingston Church, Old Church Lane
[SCS] Church with Norman nave and
chancel retaining original chancel arch
and blocked south doorway; 17th-C west
tower and north (Prestonfield) aisle and
18th- and early 19th-C additions

DUDDINGTON, NORTHANTS, 4, 1D
Church of St Mary Norman church with
north arcade built c.1150–75 (enlarged
c.1225), south doorway of c.1190–1200, and
late 12th-C south arcade; 12th- and 13th-C
tower, 14th-C clerestory, and chancel
much restored 1844

DUDLEY, W. MIDLANDS, 5, 3D
Dudley Castle Remains of castle founded
11th C with additions of 14th, 16th and 17th
C include inner gatehouse, early 14th-C
keep, barbican and chapel
Priory Remains of church and monastic
buildings of Benedictine priory founded
c.1160

DUFFUS (5 km. / 3 m. NW of Elgin),
    GRAMPIAN, 8, 3A
St Peter's Kirk and Parish Cross [HS]
Roofless medieval church much rebuilt
1700s retains work of 1226, base of 14th-C
west tower (now Sutherland burial vault),
and remains of early 16th-C rib-vaulted
porch; shaft of 14th-C parish cross in
churchyard
Duffus Castle [HS] (2.5 km. / 1 ½ m. E)
Dramatic castle with keep and bailey walls
of c.1300 stands on motte built c.1150

DUISKE ABBEY,
    CO. KILKENNY, 12, 5C
See Graiguenamanagh

DULEEK, CO. MEATH, 11, 4D
Duleek Cross [Dúchas] Small and well-
preserved 9th-C High Cross with good
sculptural scenes

St Mary's Priory [Dúchas] Impressive
14th- and 15th-C remains of church of
Augustinian priory founded 1182 with
walls of south aisle, east gable with
window of 1597, and fine tower to west
incorporating earlier Round Tower;
good 15th-C tomb chest in aisle and
fragments of carved stonework in belfry

DUMBARTON, STRATHCLYDE, 10, 4C
Dumbarton Castle [HS] Impressively
sited castle consisting of mainly 18th- and
19th-C fortifications retains 14th-C
portcullis arch
Riverside Parish Church, High Street
[SCS] Church built 1811 with interior
refurbished 1886 houses (in gallery)
11th- or 12th-C Crusader Stone

DUMFRIES, DUMFRIES AND
    GALLOWAY, 7, 1B
Lincluden Collegiate Church [HS], Abbey
Lane. Remains of late 14th- and 15th-C
collegiate buildings and church; choir
with stone pulpitum; fine mid 15th-C
monument to Princess Margaret,
Countess of Douglas
Old Bridge, from Whitesands to Mill
Road Impressive medieval bridge built
c.1430–2, reconstructed 1620 and curtailed
early 19th C

DUNAMASE (4.5 km. / 2 ¾m. WNW
    of Stradbally), CO. LAOIS, 12, 4B
Dunamase Castle [Dúchas] Scant remains
of large castle built 13th C and reworked
14th and 17th C on impressive, defensive
Rock of Dunamase

DUNBAR, LOTHIAN, 8, 4E
Trinitarian Priory, Friarscroft Surviving
late medieval crossing tower (now
converted to dovecot) of church
of friary founded c.1240–8

DUNBLANE, CENTRAL, 8, 2D
Dunblane Cathedral [HS] Important
cathedral built mainly 13th C (restored
19th and 20th C) incorporating lower
stages of mid 12th-C tower has fine west
front with lancet windows, clerestoried
nave, and good choir; sculpted stone of
c.900 (north aisle), effigies of 1271, 15th-C
figure of Bishop Ochiltree, and finely
carved stalls provided 1486
Old Bridge Bridge dating from 1409
crosses Allan Water

DUNBOYNE, CO. MEATH, 11, 4D
Dunboyne Old Castle Remains of tower
house built 1476 (now situated in churchyard); fragments of building survive in
nearby 20th-C church (SS Peter and Paul)

DUNBRODY, (1.5 km. / 1 m. WSW of Campile), CO. WEXFORD, 12, 4C
Dunbrody Abbey [Dúchas] Imposing remains of fine, mainly early 13th-C buildings of Cistercian abbey (founded between 1175 and 1178) include long church with chancel, transepts, five-bay nave and low 15th-C central tower, and cloister garth with sacristy, groin-vaulted chapter house, book-store and refectory

DUNDALK, CO. LOUTH, 11, 4C
Church of St Nicholas Church founded 13th C with 16th- to 20th-C alterations retains original tower with later spire
Franciscan Friary, "Seatown Castle" Surviving late medieval tower of church of monastery founded 1200s
Castletown Bellew Big tower house with corner turrets built c.1475 and restored 1950s; Castletown Church; Remains of small late medieval church

DUNDAS CASTLE, (1.5 km. / 1 m. S of South Queensferry), LOTHIAN, 8, 2E
Dundas Castle Late medieval castle licensed 1424 and built on L-plan has good original fireplace to upper hall

DUNDEE, TAYSIDE, 8, 3D
St Mary's Tower (or Old Steeple) (part of so-called City Churches) Impressive later 15th-C tower, originally at west end of lost medieval Church of St Mary, has elaborate tracery and telescopes upwards culminating in fine pinnacled parapet and later cap-house (small chamber); churches adjoining added 18th and mid 19th C

DUNDONALD (5.5 km. / 3 ½ m. NE of Troon), STRATHCLYDE, 10, 4C
Dundonald Castle [HS] Ruins of castle built 13th C on hilltop, rebuilt c.1370 as large tower house by Robert II

DUNDRENNAN (10 km. / 6 m. SE of Kirkcudbright), DUMFRIES AND GALLOWAY, 10, 5E
Dundrennan Abbey [HS] Substantial, beautiful remains of Cistercian monastery founded 1142 and restored 19th C include fine church completed c.1200, chapter house, and west range of cloister; good medieval monuments

DUNDRUM, CO. DOWN, 11, 5C
Dundrum Castle [EHS] Remains of impressive medieval castle on hilltop site with polygonal upper ward and circular keep built late 12th C to early 13th C, later 13th-C gatehouse, and lower ward added probably 13th to late 15th C; ruined 17th-C house in south-west corner

DUNDURN PARISH CHURCH, TAYSIDE, 8, 2D
See St Fillans

DUNFALLANDY STONE, (1.5 km. / 1 m. S of Pitlochry), TAYSIDE, 8, 2C
Dunfallandy Stone [HS] (behind glass) Fine 8th-C Pictish stone with carved figures and cross

DUNFERMLINE, FIFE, 8, 3E
Dunfermline Abbey and Palace [HS] [SCS] Impressive remains of Benedictine abbey founded soon after 1070 by Queen Margaret include fine mid 12th-C nave with attached church built 1818–21 on chancel foundations, reredorter, refectory rebuilt 1329, and gatehouse; fragment of mid 13th-C shrine chapel of St Margaret at east end of 19th-C church; 14th-C guest house reworked as royal palace c.1540 and 1590–1600

DUNGIVEN, CO. LONDONDERRY, 11, 4B
St Mary's Priory (1 km. / ½ m. S) [EHS] Medieval priory church adapted for Protestant use 17th C and abandoned c.1720 retains late 10th- or 11th-C nave and chancel added early 1300s; well-preserved O'Cahan tomb has fine traceried canopy, effigy and arcaded base

DUNGLASS (1.5 km. / 1 m. NW of Cockburnspath), LOTHIAN, 8, 4E
Collegiate Church of St Mary [HS] Ruined church of college founded 1450, formerly used as barn, retains nave and chancel with slightly later transepts and crossing tower; good triple sedilia in chancel, tomb recess in north sacristy, and consecration crosses

DUNGLOE, CO. DONEGAL, 11, 3A
Templecrone Old Church (5.5 km. / 3 ½ m. WSW) Surviving walls of medieval church abandoned 1829 with good late 12th or early 13th-C east window

DUNGORY/DUNGUAIRE, CO. GALWAY, 12, 5A
Dungory Castle (or Dunguaire Castle), Kinvara. Handsome castle built probably 16th C on picturesque site in Galway Bay (joined to mainland by small causeway) has large tower and well preserved bawn

DUNHAM MASSEY, CHESHIRE, 5, 2A
White Cottage [NT] (pre-booked visits only) Restored timber-framed cottage built c.1500

DUNKELD, TAYSIDE, 8, 2C
Dunkeld Cathedral [HS] [SCS] Mainly 14th- to 15th-C cathedral on banks of River Tay with choir built 1318-1400 (restored 19th C and 1908, now parish church) and roofless nave and aisles begun 1406; large tower at end of north aisle added 1469–c.1501 contains 15th-C wall paintings; good tracery, west window, sedilia, and fragments of effigy of founder (d.1338)

DUNKINEELY, CO. DONEGAL, 11, 3B
Killaghtee Old Church and Cross (1.5 km. / 1 m. WSW) Fragmentary remains of medieval church with mid 12th-C east window; small cross slab of c.650–700 survives to south
Rahan Castle (2 km. / 1 ¼ m. SW) Scanty ruins of late medieval castle on promontory site

DUNLUCE CASTLE (4 km. / 2 ½ m. WNW of Bushmills), CO. ANTRIM, 11, 4A
Dunluce Castle Remains of castle of 14th-C origin built on spectacular headland site with extensive 16th- and early 17th-C additions; original work includes south curtain and south-east and north-east towers

DUNMAHON CASTLE CO. LOUTH, 11, 4C
See Blackrock

DUNMOE CASTLE, CO. MEATH, 11, 4D
See Donaghmore

DUNMORE, CO. GALWAY, 12, 3A
Dunmore Castle [Dúchas] Remains of imposing early 14th-C four-storeyed tower-keep built on earlier motte with some late 16th- or early 17th-C alterations
Friary [Dúchas] Surviving church of small Augustinian friary founded 1425 with fine 15th-C west doorway; chancel later used as Protestant parish church

DUNMULLAN (8 km. / 5 m. N of Omagh), CO. TYRONE, 11, 4B
Cappagh Church Ruins of medieval church with later alterations

DUNNING, TAYSIDE, 8, 2D
St Serf's Church [HS] (view exterior only) Church of Norman origin rebuilt 1810 retains fine, lofty square tower and tower arch of c.1210

DUNNOTTAR (3 km. / 2 m. S of Stonehaven), GRAMPIAN, 8, 4C
Dunnottar Castle * Ruined castle set on spectacular, isolated promontory site approached by ravine has late 14th- or early 15th-C L-shaped tower house and extensive 16th- and 17th-C buildings including gatehouse of c.1575

DUNROBIN (2.5 km. / 1 ½ m. NE of Golspie), HIGHLAND, 9, 4C
Dunrobin Castle * Fine, mainly post medieval castle cum country house (17th- to early 20th-C) encloses massive 13th-C inner keep or tower house; museum in grounds contains, among other finds, good Pictish stones

DUNS, BORDERS, 8, 4E
Duns Castle * Castle incorporates parts of altered 14th C keep much extended 18th and 19th C

DUNSANY, CO. MEATH, 11, 4D
Church of St Nicholas and Cross [Dúchas] Ruins of impressive mid 15th-C church built by Plunkett family (almost identical to that at Killeen) with towers at west end, and large tower house attached to chancel; fine tracery, octagonal apostle font of c.1460, and Plunkett altar tomb c.1470; fragment of 15th-C cross to north

DUNSFOLD, SURREY, 3, 1D
Church of St Mary and All Saints Well preserved church built c.1270 with additions of 15th and 19th C has aisleless nave and chancel, and transepts; 13th-C pews, piscina and sedilia

DUNSHAUGHLIN, CO. MEATH, 11, 4D
Church of St Seachnaill [Dúchas] Early 19th-C church retains former lintel of 10th- or 11th-C church with carved Crucifixion, and arch from late medieval arcade

DUNSOGHLY, CO. DUBLIN, 11, 4D
Castle [Dúchas] Castle built c.1450 with square corner towers; original 15th- to 16th-C timber roof on top floor (last to survive in Ireland)

DUNSTABLE, BEDS, 3, 1D
Church of St Peter Church of Augustinian priory founded 1131 retains seven bays of late 12th-C nave and west front with ornate Norman portal; fine Norman font, partly re-cut
Dunstable Priory Fragments of priory buildings include house with medieval rib-vaulted room and 15th-C gatehouse

DUNSTAFFNAGE (5.5 km. / 3 ½ m.
NE of Oban), STRATHCLYDE, 10, 3A
Dunstaffnage Castle and Chapel [HS]
Ruins of mainly 13th-C castle on rocky
promontory in Firth of Lorn with
remains of fine contemporary
chapel nearby (c.1225–50); 17th-C
tower house above entrance

DUNSTANBURGH CASTLE,
NORTHUMBERLAND, 7, 1A
Dunstanburgh Castle [EH / NT] Vast
promontory site with remains of dramatic
castle licensed 1315 and enlarged 1380–4
retaining gatehouse and towers

DUNSTER, SOMERSET, 1, 5B
Church of St George Former church of
Norman Benedictine priory with
medieval rebuilding and restoration
of 1875–7 retains 13th-C chancel, mid
15th-C crossing tower and transepts;
good monuments, roofs, octagonal
font, and fine screen erected c.1498
Prior's House Medieval prior's house and
dovecot with surviving potence stand
close to church
Dunster Castle [NT] Fortified manor
house on elevated site has late 13th-C gateway, gatehouse built 1420–2, and main
range much remodelled 16th to 17th C
and c.1870
Luttrell Arms, Market Place. Timber-
framed house of c.1500 altered 1622–9
Nunnery, Church Street. 14th-C building
with jettied upper storeys and later
additions
Gallox Bridge [EH] Medieval packhorse
bridge spanning mill stream
Butter Cross [EH] Medieval stone cross

DUNTON, BUCKS, 2, 5A
Church of St Martin Church has Norman
nave retaining original north doorway
with carved figures flanking lintel, 13th-C
chancel, and later medieval west tower

DUNTULM CASTLE (2 km. / 1 ¼ m.
W of Kilmaluag), HIGHLAND
(Skye and Lochalsh)
(Inner Hebrides), 9, 2D
Duntulm Castle Remains of medieval
castle on defensive promontory site with
curtain walls, sea gate, and 17th-C
additions

DUNURE (8 km. / 5 m. NW of
Maybole), STRATHCLYDE, 10, 4D
Dunure Castle Cliffside ruin of 13th-C
keep with curtain wall and lower 15th-C
block containing hall and private lodgings

DUNVEGAN, HIGHLAND
(Skye) (Inner Hebrides), 9, 2D
Dunvegan Castle [HHA] Substantial
remains of medieval castle on impressive
site converted to mansion 18th and 19th C
with 13th-C curtain walls, sea gate, 14th-C
keep, and Fairy Tower of c.1500 (enlarged
1684–90); beautiful 10th-C Dunvegan
Cup, Irish drinking vessel with later
silver ornamentation

DUNWICH, SUFFOLK, 4, 5E
Friary Ruins of Franciscan friary built
after 1290
Hospital Chapel, St James' Churchyard
Surviving Norman apse of ruined leper
hospital

DUPATH WELL,
CORNWALL, 1, 3D
See Callington

DURHAM, CO. DURHAM, 7, 3C
Cathedral * Imposing cathedral restored
18th and 19th C retains Norman nave with
rich arcades, transepts, spacious late
12th-C west galilee, west towers, choir
with mid 13th-C vault, and crossing tower
rebuilt 1400s; Chapel of Nine Altars
begun 1242 has fine Joseph window of
c.1280; many medieval wall paintings,
monuments and fittings including
Neville Screen of 1372–80
Cathedral Precinct Lavish buildings
by cathedral include chapter house
completed between 1133 and 1141, deanery
with prior's chapel of 1244–54, fine
octagonal kitchen built 1366–74,
dormitory, slype, and cloister arcades
rebuilt early 15th C; Norman sculpture
and medieval wall paintings
College College rebuilt 1700s incorporates
late 15th- to early 16th-C gatehouse and
other medieval work
Castle * Extensive, well-preserved
Norman castle with later alterations
retains chapel built late 1000s, Norman
gallery with rich arcade, medieval hall
on 11th-C undercroft, kitchen converted
1499 with timber louvre, and octagonal
keep reworked 1839–40
Church of St Giles Gilesgate. Church
consecrated 1112 as chapel to hospital
and reworked 1873–6 retains good early
Norman work, early 13th-C west tower
with 15th-C upper levels, and wide
14th-C south aisle
Church of St Oswald, Church Street
Medieval church on early site much
altered 1834 retains four bays of late 12th-C
arcades, Norman chancel arch, and 15th-C

west tower; early 15th-C choir stalls and
unusual sedilia
Framwellgate Bridge Bridge begun c.1401
and reworked 1856
Elvet Bridge Bridge of c.1170 with 13th-,
14th- and 19th-C rebuildings
Medieval defences and Town Plan
Remains of medieval walling with
14th-C bastion near Owengate and
well-preserved street pattern
Kepier Hospital, Providence Row
Surviving 14th-C gatehouse of hospital
founded 1112
Crook Hall Medieval manor house
with adjoining section of 1671 retains
14th-C hall
Sherburn Hospital (3 km. / 2 m. ESE)
Hospital incorporates surviving south
wall of original chapel belonging to
lazar-house founded c.1181 with medieval
west tower (in building of 1868); medieval
gatehouse on south side of quadrangle

DURLEIGH, SOMERSET, 2, 1C
Church Norman church with early 14th-C
west tower
West Bower Manor House Small medieval
manor house retains entrance flanked by
two polygonal towers with upper rooms

DURROW, CO. OFFALY, 11, 3E
High Cross and Graveslabs [Dúchas]
Excellent 10th-C High Cross with carved
biblical scenes, medieval gravestones
(possibly 9th- to 11th-C) and other
fragments mark site of important
monastery, later abbey

DUSTON, NORTHANTS, 5, 5E
See Northampton

DUXFORD, CAMBS, 3, 2A
Church of St Peter Norman church rebuilt
13th to 15th and 19th C has original west
tower; font with 14th-C stem
Church of St John [CCT] Redundant
Norman church with 14th-, 15th- and
17th-C additions retains crossing tower
and original south doorway
Chapel of St John's Hospital [EH]
Simple 13th-C chapel with chancel
and nave has original windows,
piscina and sedilia

DYCE (10 km. / 6 m. W of Aberdeen),
GRAMPIAN, 8, 4B
Dyce Symbol Stones [HS] Two good
Pictish stones with carved work survive
in ruined parish church (probably built
mainly 14th C)

DYMOCK, GLOS, 2, 2A
Church of St Mary Early Norman church
with additions of c.1120–40, 14th and
15th C has original blank arcading, mid
12th-C chancel arch and handsome
south doorway with tympanum

DYSART (Kirkcaldy),
FIFE, 8, 3D
Church of St Serf, Shore Road Remains of
church built c.1500 and abandoned 1802
with tall, fortified projecting tower

DYSERTH / DISERTH, CLWYD, 6, 5A
Church of St Ffraid, Waterfall Road
Medieval church with restoration and
additions of 1873–5 retains east window
with good stained glass of 1450 and
1530s; 12th- or 13th-C churchyard cross
with crude carving (now inside),
cross base, and fragment of early
14th-C incised slab

DYSERT O'DEA, CO. CLARE, 12, 2B
Church, Round Tower and High Cross
[Dúchas] Early Christian monastic site
has remains of 12th-C Round Tower and
church (much reconstructed late 17th C)
with finely carved original west doorway
now in south wall; beautiful 12th-C High
Cross re-erected 1683 and 1871 to east of
church has excellent figure carving

EARDISLAND, HEREFS, 5, 2E
Church of St Mary Medieval church
extensively restored 1864 has early 13th-C
nave, south and north doorways, 14th-C
south porch and west tower; sedilia of
c.1300 and early 14th-C tomb recesses
Burton Court [HHA] 18th-C house
rebuilt 19th and 20th C incorporates early
14th-C hall with open timber roof

EARDISLEY, HEREFS, 5, 1E
Church of St Mary Magdalene Church
of Norman origin has 12th- and 13th-C
arcades, work of c.1300, and north-west
tower rebuilt 1707; splendid circular
carved font of c.1150

EARLS BARTON, NORTHANTS, 5, 5E
Church of All Saints Church famous for
its Saxon tower (c.1020) with lesene strip
decoration and ornamental bell openings;
Norman chancel with richly carved
embellishment

EARL STONHAM, SUFFOLK, 3, 4A
Church of St Mary the Virgin [OCT]
Cruciform church with early 14th-C
crossing arches, transepts, south porch,
east part of chancel, and late medieval
clerestory and tower; splendid
hammerbeam roof to nave

EASBY, N. YORKS, 7, 4C
Easby Abbey [EH] Extensive remains of church and domestic buildings of Premonstratensian abbey founded *c.*1155 in picturesque setting; impressive gatehouses, and west range of cloister with east window of *c.*1300
Church of St Agatha Mainly 13th-C church set within abbey precinct has 15th-C south porch and south aisle; Norman font, mid 13th-C wall painting in chancel, and good screens; cast of Easby Cross of *c.*800 (original in Victoria and Albert Museum, London)

EASINGTON, E. RIDING OF YORKS, 4, 2A
Church of All Saints Church of Norman origin has north aisle and arcade of *c.*1200, late 14th-C west tower and clerestory, and well lit chancel rebuilt late 1400s; 12th-C pillar piscina
Tithe Barn, Rectory Farm Spacious timber-framed aisled barn of late 15th or early 16th C has thatched roof and mid 18th-C brickwork

EASSIE (4 km. / 2 ½ m. N of Glamis), **TAYSIDE, 8, 3C**
Eassie Sculptured Stone [HS] Churchyard contains fine, richly carved early Christian stone with Celtic cross and Pictish symbols

EAST BARNET, GREATER LONDON, 3, 2B
Church of St Mary Mainly 19th-C church retains early Norman nave walls and small north windows

EAST BERGHOLT, SUFFOLK, 3, 4A
Church of St Mary 15th- and early 16th-C church with five-bay arcades, rich north doorway, two-storeyed south porch, and incomplete west tower begun 1525; wall painting of 1400s; unusual 16th-C bell house in churchyard with pyramidal roof

EASTDEAN, E. SUSSEX, 3, 2E
Church of St Simon and St Jude Surviving Norman north tower was originally tower-nave of 11th-C church with 12th-C and medieval additions, and lengthenings of 1885 and 20th C; beside south door, stoup in trefoil-headed niche with ballflower ornament

EAST DEREHAM, NORFOLK, 4, 4D
Church of St Nicholas [OCT] Church of Norman origin rebuilt 13th to 15th C with chancel of late 1200s, 14th-C crossing tower, and detached early 16th-C bell tower; fine 15th-C ceilings and font

EASTERHOUSE, STRATHCLYDE, 10, 5C
See Glasgow

EAST HAGBOURNE, OXON, 2, 5B
Church of St Andrew Mainly 13th-C church with 15th-C west tower, clerestory and north chapel; early 14th-C stained glass in north window

EAST HARLING, NORFOLK, 4, 4E
Church of St Peter and St Paul [OCT] Medieval church retains 14th-C chancel and arcades, and clerestory and south porch of *c.*1440–75; fine west tower with lower parts of *c.*1300 and 15th-C lead spire; hammerbeam roof to nave and stained glass of *c.*1475

EAST HENDRED, OXON, 2, 4B
Church of St Augustine of Canterbury Medieval church has 13th-C nave arcades with stiff-leaf capitals and 14th-C piscina with shelf
Jesus Chapel (at east end of village) Late medieval stone chapel with attached timber-framed priest's house

EASTHORPE, ESSEX, 3, 3B
Church of St Edmund Small Norman church with chancel altered 13th C

EASTLEACH, GLOS, 2, 4A
Church of St Andrew Church of Norman origin with 17th-C work retains south doorway of *c.*1130, 13th-C lancet windows and chancel, and early 14th-C west tower; canopied tomb of 1300s
Church of St Michael and St Martin [CCT] Norman church rebuilt 13th and 14th C has tower with hipped roof, porch of *c.*1300 and some fine windows; 13th-C piscina and 14th-C churchyard cross

EAST LINTON, LOTHIAN, 8, 3E
Church of St Baldred (Prestonkirk Parish Church) [SCS] Church built 1770 and reworked 1891–2 retains fine 13th-C chancel with lancets in east wall

EAST MARKHAM, NOTTS, 5, 5B
Church of St John the Baptist Mainly 15th-C church with spacious nave and chancel, clerestory and west tower; good late medieval tomb chest and brass

EAST MEON, HANTS, 2, 5D
Church of All Saints Cruciform Norman church with medieval additions has tower of *c.*1150 and late 12th-C west and south doorways; carved black marble font of *c.*1130–40
Court House House of *c.*1400 restored

early 20th C has original hall with open roof and fireplace of *c.*1500

EASTON-ON-THE-HILL NORTHANTS, 4, 1D
Church of All Saints Church of Norman origin with 19th-C additions retains south aisle of late 12th C, early 13th-C vestry and south chapel, and good late medieval west tower; stone screens to north and south chapels
Priest's House [NT] (by appointment only) Late 15th-C priest's lodge has upper room with open timber roof and fireplace

EAST WELLOW, HANTS, 2, 4D
Church of St Margaret Church of Norman origin rebuilt 1200s has arch of *c.*1180 in chancel; early 13th-C south doorway to nave and wall paintings

EAST WEMYSS, FIFE, 8, 3D
Macduff's Castle off Shand Terrace; Ruins of medieval castle on cliff-top site with 16th-C south tower

EASTRINGTON, E. RIDING OF YORKS, 7, 4E
Church of St Michael Church of Norman origin with medieval alterations has original frieze to south porch, chancel rebuilt 1632, 15th-C west tower and clerestory; good monuments

EATON BISHOP, HEREFS, 5, 2E
Church of St Michael Church of Norman origin restored 1885 has early 13th-C arcades and chancel arch; fine stained glass of *c.*1330

EATON BRAY, BEDS, 3, 1B
Church of St Mary 13th-C church with richly carved arcades of *c.*1220 and *c.*1235–40; exquisite stone font of *c.*1235–40 and mid 13th-C ironwork on south door

EATON SOCON, CAMBS, 3, 1A
Church of St Mary Long, mainly 15th-C church reworked 1930–2 has tall west tower, south porch, clerestory, and projecting chancel; south arcade retains early 14th-C arches; Norman font

ECCLESFIELD, S. YORKS, 5, 4A
Church of St Mary Embattled 15th-C church with clerestory, transepts and crossing tower retains work of *c.*1200; Saxon cross shaft, fine 15th-C roofs to chancel chapels, good screens and stalls
The Priory Post-medieval house incorporates remains of Benedictine cell founded early 12th C with chapel of *c.*1300

ECCLESHALL, STAFFS, 5, 3C
Church of the Holy Trinity Good 13th-C church restored 1866–9 retains original five-bay arcades, north vestry, west tower, and 15th-C clerestory; 13th-C font, sedilia and piscina
Eccleshall Castle Moated medieval castle slighted 17th C with late 13th-C corner tower and 14th-C bridge

ECKINGTON, DERBYS, 5, 4A
Church of St Peter and St Paul [OCT] Mainly 13th- and 14th-C church remodelled 15th and 18th C with imposing tower and tall nave arcades

EDDERTON, HIGHLAND, 9, 4D
Edderton Cross-Slab (1 km. / ½ m. E of crossroads at Edderton) Carved cross slab survives in graveyard of 18th-C church

EDGEWORTH, GLOS, 2, 3A
Church of St Mary Church of Saxon origin enlarged 12th C and poorly restored 1800s has Norman south doorway, chancel with original corbel table, and 15th-C west tower

EDINBURGH, LOTHIAN, 8, 3E
Edinburgh Castle [HS] Famous medieval castle on imposing rocky site with extensive 16th- to 20th-C additions and alterations retains St Margaret's Chapel [SCS] of *c.*1110 with apsidal chancel within, David's Tower of 1368–77 enclosed by 16th-C Half Moon Battery, 15th-C palace block with 17th-C remodelling, and Great Hall with early 16th-C hammerbeam roof
St Giles' Cathedral (High Church) * Large church built 14th to early 16th C with exterior recased 1829–33 and further 19th- and 20th-C additions retains fine choir of *c.*1400 remodelled *c.*1453, transepts, crossing and tower of *c.*1400 with impressive late 15th-C upper stages and crown spire, nave, aisles, and chapels
Holyrood Abbey [HS] (in grounds of Palace of Holyroodhouse). Ruined nave of abbey church rebuilt *c.*1195–*c.*1230 and altered 15th, early 16th C and early 17th C with handsome west front and blind arcading
Holyrood Park [HS] Park contains late medieval St Margaret's Well with fine vaulted room (originally at Restalrig) and ruins of St Anthony's Chapel
Trinity College Church, Chalmers Close Surviving chancel of church begun *c.*1460, completed 16th C, dismantled 1848 and rebuilt piecemeal 1872 has fine interior

with apse; 15th-C fireplace from
demolished house in west wall
Liberton Tower (5 km. / 3 m. SE of
Edinburgh Castle) Plain, well preserved
15th-C keep with pitched roof

EDINGTON, WILTS, 2, 3C
**Church of St Mary, St Katherine, and All
Saints** Handsome church of Augustinian
priory built 1351–61 has west front with
double portal, three-storeyed south
porch, clerestory, transepts, crossing
tower, and fine chancel with niches
and statues; good monuments and
stained glass

EDITH WESTON, RUTLAND, 4, 1D
Church of St Mary Church rebuilt 18th
and 19th C retains late Norman chancel
arch, early 13th-C south arcade, and
14th-C tower

EDLESBOROUGH, BUCKS, 3, 1B
Church of St Mary Embattled medieval
church has 13th-C nave and arcades,
chancel with fine east window of
c.1290, 14th-C west tower, and north
chapel of between 1342 and 1350;
15th-C screen and pulpit with tall
elaborate canopy

EDLINGHAM,
    NORTHUMBERLAND, 7, 3A
Church of St John the Baptist Plain
church with 11th-C nave, 12th-C chancel
arch and north aisle, and tower built
c.1300; fragments of Saxon cross shaft and
14th-C cross slab
Edlingham Castle [EH] Ruins of fortified
castle in attractive setting include mid
14th-C tower with fine fireplace

EDROM (5.5 km. / 3 ½ m. NE of Duns),
    BORDERS, 8, 4E
Edrom Church [HS] Churchyard contains
richly carved Norman doorway or chancel
arch of old parish church, now reset in
burial vault

EDSTASTON, SHROPS, 5, 2C
Church of St Mary Late Norman church
retains original nave and chancel with
corbel table, fine south doorway, and
ironwork on south door; 19th-C
bellcote

EDVIN LOACH, HEREFS, 5, 2E
Old Church [EH] Ruins of early Norman
church with good south doorway

EDZELL, TAYSIDE, 8, 4C
Edzell Castle and Garden [HS] Remains
of late medieval castle near Glen Esk with

L-plan tower house of c.1530 retaining
great hall on first floor and mansion
added 1580; well-known pleasance or
walled garden of 1604

EGGLESTONE ABBEY,
    CO. DURHAM, 7, 3C
Egglestone Abbey [EH] Ruins of church
and monastic buildings of
Premonstratensian abbey founded c.1196
include reredorter with drainage channel;
east range of cloister converted to house
mid 16th C

EGILSAY (island E. of Rousay),
    ORKNEY, 9, 5A
St Magnus Church [HS] Remains of
roofless shrine church built c.1135–8
on dramatic site with slender round
tower to west of nave and rectangular
tunnel-vaulted chancel

EGLETON, RUTLAND, 4, 1D
Church of St Edmund Church of
Saxo-Norman origin with medieval
work retains early chancel arch and
south doorway with fine carved
tympanum; 13th-C font

EGLISH, CO. ARMAGH, 11, 4C
Crosses Heads of two fine High Crosses
and base of another survive in ancient
graveyard

EGLOSKERRY, CORNWALL, 1, 3C
Church of St Keria Norman church with
15th-C west tower retains original north
transept and north and south doorways
with tympana; Norman piscina

EGREMONT, CUMBRIA, 7, 1C
Egremont Castle Remains of castle
founded c.1130–40 with Norman
gatehouse refaced 1300s, curtain
walling, and ruined 13th-C hall

EILEACH-AN-NAOIMH
    (island in Garvellach group, N of Jura,
    accessible only by hired boat from
    Ardfern or Easdale), STRATHCLYDE
    (Inner Hebrides), 10, 3B
Monastery [HS] Remains of early
monastery reputedly founded by
St Columba with chapel, stone-roofed
beehive cells and graveyard inside
circular enclosure

EILEAN DONAN CASTLE
    (nr Dornie, 13 km. / 8 m. E of Kyle of
    Lochalsh) HIGHLAND, 9, 3E
Eilean Donan Castle * Castle built 1220
and restored 1932 on beautiful island site
at end of causeway near confluence of
three lochs

EILEAN MOR (on islet off coast of
    Knapdale), STRATHCLYDE, 10, 3C
St Cormac's Chapel [HS] Vaulted chancel
of chapel built c.1200 and repaired c.1350
contains good effigy of priest (probably
12th-C)

ELFEET CASTLE
    CO. LONGFORD, 11, 3D
See Inchcleraun

ELGIN, GRAMPIAN, 8, 3A
Friary, Abbey Street Rectangular church
of Franciscan friary probably founded late
15th C, complete because of restoration of
1896 and now serving adjacent Convent of
the Sisters of Mercy
Elgin Cathedral [HS] Impressive ruins of
large cathedral founded 1224, rebuilt 13th
and 14th C, include twin-towered west
front, transepts, choir with lancets and
clerestory of c.1270, and south choir aisle
retaining 15th-C vault; 9th- to 10th-C
cross slab and 15th-C monuments; well-
preserved, groin-vaulted octagonal
chapter house built 1200s and reworked
after 1390; precinct wall retains original
east gate (Pann's Port)

ELKSTONE, GLOS, 2, 3A
Church of St John Well-preserved
Norman church of c.1160–70 rebuilt 13th
to 14th C has fine interior, south doorway
with tympanum and west tower added
c.1370; late medieval octagonal font
Priest's House Former rectory built
late 15th to early 16th C

ELM, CAMBS, 4, 2D
Church of All Saints 13th-C church
remodelled 14th C has fine west tower
with later top and 19th-C refacing to lower
parts, good doorways and chancel, and
chancel arch with unusual blind tracery
above; late medieval double hammerbeam
roof with angels

ELMLEY CASTLE, WORCS, 5, 3E
Church of St Mary Saxo-Norman church
with much medieval rebuilding retains
11th-C chancel and 13th-C west tower;
font with carved early 13th-C base and
15th-C bowl
Village Hall Medieval Hall with stone base
and timber-framed upper storey
Village Cross Late medieval village cross

ELMSTEAD, ESSEX, 3, 4B
Church of St Ann and St Laurence Mainly
early 14th-C church retaining Norman
north doorway has tower over porch and
good south chapel; fine sedilia and piscina

ELSDON,
    NORTHUMBERLAND, 7, 3B
Church of St Cuthbert Church of 12th-C
origin with medieval and 19th-C rebuilding has 14th-C arcades, chancel, narrow
aisles, and bellcote added c.1720; triple
sedilia of 1300s
Elsdon Tower 14th-C tower rebuilt 16th C
with 19th-C additions
Elsdon Castle Impressive earthworks
of early 12th-C castle with ringwork
and bailey

ELSING, NORFOLK, 4, 4D
Church of St Mary Church of c.1330 with
west tower, wide nave and tiled floor;
lavish brass to Sir Hugh Hastings
(d.1347); good 14th-C stained glass
and 15th-C font canopy
Elsing Hall Hall-house built c.1460–70
and extensively restored 19th and 20th C

ELSTON, NOTTS, 5, 5B
Chapel [CCT] Simple chapel of Norman
origin with nave, chancel and 14th-C
windows

ELSTOW, BEDS, 3, 1A
Church of St Mary and St Helen Church
of Benedictine nunnery founded c.1075
and rebuilt 12th, 13th, 16th and 19th C;
free-standing 15th-C bell tower, font
and pulpit
Hillersden Hall Remains of 17th-C house
with fragments of 13th-C abbey cloister
Moot Hall Timber-framed hall of c.1500
with overhanging upper floor and
tiebeam roof

ELTHAM,
    GREATER LONDON, 3, 2C
Eltham Palace [EH] Great Hall of 13th-C
royal palace with impressive hammerbeam roof

ELTON, CAMBS, 4, 1E
Church of All Saints Church with late
13th-C chancel arch, four-bay arcades, and
mainly late medieval exterior; sedilia,
piscina and aumbry; two Anglo-Danish
crosses in churchyard
Elton Hall * Medieval house much
reworked 18th and 19th C retains late
15th-C gatehouse and chapel undercroft

ELY, CAMBS, 4, 2E
Cathedral * Important Norman cathedral
restored 19th C retains nave started c.1100
and later 12th-C west tower and transepts;
early 13th-C west porch and retrochoir
added 1234–52; remarkable octagonal
crossing tower with lantern of 1322–42

and detached Lady Chapel built c.1335–53; fragments of shrine of St Etheldreda, fine 12th and 13th-C monuments, 14th-C sculpture, and roof bosses
Cathedral Precinct Precinct with remains of former monastery (partially incorporated into school) including dormitory, refectory, monks' kitchen, late 12th-C infirmary, and late 15th-C bishop's palace; three carved doorways include lavish prior's doorway of c.1135 connecting cloister and cathedral south aisle; Ely Porta (gatehouse) begun 1397
Prior Crauden's Chapel *, King's School (part of cathedral precinct) (key obtainable nearby) Fine chapel of c.1325 restored to show interesting medieval wall paintings
Church of St Mary Church of c.1200 rebuilt 14th and 15th C retains original nave and north doorway
Oliver Cromwell's House *, 29 St Mary's Street. 14th-C house with timber-framed upper level and stone ground floor
White Hart Inn 15th-C inn rebuilt 17th and 18th C retains original timber-framed entrance passage and first floor gallery
Bishop's Palace Late 15th-C palace of Bishop Alcock facing green with original red brick east gate tower and 16th- to 18th-C alterations

EMBERTON, BUCKS, 3, 1A
Church of All Saints Church built mainly 14th C and restored 19th C with fine east window and late medieval west tower; brass to priest (d.1410)

EMLAGH, CO. ROSCOMMON, 11, 2D
Cross [Dúchas] Fragments of possibly 11th-C High Cross with fine carved ornament

EMPINGHAM, RUTLAND, 4, 1D
Church of St Peter Medieval church remodelled 15th C with 13th-C arcades, transepts and chancel, and imposing 14th-C west tower; good 15th-C roof with angel figures; mid 13th-C sedilia and piscina in chancel

ENFORD, WILTS, 2, 4C
Church of All Saints and St Margaret Spacious Norman church retains 12th-C arcades and chancel arch, chancel with late 13th-C blind arcading to north wall, octagonal vestry, and 15th-C west tower

ENGLISHCOMBE, SOMERSET, 2, 2C
Church of St Peter Norman church with medieval rebuilding retains 12th-C central tower and part of original chancel

Tithe Barn, Rectory Farmhouse *** Early 14th-C cruck-framed tithe barn built by Bath Abbey

ENNIS, CO. CLARE, 12, 2B
Ennis Friary [Dúchas] Remains of Franciscan friary founded c.1240 include church enlarged 1287 and 1306 with fine east window, rich screen, 15th-C nave, tower and additions, and cloister added c.1400; important medieval sculpture includes archbishop and Virgin with Child (15th-C), figure of St Francis, and remarkable Creagh tomb of 1843 incorporating splendid carved panels from MacMahon tomb (c.1460 or 1470)

ENNISCORTHY, CO. WEXFORD, 12, 5A
Enniscorthy Castle * (museum) Rectangular castle with four rounded corner towers built probably 15th or 16th C on elevated site and altered 19th and early 20th C

ENSTONE, OXON, 2, 4A
Church of St Kenelm 12th-C church with medieval, 16th- and 19th-C work retains south aisle of c.1180, 12th- and 13th-C arcades, and 14th-C two-storeyed porch
Barn Medieval tithe barn with roof of cruck construction

EOLIGARRY / EOLAIGEARRAIDH (Barra) WESTERN ISLES (Outer Hebrides), 9, 1E
Church (Cille Bharra) Ruined 12th-C church with two nearby late medieval mausolea, the north-east containing a cast of 10th- or early 11th-C Kilbar Stone (original in Royal Museum of Scotland, Edinburgh) and 15th- and 16th-C grave slabs

EOROPIE / EORROPAIDH (Lewis), WESTERN ISLES (Outer Hebrides), 9, 2B
St Moluag's Church (Teampull Mholuidh) [SCS] 13th-C church restored 1912 on early site with main block, north sacristy, and south chapel; collection of stone objects includes Celtic cross head

ERPINGHAM, NORFOLK, 4, 4C
Church of St Mary [OCT] 15th-C church with fine west tower of 1484–5 contains military brass of c.1415

ERREW ABBEY AND TEMPLENAGALLIAGHDOO (10 km. / 6 m. SE of Crossmolina) CO. MAYO, 11, 1C
Abbey [Dúchas] Augustinian abbey founded 1413 with earlier (late 13th-C)

church and fragmentary remains of domestic buildings
Templenagalliaghdoo [Dúchas] Small much-reconstructed oratory, all that survives of medieval nunnery built on site of early monastery

ERRIGAL KEEROGUE (6.5 km. / 4 m. NE of Augher), CO. TYRONE, 11, 4B
Monastic Site [EHS] Graveyard on fine, elevated early monastic site houses traces of Round Tower, unfinished cross, and remains of medieval St Kiernan's Church

ESCOMB, CO. DURHAM, 7, 3C
Church of St John the Evangelist * Remarkable survival of almost complete early Saxon stone church (built c.680)

ETAL, NORTHUMBERLAND, 7, 3A
Etal Castle [EH] Remains of border castle licensed 1342 include four-storeyed Great Tower, gatehouse and part of curtain wall

ETON, BERKS, 3, 1C
Eton College * School founded 1440 by Henry VI with extensive 18th- to 20th-C work retains fine original chapel (built mainly 1449–c.1460 and c.1469–c.1475) with exquisite wall paintings of c.1479–88, hall, and parts of cloister; Long Building and Lower School added late 15th C; Lupton's Tower gatehouse built 1517–c.1520

EVERCREECH, SOMERSET, 2, 2C
Church of St Peter Medieval church remodelled 19th C has 14th-C chancel, rich exterior, and fine 15th-C west tower with tall bell openings; good roof
Village Cross Medieval cross, probably 15th-C

EVERTON, BEDS, 3, 1A
Church of St Mary Mainly late Norman church, unusually complete, with 14th-C west tower and later medieval south porch and clerestory

EVERTON, NOTTS, 5, 5A
Church of the Holy Trinity Church of Norman origin with later medieval clerestory, upper parts of tower, and south porch retains original chancel and tower arches; south door with early Norman carved tympanum

EVESHAM, WORCS, 5, 3E
Abbey Surviving fragments of abbey founded 714 include Norman gateway, chapter house with arch of c.1285–90, and well-preserved early 16th-C bell tower
Church of All Saints Norman church rebuilt 14th and 15th C retains west doorway of c.1200, 14th-C chancel arch,

and early 16th-C fan-vaulted Lichfield Chapel; small late 13th- or early 14th-C figure of Moses
Church of St Lawrence [CCT] Mainly 15th-C church much restored 1836 has west tower and fine fan-vaulted south chapel of c.1520
Booth Hall Large late 15th-C timber-framed inn has projecting upper storeys and shops on ground floor

EWELME, OXON, 2, 5B
Church of St Mary Church extensively rebuilt c.1432 has early 14th-C tower, rich St John's Chapel with timber roof, and 15th-C tomb of Duchess of Suffolk; fine late 15th-C font and cover
Almshouses Almshouses founded 1437 and built around quadrangle with later internal remodelling
School Two-storeyed school founded 1437 with later additions and alterations

EWENNY, GLAMORGAN, 6, 4E
Ewenny Priory [CADW] Remains of medieval priory include well-preserved cruciform church built c.1126 or 1140s with vaulted presbytery, 12th-C north arcade, and fine monuments; early 14th-C precinct walls retain towers and gatehouses

EWERBY, LINCS, 4, 1C
Church of St Andrew 14th-C church with original arcades, aisles, tall west tower and rich entrance to south porch; fine rood screen of 1300s, carved chest and monument with effigy of c.1360

EWLOE, CLWYD, 6, 5A
Ewloe Castle [CADW] Picturesque ruins of 13th-C castle on secluded promontory site with free standing D-plan Welsh Tower, circular west tower, and curtain walls

EXETER, DEVON, 1, 5C
Cathedral * Cathedral established 1050 and rebuilt late 13th and early 14th C with magnificent vaulting and superb carved corbels and bosses has surviving Norman towers incorporated into north and south transepts; west front with important programme of 14th-C sculpture; 13th-C misericords; carved and pinnacled bishop's throne of 1313–16; splendid pulpitum of 1324; 14th-C minstrels' gallery in nave; fine medieval monuments
Church of St Mary Arches Norman church with 12th-C nave arcades, restored after war damage and now used as Diocesan Educational Resource centre
Rougemont Castle Well-preserved Norman gatehouse keep

City walls (best stretch can be seen from Northernhay Gardens) Greater part of circuit of Roman city walls repaired and strengthed 13th and 14th C
Guildhall Hall of 1468–70 with handsome timber roof, refronted 1593–5
Bowhill [EH] (2.5 km. / 1 ½ m. SW) Substantial remains of 15th-C manor house including great hall with impressive timber roof

EXTON, RUTLAND, 4,1D
Church of St Peter and St Paul Late 13th- to early 14th-C church extensively restored 19th C retains fine 14th-C steeple with battlements; good medieval tomb chests; matrix of 15th-C brass in churchyard

EYAM, DERBYS, 5,4A
Church of St Lawrence Mainly 15th-C church retains 13th-C chancel and north arcade; 17th and 19th-C restoration; early 9th-C carved cross in churchyard

EYE, HEREFS, 5,2E
Church of St Peter and St Paul Church of Norman origin has late 12th- and early 13th-C arcades, north and south doorways, and late 14th-C timber porch; west tower added 1874

EYE, SUFFOLK, 4,4E
Church of St Peter and St Paul 14th-C church with later medieval remodelling retains original chancel chapels and arcades, 15th-C two-storeyed porch, and fine west tower with flushwork panelling; rood screen has dado with paintings of c.1500
Guildhall Early 16th-C timber-framed guildhall with oriel windows

EYE / AIGINISH (Lewis) WESTERN ISLES (Outer Hebrides), 9,2C
St Columba's Church Ruined 14th- and 15th-C church with west chapel; three good carved late medieval graveslabs

EYNESBURY, CAMBS, 3,1A
Church of St Mary Mainly 15th-C church rebuilt 1688 and 1857 retains Late Norman and early 13th-C north arcade

EYNHALLOW, ORKNEY, 9,5A
Eynhallow Church [HS] Ruins of 12th-C church on island site converted to cottages 1500s and abandoned 1851

EYNSFORD, KENT, 3,2C
Church of St Martin Church of Norman origin with medieval and 19th-C rebuilding has fine reset west doorway of late 1100s, 13th-C south transept,

west porch, tower, and apsidal chancel
Eynsford Castle [EH] Imposing boundary wall built c.1100 and remains of 12th-C hall-house on motte

FAHAN, CO. DONEGAL, 11,3A
St Mura's Cross [Dúchas] Splendid mid or late 7th-C cross with carved Greek crosses on both faces stands near site of important early Christian monastery; another set into cemetery wall

FAIRFORD, GLOS, 2,4B
Church of St Mary Medieval church completely rebuilt c.1480–1500 has fine roofs and south porch; excellent set of original stained glass, carving and woodwork including screens and stalls

FAIRLIE (5 km. / 3 m. S of Largs), STRATHCLYDE, 8,1E
Fairlie Castle Well-preserved remains of plain 15th-C keep with vaulted basement and upper hall

FAKENHAM, NORFOLK, 4,4D
Church of St Peter and St Paul Medieval church, much restored 19th C, has 13th-C north door, 14th-C arcades and 15th-C porch and tower; octagonal font with Signs of the Evangelists, Instruments of the Passion and Symbol of the Trinity; 15th- and early 16th-C brasses

FALA AND SOUTRA, LOTHIAN, 8,3E
South Aisle, Soutra Hill (3 km. SE) Surviving part of church and hospital of Holy Trinity founded c.1164, later used as burial place by Pringles of Soutra

FALKLAND (16 km. / 10 m. N of Kirkcaldy), FIFE, 8,3D
Falkland Palace [NTS] Handsome fortified palace begun c.1500 and completed 1525–42 on site of 12th-C predecessor, favourite country residence of Stuart monarchs; Britain's oldest royal tennis court (1539) survives in garden

FALLMORE, CO. MAYO, 11,1C
St Dairbhile's Church [Dúchas] Small primitive church (possibly founded for nuns) has simple 12th-C west doorway with carved ornament, and later alterations; St Dairbhile's Bed (grave) to north-east with early cross-slab

FARINGDON, OXON, 2,4B
Church of All Saints Cruciform church of Norman origin rebuilt 15th, 17th and 19th C with 12th-C nave and arcades; lavish scrollwork on 13th-C south door and 14th- and 15th-C brasses

Crown Hotel Georgian hotel incorporates courtyard with early 14th-C range

FARLEIGH, SURREY, 3,2C
Church of St Mary Simple, well-preserved church of c.1100 with original windows and chancel extended c.1250

FARLEIGH HUNGERFORD SOMERSET, 2,3C
Church of St Leonard Church consecrated 1443 and remodelled 19th C with older west tower
Farleigh Hungerford Castle [EH] Ruins of extensive 14th-C castle with walling, towers, and exposed foundations; chapel built c.1380–90 has 14th-C Hungerford tomb and wall painting of c.1440

FARNHAM, SURREY, 2,5C
Church of St Andrew Norman church much rebuilt 15th C and restored 19th C has late 12th-C north and south chapels, chancel lengthened late 1300s, 15th-C west tower and five bay nave arcades; fine sedilia and piscina of 1390s
Farnham Castle [Keep – EH] Remains of Norman motte and bailey castle used as palace by Bishops of Winchester include large keep, 12th-C chapel enlarged 1200s, and brick Waynflete (Fox's) Tower of 1470–5 (altered 18th C)

FARNWORTH, CHESHIRE, 5,2A
Church of St Luke Norman church with medieval, 17th- and 19th-C additions retains 14th-C tower, south doorway and arcades; late 15th-C chancel with fine panelled roof

FARRANACOUTH ABBEY CO. CORK, 12,2E
See Sherkin Island

FASSAROE (1.5 km. / 1 m. E of Enniskerry), CO. WICKLOW, 11,5E
St Valery's Cross [Dúchas] Small granite cross (probably 12th-C) with carved Crucifixion

FAUGHART, CO. LOUTH, 11,4C
See Kilcurry

FAULKBOURNE, ESSEX, 3,3B
Church of St Germans Norman church has original chancel, nave with good south doorway, and porch added early 19th C
Faulkbourne Hall Early 15th-C mansion enlarged in brick from 1439 and remodelled 17th and 19th C

FAVERSHAM, KENT, 3,4C
Church of St Catherine, Preston Church much reworked 19th C retains

13th-C chancel and fine piscina and sedilia of c.1320; 15th-C monuments
Davington Priory Surviving buildings of Benedictine nunnery founded 1153 and much altered 19th C include 12th-C church with lavish west doorway, and west range of cloister (now house)
Stone Chapel [EH] Ruins of medieval church incorporating part of 4th-C "Romano-British" mausoleum

FAWLEY, HANTS, 2,4D
Church of All Saints [OCT] Late 12th-C church with medieval additions retains Norman chancel arch and fine west door

FEARN ABBEY (1 km. / ½ m. E of Hill of Fearn), HIGHLAND, 9,4D
Fearn Abbey [SCS] Church of medieval Premonstratensian abbey built 1300s, known as "The Lamp of the North", with later alterations (one of oldest Scottish churches still used for parish worship)

FEENY, CO. LONDONDERRY, 11,4B
Banagher Old Church (5 km. / 3 m. ENE) [EHS] Important early medieval church founded probably 10th C has original nave with impressive flat headed west doorway and 12th-C chancel with round-headed window of c.1150; remarkable 12th-C tomb of St Muriedach O'Heney outside building takes form of church with highly pitched roof; good medieval cross slab to east

FELMERSHAM, BEDS, 3,1A
Church of St Mary Remarkably intact cruciform church of c.1220–30/40 with monumental west front, crossing tower and chancel; 13th-C double piscina and richly carved screen

FENAGH, CO. LEITRIM, 11,3C
Churches [Dúchas] Remains of two medieval churches on early monastic site, the south with good west doorway and fine 14th or 15th-C east window; both buildings retain barrel-vaulted west ends

FENNY BENTLEY, DERBYS, 5,4B
Church of St Edmund Medieval church with much 19th-C work retains interesting early 16th-C screen probably from former Beresford Chantry founded 1511; medieval chest and parclose screen possibly dating from 1519

FENSTANTON, CAMBS, 4,2E
Church of St Peter and St Paul Church of 13th-C origin has tall chancel built c.1350 with good sedilia, piscina and east

window; mid 14th-C west tower with late medieval spire; 15th-C aisles and arcades

FERNIEHIRST (2.5 km. / 1½ m. S of Jedburgh), BORDERS, 7, 2A
Ferniehirst Castle (now youth hostel) Large building incorporates altered late medieval tower house to one corner

FERNS, CO. WEXFORD, 12, 5C
Churches [Dúchas] Remains of buildings include St Mary's Abbey (church of Augustinian abbey founded 1152), chancel of early 13th-C cathedral incorporated 1817 in Church of Ireland successor, and fragment of fine early 13th-C church to east (possibly monks' choir); parts of good High Crosses in churchyard; excellent effigy of bishop in cathedral
Castle [Dúchas] Ruined castle built probably c.1200 or c.1226 with rounded angle towers and circular chapel

FERTAGH (7.5 km. / 4½ m. NE of Urlingford) CO. KILKENNY, 12, 4B
Abbey Fragmentary remains of church of 13th-C Augustinian priory (used for Protestant worship until 1780); 15th to 16th-C Kilpatrick Chapel contains excellently carved tomb of MacGillapatrick knight and wife (c.1510–40); other fine fragments incorporated in Protestant church (1799) and St Kiernan's Church (1832) at nearby Johnstown include lavish font and well preserved crucifix

FETHARD, CO. TIPPERARY, 12, 4C
Churches [Dúchas] Holy Trinity church incorporates west tower, windows and other work from late 15th-C parish building; remains of church (still in use) of Augustinian abbey founded early 1300s and restored 1820
Town Walls and Tower Houses [Dúchas] Well-preserved late 14th-C town walling with five towers and one of original five gates surviving, and four tower houses (possibly 15th-C)

FIDDAUN, CO. GALWAY, 12, 3B
Castle [Dúchas] Well-preserved early 16th-C castle with fine bawn; ruins of small gatehouse of outer bawn survive nearby

FIDDLEFORD, DORSET, 2, 3D
Fiddleford Manor [EH] Late 14th-C manor house remodelled mid 16th C has outstanding open timber roofs in hall and two-storeyed solar wing

FILEY, N. YORKS, 7, 5D
Church of St Oswald Handsome Norman church restored 19th C retains original clerestory, nave and aisles with 13th-C transepts, chancel, and fine crossing tower; font of early 1200s

FINCHALE PRIORY CO. DURHAM, 7, 3C
Finchale Priory [EH] Surviving buildings of 12th-C Benedictine monastery by River Wear include mid 13th-C church, cloister, chapter house and prior's house

FINCHAM, NORFOLK, 4, 3D
Church of St Martin Mainly 15th-C church with good south front, clerestory, vestry, and hammerbeam roof; fine Norman font and medieval screen
Fincham Hall Early 16th-C house with additions of later 1500s retains original brick north-east tower

FINCHINGFIELD, ESSEX, 3, 3A
Church of St John Church of Norman origin with 18th- to 19th-C work retains original west tower, 13th- and 14th-C arcades and clerestoried chancel; fine 14th-C south door and rood screen
Guildhall Timber-framed former guildhall built c.1500

FINEDON, NORTHANTS, 4, 1E
Church of St Mary Spacious 14th-C church retains three-bay arcades, clerestory, two-storeyed south porch and west tower with fine spire

FINGEST, BUCKS, 2, 5B
Church of St Bartholomew Unusual Norman church with large tower and 13th-C chancel; 14th-C octagonal font

FINNEA, CO. WESTMEATH, 11, 3D
Ross Castle (6 km. / 3¾ m. ENE) [Dúchas] Dramatically set late medieval tower house by Lough Sheelin reconstructed 1864 and 1970
Foyran Church (6.5 km. / 4 m. SE) Scanty remains of medieval church with triple-arched bellcote to west

FISHLAKE, S. YORKS, 7, 4E
Church of St Cuthbert Church much rebuilt 14th and 15th C with fine west tower and clerestory retains ornate south doorway of c.1170 with splendid carving, and 13th-C arcades; good font and early 16th-C tomb chest

FLAMBOROUGH, E. RIDING OF YORKS, 7, 5D
Church of St Oswald Norman church with medieval and extensive 19th-C

additions retains splendid early 16th-C rood loft and screen restored 1908

FLAMSTEAD, HERTS, 3, 1B
Church of St Leonard Church of Norman origin with medieval additions has original west tower, early 13th-C aisles, and 15th-C nave roof; fine wall paintings of 13th to 15th C, monuments and late medieval screen

FLANESFORD PRIORY, HEREFS, 2, 2A
See Goodrich

FLEDBOROUGH, NOTTS, 5, 5B
Church of St Gregory Church of Norman origin has original west tower with top added 1200s, 13th-C arcades, and 14th-C clerestory; carved panels of 1300s, Easter Sepulchre and much 14th-C stained glass

FLEET, LINCS, 4, 2D
Church of St Mary Magdalen Mainly 14th-C church much restored 18th and 19th C retains 13th-C arcade piers, good roof corbels of 1300s and detached steeple

FLEMINGTON / TREFFLEMIN, GLAMORGAN, 1, 5A
Church of St Michael the Archangel Medieval church with restoration and additions of 1858 retains early 14th-C south transept (former funerary chapel) and 15th-C roof; late 13th-C font and good early 14th-C effigy
Flemingston Court Well-preserved manor house built early 1500s

FLETTON, CAMBS, 4, 1D
Church of St Margaret Church of c.1160 reworked 13th, 14th and 19th C incorporates early 9th-C carved friezes; Norman panels with saints; Saxon cross in churchyard

FLINT, CLWYD, 6, 5A
Flint Castle [CADW] Important medieval castle begun 1277 by waters of Dee estuary and dismantled mid 17th C retains curtain walling and corner towers to inner bailey; free-standing tower to south-east has unusual, circular plan and traces of chapel on upper floor
Town Plan Town has fairly well-preserved 13th-C plan

FLORE, NORTHANTS, 5, 5E
Church of All Saints 13th-C church with some 14th-C work has fine three-bay arcades and west tower begun c.1300

FOLKINGHAM, LINCS, 4, 1C
Church of St Andrew Medieval church restored 19th C with late 13th-C chancel, 14th-C aisles and arcades, and 15th-C west tower; good screen

FONMON CASTLE (1.5 km. / 1 m. SW of Penmark), GLAMORGAN, 6, 4E
Fonmon Castle * Medieval castle extensively remodelled from 1762 incorporates early 12th-C keep extended 1200s, and tall south-east tower

FORD, NORTHUMBERLAND, 7, 3A
Church of St Michael and All Angels 13th-C church much altered 1853 retains south arcade and unusual bellcote; medieval cross slabs
Ford Castle Castle licensed 1338 has King James' Tower and Cow Tower; north range incorporated in mansion built 1589, 17th and 18th C

FORD, W. SUSSEX, 3, 1E
Church of St Andrew Simple church built 11th and 12th C with steeply pitched nave roof, bellcote and brick porch added 1637; 11th-C font

FORDE ABBEY, DORSET, 2, 1D
Forde Abbey [HHA] House of c.1650–60 incorporates parts of Cistercian abbey founded 1136 including mid 12th-C chapter house (now chapel), 13th-C dormitory and abbot's house of c.1525–35

FORDHAM, CAMBS, 4, 3E
Church of St Peter Norman and medieval church has fine though altered 14th-C Lady Chapel built above rib-vaulted undercroft used as north porch; 15th-C south porch, west tower and chancel roof; choir stalls of c.1350 and pews with carved poppyheads

FORDINGBRIDGE, HANTS, 2, 3D
Church of St Mary 13th-C church with late medieval additions has fine hammer-beam roof with angels in north chapel and painted panels from dado of screen

FORDINGTON (Dorchester), DORSET, 2, 2E
Church of St George Church of Norman origin much altered and enlarged 1906–27 retains original south arcade and fascinating tympanum of c.1100 with St George in centre; 15th-C west tower with top of c.1900

FORDWICH, KENT, 3, 4D
Church of St Mary the Virgin [CCT] 13th-C church with 14th-C south aisle

contains rare and important Norman stone tomb with hipped roof carved with scale pattern to represent wooden shingles; 14th- and 15th-C stained glass
Town hall 16th-C timber-framed town hall, with jetties on all four sides

FORE, CO. WESTMEATH, 11,3D
Church of St Fechin [Dúchas] Ruins of rare surviving 10th-C church on hillside site with fine west gable and 12th-C chancel; 13th-C font, and carving of seated monk on north side of chancel arch
Anchorite's Cell Late medieval tower reworked 19th C on elevated site with attached mausoleum built 1867 and enclosing wall
Town Gates [Dúchas] North and south gate towers to town built probably mid 1400s
Abbey of SS Taurin and Fechin [Dúchas] Substantial remains of Benedictine abbey remodelled and fortified 1400s include part of 13th-C west range, ruins of kitchen, and original church with imposing 15th-C east and west towers; aumbry-piscina in chancel retains traces of original painted decoration; late medieval cloister reconstructed from work found in 1912 excavations; semi-circular dovecot to north-east of enclosure

FORNCETT ST PETER, NORFOLK, 4,4E
Church of St Peter Saxon church rebuilt 14th and 15th C has complete original round tower; 15th-C tomb chest

FORRES, GRAMPIAN, 8,2A
Sueno's Stone [HS] (covered by glass enclosure) Oustanding monument, probably cenotaph and dating from late 10th C, stands at 7 metres (23 feet) tall and has cross and martial carvings including mounted and foot soldiers

FORSE CASTLE (2.5 km. / 1 ½ m. E of Latheron), HIGHLAND, 9,5C
Forse Castle Remains of medieval castle on promontory site include walls of 12th- or 13th-C keep

FORTROSE, HIGHLAND, 9,4D
Fortrose Cathedral [HS] Remains of 13th-C sacristy or chapter house and vaulted 14th- to 15th-C south aisle, all that survives of medieval cathedral; plan of other buildings laid out in grass

FOSTON, N. YORKS, 7,4D
Church of All Saints Norman church with north aisle and bellcote of 1911 retains fine 12th-C south doorway with carved medallions, and pillar piscina

FOTHERINGHAY, NORTHANTS, 4,1E
Church of St Mary and All Saints Former collegiate church much rebuilt 15th C has west tower with octagonal upper storey and spacious interior with clerestory and good roof; 15th-C font, pulpit and tester
Old Inn Medieval inn, now cottages
New Inn Medieval inn with 15th-C gateway

FOULDEN (6.5 km. / 4 m. SE of Chirnside), BORDERS, 8,4E
Foulden Tithe Barn [HS] (view exterior only) Attractive two-storeyed barn with outside stair

FOUNTAINS ABBEY, N. YORKS, 7,3D
Fountains Abbey [NT] Outstandingly preserved and picturesque remains of major 12th-C Cistercian monastery in superb 18th-C landscape garden setting

FOWEY, CORNWALL, 1,3D
Church of St Nicholas Church rededicated 1336 has plain early 14th-C arcades, clerestory, wide late 15th-C aisles, handsome wagon roof, and rich four-stage west tower; good Norman font
Fowey Place House built between 1813 and 1845 incorporates sumptuous early 16th-C bay window in courtyard

FOWLIS EASTER, TAYSIDE, 8,3D
Church of St Marnock Church of Norman origin rebuilt 1453 has fine west window; sacrament house with scene of Annunciation and good late medieval paintings on oak

FOWLIS WESTER (10 km. / 6 m. NE of Crieff), TAYSIDE, 8,2D
Church of St Bean [SCS] **and Fowlis Wester Sculptured Stone** [HS] Simple 13th-C church with later alterations and restoration of 1927 contains tall Pictish symbol stone with fine carved work (probably 8th-C, replica in village square); leper squint in churchyard

FOWNHOPE, HEREFS, 2,2A
Church of St Mary Norman church rebuilt 13th to 14th C retains original central tower and tympanum, 13th-C north doorway and south doorway of c.1300

FOYRAN, CO. WESTMEATH, 11,3D
See Finnea

FRAMLINGHAM, SUFFOLK, 3,4A
Framlingham Castle [EH] Important Norman castle with well-preserved curtain walls and towers (c.1190), and remains of earlier chapel and great hall (c.1150) incorporated into Tudor Poor House inside inner bailey
Church of St Michael Large late medieval parish church (15th- to 16th-C) retains 12th-C chancel arch

FRAMPTON-ON-SEVERN, GLOS, 2,2A
Church of St Mary Church consecrated 1315 with 15th-, 18th- and 19th-C additions; ornate lead font of c.1150–75 and 14th-C monuments
Frampton Manor (open by written appointment only) Mid 15th-C manor house restored 1925 with jettied timber-framed upper storeys on stone lower level; 15th-C barn

FRASERBURGH, GRAMPIAN, 8,4A
Kinnaird Head Lighthouse [HS] Massive 15th- to 16th-C keep with lighthouse built into upper floor 1787; nearby Wine Tower (possibly 16th-C) retains carved pendants to upper room, probably former chapel; outbuildings added 1820

FREISTON, LINCS, 4,2C
Church of St James Church of Norman origin with medieval and 19th-C work retains 12th-C monastic nave lengthened 13th C; 15th-C nave roof and west tower; good late medieval font, cover and screens

FRESHFORD, CO. KILKENNY, 12,4B
Church [Dúchas] Protestant parish church built 1730 incorporates (in west gable) fine 12th-C doorway with good but weathered carving

FRESSINGFIELD, SUFFOLK, 4,4E
Church of St Peter and St Paul 14th-C church remodelled 15th C with original west tower, north chapel, and fine later medieval hammerbeam roof; good set of benches

FRITHELSTOCK, DEVON, 1,4B
Frithelstock Priory Substantial remains of church of Augustinian priory founded c.1229

FRITTON, NORFOLK, 4,5D
Church of St Edmund Norman church retains original round tower,

tunnel-vaulted chancel with apse, and thatched nave enlarged 14th C; screen of 1300s

FROCESTER, GLOS, 2,3B
Tithe Barn Important and well-preserved barn built c.1300 with wagon porches

FROSTENDEN, SUFFOLK, 4,5E
Church of All Saints Medieval church with round tower has 13th-C angle piscina, octagonal font with carved bowl supported by heads, and traceried bench ends

FULBOURN, CAMBS, 3,2A
Church of St Vigor Medieval church with 13th-C tower and restoration and additions of 1869–70; late medieval pulpit has two paintings from former early 15th-C rood screen; good 15th-C brasses

FURNESS (5 km. / 3 m. E of Multyfarnham), CO. KILDARE, 11,4E
Church [Dúchas] (behind Furness House) Remains of small manorial church founded c.1210; contemporary font

FURNESS ABBEY, CUMBRIA
See Barrow-in-Furness

FYFIELD, OXON, 2,4B
Church of St Nicholas Norman church with 14th-C chancel, 15th-C north arcade and extensive 19th-C additions to south side; ornate 15th-C piscina and credence table
Fyfield Manor Rare surviving stone manor house of c.1320 and 16th C retains original doorways in porch and hall; solar above service wing
White Hart Inn Original 15th-C chantry attached to two-storeyed priest's house; full height hall with wooden roof

FYFIELD, ESSEX, 3,2B
Fyfield Hall Medieval timber-framed house retains traces of original late 13th-C aisled hall

FYVIE (13 km. / 8 m. SE of Turiff), GRAMPIAN, 9,5D
Fyvie Castle [NTS] Impressive castellated mansion much remodelled 16th C onwards and with mainly early 20th-C interior retains medieval work including Preston (south-east) Tower of c.1400

GADDESBY, LEICS, 5,5C
Church of St Luke Church of mid 13th to mid 14th C with earlier and 18th- to 19th-C work retains tower of 1200s and lavish south aisle built c.1320–30

GAERWEN (ANGLESEY),
GWYNEDD, 6, 3A
**Church of St Michael, LLanfihangel
Esceifiog** (1 km. / ½ m. NW) Ruins of 15th
and 17th-C church with late medieval
inscriptions in Welsh on east wall and
around west door; 9th- to 11th-C cross
slab in chancel

GAINFORD, CO. DURHAM, 7, 3C
**Church of St Mary (formerly
St Cuthbert)** Attractive church built
mainly early 13th C near River Tees; parts
of two cross shafts in nave (early 10th- and
late 11th-C respectively), font of probably
early 1200s, and original ironwork to
north and south doors

GAINSBOROUGH, LINCS, 4, 1B
Gainsborough Old Hall [EH] 15th-C
hall-house with 16th- to 20th-C alterations
retains fine timber-framed hall with open
roof, and brick north-east tower

**GAINSTHORPE MEDIEVAL
VILLAGE,** (8 km. / 5 m. SW of
Brigg), LINCS, 4, 1A
Gainsthorpe Deserted Medieval Village
[EH] Earthworks of deserted medieval
village, best seen from air

GALLARUS (Dingle Peninsula),
CO. KERRY, 12, 1C
Gallarus Oratory [Dúchas] Perfectly
preserved boat-shaped drystone early
Christian oratory, possibly as early as
6th-C (one of many early Christian
monuments on Dingle Peninsula, perhaps
associated with pilgrimage route to
Mount Brandon); cross-inscribed stone
survives nearby
Castle [Dúchas] Remains of four-storeyed
tower built 15th and 16th C commanding
impressive view

GALLEN, CO. OFFALY, 11, 3E
Gallen Priory and Graveslabs [Dúchas]
(1 km. / ½ m. S of Ferbane) Collection of
fine early gravestones (mainly 8th- to
11th-C, discovered 1934–5) displayed in
ruined 15th-C parish church on monastic
site near 18th-C house (now convent)

GALLOON ISLAND (5 km. / 3 m. SW
of Newtownbutler)
CO. FERMANAGH, 11, 3C
Crosses Two crosses (possibly late 10th-C)
carved with biblical scenes survive in
graveyard

GALWAY, CO. GALWAY, 12, 2A
Collegiate Church of St Nicholas of Myra
[Dúchas] Much-restored church

incorporates shell of medieval building
with 15th- and 16th-C alterations; fine
15th-C reader's desk (removed from
refectory), rich canopied Joyce tomb
of late 1400s or early 1500s and
contemporary font
Lynch's Castle [Dúchas] Late 15th- or early
16th-C tower house extensively altered
1966 when converted into bank; some
original gargoyles on exterior and
various armorial carvings

GAMLINGAY, CAMBS, 3, 2A
Church of St Mary Handsome medieval
church with west tower, two-storeyed
porch, north sacristy and north transept;
font of c.1200, late 14th- or early 15th-C
rood screen, and 15th-C stalls

GARLIES CASTLE (4 km. / 2 ½ m.
NE of Newton Stewart), DUMFRIES
AND GALLOWAY, 10, 4E
Garlies Castle Ruined tower house built
c.1500 with original fireplace

GARLINGE, KENT, 3, 5C
Dent-de-Lion Gatehouse Square gatehouse built before 1445 with unusual
striped flint and brickwork retains four
large angle turrrets, two outer arches
and tall inner arch

GARTAN, CO. DONEGAL, 11, 3A
Church of St Columba Remains of small
chapel with east window of possibly late
12th or early 13th C and late medieval
work; two pillar cross slabs mark borders
of holy ground
Temple Douglas Abbey (4.5 km. / 2 ¾ m.
SSW of Gartan Bridge) Remains of
medieval church with good lancet of
possibly 13th-C in east gable and credence
cavities; vaulted McDavit tomb to east

GARTON-ON-THE-WOLDS
E. RIDING OF YORKS, 7, 5D
Church of St Michael Norman church
restored 1856–7 has original west tower
with 15th-C top; complete scheme of wall
paintings and stained glass by Clayton
and Bell, 1873–6 (see p. 213)

GARWAY, HEREFS, 2, 2A
Church of St Michael 12th-C church of
Knights Templar retains chancel arch
of late 1100s, early 13th-C west tower,
and late 13th-C nave
Dovecot Circular dovecot dated
1326

GATCOMBE COURT,
SOMERSET, 2, 2B
See Long Ashton

**GATESHEAD, TYNE AND
WEAR,** 7, 3B
Church of the Holy Trinity (now Trinity
Community Centre) Church restored 1837
and converted 1980 incorporates 13th-C
chapel of St Edmund and has fine front
with lancet arches

GAWSWORTH, CHESHIRE, 5, 3B
Church of St James Church of 15th and
16th C has west tower with battlements
and pinnacles, wide nave, ornate south
porch and chancel
Old Rectory Late 15th-C timber-framed
house with 19th-C additions
Old Hall 15th-C timber-framed Hall
rebuilt c.1700

GEDDINGTON, NORTHANTS, 4, 1E
Church of St Mary Magdalene Church
of Saxon origin retains late 12th-C north
aisle, chancel of c.1300, and late medieval
west tower; 13th-C effigy of priest, 14th-C
screen and 15th-C reredos
Eleanor Cross [EH] Well-preserved
Eleanor Cross erected soon after 1294
(one of three surviving crosses marking
resting places of body of Eleanor, Queen
of Edward I, on route to Westminster
Abbey)
Bridge 13th-C bridge with later
rebuilding

GEDLING, NOTTS, 5, 5B
Church of All Hallows Medieval church
with west front begun c.1200 and fine
projecting steeple of c.1300–20 with
broach spire; mid 13th-C sedilia,
piscina and double aumbry

GEDNEY, LINCS, 4, 2D
Church of St Mary Magdalen Mainly
14th-C church retains 13th-C (and later)
west tower, 14th-C south door with
insctiptions and fine 15th-C clerestory;
pillar piscina of 1200s and parts of early
14th-C Jesse window

GESTINGTHORPE, ESSEX, 3, 3A
Church of St Mary Church of Norman
origin rebuilt 14th and 15th C has brick
west tower added c.1498 and fine double
hammerbeam roof of c.1500 to nave

GIFFORDS HALL, SUFFOLK, 3, 4A
See Stoke-by-Nayland

GILLISTOWN CÁSTLE
CO. WESTMEATH, 11, 4D
See Castletown-Delvin

GILSTON, HERTS, 3, 2B
Church of St Mary 13th-C church with
19th-C work has original west and north

doorways and important screen of late
1200s; 12th-C hexagonal font

GIPPING, SUFFOLK, 4, 4E
Chapel of St Nicholas Former private
chapel built c.1483 with light interior and
flushwork decoration to nave, chancel,
and north annexe; west tower added 19th
C; one original kneeling bench survives

GISSING, NORFOLK, 4, 4E
Church of St Mary Saxo-Norman church
much rebuilt 15th C retains original round
tower and south doorway to nave; fine
15th-C double hammerbeam roof to nave

GLADESTRY, POWYS, 6, 5D
Church of St Mary 13th-C church
enlarged 1300s has tall nave, fine chancel
with bellcote, west tower with 16th-C
upper levels, and 15th-C south porch;
capital of c.1200 made into piscina
and good late medieval roofs

GLAMIS (9 km. / 5 ½ m. SW of Forfar),
TAYSIDE, 8, 3C
Malcolm Stone (in manse garden) Tall
stone with fine carved work, said to be
graveslab of Malcolm II (d.1034) but probably earlier
Glamis Castle * Famous castle started
before 1484 on site occupied by royal
residence since 11th C retains some
15th-C work but was thoroughly
remodelled 17th C and later; visitors see
crypt (lower hall of medieval tower
house) and "Duncan's Hall" (possibly
guardroom)

GLANWORTH, CO. CORK, 12, 3C
Castle Fragmentary remains of castle built
later 1200s and destroyed 1649
Friary Ruins of church of Dominican
friary founded 1475

GLASBURY / Y CLAS-AR-WY
POWYS, 6, 5D
Old Vicarage House of c.1400 reworked
early 17th C has fine timberwork

GLASCWM, POWYS, 6, 5D
Church of St David Good medieval
church has 13th to 14th-C nave with fine
roof and shingled belfry to west; chancel
added 1400s

GLASGOW, STRATHCLYDE, 8, 2E
Cathedral Church of St Mungo [HS]
[SCS] Cathedral built mid to later 13th C
on hillside site, largest and best preserved
of Scotland's medieval cathedrals still in
use, has extensive vaulted crypt under fine
eastern arm, Blackadder aisle furnished

mid 1400s, non-projecting transepts, two-storeyed chapter house, and 15th-C crossing tower; mid 13th-C base possibly from St Kentigern's shrine reconstructed in south-east chapel; splendid early 15th-C pulpitum with altar platforms added 1503; 19th-C restoration and remodelled west front

Bishop's Castle Excavated walling of medieval castle demolished 18th C

Provand's Lordship *, 3 Castle Street (now museum) Well preserved prebendal house built 1471, extended 1670 and restored 1906

Provan Hall [NTS], Auchinlea Road, Auchinlea Park, Easterhouse (5 km. / 3 m. E of city centre) Excellent 15th-C mansion house

GLASPISTOL CASTLE
  CO. LOUTH, 11, 4D
See Clogher Head

GLASTONBURY, SOMERSET, 2, 2C
Glastonbury Abbey * Remains of abbey founded c.700 include St Mary's Chapel and impressive abbey church begun 1184, monastic buildings, well-preserved 14th-C abbot's kitchen with octagonal roof and lantern, gatehouse, and barn of c.1500

Church of St John Mainly 15th-C church retains tall west tower with elaborate crown, transepts, and roof of c.1495–1500; late medieval monuments, stained glass and chest

Church of St Benedict Medieval church rebuilt c.1520 and 1860s retains late 14th-C chancel

Church of St Michael / Glastonbury Tor [NT] Late 13th-C tower of chapel destroyed 1271 survives on ancient hilltop site

George Hotel, High Street. Medieval pilgrims' inn has rich stone façade with canted bay and battlemented parapet

Glastonbury Tribunal [EH] Well-preserved 15th-C courthouse of abbey has stone front remodelled c.1500 and later 16th-C kitchen wing

St Patrick's Almshouses, Magdalene Street Almshouses founded 1517 with later additions and adjacent medieval chapel

St Mary's Almshouses 14th-C almshouses retain 13th-C chapel with bellcote

GLENCOLUMBKILLE,
  CO. DONEGAL, 11, 2B
Crosses and Stations [Dúchas] Stations of tura or penitential pilgrimage which takes place here on Saint's Day (9 June) are marked by various good early medieval

pillar stones and slab crosses associated with monastery founded 6th C

St Columcille's Chapel and Well (1.5 km. / 1 m. NW of church); Remains of small stone building with cairns and cross slabs

GLENDALOUGH,
  CO. WICKLOW, 12, 5B
Monastic site [Dúchas] Remains of remarkable buildings (much reconstructed 19th and 20th C) of important and extensive monastery founded 6th C in picturesque "Valley of the Two Lakes" include 10th- to 12th-C churches, impressive Round Tower, Ireland's sole surviving early monastic gatehouse, and Cathedral of St Peter and St Paul with 10th-C nave and 12th-C chancel; fine crosses, graveslabs and sculptural work

GLENFAHAN (Dingle Peninsula),
  CO. KERRY, 12, 1C
Beehive Huts [Dúchas] Remains of several clusters of beehive huts surrounded by walls

GLENINAGH, CO. CLARE, 12, 2B
Gleninagh Castle [Dúchas] Handsome L-shaped four-storeyed tower house built probably 16th C by Galway Bay (occupied until later 1800s); simple medieval church and holy well (enclosed 1500s) survive nearby

GLENLUCE, DUMFRIES AND
  GALLOWAY, 10, 4E
Glenluce Abbey [HS / NTS] (3 km. / 2 m. N) Ruins of Cistercian abbey founded early 1190s with late medieval remodelling include fragments of church built c.1200 and well-preserved vaulted chapter house of later 15th or early 16th C; reconstructed sections of cloister arcade

GLOUCESTER, GLOS, 2, 3A
Cathedral Norman cathedral with medieval additions retains crypt of c.1089, nave finished c.1120 with arcades and triforium, original transepts remodelled 1300s, choir begun c.1337, west end rebuilt 1420, and tall mid 15th-C crossing tower; late 12th-C lead font in Lady Chapel, good monument to Edward II of c.1330, and splendid, large chancel east window finished 1350

Cathedral Precinct Monastic buildings include 11th-C chapter house reworked 1300s, Old Deanery with abbot's chapel of c.1120–35, early 13th-C St Mary's Gate, well preserved cloisters with handsome

fan vaulting (mainly 14th-C), and 14th-C library and vestry over Norman passage

Blackfriars [EH], Ladybellegate Street (access restricted) Remains of Dominican friary established by 1239 with church converted to rich merchant's house mid 16th C

Greyfriars [EH] Surviving parts of late 15th- and early 16th-C Franciscan church attached to house of c.1800

Lanthony Priory Remains of 14th-C gatehouse and tithe barn surviving from 12th-C Augustinian priory

St Oswald's Priory Scanty ruins of Norman Augustinian priory

Church of St Mary de Crypt [OCT], Southgate Street Cruciform church of Norman origin with medieval and 19th-C reworking has two-storeyed south porch, tall nave and central tower; 15th-C sedilia, piscina, Easter Sepulchre and stone screens

Church of St Mary de Lode Norman church with nave of 1826 retains imposing 12th-C arch to central tower and 13th-C chancel; early 14th-C effigy of priest

Church of St Nicholas [CCT], Westgate Street. Church of Norman origin has original south doorway with tympanum, 12th- and 13th-C arcades, clerestory, and 15th-C tower with top added 1783; 14th-C knocker to south door

Bishop Hooper's Lodging Timber-framed house of c.1500

The New Inn Pilgrims' inn of c.1457 with 18th-C alterations retains timber-framing and courtyard plan

Church of St Margaret, Wotton. Original chapel of leper hospital built 13th to early 14th C and restored 1875

Church of St Mary Magdalene, Wotton 12th-C chapel of leper hospital reworked 1861

GNOSALL, STAFFS, 5, 3C
Church of St Laurence Church of Norman origin rebuilt 13th to 15th C has fine 12th-C crossing arches, tower with late medieval top, and arch between south transept and south aisle of c.1200

GODMANCHESTER, CAMBS, 4, 2E
Church of St Mary Medieval church with good 13th-C chancel, 15th-C north and south porches, and west tower added 1623; remarkable Mass dial carved on buttress of chancel takes form of incised rose window; stalls retain 15th-C misericords said to come from Ramsey Abbey

GODSHILL, ISLE OF WIGHT, 2, 4E
Church of St Lawrence Early 14th-C church with 16th- to 18th-C additions has west tower, transepts and late medieval wall painting; fine monument to Sir John Leigh (d.1529)

GOODMANHAM, E. RIDING OF
  YORKS, 7, 4E
Church of All Saints Norman church with medieval additions has original south doorway, chancel arch, north aisle and arcade of c.1190, and tower with top added 1400s; good 15th-C roof and lavish font of c.1530

GOODRICH, HEREFS, 2, 2A
Church of St Giles Spacious medieval church has 14th-C south porch and west tower with broach spire; late 13th-C shrine

Goodrich Castle [EH] Impressive moated castle built mid 12th to late 13th C with Norman keep, barbican, courtyard and Great Hall

Flanesford Priory (1 km. / ½ m.NE) Surviving refectory range of Augustinian priory founded 1346

GOSFORTH, CUMBRIA, 7, 1C
Cross Tall, late 10th-C carved cross in churchyard of St Mary

GOUDHURST, KENT, 3, 3D
Church of St Mary Church with west tower added 1638–40 and restoration and additions of c.1865–70 has 13th- and 14th-C arcades, and 14th- and 15th-C south chapel; late medieval monuments

Pattenden Manor * (1.5 km. / 1 m. S) Wealden timber-framed house begun c.1470 and altered 16th C

GOVAN (S of Clyde, Greater Glasgow)
  STRATHCLYDE, 8, 1E
Parish Church (St Constantine's), 866 Govan Road [SCS] Church built 1883–8 houses splendid collection of early Christian sculpture including 10th- to 11th-C sarcophagus, cross shafts, hogbacked tombstones, and slabs

GOWRAN, CO. KILKENNY, 12, 4C
Collegiate Church of St Mary [Dúchas] Collegiate church built c.1275 with now roofless nave and aisles, and massive 14th- or 15th-C central tower incorporated in 19th-C Protestant church on site of original chancel; unusual windows and splendid 14th- to 17th-C sculpture including effigies possibly of James le Butler and Eleanor de Bohun (c.1320–40), early 16th-C effigy of Butler knights, and richly carved tomb chests

GRAIGUENAMANAGH,
CO. KILKENNY, 12, 5C
Duiske Abbey and Crosses [Dúchas]
Interesting though much-restored and
altered remains (smothered by modern
buildings) of Cistercian abbey founded
1207; large church built 1212–40 (well
restored 1974–80) retains good chancel
and fine early 13th-C doorway to 1916
baptistery; effigy of knight of c.1310;
two small High Crosses re-erected
in graveyard

GRANAGH, CO. KILKENNY, 12, 4C
Castle [Dúchas] Remains of castle by
River Suir include 13th-C turrets and
curtain wall, and tall keep built possibly
14th C (15th- and 17th-C additions)

GRANARD, CO. LONGFORD, 11, 3D
Abbeylaragh [Dúchas] (3 km. / 2 m. SE)
Remains of crossing tower built later 16th
C with materials from demolished church
of medieval abbey; carving built into
south wall

GRANGE, CO. LOUTH, 11, 5C
Ballug Castle (1.5 km. / 1 m. S, on edge
of Cooley Peninsula) Remains of small
late medieval tower house with attached
dwelling built probably late 1600s
Templetown Church (3 km. / 2 m S) Ruins
of modest medieval church with some
original cutstone work and traces of
timber rood screen

GRANGEFERTAGH,
CO. KILKENNY, 12, 4B
Round Tower and Church [Dúchas] Tall
Round Tower, all that survives of 6th-C
monastery; nearby church of Augustinian
monastery founded 13th C (in use until
1780 and now incorporated in later
building) retains Mac Gillapatrick
chapel with good tomb of c.1511

GRANTHAM, LINCS, 4, 1C
Church of St Wulfram Fine church of
Norman origin with medieval and 19th-C
rebuilding has ornate north doorway of
c.1280, west doorway of early 1300s, and
tall 14th-C steeple; crypt beneath south
chapel; 14th-C Harrington tomb and
15th-C octagonal font
Angel and Royal Hotel Late 15th-C inn has
lavish façade with central archway and
canted bay windows
Grantham House [NT], Castlegate. House
built 1380 with later alterations

GRAVESEND, KENT, 3, 3C
Milton Chantry [EH], New Tavern Fort
Gardens. Chantry chapel refounded 1322

in Milton Hospital retains original roof
and east wall; part of 16th-C cross wing
to south

GREAT BARDFIELD, ESSEX, 3, 3A
Church of St Mary the Virgin Mainly
14th-C church with west tower, arcades
and fine south door; splendid late 14th-C
stone rood screen under chancel arch

GREAT BEDWYN, WILTS, 2, 4C
Church of St Mary Church built 12th to
14th C with west front of 1843 retains rich
arcades of late 1100s, late 13th-C chancel,
early 14th-C transepts and crossing tower;
tomb recess of early 1300s in south
transept; churchyard cross with later head

GREAT BOOKHAM, SURREY, 3, 1D
Church of St Nicholas Norman church
reworked 19th C has 12th-C arcades,
chancel built 1341, good south aisle with
east part of c.1440, and weatherboarded
west tower

GREAT BOWDEN (Market
Harborough), LEICS, 5, 5D
Church of St Peter and St Paul Mainly
15th-C church restored 1886–7 retains
south chancel aisle arcade of c.1300 and
14th-C west tower; 13th-C piscina in
chancel and late medieval wall painting

GREAT BRICETT, SUFFOLK, 3, 4A
Church of St Mary and St Laurence
Surviving part of church of former
Augustinian priory founded c.1115 with
good Norman north doorway and later
medieval roof; 12th-C font

GREAT BROMLEY, ESSEX, 3, 4B
Church of St George Medieval church
with tall west tower and ornate south
porch, south chapel and doorways; fine
double hammerbeam roof over nave
and brass of c.1432

GREAT BUDWORTH,
CHESHIRE, 5, 2A
Church of St Mary Embattled church of
14th-C origin rebuilt 15th and 16th C with
original transept, later west tower, chancel
chapels and good nave roof

GREAT CANFIELD, ESSEX, 3, 3B
Church of St Mary Norman church
remodelled 15th C retains original north
and south doorways and fine chancel arch;
belfry and south porch added 1400s; good
wall painting of c.1250 depicting Virgin
and Child
Castle Remains of motte and bailey castle
to south-east of church

GREAT CASTERTON, RUTLAND, 4, 1D
Church of St Peter and St Paul Well-
preserved embattled 13th-C church
has chancel with lancet windows, south
porch and 14th-C tower; Norman font,
13th-C effigy of priest, and 14th-C
ironwork on south door

GREAT CHALFIELD, WILTS, 2, 3C
Church of All Saints Modest medieval
church has west porch and fine Tropenell
Chapel built c.1480 with stone screen, wall
paintings and wagon roof; Neale Chapel
added 1775
Great Chalfield Manor [NT] Well-
preserved moated manor house of late
15th C retains oriel windows, vaulted
porch, and hall with spy windows
and fine ceiling

GREAT CHART, KENT, 3, 4D
Church of St Mary 14th- and 15th-C
church of Norman origin has west
tower and chancel with chapels; good
late medieval brasses; rare surviving
timber-framed pesthouse in
churchyard
Court Lodge Stone house of 1313 with
later additions retains original hall
and hipped roof
Yardhurst Medieval "Wealden" house with
original tracery in windows on end bays

GREAT COXWELL, OXON, 2, 4B
Tithe Barn [NT] Large, fine 13th-C
stone-built monastic barn

GREAT CRESSINGHAM,
NORFOLK, 4, 3D
Church of St Michael Medieval church
with chancel of c.1300, 15th-C clerestory,
south porch and west tower; fine roofs
and brasses
Great Cressingham Priory Remaining
part of house of c.1545 with brick faced
upper floor and medieval detailing

GREAT DIXTER HOUSE,
E. SUSSEX, 3, 3D
See Northiam

GREAT DRIFFIELD, E. RIDING
OF YORKs, 7, 5D
Church of All Saints, Middle Street North
Church of Saxon origin with 19th- and
early 20th-C additions retains early 12th-C
four-bay arcades, clerestory, and fine mid
15th-C west tower; font of c.1180

GREAT DUNHAM, NORFOLK, 9, 3D
Church of St Andrew Church of late 11th
C has original nave with blind arcading,
central tower, and 15th-C chancel

GREAT GLEMHAM, SUFFOLK, 3, 5A
Church of All Saints Medieval church
renewed 19th C retains chancel built
c.1300, 15th-C west tower with flushwork
decoration, rood loft doorway, and early
16th-C priest's doorway; good late 15th-C
font and nave roof

GREAT HASELEY, OXON, 2, 5B
Church of St Peter Church of Norman
origin with medieval rebuilding has west
doorway and arcades of c.1200, early
14th-C chancel with lavish tomb
recess, and 15th-C west tower

GREAT LEIGHS, ESSEX, 3, 3B
Church of St Mary Norman church with
rich early 14th-C recess and sedilia and
piscina in chancel retains unusual
round tower with spire added 1882

GREAT LUMLEY, CO. DURHAM, 7, 3C
Lumley Castle Well-preserved castle
licensed 1389 (altered 1570–80 and early
18th C) has four-storeyed corner towers,
ranges around courtyard, and
imposing gatehouse

GREAT MALVERN, WORCS, 5, 3E
Malvern Priory Church of Benedictine
priory extensively rebuilt c.1420–60
adding chancel, clerestory and impressive
crossing tower retains six-bay nave of
c.1120; important stained glass of
c.1440–c.1506 and rare surviving 15th-C
wall tiles in chancel
Gatehouse Medieval priory gatehouse
reworked late 19th C with oriel window
and rich panelling
Pickersleigh Court Pickersleigh Road
Timber-framed house of c.1500

GREAT MASSINGHAM,
NORFOLK, 4, 3D
Church of St Mary Medieval church
retains fine 13th-C south porch with
open arcading, and chancel arch; 15th-C
west tower and clerestory; 14th-C font
and screen of late 1400s
Abbey House Early 19th-C house
incorporates fragments of Augustinian
priory founded before 1260

GREAT MILTON, OXON, 2, 5B
Church of St Mary Norman and 13th-C
church rebuilt after 14th-C fire and
restored 19th C has nave arcades of 1200s,
vaulted 14th-C south porch, and 15th-C
west tower; two late 13th-C carved slabs
Manor House House rebuilt 17th
and enlarged c.1908 retains 15th-C
main block

GREAT MISSENDEN, BUCKS, 3, 1B
Church of St Peter and St Paul Church with 14th-C arcades, chancel with rich 14th-C details, transepts, and later medieval clerestory and nave roof; tower widened 1732; two good 15th-C brasses
Missenden Abbey Remains of house of Arroasian canons founded 1133, with later dwelling occupying site of cloister, include 15th-C timber roof of dormitory in east range

GREAT PAXTON, CAMBS, 4, 1E
Church of the Holy Trinity Church retaining splendid Saxon interior with aisled nave and regular crossing (c.1020)

GREAT SHEFFORD, BERKS, 2, 4B
Church of St Mary Norman church has original south doorway, round tower with octagonal upper stage, and early 13th-C lancets in chancel; Norman font

GREAT SNORING, NORFOLK, 4, 4C
Church of St Mary Church of 13th to 15th C with original south doorway, late 13th-C priest's doorway, and late medieval west tower; marble font, 14th-C sedilia and piscina, and good early 15th-C brasses
Rectory Surviving ranges of brick manor house built c.1525 with turrets and fine terracotta friezes

GREAT TEY, ESSEX, 3, 3B
Church of St Barnabas Norman church with good 14th-C chancel, transepts, and nave built 1829 retains fine original four-stage crossing tower

GREAT WALSINGHAM, NORFOLK, 4, 4C
Church of St Peter Well-preserved 14th-C church has tall west tower with later pyramid roof, fine windows, and 15th-C porches; tiled floor, good roofs, and complete set of original benches

GREAT YARMOUTH, NORFOLK, 4, 5D
Church of St Nicholas Large church of Norman origin with medieval additions and extensive restoration of 19th C and 1957–60 retains nave of c.1190, crossing tower, and 13th-C west front; 15th-C pulpitum re-erected in vestry
Tolhouse * (museum), Tolhouse Street Medieval house restored 19th and 20th C has 13th-C tracery and doorways
Greyfriar's Cloister [EH] South Quay. Fragment of 14th-C cloister of Franciscan house founded 1226
Town Walls Well-preserved remains of town walls begun c.1260 and completed 14th C

GREENCASTLE, CO. DONEGAL, 11, 4A
Castle [Dúchas] Ruins of castle built 1305 on strategic site by entrance to Lough Foyle reworked 15th and 17th C include original gatehouse tower and late medieval O'Doherty Tower

GREEN CASTLE (6.5 km. / 4 m. SW of Kilkeel), CO. DOWN, 11, 5C
Green Castle [EHS] Royal castle built 13th C on rocky outcrop by Carlingford Lough retains imposing rectangular keep (much reworked 15th to 16th C) and ruined curtain wall
Church Ruins of medieval church survive close to castle

GREENFIELD, CLWYD, 6, 5A
Basingwerk Abbey [CADW] Remains of conventual buildings and early 13th-C church of abbey founded 1131 include 12th-C chapter house extended 1200s, novices' lodging, and mid to late 13th-C refectory with arcading to west wall

GREENKNOWE TOWER, BORDERS, 6, 5A
Greenknowe Castle [HS] (1 km. / ½ m. W of Gordon) L-plan tower house built 1581

GREENSTED, ESSEX, 3, 2B
Church of St Andrew Unique surviving wooden church built c.1013 or earlier and rebuilt 16th, 18th and 19th C has weatherboarded timber tower and nave constructed with oak logs; painted panel of c.1500

GRESFORD, CLWYD, 6, 5A
Church of All Saints Handsome church remodelled late 15th C with fine panelled camberbeam roofs, tall clerestory, and south-east chapel; 14th-C crypt, and west tower with 16th-C upper stage and elaborate crown; late 15th-C screens, stalls, misericords, and good stained glass

GREY ABBEY, CO. DOWN, 11, 5B
Grey Abbey [EHS] Impressive remains of important Cistercian abbey founded 12th C (now set amid fine parkland) include church with rich west doorway (c.1225), transepts and short chancel together with cloisters, chapter house and attractive refectory

GREYS COURT, OXON, 2, 5B
See Rotherfield Greys

GREYSTOKE, CUMBRIA, 7, 2C
Church of St Andrew Early 13th-C church rebuilt 14th, 15th, 17th and 19th C has original arcades and two-storeyed

sacristy; alabaster effigies of 14th and 15th C, and 15th-C stained glass in east window
Greystoke Castle Medieval castle rebuilt 17th to 19th C retains original 14th-C pele tower

GRIMSBY, LINCS, 7, 5E
Church of St James, St James' Square Cruciform church of early 13th-C origin extensively remodelled 19th and 20th C retains original nave with wall passage screen and clerestory windows above arcades; 13th and 14th-C font

GRINTON, N. YORKS, 7, 3D
Church of St Andrew Medieval church much rebuilt 14th and 15th C retains late 12th-C tower arch and Norman west window

GROSMONT, GWENT, 2, 2A
Church of St Nicholas Impressive cruciform early medieval church with aisled nave has fine 14th-C octagonal tower and spire; Norman font; 14th-C double piscina
Grosmont Castle [CADW] Ruins of Norman castle with surviving remains of medieval buildings including hall-keep (1201–4), curtain wall and towers (1219–32), and residential accommodation remodelled 1320–60; remarkable surviving stone chimney with elaborate chimney pot

GUILDFORD, SURREY, 3, 1D
Church of St Mary, Quarry Street Church of Saxon origin with medieval and 19th-C rebuilding has 11th-C central tower, arcades and apsidal north and south chapels of c.1180, and chancel with rib-vault of c.1220
Guildford Castle Remains of Norman castle with early 12th-C shell keep and monumental Tower Keep built c.1170

GUILSFIELD / CEGIDFA, POWYS, 6, 5B
Church of St Aelhaiarn Medieval church restored 1877–9 has west tower built c.1300 with later reworking, south porch of c.1400 with 15th-C door and early 16th-C stoup, late 14th- or early 15th-C nave, and fine ceiling of c.1500

GUISBOROUGH, N. YORKS, 7, 4C
Guisborough Priory [EH] Ruins of Augustinian priory founded c.1120 and damaged by fire 1289 include gatehouse built c.1200, imposing late 13th-C east wall of chancel, and octagonal dovecot
Church of St Nicholas Church built

c.1500 restored 1903–8 retains six-bay arcades, west tower, and fine Brus Cenotaph of c.1520–30 with lively carved knights

GUMFRESTON, DYFED, 6, 3E
See Tenby

GURNEY MANOR, SOMERSET, 2, 1C
See Cannington

GUY'S CLIFFE, WARWS, 5, 4E
Manor House Chapel House of 1751 has unusual attached chapel rebuilt 1422–3 with projecting tower, fan vault, rock-hewn statue of Guy of Warwick, and late 18th-C façade

GWAUNYSGOR, CLWYD, 6, 5A
Church of St Mary Simple medieval church reworked 15th C retains timber roof exposed 1931; early 13th-C font, and parts of 13th- to early 14th-C cross slabs

GYFFIN, GWYNEDD, 6, 4A
See Conway

HACCOMBE, DEVON, 1, 5D
Church of St Blaise (in grounds of Haccombe House) Early medieval church refurbished for college established 1335 retains fine early 14th-C pavement in chancel and north chancel chapel; some early 14th-C stained glass and excellent monuments

HACKNESS, N. YORKS, 7, 5D
Church of St Peter Church of Saxon origin has original chancel arch, mid 12th-C south arcade, north arcade built c.1200, and 13th-C west tower with later spire; fragments of fine Saxon cross, good 15th-C font cover and stalls

HADDENHAM, BUCKS, 2, 5A
Church of St Mary Mainly 13th-C church with handsome west tower and original chancel; Norman font, 13th-C piscina and three 15th-C screens

HADDINGTON, LOTHIAN, 8, 3E
St Mary's Collegiate Church, Sidegate [Lauderdale Aisle – HS] [SCS] Large, handsome church built 15th and early 16th C with transepts and chancel restored 1971–3; fine west front of c.1500, incomplete crossing tower, and sacristy converted to Lauderdale Mausoleum 1595; spacious interior with nave reworked 1811
St Martin's Kirk [HS] Ruined nave of late 12th-C church with medieval alterations

HADDISCOE, NORFOLK, 4, 5D
Church of St Mary Saxo-Norman church with medieval additions retains original round tower and rich south doorway with carved figure above; good ironwork on south door and wall painting of c.1400

HADDON HALL (3 km. / 2 m. SE of Bakewell), DERBYS, 5, 4B
Haddon Hall [HHA] Handsome 12th-C manor house enlarged and remodelled 13th to 17th C includes great hall of c.1370 with splendid screen of c.1450, parlour altered c.1500, and chapel with 15th-C wall paintings

HADLEIGH, ESSEX, 3, 3C
Church of St James the Less Small, well-preserved Norman church with nave, apsidal chancel and 15th-C boarded belfry; fragments of good medieval painting
Hadleigh Castle [EH] Castle of c.1232 rebuilt 14th C with surviving remains of curtain wall, barbican and towers

HADLEIGH, SUFFOLK, 3, 4A
Church of St Mary Mainly 15th-C church with two-storeyed vestry retains early 14th-C tower with tall lead spire; 15th-C screens and early 16th-C Easter Sepulchre
Deanery Tower Surviving brick gatehouse of archdeacon's palace built 1495 has elaborate six-stage polygonal turrets
Guildhall Timber-framed guildhall built 15th C with two overhanging levels and Long Room on first floor; ground storey originally almshouses

HADSTOCK, ESSEX, 3, 2A
Church of St Botolph Church of 11th-C origin rebuilt 13th to 15th C has Saxon nave windows, arch to south transept, oak north doorway and late medieval west tower; 15th-C screen, lectern and benches

HAGGARDSTOWN, CO. LOUTH, 11, 4C
See Blackrock

HAIL WESTON, CAMBS, 8, 1E
Church of St Nicholas 13th-C church with timber-framed, shingled west tower built c.1500 or earlier

HAILES, GLOS, 2, 3A
Hailes Abbey [NT / EH] Remains of abbey founded 1246 include part of 13th-C cloister; 13th and 15th-C bosses in museum
Church Church built c.1130 with medieval and 20th-C additions has timber-framed west belfry and 12th-C chancel arch; good

13th-C font, wall paintings of c.1300, 15th-C stained glass and rood screen

HAILES CASTLE (2 km. / 1 ¼ m. S of East Linton), LOTHIAN, 8, 3E
Hailes Castle [HS] Castle of enclosure built 13th to 14th C by River Tyne retains curtain walls, two towers with pit prisons, and range added 1400s

HALES, NORFOLK, 8, 5D
Church of St Margaret [CCT] Well-preserved Norman church with ornate north doorway, round tower, and apsidal end to chancel; medieval wall painting
Hales Court Remains of early 16th-C mansion, now farmhouse

HALESOWEN, W. MIDLANDS, 5, 3D
Church of St John the Baptist Spacious church of Norman origin much rebuilt 15th C and 1883 retains two bays of nave built c.1150–60, south doorway with zig-zag enrichment and late medieval crossing tower; large carved Norman font
Halesowen Abbey [EH] Remains of abbey founded 1218 include walling of 1220–30 and 13th-C abbots house with 13th and 14th-C monuments

HALFORD, WARWS, 5, 4E
Church of St Mary Church of Norman origin remodelled 19th C retains original chancel arch and north doorway with finely carved tympanum; early 16th-C font cover

HALIFAX, W. YORKS, 7, 3E
Church of St John, Church Street Church built mainly 15th to early 16th C with large west tower of c.1450–80, long chancel over crypt, and aisle chapels; fine late medieval font cover
Shibden Hall * Early 15th-C hall-house with 16th-C additions has fine south front with gables and timber-framing

HALLATON, LEICS, 5, 5D
Church of St Michael Church of Norman origin with much 13th- and 14th-C work retains three bays of 12th-C north arcade, 13th-C west tower, and rich north aisle added c.1320–40; reset Norman tympanum in porch and 13th-C font

HALSALL, LANCS, 7, 1E
Church of St Cuthbert Medieval church of 14th to 15th C rebuilt 1886 has west tower with octagonal upper storey and spacious chancel; early 14th-C effigy and late 15th-C stalls with misericords

HALSE, SOMERSET, 2, 1D
Church of St James Church of Norman origin much remodelled 15th C retains original south doorway and 13th- to 14th-C west tower; Norman font and good rood screen

HALSHAM, E. RIDING OF YORKS, 7, 5E
Church of All Saints Church of Norman origin has north arcade of c.1180, 13th-C arcade to north chapel, chancel rebuilt 14th C with arcading on south side, and 15th-C west tower; rich sedilia and piscina of 1300s, and good 15th-C effigy on tomb chest

HALTWHISTLE, NORTHUMBERLAND, 7, 2B
Church of the Holy Cross 13th-C church remodelled 1870 has tall nave and long chancel with lancet windows; sedilia, piscina and 14th-C cross slabs

HAMBLEDON, HANTS, 2, 5D
Church of St Peter and St Paul Church of Saxon origin with Norman and medieval additions and 19th-C restoration has 13th-C chancel and two-storeyed 15th-C vestry

HAMILTON, STRATHCLYDE, 8, 2E
Netherton Cross Hamilton Old Parish Church, Strathmore Road [SCS] Fine 10th-C sculptured cross survives in graveyard of church built 1732–4

HAMPNETT, GLOS, 2, 3A
Church of St George Norman church rebuilt 15th C with original rib-vaulted sanctuary and choir and sanctuary arches (painted c.1871)

HAMPSTEAD NORRIS, BERKS, 2, 5B
Church of St Mary Spacious medieval church with south and north doorways of c.1200 and 13th-C chancel; nave roof added 1635 and chancel arch 1879–80; fine relief carving of knight on horseback (late 13th-C) and painted figure of Virgin

HAMPTON COURT (1.5 km. / 1 m. SE of Hope-under-Dinmore) HEREFS, 5, 2E
Hampton Court House licensed 1434 and much remodelled 18th and 19th C retains 15th-C gatehouse and handsome chapel with panelled ceiling

HAMPTON COURT, LONDON
Hampton Court Palace * Ambitious courtyard house begun 1514 by Cardinal Wolsey, which became royal palace of Henry VIII

HAMSTALL RIDWARE, STAFFS, 5, 3C
Church of St Michael Church of Norman origin with 14th-C chancel, tower, north chapel, and 15th-C clerestory; Norman font, paintings on reredos of late 1400s, and good monument of 1502

HANNINGTON, NORTHANTS, 5, 5D
Church of St Peter and St Paul Unusual two-naved church of late 13th C retains south doorway of c.1180–90; 15th-C screen and pulpit

HANSLOPE, BUCKS, 5, 5E
Church of St James Medieval church has late Norman chancel with rich corbel table, wide early 13th-C aisles, and fine 15th-C tower with pinnacles and recessed spire; 13th-C sedilia and piscina

HANWELL, OXON, 5, 4E
Church of St Peter Medieval church rebuilt early 14th-C retains 13th-C north and south doorways, chancel of early 1300s, west tower, and fine carving of c.1340
Hanwell Castle Farmhouse built into remains of hall-house begun c.1498 with original south-west tower and south wing

HAPPISBURGH, NORFOLK, 4, 5C
Church of St Mary Medieval church restored 19th C with tall west tower and 15th-C arcades, south porch and additions; good font and screen of 1400s

HARBERTON, DEVON, 1, 5D
Church of St Andrew Medieval church restored 1861 and 1871–2 with west tower, vaulted south porch and ceiled wagon roofs; Norman font and fine rood screen

HARBLEDOWN, KENT, 3, 4C
Hospital of St Nicholas 12th-C church of former leper hospital founded c.1084 with 14th-C work incorporates Norman north aisle with arches, west doorway and part of original apse; wall painting of c.1350

HARDHAM, W. SUSSEX, 3, 1E
Church of St Botolph Modest 11th-C church with 19th-C porch and bell turret has extensive cycle of faded wall paintings of c.1120–40
Hardham Priory Ruins of monastic buildings of Augustinian priory founded after 1248 with fine entrance front to 13th-C chapter house

HARDINGSTONE,
NORTHANTS, 5, 5E
See Northampton

HAREWOOD, W. YORKS, 7, 3E
Church of All Saints [CCT] 15th-C church
with 18th- and 19th-C additions has west
tower and fine collection of alabaster
monuments
Harewood Castle Castle licensed 1367
retains angle towers, portcullis chamber,
Great Hall and projecting kitchen

HARLECH, GWYNEDD, 6, 4B
Harlech Castle [CADW] Virtually
impregnable castle built by Edward I
1283–90 on rocky coastal promontary
has inner and outer wards, massive
gatehouse keep and double concentric
fortifications

HARLINGTON, GREATER
LONDON
Church of St Peter and St Paul Norman
and medieval church with fine carved
12th-C south doorway

HARLTON, CAMBS, 3, 2A
**Church of the Assumption of the Blessed
Virgin Mary** 13th-C church with later
medieval additions retains original but
damaged stone rood screen and stoup
with scalloped bowl set on shafted
column

HARMONDSWORTH, GREATER
LONDON
Church of St Mary Norman church
enlarged during medieval period retains
12th-C south arcade; many pews of c.1500
Manor Farm Barn Huge, impressive
timber-framed barn of c.1427, formerly
belonging to Winchester College

HARPLEY, NORFOLK, 4, 3D
Church of St Lawrence Late 13th to early
14th-C church with later medieval
additions retains traceried rood screen,
benches decorated with animals and
poppyheads, and fine south door
carved with figures of saints

HARPSWELL, LINCS, 4, 1B
Church of St Chad Saxon church
reworked 13th and 14th C and restored
1891–2 retains original west tower and late
13th-C south arcade; late 12th-C font and
good medieval monuments

HART, CO. DURHAM, 7, 4C
Church of St Mary Magdalene Church of
Saxon origin has Norman west tower with
upper part of c.1200, 15th-C chancel arch

and north arcade, and minor post-
medieval additions; fragments of
mainly 10th- and 11th-C cross shafts,
Norman font, and lavish late
15th-C font

HARTBURN,
NORTHUMBERLAND, 7, 3B
Church of St Andrew Church of Saxon
origin with 12th- and 13th-C additions has
west tower, four-bay arcades and long
chancel; sedilia, piscina and medieval
stone coffins

HARTLAND, DEVON, 1, 3B
Church of St Nectan 14th-C church
restored and enlarged 1848 has original
arcades, early 16th-C tower and wagon
roofs; ornate Norman font and 15th-C
tomb chest
Hartland Abbey * 16th-, 18th- and 19th-C
house incorporates fragments of
12th-C abbey

HARTLEBURY, WORCS, 5, 3D
Hartlebury Castle * Moated castle begun
1255, damaged 1646 and much rebuilt 17th
to 18th C retains 14th-C chapel and 15th-C
great hall; former residence of Bishops of
Worcester

HARTLEPOOL, CO. DURHAM, 7, 4C
Church of St Hilda [OCT] Early 13th-C
church much rebuilt 19th and 20th C
retains fine nave and chancel arch of
c.1200, and west tower with monumental
buttresses; late 7th- or early 8th-C
gravemarker and 14th-C monuments
Sandwellgate Early 14th-C gate with
turrets leading to harbour beach

HARTLEY WESPALL, HANTS, 2, 5C
Church of St Mary Medieval church
extensively rebuilt 1868–9 has splendid
west wall with large early 14th-C timbers

HARTLEY WINTNEY, HANTS, 2, 5C
Church of St Mary [CCT] Medieval
church rebuilt 19th C has late 13th- to early
14th-C chancel and nave with original
west doorway; late 12th-C pillar piscina

HASTINGS, E. SUSSEX, 3, 3E
Church of St Clement Croft Road
Church of late 14th C has seven-bay
arcades, and south-west tower with
pyramidal roof
Church of All Saints, All Saints Street
Early 15th-C church retains four-bay
arcades, west tower, medieval wall
paintings and monuments
Hastings Castle Ruins of Norman
castle include church begun before

1094, keep of 1172, 13th-C gatehouse and
curtain walling

HATFIELD, HERTS, 3, 2B
Bishop's Palace (within grounds of
Hatfield House) * Substantial remains
of bishop's palace built c.1480–90 (now
situated between church and important
17th-C house) include gatehouse range
and hall with handsome roof

HATFIELD, S. YORKS, 7, 4E
Church of St Lawrence Imposing
cruciform church restored 19th C retains
Norman west front, early 13th-C arcades,
large late 15th-C crossing tower, and good
clerestory; original ceilings to north and
south chapels; fine screen

HATFIELD BROAK OAK,
ESSEX, 3, 2B
Church of St Mary the Virgin Medieval
church with late 14th-C clerestoried
nave and mainly 15th-C exterior
incorporates western parts of church
of Benedictine priory founded 1135; late
17th-C vestry and library added 1708

HATHERLEIGH, DEVON, 1, 4C
Church of St John the Baptist Late
medieval church with ceiled wagon roof
and celure above former rood screen;
Norman font

HATHERSAGE, DERBYS, 5, 4A
Church of St Michael Church rebuilt 1381
and restored 1849–52 retains original
chancel, south arcade, 15th-C west tower
with crocketed spire, and north chancel
chapel added 1463; fine collection of
brasses to Eyre family

HAUGHMOND, SHROPS, 5, 2C
Haughmond Abbey [EH] Extensive
remains of Augustinian priory converted
to house 16th C include impressive late
12th-C chapter house, 14th-C infirmary,
and abbot's lodgings of c.1500

HAUGHTON CASTLE,
NORTHUMBERLAND, 7, 2B
Haughton Castle 13th- and late 14th-C
tower house with embattled parapets
and turrets; west wing added 1876

HAUGHTON-LE-SKERNE
(Darlington), CO. DURHAM, 7, 3C
Church of St Andrew Norman church
remodelled late 14th to early 15th C
retains original chancel arch and
west tower; extensive additions of 1895;
fragments of Saxon sculpture in nave
and porch

HAUXWELL, N. YORKS, 7, 3D
Church of St Oswald Church built late
11th C retains original chancel arch,
north doorway made up of early work,
12th-C south doorway with tympanum,
west tower of c.1200, and 13th-C
chancel; Anglo-Danish cross shaft
in churchyard

HAVERFORDWEST, DYFED, 6, 2D
Church of St Martin 12th-C church with
south chapel and porch added 14th C
Church of St Mary Spacious 13th-C
church with vigorously carved chancel
arch and fine north arcade, enlarged c.1500
with clerestory and handsome timber
roof; effigy of 15th-C pilgrim
Vaulted basement (upper storeys
demolished), Opposite St Mary's Church
One of the town's many surviving
medieval vaulted basements
Haverfordwest Priory [CADW] Ruins
and excavations of church and claustral
buildings of Augustinian priory founded
c.1200
Higgon's Well (south-east edge of town
off road to Uzmaston) Vaulted stone
structure above medieval holy well with
built-in stone benches around sides
Castle Surviving outer walls and angle
towers of Norman and medieval castle
built late 12th and 13th C

HAWARDEN / PENARLAG,
CLWYD, 6, 5A
Hawarden Old Castle Ruins of medieval
castle close to house remodelled 1809–10
with interesting 13th-C circular keep on
motte and earlier earthworks

HAWKCHURCH, DEVON, 2, 1D
Church of St John Norman church rebuilt
13th C and 1859–61 has original north
arcade, chancel arch with good north
respond, south arcade built c.1200 with
fine capitals, and 15th-C west tower

HAWKSHEAD, CUMBRIA, 7, 1D
Hawkshead Courthouse [NT] Remaining
part of 15th-C manorial buildings once
held by Furness Abbey

HAWKSWORTH, NOTTS, 5, 5B
Church of St Mary and All Saints Church
with extensive 19th-C rebuilding retains
ornate early 12th-C tympanum in south
wall of 13th- and 17th-C tower; tall Saxon
cross shaft

HAWSTEAD, SUFFOLK, 3, 3A
Church of All Saints Church of Norman
origin with medieval rebuilding has
12th-C north and south doorways, chancel

of *c*.1300, 15th-C west tower, and good roofs; fine collection of monuments, late 15th-C screen and early 16th-C pulpit

HAWTHORNDEN CASTLE (0.5 km. / ¼ m. NW of Rosewell), LOTHIAN
Hawthornden Castle Castle by River North Esk mainly rebuilt 17th to 18th C retains ruined 15th-C tower at south-east; caves dating back to 1341 survive beneath former south range

HAWTON, NOTTS, 5,5B
Church of All Saints Medieval church with late 13th-C north arcade, fine 14th-C chancel, and west tower built 1482; superb elaborately carved Easter Sepulchre, sedilia and founder's tomb recess in chancel

HAY-ON-WYE / Y GELLI, POWYS, 5,1E
Chapel of St John, Lion Street Mid 13th-C chapel restored 1930
Castle Ruins of Norman castle rebuilt 1233 with adjoining mansion of *c*.1660; 13th-C gateway with medieval wooden doors
Town Walls Fragmentary remains of town walls built *c*.1236

HAYDON BRIDGE NORTHUMBERLAND, 7,2B
Haydon Old Church 12th-C chancel and 14th-C chapel, all that survives of demolished medieval church; font made of recut Roman altar

HEADBOURNE WORTHY, HANTS, 2,4D
Church of St Swithun Saxon church with mutilated remains of monumental sculptured Crucifixion group (*c*.1000) on west wall; 13th-C south-west tower and piscina

HEALAUGH, N. YORKS, 7,4E
Church of St John Norman church built *c*.1130–50 with original corbel tables, west tower, nave, lavish south doorway, north aisle of *c*.1175 and late 12th-C priest's doorway
Healaugh Priory 15th- and early 16th-C fragments of Augustinian priory founded before 1190, now incorporated in two farmhouses

HEANTON PUNCHARDON, DEVON, 1,4B
Church of St Augustine Medieval church restored 1889–90 has west tower with 14th-C bell openings and 15th-C work; lavish monument to Richard

Coffin (d.1523) forms recess probably intended as Easter Sepulchre

HEATH, SHROPS, 5,2D
Chapel Small, well-preserved Norman church with good south doorway and 12th-C font

HECKINGHAM, NORFOLK, 8,5D
Church of St Gregory [CCT] Norman church with 13th-C work has round tower, thatched nave, chancel and apse; fine Norman doorway and font

HECKINGTON, LINCS, 4,1C
Church of St Andrew Large dignified church of 14th C with west tower, transepts, lavish south porch and four bay arcades; big traceried east window of *c*.1330; ornate sedilia, piscina, Easter Sepulchre and tomb recess in chancel

HEDDON-ON-THE-WALL NORTHUMBERLAND, 7,3B
Church of St Andrew Church of Saxon origin with medieval and 19th-C rebuilding retains square 12th-C sanctuary, north aisle of *c*.1200, and 13th-C south aisle

HEDON, E. RIDING OF YORKS, 7,5E
Church of St Augustine Church built mainly early 13th to early 14th C with 18th- and 19th-C alterations has lancet windows, transepts, clerestoried chancel, 15th-C vestry retaining 13th-C wall arcading, and noble crossing tower of *c*.1427–37; fine 14th-C font

HEIGHINGTON, CO. DURHAM, 7,3C
Church of St Michael Early church much altered *c*.1160–70 with Norman sanctuary, chancel arch and tower arch; vestry built probably 13th C and later medieval and 19th-C additions; early 16th-C pulpit and chancel stalls

HELMSLEY, N. YORKS, 7,4D
Helmsley Castle [EH] Imposing remains of Norman castle with earthworks, curtain walls with towers, barbican, keep enlarged 14th C, and range reworked between 1563 and 1587

HEMEL HEMPSTEAD, HERTS, 3,1B
Church of St Mary Spacious, well-preserved Norman church with rib-vaulted chancel of *c*.1150, crossing tower, transepts, nave and clerestory of *c*.1175; ornate west doorway and good late 14th-C brass

Picotts End Cottage has religious wall paintings of *c*.1500, originally behind dais of great hall

HEMINGBROUGH, N. YORKS, 7,4E
Church of St Mary Mainly 13th-C church with 14th-C south aisle, 15th-C upper storey to sacristy, north (Babthorpe) chapel, remarkably tall spire to original crossing tower, and rich south chapel built *c*.1520; font of *c*.1200, 13th-C gravestones, fine screens, stalls and bench ends

HEMINGFORD GREY, CAMBS, 4,2E
Church of St James Norman church with 13th- to 15th- and 18th-C additions retains north arcade of *c*.1180; mid 13th-C double piscina and double aumbry in chancel
Manor House (garden open * visit house by appointment only) Remarkable survival of moated Norman manor house still in domestic occupation; blocked first-floor entrance and hall with massive stone fireplace

HEMSBY, NORFOLK, 8,5D
Hall Farm Barn Rare surviving early 14th-C aisled barn retains fine interior with original timber work

HEMYOCK, DEVON, 2,1D
Hemyock Castle * Medieval castle reworked *c*.1380 and early 1800s retains moat, gateway with circular towers, and enclosing wall
Culm Dary (1.5 km. / 1 m. N) Simple late medieval chapel much restored 1860
Culm Dary Farm Farm with medieval hall-house and later additions

HENBURY, SOMERSET, 2,2B
See Bristol

HENLEY-IN-ARDEN, WARWS, 5,4D
Church of St John the Baptist Late 15th-C church and adjoining Guildhall, much restored. See also: Beaudesert

HEREFORD, HEREFS, 5,2E
Cathedral * Norman cathedral with extensive medieval and 18th- to early 20th-C rebuilding retains east wall of south transept of *c*.1110, 12th-C chancel remodelled 13th C, good 12th-C nave arcade, crypt beneath lavish Lady Chapel of *c*.1220–40, fine north transept begun *c*.1250–5, early 14th-C crossing tower, and two-storeyed north porch; excellent monuments and early 14th-C chancel stalls
Cathedral Precinct Precinct includes Bishop's Palace (altered 18th to 20th C)

with remains of 11th-C chapel and late 12th-C timber great hall, 15th-C Bishop's Cloister incorporating important 14th-C decagonal chapter house, and well-preserved College of Vicars Choral (founded 1396)
Church of All Saints, High Street. Church rebuilt late 13th to early 14th C has imposing north-west tower with spire and good roofs; fine chest and early 14th-C stalls with misericords
Church of St Peter Church built mainly *c*.1300 much reworked 1880–5 retains fine late 13th-C south-east tower with recessed spire; 13th-C gable cross and 15th-C stalls
Coningsby Hospital Hospital founded *c*.1614 incorporates 13th- to 14th-C remains of house of Knights of St John
Blackfriars Remains of house of Blackfriars begun 1322 include west range reworked 1600s; rare surviving hexagonal preaching cross
Booth Hall Hotel Hotel incorporates upper hall of merchant's guild of *c*.1400 with fine timber roof

HERGEST COURT, HEREFS, 5,1E
See Kington

HERMITAGE (8 km. / 5 m. N of Newcastleton), BORDERS, 7,2B
Hermitage Castle [HS] Restored remains of mainly late 14th-C castle beside haunting Hermitage Water with large keep and corner towers; traces of 13th-C work to interior; nearby 14th-C Hermitage Chapel

HERNE, KENT, 3,4C
Church of St Martin Early 14th-C church with medieval additions has handsome three-stage west tower, large east window and north porch with stoups of *c*.1350; sedilia, font of *c*.1405–14 and 15th-C brasses

HERRINGFLEET, SUFFOLK, 8,5D
Church of St Margaret Norman church with original round tower, south doorway, and 13th-C nave

HERSTMONCEUX, E. SUSSEX, 3,3E
Church of All Saints Church built *c*.1180–1200, remodelled mid 15th and 19th C, has 12th-C north arcade, north-west tower with later spire, and brick north chapel added *c*.1440; Norman font and good early 15th-C brass
Herstmonceux Castle (garden open*) Impressive moated brick mansion licensed 1440 with bridge, gatehouse and turrets

HERTFORD, HERTS, 3, 2B
Hertford Castle Remains of medieval motte and bailey castle include part of 12th-C flint curtain walling and brick gatehouse of 1461–5
Fountain, Old Cross Fountain composed of 13th-C lancet windows from demolished medieval church

HESSETT, SUFFOLK, 3, 3A
Church of St Ethelbert Mainly 15th-C church with two-storeyed vestry, handsome south porch, and west tower retains 14th-C chancel; set of medieval benches in nave; wall paintings, good stained glass, screen and font

HEVER CASTLE, KENT, 3, 2D
Hever Castle [HHA] Impressive moated manor house licensed 1384 with work of c.1584 and 1903–7 retains three-storeyed gatehouse, courtyard and timber-framed ranges; oratory with 13th-C stained glass

HEVERSHAM, CUMBRIA, 7, 2D
Church of St Peter Church of Norman origin much rebuilt 15th to early 16th C and 1800s retains late 12th-C pier in south arcade; fragment of Saxon cross shaft of late 9th C
Heversham Hall Incomplete 14th-C hall-house with alterations of 1500s and 1600s

HEXHAM, NORTHUMBERLAND, 7, 3B
Hexham Priory Augustainain priory with work of c.1850–1910 retains church of c.1180–1250 replacing 7th-C church, whose crypt survives beneath present nave; 13th-C slype, night stair, and fine medieval furnishings including 7th-C "Wilfred's Chair"; remains of monastic buildings with Priory Gate of c.1160
Moot Hall Imposing 14th-C moot hall with later additions and restoration
Prison Prison built 1330–2 for Archbishop of York

HEYNESTOWN CASTLE, CO. LOUTH, 11, 4C
See Blackrock

HEYSHAM, LANCS, 7, 2D
Church of St Peter Saxon church with medieval and later additions has original west and north doorways and 15th-C screen; hogback tombstone and 13th-C coffin lid; carved shaft of Saxon cross in churchyard
St Patrick's Chapel Small oblong chapel with south doorway of 8th to 9th C

HEYTESBURY, WILTS, 2, 3C
Church of St Peter and St Paul Mainly 13th-C church completed early or mid 14th C and much restored 1865–7 retains crossing tower, north and south chapels, and good chancel with lancet windows to clerestory; early 16th-C stone screen to north transept

HIGHAM, KENT, 3, 3C
Church of St Mary Norman and early medieval church remodelled 14th-C retains 13th-C font, 14th-C pulpit and handsome carved door, and 15th-C screen

HIGHAM FERRERS, NORTHANTS, 8, 1E
Church of St Mary Handsome church of c.1220–80 enlarged 1300s retains fine west tower and portal with carved tympanum; spacious 14th-C north aisle and Lady Chapel; some original stalls, and good medieval brasses and tomb chest; early 14th-C cross in churchyard
Archbishop Chichele's School School refounded 1422 with battlements and pinnacles
Archbishop Chichele's Bede House Bede house refounded 1428 has banded stonework, raised chapel and bellcote
Archbishop Chichele's College [EH] Remains of south range, west range and gatehouse of college founded 1431
Market Cross Tall 14th-C market cross

HIGHAM-ON-THE-HILL, LEICS, 5, 4D
Church of St Peter Norman church largely rebuilt 1791 and 19th C retains fine original tower

HIGH BICKINGTON, DEVON, 1, 4B
Church of St Mary Church of Norman origin with 14th- and 15th-C additions has original south door and tall 15th-C west tower; ceiled wagon roofs and many fine bench ends

HIGH HAM, SOMERSET, 2, 1D
Church of St Andrew Medieval church with extensive 15th-C rebuilding retains early 14th-C lower parts to west tower; good roofs and rood screen

HIGH ISLAND / ARDOILEAN (11 km. / 7 m. W of Cleggan, accessible by boat) CO. GALWAY, 12, 1A
Monastery [Dúchas] Remains of monastery founded probably 7th C on (now uninhabited) island include rectangular church with flat-headed doorway, enclosing wall, and beehive huts

HIGH ONGAR, ESSEX, 3, 2B
Church of St Mary Medieval church has Norman nave with splendid doorway and 13th-C chancel; south tower added 1858

HILL CROOME, WORCS, 5, 3E
Church of St Mary 13th-C church with saddleback tower
Dovecot Cruck-built dovecot, possibly as early as 15th C, survives at farm to west of church

HILLESDEN, BUCKS, 2, 5A
Church of All Saints Late 15th-C church with lavish west tower and interior; tall north porch, two-storeyed north vestry and chancel adorned with carved stone angels

HILLS TOWER (1.5 km. / 1 m. SE of Lochfoot), DUMFRIES AND GALLOWAY, 10, 5E
Hills Tower Attractive early 16th-C tower house with gatehouse of 1598 and adjoining wing added 1721

HILTON, DORSET, 2, 2D
Church of All Saints Mainly 15th-C church with vaulted south porch incorporates windows and painted panels of c.1500 from Milton Abbey; 12th-C font

HINCHINGBROOKE, CAMBS, 4, 2E
Hinchingbrooke House built 16th, 17th and 19th C with materials from 11th-C Augustinian nunnery; medieval walling and fine gatehouse of c.1500 from Ramsey Abbey

HINGHAM, NORFOLK, 8, 4D
Church of St Andrew Spacious mainly 14th-C church has west tower, clerestory, and long chancel with 15th-C chapels; splendid Morley monument of 1400s and hammerbeam roofs; glass in east window of c.1500

HINTON CHARTERHOUSE, SOMERSET, 2, 2C
Hinton Priory Carthusian monastery founded 1232 and converted to dwelling late 16th C with remains of sacristy, rib-vaulted chapter house, and refectory undercroft of c.1300
Church of St John the Baptist Norman church with 19th-C additions retains early 13th-C west tower remodelled 1770, and much work of 1200s; Norman font

HINTON ST GEORGE, SOMERSET, 2, 1D
Church of St George 15th-C church has four-storeyed tower with pinnacles,

embattled south porch, and Poulett Chapel rebuilt 1814; 15th-C monuments and brasses

HISTON, CAMBS, 4, 2E
Church of St Andrew Cruciform church reworked 19th C retains splendid transepts built c.1275 with nook-shafting, blind arcading, and double piscinas; crossing of c.1300 and tower with 14th-C upper stages

HITCHIN, HERTS, 3, 1A
Church of St Mary Restored medieval church with low west tower of 12th to 13th C; early 14th-C nave arcades, south chapel of 1450s and vaulted south porch; some fine original roofs and screens
The Priory House much rebuilt 18th C incorporates 14th- to 16th-C fragments of original Carmelite priory
Medieval Buildings 15th-C timber-framed houses on Bridge Street, Tilehouse Street and corner of Market Square

HODNET, SHROPS, 5, 2C
Church of St Luke Church of Norman origin with original priest's door, octagonal west tower, and wide south aisle; 19th-C Heber Chapel and restoration

HOGNASTON, DERBYS, 5, 4B
Church of St Bartholomew Church mainly rebuilt 1879–81 retains fine Norman doorway with unusual carved figures in tympanum, possibly on Agnus Dei theme; 13th-C west tower with later medieval top

HOLBEACH, LINCS, 4, 2D
Church of All Saints Mainly 14th-C church restored 19th C with tall nave arcades, good windows, porches and west tower; fine effigy of late 1300s on tomb chest, and late medieval font

HOLCOMBE ROGUS, DEVON, 1, 5B
Church of All Saints Attractive late medieval church restored 19th C; south porch has arcading and fan vault
The Priest's House [LT] Fine church house built c.1500 (converted 1984–5)
Holcombe Court Handsome courtyard house with impressive early 16th-C south (entrance) front retaining bay windows and big gatetower and fine early 16th-C screens passage; extensive alterations and additions of later 16th C and c.1859–68

HOLDGATE, SHROPS, 5, 2D
Church of the Holy Trinity Norman church with original nave, ornate south

doorway, 13th-C chancel and short west tower; fine 12th-C font

HOLME, NOTTS, 5,5B
Church of St Giles Medieval church with much late 15th-C rebuilding has spacious chancel, south chancel chapel, and rich south porch; good monument to John Barton (d.1491) and 15th-C bench ends

HOLME PIERREPONT, NOTTS, 5,5C
Church of St Edmund Church with much work of 1666 retains 13th-C arcade and good medieval monuments
Holme Pierrepont Hall * House with 18th- and 19th-C additions has impressive brick-built south (gatehouse) range of early 1500s

HOLMES CHAPEL, CHESHIRE, 5,3B
Church of St Luke Spacious timber church of 15th C encased in brick early 1700s retains four-bay arcades, fine nave roof, and west tower

HOLT, CLWYD, 6,5A
Church of St Chad Medieval church remodelled late 1400s and restored 1871–3 retains 14th-C nave arcades; west tower added 1679; font of c.1493
Castle Scanty remains of late 13th-C castle by river
Bridge 15th- or early 16th-C bridge of eight arches crosses River Dee

HOLT, WORCS, 5,3E
Church of St Martin Well-preserved Norman church has original north and south doorways with carved capitals, chancel and arch of c.1160–75, and 15th-C west tower; fine Norman font
Castle medieval castle with four-stage 14th-C tower and 15th-C hall

HOLWELL, DORSET, 2,2D
Church of St Laurence 15th-C church restored 1885 with west tower, south chapel and ceiled wagon roof in nave

HOLY CROSS, CO. TIPPERARY, 12,4C
Holy Cross Abbey [Dúchas] Remains of Cistercian abbey founded 12th C by River Suir include 13th-C church much remodelled 1450–75 and reconstructed 1971–5 (in use) with superb chancel, transepts, low central tower, and exquisite rib vaulting; fine 15th-C triple sedilia in choir, unique open arcaded structure in south transept (probable shrine for monastery's relic of True Cross), and late medieval wall painting with hunting scene in north transept; remnants of reworked cloister

HOLYHEAD / CAER GYBI (ANGLESEY), GWYNEDD, 6,3A
Church of St Cybi Lofty 13th-C church almost entirely rebuilt late 15th and early 16th C survives within walls of 3rd- to 4th-C Roman fortlet [CADW]

HOLY ISLAND (accessible by causeway at low tide) **NORTHUMBERLAND, 7,3A**
Lindisfarne Priory [EH] Ruins of important priory refounded 1083, once major pilgrimage centre, include 12th-C church (rebuilt 1855–6 and early 20th C) with carved "rainbow" arch and medieval monastic buildings
Church of St Mary Church of Saxon origin with much 13th- and some 19th-C work retains fine chancel of c.1200 and bellcote

HOLYWELL, CLWYD, 6,5A
St Winefride's Chapel and Holy Well [CADW] Handsome early 16th-C chapel over vaulted well chamber, site of reputed martyrdom of St Winefride and place of pilgrimage; chancel with three-sided apse, north aisle, and fine camberbeam roof with bosses; well chamber has good carved decoration and north narthex lwith elaborate niche

HOLYWELL (1.5 km. / 1 m. NW of Belcoo), **CO. FERMANAGH, 11,3C**
Templerushin Church Remains of parish church built late 15th and early 16th C

HOLYWOOD, CO. DOWN, 11,5B
Church Remains of small late 12th- to early 13th-C parish church on site of Franciscan friary (close to Norman motte); fine cut stonework and gravestone with foliate cross and shears

HONEYCHURCH, DEVON, 1,4C
Church of St Mary Church of 12th-C origin rebuilt 15th C has west tower, north-east stair turret, and low chancel; Norman font

HOOK NORTON, OXON, 2,4A
Church of St Peter Large Norman church with 13th- to 15th-C additions has original chancel and north transept, north arcade of c.1300, and 15th-C west tower; good Norman font with carved figures

HOPE, CLWYD, 6,5A
Church of St Cyngar Medieval church with north nave added 1400s retains crypt and part of 13th-C double piscina to east of original (now south) nave; good 15th-C east windows

HOPE CASTLE, CLWYD, 6,5A
See Caergwrle

HOPESAY, SHROPS, 5,1D
Church of St Mary Modest church has nave and chancel of c.1200, priest's doorway, and west tower with pyramidal roof; good timber roof to nave

HOPTON CASTLE, SHROPS, 5,2C
Hopton Castle Surviving Norman keep of ruined castle

HORLEY, OXON, 5,4E
Church of St Ethelreda Late Norman church with medieval remodelling retains original central tower, chancel, nave rebuilt 13th C, and clerestory of c.1320; 15th-C wall painting of St Christopher
Park House Modest house built early 1300s

HORNBY, LANCS, 7,2C
Church of St Margaret Church rebuilt 1817 and 1899 retains early 16th-C octagonal west tower and polygonal apse to chancel; remains of carved Saxon cross shaft
Hornby Castle 19th-C castle reworked 20th C incorporates 13th- and early 16th-C pele tower to rear

HORNBY, N. YORKS, 7,3D
Church of St Mary Church of Norman origin retains 11th-C west tower with later top, rich north arcade of late 1100s, chancel with east wall built 1877, and 15th-C south arcade; screen with fine ornamental paintings of 1400s and good monuments

HORNING, NORFOLK, 8,5D
Church of St Benedict Surviving nave of 13th-C church with 14th-C tower and later medieval additions retains staircase to rood loft; early 14th-C font and benches with lively carvings
St Benet's Abbey Ruined 14th-C gatehouse of abbey founded c.800

HORNSEA, E. RIDING OF YORKS, 7,5E
Church of St Nicholas Spacious medieval church has 13th-C west tower, fine interior with 14th-C arcades, well-lit 15th-C chancel above vaulted crypt, and clerestory; fine monuments of 1200s and 1300s

HORSHAM ST FAITH, NORFOLK, 8,4D
Church of St Mary and St Andrew Spacious mainly 15th-C church retains 13th-C east wall to chancel and 14th-C

west tower; 19th-C arcades; pulpit dated 1480 and screen of 1528
Priory of St Faith Abbey Farm. Remains of priory founded 1105 with walls of cloister and rectory, now part of farm
Mission Room Mission room incorporating late Norman work from priory

HORTON, GLOS, 2,2B
Church of St James 14th-C church remodelled 1400s and 1500s has original north arcade, three-stage west tower, south porch and north chapel; pillar piscina in chancel and good wagon roof
Horton Court [NT] Manor house built 1521 and reworked 18th to 20th C retains north wing of c.1140 (former prebendal house) with hall and timber roof; detached late medieval ambulatory

HOSPITAL, CO. LIMERICK, 12,3C
Church [Dúchas] Remains of church of once important commandery of Knights Hospitaller founded 1215; three fine 13th- to 14th-C effigy tombs

HOUGH-ON-THE-HILL, LINCS, 4,1C
Church of All Saints Saxon church extensively remodelled 15th C with original lower parts to west tower and projecting stair; 13th-C arcades and chancel arch; late medieval clerestory and upper level to west tower

HOUGHTON CONQUEST, BEDS, 3,1A
Church of All Saints Good medieval church with uncommonly tall 14th-C arcades, west tower begun late 1300s, and renewed chancel with two-storeyed vestry; 14th-C painting of Doom over chancel arch and 15th-C St Christopher over north doorway; 15th-C roof with carved bosses and fine tomb chest in chancel with brasses to Isabel Conquest (d.1493) and husband and son

HOUGHTON-LE-SPRING, TYNE AND WEAR, 7,3C
Church of St Michael and All Angels Church of Norman origin largely rebuilt 13th to 14th C and restored 17th and 19th C has arcades of c.1300, crossing tower, and fine mid 14th-C west and east windows

HOUND TOR MEDIEVAL VILLAGE, DEVON, 1,5C
See Manaton

HOWDEN, E. RIDING OF YORKS, 7,4E
Church of St Peter (Chancel and Chapter House [EH], visitors see outside only)

Impressive church built c.1270–c.1320 has fine west front with hexagonal turrets, six-bay nave, tall crossing tower, transepts, and attached grammar school of c.1500; ruinous 14th-C chancel and octagonal chapter house; important medieval monuments and good 15th-C pulpitum (now reredos) with statues
Bishop of Durham's Manor House Remains of medieval bishop's house converted to private house 17th and 18th C with late 14th-C great hall, two-storeyed porch, and original screens passage

HOWELL, LINCS, 4, 1C
Church of St Oswald Church of Norman origin with original south doorway, north arcade of c.1200, 13th-C double bellcote, and 14th-C north chapel; 15th-C font and good medieval monuments

HOWMORE / TOBHA MOR
(South Uist), WESTERN ISLES (Outer Hebrides), 9, 1D
St Mary's Church, St Dermot's Chapel, and The Priest's Chapel (Teampull Mor, Caibeal Dhiarmaid, and Caibeal Nan Sagairt) Remains of three medieval buildings survive in old parish churchyard

HOWTH, CO. DUBLIN, 11, 5E
Church of St Mary (or St Mary's Abbey) [Dúchas] Ruined mainly 14th-C collegiate church with 15th- to 16th-C additions houses well-preserved tomb of Sir Christopher St Lawrence (d.1462) and wife with excellent carved panels; remains of late medieval college or priest's house to south

HUGHLEY, SHROPS, 5, 2D
Church of St John the Baptist Medieval church with 13th-C south doorway, 14th-C chancel, and timber-framed belfry; fine 15th- or early 16th-C rood screen

HUISH EPISCOPI, SOMERSET, 2, 1D
Church of St Mary Church of Norman origin rebuilt 14th and 15th C has tall west tower with rich decoration; late medieval font

HULL (KINGSTON-UPON-HULL)
E. RIDING OF YORKS, 7, 5E
Church of Holy Trinity, Market Place Large cruciform church begun c.1300 and consecrated 1425 has brick transepts and chancel, and handsome crossing tower with upper levels added c.1500–30; fine 14th-C font with lively carvings, screen and monuments

Church of St Mary Lowgate Former chapel of ease begun c.1400 with west tower rebuilt 1697 and 19th-C restoration and additions
Church of St James, Church Street, Sutton (Outer Hull) Church consecrated 1349 has stone chancel and 14th- to 15th-C west tower and south side with brickwork; good late medieval screen

HULNE PRIORY,
NORTHUMBERLAND, 7, 3A
Hulne Priory Well-preserved remains of Carmelite priory founded 1242 include church with original sedilia, two-storeyed sacristy and tower of 1486

HUNTINGDON, CAMBS, 4, 2E
Church of St Mary Norman church rebuilt 17th C and 1876 has early 13th-C chancel and priest's doorway, and lavish 15th-C west tower
Bridge Early 14th-C bridge with cutwaters on site of former bridge chapel
Cromwell Museum * Surviving west end of infirmary hall built c.1170–90 (formerly used as grammar school) retains doorways and arcading; heightened 1878

HUNTINGTOWER (5 km. / 3 m. NW of Perth), TAYSIDE, 8, 2D
Huntingtower Castle [HS] Partly restored tower house (known until 1600 as Ruthven Castle) with two, closely set 15th-C towers joined by 17th-C building; first-floor hall retains wall and ceiling paintings of c.1540

HUNTLY, GRAMPIAN, 8, 3A
Huntly Castle [HS] Norman motte and bailey on defensive site near Rivers Deveron and Bogie with imposing, well-preserved palace built mainly 1552 (enriched 1602) retaining 15th-C vaulted dungeon below; foundations of massive 15th-C tower house to north of court

HURLEY, BERKS, 2, 5B
Hurley Priory (St Mary's) Long, narrow nave of church originally belonging to Benedictine house founded before 1087 (restored 1852, now used for parish worship); round dovecot and barn, probably built 14th C, survive to west; refectory range incorporated in house to north

HURSTBOURNE TARRANT
HANTS
Church of St Peter Early medieval church with arcades of c.1230 and 14th-, 15th- and 17th-C additions retains late Norman

carved doorway and early 14th-C wall paintings

HYLTON CASTLE
TYNE AND WEAR, 7, 3B
Hylton Castle [EH] Well-preserved shell of castle completed 1410 and altered 16th and 18th C; impressive west front with towers and machicolated parapet
Chapel Remains of chapel built possibly mid 15th C with much later alteration

HYTHE, KENT, 3, 4D
Church of St Leonard Interesting early church reworked 12th, 13th, 18th and 19th C retains handsome chancel raised on vaulted passage with arcades, gallery and clerestory; piscina and sedilia of c.1230 and 14th-C font

ICKLESHAM, E. SUSSEX, 3, 3E
Church of All Saints Early Norman church restored 1848–9 has 11th-C north tower and doorway, arcades built c.1175, and north and south chapels of c.1200; piscina in 14th-C chancel

ICKLETON, CAMBS, 3, 2A
Church of St Mary Early Norman church with reused Roman columns in nave arcades; medieval broach spire, rood screen and bench ends; important cycle of wall paintings on north wall of nave (12th-C) and Doom (14th-C) painted above chancel arch

ICKLINGHAM, SUFFOLK, 4, 3E
Church of All Saints [CCT] Thatched church of Norman origin much rebuilt late 1200s to early 1300s has south-west tower and plain interior; early 14th-C chest, octagonal font, and medieval benche
Church of St James Mainly 15th-C church retains chancel of c.1300; late medieval font

IDSWORTH, HANTS, 2, 5D
Church of St Hubert Church of 12th-C origin carefully restored 1912 with simple nave, chancel and bell-turret; important and extensive wall paintings of c.1330

IFFLEY, OXON, 2, 5B
Church of St Mary Exceptionally complete and well-preserved Norman church with rich sculptured decoration
The Old Parsonage [LT] Rectory of Norman origin has wing added c.1500 and later additions and alterations

IFORD, E. SUSSEX, 3, 2E
Church of St Nicholas Norman church retains original chancel, nave, and central tower with later roof; 13th-C font
Swanborough Manor Medieval manor house has hall built c.1200 with 15th-C alterations

IGHTHAM MOTE, KENT, 3, 3D
Ightham Mote [NT] Handsome moated medieval manor house retaining much good 14th- to 16th-C work has timber-framing and jettied upper floors; fine early 14th-C hall and well-preserved early 16th-C chapel

ILAM, STAFFS, 5, 4B
Church of the Holy Cross Medieval church with extensive 19th-C additions has Norman font and two late Saxon crosses in churchyard

ILFRACOMBE, DEVON, 1, 4A
Church of the Holy Trinity Medieval church with additions of c.1321, 15th and 19th C has low north tower and ceiled wagon roofs with unusual corbels and celures
Church of St Nicholas Small medieval church used 16th C as lighthouse with lantern at west end

ILKESTON, DERBYS, 5, 4B
Church of St Mary Church of c.1200 rebuilt 14th, 18th and 19th C and enlarged 1909–10; fine sedilia and double piscina of c.1280 and early 14th-C stone screen

ILKLEY, W. YORKS, 7, 3E
Church of All Saints Medieval church with chancel of 1860 retains good 13th-C south doorway, 15th-C west tower, and low nave and aisles; three important Saxon crosses in churchyard

ILLAUNTANNIG (Maharee Islands off Dingle Peninsula, accessible by boat), CO. KERRY, 12, 1C
Monastic Site [Dúchas] Remains of monastery founded 6th or 7th C and enclosed by old stone wall include two oratories, three beehive huts, three burial monuments, and stone cross

ILMINSTER, SOMERSET, 2, 1D
Church of St Mary Spacious 15th-C church altered 19th C with rich north chapel, south porch, and fine fan-vaulted crossing and tower; 15th-C font and tomb chest

INCH ABBEY / INIS CUMHSCRAIGH (1.5 km. / 1 m. NW of Downpatrick), CO. DOWN, 11, 5C
Inch Abbey (or St Mary's Abbey de Insula) [EHS] Surviving buildings (mainly late 12th- and 13th-C) of important Cistercian abbey founded 1180s by River Quoile include church altered 1400s with fine lancets to chancel, bakehouse and infirmary

INCHAFFRAY (3 km. / 2 m. SE of Fowlis Wester), TAYSIDE, 8, 2D
Inchaffray Abbey Fragments of Augustinian abbey founded c.1200 on site of earlier church include part of west range (probably converted 16th C as residence for commendators)

INCHAGOILL (island in Lough Corrib, 8 km. / 5 m. SW of Cong, Co. Mayo), CO. GALWAY, 11, 2A
Monastic Site [Dúchas] Remains of two churches on site of early monastery, St Patrick's with later chancel and nearby inscribed pillar-cross (Luguaedon Stone), and 12th-C Templenaneeve or Saints' Church with fine original west doorway (incorrectly reassembled 1860)

INCHBOFIN (3 km. / 2 m. NE of Inchmore, accessible by boat) CO. WESTMEATH, 11, 3D
Early Christian Monastery [Dúchas] Site of monastery founded c.530 on island in Lough Ree with remains including two small churches, that to north (Augustinian) with good 12th-C north-east window of nave, large later medieval north transept and sacristy; some fine early grave slabs

INCHCLERAUN, CO. LONGFORD, 12, 4A
Elfeet Castle (2.5 km. / 1½ m.E, on shore of Lough Ree) Remains of late medieval tower house on defensive site with good fireplace on upper floor

INCHCLERAUN ISLAND CO. LONGFORD, 12, 4A
Teampull Dhiarmada Earliest of churches (built probably 8th C) of monastery founded 6th C on island;
Teampull Mor Spacious medieval church with good east gable, 15th-C vaulted sacristy, and chapter house;
Churches Remains of two further churches (Chancel Church and Church of the Dead), with Women's Church to south

Clogar Medieval bell tower on elevated site south of churches

INCHCOLM (island in Firth of Forth, 2 km. / 1¼ m. S of Aberdour, accessible by ferry from South Queensferry), FIFE, 8, 3E
Inchcolm Abbey [HS] Unusually well-preserved remains of Augustinian monastery founded 1123 and abandoned after 1560 (known as "Iona of the east") include church with tower, cloister with tunnel-vaulted ambulatory, 13th-C octagonal chapter house with 14th-C upper floor, and 15th-C infirmary

INCHICRONAN, CO. CLARE, 12, 3B
Inchicronan Abbey [Dúchas] Church of Augustinan abbey in picturesque location by lake retains unusual east window (probably late 12th-C); 15th-C additions and remains of conventual buildings

INCHINNAN, STRATHCLYDE, 8, 1E
Inchinnan Early Christian Stones Carved sarcophagus, cross-shaft and grave slab survive in covered area between church and bell-tower

INCH ISLAND (2.5 km. / 1½ m. S of Fahan, in Lough Swilly), CO. DONEGAL, 11, 3A
Inch Castle Remains of late medieval tower house on island accessible via causeway

INCHKENNETH (island to W of Mull), STRATHCLYDE (Inner Hebrides), 10, 3A
Inchkenneth Chapel [HS] Remains of simple 13th-C chapel with Celtic cross and good medieval monuments in graveyard

INCHMAHOME PRIORY (on island in Lake of Menteith, accessible by boat from Port of Menteith) CENTRAL, 8, 1D
Inchmahome Priory [HS] Ruins of Augustinian priory founded c.1238 on beautiful island with fragments of 13th-C church retaining tomb of Sir John Drummond (d.1390); 13th-C monuments in chapter house partly rebuilt 1600s as mausoleum include double effigy of Countess Mary of Menteith and Walter Stewart

INCHNAMEO ABBEY, CO. TIPPERARY, 12, 4B
See Monaincha

INCHTALLA CASTLE (W of Inchmahome Priory), CENTRAL, 8, 2D
Inchtalla Castle Ruined 15th-C castle on island in Lake of Menteith

INGLESHAM, WILTS, 2, 4B
Church of St John the Baptist [CCT] Mainly 13th-C church has south doorway of c.1200, double bellcote, and good blind arcading to north side of chancel; fine late Saxon sculpture of Virgin and Child, and 15th-C parclose screens

INGOLDMELLS, LINCS, 4, 2B
Church of St Peter and St Paul Spacious church has late 12th-C arcades with carved capitals and 14th- and 15th-C west tower; late medieval font

INISHCALTRA (or Iniscealtra) (accessible only by boat), CO. CLARE, 12, 3B
Churches and Round Tower [Dúchas] Remains of buildings on peaceful island in Lough Derg (site of monastery founded 7th C) include Round Tower, fragment of carved "Cross of Cathasach", tiny anchorite's cell, ruined oratory (St Michael's Church), and other 12th- and 13th-C churches

INISHEER, CO. GALWAY, 12, 2B
See Aran Islands

INISHGLORA (2.5 km. / 1½ m. offshore, accessible by boat) CO. MAYO, 11, 1C
Early Monastery [Dúchas] Remains of monastery founded 6th C on island include three churches (St Brendan's Oratory, Saints' Church, and Nun's Church), beehive huts, traces of monastic cashel, and early cross-slabs and pillars

INISHKEA NORTH (accessible by boat), CO. MAYO, 11, 1C
Early Monastery [Dúchas] Early monastic island site with remains including tiny church of St Colmcille, ancient houses, and early cross-slabs, pillars and fragments found on large mound (Bailey Mor)

INISHKEEL, CO. DONEGAL, 11, 2B
See Portnoo

INISHKEEN, CO. MONAGHAN, 11, 4C
Round Tower [Dúchas] Stump of Round Tower marks site of monastery founded 6th C

INISHMAAN, CO. GALWAY, 12, 2B
See Aran Islands

INISHMACSAINT (island near west shore of Lower Lough Erne, 9 km. / 5½ m. NW of Devenish), CO. FERMANAGH, 11, 3B
Monastic Site [EHS] Ruined church with west end of possibly 10th or 11th C and east end added c.1200 survives on site of 6th-C monastery; plain tall cross to south-west

INISHMAINE (7.5 km. / 4½ m. SW of Ballinrobe by Lough Mask), CO. MAYO, 11, 1D
Augustinian Abbey [Dúchas] Ruined early 13th-C church on peninsula (originally island site of 7th-C monastery) has flat-headed north doorway and incomplete chancel arch with fine capitals; small gatehouse built probably 15th C survives to north-east

INISHMORE, CO. GALWAY, 12, 2B
See Aran Islands

INISHMURRAY (accessible by boat from Rosses Point, 8 km. / 5 m. NW of Sligo), CO. SLIGO, 11, 2B
Monastic Site [Dúchas] Interesting and extensive remains of early Christian monastery (founded 6th C on island in Atlantic) with churches and beehive huts in roughly circular walled enclosure; "altars" with cross-decorated stones, pillar stones, and cross slabs used as pilgrimage stations survive within and without monastic walls

INSTIOGE, CO. KILKENNY, 12, 4C
Priory Roofless ruin of medieval church of Augustinian priory and tower with crow-stepped battlements, now attached to adjacent Church of Ireland church of 1824

INISHTOOSKERT (off Dingle Peninsula, accessible by boat) CO. KERRY, 12, 1C
Oratory, Crosses and Huts [Dúchas] Ruins of small church dedicated to St Brendan the Navigator, three crosses, and several beehive huts (one very well preserved)

INISHVICKILLANE (off Dingle Peninsula, accessible by boat) CO. KERRY, 12, 1C
Oratory, Cell and Cross [Dúchas] Remains of small stone church (St Brendan's Oratory), beehive cell and early cross on site of early anchoritic settlement

INNERPEFFRAY (6.5 km. / 4 m. SE of Crieff), TAYSIDE, 8, 2D
Innerpeffray Chapel [HS] Remains of low, rectangular collegiate church founded c.1508; altar, traces of furnishings, and Laird's Loft; adjoining library founded 1691

INNIS CHONNEL (on island W of shore of Loch Awe) STRATHCLYDE, 8, 1D
Innis Chonnel Castle Remains of rectangular 13th-C castle of enclosure on island site

INNISFALLEN (accessible by boat), CO. KERRY, 12, 2D
Church and Abbey [Dúchas] Early monastic site on picturesque island in Lough Leane has 12th-C oratory on cliff by shore with good west doorway, and nearby remains of abbey including church with 12th-C nave and 13th-C chancel

INVERKEITHING, FIFE, 8, 3E
Church of St Peter [SCS] Church built 1826–7 retains imposing 14th-C tower with 19th-C spire and dormered clocks; splendid font of c.1398
Greyfriar's Convent * (Inverkeithing Museum) Former guesthouse and late 14th-C vaulted cellars of Franciscan house founded c.1350 with much post-medieval alteration and reconstruction
Mercat Cross Townhall Street. Late 14th-C cross with sundial and finial added 1688

INVERLOCHY CASTLE (Fort William), HIGHLANDS, 8, 1C
Inverlochy Castle [HS] Ruins of 13th-C quadrangular castle with corner towers and later alterations

INVERMARK (22 km. / 14 m. NW of Edzell), TAYSIDE, 8, 3C
Invermark Castle Ruins of plain 14th-C keep with parapet added late 1500s

INVERNESS, HIGHLAND, 8, 2A
Graveyard, Friars Street Scanty remains of church of Dominican convent founded early 1200s survive in graveyard; part of early 15th-C effigy built into south wall
Knocknagael Boar Stone [HS] Highland Regional Council Offices, Glenurquhart Road. Rough Pictish block of 7th or 8th C incised with mirror-case and wild boar

INVERURIE, GRAMPIAN, 8, 4B
Brandsbutt Symbol Stone [HS] (1.5 km. / 1 m. NW) Early Pictish stone with carved symbols and ogham inscription

IONA, STRATHCLYDE (Inner Hebrides), 12, 2A
High Crosses [Maclean's Cross – HS] Site of most important early monastery in Scotland founded 563 or 565 by St Columba houses fine 10th-C St Martin's Cross near west façade of cathedral and 15th-C Maclean's Cross
Nunnery [Iona Cathedral Trust] Remains of Augustinain nunnery founded soon after 1203 include impressive original church with virtually complete north arcade and west gable; fragments of cloister court with chapter house and fine refectory; good collection of tombs and monuments
Church of St Ronan [ICT] Church built 13th to 14th C retains fine collection of monuments; glass roof added 1923
St Oran's Chapel [ICT] Small, restored chapel built possibly 1080 contains tombs of first two Lords of the Isles (d.1386 and 1420) and canopy of tomb of Lachlan Mackinnon (d.1489)
Iona Cathedral or Abbey [ICT] [SCS] Mainly early 16th-C cruciform cathedral (still in use), formerly church of Benedictine abbey founded before 1203, with extensive additions and restorations completed 1910; 9th-C St Columba's Shrine in north-west angle of nave and section of possibly 13th-C roadway to front (Street of the Dead); well-restored monastic buildings include chapter house and reredorter; infirmary now serves as museum housing fine collection of stones and fragments

IPSWICH, SUFFOLK, 3, 4A
Church of St Margaret Imposing medieval church with 14th-C arcades, low chancel, lavish clerestory, west tower, and fine double hammerbeam roof
Church of St Mary at the Elms, Elm Street Church of Norman origin has original south doorway, 15th-C nave, early 16th-C brick west tower and chancel added 1883
Church of St Mary at the Quay [CCT], Foundation Street. Medieval church with good hammerbeam roof, west tower, and 15th-C exterior
Church of St Nicholas, Friars Road Medieval church with early 14th-C aisles, 15th-C chancel chapels, and west tower rebuilt 1886; early 12th-C panels and two good brasses
Church of St Peter Medieval church reworked 1800s has 14th-C aisles and arcades, and 15th-C west tower and east end; fine Norman font of Tournai marble

Gateway, Northgate Street. 15th-C brick gateway to former archdeacon's mansion

IRNHAM, LINCS, 4, 1D
Church of St Andrew Norman church rebuilt 13th to 15th C has late 13th-C chancel and north arcade, and late medieval clerestory; late Norman west tower with 13th- and 14th-C upper parts; ornate 14th-C monument, probably former Easter Sepulchre
Irnham Hall Manor house built between 1510 and 1531, altered late 16th C, 1765 and 19th C, retains 14th-C doorways and open hall

IRON ACTON, GLOS, 2, 2B
Church of St James 15th-C church has three-stage west tower and spacious nave with wagon roof; pillar stoup in north porch and good medieval monuments; fine early 15th-C cross in churchyard

IRTHLINGBOROUGH NORTHANTS, 4, 1E
Church of St Peter Spacious 13th-C former collegiate church enlarged c.1300–50 has transepts, mid 13th-C arcades, and good monuments; detached tower to west begun soon after 1354 with octagonal stages
College Remains of college founded 1388 adjoining church
Bridge 14th-C bridge crossing River Nene with cutwaters and pointed arches

IRTON, CUMBRIA, 7, 1C
Cross Carved 9th-C cross shaft in churchyard of St Paul
Irton Hall Largely 19th-C house retains 14th-C pele tower

ISLE ABBOTS, SOMERSET, 2, 1D
Church of St Mary Church built c.1300 with elaborate additions of c.1500 retains original chancel with piscina and sedilia, and stoup in south porch; early 16th-C west tower has original figures in niches

ISLE OF WHITHORN, DUMFRIES AND GALLOWAY, 10, 5E
St Ninian's Chapel [HS] Roofless remains of church built c.1300 and restored 1898, probably used by pilgrims on way to Whithorn

ISLEHAM, CAMBS, 4, 3E
Church of St Andrew Early 14th-C cruciform church with clerestory and roof of c.1495 and 19th-C west tower; fine 14th-C porch, 15th-C brasses and chancel stalls of c.1450; late medieval lychgate

Isleham Priory Church [EH] Small, unaltered chapel of 11th-C Benedictine priory with nave, chancel and apse

IVINGHOE, BUCKS, 3, 1B
Church of St Mary Large cruciform church with 13th-C west doorway and arcades, 14th-C crossing tower and north doorway, and 15th-C roofs and west porch

IWADE, KENT, 3, 3C
Church of All Saints Early 14th-C church with 13th-C tower retains original south door with iron ring handle decorated with two winged dragons

JARLSHOF (1 km. / ½ m. S of Sumburgh), SHETLAND, 9, 1B
Prehistoric and Norse Settlement [HS] Fragmentary remains of structures on promontory site occupied since c.2000 BC include Viking farm buildings of 9th and 10th C, medieval farmstead built early 1300s, and 16th- to 17th-C Old House of Sumburgh

JARROW, TYNE AND WEAR, 7, 3B
Church of St Paul Saxon chancel and tower of church (founded 681) belonging to monastery where Bede lived and died; nave rebuilt 19th C; fragments of 7th- and 8th-C sculpture displayed inside building
St Paul's Monastery and Bede's World Museum [EH] Remains of 7th-C church (partly surviving as chancel of parish church) and later monastic buildings, former home of Venerable Bede, on important Anglo-Saxon site; museum houses excavated finds

JEDBURGH, BORDERS, 7, 2A
Jedburgh Abbey [HS] Impressive ruins of mainly 12th- to 15th-C sandstone buildings of Augustinian priory founded c.1138 (abbey after 1147) include well-preserved Norman church with crossing tower, nine-bay nave and splendid west front (west end used as parish church until 1875); excavated remains of monastic buildings to south by Jed Water and finds displayed in visitor centre
Canongate Bridge 15th-C bridge, unusual as still in use

JERPOINT, CO. KILKENNY, 12, 4C
Jerpoint Abbey [Dúchas] Remains of important Cistercian abbey founded 1158, one of finest ruins in Ireland, include 12th-C church with 15th-C rebuilding and tall central tower,

15th-C cloister (recently restored) with splendid figural sculpture, and domestic buildings; fine collection of monuments includes effigy of bishop (possibly Felix O Dulany d.1202), late 13th-C incised slab known as "The Brethren", and altar tomb of Katerine Poher and Robert Walsh (1501) with wonderfully carved weepers by Rory O'Tunney

Newtown Jerpoint Church 0.5 km. / ¼ m. NW) 12th- to 13th-C church with later medieval additions retains good effigy of ecclesiastic in graveyard

JERVAULX ABBEY, N. YORKS, 7,3D
Jervaulx Abbey Ruins of church and monastic buildings of Cistercian abbey moved to Jervaulx 1156

JESMOND, TYNE AND WEAR, 7,3B
See Newcastle upon Tyne

JEVINGTON, E. SUSSEX, 3,2E
Church of St Andrew Saxon church retains original west tower, south doorway of c.1200, and 13th-C north aisle; late Saxon carved Christ
Filching Manor Timber-framed manor house built 15th C

JOHNSTOWN, CO. KILKENNY, 12,4B
See Fertagh

JULIANSTOWN, CO. MEATH, 11,4D
Ballygarth Castle (1.5 km. / 1 m. E) Country seat built 18th and 19th C incorporates large medieval tower house at west end of entrance front
Ballygarth Old Church Remains of medieval manorial chapel in grounds of castle
Dardistown Castle (2 km. / 1 ¼ m. SW); Large 15th-C tower house extended 1500s with corner towers, 18th-C range, and 19th-C remodelling

JURBY, ISLE OF MAN, 6,1A
Crosses Celtic and Norse crosses with fine carved decoration and mythological figures survive in church porch

KAMES (Isle of Bute), STRATHCLYDE, 10,4C
Kames Castle (now part of holiday centre) Massive keep built 14th C at head of Kames Bay with lower buildings added 18th C

KEDINGTON, SUFFOLK, 3,3A
Church of St Peter and St Paul [OCT] Medieval church with later alterations retains 13th-C chancel, nave, and 14th-C

west tower; part of Saxon cross, 15th-C font, and wooden poor box

KEDLESTON, DERBYS, 5,4B
Church of All Saints Cruciform church built mainly late 1200s has Norman south doorway, late medieval top to crossing tower, east end reworked late 17th C, and north aisle added 1907–13; fine medieval monuments include tomb chest for Sir John Curzon (d.c.1450)

KEGWORTH, LEICS, 5,4C
Church of St Andrew Mainly 13th-C church rebuilt 14th C has west tower, chancel with sacristy and early 14th-C arcade piers; fragments of medieval glass

KEIL CHURCH, HIGHLAND, 10,3A
See Lochaline

KEILLS (10 km. / 6 m. SW of Tayvallich), STRATHCLYDE, 10,3B
Keills Chapel [HS] Modest 12th-C chapel re-roofed 1978 to house collection of grave slabs and fine Keills Cross

KELLAWAYS, WILTS, 2,3B
Maud Heath's Causeway Stone causeway erected after 1474 carried on sixty-four segmental arches

KELLIE (4 km. / 2 ½ m. W of Arbroath), TAYSIDE, 8,3C
Kelly Castle Fortified house (still occupied) built mainly early 1600s incorporates fine, five-storeyed 15th-C keep at corner of courtyard

KELLIE CASTLE (1 km. / ½ m. E of Arncroach), FIFE, 8,3D
Kellie Castle [NTS] (gardens also open) Fine mansion house with extensive additions of late 16th C and c.1603–6 retains 14th- or 15th-C north-west tower

KELLOE, CO. DURHAM, 7,3C
Church of St Helen Norman church with original west tower and 13th-C chancel refitted 1901; remarkable late 12th-C cross with carved figurework
Town Kelloe Remains of deserted medieval village

KELLS, CO. KILKENNY, 12,4C
Kells Priory [Dúchas] Impressive ruins of mainly 14th- and 15th-C fortified buildings of vast Augustinian priory founded c.1193; cruciform church has large north-east Lady Chapel, and central and north-west towers (latter possibly prior's residence or sacristy); remains of extensive domestic buildings and towered enclosure walls

KELLS, CO. MEATH, 11,4D
Monastic Site [Dúchas] Site of early monastery, original home of celebrated Book of Kells; surviving structures include remarkable St Colmcille's House (built probably early 800s as residential oratory), tall Round Tower (11th-C or earlier), and four impressive High Crosses with ornately carved religious scenes (8th- and 9th-C) Dulane Church (2.5 km. / 1 ½ m. N); Remains of small, possibly 8th-C church

KELMSCOTT, OXON, 2,4B
Church of St George Small cruciform church of Norman origin retains nave and chancel of c.1190, transepts of c.1260, and 13th-C bellcote; font of early 1200s

KELSALE, SUFFOLK, 4,5E
Church of St Mary and St Peter Church of Norman origin with medieval and later additions includes 12th-C north doorway, south-west tower built 1300s, and good 15th-C south porch with flushwork panelling
Guildhall Timber-framed guildhall of c.1500 with jettied upper level

KELSO, BORDERS, 7,2A
Kelso Abbey [HS] Surviving western parts of remarkable 12th- to 13th-C church of large and important Tironensian abbey moved 1128 from Selkirk (mainly destroyed 1545); two bays of nave with arcading to triforium and clerestory, large tower, and north-west transept with excellent doorway surmounted by arcading and gabled hood

KEMEYS COMMANDER, GWENT, 6,5E
Church of All Saints Little 15th-C church with timber west porch, screen and wagon roof

KEMPLEY, GLOS, 2,2A
Church of St Mary [EH / CCT] Norman church reworked 17th C has tunnel-vaulted chancel with excellent frescoes of c.1130–40 and medieval tempera paintings in nave; defensive west tower built c.1276 and carved tympanumn over south doorway

KENDAL, CUMBRIA, 7,2D
Church of the Holy Trinity Medieval church extensively restored 1850–2 contains fragment of 9th-C cross shaft, fine late 13th-C coffin lid (in Bellingham Chapel), late 15th-C black marble font, and plain early 16th-C tomb chest

Castle Fragmentary remains of medieval castle on Norman earthwork
Castle Dairy Wildman Street. 14th-C hall-house with later additions and alterations

KENILWORTH, WARWS, 5,4D
Church of St Nicholas Mainly 15th-C church restored 1864 retains fine Norman doorway and tower with 14th-C upper stage; architectural fragments and tiles from priory
Abbey Extensive remains of church and domestic buildings of Augustinian priory founded c.1122 (raised to abbey status after mid 15th C)
Kenilworth Castle [EH] Impressive remains of medieval castle (largest castle ruin in England) with extensive 16th-C additions include keep of c.1170–80, curtain wall and towers of c.1205–15, and great hall on undercroft of c.1390–3

KENTISBEARE, DEVON, 1,5C
Church of St Mary Medieval church with 14th-C west tower and chancel, and work of early 16th C and 1865–6; wagon roofs and early 16th-C screen
Priest Hall Late medieval priest's house converted to cottages 19th C and restored 1950s retains screens passage, parlour and original window at back of open hall

KENTON, DEVON, 1,5C
Church of All Saints Late 15th- and early 16th-C church restored 19th C with west tower and embattled south porch; 15th-C pulpit and fine screen

KENTSTOWN (11 km. / 7 m. ESE of Navan), CO. MEATH, 11,4D
Church Protestant church built 1797 contains excellent effigy of Sir Thomas de Tuite (d.1363), formerly in Danestown medieval church

KERRY / CERI, POWYS, 6,5C
Church of St Michael Medieval church restored 19th C has interior with 12th- and early 14th-C work, north chancel and aisle, good roofs, and imposing west tower with wooden bell stage; octagonal font of early 1500s

KERSEY, SUFFOLK, 3,4A
Church of St Mary Medieval church restored 19th C with north aisle completed 1335, 14th-C north arcade, large 15th-C south porch, and west tower completed 1481; good roof to nave and late medieval font

Priory Remains of church of Augustinian priory founded early 13th C with attached monks' kitchen and early 19th-C front

KETTERING, NORTHANTS, 4, 1E
Church of St Peter and St Paul Mainly 15th-C church has four-stage tower and good interior with clerestory, six-bay arcades and tall chancel arch

KETTON, RUTLAND, 4, 1D
Church of St Mary Church of Norman origin with medieval, 18th- and 19th-C additions retains west front of c.1190, arcades built c.1300 and fine tower with broach spire

KEYWORTH, NOTTS, 5, 5C
Church of St Mary Magdalene Medieval church has 14th-C chancel, north arcade and unusual square tower with recessed octagonal upper stage and spire

KIDLINGTON, OXON, 2, 4A
Church of St Mary Church of 13th-C origin enlarged 14th and 15th C has transepts, central tower with top of 1400s, and 14th-C arcades; 13th-C misericords and good late medieval screens; 13th-, 14th- and 15th-C stained glass

KIDWELLY, DYFED, 6, 3D
Kidwelly Castle [CADW] Impressive ruins of Norman fortress enlarged late 12th and rebuilt 13th to 14th C as concentric castle, with Great Gatehouse completed 1422 and large late 15th-C hall and kitchen
Church of St Mary Norman Benedictine priory church rebuilt 14th C with medieval and later alterations has fine tower with broach spire built above north-west porch
Pont Spwdwr (Spudder's Bridge) Stone bridge with pointed arches and cutwaters, believed to be 15th-C

KILBARRON, CO. DONEGAL, 11, 3B
Church of St Barron Ruined 15th- or 16th-C church
Kilbarron Castle Scanty remains of late medieval castle on impressive promontory site

KILBERRY CASTLE (27 km. / 17 m. SSW of Lochgilphead on W. coast of Knapdale), STRATHCLYDE, 10, 3C
Kilberry Sculptured Stones [HS] Group of late medieval stones collected during 19th C from Kilberry Estate

KILBIRNIE, STRATHCLYDE, 10, 4C
Auld Kirk of Kilbirnie [SCS] Dalry Road Church with 15th-C nave (1470) and tower

(1490), north (Glengarnock) aisle added 1597, and rich Crawfurd aisle of 1642 with laird's loft

KILBOLANE, CO. CORK, 12, 3C
Castle [Dúchas] Remains of square moated castle with corner turrets built 15th or 16th C

KILBRIDE, CO. MEATH, 11, 4D
See Kildalkey

KILBRIDE CASTLE, STRATHCLYDE, 10, 5C
See Law

KILBRONEY (1.5 km. / 1 m. NE of Rostrevor), CO. DOWN, 11, 5C
Bronach's Church and Crosses Ruins of medieval church; large High Cross to south-east has rich ornament to west face; smaller cross with Crucifixion survives nearby

KILCHURN (4 km. / 2½ m. W of Dalmally), STRATHCLYDE, 10, 4A
Kilchurn Castle [HS] Substantial ruins of castle in picturesque setting at north-east end of Loch Awe with square keep built mid 1400s, 16th-C work, and extensive additions of 1690s

KILCLIEF CASTLE, (4 km. / 2½ m. S of Strangford) CO. DOWN, 11, 5C
Kilclief Castle [EHS] Well-preserved tower house built supposedly 1413–41 by sea has projecting corner turrets, battlements, and barrel vault to lower chamber; 13th-C coffin lid used as fireplace lintel on second floor

KILCLISPEEN, CO. TIPPERARY, 12, 4C
See Ahenny

KILCONNELL, CO. GALWAY, 12, 3A
Friary [Dúchas] Remains of Franciscan friary founded 1353 on site of earlier monastery include church with good west doorway, south transept of c.1450–75 and later central tower and sacristy; two fine 15th- or 16th-C canopied tombs survive in north wall of nave (one with carved figures of saints)

KILCOOLE, CO. WICKLOW, 11, 5E
Church of St Mary [Dúchas] Ruins of small plain church built probably 12th C with later two-storeyed residential quarters to west

KILCOOLY, CO. TIPPERARY, 12, 4C
Kilcooly Abbey [Dúchas] Remains of small Cistercian abbey founded c.1182 with interesting church of c.1200 (much reconstructed c.1445–70); pair of fine, unusual

15th-C stalls at east end of nave (possibly for abbot and prior) and excellent sculpted screen between south transept and sacristy; good monuments include those to Abbot Philip (d.1463) and Piers Fitz Oge Butler (d.1526, superbly carved by Rory O'Tunney); rare surviving circular dovecot to north-east

KILCREA, CO. CORK, 12, 3D
Friary [Dúchas] Remains of Franciscan friary founded 1465 include church with tower and south transept, well-lit sacristy and scriptoria to north of chancel, and well-preserved conventual buildings
Kilcrea Castle Ruined 15th-C castle, formerly moated, with tower and small court

KILCRONEY (3 km. / 2 m. ESE of Enniskerry), CO. WICKLOW, 12, 5B
Church of St Croine [Dúchas] Ruins of medieval church on high plinth (possibly earlier) with good flat-headed doorway

KILCULLEN, CO. KILDARE, 12, 5B
New Abbey (1.5 km. / 1 m. E) Graveyard occupying site of Franciscan friary founded 1486 retains fine fragments of tomb of Sir Roland FitzEustace, Baron of Portlester (d.1496) and wife; carved panels built into wall of 18th-C 'Mass House'

KILCURRY, CO. LOUTH, 11, 4C
Faughart Church (6.5 km. / 4 m. NE) Ruined church built probably 12th C on dramatic elevated site
Roche Castle [Dúchas] (3.5 km. / 2¼ m. NW) Impressive remains of castle begun 1230s on rocky outcrop (slighted 1649) with battlemented curtain walls and gatehouse with round bastions

KILDALKEY, CO. MEATH, 11, 4D
Kildalkey Church Scanty remains of small medieval church
Kilbride Old Mansion (5 km. / 3 m. NE) Ruins of three-storeyed medieval tower house reworked 1700s; adjoining 19th-C mansion
Moyrath Castle (1 km. / ½ m. S) Medieval tower house with later alterations and additions

KILDALTON CROSS (on island of Islay, 3 km. / 2 m. ENE of Port Ellen) STRATHCLYDE (Inner Hebrides), 10, 3C
Kildalton Cross [HS] Splendid, well-preserved late 8th-C High Cross, possibly finest in Scotland and probably work of sculptor from Iona, survives in

churchyard of ruined 12th- or 13th-C chapel; 15th-C Thief's Cross and carved grave slabs nearby

KILDARE, CO. KILDARE, 11, 4E
St Brigid's Cathedral and Round Tower [Dúchas] Handsome cathedral begun c.1223 on site of great monastery (repaired 1484, rebuilt 1875–96) retains original south transept with good floor tiles and tombs; early font, fine 13th-C effigy (possibly Bishop John of Taunton d.1258) and excellent Wellesly tomb of c.1539; Round Tower to south-west with 12th-C doorway and 18th-C top; remains of Fire House to east
Castle 15th-C tower of castle mostly destroyed 16th C

KILDAVNET CASTLE (3.5 km. / 2¼ m. S of Achill Island), CO. MAYO, 11, 1C
Kildavnet Castle [Dúchas] Well-preserved tower of small castle built probably early 1500s

KILDEMOCK, CO. LOUTH, 11, 4D
See Ardee

KILDRUMMY, GRAMPIAN, 8, 3B
Church of St Bride Ruins of medieval church by later buildings with 14th-C tomb of Forbes of Brux
Kildrummy Castle [HS] (1.5 km. / 1 m. SW) Impressive and extensive ruins of early 13th-C castle, unusual in retaining complete layout of domestic buildings; massive curtain wall, east gable of mid 13th-C chapel, keep, and twin-towered gatehouse dating from alterations of 1296–1303

KILFANE, CO. KILKENNY, 12, 4C
Church [Dúchas] 14th-C church contains large, impressive and important effigy of Cantwell knight (c.1320)

KILFENORA, CO. CLARE, 12, 2B
Cathedral and Crosses [Dúchas] Cathedral church built late 12th C on site of early monastery, the west part of which is still used; ruined chancel houses fine sculpture including 13th- and 14th-C effigies of bishops, incised slab, carved figure capitals to window, and triple sedilia; parts of good High Crosses survive nearby

KILINCOOLE CASTLE (0.5 km. / ¼ m. NW of Readypenny Crossroads) CO. LOUTH, 11, 4C
Kilincoole Castle (0.5 km. / ¼ m. NW) Unusual four-storeyed tower house built possibly mid 13th-C with curved walls,

two round stair towers, and well-preserved barrel-vault to ground floor

KILKEERAN, CO. KILKENNY, 12, 4C
High Crosses [Dúchas] Three High Crosses (possibly 9th-C) on site of early monastery, the west with important carved ornament

KILKENNY, CO. KILKENNY, 12, 4C
Kilkenny Castle [Dúchas] Impressive castle begun *c.*1192 and greatly altered 17th to 20th C retains massive original corner bastions and north wall
Cathedral of St Canice [Dúchas], Irishtown. Large cruciform cathedral built 1250s to *c.*1280 on site of early monastery and much restored 1863–4 (with new roof) retains chancel with fine lancet windows, good west doorway, late 13th-C south porch, and 14th-C central tower over crossing with elaborate 15th-C star vaulting; 13th-C font and St Kiernan's Chair, effigy of Bishop de Ledrede (*c.*1361) and splendid collection of 16th and 17th-C monuments; tall Round Tower survives to south
Friary of St Francis [Dúchas], Bull Ring Remains of Franciscan friary founded *c.*1232 include ruined choir extended 1321 with unusual east window, and tall central tower of *c.*1350 (good carved corbels under vaulting)
Black Friar's Church (or Black Abbey Church) [Dúchas], Abbey Street Surviving 13th-C aisled nave and 14th-C south transept of Dominican friary founded 1226 (altered and restored for worship 18th and 19th C); central tower added 15th or early 16th C; late medieval alabaster statue of Trinity in adjoining convent
St John's Priory [Dúchas], Lower John Street. Roofless chancel of Augustinian priory founded *c.*1211 has fine east window of *c.*1250 and contains double Purcell tomb of *c.*1500 with excellently carved surrounds; Lady Chapel (*c.*1290) rebuilt 1817 and still used as church (St John's); fragments of nave and domestic buildings
Town Walls Fragments of medieval town walls include Blackfriars or Trinity Gate (near Black Abbey)

KILKHAMPTON, CORNWALL, 1, 3B
Church of St James Church of Norman origin rebuilt 16th C retains original south doorway, wagon roofs, and south porch of 1567

KILLADEAS,
CO. FERMANAGH, 11, 3B
Parish Church Church built 1864 retains 9th- or 10th-C sculpted stone and two carved stone slabs in churchyard

KILLAGHA, CO. KERRY, 12, 2C
Abbey [Dúchas] Surviving 13th-C church of Augustinian abbey built after 1216 with 15th-C work including fine east window

KILLAGHTEE, CO. DONEGAL, 11, 3B
See Dunkineely

KILLALA, CO. MAYO, 11, 2C
Round Tower [Dúchas] Well-preserved Round Tower repaired *c.*1840

KILLALIATHAN,
CO. LIMERICK, 12, 2C
Church [Dúchas] 15th-C church with unusual east window and good tomb niche in north wall

KILLALOE, CO. CLARE, 12, 3B
Cathedral of St Flannan and Churches [Dúchas] Restored medieval cathedral on early monastic site near Lough Derg incorporates rich doorway (*c.*1200) of earlier church; rare surviving stone with Viking Runic inscription, carved cross (removed 1821 from Kilfenora), and "unfinished" font; churchyard contains 12th-C nave of St Flannan's Oratory
St Molua's Church (early oratory removed 1929 from Friar's Island) survives in grounds of Catholic church

KILLAMERY, CO. KILKENNY, 12, 4C
High Cross [Dúchas] Fine 9th-C High Cross with richly carved ornament

KILLARNEY, CO. KERRY, 12, 2D
Muckross Friary [Dúchas] Well-preserved remains of Franciscan friary founded 1448 (built mainly 1448 to 1500), beautifully set near lakes of Killarney in National Park, include church with later tower and south transept, and remarkable cloister surrounding old yew tree; good tombs in chancel
Ross Castle [Dúchas], Ross Island Picturesque ruins of massive 15th- or 16th-C tower house and bawn beside Lough Leane (well restored 1990s)

KILLARY CROSS, CO. MEATH, 11, 4D
See Lobinstown

KILLEAN, STRATHCLYDE, 10, 3C
Killean Old Parish Church Ruins of church with 12th-C nave, 13th-C chancel (*c.*1220), and north aisle added 15th;

several finely carved slabs in church and graveyard

KILLEEN, CO. MEATH, 11, 4D
Killeen Castle Remains of 15th-C castle reworked as country house 19th C and burnt out 1981
Church of St Mary [Dúchas] Well-preserved remains of church built *c.*1425 by Plunkett family (imitated at Dunsany and Rathmore) with square turrets at west end, long nave and chancel, and residential north-east tower; elaborate tracery, triple sedilia, and good font; fine monuments include Plunkett box-tomb and effigies of knight and bishop

KILLEEN COWPARK (5 km. / 3 m. SSW of Pallaskenry or Shanpallas)
CO. LIMERICK, 12, 3C
Church [Dúchas] Well-preserved remains of small church built 15th C

KILLESHIN, CO. LAOIS, 12, 5B
Church [Dúchas] Fragments of early 12th-C church on site of monastery founded late 5th C include splendid, well-preserved west doorway with partly modern hood above; 15th-C chancel

KILLEVY CHURCHES,
BALLINTEMPLE,
CO. ARMAGH, 11, 4C
Killevy Churches [EHS] Remains of two churches linked by post-medieval walling on site of early Irish convent; west church (mainly 12th-C) retains monumental west doorway of 10th- or 11th-C; east church has 15th-C east window

KILLINABOY, CO. CLARE, 12, 2B
Round Tower and Church [Dúchas] Medieval church built 11th to 12th C and later on early monastic site has well-preserved sheila-na-gig above south doorway and double armed cross on west gable (*c.*1200); stump of Round Tower survives nearby

KILLINEY, CO. DUBLIN, 11, 5E
Church [Dúchas] Ruins of early nave and chancel of church (possibly 11th- or 12th-C) with flat-headed west doorway and later north aisle

KILLODIERNAN (Johnstown),
CO. TIPPERARY, 12, 3B
Church [Dúchas] Late medieval church with 15th-C door incorporates good 12th-C east window and west doorway with scroll work and spirals

KILL OF THE GRANGE,
CO. DUBLIN, 11, 4E
Church [Dúchas] Remains of small early Christian church with antae, flat-headed doorway, and 16th-C chancel; fragments of crosses and cross-inscribed slab

KILLONE, CO. CLARE, 12, 2B
Augustinian Convent [Dúchas] Rare surviving Irish convent probably founded *c.*1190 on picturesque site by lake has church (curtailed 1400s) with fine east windows and crypt of *c.*1225, and 15th-C domestic buildings

KILLOUGHTERNANE
CO. CARLOW, 12, 5C
Church [Dúchas] Modest church of early Christian period with round east window and antae; baptismal font

KILLUCAN,
CO. WESTMEATH, 11, 4D
Church of St Etchen Remains of tower and chancel of medieval church survive to east of present mainly 19th-C building containing good mid 13th-C font and 15th-C work

KILLULTA, CO. LIMERICK, 12, 3C
Church [Dúchas] Remains of small, primitive church (possibly 9th- or 10th-C), said to be oldest in Ireland

KILLURSA (3 km. / 2 m. W of Headford), CO. GALWAY, 12, 2A
Church [Dúchas] Church built mainly 15th C incorporates possibly 10th-C part to south-west with flat-headed west doorway

KILLYDONNELL FRIARY (3.5 km. / 2 ¼ m. SW of Ramelton, in grounds of Fort Stewart), CO. DONEGAL, 11, 3A
Killydonnell Friary Fragmentary ruins of church and conventual buildings of Franciscan tertiary house founded 1471, partly used as family burial ground

KILLYLEAGH (on shore of Strangford Lough), CO. DOWN, 11, 5C
Killyleagh Castle Castle built 13th and 14th C on Anglo-Norman motte and bailey, restored and enlarged 1666 and remodelled 1850–62, retains original south-west tower and adjacent parts
Church Fine 12th-C fragments of lost early Christian church

KILMACDUAGH,
CO. GALWAY, 12, 3B
Churches and Round Tower [Dúchas] Site of monastery founded early 7th C

houses well-preserved, leaning Round Tower next to cathedral with nave of mainly *c*.1200 and 15th-C transepts and additions; small nearby churches of St John the Baptist and St Mary's (early 13th-C); two-storeyed Glebe House (or Seanchloch) to north, possibly former abbot's house; O Heyne's Church or Monastery built late 12th to early 13th C to north-west retains finely carved chancel arch and details

KILMALKEDAR (Dingle Peninsula), CO. KERRY, 12, 1C
Church [Dúchas] Remains of 12th-C church on site of important early monastery with parts of original stone roof and finials, antae, tympanum (carved on inside), fine chancel arch, and blind arcading to interior walls; churchyard contains stone cross and excellent early sundial; medieval St Brendan's House nearby (probably priest's residence
St Brendan's Oratory [Dúchas] Remains of stone oratory of Gallarus type

KILMALLOCK, CO. LIMERICK, 12, 3C
Collegiate Church of St Peter and St Paul [Dúchas] Church built 13th to 15th C incorporating earlier Round Tower to south-west has chancel of *c*.1300 used as Protestant parish church until 20th C and ruined south transept and nave; fine 15th-C south door
Friary [Dúchas] Well-preserved remains of Dominican friary founded *c*.1291 on bank of River Loobagh, restored and enlarged 14th and 15th C; fine church has five-light window to choir, good 15th-C window to south transept and slender tower
King's Castle Altered four-storeyed castle, probably built 1400s
Blossom Gate Emmet Street. Sole survivor of four medieval town gate defences

KILMARTIN GLEN, STRATHCLYDE, 10, 3B
Kilmartin Sculptured Stones [HS] Church opened 1835 [SCS] has splendid collection of tomb slabs and two outstanding crosses housed both inside building and in mausoleum of Bishop Neil Campbell

KILMODAN SCULPTURED STONES, STRATHCLYDE, 10, 4B
See Clachan of Glendaruel

KILMORE, CO. CAVAN, 11, 3C
Cathedral of St Feidhlimidh [Dúchas] Modern building incorporates fine 12th-C doorway removed from monastery remains on Trinity Island in Lough Oughter

KILMORY KNAP CHAPEL (South Knapdale, on shore between Lochs Sween and Caolisport), STRATHCLYDE, 10, 3C
Kilmory Knap Chapel [HS] Small ruined church dating from 13th C with later glass roof houses notable collection of Celtic and medieval sculptured stones and grave slabs; excellent Macmillan's Cross, richly carved during 15th C

KILMUN (nr Dunoon), STRATHCLYDE, 10, 4B
Kilmun Parish Church [SCS] Ruined west tower of collegiate church founded 1441 survives by church built 1841 near Holy Loch; tomb with effigies of founder Sir Duncan Campbell and wife

KILNARUANE, CO. CORK, 12, 2D
Pillar Stone [Dúchas] Early Christian pillar stone with good carved panels

KILNASAGGART PILLAR STONE, EDENAPPA (2 km. / 1¼ m. S of Jonesborough) CO. ARMAGH, 11, 4C
Kilnasaggart Pillar Stone [EHS] Fine tall pillar stone of *c*.700 with inscriptions and crosses marks site of cemetery on important early road (Slighe Miodhluachra)

KILPECK, HEREFS, 2, 2A
Church of St Mary and St David Well-preserved Norman church begun *c*.1135 with nave, chancel and rib-vaulted apse; splendid carved south doorway of *c*.1140–5 and chancel arch of *c*.1145; stoup and large font; bell-cote rebuilt 1864
Castle Ruins of motte and bailey castle with 12th-C shell keep

KILRAVOCK CASTLE (1.5 km. / 1 m. E of Croy), HIGHLAND, 8, 2A
Kilravock Castle Castle retains big late 15th-C tower-keep with 20th-C additions, and adjoining house built 1665–7; smaller mid 16th-C tower to south-west with upper floor converted to dovecot early 1800s

KILREE, CO. KILKENNY, 12, 4C
Church, Round Tower and High Cross [Dúchas] Round Tower, ruined church and possibly 9th-C cross with richly

carved work survive on site of early monastery

KILRENNY, FIFE, 8, 3D
Parish Church Church of 1807–8 retains big 15th-C north-west tower with 16th-C spire

KILTARTAN, CO. GALWAY, 12, 3B
Kiltartan or Ballinamantain Castle [Dúchas] Much ruined 13th-C castle with three-storeyed tower and walled enclosure

KILTEEL, CO. KILDARE, 12, 5B
Church and Castle Castle [Dúchas] Remains of medieval church retaining partly re-erected 12th-C chancel arch with fine figure sculpture; 15th-C gateway and flanking tower (Kilteel Castle) forms one of surviving fragments of commandery of Knights Hospitaller of St John of Jerusalem

KILWINNING, STRATHCLYDE, 10, 4C
Kilwinning Abbey [HS] Fragmentary remains of Tironensian abbey founded *c*.1150, mainly destroyed 1561, include south transept wall, part of twin-towered west front, and well-preserved late medieval entrance front of chapter house

KIMBOLTON, CAMBS, 4, 1E
Church of St Andrew Mainly 14th- and 15th-C church with respond of *c*.1200, 13th-C arcades, and fine 15th-C south porch; 12th-C font

KINAWLEY, CO. FERMANAGH, 11, 3C
Church of St Naile Surviving east gable of late medieval church with good mid 15th-C traceried window

KINCARDINE, GRAMPIAN, 8, 4B
Kincardine Church Surviving part of large 13th-C church with 18th-C east wall and additions

KINCARDINE-ON-FORTH, FIFE, 8, 2E
Tulliallan Castle Remains of large early 14th-C house reworked late 1500s

KINDELESTOWN, CO. WICKLOW, 12, 5B
Castle Ruins of halled castle probably built 13th C, with continuous barrel vault on ground floor and upper storey divided into rooms

KINGARTH (Isle of Bute), STRATHCLYDE, 10, 4C
St Blane's Church [HS] Small chapel built mid 12th C on site of early monastery retains rich chancel arch; enclosure wall and remains of other medieval buildings

KINGSBURY EPISCOPI, SOMERSET, 2, 2D
Church of St Martin Medieval church with 13th-C nave and sumptuous 15th- and early 16th-C additions; tall rich west tower, well-lit chancel and south porch; rood screen

KING'S LYNN, NORFOLK, 4, 3D
Church of St Margaret, Saturday Market Church of Norman origin reworked 13th C, 15th C, 1745–6 and 1875 retains twin west towers begun mid 1100s with chapel attached to north, and short crossing tower; 14th-C screens and two large brass plates
Church of St Nicholas [CCT], St Ann's Street. Chapel of ease founded 1146 with medieval additions retains 13th-C tower and fine vaulted south porch of *c*.1410; 15th-C stoup and two bench ends
Church of All Saints Church of Norman origin rebuilt 15th and 19th C retains fine nave roof
Greyfriars Surviving late 14th-C hexagonal tower built into 13th-C church of friary founded *c*.1230–5; 13th-C cross beneath vault
Red Mount Chapel Unusual octagonal pilgrims' chapel built *c*.1485 with red brick and stone dressings has cruciform stone upper level and vaulted chapel
St George's Guildhall [NT], 27 King Street (now arts centre) Big 15th-C guildhall (largest surviving in England) with 20th-C restoration
Guildhall, Saturday Market. Lavish guildhall built 1421 with flint chequer work and later 16th-C addition
Priory Lane Surviving range of Benedictine priory established *c*.1100 with internal work of 14th C and king-post roof
South Gate Sole surviving town gate built *c*.1520

KING'S NORTON, W. MIDLANDS, 5, 3D
See Birmingham

KING'S SUTTON, NORTHANTS, 5, 4E
Church of St Peter and St Paul Mainly 14th-C church with fine west tower and crocketed spire retains chancel and south arcade of 12th C origin; Norman font

Court House Courthouse of *c.*1500 altered 16th and 18th C has jettied upper storey and Great Chamber with fireplace

KINGSTHORPE, NORTHANTS, 5,5E
See Northampton

KINGSTON, CAMBS, 3,2A
Church of All Saints and St Andrew
Church repaired after 1488 has blank arcading in chancel, and 15th-C clerestory and arcades; many good medieval wall paintings

KINGSTON, SOMERSET, 2,1D
Church of St Mary 13th-C church with late medieval additions retains original arcade, 15th-C north and south chapels, and splendid ornate west tower; large set of carved benches, one dated 1522

KINGSTON-UPON-HULL
E. RIDING OF YORKS, 7,5E
See Hull

KINGSWINFORD,
W. MIDLANDS, 5,3D
Church of St Mary Church of uncertain date retains fine Norman carved tympanum with St Michael and Dragon

KINGTON, HEREFS, 5,1E
Church of St Mary Spacious medieval church with south tower of *c.*1200, good early 13th-C chancel, and nave rebuilt *c.*1300 with aisles; 19th-C outer north aisle and reworking; Norman font and 15th-C effigies on tomb chest
Hergest Court * (2 km. / 1¼ m. SW) Imposing medieval house with good 15th-C timberwork

KINKELL (3 km. / 2 m. S of Inverurie),
GRAMPIAN, 8,4B
Kinkell Church (St Michael's) [HS]
Ruined early 16th-C church with tombstone of Gilbert de Greenlaw (d.1411) and rich sacrament house dated 1524 (designed by parson, Alexander Galloway)

KINLET, SHROPS, 5,2D
Church of St John the Baptist Church of Norman origin with late 12th-C north aisle and early 13th-C south arcade, porch and west tower; chancel and transepts built *c.*1310-20; 15th-C timber-framed clerestory; good medieval monuments

KINLOCHALINE CASTLE,
HIGHLAND, 10,3A
See Lochaline

KINLOSS, GRAMPIAN, 8,2A
Kinloss Abbey Fragmentary remains of once important abbey founded *c.*1150 by

David I include south transept with adjacent sacristy or parlour and part of abbot's house

KINNAIRD (14 km. / 9 m. NE of Perth),
TAYSIDE, 8,3D
Kinnaird Castle Tall, imposing 15th-C keep restored 1855 with machicolations, pit prison, and first-floor hall; small 17th-C range nearby

KINNAIRD HEAD LIGHTHOUSE,
GRAMPIAN, 8,4A
See Fraserburgh

KINNAIRDY 3 km. / 2 m. SW of
Aberchirder), GRAMPIAN, 8,4A
Kinnairdy Castle 14th-C keep with later alterations and extensions (still occupied) retains hall with beautifully carved work to oak-panelled aumbry including heads of Sir Alexander Innes and wife Christine Dunbar (dated 1493)

KINNEIGH, CO. CORK, 12,2D
Round Tower [Dúchas] Unusual Round Tower with hexagonal lower stages marks site of early monastery

KINNEIL, LOTHIAN
Church Remains of 12th-C church formerly belonging to Holyrood Abbey
Kinneil House 16th-C house reworked *c.*1677 contains remarkable stone cross from Kinneil church in basement room

KINNERSLEY, HEREFS, 5,1E
Church of St James Church of Norman origin reworked *c.*1300 and 1868 with imposing early 14th-C north-west tower; pulpit with panels of *c.*1530

KINNITTY, CO. OFFALY, 11,3E
High Cross and Church [Dúchas] grounds of Castle Bernard (2 km. / 1¼ m. NE); Terrace of castle (original site of early monastery) houses shaft of 10th-C High Cross with fine figural carvings; south wall of stable yard behind castle incorporates part of 15th-C church

KINORD (5 km. / 3 m. W of Aboyne),
GRAMPIAN, 8,3B
Kinord Cross-Slab Fine cross slab with knotwork dates from 9th C

KINSALE, CO. CORK, 12,3D
Church of St Multose [Dúchas] Church built *c.*1200 with original north-west tower and extensive 17th- to 19th-C alterations;
Desmond Castle (French Prison) Cork Street [Dúchas] Small three-storeyed tower built *c.*1500 as custom house and used as prison 1630–1800

KINWARTON, WARWS, 5,3E
Church of St Mary Small medieval church with 16th- to 17th-C bell turret; sedilia and piece of early 14th-C stained glass in chancel
Dovecot [NT] Circular dovecot built 14th C retains potence and still houses doves

KIPPAX, W. YORKS, 7,3E
Church of St Mary Well-preserved Norman church has spacious interior, west tower with late medieval top, and north and south doorways of *c.*1300; part of good late 10th-C cross shaft

KIRBY BELLARS, LEICS, 5,5C
Church of St Peter Mainly 14th-C church with some late 17th-C work has wide south aisle, fine west tower and 15th-C clerestory; effigies of *c.*1360–70 in early 14th-C recess

KIRBY MUXLOE, LEICS, 5,5D
Church of St Bartholomew Medieval church extensively restored 19th C has nave and chancel of *c.*1300 and south-west tower
Kirby Muxloe Castle [EH] Surviving brick gatehouse and west tower of moated manor house built 1480–4

KIRKBURN, E. RIDING OF
YORKS, 7,5D
Church of St Mary Fine Norman church reworked 19th C retains nave with original corbel table, north and south doorways, and west tower with later medieval upper parts; Norman font with splendid carvings

KIRKBY LONSDALE,
CUMBRIA, 7,2D
Church of St Mary Church of Norman origin with north arcade of *c.*1115 and south arcade, west tower, west portal and priest's doorway all of *c.*1200; 14th to 16th-C additions
Devil's Bridge 15th-C bridge with three imposing round arches

KIRKCALDY, FIFE, 8,3D
Old Parish Church, Kirk Wynd [SCS] Church of 1806–8 retains ashlar-faced west tower built *c.*1500

KIRKCONNELL HOUSE (2.5 km. /
1½ m. NE of New Abbey)
DUMFRIES AND
GALLOWAY, 7,1B
Kirkconnell House House of 15th to 19th C retains tower built *c.*1450 (enlarged early to mid 1500s)

KIRKDALE, N. YORKS, 7,4D
Church of St Gregory Late Saxon church with original nave and Norman north aisle added *c.*1200; sundial with interesting inscription (*c.*1060) above south door

KIRKHAM, N. YORKS, 7,4D
Kirkham Priory [EH] Remains of church and domestic buildings of Augustinain priory founded *c.*1125 by River Derwent include fine late 13th-C lavatorium with blind arcading and splendid carved gatehouse built *c.*1290–5

KIRK HAMMERTON,
N. YORKS, 7,4D
Church of St John Church built 1891 incorporates complete Saxon church to south with narrow tower, south aisle, nave, chancel, and north aisle added *c.*1200

KIRKLAND (nr Garstang), LANCS, 7,2E
Church of St Helen Churchtown Medieval church with 13th-C north arcade, 14th-C chancel arch and 15th-C west tower

KIRKLISTON, LOTHIAN, 8,3E
Parish Church, The Square [SCS] Late 12th-C church with 19th-C additions on elevated site retains much of nave with rich original south door, reset north door, and shortened west tower

KIRKMADRINE (Rhinns of Galloway,
3 km. / 2 m. SW of Sandhead),
DUMFRIES AND
GALLOWAY, 10,4E
Kirkmadrine Early Christian Stones [HS] Porch of 19th-C former chapel contains three fine 5th- or early 6th-C stones, generally accepted as being Britain's earliest Christian memorials

KIRKMAIDEN, DUMFRIES AND
GALLOWAY, 10,4E
See Monreith

KIRK MICHAEL,
ISLE OF MAN, 6,1A
Crosses Church contains Island's largest collection of Norse crosses together with Celtic examples; Joalf's Cross has particularly fine figure carving and runic inscription
Bishopcourt (2.5 km. / 1½ m. N) Residence of Lord Bishop of Sodor and Man with extensive additions and alterations of 18th and 19th C retains imposing medieval tower built probably later 1300s

KIRKNEWTON,
NORTHUMBERLAND, 7,3A
Church of St Gregory the Great Mainly
19th-C church retains fine 13th- or 14th-C
tunnel-vaulted south transept and
chancel; good Norman sculpture
depicting Adoration of Magi

KIRKOSWALD, CUMBRIA, 7,2C
Church of St Oswald Plain church of
Norman origin altered 13th to 15th C with
late 12th-C south arcade and chancel
of c.1523
Kirkoswald Castle Remains of moated
medieval castle include angle and
north towers

KIRKSTALL (outer Leeds),
W. YORKS, 7,3E
Kirkstall Abbey Impressive, well-
preserved remains of Cistercian abbey
founded 1152 include church completed
c.1175 with crossing tower, rib-vaulted
chancel and aisles, fine 13th-C abbot's
lodging, guest house, and chapter house
Abbey House Museum * Museum
incorporates gatehouse of abbey with
rib-vaulted archway and 19th-C work

KIRKSTEAD, LINCS, 4,1C
Kirkstead Abbey Surviving remains of
Cistercian abbey founded 1139
Church of St Leonard Original chapel of
abbey built c.1230–40 and restored completed
1913–14 has fine vaulted interior with carved
bosses and original wodden screen;
effigy of knight of c.1250
Old Hall 15th-C hall-house with 17th-C
brick facing

KIRKWALL, ORKNEY, 9,5B
St Magnus Cathedral [SCS] *, Broad
Street Important cathedral built 12th C
on model of Durham with medieval,
19th- and 20th-C rebuildings retains
original choir with presbytery added
c.1190, transepts, and crossing tower of
c.1200 (14th-C belfry)
Bishop's and Earl's Palaces [HS],
Watergate. Remains of medieval bishop's
palace include important hall undercroft
of c.1550 (remodelled c.1550 and c.1660)
and round north-west tower built
1541–48; adjacent Earl's Place
of 1607

KIRKWHELPINGTON,
NORTHUMBERLAND, 7,3B
Church of St Bartholomew Medieval
church restored 1896 has long chancel
with 13th-C arch, and 15th-C west tower

KIRTLING, CAMBS, 3,3A
Church of All Saints Church of Norman
origin extensively rebuilt c.1500 retains
original south doorway and ironwork;
16th-C tomb chest to First Baron North,
builder of south-east chapel
Kirtling Tower Red brick gatehouse of
c.1530 with tall turrets and semi-circular
oriel window

KIRTON-IN-LINDSEY,
LINCS, 4,1B
Church of St Andrew Norman church
with medieval and 19th-C remodelling has
original priest's doorway, late 12th-C
north arcade, large 13th-C west tower
and fine west doorway

KISIMUL CASTLE, WESTERN
ISLES (Outer Hebrides), 9,1E
See Castlebay

KNAPTON, NORFOLK, 4,5C
Church of St Peter and St Paul Medieval
church has 14th-C chancel, west tower and
south porch, and splendid double
hammerbeam roof of 1504 with carved
angels; 13th-C octagonal font

KNARESBOROUGH,
N. YORKS, 7,3D
Church of St John Church of Norman
origin retains late 12th-C crossing tower
with later upper levels, late 13th-C north
chapel, south chapel and east end rebuilt
c.1330–50; embattled nave and aisles
reworked 15th C
Chapel of Our Lady of the Crag
Remarkable little rib-vaulted chapel
founded 1409 survives carved into cliff
Knaresborough Castle * Remains of castle
with well-preserved keep built c.1310–40

KNOCK ABBEY, CO. LOUTH, 11,4D
See Tallanstown

KNOCKGRAFFON,
CO. TIPPERARY, 12,3C
Church and Castle [Dúchas] Remains of
simple 13th-C church with 15th-C east
window; 16th-C tower survives nearby

KNOCKMOY, CO. GALWAY, 12,3A
Knockmoy Abbey [Dúchas] Remains of
Cistercian abbey founded 1189–90 include
church with simple nave, fine rib-vaulted
chancel and 15th-C central tower; rare
surviving medieval fresco (c.1400) in
chancel; well preserved east wing of
domestic buildings

KNOCKNAGAEL BOAR STONE,
HIGHLAND, 9,4D
See Inverness

KNOCKTOPHER,
CO. KILKENNY, 12,4C
Church of St David [Dúchas] Surviving
fragments and west tower of medieval
church mainly demolished 1870; good
double effigy of later 14th C survives
in tower base
Knocktopher House House incorporates
remains of important Carmelite friary
of St Saviour (founded 1356)

KNOLE, KENT, 3,2D
Knole [NT] Vast and impressive 15th- to
16th-C palace extensively remodelled
c.1605 retains much original work
including 15th-C Bourchier's Tower
and Great Hall

KNOOK, WILTS, 2,3C
Church of St Margaret Norman church
with carved south tympanum, chancel
arch with fine capitals, and later two-
storeyed south porch

KNOWLE, W. MIDLANDS, 5,4D
**Church of St John the Baptist, St
Lawrence and St Anne** Embattled church
built c.1400 has west tower, five-bay
arcades, clerestory, high chancel, and later
north chapel; 15th-C screen, font and stalls
Guildhouse Timber-framed guildhall
of 15th C

KNOWLTON, DORSET, 2,3D
Knowlton Church and Earthworks [EH]
Ruins of Norman church in neolithic
earthworks

LABBAMOLAGA, CO. CORK, 12,3C
Monastic Site [Dúchas] Remains of small
oratory with antae and 12th-C church
nearby occupy site of early monastery;
stone near south wall of oratory
supposedly marks tomb of St Molaga;
early cross-slab in enclosure

LACKEN, CO. WESTMEATH, 11,3D
See Multyfarnham

LACOCK, WILTS, 2,3B
Church of St Cyriac Mainly 15th-C church
with west tower, vaulted west porch, rich
vaulted north-east chapel of c.1430 and
tall nave retains transepts built c.1300
Lacock Abbey [NT] Mid 16th-C mansion
incorporates extensive remains of
Augustinian nunnery with well-
preserved cloisters, sacristy, and
chapter house
Village [NT] Village dating from 13th C
has 14th-C tithe barn with cruck trusses
and good half-timbered houses

LADYKIRK, BORDERS, 8,4E
Ladykirk Church Fine and well-preserved
collegiate church built 1500–4 with apsidal
transepts and apsidal east end to chancel;
small west tower has upper stage added
1743; good tracery

LAKENHEATH, SUFFOLK, 4,3E
Church of St Mary Church of Norman
origin retains original chancel arch,
chancel extended 13th C, west tower with
lower parts of late 1200s, 14th-C arcades,
and splendid hammerbeam roof; fine
13th-C font, 14th-C wall paintings,
15th-C pulpit and set of carved
bench ends

LALEHAM, SURREY, 3,1C
Church of All Saints Norman church
much remodelled 19th C retains original
arcades, 16th-C north chancel chapel, and
west tower dated 1732

LAMBETH PALACE, LONDON
See London

LAMBLEY, NOTTS, 5,5B
Church of the Holy Trinity Church of
mostly 15th C with 12th- to 14th-C west
tower and rood stair; rood screen
dated 1377

LAMBOURN, BERKS, 2,4B
Church of St Michael Large church of late
Norman origin with crossing tower and
additions of 13th to 15th C; ornate 15th-C
south chapel; Norman pillar piscina and
good 14th-C monuments

LAMLASH (Isle of Arran),
STRATHCLYDE, 10,4C
St Bride's Church Shell of church dating
from 14th C has sculptured stones built
into walls and in graveyard

LAMPHEY, DYFED, 6,2E
Bishop's Palace [CADW] Luxurious
country house of Bishops of St David's
with 13th-C banqueting hall and private
apartments, 14th-C Great Hall and
16th-C chapel

LANARK, STRATHCLYDE, 10,5C
Church of St Kentigern Ruins of medieval
church abandoned 1777 with early
13th-C chancel arch and north arcade
(reconstructed 1954)

LANCASTER, LANCS, 7,2D
Church of St Mary Church of
Saxo-Norman origin has 13th-C south
doorway and fine late 14th-C chancel
and nave; west tower rebuilt 1754 and
work of 1903; Saxon sculpture and

14th-C stalls with splendid canopies

Lancaster Castle * Norman castle extensively rebuilt 18th to 19th C retains part of 11th-C keep, Adrian's Tower of *c.*1210 and great gatehouse added *c.*1400

LANCHESTER, CO. DURHAM, 7, 3C
Church of All Saints Medieval church with Norman chancel arch, late 12th-C nave, mid 13th-C chancel and 15th-C west tower; 13th-C stained glass and fine carved tympanum in chancel

LANDWADE, CAMBS, 4, 3E
Church of St Nicholas Church built *c.*1445 with low west tower, nave, transepts and chancel; 15th-C stained glass, rood screen and good monuments

LANEAST, CORNWALL, 1, 3C
Church of St Sativola Virgin or St Michael Cruciform Norman church with 14th-C tower; 15th-C south porch and south aisle retain fine wagon roofs; medieval benches and rood screen

LANERCOST, CUMBRIA, 7, 2B
Lanercost Priory [EH – except church] Remains of priory founded 1166 include well-preserved church (now used by parish) with complete west front of *c.*1250–75, ruined chancel, transepts, walls of cloister, and chapter house
Bridge Medieval bridge of two arches

LANGFORD, OXON, 2, 4B
Church of St Matthew Saxon church with mid 11th-C tower, nave aisles added *c.*1200, and 13th-C chancel; sophisticated sculpture (perhaps as early as 10th C) reset in south porch

LANGHAM, RUTLAND, 5, 5C
Church of St Peter and St Paul Spacious church built 13th to 15th C has fine mid 14th-C south façade with porch and transept, tall west tower, and 15th-C clerestory

LANGLEY CASTLE, NORTHUMBERLAND, 7, 2B
Langley Castle Late 13th- or early 14th-C tower house remodelled *c.*1350 and restored late 19th C has corner towers and embattled parapet

LANGLEY BURRELL, WILTS, 2, 3B
Church of St Peter Medieval church with north arcade of *c.*1200 retains much work of *c.*1300–20 including west front, south tower and chancel

LANGPORT, SOMERSET, 2, 1D
Church of All Saints 15th-C church with

west tower and embattled aisles and chapels retains fine carved lintel stone of *c.*1190–1200 above south doorway; medieval stained glass in east window
Hanging Chapel 15th-C guild or corporation chapel over gateway

LANREATH, CORNWALL, 1, 3D
Church of St Manarck (Marnach) and St Dunstan Church of Norman origin rededicated 1321 and extensively rebuilt 15th C has west tower, north transept, south porch, and fine wagon roofs to nave and south aisle; Norman altar stone, elaborate font, and rood screen with painted saints of *c.*1520

LANTEGLOS-BY-FOWEY CORNWALL, 1, 3D
Church of St Willow Mainly 14th-C church restored 1904 with four-storeyed tower and fine roofs in nave and aisles; Norman south doorway incorporates 8th-C stone; early 13th-C font

LAPLEY, STAFFS, 5, 3C
Church of All Saints Norman church retains nave, chancel enlarged 13th C, and central tower with 15th-C upper stage; good sedilia, piscina and screens

LAPWORTH, WARWS, 5, 4D
Church of St Mary Mainly 15th-C church retains Norman work, 13th-C arcades, fine detached north tower of 14th C, west porch, and clerestory with pinnacles; early 14th-C font and good timber roof

LASTINGHAM, N. YORKS, 7, 4D
Church of St Mary Church of monastery refounded 1078 with later additions retains remarkable vaulted crypt built *c.*1078–*c.*1085 with monumental columns, chancel, apse, and fragments of Saxon sculpture

LAUGHARNE, DYFED, 6, 3D
Laugharne Castle [CADW] Substantial ruins, including two round towers, of medieval fortress overlooking Taf estuary, built mainly 13th to 14th C and converted into mansion during 16th C
Church of St Martin Large 14th-C church with central tower and 19th-C additions; sculptured cross of 9th to early 10th C

LAUGHTON-EN-LE-MORTHEN, S. YORKS, 5, 5A
Church of All Saints Church of Saxon origin retains original north doorway, north arcade built *c.*1190, 15th-C south

arcade, and tower with octagonal stage and fine spire; late medieval font and carved hood moulds in aisles

LAUNCELLS, CORNWALL, 1, 3C
Church of St Andrew and St Swithin Medieval church rebuilt 15th and 19th C with west tower and white-washed interior; good 15th-C carved bench ends and tiles

LAUNCESTON, CORNWALL, 1, 3C
Church of St Mary Magdalene Church built 1511–24 has lavish carved granite facing, late 14th-C south-west tower and elaborate wooden pulpit
Church of St Thomas Church of Norman origin rebuilt 14th to 15th C and much restored 1874 has west tower and Norman tympanum built into south porch; carved Norman font and 13th-C ironwork
White Hart Hotel Hotel incorporates simple Norman doorway from Augustinian priory founded 1136
Launceston Castle [EH] Remains of important medieval castle include bailey, keep, and 12th- and 13th-C gates
Bridges Medieval bridge of five arches crossing River Kensey and early 16th-C New Bridge across River Tamar

LAVENHAM, SUFFOLK, 3, 3A
Church of St Peter and St Paul Noble church of 14th to 16th C retains original chancel, west tower built *c.*1486–95 with later upper parts, fine nave of *c.*1500, and early 16th-C north and south chapels; rood screen of *c.*1330–40 and good 16th-C screens to chantries
The Old Wool Hall, Water Street. Fine 15th-C timber-framed hall house incorporated in Swan Hotel
De Vere House, Water Street. 15th-C house with later restoration has ornate gables and oriel windows
Guildhall of Corpus Christi [NT], Market Place. Timber-framed guildhall built late 1400s
Medieval Buildings Good medieval timber-framed buildings include: The Little House (Market Place) Mullet House (Water Street); Shilling Old Grange (Shilling Street); Woolstaplers (Prentice Street)

LAW, STRATHCLYDE, 10, 5C
Law Castle (or Kilbride Castle) (1 km. / ½ m. NE of West Kilbride) Large, recently restored 15th-C keep has vaulted basement and first floor hall with screened-off kitchen

LAWFORD, ESSEX, 3, 4A
Church of St Mary Mainly 14th-C church with 19th-C additions retains lavish chancel of *c.*1330, west tower, sedilia and piscina

LAXTON, NOTTS, 5, 5B
Church of St Michael Handsome church restored 1859–60 with mainly 14th-C interior and fine late 15th-C nave clerestory; 13th- and 14th-C monuments

LAYD CHURCH, CO. ANTRIM, 11, 5A
See Cushendall

LAYER MARNEY, ESSEX, 3, 3B
Church of St Mary the Virgin Late medieval brick church has west tower, priest's chamber with chimney, and south porches; 15th-C wall painting, iron bound chest, and good monuments to Marney family
Layer Marney Tower [HHA] Splendid brick gatehouse built *c.*1520–30 with seven- and eight-storeyed towers and terracotta detailing

LEA, CO. LAOIS, 11, 3E
Lea Castle [Dúchas] Remains of square medieval castle (probably 13th-C) with corner towers and enclosing wall; gatehouse (*c.*1297) to east

LEACANABUAILE, CO. KERRY, 12, 1D
Stone Fort [Dúchas] Round fort on hilltop, dated by excavation to 9th or 10th C, containing remains of four dry-stone huts

LEAMANEH, CO. CLARE, 12, 2B
Leamaneh Castle [Dúchas] Five-storeyed tower house built *c.*1480 with mansion added to west 17th C

LEATHERHEAD, SURREY, 3, 1D
Church of St Mary and St Nicholas Medieval church much remodelled 19th C retains good internal work of *c.*1210 with mid 13th-C chancel arch; 15th-C font

LECKHAMPSTEAD, BUCKS, 2, 5A
Church of the Assumption Church of Norman origin has good 12th-C south and north doorways, carved tympanum, and reset west window in 13th-C west tower; 14th-C chancel; mainly 14th-C font retains one Norman panel; carved effigy of knight of *c.*1325

LEDBURY, HEREFS, 2, 2A
Church of St Michael Church of Norman origin with medieval and 18th-C additions has detached early 13th-C tower, rich

north chapel built mid 14th C, and 15th-C arcades; fine late 13th-C monument of priest

Medieval Buildings Good buildings include 15th-C council offices and Old Grammar School of c.1500 in Church Lane, St Katherine's Hospital with early 14th-C south range, and timber-framed house in New Street

LEDSHAM, W. YORKS, 7, 4E

Church of All Saints Saxon church with medieval and 19th-C additions retains original chancel arch, two-storeyed west porch heightened 12th C as tower; and north chapel built 1400s; Saxon stone in north wall of 15th-C north aisle

LEEDS, KENT, 3, 3D

Church of St Nicholas Church of Saxo-Norman origin with medieval and 19th-C additions retains 11th-C west tower and fine tower arch; 15th-C rood screen

Leeds Castle * Imposing castle of Norman origin with medieval additions and main building of 1822 retains original mill, gatehouse and 16th-C Maiden's Tower

Battel Hall 14th-C stone house with 17th-C range has original doorways, walls to hall and unusual laver

LEEDS, W. YORKS, 7, 3E
See Adel

LEEK, STAFFS, 5, 3B

Church of St Edward the Confessor Spacious church rebuilt c.1297 with later additions and major restoration of 1865–7 has 14th-C west tower with 15th-C upper stage; fragments of two 11th-C crosses in churchyard

Market Cross (in cemetery) Cross of early 1400s moved to cemetery 1806

LEES HALL, W. YORKS, 7, 3E
See Thornhill

LEICESTER, LEICS, 5, 5D

Church of All Saints, Highcross. Church of Norman origin much rebuilt c.1300 with six-bay arcades, and chancel reworked c.1830; handsome late 13th-C font, 14th-C tiles and late medieval pulpit

Church of St Margaret Medieval church restored 19th C with impressive tower, south porch and fine chancel (all built c.1444)

Church of St Mary de Castro, Castle Yard. Church of Norman origin with medieval and 19th-C rebuilding retains 12th-C blind arcading, fine sedilia of late 1100s, and good early 14th-C west tower; 13th-C font and 14th-C tiles

Church of St Nicholas Saxon church adjoining Roman remains has original nave with Norman north arcade, late 11th-C central tower raised 1100s, and chancel with Norman string course

Castle Remains of Norman castle with later additions above River Soar include large 12th-C great hall with fine timber roof (used as courthouse until 1980) and timber-framed gatehouse built 1446–7

Trinity Hospital Almshouses, The Newarke. Remains of hospital founded 1331 with aisled hall reworked 1776 and 1898–1902 retaining late 14th-C chapel

Newarke House Museum * Museum built into two late medieval chantry houses of Trinity Hospital with extensive later alterations

Magazine Gateway Regimental Museum *, Southgate. Town gateway built c.1410 and used as magazine store 17th C

Guildhall *, Guildhall Lane Guildhall begun c.1343 on courtyard plan and restored 1922–6 retains fine great hall

Wygston's House * (Museum of Costume), Applegate. Timber-framed house of c.1480 with adjoining late 18th- and 19th-C ranges

Leicester Abbey Ruins of Augustinian abbey founded 1143 survive in park laid out 1878–82

Church of St Andrew, Aylestone (Outer Leicester) Medieval church with 13th-C west tower, spacious chancel of c.1300-10, and 15th-C clerestory

Aylestone Old Bridge (Outer Leicester) 15th-C packhorse bridge and causeway with cutwaters

Church of St Peter, Belgrave (Outer Leicester) Church of Norman origin restored 19th C retains original south doorway, 13th-C arcades, and 14th-C chancel

LEIGH, WORCS, 5, 3E

Church of St Eadburga Norman church rebuilt 13th, 14th and 19th C has original nave and chancel, and west tower added 1300s; figure of Christ of c.1220 in blank north window

Leigh Court Barn [EH] Long and well preserved early 14th-C cruck barn built for monks of Pershore Abbey with two wagon porches

LEIGH BARTON (3 km. / 2 m. NW of Kingsbridge at Leigh), DEVON, 1, 4D

Leigh Barton [EH] Late medieval complex of buildings with farmhouse, ranges around courtyard and handsome gatehouse

LEIGHLINBRIDGE, CO. CARLOW, 12, 5C

Bridge [Dúchas] Bridge on important crossing over River Barrow, protected by mid 16th-C "Black Castle", retains much work of 1320

LEIGH-ON-MENDIP, SOMERSET, 2, 2C

Church of St Giles Medieval church has rich 15th- to early 16th-C west tower and nave, clerestory, plain chancel, and fine roofs with angels and bosses; Norman font and good set of benches

LEIGHTON BROMSWOLD, CAMBS, 4, 1E

Church of St Mary 13th-C church extensively rebuilt 17th C retains chancel of late 1200s with fine double piscina and aumbry; west tower and furnishings of 1634

LEIGHTON BUZZARD, BEDS, 3, 1B

Church of All Saints Church consecrated 1288 and rebuilt 15th C retains 13th-C crossing steeple, arcades, ironwork and lectern; sgraffiti on crossing piers

Market Cross Fine pentagonal cross of 15th C with recessed upper stage, statues and central pinnacle

Church of St Mary, Linslade (1.5 km. / 1 m.N) Church with early 12th-C nave, 15th-C west tower and simple early 16th-C chancel; Norman font and remains of 15th-C screen

LEIGHTON LINSLADE, BEDS, 3, 1B
See Leighton Buzzard

LEISTON, SUFFOLK, 3, 5A

Leiston Abbey [EH] Extensive remains of church and monastic buildings of Premonstratensian abbey founded 1182 with restored chapel and early 16th-C gatehouse

LENNOXLOVE (1.5 km. / 1 m. S of Haddington), LOTHIAN, 8, 3E

Lennoxlove * 15th-C tower house with post-medieval additions and adjoining ranges retains large hall, parapet walk, gargoyles, and penthouse

LENTON (Nottingham), NOTTS, 5, 5B

Church of the Holy Trinity Church built 1842 houses splendid mid 12th-C narrative font from Norman priory

LEOMINSTER, HEREFS, 5, 2E

Priory of St Peter and St Paul Church of Benedictine priory begun 1120 and remodelled 13th, 15th and 19th C retains original nave and north aisle, west doorway of c.1150, fine 13th-C south porch,

south aisle richly decorated with ballflower ornament and 15th-C west tower; 13th-C piscina and late 15th-C chalice

Medieval Buildings Good medieval buildings include late 13th-C Forbury Chapel, late 14th-C Grafton House and early 16th-C White Lion.

LEONARD STANLEY, GLOS, 2, 3A

Church of St Swithin Cruciform church of former Augustinian priory founded between 1121 and 1129 has fine Norman central tower with later top, wide nave with original doorways and later medieval wagon roof, chancel with fine early 12th-C capitals to vaulting shafts, and much Norman carving

Priory Buildings Late 10th- or early 11th-C church enlarged 1300s (now used as farm building); medieval barn

LESNES ABBEY, GREATER LONDON

Lesnes Abbey * Abbey Road, Abbey Wood, Belvedere. Ruins of abbey founded 1178 survive in public park

LETTAFORD, DEVON, 1, 4C

Sanders [LT] Unusually well-preserved stone-built Dartmoor long-house of c.1500 (repaired 1975–7 for Landmark Trust)

LEUCHARS, FIFE, 8, 3D

Church of St Athernase, Schoolhill [SCS] Church with nave of mainly 1857–8 retains splendid mid 12th-C chancel and apse with rich external blind arcading; belfry added to apse c.1700

LEVERINGTON, CAMBS, 4, 2D

Church of St Leonard 13th-C church rebuilt 14th and 15th C retains handsome west tower and early 14th-C south porch; fine 15th-C font and Jesse window in north aisle

LEWES, E. SUSSEX, 3, 2E

Priory of St Pancras, Southover. Ruins of church and monastic quarters of 11th-C Cluniac priory with 13th-C Great Gate

Church of St Anne, High Street. Norman church with 13th-C chancel and 19th-C work retains original west tower, nave with late 12th-C south arcade, and south transept; Norman font

Church of St Michael, High Street. Medieval church with 13th-C round tower, 14th-C south arcade, and street front of 1748; 15th-C brasses

Church of St Thomas Becket, Cliffe High

Street Medieval church with later restoration has 14th-C arcades and 15th-C west tower

Lewes Castle and Barbican House * Remains of castle started *c.*1100 include early Norman gatehouse, shell keep with 13th-C turrets, and imposing early 14th-C barbican with portcullis groove

Anne of Cleves' House and Museum * House has early 16th-C front with later back wing

Town Walls Remains of walls built *c.*1266–9

LEWKNOR, OXON, 2, 5B
Church of St Margaret Church built *c.*1200 with rebuilding of 14th and 15th C has original chancel arch and later medieval south aisle and west tower; 12th-C font and ornate piscina, sedilia and tomb recess in chancel

Church Farm Barn Aisled timber structure of late 14th to 15th C inside weather-boarded barn

LIATHMORE, CO. TIPPERARY, 12, 4C
Churches [Dúchas] Early monastic site houses remains of two churches, one small with antae, the other larger building begun 12th C and considerably altered 1400s (original chancel demolished and 12th-C nave made into chancel)

LIBERTON TOWER, LOTHIAN, 8, 3E
See Edinburgh

LICHFIELD, STAFFS, 5, 3C
Cathedral * Imposing 13th- to 14th-C cathedral with later additions and restoration retains transepts built *c.*1230–40, octagonal chapter house started *c.*1240, nave of *c.*1260–80, and crossing tower; splendid west front begun *c.*1280 with twin towers and tiers of statues

Church of St Chad Medieval church with 19th-C remodelling retains 13th-C chancel, south arcade, and 14th-C west tower; 15th-C font

St John's Hospital 12th-C hospital refounded 1495 with 19th- to 20th-C additions has chapel and fine east range with chimneybreasts

LIFTON, DEVON, 1, 4C
Wortham Manor [LT] Well-preserved manor house of 15th and 16th C with good carved granite doorway, ceiling to hall, and fine arch-braced roof to chamber above (all dating from soon after 1500)

LILLESHALL, SHROPS, 5, 2C
Church of St Michael Church with late Norman nave, good south doorway, 13th-C chancel enlarged 1300s, and 15th-C west tower; Norman font

Lilleshall Abbey [EH] Picturesque remains of abbey founded *c.*1148 include 12th- to 13th-C church with good west front and cloister buildings

LILLINGSTONE DAYRELL, BUCKS
Church of St Nicholas Interesting church retains early Norman chancel arch, 12th-C tower with 14th-C top, ornate 13th-C chancel, and fine south doorway; late 13th-C Easter Sepulchre and good brass figures on 15th-C tomb chest

LIMEKILNS, FIFE, 8, 2E
King's Barn, Academy Square Well-preserved early 16th-C warehouse

LIMERICK, CO. LIMERICK, 12, 3C
King John's Castle [Dúchas] Altered but impressive remains of castle built 1200–2 by Shannon Estuary include curtain wall with rounded towers and fine gatehouse; interior used as barracks 18th to 19th C

Cathedral of St Mary [Dúchas], Nicholas Street (English Town) Fine cathedral church built late 12th C, remodelled 13th to 16th C, and restored 19th to 20th C retains original west doorway (renewed 1895), 13th-C tower with later medieval upper stages, transepts and 15th-C chapels; late 15th-C oak stalls with excellent misericords (only surviving carved examples in Ireland); fine monuments include Bultingford-Galway canopied niche of *c.*1500 incorporating mensa of earlier tomb

Kilrush Church (or St Mainchin's) [Dúchas], near Barrington's Pier. Church with flat-headed west doorway and reused 15th-C window in south wall (from Franciscan church in St Mary's Lane)

Cathedral of St John Cathedral built 1856–61 contains (in Treasury) exquisite mitre and crozier commissioned 1418 by Bishop Cornelius O'Dea

Dominican Friary of St Saviour, grounds of Convent of Mercy. Fragmentary remains of friary founded 1227 and rebuilt 15th C

LINCLUDEN, DUMFRIES AND GALLOWAY, 7, 1B
See Dumfries

LINCOLN, LINCS, 4, 1B
Cathedral * Cathedral rebuilt 1192–1250 to incorporate earlier Norman west front; eastern extension with "Angel Choir" added 1256–1280; later medieval work includes Easter Sepulchre (1290s) and tracery (*c.*1330) in circular "Bishop's Eye" window in south transept (13th-C), heightening of both crossing tower (early 14th-C) and two western towers (15th-C); 13th-C chapter house and cloisters

Cathedral Close Exchequer and Potter Gates and parts of 14th-C precinct walls

Lincoln Castle *, Castle Hill. Remains of castle built 1086 by William the Conqueror on Roman site with shell keep (*c.*1200), medieval towers (*c.*1400) and gateway refaced 15th C

City Walls Parts of walls and gates of Roman city including Newport Arch at north end of Bailgate

Norman Town Houses Buildings with good 12th-C work include: St Mary's Guildhall (High Street); two houses in Steep Hill known as Norman House (at corner of Christ's Hospital Terrace) and Jew's House (near Well Lane); Deloraine Court (James Street)

Medieval Bishop's Palace [EH] Minster Yard. Ruins of Bishop's Palace (south of Minster Yard) and Monks Abbey (Monks Road) (12th and 13th-C with medieval alterations)

Norman Churches Two churches of Norman origin survive in High Street: St Peter and St Andrew has 11th-C nave and both it and St Mary le Wigford have Saxo-Norman towers

Medieval Buildings Surviving medieval buildings include: Greyfriars Museum * (Broadgate), probably infirmary of 13th-C friary; Burghersh Chantry (James Street), founded 1345; late medieval timber-framed Harlequin Inn (nos. 21–22) and houses and shops (nos. 27–30) in Steep Hill; two fine late 15th-C houses in High Street are Cardinal's Hat (on corner with Grantham St) and Dernstall House (at junction with St Martin's Lane), rebuilt 1969–70; late 15th to early 16th-C Guildhall and Stonebow (arched gateway) (High St)

Medieval Churches Churches with good medieval work are: 13th-C St Mary le Wigford (High Street) and St Benedict (St Benedict's Square)

LINDISFARNE PRIORY, NORTHUMBERLAND, 7, 3A
See Holy Island

LINDORES ABBEY, FIFE, 8, 3D
See Newburgh

LINDSEY, SUFFOLK, 3, 4A
Church of St Peter Church built mainly early 14th C with original arcade, timber south porch, and fine two-light window on north side of nave; good font of *c.*1300

St James's Chapel [EH] Modest early 13th-C chapel has lancet windows, thatched roof, and late 13th-C piscina

LINGFIELD, SURREY, 3, 2D
Church of St Peter and St Paul Medieval church rebuilt *c.*1431 with four-bay nave and north and south chancel chapels retains 14th-C south-west tower; good late medieval fittings and monument

Old Guest House Timber-framed collegiate building of 15th C with later restoration

Old Surrey Hall (3 km. / 2 m. SE) Timber-framed hall-house built *c.*1450 with remodelling and additions of 1922; fine roof to hall

LINLEY, SHROPS, 5, 1D
Church of St Leonard Norman church with carved tympana to north and south doorways, west tower and 12th-C font

LINLITHGOW, LOTHIAN, 8, 2E
Parish Church of St Michael, Kirkgate [SCS] Large church built early 15th to early 16th C on promontory by loch and much restored 1800s retains chancel with apse, two-storeyed south porch with oriel and image niches, and west tower with spire added 1964; fine tracery (particularly that of window in south transeptal chapel); relief slabs from 15th-C Passion retable survive in vestry

Linlithgow Palace [HS] Important royal palace built 15th to early 16th C on simple courtyard plan with north range remodelled 1618–20 retains front east (original entrance) front with niches and angels on inner side, great hall with vaulted screens passage and minstrels' gallery, remarkable chapel, and royal chambers; good original fireplaces

LINTON (nr Morebattle), BORDERS, 7, 2A
Linton Kirk [SCS] Church of 12th-C origin almost wholly rebuilt 1616, 1774, 1813 and 1912 retains unique Norman tympanum to porch with carving of knight on horseback lancing two creatures

LISCARROLL, CO. CORK, 12, 3C
Liscarroll Castle [Dúchas] Remains of square 13th-C castle (third largest in Ireland) with round angle turrets, gatehouse in south wall, and rectangular tower to north

LISCARTON (3 km. / 2 m. NW of Kells), CO. MEATH, 11, 4D
Castle Ruins of two substantial medieval tower houses, that north particularly well preserved and retaining impressive central hall; fortified gate tower to south-east
Church Remains of narrow medieval church (separated from castle ruins by farm buildings) with late 15th-C carved label stops

LISGOOLE ABBEY, CO. FERMANAGH, 11, 3C
Lisgoole Abbey Early 19th-C villa incorporates much reworked square tower of important medieval abbey

LISLAUGHTIN, CO. KERRY, 12, 2C
Friary [Dúchas] Ruins of church, domestic buildings, and gatehouse of Franciscan friary founded 1478; church contains triple sedilia and two good tomb niches

LISMORE, CO. WATERFORD, 12, 3D
St Mochuda's or Carthage's Cathedral [Dúchas] Cathedral church built 1633 incorporates medieval work of predecessor (eg. 13th-C chancel arch and south transept windows) and houses fine MacGrath tomb of 1557
Castle [Dúchas] Attractive castle built 1800s using work from medieval building; 12th-C gateway removed from nearby church

LISMORE (island), STRATHCLYDE, 10, 3A
Cathedral of St Moluag (4 km. / 2 ½ m. from Achnacroish) Choir of 14th-C cathedral of Argyll and Isles (restored 1749) survives as parish church; foundations of nave and tower; medieval carved slabs in graveyard

LISNASKEA, CO. FERMANAGH, 11, 3C
Cross Cross in Cornmarket incorporates fragments of High Cross from early monastery with bosses and carving
Aghalurcher Church [EHS] (2.5 km. / 1 ½ m. S) Remains of medieval parish church on site of early monastery with fine gravestones and effigy of bishop in vaulted sacristy or chapel

LISTOWEL, CO. KERRY, 12, 2C
Listowel Castle [Dúchas] Surviving half of 15th-C castle with two towers and modern entrance

LITLINGTON, CAMBS, 3, 2A
Church of St Catherine Church of Norman origin has fine 14th-C interior with arcades and clerestory, and west tower with bell stage added 1300s; 15th-C pulpit, good font and screen

LITTLEBOROUGH, NOTTS, 5, 5A
Church of St Nicholas Small Norman church with original chancel arch

LITTLE BOWDEN (Market Harborough), LEICS, 5, 5D
Church of St Nicholas 13th- and early 14th-C church rebuilt 1776, 19th C and 1900–1 has original nave, north aisle and north chapel

LITTLEBURY, ESSEX, 3, 2A
Church of the Holy Trinity 12th- and 13th-C church remodelled 1870–5 has south doorway of late 1100s and two fine porches; good brasses and early 16th-C font case

LITTLE BYTHAM, LINCS, 4, 1D
Church of St Medard Church of Saxon and Norman origin remodelled 13th to 14th C retains rich priest's doorway with tympanum and late 12th-C north doorway to nave; piscinas and Easter Sepulchre

LITTLE CASTERTON, RUTLAND, 4, 1D
Church of All Saints Mainly 13th-C church with 19th-C additions and restoration retains Norman tympanum in north aisle, north arcade and north doorway of c.1200, 13th-C bellcote, and fine 15th-C nave roof; late 13th-C tomb recess in south aisle with coffin lids and late 14th-C brass

LITTLE COGGESHALL, ESSEX, 3, 3B
Abbey Remains of abbey founded c.1140 include dormitory undercroft built c.1180, abbot's lodging of c.1185–90, well preserved corridor with early 13th-C vaulting, detached gate chapel of c.1225, and late 16th-C work

LITTLEDEAN, GLOS, 2, 2A
Church of St Ethelbert Good mainly 14th-C church retains Norman jambs and capitals to chancel arch; north chapel added c.1411; original 14th- to 15th-C wagon roofs

LITTLE DUNMOW, ESSEX, 3, 3B
Church of St Mary Surviving Lady Chapel of Augustinian priory founded 1106, remodelled 1360 and with turret of 1872, retains arcade of c.1200 in north wall and

five fine windows; Dunmow Flitch Chair (incorporating part of 13th-C stall) in chancel and two well-preserved 15th-C effigies
Priory Place Medieval timber-framed building in priory precinct, probably former gatehouse

LITTLE KIMBLE, BUCKS, 2, 5A
Church of All Saints Modest medieval church contains fine but poorly-preserved series of wall paintings of c.1300; good 13th-C tiles in chancel

LITTLE MALVERN, WORCS, 5, 3E
Church of St Giles Remains of priory church founded 1171 (rebuilt 14th C and c.1480–2) with Norman central tower, transepts and chancel, and ruinous 15th-C chapels; pillar piscina and part of late 14th-C tomb chest
Little Malvern Court [HHA] Medieval house with 16th- and 19th-C additions has fine early 14th-C double purlin roof; east range incorporates original prior's hall or refectory of former Benedictine monastery

LITTLE MAPLESTEAD, ESSEX, 3, 3A
Church of St John the Baptist Circular church built c.1335 and restored 1851–7 has chancel with apse and 11th-C saltire cross

LITTLE MISSENDEN, BUCKS, 3, 1B
Church of St John the Baptist Saxon church greatly reworked from 12th to 15th C and 18th C retains 13th-C chancel and 15th-C timber porch and west tower; Norman font and handsome wall paintings

LITTLE MORETON HALL, CHESHIRE, 5, 3B
Little Moreton Hall [NT] Handsome 15th-C timber-framed moated manor house (begun 1450) with additions of c.1559– 1600; fine wall paintings and roof to hall

LITTLE SAXHAM, SUFFOLK, 3, 3A
Church of St Nicholas Norman church has fine original round tower, tower arch, and south doorway; 14th-C north aisle and 15th-C south side

LITTLE STAUGHTON, BEDS, 4, 1E
Church of St Margaret Medieval church has south arcade of c.1300, west tower, and 15th-C chancel, south porch, south aisle, clerestory and roof to nave; chancel retains 14th-C tomb recess

LITTLE STUKELEY, CAMBS, 4, 2E
Church of St Martin Church with late medieval arcades, north and south chapels, and south porch; fragments of Norman work collected and displayed by restorer include arch with beakhead, window heads and frieze (inside tower) and corbel table (north wall of north aisle)

LITTLE TEY, ESSEX, 3, 3B
Church of St James the Less Small Norman church with restored 13th- and 14th-C wall paintings

LITTLETON, SURREY, 3, 1C
Church of St Mary Magdalene Medieval church restored 19th C retains 13th-C nave and chancel, early 16th-C brick west tower (top added early 1700s), brick clerestory, and north chapel dated 1705; good late medieval pews, choir stalls, and rood screen of c.1500

LITTLE WALSINGHAM NORFOLK, 4, 4C
Church of St Mary 14th- and 15th-C church gutted by fire 1961 retains west tower and two-storeyed south porch; 15th-C font and good monuments; **Priory** Surviving fragments of church, late 13th-C refectory, and 15th-C gatehouse of important 12th-C priory
Walsingham Abbey [HHA] (public access to grounds only) 18th- and 19th-C house built into dormitory range of 12th-C priory
Greyfriars Ruins of friary founded 1347

LITTLE WENHAM, SUFFOLK, 3, 4A
Church of All Saints [CCT] Flint church built c.1300 has west tower with 16th-C top; good original wall paintings and large font
Little Wenham Hall Well-preserved fortified hall-house built of brick c.1270–80 with battlements, staircase tower, and rib-vaulted chapel of c.1285

LIVERPOOL, MERSEYSIDE, 6, 5A
Church of All Saints [OCT] Childwall; Medieval church with 14th- to 15th-C masonry and work of 19th and 20th C; part of Saxon cross shaft on west wall and Norman capital in chancel
Speke Hall [NT], The Walk. Splendid timber-framed manor house of 15th and 16th C with moat and inner courtyard; double-height hall of possibly c.1500 has fragments of 15th-C stained glass

LLANABER, GWYNEDD, 6, 4B
Church of St Mary and St Bodfan Large exceptionally well-preserved 13th-C

church with original raised chancel, chancel arch, nave arcades and south doorway; late medieval chancel roof and font and 19th-C additions

LLANANNO, POWYS, 6,5C
Church of St Anno Church built 1876–7 retains splendid late 15th to early 16th-C rood screen with rich carving and figures of c.1880

LLANBABO (ANGLESEY), GWYNEDD, 6,3A
Church of St Pabo Small medieval church in circular graveyard contains beautiful 14th-C low-relief carving of St Pabo

LLANBADARN FAWR, DYFED, 6,4C
Church of St Padarn Austere and massive 13th-C cruciform church on site of clas church founded 6th C; two carved Celtic crosses of 9th to 11th C in south transept

LLANBADARN FAWR, POWYS, 6,5C
Church of St Padarn or Paternus Church completely rebuilt 1878 retains tympanum of south doorway with reset carved stone of c.1100–1150

LLANBADRIG (ANGLESEY), GWYNEDD, 6,3A
Church of St Patrick Simple church with 14th-C nave and 16th-C chancel contains crudely carved gravestone of 9th to 11th C and 12th-C font

LLANBEBLIG, GWYNEDD, 6,3A
Church of St Peblig Medieval church of 13th, 14th and 15th C with 16th-C north chapel and 19th-C chancel contains small memorial brass of c.1500 showing man lying in bed

LLANBEDR YSTRAD YW, POWYS, 6,5D
Church of St Peter Church consecrated 1060 and much rebuilt late 15th or early 16th C with north aisle, good south porch, and priest's doorway; 14th-C west tower; font of c.1500 and traces of wall paintings

LLANBLETHIAN, GLAMORGAN, 1,5A
Church of St John the Baptist Church of Norman origin has low chancel, south transept with vaulted crypt, nave, and imposing west tower built c.1477
St Quintin's Castle [CADW] Remains of medieval castle include early 14th-C gatehouse with south tower converted to prison by early 16th C

LLANCARFAN, GLAMORGAN, 2,1B
Church of St Cadoc Medieval church much reworked 1877 retains chancel arch of c.1200, early 13th-C south aisle enlarged 1300s, and elaborate wagon roofs to nave and south chapel; 15th-C screen and reredos with fine canopywork
Garnllwyd House built 1400s with upper-floor hall

LLANDAFF (Cardiff), GLAMORGAN, 2,1B
Llandaff Cathedral * Medieval cathedral extensively reworked 19th and mid 20th C retains rich early 12th-C sanctuary arch, fine early 13th-C west front with lancet windows, small chapter house, Lady Chapel, and late 15th-C north-west (Jasper) tower; 14th-C stone reredos
Bell Tower, The Green Remains of large bell tower built 1200s;
Bishop's Castle, The Green Well-preserved fortified house of late 13th C with imposing gatehouse

LLANDANWG, GWYNEDD, 6,4B
Church of St Tanwg Simple church on sea shore, thought to have been chapel of rest for corpses awaiting burial on Bardsey Island, has original rood beam, doorway and windows, and early 15th-C east window with external protective hood

LLANDDEW, POWYS, 6,4D
Church of the Holy Trinity or St David Cruciform church of mainly late 13th C has transepts, chancel with lancet windows, 14th-C priest's doorway, and crossing tower of 1620 (with 18th-C roof); Norman font and good stoups
Bishop's Palace Bishop's palace with ruins of early 14th-C hall, defensive wall, and Bishop Gower's well of c.1340

LLANDEFALLE, POWYS, 6,5D
Church of St Matthew or Maelog Church built late 15th C with west tower, south aisle, and barrel-ceiled roofs retains south doorway of c.1300; 13th-C font and screen of c.1500

LLANDEWI BREFI, DYFED, 6,4C
Church of St David Much rebuilt clas church has inscribed early Christian stones of 6th to 9th C set in floor beneath surviving 12th-C crossing tower

LLANDOUGH / LLANDOCHAU GLAMORGAN, 2,1B
Church of St Dochdwy Church built 1865–6 with impressive Saxon Irbic cross in churchyard

LLANDOVERY, DYFED, 6,4D
Llanfair-ar-y-Bryn Church (St Mary's) 12th-C church, built like tithe barn, survives on site of Roman fort; 13th-C tower and later medieval additions
Castle Fragmentary remains of early medieval castle on site of Norman motte and bailey above town

LLANDRILLO-YN-RHOS (Colwyn Bay), CLWYD, 6,4A
Church of St Trillo Llandudno Road Medieval church enlarged 16th C with west tower of 1552 adapted c.1600 as beacon watch-tower; early 14th-C sepulchral slab in porch
Capel Trillo below Rhos Promenade Little medieval chapel, possibly Saxon, built over spring with roof incorrectly restored c.1892
Llys Euryn, Bryn Euryn Ruins of late medieval house

LLANDRINIO, POWYS, 6,5B
Church of St Trunio or St Peter Church of Norman origin with medieval rebuilding has 12th-C east end to chancel, original south doorway, south porch, and west tower with bell turret of 1829; part of possibly 10th-C cross, and late Norman font

LLANDYSUL, DYFED, 6,3D
Church of St Tysul 13th-C church with later medieval additions including handsome west tower; ancient altar stone with incised crosses and carved Crucifixion survive in Lady Chapel

LLANEFYDD, CLWYD, 6,4A
Church of St Nefydd and St Mary Late medieval double-naved church with west bellcote reworked 1859; fragments of 14th-C crosses

LLANEGRYN, GWYNEDD, 6,4B
Church of St Mary and St Egryn Medieval church heavily restored 19th C has magnificent early 16th-C carved rood loft and screen, said to have come from Cymer Abbey; medieval font

LLANEILIAN (ANGLESEY), GWYNEDD, 6,3A
Church of St Eilian Late 15th-C church linked by passageway to St Eilian's Chapel retains contemporary rood screen and loft; 12th-C tower

LLANELIEU, POWYS, 6,5D
Church of St Ellyw Simple 13th-C church with work of c.1600 and 1905 retains parts of 14th-C screen with rood beam and

boarded partition; two pillar stones of 7th to 9th C

LLANELLY, GWENT, 6,5D
Church of St Elli or Ellyw or Almeda 13th-C church with broad west tower and late medieval additions to nave and chancel; primitive 11th- or 12th-C font

LLANENGAN, GWYNEDD, 6,3B
Church of St Engan Large handsome late medieval pilgrimage church with double nave and 16th-C tower and porch; original roofs, screens and stalls survive

LLANERFYL, POWYS, 6,4B
Church of St Erfyl Medieval church rebuilt 1870 retains nave roof trusses of c.1400, late 15th-C reliquary, and wooden shrine

LLANFAIR CAEREINION, POWYS, 6,5B
Church of St Mary Medieval church extensively rebuilt 1868 and with tower added 1884 retains fine south doorway with capitals of c.1200; font of c.1300 and effigy of knight of c.1400

LLANFARCHELL (Whitchurch), CLWYD, 6,5A
See Denbigh

LLANFECHAIN, POWYS, 6,5B
Church of St Garmon Good Norman church with 19th-C shingled spire retains late 12th-C south doorway and 15th-C nave roof; font of c.1500

LLANFIGAN, POWYS, 6,4D
Church of St Meugan Church built c.1273 with 14th-C north aisle, four-bay arcade, and later additions; west tower and late medieval nave roof; font of late 1200s and late 14th-C screen

LLANFIHANGEL-Y-PENNANT GWYNEDD, 6,4B
Castell-y-Bere [CADW] Ruined site showing layout of fortress built on rocky spur above Dysinni valley by Llywelyn ap Iorwerth (Llewelyn the Great) c.1221

LLANFILO, POWYS, 6,5D
Church of St Bilo or St Milburg Church of Norman origin with medieval and 18th- to 20th-C rebuilding retains two lintels of c.1100, 15th-C roof to south porch, and barrel-ceiling to nave; two altar slabs (mensae) of c.1200 and fine early 16th-C rood screen

LLANFROTHEN, GWYNEDD, 6, 4B
Church of St Brothen Primitive 13th-C church with simple bellcote, altered 17th and early 18th C, still has crude medieval screen and rood beam; 15th-C font

LLANGADWALADR (ANGLESEY), GWYNEDD, 6, 3A
Church of St Cadwaladr Much-restored Welsh royal church with 12th-C nave, 14th-C chancel and 15th-C east window showing Saint below Crucifixion

LLANGAFFO (ANGLESEY), GWYNEDD, 6, 3A
Cross and Gravestones Cross and several inscribed gravestones dating from 7th to 12th C survive in sacristy and graveyard of 19th-C Church of St Gaffo

LLANGAN, GLAMORGAN, 1, 5A
Church of St Canna Mainly 19th-C church has late 9th- or early 10th-C wheel cross head in churchyard and fine 15th-C cross with original features to front of building

LLANGAR, CLWYD, 6, 3B
See Corwen

LLANGELYNIN, GWYNEDD, 6, 4B
Church of St Celynin (2 km. / 1¼ m. W) Simple early medieval church with 15th-C timber roof in chancel and Holy Well in south corner of churchyard

LLANGENNITH / LLANGYNYDD, GLAMORGAN, 6, 3E
Church of St Cennydd Church of mainly 13th C restored 1882–4 and built into hillside has north tower and long chancel; part of 9th-C cross shaft in west wall and 14th-C effigy of knight
Burry Holms (tidal island off coast – 3 km. / 2 m. NW) Picturesque ruins of medieval hermitage supposedly founded 6th C, set on island off tip of penninsula

LLANGENNY, POWYS, 6, 5D
Church of St Cenau Medieval church enlarged late 15th to early 16th C retains north aisle (original nave), north chancel, and nave with south porch and barrel-ceilings

LLANGOLLEN, CLWYD, 6, 5B
Church of St Collen Church with mid 18th-C west tower and 19th-C additions retains 13th-C south doorway and 15th-C north arcade; splendid late medieval roofs to nave and north aisle, and panelled ceiling with carving
Bridge Bridge built c.1500 with later widening and alterations

Castell Dinas Bran Ruins of 13th-C hilltop castle include gatehouse and curtain walls

LLANGRISTIOLUS (ANGLESEY), GWYNEDD, 6, 3A
Church of St Cristiolus Medieval church with fine 13th-C chancel arch, 12th-C font and 16th-C east window

LLANGWM UCHAF, GWENT, 6, 5E
Church of St Heirom or St Jerome 13th-C church with late medieval tower, on site of 8th-C foundation, has fine early 16th-C rood screen and loft, carved with vine leaves and tracery, restored 1870 with colouring; 17th-C tower

LLANGWNNADL, GWYNEDD, 6, 3B
Church of St Gwynhoydl Spacious medieval church with north and south aisles and three-bay arcades added early 16th C; font of c.1520

LLANGYBI, GWYNEDD, 6, 3B
Church of St Cybi 14th- and 15th-C church with 19th-C alterations
St Cybi's Well [CADW] Medieval holy well, restored 1879; 18th-C buildings on site built to provide facilities for sick people seeking treatment based on supposedly curative properties of the water

LLANIDAN (ANGLESEY), GWYNEDD, 6, 3A
See Brynsiencyn

LLANIDLOES, POWYS, 6, 4C
Church of St Idloes Medieval church with late 14th-C west tower and lavish timber roof of 1542; splendid early 13th-C arcade from Cwmhir Abbey
Town Plan Town retains 13th-C street plan and earthwork defences

LLANIESTYN (ANGLESEY), GWYNEDD, 6, 4A
Church of St Iestyn Simple 14th-C church with large 15th-C south chapel containing beautiful low-relief carving of St Iestyn; Norman font
Hafotty (2 km. / 1¼ m. SW) 14th-C hall-house altered 16th and 17th C

LLANMAES, GLAMORGAN, 1, 5A
Church of St Catwg 13th-C church with west tower added 1632 retains 15th-C rood loft arrangement and timber screen

LLANRHAEADR-YM-MOCHNANT, POWYS, 6, 5B
Church of St Dogfan Church on early site much reworked 19th C retains late medieval panelled wagon ceiling at east

end of chancel; 9th or 10th-C sepulchral slab and fragments of 12th-C shrine

LLANRHAEADR-YNG-NGHINMEIRCH, CLWYD, 6, 5A
Church of St Dyfnog Late medieval double-naved church restored 1800s has timber-framed north porch, battlemented west tower, and good roofs; splendid Jesse window dated 1533 at east of north nave

LLANRHIDIAN, GLAMORGAN, 6, 3E
Church of St Rhidian and St Illtyd Medieval church with 19th-C rebuilding retains 15th-C work in chancel and tall west tower; carved stone of 9th or 10th C in porch
Weobley Castle [CADW] Well-preserved 14th-C fortified manor house set by marshes of estuary (reworked 15th to 16th C) retains fine hall with kitchen beneath

LLANRHWYDRYS (ANGLESEY), GWYNEDD
Church of St Rhwydrys Tiny 12th-C church with 13th-C chancel and 15th-C east window; Norman font

LLANRWST, GWYNEDD, 6, 4A
Church of St Gwrst [OCT] Medieval church much restored 19th-C retains fine traceried rood screen and loft of c.1500 carved with Emblems of the Passion and pigs eating acorns, with vine trails and acorn and oakleaf bands on loft parapet; stone coffin of c.1240 survives in Gwydir chapel (added 1633–4), traditionally believed to be that of Llywelyn the Great; tomb effigy of c.1440

LLANSANNOR / LLANSANWYR, GLAMORGAN, 1, 5A
Church of St Senwyr Small medieval church with west tower retains fine nave roof of 15th or early 16th C; good effigy of knight of c.1400

LLANSILIN, CLWYD, 6, 5B
Church of St Silin Double-naved church of 13th-C origin with late medieval remodelling and 19th-C west tower; good roofs
Hafod (4 km. / 2½ m. N) 15th-C house with 16th and early 17th-C range
Pen-y-Bryn (1 km. / ½ m. W of Ty-Newydd) Hall-house built 1400s, reworked 17th C and restored 1970–2

LLANSTEFFAN, DYFED, 6, 3D
Old Church of St Michael Ruined Norman church with 15th-C chancel; churchyard contains six graves with

decorated grave slabs and headstones dating from late 12th to early 13th C
LLansteffan Castle [CADW] Remains of 12th-C castle remodelled 13th C on promontory site of 6th-C Iron Age fort above Towy estuary include curtain walls, D-shaped towers and Great Gatehouse

LLANSTEPHAN, POWYS, 6, 5D
Church of St Stephen or Ystyffan 13th- and 14th-C church with work of 1867–8 has low west tower rebuilt 1500s; 17th-C roof to chancel

LLANTHONY, GWENT, 6, 5D
Llanthony Priory [CADW] Surviving ruins of great priory church built 1180–1230 include north nave arcade, crossing and western towers; surviving parts of monastic buildings converted to other uses include 13th-C Church of St David, perhaps original infirmary

LLANTILIO CROSSENNY, GWENT, 2, 2A
Church of St Teilo Large 13th-C church with central tower and later medieval additions; spire rebuilt 1708–9; Norman font
Hen Gwrt (Old Court) [CADW] Moated site (with no remaining structures) of both 13th- to 14th-C manor house belonging to Bishops of Llandaff and 16th- to 17th-C building, possibly hunting lodge

LLANTWIT MAJOR / LLANILLTUD FAWR, GLAMORGAN, 1, 5A
Church of St Illtyd Church of Norman origin retains original "western church" and tower with aisled nave and chancel added late 1200s; ruined late 15th-C chantry chapel to west; important group of 9th- and 10th-C crosses, early 13th-C niche with Jesse tree, and splendid 14th-C stone reredos; remains of chantry priest's house in churchyard
Grange Remains of grange of Tewkesbury Abbey with 13th-C gatehouse, circular dovecot, and poorly-preserved barn

LLANVAIR DISCOED, GWENT, 6, 5E
LLanvair Castle Remains of 13th-C castle including east tower and south curtain wall survive beside modern house built on part of site

LLANWENOG, DYFED, 6, 3D
Church of St Gwenog Medieval church with tall 15th-C tower and 18th-C barrel roof in nave; south chapel contains Norman font powerfully carved with twelve faces

LLANWNNOG, POWYS, 6, 4C
Church of St Gwynnog Simple medieval church much restored 1863 retains fine well-preserved screen and rood loft of c.1500

LLANYNYS, CLWYD, 6, 5A
Church of St Saeran 13th-C church with south nave added 15th or early 16th C and reworking of c.1768 and 19th C; rare mid 14th-C sepulchral cross, 15th-C wall painting, and early 16th-C south door

LLAWHADEN, DYFED, 6, 3D
LLawhaden Castle [CADW] Impressive 14th-C gatehouse and other ruins of 12th-C castle of bishops of St David's, transformed into great fortified mansion during late 13th to early 14th C, and with later 14th and 16th-C additions
Hospital Plain stone-vaulted building, believed to be remains of chapel of hospital founded 1287, survives behind village hall at other end of village street

LLYWEL, POWYS, 6, 4D
Church of St David Church founded 5th C and extensively rebuilt 1480s with west tower, low chancel arch, priest's doorway, and barrel vaults; replica of Llywel Stone (original in British Museum) with 8th-C or later inscriptions

LOBINSTOWN, CO. MEATH, 11, 4D
Killary Cross [Dúchas] (1.5 km. / 1 m. W) Surviving shaft of medieval cross with rich figural carving

LOCHALINE, HIGHLAND, 10, 3A
Keil Church [SCS] Church built 1898 contains fine set of medieval gravestones at west end; 15th-C cross to front
Kinlochaline Castle (3.5 km. / 2¼ m. NE) 15th-C tower house remodelled c.1600 and restored c.1890

LOCHANEILEAN CASTLE (2 km. / 1¼ m. SE of Rothiemurchus), HIGHLAND, 9, 2B
Lochaneilean Castle Remains of medieval castle set on island in loch with late 15th-C north tower, early 16th-C hall block, mid 16th-C curtain walling, and 17th-C additions

LOCHBUIE (Island of Mull) STRATHCLYDE (Inner Hebrides), 10, 3A
Castle of Moy Substantial ruins of plain 15th-C keep prettily set on rock by seashore

LOCH DOON CASTLE (16 km. / 10 m. S of Dalmellington) STRATHCLYDE, 10, 5D
Loch Doon Castle [HS] Ruins of castle built early 14th C on polygonal plan, originally island in loch but moved to present position mid 1930s when water level raised

LOCHINDORB CASTLE (10 km. / 6 m. NW of Grantown-on-Spey) HIGHLAND, 9, 4D
Lochindorb Castle Ruins of 13th-C castle dismantled 1450s survive on island in loch

LOCH LEVEN (1.5 km. / 1 m. E of Kinross), TAYSIDE, 8, 3D
Lochleven Castle [HS] (on Castle Island) Island in loch houses remains of 14th- or 15th-C tower house in curtain-walled enclosure with early 16th-C additions and alterations
Priory (on St Serf's Island) Small 12th-C nave, all that survives of Augustinian priory founded c.1150 by David I

LOCHMABEN, DUMFRIES AND GALLOWAY, 7, 1B
Lochmaben Castle [HS] (1 km. / ½ m. SE) Fragmentary remains of late 13th- and 14th-C castle built on promontory site jutting into Castle Loch

LOCHNAW CASTLE (3 km. / 2 m. W of Leswalt), DUMFRIES AND GALLOWAY, 10, 4E
Lochnaw Castle House with post-medieval alterations retains 15th-C tower at north-east with well preserved interior

LOCHORE, FIFE, 8, 3D
Lochore Castle Ruined 14th-C tower and late medieval curtain wall

LOCHRANZA (Isle of Arran) STRATHCLYDE, 10, 4C
Lochranza Castle [HS] Remains of 13th- to 14th-C hall castle enlarged as tower house during 1500s

LOCHWOOD TOWER (5 km. / 3 m. S of Beattock), DUMFRIES AND GALLOWAY, 7, 1B
Lochwood Tower Scanty but extensive remains of late 13th- or 14th-C castle remodelled 1400s include tower house built late 15th C with alterations of 1603

LOCKINGTON, E. RIDING OF YORKS, 7, 5E
Church of St Mary Church of Norman origin has original south doorway, north wall of nave, low 13th-C west tower, high chancel, and late 14th-C south chapel (reworked 1635)

LOCKINGTON, LEICS, 5, 4C
Church of St Nicholas Well-preserved church of 13th to 15th C retains chancel with lancet lights and fine east window to north aisle; fragments of Saxon and Norman sculpture, 15th-C screens and benches of c.1500

LODDON, NORFOLK, 4, 5D
Church of the Holy Trinity Spacious 15th-C church restored 19th C has west tower, embattled aisles and clerestory, and fine south porch with flushwork decoration; good font, early 16th-C screen and hammerbeam roof

LODE, CAMBS, 3, 2A
Anglesey Abbey [NT] Buildings of late Norman priory incorporated into mansion of c.1600, restored and altered 19th and 20th C

LONAN, ISLE OF MAN, 6, 1A
Old Parish Church Medieval church built on site of earlier structure retains traces of 12th-C work in west wall; collection of important later Celtic crosses with finely carved work

LONDON (Inner London areas, including Cities of London and Westminster), 3, 2C
Tower of London, Tower Hill, EC3 * Late 11th-C four-storeyed Norman keep known as White Tower (now museum), containing St John's Chapel (c.1090); curtain walls date from 13th C
Norman Churches Surviving parts of Norman churches include: crypt beneath Wren's St Mary-le-Bow (Cheapside, EC4); chancel and crossing of St Bartholomew the Great (Smithfield Street, EC1); circular nave of Temple Church (off Fleet Street, EC4) which has 13th-C aisled chancel
Palace of Westminster Fragmentary remains of Old Palace of Westminster include Westminster Hall (Parliament Square, SW1) built 1097–9 and remodelled 1394–1402 with magnificent hammerbeam roof, undercroft of St Stephen's Chapel (begun 1292) and Jewel Tower built c.1365 ([EH], Old Palace Yard, SW1, now museum)
Guildhall, EC2. Guildhall retains medieval porch, great hall and vaulted undercroft (c.1411–1440), much restored and rebuilt
Lincoln's Inn, Chancery Lane, WC2. Old Buildings (c.1490–1520) are east court and gatehouse of original college of lawyers founded 14th C
The Savoy Chapel, off Strand, WC2. Cruciform building which once formed part of Hospital of St John (1503)
Lambeth Palace, Palace Road, SE1. Late 15th- and early 16th-C residence of Archbishops of Canterbury with early 13th-C crypt and chapel
Winchester Palace [EH], Clink Street, SE1. Fragmentary early 14th-C remains of great hall of residence of Bishops of Winchester
Westminster Abbey *, SW1 [Chapter House, Pyx Chamber and Abbey Museum – EH] Great 13th-C royal church on site of Norman predecessor, built in a style inspired by contemporary French Gothic and richly ornamented with sculpture to house shrine of Edward the Confessor; nave and west end continued 14th to 16th C with west towers completed 18th C; chapter house of c.1245–50 and 13th- to 14th-C cloisters; Henry VII's Chapel built 1503–c.1512 with superb fan vaulting and royal monuments
Southwark Cathedral, SE1. Traces of original 12th-C priory church (founded 1106); 13th-C choir and retrochoir; 13th to 14th-C transepts and crossing; much restoration and nave rebuilt 19th C
Medieval Churches medieval churches surviving both 17th-C Fire of London and 20th-C conflict include: St Helen's, Bishopsgate (EC2) (mainly 14th and 15th-C); St Olave (Hart Street, EC3) (15th-C with 13th-C crypt); St Sepulchre (Holborn, EC1) (mid 15th-C with interior probably by Wren); aisles of All Hallows Barking by the Tower (Great Tower Street, EC3) (15th-C); St Margaret's, Westminster (Parliament Square, SW1) (late 15th- to early 16th-C)
London Wall [EH], Tower Hill. Well preserved section of Roman city wall heightened during medieval period
St John's Gate (Museum of Order of St John) *, Clerkenwell, EC1M. Norman crypt of 12th-C Priory of Clerkenwell survives under St John's Church; choir rebuilt 1721–3 for parish worship retains medieval walling; 16th-C gatehouse
Crosby Hall, Cheyne Walk and Danvers Street, Chelsea. Collegiate buildings of 1926–7 and 1950s incorporate sumptuous 15th-C hall on undercroft (re-erected 1908–10) from Bishopsgate house of rich wool merchant, Sir John Crosby; rich oriel window at dais end and excellent timber roof
See also: Beckenham, Beddington, Cheam, Coulsden, Croydon, East Barnet, Eltham, Hampton Court, Harlington, Harmondsworth, Lesnes Abbey, Rainham

LONG ASHTON, SOMERSET, 2,2B
Church of All Saints Late 14th-C embattled church with four-bay arcades and three-stage west tower; fine screen and late 15th-C monument to Sir Richard Choke (d.1486)
Gatcombe Court, Ashton Watering (open by written appointment only) Medieval manor house with 16th-C, 17th-C and later remodelling and additions

LONG CRENDON, BUCKS, 2,5A
Church of St Mary Substantial 13th-C church rebuilt 15th and 17th C retains 15th-C crossing tower and fine chancel roof
Courthouse [NT] House of 15th C with timber-framed upper floor overhanging stone base; main upper room has open queen-post roof
Long Crendon Manor 15th-C manor house extensively rebuilt 1920s retains hall and 16th-C west wing; 15th-C hall screen from Kentish house
Gatehouse 15th-C stone gatehouse, altered 17th and 18th C

LONGDON, STAFFS, 5,3C
Church of St James Church of Norman origin with medieval and 19th-C additions retains original south doorway, chancel arch, late 13th-C chancel, and south chapel added c.1500; font has Norman bowl and 13th-C stem

LONGFIELD, KENT, 3,3C
Church of St Mary Magdalene Medieval church enlarged 1889 has 13th-C chancel with attached piscina and aumbry

LONG MARTON, CUMBRIA, 7,2C
Church of St Margaret and St James Church built 11th and 12th C has original south and west doorways with lively tympana, Norman west tower, and 12th-C east end to 14th-C chancel

LONG MELFORD, SUFFOLK, 3,3A
Church of the Holy Trinity Large handsome church of mainly c.1460–c.1495 has projecting chancel, low Lady Chapel with fine roofs, and rich south front with tall porch; lavish Clopton Chantry built c.1500 with sedilia, piscina and tomb chest; much late 15th-C stained glass and good monuments

LONGNOR, SHROPS, 5,2D
Church of St Mary the Virgin Small well-preserved church built c.1260–70 with later belfry
Moat House [HHA] Medieval black-and-white house dating from 1467 with fine timberwork and remains of hall roof

LONGSTANTON, CAMBS, 4,2E
Church of All Saints Church with 19th-C work retains fine south transept of c.1340, 14th-C arcades, and later medieval west tower; good east chancel window of c.1320–40 and interesting 15th-C font
Church of St Michael Fine church built mainly c.1230 with impressive west front and higher chancel; exquisite double piscina

LONG STRATTON, NORFOLK, 4,4E
Church of St Mary [OCT] Medieval church with 14th-C arcades, round tower, 15th-C font, and rare surviving sexton's wheel (used for determining day of Lady Fast)

LONG SUTTON, LINCS, 4,2D
Church of St Mary Church of Norman origin much reworked 13th to 15th and 19th C retains original nave and chancel arch, and early 13th-C tower with lead spire

LONG SUTTON, SOMERSET, 2,2C
Church of the Holy Trinity Church built c.1490 with embattled clerestory and chancel chapels, and high west tower; good nave roof, octagonal font and rood screen

LONGTHORPE, CAMBS, 4,1D
Longthorpe Tower [EH] Square tower of c.1300 with two vaulted rooms adjoins late 13th-C hall (part of fortified manor house); extensive wall paintings of c.1330, among finest in northern Europe

LONGTOWN, HEREFS, 2,1A
Longtown Castle [EH] Norman motte and bailey castle with circular keep of c.1200

LONG WITTENHAM, OXON, 2,5B
Church of St Mary Norman church retains original chancel arch, chancel and south arcade of c.1250, south chapel built c.1275, 15th-C clerestory and timber south porch; late Norman lead font and fine late 13th-C piscina-monument

LORRHA, CO. TIPPERARY, 12,3B
Priory [Dúchas] Ruined church of Dominican friary founded c.1269; adjacent Catholic church (1812) occupies site of conventual buildings and incorporates medieval fragments
St Ruadhan's Church (or Abbey) [Dúchas] Remains of 15th-C church of Augustinian priory with fine windows and rich west doorway
Church of Ireland Church [Dúchas] Medieval church (in partial use) has roofless nave and ornamented 15th-C south doorway

LOSTWITHIEL, CORNWALL, 1,3D
Church of St Bartholomew Church of 13th and 14th C has impressive tower with octagonal screen, and rich traceried east window; 14th-C octagonal font with fine carved figures
Bridge Bridge of early 14th and late 17th C with five pointed arches

LOUGHBOROUGH, LEICS, 5,5C
Church of All Saints Spacious early 14th-C church with additions of early 16th C and 1860–3 retains imposing west tower, fine nave roof, transepts, aisles and outer south aisle; early 14th-C piscinas and 15th-C brasses
Old Rectory Substantial remains of early 14th-C rectory altered 16th to 18th C and partially demolished 1962

LOUGHCREW, CO. MEATH, 11,4D
Loughcrew Church Well-preserved late medieval manorial church remodelled 18th C and abandoned 1843 retains large residential tower to west, and long body with projecting south chapel

LOUGHINISLAND, CO. DOWN, 11,5D
Churches [EHS] Former island in lake has remains of three churches; the middle one built probably 13th C, the large north building of 15th C, and the south (MacCartan's) church dated 1636

LOUGHMOE, CO. TIPPERARY, 12,4B
Castle [Dúchas] House (known as "The Court") built 17th C incorporates 15th- or 16th-C tower house at south end

LOUGHOR / CASLLWCHWR
GLAMORGAN
Loughor Castle [CADW] Small early 14th-C rectangular tower house on mound

LOUGHREA, CO. GALWAY, 12,3B
Loughrea Priory [Dúchas] Well-preserved church of Carmelite priory founded 13th or early 14th C with south transept, lancet windows, and 15th-C tower and additions
Gate * Fragment of 15th-C town gate converted into museum of ecclesiastical art

LOUTH, CO. LOUTH, 11,4C
St Mochta's House [Dúchas] Stone oratory built 10th or 11th C with steeply pitched roof and internal barrel-vault
Louth Abbey Roofless medieval church, all that survives of extensive and wealthy Augustinian abbey founded 1148, with large windows to chancel, fine early 14th-C capitals to rere-arch on south wall, and fragment of rood screen

LOUTH, LINCS, 4,2B
Church of St James Church built c.1430–40 and restored 19th C has splendid tower of c.1440–50 partly open to interior, and spire of 1501–15; good nave roof with angel figures and 15th-C chest

LOWER BROCKHAMPTON
HEREFS, 5,2E
Lower Brockhampton [NT] Handsome timber-framed house and gatehouse built late 14th and late 15th C in picturesque setting with moat; ruins of 12th-C chapel

LOWER PEOVER, CHESHIRE, 5,2B
Church of St Oswald Important 14th-C timber-framed church with 13th-C origins has original timbers in nave roof; west tower of 1582; 17th-C chancel chapels and alterations of 1852

LOWER WINCHENDON,
BUCKS, 2,5A
Church of St Nicholas Medieval church with late 13th-C chancel arch, west tower added 1400s, and later work; 15th-C brasses
Nether Winchendon House * House remodelled 16th C and 1798–1803 and much restored 20th C retains good 15th-C timber-framed core

LOWESTOFT, SUFFOLK, 4,5E
Church of St Margaret Spacious late 15th-C church with much flushwork decoration retains tall west tower built c.1300 and 14th-C crypt; font of 1400s and lectern dated 1504

LOWICK, NORTHANTS, 4,1E
Church of St Peter Church built mainly late 14th to late 15th C has west tower with recessed octagonal top storey, south transept, north chapel and tall windows; good monuments and stained glass of c.1310–30

LOWTHORPE, E. RIDING OF
YORKS, 7,5D
Church of St Martin Medieval church altered 1776–7 and 1859 with ruined chancel of mid 1300s; part of Saxon cross and fine 14th-C monument; cross in churchyard possibly dating from 12th C

LUBENHAM, LEICS, 5,5D
Church of All Saints Mainly 13th-C church has early north doorway and chancel of late 1200s; late 13th-C lower parts of west tower with upper levels added 16th C

LUDGERSHALL, WILTS, 2,4C
Church of St James Church of Norman origin with medieval reworking retains 13th-C chancel and north and south chapels; 17th-C west tower
Ludgershall Castle [EH] Earthworks and ruins of 12th-C royal castle enlarged 13th and 14th C as hunting palace
Cross [EH], Castle Street. Late medieval cross with well-preserved head

LUDHAM, NORFOLK, 4,5D
Church of St Catherine Medieval church with 14th-C west tower and chancel, 15th-C arcades and hammerbeam roof to nave; rich 14th-C sedilia, good font, screen dated 1493 and 15th-C poor box
St Benet's Abbey Fragments of Saxon priory with ruins of church and gatehouse

LUDLOW, SHROPSHIRE, 5,2D
Ludlow Castle *, Castle Square Substantial remains of Norman Castle built c.1085 with impressive early 12th-C gatehouse keep and circular chapel of c.1140; medieval work includes 14th-C hall range
Church of St Laurence Large cruciform church of mainly 15th C retains Norman work, 13th-C south doorway, and hexagonal south porch of c.1300–20; tall crossing tower built c.1453–79; furnishings include choir stalls with lively misericords of c.1447 and carved poppyheads
Town Plan and Buildings Town's 12th-C grid plan can be traced in present streets; surviving parts of 13th-C town walls are best seen at lower end of Old Street; good medieval buildings include 13th-C Broad Gate, 15th-C Guildhall with 18th-C additions, and Hosyer's Almshouses founded 1486 and rebuilt 1758

LULLINGSTONE, KENT, 3,2C
Church of St Botolph Modest early 14th-C church with early 16th- and early 18th-C additions retains fine rood screen of 1510–1522 and monument of c.1522
Lullingstone Castle [HHA] Medieval and 16th-C house rebuilt early 18th C

LULLINGTON, SOMERSET, 2,2C
Church of All Saints Well-preserved Norman church retains fine north doorway with carved tympanum and central tower with 15th-C upper levels; richly carved Norman font

LUMLEY CASTLE, CO. DURHAM
See Great Lumley

LUNDA WICK (Unst), SHETLAND
Church Ruins of 12th-C church with later remodelling survive in graveyard

LUPPITT, DEVON, 2,1D
Church of St Mary Medieval church with late 13th- to early 14th-C chancel, 15th-C west tower and original wagon roofs meeting in impressive crossing; Norman font and pillar piscina

LUSK, CO. DUBLIN, 11,5D
Round Tower and Tower House [Dúchas] Splendid five-storeyed Round Tower with original conical roof, sole survivor of monastery founded c.500, stands adjacent to fine later medieval square tower (c.1500) and 19th-C church

LUSS, STRATHCLYDE, 10,4B
Luss Parish Church [SCS] Ancient graveyard of pretty church built 1875 by Loch Lomond contains several good monuments including old stone font and medieval effigy of St Kessog

LUSTLEIGH, DEVON, 1,5C
Church of St John Church with 13th-C chancel and later medieval west tower and south transept; inscribed stone of probably c.550–600, effigies, and lavishly carved 16th-C screen
Uphill and Great Hall, Mapstone Hill Medieval house restored and enlarged 19th C and subdivided 20th C retains excellent 15th-C open roofs to hall and solar

LUTON, BEDS
Church of St Mary Large cruciform church of 13th to 15th C with fine early 14th-C work, including font with ornate octagonal stone canopy, and splendid 15th-C Wenlock and Barnard Chapels; medieval monuments and brasses
Moat House Late 14th-C house with hall roof of c.1500
Someries Castle Remains of late 15th-C manor house with brick gatehouse and chapel

LUTTERWORTH, LEICS, 5,5D
Church of St Mary Large mainly 13th-C church with 18th- and 19th-C work retains

fine 14th-C aisle roofs and two wall paintings; 15th-C pulpit, tomb chest and brasses

LYDBURY NORTH, SHROPS, 5,1D
Church of St Michael Norman church restored 1901 with early nave, priest's door and chancel of c.1175–80, long transepts and early 13th-C west tower; early 16th-C timber porch and good screens

LYDD, KENT, 3,4E
Church of All Saints Church of Saxon and earlier origin with much work of 13th and 15th C retains high west tower built 1442–6 and chancel rebuilt mid 20th C; numerous medieval brasses

LYDDINGTON, RUTLAND, 4,1D
Church of St Andrew 14th-C church reworked 15th and 19th C has original west tower and tall 15th-C arcades; rood screen with painted panels, late medieval wall paintings and good monuments
Bede House [EH] Blue Coat Lane Surviving range of 15th-C palace of Bishops of Lincoln altered 16th to 18th C with fine south front; presence and privy chambers have early 16th-C ceilings with carved coving and medieval painted glass; early 16th-C summerhouse

LYDFORD, DEVON, 1,4C
Lydford Castles and Saxon Town [EH / NT] Remains of two castles, one early Norman, the other late 12th-C (rebuilt 13th and 17th C), on dramatic promontory site by gorge of River Lyd; defences and street plan of Saxon town
Church of St Petrock 13th-C church reworked 15th and 19th C with west tower and early Norman font

LYMINGE, KENT, 3,4D
Church of St Mary and St Ethelburga Spacious church built c.965 with medieval remodelling has 14th-C chancel arch, good 15th-C nave roof, early 16th-C north aisle and short west tower

LYMPNE, KENT, 3,4D
Church of St Stephen Ragstone church of Norman origin restored 1878–80 retains original four-stage central tower, 12th-C nave and 13th-C chancel with stone benches; Norman font
Lympne Castle * Medieval castle with 13th-C east tower, 14th-C main range and 15th-C west tower; crown-post roofs in hall and great chamber

LYTES CARY MANOR, SOMERSET, 2,2D
See Charlton Mackrell

MACCLESFIELD, CHESHIRE, 5,3B
Church of St Michael (formerly All Hallows) Church of 13th-C origin almost totally rebuilt 1898–1901 retains Savage (south) Chapel built between 1501 and 1507; fine collection of medieval monuments including many to Savage family and excellent Pardon Brass of Roger Legh (d.1506)
West Park Park contains three Anglo-Danish cross shafts

MACHYNLLETH, POWYS, 6,4C
Owain Glyndwr's Parliament House Rare surviving town house built 15th C

MACOSQUIN, CO. LONDONDERRY, 11,4A
High Cross of St Comgal (4.5 km. / 2 ¾ m. E) Base and shaft of tall late 9th- or early 10th-C cross survive in graveyard by Camus House (site of former monastery and possibly of early 13th-C abbey)

MADLEY, HEREFS, 5,2E
Church of Nativity of the Virgin Church of Norman origin has original north transept (now porch), fine early 13th-C west tower and early 14th-C chancel with apse; rib-vaulted crypt, 13th-C ironwork and medieval stained glass; churchyard cross

MAGHERA, CO. LONDONDERRY, 11,4B
Maghera Old Church [EHS] Shell of medieval church with 17th-C tower and additions; remarkable flat-headed west doorway of c.1100 with lintel carved with Crucifixion; part of sheila-na-gig built into north of tower

MAGHERA (5 km. / 3 m. N of Newcastle), CO. DOWN, 11,5C
Maghera Round Tower and Church [EHS] Stump of Round Tower survives on site of monastery founded 6th C; ruined medieval parish church (possibly 13th-C) in graveyard to east of present building

MAGHERABEG ABBEY CO. DONEGAL, 11,3B
See Donegal

MAGHERALIN (3 km. / 2 m. SW of Moira), CO. DOWN, 11,5C
Church Remains of 15th-C parish church (dismantled 1845) on site of monastery founded 600s; residential tower added 17th C and later church incorporated as side chapel

MAGHULL, MERSEYSIDE, 5,2A
Church of Old St Andrew Remains of late 13th-C chancel and north chapel of medieval church

**MAGILLIGAN,
  CO. LONDONDERRY, 11,4A**
Tamlaghtard Church (4 km. / 2 ½ m.SW) Remains of narrow medieval church restored 1660 with incomplete mortuary house in churchyard (possibly 12th-C and said to contain grave of St Aidan, Bishop of Lindisfarne)
Cross (0.5 km. / ¼ m. NW of St Cadan's Church) Tall late medieval stone with relief carving of cross

MAGOR, GWENT, 6,5E
Church of St Mary Large cruciform 13th-C church of Norman origin enlarged during later Middle Ages has late medieval capitals of nave arcades decorated with carved angels, and splendid two-storeyed 15th-C porch; fragmentary remains of priory buildings in churchyard

MAHEE ISLAND (11 km. / 7 m. SE of Comber), CO. DOWN, 11,5C
Nendrum Monastic Site (or Abbey) [EHS] Important early Christian monastic site excavated 1922–4 has restored walled enclosures on hill with fragmentary remains of Round Tower, 12th-C church (west wall reconstructed with sundial 1920s) and other buildings

MAIDEN STONE (nr Chapel of Garioch, 7.5 km. / 4 ½ m. NW of Inverurie), GRAMPIAN, 8,4B
Maiden Stone [HS] Magnificent 9th-C cross slab with Celtic cross and carved Pictish symbols

MAIDS MORETON, BUCKS, 2,5A
Church of St Edmund Mid 15th-C church has large windows, wide nave with fan-vaulted porches, and good west tower; Norman font and rich sedilia in chancel

MAIDSTONE, KENT, 3,3D
Church of All Saints Handsome church begun 1395 has south-west tower, tall nave and chancel arcades, and 19th-C roofs; fine sedilia with attached 15th-C monument
Church of St Peter Mid 13th-C chapel of hospital founded after 1244, rebuilt as parish church 1836–7
Archbishop's College Late 14th-C college incorporates three-storeyed gate tower, River Tower, and Master's House
Archbishop's Palace * Mid 14th-C palace with 16th and early 20th-C work; associated 13th-C gatehouse

Tithe Barn (or stables) Large, handsome 15th-C stone tithe barn with outer staircase to upper floor and porch with timber-framed upper storey
Corpus Christi Hall 15th-C hall of Fraternity much restored 19th and 20th C retains crown-post roof

MALAHIDE, CO. DUBLIN, 11,5D
Malahide Castle * Handsome castle much rebuilt late 18th and early 19th C encloses original 15th-C tower house with well preserved medieval Great Hall; castle houses fine collection of art works and furniture
Abbey Ruins of 15th- to 16th-C manorial church survive to east of castle; two sheila-na-gigs and fine 15th-C effigy of Maud Plunket

MALBOROUGH, DEVON, 1,4E
Church of All Saints Medieval church restored 1870 has 13th-C tower arch and good two-storeyed south porch; Norman font
Yarde Medieval Farmhouse * Medieval farmhouse on courtyard plan with front dated 1718

MALDON, ESSEX, 3,3B
Moot Hall, High Street. 15th-C brick tower used as moot hall after 1576; porch added c.1830
Inns Blue Boar Hotel retains 15th-C stabling behind front of c.1800; timber-framed 16th-C Swan Hotel (front much reworked)
St Giles's Hospital Remaining part of east end of 12th-C leper hospital chapel
Church of All Saints 13th-C church with unique triangular tower and hexagonal spire; rich south aisle of c.1340 with crypt beneath
Vicarage Handsome 15th-C timber-framed building

MALMESBURY, WILTS, 2,3B
Malmesbury Abbey Surviving church of abbey built c.1160–70, damaged and converted to parish church 16th C, retains original nave with gallery and early 14th-C vault, south porch with splendid figural carving, and part of west front; 15th-C stone screens to rib-vaulted aisles and tomb chest of King Athelstan
Market Cross Fine octagonal market cross of c.1500 with battlements and vaulted lantern

MALPAS, CHESHIRE, 5,2B
Church of St Oswald Church of early 14th C rebuilt in late 15th C, early 16th C and

c.1864 retains original outer walls and chancel arch; fine nave roof has carved angels with outspread wings; iron bound chest, good screens and alabaster effigies of 1522

MALTON, N. YORKS, 7,4D
Church of St Mary Western part of nave and most of west front of church belonging to Gilbertine priory founded c.1150; lavish west doorway, south-west tower, and remodelling of c.1500

MANAAN CASTLE [Dúchas], CO. MONAGHAN, 11,4C
See Donaghmoyne

MANATON, DEVON, 1,5C
Upper Hall, Neadon Small late 15th-C house restored 1982–3 retains fine first floor hall with garderobe and fireplace at dais end
Hound Tor Deserted Medieval Village [EH] (2.5 km. / 1 ½ m. S) Remains of deserted medieval farmsteads

MANCHESTER, GREATER MANCHESTER, 5,3A
Cathedral * Ornate cathedral built as parish church c.1420–c.1520 (much reworked 19th and 20th C) with chantry chapels, octagonal chapter house and fine roofs; splendid stalls of c.1505–10 with canopies and misericords
Chetham's Hospital Long Millgate; Well-preserved 15th-C collegiate buildings converted to hospital mid 17th C
Wellington Inn, Old Shambles Sole surviving timber-framed building in central Manchester

MANISTERNAGALLIAGHDUFF ABBEY, CO. LIMERICK, 12,2C
See Shanagolden

MANNINGFORD BRUCE, WILTS, 2,3C
Church of St Peter Complete Norman church with apse, 13th-C west window, and 15th-C west tower; bell turret, wagon roof, and chancel ceiling added 1882

MANNINGTON HALL, NORFOLK, 4,4C
Mannington Hall Moated manor house licensed 1451 and remodelled mid 19th C with fine south front

MANORBIER, DYFED, 6,2E
Manorbier Castle [CADW] Norman castle with 12th-C hall and Round Tower and extensive 13th and 14th-C additions including gatehouse and chapel built around inner ward; further accretions

of 16th to 17th and late 19th to 20th C
Dovecot (N of castle car park) Circular medieval dovecot with corbelled roof and surviving nesting boxes
Church of St James Norman church greatly enlarged 13th C has tunnel-vaulted nave and arcades with square pillars and pointed arches

MANSFIELD, NOTTS, 5,5B
Church of St Peter Norman church with 13th- to 15th-C additions retains original west tower with 14th-C top, arcades of c.1300, and east end of c.1475

MANTON, RUTLAND, 4,1D
Church of St Mary Medieval church with north doorway and aisle arcades of c.1200, and imposing 13th-C west front; 15th-C transepts and chancel added 1796

MARCH, CAMBS, 4,2D
Church of St Wendreda Church rebuilt early 16th and 19th C retains mid 14th-C chancel arch and south arcade; rich 16th-C additions include remarkable double hammerbeam roof with carved angels

MARGAM, GLAMORGAN, 6,4E
Stones Museum [CADW] Early 19th-C school room houses splendid collection of early Christian and monastic crosses, tomb slabs and monuments and includes important Saxon Conbelin Stone
Church of St Mary Surviving nave of church of Cistercian abbey built c.1150–70 and much remodelled c.1805–10 retains fine arcades and west front
Monastic Buildings, Margam Park * Remains of monastic buildings include fine, roofless polygonal chapter house of c.1200 with vaulted vestibule and fragments of 13th-C church

MARGARETTING, ESSEX, 3,3B
Church of St Margaret Late medieval church retains fine 15th-C timber north porch, and timber west tower with shingled broach spire and ten free-standing supporting posts; good octagonal font and Tree of Jesse in east window

MARGATE, KENT, 3,5C
Church of St John the Baptist High Street Church of Norman origin restored 19th C has 12th-C arcades, chancel, north doorway of c.1300, 14th-C north-west tower, and low north-east vestry; unusual late medieval brasses
Salmestone Grange Nash Road. Surviving buildings of grange of St Augustine's Abbey include early 14th-C hall, kitchen range, and chapel consecrated 1326

MARKENFIELD HALL (5 km. / 3 m. SSW of Ripon), N. YORKS, 7, 3D
Markenfield Hall, Hell Wath Lane * Fortified house licensed 1310 with moated forecourt and impressive south front

MARKET BOSWORTH, LEICS, 5, 4D
Church of St Peter Church of early 14th and 15th C much restored 1893 with tall west tower; fine vaulted sedilia and mid 14th-C font

MARKET HARBOROUGH, LEICS, 5, 5D
Church of St Dionysius 14th-C church rebuilt 15th and 19th C has impressive west tower begun c.1300 and embattled body; fine traceried windows in chancel of c.1320–30 and 15th-C nave arcades

MARKET OVERTON, RUTLAND, 4, 1D
Church of St Peter and St Paul Church of Saxon origin almost wholly rebuilt 14th C retains original tower arch; chancel remodelled 1857

MARKINCH, FIFE, 8, 3D
Parish Church, Kirk Brae Church rebuilt 1786 with 19th-C additions retains tall west tower of c.1200 with spire added 1807

MARLFIELD, CO. TIPPERARY, 12, 4C
Church [Dúchas] 19th-C church occupying site of Cistercian abbey of Inishlounaght (founded before 1148, re-endowed 1187) incorporates medieval fragments including doorway of c.1200 and 15th-C east window

MARNHAM, NOTTS, 5, 5B
Church of St Wilfrid Medieval church with fine early 13th-C south arcade, chancel arch and north chancel chapel

MAROWN, ISLE OF MAN, 6, 1A
Chapel of St Trinian (1.5 km. / 1 m. W of Crosby, near Highlander Hotel) Roofless ruins of church built c.1200 and enlarged 14th C (formerly belonging to Whithorn Priory, Scotland);

MARSTON MORETAINE, BEDS, 3, 1A
Church of St Mary 14th-C church rebuilt 15th C retains early chancel and vaulted vestry; nave roof and fine north porch of early 1400s; 15th-C brasses

MARTINSTOWN CASTLE, CO. WESTMEATH, 11, 4D
See Castletown-Delvin

MARTOCK, SOMERSET, 2, 2D
Church of All Saints Mainly 15th-C church with embattled south porch, aisles, chancel chapels, and large west tower; fine interior with nave roof dated 1513
Treasurer's House [NT] Small 13th- and 14th-C house has hall with open roof and 15th-C kitchen

MARTON, CHESHIRE, 5, 3B
Church of St James and St Paul Timber-framed church founded mid 14th C and altered 19th C with unusual tower; 14th-C effigies of knights and remains of wall paintings

MARWOOD, DEVON, 1, 4B
Church of St Michael 13th-C church remodelled 14th, 16th and 19th C has wagon roofs and fine 16th-C screen; back of rood loft survives

MASHAM, N. YORKS, 7, 3D
Church of St Mary Church of Norman origin much reworked 19th C has original west tower with late 14th- or 15th-C octagonal bell stage and late medieval south porch; good Saxon cross shaft with carved figures survives outside church

MATHERN, GWENT, 2, 2B
Manor House Site (S of Moynes Court) Moated site of palace, used by Bishops of Llandaff from early 15th to 18th C and restored as private house during late 19th to early 20th C
Church of St Tewdric Early medieval church enlarged 15th C with south porch and tall tower

MATHON, HEREFS, 5, 2E
Church of St John the Baptist Church retains early Norman nave with original doorways, later Norman chancel with priest's doorway, and 14th-C west tower

MATTERSEY, NOTTS, 5, 5A
Mattersey Priory [EH] Remains of Gilbertine priory founded c.1185 with 13th-C dorter and refectory ranges
Church of All Saints Medieval church with 13th-C arcade to north chancel chapel and 14th-C aisle arcades; two finely carved panels of 1300s

MAUCHLINE, STRATHCLYDE, 10, 5C
Abbot Hunter's Tower Handsome tower house with rib-vaulted first floor hall, all that survives of residence built c.1444–71 by Abbot Hunter on grange of Melrose Abbey

MAUGHOLD, ISLE OF MAN, 6, 1A
Church of St Maughold Crosses and Chapels; Medieval church built on site of early Christian monastery has reset 11th- or 12th-C arch to west doorway and small 13th-C windows to nave; fragments of 14th-C east window survive behind altar; churchyard contains fine and extensive collection of Celtic and Norse crosses (7th- to 12th-C) with good carving and handsome 14th-C pillar cross; ruins of three restored chapels or keeills (possibly 8th to 12th-C)

MAUNSEL HOUSE, SOMERSET, 2, 1D
See North Newton

MAWGAN-IN-MENEAGE CORNWALL, 1, 2E
Church of St Mawgan Medieval church retains two 13th-C windows in chancel, fine west tower, transepts, and 15th-C north aisle with wagon roof; inscribed Saxon cross
Trelowarren House built c.1450 with bay window of 1662, chapel wing extended c.1750, and 19th-C alterations

MAWGAN-IN-PYDAR CORNWALL, 1, 2D
Church of St Mawgan Spacious medieval church reworked 1860–1 has 13th-C nave with 15th-C south aisle, south tower with later upper levels, and transepts; good font, rood screen, 15th-C bench ends, and pulpit of c.1530
Lanherne Cross Fine Saxon cross with rich carving survives in garden of post medieval convent

MAXEY, CAMBS, 4, 1D
Church of St Peter Church of Norman origin retains early 12th-C west tower (15th-C top), south arcade of c.1175–95 and 12th-C north arcade; small late 13th-C treasury adjoining chancel; fine north chancel chapel founded 1367 as chantry; 15th-C Easter Sepulchre

MAXSTOKE, WARWS, 5, 4D
Maxstoke Castle Moated castle licensed 1346 with later alterations has polygonal corner towers, imposing gatehouse, and 16th-C timber-framing on north side
Priory Remains of Augustinian priory consecrated 1342 with imposing crossing tower of church, part of infirmary, and two gatehouses
Church of St Michael Simple church built mid 14th C and remodelled 18th C with later bell turret

MAYBOLE, STRATHCLYDE, 10, 4D
Maybole Collegiate Church [HS] (view exterior only) Remains of building established 1371 as chapel (associated college founded 1373) with barrel-vaulted sacristy on north later enlarged as Kennedy burial place

MAYFIELD, E. SUSSEX, 3, 2D
Church of St Dunstan Spacious church built mainly late 14th to 15th C retains short west tower of 1200s with later spire
Convent of the Holy Child Jesus Convent incorporates remains of medieval archbishop's palace with fine 14th-C hall converted to chapel 1863–6 and 15th-C gatehouse

MAYFIELD, STAFFS, 5, 4B
Church of St John the Baptist Late Norman church with medieval and mid 19th-C remodelling retains 12th-C south doorway, south arcade, early 14th-C chancel, and west tower dated 1515

MAYNOOTH, CO. KILDARE, 11, 4D
Maynooth Castle [Dúchas] Remains of massive castle begun probably 1203 and enlarged 1426 include large tower, fine gatehouse and parts of curtain wall

MEARE, SOMERSET, 2, 2C
Church of St Mary Church dedicated 1323 with 15th-C additions retains original chancel, west tower and south door; 15th-C font and stone pulpit
Manor House Manor house built c.1340, formerly used as summer palace by Abbots of Glastonbury
Fish House [EH] Plain and well-preserved fisherman's house of early 14th C

MEARNS (E of Newton Mearns), STRATHCLYDE, 10, 5C
Mearns Castle Plain, well-preserved 15th-C tower house with fine machicolation projecting from wall head

MEELICK, CO. GALWAY, 12, 3B
Friary [Dúchas] Church (re-roofed and still in use) of Franciscan friary founded 1414 on hill near River Shannon with later alterations

MEELICK, CO. MAYO, 11, 2C
Round Tower [Dúchas] Good Round Tower on monastic site; nearby gravestone with inscription

MEIFOD, POWYS, 6, 5B
Church of St Tysilio and St Mary Church of Norman origin on important early site retains 12th-C work at west of building, 14th-C south doorway, 15th-C west tower, and north aisle rebuilt 1871–2; fine 9th- or 10th-C cross slab

MEIGLE, TAYSIDE, 8, 3C
Meigle Sculptured Stones Museum [HS]
Museum (old school) houses outstanding
collection of early Christian stones of 7th
to 10th C with carved and inscribed work,
all found at and around old churchyard

MELBOURN, CAMBS, 3, 2A
Church of All Saints 13th-C church with
west tower, clerestory, nave roof and other
additions of early 16th C; 13th-C font, rood
screen of 1504 and choir stalls with tracery
and poppyheads
Cottages Row of small late medieval
houses built as terrace under single
thatched roof

MELBOURNE, DERBYS, 5, 4C
Church of St Michael and St Mary
11th- or early 12th-C church retains fine
nave, crossing, and west front with two
incomplete towers; Norman font,
13th-C monuments and 14th-C
painting on arcade piers

MELBURY BUBB, DORSET, 2, 2D
Church of St Mary 15th-C church rebuilt
19th C has superb cylindrical Saxon font
carved with barbaric intertwined animals
and fragments of 15th-C stained glass

MELBURY SAMPFORD,
DORSET, 2, 2D
Church of St Mary Mainly 15th-C church
with handsome marble and alabaster
monument of 1467 and heraldic stained
glass of c.1440

MELLIFONT ABBEY (10 km. / 6 m.
NW of Drogheda)
CO. LOUTH, 11, 4D
Mellifont Abbey [Dúchas] Fragmentary
remains of important Cistercian abbey
founded 1142 with ambitious octagonal
lavabo of c.1200, chapter house of c.1220,
and extensive foundations showing plan
of church and monastic buildings; ruined
15th-C parish church and late medieval
gatehouse survive to north

MELLS, SOMERSET, 2, 2C
Church of St Andrew Embattled church
built mainly 15th and early 16th C has tall
west tower, vaulted south porch, and
polygonal chapel of 1485

MELROSE, BORDERS, 7, 2A
Melrose Abbey [HS] Ruined mainly late
14th- and mid 15th-C buildings of beautiful
Cistercian abbey founded c.1136, successor
of early monastery and burial place of
heart of Robert Bruce, include church
with transepts (fine window to south),

remains of tower, unusual Monk's Choir,
sacristy, and traces of domestic quarters;
excellent bosses, capitals and figure sculpture; restored Commendator's House
(remodelled from abbot's house c.1590)

MELTON MOWBRAY, LEICS, 5, 5C
Church of St Mary Large church of 13th
to 15th C restored 19th C has nave, aisles,
transepts, and chancel of c.1280–c.1330 and
rich west porch built 1320–30; impressive,
high tower and 15th-C clerestory
Anne of Cleves' House, Burton Street
14th-C house with later additions retains
buttresses of original hall on street façade

MELVERLEY, SHROPS, 5, 1C
Church of St Peter Small black-and-white
timber-framed church built 15th or early
16th C and restored 1878; belfry, and fine
interior and roof

MENDLESHAM, SUFFOLK, 4, 4E
Church of St Mary 13th- and 15th-C
church has original six-bay arcade,
south and north doorways, and
elaborate later west tower; north
porch with armoury above

MERCHISTON (Edinburgh),
LOTHIAN, 8, 3E
Merchiston Castle, Napier College
College built 1961 around late medieval
tower house

MERE, WILTS, 2, 3D
Church of St Michael Large mainly 14th-C
church retains chancel of 1200s, rich north
chapel built c.1325, south chapel of c.1350,
two-storeyed north porch, and 15th-C
aisle arcades; fine chapel and rood screens,
stalls with misericords, and monuments;
Chantry House Late medieval house with
hall and two storeyed solar end
Woodlands Manor (1.5 km. / 1 m. SSE)
Medieval manor house retains 14th-C
chapel restored 1921 and hall with
good roof

MEREVALE, WARWS, 5, 4D
Merevale Abbey Surviving walls of 13th-C
refectory of Cistercian abbey founded 1148
Church of Our Lady Medieval church
(original "chapel at the gate" of monastic
precinct) has late 13th-C chancel arch,
short nave, and chancel added c.1500; early
14th-C Jesse tree in east window, unusual
wooden screen, and good monuments
and brasses

MERIDEN, WARWS, 5, 4D
Church of St Lawrence Medieval church
reworked 19th C retains Norman chancel

enlarged 13th C, south arcade of c.1400,
15th-C north arcade and west tower
Walsh Hall Timber-framed hall-house
built c.1500 with additions of 1938

MERKLAND SMITHY
(nr Ecclefechan), DUMFRIES AND
GALLOWAY, 7, 1B
Merkland Cross [HS] Fine tall 15th-C
wayside cross with carved work,
supposedly erected to commemorate
death of a Maxwell in battle

MERSHAM, KENT, 3, 4D
Church of St John the Baptist Church of
Norman origin with late 13th-C tower and
fine west window of c.1396
Court Lodge 14th-C stone house with tall
hipped roof

MERSTHAM, SURREY, 3, 2D
Church of St Katharine 13th-C church
remodelled 15th C retains tower built
c.1220, west doorway, arcades, and
clerestory; remains of blank arcading
in chancel

MERTHYR CYNOG, POWYS, 6, 4D
Church of St Cynog Church built 12th to
14th C with low west tower and long
chancel; 12th-C font, stoup, and fine
timber screen of 1300s

MERTHYR MAWR,
GLAMORGAN, 6, 4E
Church of St Teilo Church built 1849–51
with Lapidary Collection of 11th- to
12th-C crosses and headstones housed
in shelter to north
St Roch Chapel Small 15th-C chapel
containing two fine 11th-C cross shafts
New Inn Bridge Late medieval bridge
Candleston Castle Ruined 14th-C fortified
manor house has tower and first floor hall
with well-preserved chimneypiece of
c.1500

MERTHYR TYDFIL,
GLAMORGAN, 6, 4E
Morlais Castle Remains of hilltop castle
built 1288–94 include impressive vaulted
undercroft of south keep

MERTON, NORFOLK, 4, 3D
Church of St Peter Church of Norman
origin rebuilt c.1300 and mid 19th C
retains original round tower; fine tracery,
sedilia and piscina, font and 14th-C screen

MEYSEY HAMPTON, GLOS, 2, 3B
Church of St Mary Cruciform church
built by Knights Templar (consecrated
1269) retains transepts, chancel
remodelled 14th C, and central tower

with 15th-C parapet; fine tomb of 1300s
and crocketed canopies in chancel

MICHAELCHURCH-ON-ARROW,
POWYS, 6, 5D
Church of St Michael 13th and 14th-C
church reworked 1869 has original nave,
chancel and low west tower; remains of
ciborium in sanctuary, Easter Sepulchre,
reredos of c.1410 with later restoration,
and late medieval screen

MICHAELSTON-LE-PIT /
LLANFIHANGEL-Y-PWLL
GLAMORGAN, 2, 1B
Church of St Michael and All Angels
Medieval church has small transepts,
crossing tower, and stoup beside 14th-C
south doorway

MICHELHAM PRIORY
(nr Hailsham), E. SUSSEX, 3, 2E
Michelham Priory [HHA] Remains of
Augustinian priory founded 1229
incorporated into house; tall 15th-C
gatehouse

MIDDLEHAM, N. YORKS, 7, 3D
Church of St Mary and St Alkelda Church
built 14th and 15th C retains four-bay
arcades, south chapel, clerestory, and west
tower; tall 15th-C font cover and good
monument to Abbot Thornton (d.c.1533)
Middleham Castle [EH] Well-preserved
medieval castle has 12th to 13th-C walls
with angle towers, and 14th to 15th-C
ranges enclosing large keep built 1170s

MIDDLE LITTLETON, WORCS, 5, 3E
Church of St Nicholas Church has 13th-C
lancets to nave and chancel, 13th-C tower
with late medieval upper parts, north
transept of c.1300 with later alterations,
and good early 16th-C south chapel;
Norman font
Middle Littleton Tithe Barn [NT]
Handsome, spacious tithe barn built 1200s
for Abbey of Evesham (still in use as
farmbuilding)

MIDDLETON, GREATER
MANCHESTER, 5, 3A
Church of St Leonard [OCT] Church
consecrated 1412, remodelled 1524 and
later, retains Norman work, late 13th-C
priest's doorway and lavish 15th-C south
porch; late medieval west tower with
weatherboarding of c.1667;
16th-C brasses

MIDDLETON, N. YORKS, 7, 4D
Church of St Andrew Medieval church
retains Saxon west tower with 13th-C bell

stage, north arcade of *c.*1140, south arcade built *c.*1200, and 13th-C chancel; fagments of three good Saxon crosses

MILBORNE PORT, SOMERSET, 2, 2D
Church of St John the Evangelist
Saxo-Norman church with medieval and 19th-C reworking has 11th-C tympanum to south doorway, crossing arches with carved capitals, and crossing tower with 15th-C upper levels; Norman font and rood screen of 1400s

MILDENHALL, SUFFOLK, 4, 3E
Church of St Mary and St Andrew Large church retains chancel and rib-vaulted north chapel of *c.*1240–1300 with fine windows; 15th-C arcades, west tower, north porch with Lady Chapel above, and fine roofs with carved angels; remains of charnel house in churchyard with upper chapel endowed 1387

MILDENHALL, WILTS, 2, 4B
Church of St John the Baptist Church of Saxon origin retains Norman west tower with 15th-C top, chancel and arcades built *c.*1150-1200, and 17th-C roofs

MILFORD HAVEN, DYFED, 6, 2D
Church of St David [OCT] Small restored Norman church retains stone-vaulted roof, piscina, sedilia and font

MILFORD-ON-SEA, HANTS, 2, 4E
Church of All Saints Early medieval church of Norman origin with 13th-C west tower, chancel, south porch and doorway

MILLOM, CUMBRIA, 7, 1D
Church of the Holy Trinity Late Norman church rebuilt early 13th to early 14th C with restorations and additions of 19th to 20th C; 15th-C tomb chest
Millom Castle Ruins of castle licensed 1335 include original hall and gatehouse and 15th- or 16th-C pele tower

MILLTOWN CASTLE,
CO. LOUTH, 11, 4D
See Dromiskin

MILTON ABBAS, DORSET, 2, 3D
Milton Abbey * Remains of abbey founded 935 including impressive church of *c.*1310–25 and abbot's hall of 1498 survive in grounds of Milton Abbey School

MILTON KEYNES, BUCKS, 3, 1A
Church of All Saints Milton Keynes Village, Middleton. Medieval church rebuilt 14th C retains chancel arch of

*c.*1200; north tower, north chapel, sedilia and double piscina
Bradwell Abbey Bradwell. Outbuilding of Abbey Farm incorporates 14th-C fragments from church of Benedictine priory founded *c.*1155
Church of St Lawrence [CCT] Broughton 14th-C church with 15th-C west tower has extensive wall paintings of 1300s to 1400s

MILVERTON, SOMERSET, 2, 1D
Church of St Michael Church of Norman origin extensively rebuilt late 14th and 15th C has base of *c.*1200 to west tower and 19th-C south arcade; Norman font, medieval rood screen and stalls
Parsonage Late 15th-C house with two-storeyed porch

MINCHINHAMPTON, GLOS, 2, 3B
Church of the Holy Trinity Cruciform church of Norman origin rebuilt 12th, 14th, 16th and 19th C with central tower and fine early 14th-C south transept; 14th-C octagonal font and good medieval monuments

MINEHEAD, SOMERSET, 1, 5B
Church of St Michael Spacious 15th-C church with chancel chapels, south porch, west tower and wagon roofs; good octagonal font, rood screen and monuments

MINGARY CASTLE (1.5 km. / 1 m. SE of Kilchoan) HIGHLAND, 10, 3A
Mingary Castle Well-preserved remains of 13th-C castle on dramatic promontory with alterations of 16th to early 18th C

MINIONS, CORNWALL, 1, 3D
See St Cleer

MINSTER ABBEY, KENT, 3, 4C
See Minster-in-Thanet

MINSTER-IN-SHEPPEY, KENT, 3, 4C
Church of St Mary and St Sexburga
Two churches in one, a nunnery church founded 7th C and an early 13th-C parochial church, both with medieval and later additions; 12th-C column under canopy, late 14th-C screen and fine 14th- and 15th-C monuments
Gatehouse Late medieval gatehouse of former nunnery

MINSTER-IN-THANET, KENT, 3, 4C
Church of St Mary Norman church enlarged *c.*1150 to *c.*1230 retains original nave, transepts, west tower, and fine 13th-C rib-vaulted chancel; 15th-C font with cover, and stalls and misericords in chancel

Minster Abbey Remains of Norman grange used as abbey since 1930s with parts of 12th-C church, ranges around quadrangle and later additions

MINSTER LOVELL, OXON, 2, 4A
Church of St Kenelm Almost unaltered mainly 15th-C cruciform church with vaulted crossing and central tower; 15th-C font, benches, stained glass and carved tomb chest
Minster Lovell Hall and Dovecot [EH] Substantial ruins of manor house built *c.*1431–42 on courtyard plan; 15th-C circular dovecot with lantern survives to north-east

MITCHELDEAN, GLOS, 2, 2A
Church of St Michael Medieval church has 13th or 14th-C tower with tall spire rebuilt *c.*1760, 14th-C nave and aisles, tunnel-vaulted ossuary, outer north aisle added *c.*1460, and fine 15th-C roofs with bosses; late medieval painting on wooden panels

MITCHEL TROY, GWENT, 2, 2A
Church of St Michael 14th-C church with fine chancel, aisled nave and south porch; medieval chuchyard cross has tapering shaft decorated with shields and ballflowers

MITFORD,
NORTHUMBERLAND, 7, 3B
Church of St Mary Magdalene Church of 12th-C origin with 13th-, 14th- and extensive 19th-C additions retains chancel built 1200s; 13th-C sedilia and piscina
Mitford Castle Remains of Norman motte and bailey castle destroyed *c.*1318 with fragments of 12th- and 13th-C keeps

MOATE, CO. WESTMEATH, 11, 3D
Moate Castle Castle built 17th and 18th C incorporates late medieval tower house with sheila-na-gig above arch

MOBBERLEY, CHESHIRE, 5, 3A
Church of St Wilfrid Church of 14th to 15th C retains piscina of *c.*1300 and west tower of *c.*1533; east end built 1889; fine rood screen dated 1500 with lavish carving

MOCCAS, HEREFS, 5, 1E
Church of St Michael Well-preserved Norman church with work of *c.*1300 retains nave, chancel and lower apse with fine arch; early 14th-C effigy and stained glass

MOELFRE (ANGLESEY),
GWYNEDD, 6, 3A
Hen Capel Lligwy [CADW] Small 12th-C chapel with upper walls and bellcote dating from 14th C; smaller chapel to south added 16th-C

MOLANA ABBEY
CO. WATERFORD, 12, 3D
See Youghal

MOLD / YR WYDDGRUG,
CLWYD, 6, 5A
Church of St Mary Handsome medieval church remodelled late 15th and early 16th C with west tower of 1768–73 and chancel added 1853–6; lively exterior ornament and gargoyles, splendid nave arcades with rich carving, and good niches at east of aisles; camberbeam roof to north aisle
The Tower, Brancoed (Outer Mold) Mid 15th-C fortified tower house with post medieval alterations

MONAINCHA,
CO. TIPPERARY, 12, 4B
Church (Inchnameo Abbey) [Dúchas] Site of monastery and later priory (once an island in bog, now drained) retains ruins of interesting church with rich 12th-C west doorway and chancel arch, unusual pilasters on external wall of chancel, and small 15th- or 16th-C sacristy to north; small High Cross (possibly 12th-C) to west

MONASTERANENAGH (4 km. / 2 ½ m. E of Croom),
CO. LIMERICK, 12, 3C
Abbey [Dúchas] Remains of once important Cistercian abbey founded between 1148 and 1151 include cruciform church (*c.*1185–1205) with well-preserved capitals, and fragments of domestic buildings; ruins of abbey mill and bridge survive nearby

MONASTERBOICE,
CO. LOUTH, 11, 4D
Monastic Site [Dúchas] Important remains of early Irish monastery (6th- to 12th-C) with ruins of two churches, Round Tower (built probably 900s) and three splendid 9th- and 10th-C High Crosses of great importance, two (south or "Muiredach's cross" and west cross) with carved scriptural scenes

MONIKIE, TAYSIDE, 8, 3C
Affleck Castle (0.5 km. / ¼ m. m.W) Perfectly preserved L-plan tower house built late 1400s with hall on third floor

and enchanting upper chapel or oratory entered off laird's private chamber

MONK BRETTON, S. YORKS, 5,4A
Monk Bretton Priory [EH] Remains of Cluniac house founded 1153 include parts of church, domestic buildings, and restored 14th-C gatehouse; cloister west range converted to house late 16th C

MONK FRYSTON, N. YORKS, 7,4E
Church of St Wilfrid Church retains Saxon west tower with 15th-C top, 13th-C arcades, chancel remodelled early 14th C, and 16th-C clerestory

MONKLEIGH, DEVON, 1,4B
Church of St George Church built 15th C has west tower and south (Annery) chapel with rich tomb chest and monument to Sir William Hankford (d.1423); unusual Norman font and fine carved screen between chapel and aisle

MONKNASH / YR AS FAWR
GLAMORGAN, 1,5A
Grange Remains of grange of Neath Abbey with large ruined barn and circular dovecot

MONKS KIRBY, WARWS, 5,4D
Church of St Edith Former church of Benedictine priory founded 1077 with medieval rebuilding retains 13th-C chancel, 14th-C south porch, imposing south-west tower, and spacious nave with six-bay arcades

MONKSTOWN, CO. DUBLIN, 11,5E
Castle [Dúchas] Remains of small 15th- or 16th-C keep-tower and gatehouse; bawn mainly 19th C

MONKWEARMOUTH (Sunderland), TYNE AND WEAR, 7,3B
Church of St Peter Remaining parts of monastic church founded c.675 with remarkable survival of late Saxon tower (c.1000) incorporating 7th-C porticus

MONMOUTH, GWENT, 6,5D
Monmouth Castle [CADW] Ruined Great Tower and Hall of 12th- to 14th-C castle
Monnow Bridge Bridge over River Monnow built 1272 with fortified gatehouse added c.1300 as toll house and defensive tower
"Geoffrey's Window" (in school in Priory Street) 15th-C window

MONREITH, DUMFRIES AND GALLOWAY, 10,4E
Kirkmaiden Churchyard Churchyard contains remains of medieval church with

chancel rebuilt as mausoleum late 19th C
Myrton Castle Castle with early 17th-C northern section retains part of tower house built c.1500 on 12th-C motte (converted to dovecot c.1870)

MONTGOMERY / TREFALDWYN, POWYS, 6,5C
Church of St Nicholas Church with 19th-C additions has long nave begun c.1223, late 13th-C transepts, lavish south doorway, and fine late medieval east window and nave roofs; late 15th-C screen with choir stalls and misericords from Chirbury Priory, Shropshire
Castle [CADW] Castle begun 1223 with impressive earthworks and remains of twin-towered gatehouse, curtain walls, circular turrets, and Well Tower rebuilt c.1359

MONYASH, DERBYS, 5,4B
Church of St Leonard Church founded c.1198 with later medieval and 19th-C additions retains original sedilia and piscina of c.1200 with dog-tooth ornament and stiff-leaf or crocket capitals; 15th-C font carved with animals

MONYMUSK, GRAMPIAN, 8,4B
St Mary's Church Interesting church built mid 12th C and well restored 1929 has original chancel arch, nave, and good west doorway; additions of 17th C and later
Monymusk Stone (Pictish symbol stone)

MOONE, CO. KILDARE, 12,5B
High Cross and Church [Dúchas] Excellent, unusually slender High Cross (9th-C, re-erected 1800s) with naively carved flat stylised figures survives on site of early Christian monastery; nearby 13th-C church with antae (possibly part of Franciscan friary founded 1258)

MORCOTT, RUTLAND, 4,1D
Church of St Mary Norman church with medieval additions retains original priest's doorway, arch to nave, and west doorway with oculus window above; 13th-C chancel arch and early 14th-C south porch

MORETON CORBET, SHROPS, 5,2C
Church of St Batholomew Church of Norman origin much altered 18th C has original chancel, south aisle built c.1330–40, and west tower begun 1530s
Moreton Corbet Castle [EH] Ruins of medieval castle with keep of c.1200,

gatehouse, and south range built c.1575–80

MORLAIS CASTLE, GLAMORGAN, 6,4E
See Merthyr Tydfil

MORLAND, CUMBRIA, 7,2C
Church of St Laurence Church retains Saxon west tower with later upper parts, late 12th-C aisles, transepts of c.1225, and 15th- or early 16th-C chancel; good coffin lid of late 1200s and top rail of late 14th- or 15th-C screen

MORLEY, DERBYS, 5,4B
Church of St Matthew Medieval church with Norman south arcade, early 14th-C chancel, north chancel chapel added c.1370, later 14th-C west tower, and south chancel chapel of mid 15th C; fine set of monuments and late medieval stained glass

MORNIN CASTLE (4.5 km. / 2 ¾ m. E of Kenagh), CO. LONGFORD, 11,3D
Mornin Castle Remains of large tower house built 15th or early 16th C

MORPETH, NORTHUMBERLAND, 7,3B
Church of St Mary Mainly 14th-C church with five-bay arcades, two-storeyed vestry and good roofs; original ironwork to chancel doors and 14th-C Jesse window renewed 19th C
The Chantry, Bridge Street Bridge chantry founded 1296 and remodelled 1738, 19th and 20th
Morpeth Castle [Gatehouse – LT] Mid 14th- and 15th-C gatehouse and curtain wall of 13th-C castle

MORTHAM, CO. DURHAM, 7,3C
Mortham Tower Late 15th-C house remodelled 17th and 18th C incorporates mid 14th-C tower house at centre

MORTLACH, GRAMPIAN, 8,3A
See Balvenie Castle

MORTON CASTLE (2.5 km. / 1 ½ m. NE of Carronbridge), DUMFRIES AND GALLOWAY, 10,5D
Morton Castle [HS] Surviving south range of castle built probably early 14th C on promontory site

MORVILLE, SHROPS, 5,2D
Church of St Gregory Norman church consecrated 1118 has original nave, chancel, west tower with later top, and late 12th-C aisles; Norman font

MORWENSTOW, CORNWALL, 1,3B
Church of St John the Baptist Norman church rebuilt 13th and 16th C retains original south door, much of carved north arcade and fine wagon roofs

MOTHEL, CO. WATERFORD, 12,4C
Mothel Abbey [Dúchas] (5.5 km. / 3 ½ m. SE of Carrick-on-Suir) Site of Augustinian abbey refounded probably 13th C replacing early monastery has fragments of medieval walls and fine tomb chest of c.1500 (by Roricus O'Comayn) with carved saints and biblical scenes

MOTTISFONT, HANTS, 2,4D
Church of St Andrew Church of Norman origin with medieval work has fine original chancel arch and south doorway; much 15th-C stained glass in chancel
Mottisfont Abbey [NT] 16th-C house rebuilt 18th to 20th C incorporates remains of Augustinian priory founded 1201

MOULTON, LINCS, 4,2D
Church of All Saints Norman church with medieval and 18th-C additions retains arcades built c.1180–90, 13th-C clerestory, and fine 15th-C west tower; sedilia of 1200s, 14th-C Easter Sepulchre and good screen
Elloe Stone Surviving fragment of 10th or 11th-C wheel cross

MOULTON, SUFFOLK, 4,3E
Church of St Peter Church of Norman origin with much later restoration has transept chapels, and west tower built late 13th C
Packhorse Bridge [EH] One of two fine 15th-C bridges crossing River Kennett

MOUNT GRACE PRIORY, N. YORKS, 7,4D
Mount Grace Priory [EH / NT] Britain's best preserved Charterhouse or Carthusian monastery (founded 1398) with buildings partly reconstructed to show individual monk's living quarters and garden; surviving structures include gatehouse, church with tower, cloisters, and guest house converted to mansion 17th C (altered c.1900)

MOVILLA ABBEY (1.5 km. / 1 m. E of Newtownards), CO. DOWN, 11,5B
Movilla Abbey [EHS] Monastery refounded 1100s as Augustinian abbey with ruins of long 13th- and 15th-C church; splendid collection of 13th-C foliate coffin lids with pre-Norman

slab from early monastery surviving at end of row

MOVILLE, CO. DONEGAL, 11, 4A
Cooley Churchyard [Dúchas] (1.5 km. / 1 m.W) Site of medieval monastery contains plain, tall cross and remarkable skull house, a tomb shrine with gabled roof (possibly 12th-C)

MOYLAGH, CO. MEATH, 11, 4D
See Oldcastle

MOYNE (1.5 km. / 1 m. ESE of Killala), **CO. MAYO, 11, 2C**
Friary (or Moyne Abbey) [Dúchas] Well-preserved remains of Franciscan friary founded 1460 include church with wide south aisle, south transept, and slender later tower, fine late 15th-C cloisters, vaulted chapter house, sacristy, and refectory with reader's desk; ruins of 18th-C house attached to east

MOYRATH CASTLE, CO. MEATH, 11, 4D
See Kildalkey

MUCHELNEY, SOMERSET, 2, 1D
Muchelney Abbey [EH] Well-preserved remains of cloister buildings and abbot's lodgings of Benedictine abbey reworked early 16th C
Church of St Peter and St Paul Medieval church retains three-bay arcades, west tower, and embattled north side with vaulted porch; stone reredos in south chapel
Priest's House [NT] Unusual thatched priest's house built 14th to 15th C

MUCH HADHAM, HERTS, 3, 2B
Church of St Andrew Church of Norman origin with medieval additions has chancel of c.1220, 14th-C piscina and Easter Sepulchre, and good 15th-C roofs; early 13th-C ironwork and 15th-C pulpit and screen
Medieval Buildings Some good early 16th-C cottages with exposed timber-framing include The Old House and Morris, Bull and Campden Cottages

MUCH MARCLE, HEREFS, 2, 2A
Church of St Bartholomew Mainly 13th-C church has arcades of c.1230–40, large north chapel and 15th-C central tower; fine 14th-C effigies; churchyard cross
Mortimer's Castle Remains of medieval motte and bailey castle

MUCH WENLOCK, SHROPS, 5, 2D
Wenlock Priory [EH] Substantial remains of Cluniac priory with late 12th-C

monastic buildings and church of c.1200–40; infirmary and splendid prior's lodge of c.1500 form part of private house
Church of the Holy Trinity Norman church with 13th- to 15th-C and later additions retains original nave, chancel, and late 12th-C west tower
Guildhall * Medieval building with overhanging upper storey and timberwork of c.1577

MUCKROSS FRIARY, CO. KERRY, 12, 2D
See Killarney

MUGDOCK (2.5 km. / 1½ m. N of Milngavie), **CENTRAL, 10, 5B**
Mugdock Castle Remains of courtyard castle extended and remodelled until 19th C include well-preserved 14th-C tower at south-west angle and parts of curtain wall

MULLABOY (7 km. / 4½ m. N of Claudy)
CO. LONDONDERRY, 11, 4B
Cross Ancient stone cross in Roman Catholic graveyard

MULLION, CORNWALL, 1, 2E
Church of St Melina 13th-C church rebuilt c.1500 with west tower and ceiled wagon roofs; 13th-C font and many carved bench ends of c.1535

MULTYFARNHAM, CO. WESTMEATH, 11, 3D
Multyfarnham Abbey [Dúchas] Church of abbey founded late 13th C, damaged 16th and 17th C, and restored by Franciscan community 1827 retains slender original crossing tower; chancel reconstructed 1971
Lacken Church (2.5 km. / 1½ m. NW) Ruins of modest medieval church built probably 1400s on site of abbey founded 7th C

MUNGRET, CO. LIMERICK, 12, 3C
Churches [Dúchas] Site of important early monastery houses remains of three churches, one small and built before 1100s, second probably 12th C with flat-headed west doorway, and third ("Abbey") built 13th to 15th C with west dwelling tower

MURRISK, CO. MAYO, 11, 1C
Monastery (or Murrisk Abbey) [Dúchas] Ruined church and domestic buildings of small Augustinian monastery founded 1456/7 in picturesque location by Clew Bay

dominated by Croagh Patrick (Ireland's Holy or Pilgrimage Mountain)

MUTFORD, SUFFOLK, 4, 5E
Church of St Andrew Church of Norman origin has round tower with octagonal top, 14th-C galilee, chancel and south aisle, and 18th-C brick chapel; font of c.1380

MUTHILL (5 km. / 3 m. S of Crieff), **TAYSIDE, 8, 2D**
Muthill Old Church and Tower [HS] Mainly 15th-C remains of important medieval parish church retaining tall 12th-C tower at west end; effigies of Sir Muriel Drummond (d.1382) and wife

MWNT (VERWICK), DYFED, 6, 3D
Church of the Holy Cross Small, plain early medieval church with timber roof and surviving parts of rood screen with traces of paint

MYLOR, CORNWALL, 1, 2E
Church of St Melorus Norman church in fine setting has two original doorways with tympana and attractive late medieval south side with unusual carving to porch doorway; well-preserved carved rood screen; tall Cornish cross in churchyard

MYRTON CASTLE, DUMFRIES AND GALLOWAY, 10, 4E
See Monreith

NANTWICH, CHESHIRE, 5, 2B
Church of St Mary Mainly 14th-C church restored 1854–61 with octagonal crossing tower and 15th-C two-storeyed south porch; 14th-C chancel with fine vaulted roof contains original sedilia, piscina and aumbry; 14th-C stalls with misericords and stone pulpit

NAPPA HALL (2 km. / 1¼ m. E of Askrigg), **N. YORKS, 7, 3D**
Nappa Hall Fortified house built c.1460 with two imposing towers, hall, and 17th-C south wing

NAPTON-ON-THE-HILL, WARWS, 5, 4E
Church of St Lawrence Church of Norman origin restored 1861 retains 12th-C chancel, south doorway of c.1200, fine transepts built c.1275, and early 14th-C west tower with 18th-C upper levels

NASSINGTON, NORTHANTS, 4, 1D
Church of All Saints Church of Saxon origin retains original nave with 13th-C aisles and chancel arch, and Norman

west tower; fragment of Saxon cross shaft and wall paintings of c.1350
Prebendal Manor House * Fine medieval manor house with later rebuilding has early 13th-C south range and hall; 15th-C dovecot; 14th-C re-created medieval gardens
Manor House Manor house built c.1500 ·

NAVAN, CO. MEATH, 11, 4D
Rathaldron Castle (3 km. / 2 m. NW, on bank of Blackwater) Small country house of mainly 18th and 19th C incorporates medieval tower house at core (built probably 1300s)
Athlumney Castle [Dúchas] (1.5 km. / 1 m. ENE) Imposing ruins of 15th-C tower house with attached three-storeyed range built c.1600

NAVENBY, LINCS, 4, 1C
Church of St Peter Medieval church reworked mid 18th C has 13th-C arcades and fine 14th-C chancel with Easter Sepulchre, founder's tomb, sedilia and piscina

NAVESTOCK, ESSEX, 3, 2B
Church of St Thomas the Apostle Norman and medieval church with timber tower believed to date from c.1250

NAWORTH CASTLE, CUMBRIA, 7, 2B
Naworth Castle (visit by appointment only) Border castle licensed 1335, altered c.1520, and converted to mansion early 17th C retains much medieval work; elaborate timber ceiling of c.1350 from Kirkoswald Castle survives in Lord William Howard's Tower

NAYLAND, SUFFOLK, 3, 4A
Church of St James 15th-C church with 14th-C west tower and west porch of 1525, rebuilt 1884; eight painted panels of former rood screen of c.1500; carved north door
Alston Court Timber-framed house built around courtyard, dating from mid 14th to 15th-C with additions of c.1500 and later

NEATH / CASTELL NEDD GLAMORGAN, 6, 4E
Church of St Illtyd, Llantwit Road Simple medieval church restored 1858–9 with west tower, nave and lower chancel
Castle Surviving three-storeyed gatehouse built c.1321 of former Norman castle
Neath Abbey [CADW] Well-preserved remains of Cistercian abbey partially incorporated into 16th-C mansion include late 12th-C lay brothers' quarters, 13th-C

dormitory undercroft, and ruins of church rebuilt c.1280–1330

NEEDHAM MARKET, SUFFOLK, 3,4A
Church of St John the Baptist Plain 15th-C church (chapel of ease until 1907) retains one of most remarkable roofs in country with hammerbeams and angels; timber clerestory

NEIDPATH (1.5 km. / 1 m. W of Peebles), BORDERS, 7,1A
Neidpath Castle Large, unspoilt 14th-C L-plan tower house remodelled 16th C, 17th C and later survives in picturesque setting by River Tweed

NENAGH, CO. TIPPERARY, 12,3B
Nenagh Castle [Dúchas] Remarkable and imposing circular donjon tower (upper part c.1860) with remains of gatehouse to south, all that remains of pentagonal castle built early 1200s
Friary [Dúchas] Abbey Street; Ruins of once important Franciscan friary founded c.1250

NENDRUM ABBEY, CO. DOWN, 11,5C
See Mahee Island

NERCWYS, CLWYD, 6,5A
Church of St Mary Medieval church with 19th-C transepts, north aisle and chancel retains late 15th- or early 16th-C pulpit, and sedilia made up of rood screen; good sepulchral slabs in south porch; east window of 1883 incorporates medieval stained glass

NETHER ALDERLEY, CHESHIRE, 5,3A
Church of St Mary Large 15th-C church with good west tower, roofs and arcades retains 14th-C west and south doorways; 17th- and 19th-C additions
Nether Alderley Mill [NT] **Congleton Road** Watermill dating from 15th C with restored 19th-C machinery

NETHER WINCHENDON HOUSE, BUCKS, 2,5A
See Lower Winchendon

NETHERAVON, WILTS, 2,4C
Church of All Saints Saxo-Norman church with original west tower and traces of 11th-C porticus; 13th-C nave, chancel and clerestory

NETLEY, HANTS, 2,4D
Netley Abbey [EH] Remains of Cistercian abbey begun 1240s and converted to house 16th C

NETTLESTEAD, KENT, 3,3D
Church of St Mary Medieval church with additions of 1858 has nave built c.1438 with impressive windows, south porch of c.1496, and earlier tower; some original stained glass survives
Nettlestead Place Medieval manor house rebuilt 16th C and 1922 retains splendid vaulted undercroft of c.1250–60 and work of c.1438

NEVERN, DYFED, 6,3D
Church of St Brynach 15th-C cruciform church with battlemented west tower; fine Celtic cross of c.1000, richly decorated with knotwork and fret-patterning, survives to south of building; nearby early Christian inscribed stones of 5th to 6th and 10th C

NEVILL HOLT, LEICS, 5,5D
Church of St Mary Late 13th-C church with later additions has aisleless nave, transepts, chancel and west tower; Norman font and late 13th-C sedilia and piscina
Nevill Holt Hall 14th-C hall-house rebuilt 15th to 19th C retains original hall with fine open timber roof, 15th-C porch and two-storeyed bay window

NEW ABBEY, CO. KILDARE, 12,5B
See Kilcullen

NEW ABBEY (11 km. / 7 m. S of Dumfries), DUMFRIES AND GALLOWAY, 7,1B
Sweetheart Abbey [HS] Picturesque 13th- and 14th-C remains of important Cistercian monastery (founded 1273) include well-preserved church with near complete crossing tower, fragments of domestic buildings and massive precinct wall

NEWARK CASTLE (5 km. / 3 m. W of Selkirk, in grounds of Bowhill) BORDERS, 7,2A
Newark Castle Ruins of large 15th-C keep with upper floor and parts of gatehouse and wall

NEWARK CASTLE, STRATHCLYDE, 8,1E
See Port Glasgow

NEWARK-ON-TRENT, NOTTS, 5,5B
Church of St Mary Magdalen Large mainly 15th-C church retains early 12th-C crypt, 13th-C crossing, and high 13th and 14th-C west tower; choir stalls of c.1500 and good rood screen of 1508

Newark Castle Norman castle restored 1845–8 with gatehouse of c.1133–9 and early 14th-C curtain wall
Beaumond Cross Slender 15th-C cross shaft restored 1778 and 1801
White Hart Inn Mainly late 15th-C timber-framed inn

NEWBALD, E. RIDING OF YORKS, 7,4E
Church of St Nicholas Well preserved cruciform Norman church has four original doorways, corbel table, good crossing arches, tower completed early 13th C, and chancel rebuilt 1400s; late 12th-C font and 14th-C chest

NEWBATTLE, LOTHIAN, 8,3E
Newbattle Abbey Fragmentary remains of important Cistercian abbey founded 1140, partially incorporated into 16th-C mansion
Maiden Bridge Bridge built late 1400s across River South Esk

NEWBIGGIN, NORTHUMBERLAND, 7,3B
Church of St Bartolomew Church of Norman origin with extensive 19th-C rebuilding retains 13th-C aisle arcades and small west tower with 14th-C spire; good collection of mainly 13th-C cross slabs

NEWBOROUGH (ANGLESEY), GWYNEDD, 6,3A
Church of St Peter Large aisleless medieval church extended 16th C contains 12th-C font and carved grave slabs in chancel

NEWBURGH, FIFE, 8,3D
Lindores Abbey Scanty and overgrown remains of Tironensian monastery founded c.1190

NEWBURGH PRIORY, N. YORKS, 7,4D
Newburgh Priory * House built mainly 18th C with early 17th-C and earlier work incorporates small fragments of Augustinian priory moved to Newburgh c.1150

NEWBURN, TYNE AND WEAR, 7,3B
Church of St Michael and All Angels Church of Saxo-Norman origin with medieval and 19th-C work retains 11th-C west tower, north arcade of c.1175, and 14th- or 15th-C transepts

NEWBURY, BERKS, 2,4C
Church of St Nicholas Large embattled church built c.1500–32 has five-bay arcades, clerestory, good nave roof, and west tower with polygonal buttresses

NEWCASTLE, CO. DUBLIN, 11,4E
Church [Dúchas] 15th-C church with west tower and eastern addition of 1724; early Christian cross in graveyard

NEWCASTLE, CO. MEATH, 12,4A
See Castlejordan

NEWCASTLE, GLAMORGAN, 6,4E
See Bridgend

NEWCASTLE EMLYN, DYFED, 6,3D
Castle Twin-towered 14th-C gatehouse dominating fragmentary ruins of 13th-C castle, rebuilt c.1500 as late medieval country house

NEWCASTLE UPON TYNE TYNE AND WEAR, 7,3B
Cathedral Church of St Nicholas * Medieval church made cathedral 1882 has mainly 14th-C interior with nave and transepts complete by c.1350, big crossing piers and clerestory, and 15th-C exterior with ambitious west tower and crown of c.1435–70; large 15th-C Flemish brass and lavish font cover of c.1500
Church of St Andrew Church of Norman origin with 19th-C rebuilding has tall chancel arch, late 12th-C west tower raised 1200s, chancel reworked c.1300, and north chapel added c.1327; fine 15th-C font cover
Church of St John Mainly 15th-C church with west tower retains 14th-C nave arcades and north transept
Castle Surviving buildings of Norman castle include well preserved keep built 1172–7 with ambitious forebuilding and rib-vaulted chapel, and Black Gate of c.1247 topped by early 17th-C house
Town Walls Extensive remains of tall 13th-C town walls with towers and turrets
Blackfriars Remains of monastic buildings of house of Dominicans founded before 1239
St Mary's Chapel, Reid Park Road, Jesmond (Outer Newcastle) Ruins of medieval chapel with 12th-C chancel arch and 14th-C chancel

NEWCASTLE WEST, CO. LIMERICK
Desmond Hall (Banqueting Hall) [Dúchas], The Square. Impressive two-storeyed banqueting hall built

15th C on remains of 13th-C structure with vaulted lower chamber and adjoining tower

NEWCHURCH, POWYS, 6, 5D
Great House Medieval house converted 17th C with wing of 1790 retains wide cruck hall built *c.*1490

NEWHAGGARD CASTLE GATEHOUSE, CO. MEATH, 11, 4D
See Trim

NEWLAND, GLOS, 2, 2A
Church of All Saints Large mainly 13th-C church restored 1861 with wide aisles and imposing tower of late 13th and late 14th C; fine 14th- and 15th-C effigies and brasses

NEWPORT, ESSEX, 3, 2A
Church of St Mary the Virgin Medieval church with 13th-C chancel, 14th-C nave arcade, and 15th-C south porch and nave clerestory; west tower added 1858; 13th-C font and chest; early 14th-C stained glass
Monk's Barn, Main St 15th-C timber-framed house retains oriel with decorative carving

NEWPORT, GWENT, 2, 1B
Cathedral of St Woolos Large 12th- to 13th-C church with fine late Norman nave and richly-carved doorway, Galilee Chapel of St Mary (an earlier Norman nave remodelled 13th C), and later medieval additions; east end extended 1961–2
Newport Castle [CADW] Fragmentary remains of 14th- to 15th-C castle of Norman origin, dominated by central tower above watergate

NEW ROMNEY, KENT, 3, 4E
Church of St Nicholas Norman church built *c.*1160–70 and enlarged to east 14th C retains four original bays of nave with clerestory windows and ornate west doorway
St John's Priory, Ashford Road Two-storeyed medieval building adorned with fragments from ruined church (Hope All Saints)

NEW ROSS, CO. WEXFORD, 12, 5C
Church of St Mary [Dúchas] Church Lane. Roofless chancel and transepts of fine church founded probably between 1207 and 1220 with early 19th-C Protestant building occupying site of crossing and nave; fragments of good head-slabs (including that to Isabella, heiress of Strongbow, d.1220), effigies, and late 13th-C Bambino Stone

NEW SHOREHAM, W. SUSSEX, 3, 2E
Church of St Mary de Haura Ambitious Norman church retains transepts, central tower built *c.*1130 with late 12th-C top, nave with fine north arcade of *c.*1200, and 13th-C vaulted choir; late Norman font
Marlipins Museum * Medieval store with 14th-C front

NEWSTEAD ABBEY, NOTTS, 5, 5B
Newstead Abbey * Augustinian priory founded 1163–73 and rebuilt as house 16th to 19th C (home of famous poet, Lord Byron) retains elaborate late 13th-C west front of priory church, undercroft of Great Hall, and chapter house

NEWTON ABBOT, DEVON, 1, 5D
Bradley Manor [NT] Small medieval house built mainly 13th and 15th C with 16th-C and later additions

NEWTON ARLOSH, CUMBRIA, 7, 1B
Church of St John the Baptist Church licensed 1304 and enlarged 19th C has defensive west tower with battlements

NEWTON NOTTAGE / DRENEWYDD YN NOTAIS GLAMORGAN, 6, 4E
Church of St John the Baptist Handsome church built *c.*1500 with nave restored 1860–1 has big west tower and chancel with priest's door; 13th-C stoup by south door and fine late medieval stone pulpit with figural carving

NEWTOWN, CO. CLARE, 12, 2B
Newtown Castle [Dúchas] Fine late medieval circular castle on unique pyramidal base (probably 16th-C, restored 1994 as centre of Burren College of Art)

NEWTOWN, POWYS, 6, 5C
Cwrt Plas-y-Dre (Quaker Meeting House) Aisled hall built 1400s with 17th-C alterations, moved from Dolgellau in 1885

NEWTOWNARDS, CO. DOWN, 11, 5B
Newtownards Priory [EHS] Extensive remains of Dominican friary founded mid 1200s include original church with 14th-C rebuilding and enlargement and 17th-C tower

NEWTOWN JERPOINT CO. KILKENNY, 12, 4C
See Jerpoint

NEWTOWN STEWART CO. TYRONE, 11, 3B
Harry Avery's Castle (1 km. / ½ m. NE) [EHS] Surviving D-shaped gatehouse

towers of 14th-C castle with rectangular block behind
Corickmore Abbey (5.5 km. / 3 ½ m. ENE) Scanty and overgrown remains of Franciscan Tertiary friary founded *c.*1465 on promontory site

NEWTOWN TRIM, CO. MEATH, 11, 4D
Victorine Abbey and Cathedral of SS Peter and Paul [Dúchas] Remains of once splendid cathedral church and monastic buildings of abbey founded 1206 on banks of River Boyne
Hospital Priory of St John the Baptist [Dúchas] Ruins of priory founded early 13th C on other side of river from abbey include good east gable of church and two 15th-C tower houses; restored late medieval bridge

NIGG, HIGHLAND, 8, 2A
Parish Church Church built 1626 and much reworked 18th C retains fine carved Pictish cross slab of *c.*800 at east end

NITH BRIDGE CROSS, DUMFRIES AND GALLOWAY, 10, 5D
See Thornhill

NOBBER, CO. MEATH, 11, 4D
Cruicetown Church (3 km. / 2 m. SW) Remains of church built *c.*1200 with well-preserved nave and chancel and original font

NORBURY, DERBYS, 5, 3D
Church of St Mary Church retains fine chancel (probably built *c.*1300–7) with large windows and late medieval timber roof, 15th-C nave, south tower, and south-west chapel completed 1517; parts of two Saxon crosses and good collections of monuments and stained glass
The Old Manor [NT] (by written appointment only) Medieval hall-house built 13th to 15th C

NORBURY, STAFFS, 5, 3C
Church of St Peter Church built *c.*1300 to *c.*1350 with wagon roofs and mid 18th-C tower; good 14th-C brass and effigies

NORHAM, NORTHUMBERLAND, 8, 4E
Norham Castle [EH] Remains of castle begun *c.*1157 with medieval rebuilding include keep, gatehouse, 15th-C Garderobe Tower, and early 16th-C walls of Great Hall
Church of St Cuthbert Norman church mainly rebuilt 1837–52 retains chancel

with original side windows, and fine south arcade of *c.*1170
Village Cross Medieval cross with cap and restoration of 1870

NORRINGTON MANOR, WILTS, 2, 3D
See Alvediston

NORTHALLERTON, N. YORKS, 7, 3D
Church of All Saints Church built 12th and 13th C with later alterations and chancel of 1885 retains original arcades, west and south doorways, transepts, and 15th-C crossing tower; fragments of good Saxon sculpture

NORTHAMPTON, NORTHANTS, 5, 5E
Church of All Saints Church totally rebuilt 1676–80 after fire retains Norman and 14th-C west tower, and 13th-C crypt
Church of St Giles Church of Norman origin enlarged 1850s with original crossing arches and tower (upper parts of 1616), chancel rebuilt 13th C, and 14th-C chapels
Church of St John the Baptist, Bridge Street Former almshouse of Hospital of St John founded *c.*1137 with early 14th-C street front (converted to church 1955) adjoins original chapel restored 1881
Church of St Peter, Marefair. Large ambitious Norman church of *c.*1150 with sumptuous interior, low west tower rebuilt early 17th C and east end reworked 1850; fragments of Saxon and mid 12th-C sculpture
Church of the Holy Sepulchre, Sheep Street Norman church founded *c.*1110 has unusual round nave with ambulatory and octagonal upper level remodelled 1300s, chancel rebuilt *c.*1180–*c.*1330 with east end of 1860–4, and good early 14th-C west tower; medieval banner-staff locker
Church of St John the Baptist, Kingsthorpe (Outer Northampton) Early Norman church with aisles added *c.*1170–80 and rib-vaulted crypt
Eleanor Cross, London Road, Hardingstone (Outer Northampton) Elaborate octagonal cross begun 1291 by John of Battle with statues by William of Ireland (one of three surviving crosses marking resting places of body of Eleanor, Queen of Edward I, on route to Westminster Abbey)
Church of St Luke, Duston (Outer Northampton) Norman church with medieval rebuilding retains late 12th-C south doorway, crossing tower with 14th-C top, late 13th-C arcades, and 14th-C chancel; Norman font

NORTH BARNINGHAM
NORFOLK, 4, 4C
Church of St Peter Mainly 14th-C
church damaged 18th C and restored
1893 has 15th-C west tower and unusual
tiling

NORTH BERWICK, LOTHIAN, 8, 3E
Cistercian Nunnery, Old Abbey Road
Remains of Cistercian nunnery founded
before 1177 survive in grounds of old
people's home

NORTHBOROUGH, CAMBS, 4, 1D
Church of St Andrew Small mainly late
12th- to 13th-C church with rich 14th-C
additions (probably incomplete)
including south transept with good
windows and two large tomb recesses
Manor House Surviving hall range
and gatehouse of manor house built
c.1330–40 with extensive alterations
of early 1600s

NORTH CERNEY, GLOS, 2, 3A
Church of All Saints Church begun early
12th C, altered c.1200 and rebuilt 15th C
and 18th to 20th C, retains Norman west
tower, south doorway with fine
tympanum, squint passage, 15th-C
transepts and elaborate nave roof;
good 12th-C tombstone, altar of c.1200
(still in use), and brass lectern and stone
pulpit of c.1480; 15th-C stained glass
and wooden statues (foreign)
Old Church House Attractive house
built c.1470

NORTH CREAKE, NORFOLK, 4, 3C
Church of St Mary Medieval church
restored 19th C retains south porch of
c.1300, and 15th-C arcade and north tower;
lavish Easter Sepulchre, sedilia and piscina
of c.1300, and fine hammerbeam roof
with angels

NORTH CURRY, SOMERSET, 2, 1D
Church of St Peter and St Paul Spacious
medieval church retains north doorway
of c.1180, octagonal crossing tower of
c.1300 with 15th-C upper parts, and lavish
south side built 1400s

NORTH ELMHAM, NORFOLK, 4, 4D
Cathedral Moated site with mainly early
11th-C ruins of Saxon cathedral (of see
later moved to Norwich), overlaid by
remains of Bishop Despenser's manor
house, licensed 1388
North Elmham Chapel [EH] Remains of
Norman chapel reworked 14th C as
fortified manor house

Church of St Mary Church of Norman
origin with medieval and 19th-C work has
13th-C nave, 15th-C west tower, and
16th-C chancel

NORTH END, ESSEX, 3, 3B
Black Chapel Timber-framed medieval
chapel restored early 19th C with
attached priest's house to west;
15th-C screen

NORTHFIELD, W. MIDLANDS, 5, 3D
See Birmingham

NORTH FRODINGHAM
E. RIDING OF YORKS, 7, 5E
Church of St Elgin Medieval church
extensively restored 1800s contains
part of shaft and head of Saxon
cross with fine decoration; good
chest of c.1530

NORTH GRIMSTON,
N. YORKS, 7, 4D
Church of St Nicholas Norman church
with medieval and 19th-C additions has
original chancel arch and 13th-C west
tower; fine Norman font with carving
depicting Last Supper, and two
medieval grave slabs

NORTH HILL, CORNWALL, 1, 3C
Church of St Torney Spacious church
with finely carved work to south aisle and
three-storeyed west tower, probably by
masons from St Neot; 15th- or early 16th-C
ceiled wagon roofs to nave and aisles;
good Easter Sepulchre

NORTH HINKSEY, OXON
Church of St Lawrence Norman church
with carved south doorway and early
medieval west tower has 14th-C octagonal
font decorated with eight different tracery
designs

NORTHIAM, E. SUSSEX, 3, 3D
Church of St Mary Church of Norman
origin with mid 19th-C additions has
original lower part of tower with
13th-C upper storey and 15th-C
spire; 13th-C arcades
Great Dixter House [HHA] 15th-C
hall-house reworked 1910 by Lutyens
retains fine timber-framing
Wellhouse Timber-framed house
built 15th C with thatched roof and
open hall

NORTHLEACH, GLOS, 2, 3A
Church of St Peter and St Paul "Wool"
church of Norman origin much rebuilt
15th C has west tower of c.1380–1400 and

lavish early 15th-C south porch with
medieval sculpture; late 15th-C nave with
unusual arcade piers; late medieval pillar
piscina, pulpit and brasses

NORTH LEIGH, OXON, 2, 4A
Church of St Mary Church with west
tower of c.1000–50, arcades of c.1200, and
fan-vaulted Wilcote Chantry begun c.1439;
north aisle added early 18th C; good
15th-C Wilcote monument and
stained glass

NORTH LUFFENHAM,
RUTLAND, 4, 1D
Church of St John the Baptist Norman
church rebuilt 13th to 15th C retains late
12th-C piers to north arcade, 13th-C west
tower and fine late medieval nave roof;
13th-C wall painting, chancel windows
and sedilia of c.1300–25

NORTH MARDEN, W. SUSSEX, 2, 5D
Church of St Mary Simple Norman
church with apsidal east end and south
doorway of c.1130–40; 13th-C piscina

NORTH MORETON, OXON
Church of All Saints Church of Norman
origin largely rebuilt from mid 13th to
early 14th C with 15th-C west tower;
unusual east window of 1299 and
fine stained glass of c.1300 in south
chapel

NORTH NEWTON, SOMERSET, 2, 1D
Maunsel House (gardens only open)*
Medieval manor house partly built
before Norman Conquest with great
hall of 1420 and reworking of c.1791
and 19th C

NORTH PETHERTON,
SOMERSET, 2, 1C
Church of St Mary Embattled medieval
church with large 15th-C windows, tall
tower arch, clerestory, and fine west
tower with pinnacles; 15th-C pulpit

NORTH RONA, WESTERN ISLES
(Outer Hebrides), 9, 3B
Church Ruins of church on remote, now
uninhabited, island with east part built
possibly 8th or 9th C and medieval west
extension

NORTH STOKE, W. SUSSEX, 3, 1E
Church Attractive cruciform church
retains spacious Norman nave, mid 13th-C
chancel, transepts of c.1290, and bell turret
on ridge of north transept roof; font of
c.1200, good 13th-C carved corbels and
wall paintings

NORTH WALSHAM,
NORFOLK, 4, 4D
Church of St Nicholas Spacious medieval
church much restored 19th C with 14th-C
arcades, chancel, rich south porch and tall
tower arch; 15th-C font canopy and rood
screen with painted dado

NORTHWICH, CHESHIRE, 5, 2A
Church of St Helen, Witton Embattled
church of 14th to 16th C much restored
1800s has clerestory, polygonal apse, west
tower, and fine panelled roofs of c.1525

NORTON, CHESHIRE, 5, 2A
Norton Priory Surviving porch of 16th-
and 18th-C house contains late 12th-C
doorway from Augustinian priory;
remains of Norman undercroft from
west range of cloister

NORTON (Stockton-on-Tees),
CO. DURHAM, 7, 4C
Church of St Mary the Virgin Embattled
church of Saxon origin restored 19th C has
crossing tower, 12th-C arcades and late
15th-C nave roof; fragments of 10th-C
cross shafts and good 14th-C
monuments

NORTON (Sheffield), S. YORKS, 5, 4A
Church of St James Medieval church
retains Norman south doorway, north
aisle built c.1200, 13th-C west tower with
later top, and much 15th-C work; 13th-C
font and alabaster monument erected
c.1510–20

NORTON, WORCS, 5, 3E
Church of St Egwin Medieval church
extensively rebuilt 1844 with 15th-C
west tower; richly carved lectern of
c.1190 and early 16th-C panelling in
chancel

NORTON ST PHILIP,
SOMERSET, 2, 2C
Church of St Philip Medieval church
with extensive 17th-C rebuilding and
restoration of 1847 retains early
14th-C south arcade, 15th-C chancel,
chancel chapels, and font
George Inn Splendid medieval inn
built 15th C with stone base and two
timber-framed overhanging upper
storeys

NORTON-SUB-HAMDON
SOMERSET, 2, 2D
Church of St Mary Attractive church of
c.1500–10 has spacious interior and tower
with tall bell openings

NORWICH, NORFOLK, 4, 4D
Cathedral Complete Norman cathedral built late 11th to mid 12th C with original apse and ambulatory, crossing and magnificent nave; cloisters (rebuilt 13th to 15th C) with tierceron vaults and nearly 400 carved bosses; clerestory of presbytery (14th-C); 15th-C stone vaults (again with exquisite bosses) replacing Norman roof; spire rebuilt after 1463
Cathedral precinct Several monastic buildings, fragment of Norman Bishop's Palace; east porch of Bishop Salmon's Hall (early 14th-C) and chapel of Canary College (founded 1316, now belonging to Norwich School; medieval precinct walls and entrances to cathedral close, including St Ethelbert's Gate of c.1316–20 (much restored 19th C) and Erpingham Gate of 1416–25
Church of St Mary at Coslany, St Mary Plain, off Oak Street. Saxon round tower of church rebuilt mid 15th C
Norwich Castle (museum) * Norman motte of 1070 with massive rectangular hall-keep decorated with blind arcading (c.1160, refaced 19th C)
Wensum Lodge (The Music House), 167 King Street. Well-preserved undercroft of Norman town house (c.1200) survives behind 17th-C facade
The Lazar House, 219 Sprowston Road (now public library) Surviving part of building of Norman hospital founded c.1180
City walls Norman city walls and towers (rebuilt 1294–1320), best seen near Carrow Bridge and along Chapelfield Gardens
Cow Tower [EH] 14th-C circular tower, formerly part of city defences
Bishop's Bridge East end of Bishopgate Bridge with three segmental arches believed to date from c.1340
Guildhall, Market Place. Medieval Guildhall built 1407–13 with Council Chamber added 1535
Bridewell Museum *, Bridewell Alley. Late 14th-C house of first Mayor of Norwich with very early example of brick vaults
Dragon Hall *, 115–123 King Street Magnificent 15th-C merchant's hall with fine timber roof
St Peter Mancroft, Market Place. Impressive late medieval church built 1430–55 has richly decorated tower with spire added 1895; 15th-C glass in east window; furnishings include rare medieval font cover and pulley wheels and boss for Lenten veil
Medieval churches The city's 35 surviving

medieval churches (some no longer in use) also include: **St George** (Tombland) [OCT]; **St Giles** (St Giles's Street) [OCT] with splendid hammerbeam roof; **St Andrew** (St Andrew Street) [OCT]; **St Gregory** (Pottergate) with fine mid 15th-C wall paintings; **St Peter Hungate** * (Elm Hill) (now museum of church history)
St Andrew's Hall, St Andrew's Plain Important former Blackfriars' church built 1440–70
Great Hospital, Bishopgate. Hospital founded 1249 retains traces of 14th- and 15th-C plan with surviving buildings including cloister, Master's Lodging, and medieval parish Church of St Helen which was incorporated into infirmary building
Strangers' Hall Museum (currently closed), Charing Cross. Mid 15th-C hall survives inside medieval merchant's house remodelled 16th and 17th C
The Briton's Arms (restaurant), 9 Elm Hill Jettied timber-framed medieval building belonging to 15th-C community of religious women, restored 1953
Town Plan Extensive survival of medieval street pattern, especially in picturesque area around Elm Hill

NOSELEY, LEICS, 5, 5D
Chapel of St Mary Long, aisleless chapel built c.1274–c.1305 with 15th-C work; lavish carved stalls of c.1473–4

NOTLEY ABBEY, BUCKS, 2, 5A
Notley Abbey Late medieval abbot's lodging of Augustinian abbey founded early 1100s, later converted to private residence; fragments of church built c.1160 with later work; part of south range with good 13th-C arcading; stone dovecot (possibly 14th-C) survives nearby

NOTTINGHAM, NOTTS, 5, 5B
Church of St Mary, High Pavement. Spacious mainly 15th-C church with west front of 1845–53 and chapter house added 1890 has rich exterior, large windows, crossing tower, transepts, clerestory and tall nave arcades
Church of St Peter Medieval church with chancel restored 1875 has west tower with tall spire, rich west portal, and nave and south aisle roofs of 1501–9
Lenton Priory, Gregory Street, Old Lenton (Outer Nottingham) Scanty remains of important Cluniac priory founded 1102–8 include priory church of 1883 with 12th-C chancel from original building

Church of the Holy Trinity, Church Street, New Lenton (Outer Nottingham) Big church built 1842 contains splendid mid 12th-C font with narrative scenes from Lenton Priory
Church of St Mary, Clifton (Outer Nottingham) Cruciform church of Norman origin restored 19th and 20th C retains late 12th-C north arcade, tall crossing tower, late 14th-C clerestory, and chancel enlarged c.1476 with good timber roof; mid 15th-C device over chancel arch
Church of St Leonard, Wollaton (Outer Nottingham) Church built mainly late 14th C with tower and slender spire retains chancel south doorway of c.1200; good brasses and monuments
Cottage, 737 Wollaton Road, Wollaton (Outer Nottingham) Medieval cottage with later alterations (possibly 15th-C chantry house)

NUNBURNHOLME,
   E. RIDING OF YORKS, 7, 4E
Church of St James Norman church restored 1872–3 retains original nave with fine tower arch, and 13th-C chancel; lavish cross shaft of c.900 with figural carvings

NUNEATON, WARWS, 5, 4D
Church of St Nicholas Spacious medieval church has fine interior with four-bay arcades, 14th-C south chapel arcade, good roofs, 15th-C clerestory and west tower; chancel extensively rebuilt 1852
Church of St Mary Manor Court Road; Former church of Benedictine nunnery founded c.1155–60, rebuilt 13th C and with extensive 19th- and 20th-C additions retains original crossing and ruined south transept; medieval tiles in chancel

NUN MONKTON, N. YORKS, 7, 4D
Church of St Mary Surviving nave of church of Benedictine nunnery founded c.1150 has good west front with large doorway, 12th-C lower walls, and rich upper levels of c.1230–40; east wall added 1873 after demolition of chancel

NUNNEY, SOMERSET, 2, 2C
Church of All Saints 13th-C church with medieval and 19th-C rebuilding has transepts added c.1330–50, arcades of c.1375–80, and 15th- or early 16th-C wagon roof; Norman font and medieval wall painting
Nunney Castle [EH] Small symmetrical moated castle begun 1373 with round angle towers

NURNEY, CO. CARLOW, 12, 5B
Cross [Dúchas] Early Christian granite cross, sole survivor of three which formerly stood on site

NURSTEAD, KENT, 3, 3C
Church of St Mildred 15th-C church with west tower, south vestry and north porch
Nurstead Court House rebuilt c.1837 retains half of original 14th-C aisled hall with hipped roof

OAKHAM, RUTLAND, 4, 1D
Church of All Saints Church of 13th to early 16th C has original south doorway and porch, and spacious interior with carved capitals to early 14th-C arcades; early 13th-C font
Oakham Castle * Remarkable, well-preserved aisled hall of c.1180–90 set within inner bailey of castle; carved capitals to arcades and good exterior sculpture
Flore's House High Street. Late 14th-C house with 15th-C timber-framed parlour wing

OAKSEY, WILTS, 2, 3B
Church of All Saints Medieval church has 13th-C clerestory, south arcade, west tower with 15th-C top, and good 14th-C north porch; 15th-C screen and wall painting

OCKHAM, SURREY, 3, 1D
Church of All Saints 13th-C church with 16th-C tower and King Chapel of c.1735 retains original north arcade, chancel arch, and fine east window of c.1260; wagon roof to nave added c.1530; good 14th-C brass

OCKWELLS MANOR HOUSE
(1.5 km. / 1 m. WSW of Bray),
   BERKS, 2, 5B
Ockwells Manor House Fine timber-framed manor house built between 1446 and 1466 and restored 20th C has original east front with gables and bay windows, cloister, and hall with timber roof

ODELL, BEDS, 3, 1A
Church of All Saints Mainly 15th-C church with four-stage west tower, south porch and spacious interior; fragments of 15th-C stained glass
Odell Castle Surviving outbuildings of motte and bailey castle

ODIHAM, HANTS, 2, 5C
Church of All Saints Medieval church with 19th-C work has early 13th-C tower

arch, early 16th-C arcades and 17th-C
tower; late 12th-C pillar piscina and good
medieval brasses
Odiham Castle Surviving octagonal keep
of medieval castle built c.1207–12

OFFLEY, HERTS, 3, 1B
Church of St Mary Magdalene Medieval
church remodelled c.1777 with west tower
of 1800 retains nave and arcades of c.1230;
14th-C font and 15th-C benches

OGMORE CASTLE,
    GLAMORGAN, 6, 4E
Ogmore Castle [CADW] Remains of
Norman castle include imposing west wall
of early 12th-C keep with chimneypiece,
early 13th-C curtain wall, and roofless
courthouse rebuilt 1454–5

OKEHAMPTON, DEVON, 1, 4C
Okehampton Castle [EH] Norman
castle on picturesque site above river
reconstructed with extensive buildings
and curtain wall early 14th C

OLD BEAUPRE CASTLE (1.5 km. /
    1 m. SW of St Hilary),
    GLAMORGAN, 1, 5A
Old Beaupre Castle [CADW] Mansion of
c.1300 much rebuilt 16th C on courtyard
plan retains original service end to east of
hall and barn of c.1500 to south-east

OLD BEWICK,
    NORTHUMBERLAND, 7, 3A
Church of the Holy Trinity Norman
church restored 1695 and 1866–7 with
good original chancel and apse arches,
south doorway and priest's door

OLD BOLINGBROKE, LINCS, 4, 2B
Church of St Peter and St Paul Mainly
14th-C church with 19th-C work has
rich south aisle (now nave and chancel)
and north-west tower; good tracery
in windows
Bolingbroke Castle [EH] Remains of
13th-C moated hexagonal castle
sacked 1643 with towers and inner
courtyard

OLDCASTLE, CO. MEATH, 11, 4D
Moylagh Church and Castle (4.5 km. /
2 ¾ m.S) Scanty remains of late medieval
castle and church with small residential
tower to south of nave

OLD KILCULLEN,
    CO. KILDARE, 12, 5B
High Crosses and Round Tower [Dúchas]
Remnants of three High Crosses (west
with good figure carving) and stump

of Round Tower mark site of early
monastery

OLD LEAKE, LINCS, 4, 2C
Church of St Mary Spacious church of
Norman origin remodelled 13th to
15th C retains 14th-C arcades and west
tower built 1490–1547; rare 15th-C
oak almsbox

OLD PLACE OF MOCHRUM
    (7 km. / 4 ¼ m. SW of Kirkcowan),
    DUMFRIES AND
    GALLOWAY, 10, 4E
Old Place of Mochrum House created late
19th and early 20th C incorporates 15th-C
Old Tower restored 1873–4 with original
kitchen on ground floor

OLD RADNOR / PENCRAIG
    POWYS, 6, 5C
Church of St Stephen Handsome church
rebuilt early 15th C has three-stage west
tower, south porch, aisles with chapels,
and good 16th-C roofs; megalithic font
(possibly 8th-C), fine wide late 15th-C
screen, and earliest organ case in
Britain (16th-C)

OLD SARUM, WILTS, 2, 4C
Old Sarum [EH] Impressive remains of
Norman stronghold on important Iron
Age earthwork include late 12th-C gate-
house, curtain walling, keep, 13th-C hall,
and foundations of cathedral

OLD SHOREHAM,
    W. SUSSEX, 3, 1E
Church of St Nicholas Mainly Norman
church restored 1839–40 retains Saxon
work, central tower of c.1140, transepts,
and chancel lengthened 14th C; carved
tie beam of c.1300 and contemporary
screen

OLD SOAR MANOR,
    KENT, 3, 3D
See Plaxtol

OLD WARDOUR, WILTS, 2, 3D
See Wardour

OLD WOKING, SURREY, 3, 1D
Church of St Peter Norman and medieval
church has tall west doorway of c.1100 and
door with original ironwork

OLNEY, BUCKS, 3, 1A
Church of St Peter and St Paul Church
built mainly early 14th C has spacious
interior with five-bay arcades, tall
windows, and tower with broach
spire; good Easter Sepulchre

ONCHAN, ISLE OF MAN, 6, 1A
Crosses Group of fine Celtic crosses and
one Norse example survive in porch of
church

ONIBURY, SHROPS, 5, 2D
Church of St Michael Medieval church
restored 1902 has Norman chancel arch,
west tower, 13th-C work, and 15th-C porch

ORCHARDTON TOWER (2 km. /
    1 ¼ m. S of Palnackie), DUMFRIES
    AND GALLOWAY, 10, 5E
Orchardton Tower [HS] Charming,
well-preserved circular tower house
built late 1400s

ORCHARD WYNDHAM
    SOMERSET, 1, 5B
Orchard Wyndham * House much rebuilt
and with west front of c.1600 retains
original great hall of c.1500 with open
timber roof

ORDSALL HALL, LANCS, 5, 3A
See Salford

ORFORD, SUFFOLK, 3, 5A
Orford Castle [EH] Experimental
polygonal keep of major Norman castle
built 1165–7
Church of St Bartholomew Ruins of
Norman chancel begun 1166
survive at eastern end of large 14th-C
parish church with good late medieval
font and brasses

ORLEIGH COURT (N of Buckland
    Brewer), DEVON, 1, 4B
Orleigh Court Late medieval hall-house
with extensive alterations and additions
of 18th to 20th C (converted to flats
1982–3) retains original two-storeyed
porch and hammerbeam roof to hall

ORMISTON, LOTHIAN, 8, 3E
Market Cross [HS], High Street. Tall
15th-C cross, a rare survival in Scotland

ORMSIDE, CUMBRIA, 7, 2C
Church of St James Medieval church
retains 11th-C south doorway, north
arcade built c.1140–50, late 12th-C west
tower, and early 16th-C chancel
Ormside Hall Medieval hall-house with
tower wing built 14th or 15th C

ORMSKIRK, LANCS, 7, 2E
Church of St Peter and St Paul Medieval
church much rebuilt 1729 and 1877–91 has
14th-C south tower with octagonal bell
stage and mid 16th-C west tower; late
15th-C monuments

ORONSAY (tidal island accessible
    by causeway from Colonsay),
    STRATHCLYDE
    (Inner Hebrides), 10, 2B
Oronsay Priory Island houses substantial
remains of Augustinian priory founded
14th C on earlier site; finely carved late
medieval Oronsay Cross; Prior's House
contains large collection of carved
grave slabs

ORPHIR (13 km. / 8 m. WSW of
    Kirkwall), ORKNEY, 9, 5B
Earl's Bu and Church of St Nicholas [HS]
Scanty remains of Scotland's only
surviving round church built possibly
c.1120 (mainly demolished 1757) with
tunnel-vaulted chancel, apse, and part
of nave; adjacent foundations may be
Earl's Palace of Viking period

ORTON LONGUEVILLE,
    CAMBS, 4, 1D
Church of the Holy Trinity Mainly
14th-C church with north chapel of
c.1275 and west tower; early 14th-C scroll
work on chancel door and early 16th-C
painting of St Christopher

OSBOURNBY, LINCS, 4, 1C
Church of St Peter and St Paul Largely
14th-C church with four-bay arcades and
good south porch; Norman font, 14th-C
sedilia and carved bench ends

OSPRINGE, KENT, 3, 4D
Maison Dieu [EH] Two houses of c.1255
and c.1300 respectively, once forming
part of hospital founded before 1234

OTHAM, KENT, 3, 3D
Stoneacre [NT] Late 15th- and 16th-C
house reworked 1920 retains open hall
with crown-post roof

OTLEY, SUFFOLK, 3, 4A
Church of St Mary 15th-C church with
west tower, south porch, clerestory, and
good hammerbeam roof to nave;
octagonal font
Otley Hall [HHA] (open bank holidays)
Handsome hall-house built 15th and early
16th C has fine entrance arch, hall with
screen, and parlour with original linenfold
panelling

OTLEY, W. YORKS, 7, 3E
Church of All Saints Church of Norman
origin has 12th-C north doorway, north
and south chancel windows, and early
14th-C west tower and transepts; fine
fragment of 9th to 11th-C Saxon
sculpture

OTTERY ST MARY, DEVON, 1, 5C
Church of St Mary Mainly mid 14th-C church restored 19th C has crossing, transept towers and long east end; fine vaulted roofs and bosses; 14th-C fittings and good monuments

OUGHTERARD,
CO. KILDARE, 12, 5B
Round Tower and Church [Dúchas] Stump of hilltop Round Tower, all that survives of 6th-C monastery; remains of church built 1009 or possibly much earlier

OUGHTMAMA, CO. CLARE, 12, 2B
Churches [Dúchas] Remains of three early Christian churches, the largest at west with flat-headed doorway and good font inserted 15th C into south-west corner

OUNDLE, NORTHANTS, 4, 1E
Church of St Peter Mainly 13th-C church has fine fine 14th-C west tower with crocketed spire, and ornate 15th-C south porch; late medieval screens and lectern

OUTWELL, NORFOLK, 4, 2D
Church of St Clement Mainly 15th-C stone-built church reworked 19th C retains west tower of 13th to 14th C and arcades of early 1300s; good roofs with angels and hammerbeams
Beaupre Hall Ruined manor house with hall range of c.1500, west front and gatehouse of c.1525, and later 16th-C work

OVER, CAMBS, 4, 2E
Church of St Mary Lavish mainly 14th- and 15th-C church, formerly belonging to Ramsey Abbey, has fine south side of c.1320–30 with porch and gargoyles, 14th-C west tower, and later medieval chancel; poorly preserved rood screen retains ribbed coving on east side; chancel stalls with misericords said to come from Ramsey Abbey

OVINGHAM,
NORTHUMBERLAND, 7, 3B
Church of St Mary Saxon church with extensive rebuilding of 1200s retains original west tower, 13th-C transepts, south porch and lancet windows; fragments of Saxon cross shafts and 13th-C font
Vicarage Medieval vicarage rebuilt 17th and 19th C with late 14th-C east end

OWLPEN, GLOS, 2, 2B
Owlpen Manor * Handsome manor house with medieval work and east wing (remodelled 1720), additions of c.1540, and west wing added 1616; early 16th-C roof and fireplace to hall; 15th-C barn

OXBOROUGH, NORFOLK, 4, 3D
Church of St John the Evangelist Mainly 15th-C church damaged 1948 has 14th-C north porch and doorway, and Bedingfeld Chapel with two lavish terracotta monuments of c.1525
Oxburgh Hall [NT] Moated manor house licensed 1482 (rebuilt 18th C and c.1835) retains remarkable late 15th-C brick gatehouse with tall flanking turrets

OXBURGH HALL,
NORFOLK, 4, 3D
See Oxborough

OXFORD, OXON, 2, 5A
St Michael's Church, Cornmarket and Ship Street. Saxon church tower (probably early 11th-C) with 13th-C and later rebuilding
Oxford Castle Remains of Norman castle include earth motte (probably 1071) and tower and crypt of chapel (inaccessible inside Oxford Prison)
Christ Church Cathedral * (also chapel of college of Christ Church), off St Aldates Great church built c.1180–1210 to house shrine of St Frideswide with medieval additions including 13th-C tower and Lady Chapel, and complex star-vault above choir (c.1500)
Norman churches Surviving parts of Norman churches are found in: **St Peter-in-the-East** (Queen's Lane) (now college library of St Edmund Hall); **St Aldate; St Cross; St Ebbe; St Andrew**, Headington; **St James**, Cowley. See also under Iffley
Town Walls Surviving parts of medieval town walls built 1226–40, best seen in gardens of New College
University Buildings Medieval College buildings include: **Merton College** – hall (13th-C), chapel (13th- to 15th-C) with contemporary stained glass, 15th-C brasses and fine brass lectern c.1500, Mob Quad and Library (14th-C); **New College** – Great Quad of William of Wykeham's College (founded 1379) with gatehouse, hall, library, cloister, bell tower and chapel, which retains some original stained glass and stalls with misericords; **Magdalen College** – hall, chapel, cloister and bell tower (late 15th- to early 16th-C) and

chapel with monument of c.1450 in the chantry and stalls with misericords in the antechapel; **Worcester College** – north-east and south ranges of quadrangle (15th-C), part of earlier medieval monastic college; **All Souls College** – Front Quad and chapel with mid 15th-C reredos, stalls with misericords and stained glass; **Lincoln College** – Front Quad, hall and kitchen (15th-C); **Balliol College** Extensively restored 15th-C buildings in north and west ranges of Front Quad, including library and former hall
Divinity School, off Broad Street. 15th-C lecture room with ornate lierne-vaulted roof and heraldic bosses
University Church of St Mary the Virgin High Street. Mainly 15th-C church with 13th-C tower, spire of 1315–25 and 14th-C Congregation House; S porch dates from 1637; 15th-C stalls, part of reredos and sedilia; late medieval stained glass in east window
Medieval Churches. Other medieval churches include: **St Aldate; St Andrew**, Headington; **St Cross; St Giles; St James**, Cowley; **St Mary Magdalen** (Magdalen Street); **St Michael** (Cornmarket)

OXWICH, GLAMORGAN, 6, 3E
Church of St Illtyd Church of Norman origin has 12th-C chancel remodelled c.1350 as funerary chapel, 14th-C west tower, and nave reworked c.1500; good 14th-C effigies of knight and lady
Oxwich Castle [CADW] Ruined castle built 1520s and enlarged by c.1580 with original gatehouse, south range, and tower

OZLEWORTH, GLOS, 2, 3B
Church of St Nicholas [CCT] Little church of Norman origin reworked 13th, 14th and 19th C retains unusual hexagonal central tower begun before 1131 and nave added c.1220; early 13th-C font

PADWORTH, BERKS, 2, 5C
Church of St John the Baptist Norman church with timber bell turret, apsed chancel and tall chancel arch; traces of wall painting in nave

PAIGNTON (Torbay), DEVON, 1, 5D
Church of St John Church of Norman origin rebuilt 13th to 15th C with large west tower; ornate late 15th-C Kirkham Chantry has stone screen with tomb chests
Kirkham House [EH] Restored stone-built medieval house

PAISLEY, STRATHCLYDE, 8, 1E
Paisley Abbey [SCS] Church of Cluniac abbey founded 1160s with 13th-, 14th- and 15th-C work (restored 1897–1928) retains fine three-storeyed nave built mainly 1445–59, restored transepts, and reconstructed choir; 10th-C Barochan Cross [HS] from nearby parish of Houston; panels depicting life of St Mirren (probably 12th-C) and choir with tombs of Stuart monarchs and six High Stewards; 15th-C monastic buildings incorporated in adjoining Place of Paisley

PALLAS, CO. GALWAY, 12, 3B
Pallas Castle [Dúchas] Remains of unusually well preserved five storeyed tower house and bawn built c.1500

PAMBER END, HANTS
Pamber Priory Surviving remnant of church of Norman Benedictine priory with crossing tower and complete chancel with fine piscina; late 12th-C coffin lid, early 14th-C oaken effigy

PAMPISFORD, CAMBS, 3, 2A
Church of St John Church of Norman origin with 19th-C restoration retains original south doorway with unusual tympanum, 13th-C north arcade, and 14th-C west tower; Norman font

PARKAVONEAR CASTLE,
CO. KERRY, 12, C
See Aghadoe

PARSONSTOWN, CO. LOUTH, 11, 4D
See Clogher Head

PARTRISHOW / PATRISIO
POWYS, 6, 5D
Church of St Ishow or Issui Small church restored 1908–9 has Norman nave, burial chapel (eglwys y bedd) at west with tomb of Issui and 14th-C roof, 15th-C porch, and chancel rebuilt 1500s; font of c.1055 and fine, well-preserved screen and rood loft of c.1500; churchyard cross of c.1300 with lantern dated 1918
Neuadd Hall-house built 15th C with 16th-C alterations

PATHHEAD (Kirkcaldy),
FIFE, 8,3D
Ravenscraig Castle [HS] Remains of medieval castle begun 1460 on promontory site with central range flanked by two impressive towers and subsidiary buildings to south

PATRINGTON,
E. RIDING OF YORKS, 7,5E
Church of St Patrick Handsome medieval church built c.1300 to mid 14th C has transepts, buttresses, pinnacles, good tracery, and fine crossing tower with late 14th-C spire; sedilia, piscina and Easter Sepulchre in chancel

PATRIXBOURNE, KENT, 3,4D
Church of St Mary Late Norman church with 15th- and much 19th-C work retains wheel window, and fine tower doorway with tympanum; late 13th-C piscina

PATTENDEN, KENT, 3,3D
See Goudhurst

PATTINGHAM, STAFFS, 5,3D
Church of St Chad Church of Norman origin with medieval and 19th-C remodelling retains 12th-C north arcade, good 13th-C chancel, and 14th-C west tower with later spire; well-preserved cross shaft in churchyard

PAUNTLEY, GLOS, 2,2A
Church of St John Norman church with medieval additions has original nave, south doorway and fine chancel arch; short early 16th-C west tower; 13th-C pillar piscina

PAVENHAM, BEDS, 3,1A
Church of St Peter Medieval church rebuilt 15th C retains 13th-C south porch and piscina of c.1300; fine corbels in north aisle and 13th-C coffin lid
Stafford Bridge 13th-C bridge of four arches crosses River Ouse

PAWLETT, SOMERSET, 2,1C
Church of St John the Baptist Church with 17th-C work retains fine Norman south doorway with good beakhead moulding, and late medieval rood screen

PEAKIRK, CAMBS, 4,1D
Church of St Pega 12th- and early 13th-C church with Norman west bellcote and rich south doorway has remarkable wall paintings dating from mainly 14th C including two-tiered Cycle of the Passion
The Hermitage (E of church) Restored chapel with chancel of c.1300 and 15th-C nave; part of Saxon cross shaft

PEASENHALL, SUFFOLK, 4,5E
Church of St Michael Late medieval church with nave and chancel rebuilt 1860–1 has good flushwork decoration to west tower and handsome north porch; Norman or early 13th-C octagonal font
New Inn [LT] Range incorporating handsome late medieval hall-house at centre (probably built as inn, certainly in use as one by 1478); fine king-post roof

PEEBLES, BORDERS, 7,1A
Cross Kirk [HS], Cross Road. Ruined 13th-C church associated with Trinitarian friary founded c.1474 retains nave and plain 15th-C residential west tower; excavated foundations of conventual buildings
Tweed Bridge 15th-C bridge widened 1834 and 1900
Mercat Cross Octagonal shaft of medieval market cross
Church of St Andrew Ruins of church founded 1195, collegiate after 1543, with tower restored 1883

PEEL, ISLE OF MAN, 6,1A
Peel Castle and Cathedral [MNH] Castle built mid 14th C on important site of St Patrick's Isle has extensive walls of c.1460 enclosing remains of buildings including Round Tower of Irish type (probably 10th-C), 10th-C church rebuilt early 1100s and later, and mainly 13th-C Cathedral of St German; round fort at north of island added mid 16th-C

PEMBREY, DYFED, 6,3E
Church of St Illtud 13th-C Benedictine priory church enlarged 14th C has 16th-C barrel roof and south nave window retaining arch carved with shields and emblems of Passion

PEMBRIDGE, HEREFS, 5,1E
Church of St Mary Church of Norman origin rebuilt c.1320–60 with low chancel, transepts and rood stair turret; unusual late 14th-C bell house with fine timber roof; 13th-C font
Castle Mainly 13th-C border castle with curtain walling, gatehouse, towers and original vaulted undercroft beneath 16th-C chapel
Medieval Buildings Good early 16th-C buildings include Market House with open lower storey, and Greyhound Inn

PEMBROKE, DYFED, 6,2E
Pembroke Castle [CADW] Impregnable late 12th- to mid 13th-C castle has inner ward with monumental Great Keep and

Outer Ward with curtain walls, towers and gatehouse
Town Plan and Defences Surviving street plan and parts of walls, including Barnard's Tower, which defended medieval town
Church of St Mary Large medieval church much restored 19th C
Monkton Priory Church of St Nicholas (1 km. / ½ m. SW of castle) Spacious Norman Benedictine priory church with long barrel-vaulted nave and early medieval south transept tower
Monkton Old Hall [LT] Attractive building dating from before 1400, probably former guest house of small priory, with later rebuilding and restoration

PENALLY, DYFED, 6,3E
Church of St Nicholas South transept of medieval church contains early Christian wheelhead cross of 9th to 10th C, carved with both Celtic interlace, spirals and key-patterning and Anglo-Saxon beasts and vine-scrolls

PENARTH, GLAMORGAN, 6,5E
Church of St Peter off Sully Road. Simple early Norman church restored 1894 has original chancel arch, south porch and west bellcote
Cosmeston Medieval Village 13th- to 14th-C village excavated 1981 with reconstructed farmstead, barn and kilnhouse

PENHALLAM (1.5 km. / 1 m. NW of Week St Mary), CORNWALL, 1,3C
Penhallam [EH] Remains of moated medieval manor house

PENHOW, GWENT, 6,5E
Church of St John the Baptist Much-restored Norman and 13th-C church
Penhow Castle * 18th-C house incorporating remains of medieval castle, including three-storeyed rectangular Norman tower and 15th-C great hall

PENKRIDGE, STAFFS, 5,3C
Church of St Michael Medieval church has 13th-C interior and embattled exterior of 14th to 16th C with west tower and two-storeyed south porch; late 15th-C stalls with misericords

PENMARK, GLAMORGAN, 2,1B
Church of St Mary Church of late Norman origin rebuilt 14th and 15th C retains original chancel arch, nave with

ceiled wagon roof, and big tower arch; chancel reworked 1860
Castle Remains of medieval castle with 13th-C curtain walling and north-west tower

PENMON (ANGLESEY),
GWYNEDD, 6,4A
Penmon Priory [CADW] Cruciform church built c.1140–c.1170 has south doorway with carved tympanum and low central tower topped by pyramid roof; 13th-C chancel rebuilt 19th C; two 10th-C carved Celtic crosses by entrance and in south transept; font made out of base of another one; 13th- and 16th-C monastic building and dovecot of c.1600
St Seiriol's Well Remains of saint's oval cell and well with stone benches beneath 18th-C superstructure

PENN, BUCKS, 3,1B
Church of the Holy Trinity Medieval church with early 14th-C west tower, fine queen-post roof added to nave early 1400s, and 15th-C north porch; work and additions of 1730s; rare surviving Doom painted on boards (c.1400 and late 15th-C, discovered 1938)

PENNANT MELANGELL,
POWYS, 6,4B
Church of St Melangell Mid 12th-C church enlarged and altered in 15th, 17th, 18th and 19th C and restored 1988–92 contains remarkable shrine of Monacella c.1165 (reconstructed 1958–9), a rare survival and believed to be oldest in Britain; 12th-C font, 14th-C effigies, 15th-C nave roof and screen; 17th-C cell-y-bedd (cell of the grave) on foundations of Norman apse

PENNARD, GLAMORGAN, 6,3E
Church of St Mary Medieval church restored 1847 with unusual west tower
Castle (2.5 km. / 1½ m. W) Surviving gatehouse and curtain walls of castle built c.1300

PENNARTH FAWR,
GWYNEDD, 6,3B
See Abererch

PENNYGOWN (Island of Mull)
STRATHCLYDE
(Inner Hebrides)
Pennygown Chapel Shell of 13th-C chapel with base of cross shaft within walls

PENRICE, GLAMORGAN, 6,3E
Church of St Andrew Church of Norman origin with 12th-C chancel arch, 13th- or

early 14th-C transepts, and west tower
Penrice Castle Inaccessible ruins of medieval castle set in 18th-C landscaped grounds with 13th-C gatehouse and curtain walling

PENRITH, CUMBRIA, 7, 2C
Penrith Castle [EH] 14th-C castle with 15th-C additions
Church of St Andrew Graveyard of church built 1720–2 contains so-called Giant's Grave made up of two tall carved crosses of c.1000 with hogback coffins between and Giant's Thumb, a similar cross

PENSHURST, KENT, 3, 2D
Church of St John the Baptist Medieval church extensively rebuilt 19th C with 13th- and early 14th-C arcades and 15th-C clerestory; two 13th-C coffin slabs
Penshurst Place * Splendid, well-preserved manor house licensed 1341 with 15th-, 16th- and 19th-C additions retains 14th-C porch, service wing, and solar; hall with fine timber roof and central hearth

PENTLOW, ESSEX, 3, 3A
Church of St George Norman church with original apse, 12th-C round tower, and vaulted 16th-C north chapel; Norman font with good late medieval cover
Pentlow Hall Timber-framed manor house built c.1500 and reworked late 1500s

PERSHORE, WORCS, 5, 3E
Abbey Norman abbey church damaged 16th C and rebuilt 19th C retains 12th-C south transept, handsome chancel consecrated 1239 with vault of c.1290–1330, and early 14th-C crossing tower; Norman font and good monuments
Church of St Andrew Norman church rebuilt 14th and 15th C has north arcade of 1190–1200 and south-west tower

PERTH, TAYSIDE, 8, 3D
Church of St John, St John Street Interesting cruciform church dating from mainly 15th, 16th and 19th C (restored 1923–6) retains fine choir of c.1440–8 with open timber roof incorporating original work, north porch with 15th-C vault (lower part of tower dismantled 1817), and central tower with steeple finished before 1511; north transept truncated and remodelled 1823

PETERBOROUGH, CAMBS, 4, 1D
Cathedral * Impressive cathedral begun 1118 and restored 1882–6, formerly part of

Benedictine abbey, retains fine 12th-C work in chancel, transepts and nave, low crossing tower of c.1325, west front with turrets, three giant recesses and porch added late 1300s, and retrochoir built c.1496–1508 with handsome fan vault; original wooden ceilings to transepts and nave, the latter with 13th-C colouring; important Hedda Stone of c.800, good monuments of abbots of c.1195–c.1225, and late 15th-C brass lectern
Cathedral Precinct Remains of gateways and domestic buildings of medieval abbey include 12th-C Outer Gate altered 1302–7, early 13th-C Abbot's Gate with good original figures, parts of refectory, and impressive infirmary; chancel of church built c.1330 survives by Outer Gate (St Thomas's Chapel)
Church of St John the Baptist Church rebuilt on present site 1402–7 with medieval material including that of demolished nave of St Thomas's has west tower, good two-storeyed south porch, and tall arcades

PETERCHURCH, HEREFS, 5, 1E
Church of St Peter Spacious Norman church retains apse, three fine internal arches, original south doorway and west tower added late 13th to early 14th C; Norman font;
Wellbrook Manor Handsome 14th-C hall-house
Snodhill Castle Ruins of Norman and medieval motte and bailey castle with keep of c.1200 and 14th-C bailey walls
Urishay Chapel Modest chapel, probably Norman, situated next to moat of castle

PETERSFIELD, HANTS, 2, 5D
Church of St Peter Church begun c.1120 and restored 1873–4 has crossing tower with upper stages of c.1130–40, late 12th-C nave arcades, and west tower with 15th-C top

PETERSTONE WENTLOOGE
GWENT, 2, 1B
Church of St Peter Large 15th-C church with grand aisled nave, south porch, and west tower with battlements and saints in niches; chancel and north aisle rebuilt 19th C

PEVENSEY, E. SUSSEX
Pevensey Castle [EH] Remains of Roman fort adapted for use as castle during early Norman period, with keep and inner bailey built inside Roman walls; inner bailey reconstructed 13th C

Church of St Nicholas High Street Mainly 13th-C church with lancet windows, original arcades, and reworked chancel arch of c.1230–40; north tower has bell stage added 1877–9

PEVERIL CASTLE, DERBYS, 5, 4A
See Castleton

PHILIPSTOWN CHURCH
CO. LOUTH, 11, 4D
See Tallanstown

PICARDY SYMBOL STONE (nr Mireton, Insch), GRAMPIAN, 8, 4B
Picardy Symbol Stone [HS] Fine Pictish stone of possibly 7th C with variety of carved symbols including mirror, serpent and double disc

PICKERING, N. YORKS, 7, 4D
Church of St Peter and St Paul Church of Norman origin with medieval additions retains 12th-C arcades, early 13th-C west tower with later upper level, chancel of 1300s, and 15th-C two-storeyed south chapel; 14th-C effigies and good set of mid 15th-C wall paintings
Pickering Castle [EH] Remains of motte and bailey castle with shell keep of c.1220–30, impressive chapel built c.1226–7, towers and walling

PIEL CASTLE, CUMBRIA, 7, 1D
See Barrow-in-Furness

PIEROWALL, ORKNEY, 9, 5A
See Westray

PILLATON, STAFFS, 5, 3C
Pillaton Hall Remains of range of late 15th-C mansion with gatehouse and stone chapel; carved wooden saint of 13th C

PILLERTON HERSEY,
WARWS, 5, 4E
Church of St Mary Medieval church with later remodelling retains fine chancel built mid 13th C with priest's doorway, double piscina and double aumbry; good 15th-C nave roof

PILTON (nr Barnstaple), DEVON, 1, 4B
Church of St Mary Church formerly belonging to Benedictine priory founded 1100s has early north tower with octagonal upper levels (restored 1696, reconstructed 1845–50), early north aisle, and later medieval additions; rood screen and early 16th-C stone pulpit
Bull House Impressive, well-preserved

15th-C house, probably former prior's lodging or guesthouse, with 16th- and 18th-C additions

PILTON, SOMERSET, 2, 2C
Church of St John the Baptist Church of Norman origin with medieval additions has original south doorway, north arcade of c.1180–90, 13th-C west tower, and 15th-C chancel; good roofs and Easter Sepulchre
Tithe Barn Medieval stone barn of Glastonbury Abbey with fine roof

PIRTON, WORCS, 5, 3E
Church of St Peter Church of Norman origin with 14th-C chancel and timber-framed north tower; fine early Norman Pirton Stone

PITCHFORD, SHROPS, 5, 2D
Church of St Michael Church of Norman origin with work of 13th C and 1719 has weatherboarded belfry; well-preserved 13th-C oaken effigy of knight

PITEADIE CASTLE (2.5 km. / 1 ½ m. NW of Kinghorn), FIFE, 8, 3E
Piteadie Castle Remains of late 15th-C tower house with upper floors reworked late 1600s

PITFIRRANE (3 km. / 2 m. W of Dunfermline), FIFE, 8, 2D
Pitfirrane (now golf club) Simple tower house built c.1500 with turrets of 1583 and 18th- and 19th-C work

PITSFORD, NORTHANTS, 5, 5E
Church of All Saints Medieval church with arcades and rebuilding of 1867 retains good Norman south doorway with carved tympanum and 14th-C west tower; octagonal font of 1300s

PITSLIGO (5.5 km. / 3 ½ m. W of Fraserburgh), GRAMPIAN, 8, 4A
Pitsligo Castle Ruins of large and imposing 15th-C courtyard castle much extended c.1570 include massive original keep; complex surrounded by walled pleasance

PITTENWEEM, FIFE, 8, 3D
Pittenweem Priory Remains of 13th-C Augustinian priory rebuilt 15th C include gatehouse, west range reworked c.1588 (now Great House), and prior's lodging with post-medieval alterations
St Filan's Cave (accessible from Cove Wynd) Cave, reputedly dwelling and chapel of 7th-C saint

PITTINGTON,
CO. DURHAM, 7, 3C
Church of St Laurence, Hallgarth Church of Saxo-Norman origin extensively rebuilt 1846–7 has ornate late 12th-C north arcade, tower and south arcade of c.1225–50; 12th-C wall paintings and 13th-C monuments

PLAS UCHAF, CLWYD, 6, 5B
See Corwen

PLAS YN RHIW,
GWYNEDD, 6, 3B
See Rhiw

PLAXTOL, KENT, 3, 3D
Old Soar Manor [EH / NT] Surviving solar block of knight's manor house built c.1290 with attached 18th-C block; solar on undercroft, and projecting chapel and garderobe

PLUSCARDEN ABBEY (10 km. / 6 m. SE of Elgin), GRAMPIAN, 8, 3A
Pluscarden Abbey [SCS] Fine, imposing remains of Valliscaulian abbey founded 1230 by Alexander II (Benedictine after 1454), well restored by Benedictine monks since 1948, include transepts, chancel and central tower of ambitious 13th-C church with traces of wall paintings of c.1500, part of cloisters, and extensive precinct wall; Lady Chapel (open on request) retains original work of 1230

PLYMPTON (Plymouth),
DEVON, 1, 4D
Castle Fragmentary remains of 12th-C motte and bailey castle
Church of St Mary, Market Road. Mainly early 15th-C church retains early 14th-C outer north aisle and chancel; lavish south side with two-storeyed porch retaining fine lierne vault of c.1400; imposing west tower
Priory Fragments of Augustinian priory founded 1121 survive in Priory Row and Tower House

PLYMTREE, DEVON, 1, 5C
Church of St John Church of Norman origin restored 19th C has 15th-C arcade and west tower; interior with splendid early 16th-C screen and bench ends

POLEBROOK, NORTHANTS, 4, 1E
Church of All Saints Church built mainly c.1175–c.1250 with south-west tower, transepts, chancel with lancet windows, and rich mid 13th-C north porch; font of c.1300

POLESWORTH, WARWS, 5, 4D
Church of St Editha Medieval church incorporates nave of Benedictine nunnery established 10th C with arcade of c.1120–30 and north aisle; imposing north tower with 17th-C top, and 19th-C chancel; effigy of abbess of c.1200 on 15th-C tomb chest
Abbey Gatehouse 14th-C stone gatehouse, once part of abbey, with timber-framed upper level

POLLOK (6.5 km. / 4 m. SW of Glasgow city centre) STRATHCLYDE, 10, 5C
Crookston Castle [HS / NTS] Remains of unusual tower house built c.1400 within ringwork defences of 12th-C castle

POLSTEAD, SUFFOLK, 3, 4A
Church of St Mary Norman church reworked 14th and 15th C has 12th-C arcades, brick clerestory, chancel arch, rich west doorway, and west tower added c.1300; 13th-C octagonal font and 15th-C brasses

PONTELAND,
NORTHUMBERLAND, 7, 3B
Church of St Mary Church of Norman origin with medieval and 19th-C work retains original west doorway, and west tower with 14th-C upper stage; 13th-C chancel, north transept and font
Blackbird Inn Inn built into surviving 13th or 14th-C wing of former hall-house with alterations and additions of 1597

PORLOCK, SOMERSET, 1, 5B
Church of St Dubricius Medieval church with work of c.1890 retains 13th-C west tower, 14th-C south arcade, and 15th-C north porch; font and Harrington monument of 1400s
Doverhay Manor House Part of 15th-C manor house reworked 1883

PORTAFERRY, CO. DOWN, 11, 5C
Portaferry Castle [EHS] Simple shell of 15th-C tower house

PORTCHESTER, HANTS, 2, 5D
Portchester Castle [EH] Roman fort adapted for use as castle when 12th-C keep and 13th-C inner bailey were built inside its walls; domestic quarters rebuilt 14th C as royal residence for Richard II
Church of St Mary 12th-C priory church in south-east corner of fort

PORT GLASGOW,
STRATHCLYDE, 10, 4C
Newark Castle [HS] Well-preserved mansion built mainly 16th to 17th C incorporating 15th-C tower house

survives beside River Clyde amidst modern shipyards and buildings; 15th-C gatehouse and remains of barmkin wall

PORTLICK CASTLE (3.5 km. / 2 ¼ m. NW of Glassan), CO. WESTMEATH, 11, 3D
Portlick Castle Four-storeyed late medieval tower house with alterations and additions of 18th and 19th C

PORTNESHANGAN,
CO. WESTMEATH, 11, 3D
Church of St Munna [Dúchas], **Taghmon** (5 km. / 3 m. NE) Imposing fortified church of mid to late 15th C with large west tower built as dwelling for clergy; inward sloping walls, and flat stone vault to interior

PORTNOO, CO. DONEGAL, 11, 2B
Inishkeel Churches and Crosses (island accessible at low tide from Tramore Strand) Site of early Christian monastery retains good cross slabs of possibly 8th C and two 13th-C and later churches

PORTSLADE (Brighton),
E. SUSSEX, 3, 2E
Church of St Nicholas 12th- and 13th-C church enlarged 1800s
Manor House (in grounds of St Mary's Convent) Fragments of 12th-C house survive partly built into churchyard wall

PORTSMOUTH, HANTS, 2, 5E
Cathedral * Church founded c.1180 (raised to cathedral status 1927) with nave and west tower built 1683–93 and 20th-C enlargement retains choir of c.1180–90 with galleried clerestory and transepts of c.1190–1220
Royal Garrison Church [EH], Old Portsmouth. Surviving part of Hospital of St John and St Nicholas founded c.1212 with 19th-C additions retains fine chancel of c.1212–20 and roofless nave (damaged 1940)
Square Tower Defensive tower built 1494 with much later remodelling

PORTSTEWART
CO. LONDONDERRY, 11, 4A
Ballywillan Old Church (4 km. / 2 ½ m. E) Well-preserved remains of large medieval church abandoned 1842 with early 13th-C aumbry in east wall

PORTUMNA, CO. GALWAY, 12, 3B
Portumna Friary [Dúchas] Surviving buildings (c.1426–1500) of Dominican Observant friary founded c.1425 include church with fine east window and

fragments of 13th-C work from earlier Cistercian building; cloister partly re-erected 1954

POTTER HEIGHAM,
NORFOLK, 4, 5D.
Church of St Nicholas Medieval church with thatched nave and chancel, round tower with 14th-C upper level, and 15th-C arcades; nave roof with angels and hammerbeams, brick font, and late 14th-C wall painting

POTTERNE, WILTS, 2, 3C
Church of St Mary Well-preserved 13th-C cruciform church retains lancet windows and crossing tower with 15th-C upper part; Saxon font and late medieval wooden pulpit
Porch House, High Street. Fine late 15th-C timber-framed hall-house with gables and original windows

POWERSTOCK, DORSET, 2, 2E
Church of St Mary Church retains richly carved Norman chancel arch of c.1150 to chancel of 1854–9; late medieval west tower and good south doorway

POWIS CASTLE, POWYS, 6, 5B
Powis Castle [NT] Impressive border castle set on tall ridge, converted to country house from 16th to 19th C, retains work of c.1200, keep of c.1300, and late 13th-C curtain walling

POYNINGS, W. SUSSEX, 3, 2E
Church of the Holy Trinity Church built late 14th C has ogee-arched decoration on sedilia, piscina and font with bowl, stem and foot all in one; 15th-C stained glass

PRESTBURY, CHESHIRE, 5, 3A
Church of St Peter Church of 13th-C origin rebuilt 15th and 17th to 19th C with original arcades and south doorway; west tower of c.1480
Chapel Norman chapel rebuilt c.1747 survives in churchyard and has west doorway with tympanum

PRESTEIGNE / LLANANDRAS
POWYS, 6, 5C
Church of St Andrew Spacious church of Saxon origin has clerestoried nave rebuilt early 1300s, south aisle enlarged and chancel rebuilt mid 15th C, and south tower; coffin lid of c.1240

PRESTON, LOTHIAN, 8, 3E
Preston Tower [NTS] Tower house built 1400s and heightened 1626

Church of St Baldred Plain church built 1770 with work of 1891–2 retains eastern part of 13th-C chancel, formerly used as burial aisle by Smeaton family

PRESTON, NORTHUMBERLAND, 7, 3A
Preston Tower [HHA] Remains of three-storeyed 14th-C hall tower, built 1392 and restored 1864, with well-preserved tunnel-vaulted rooms

PRESTON, RUTLAND, 4, 1D
Church of St Peter and St Paul Church with Norman north arcade, south arcade of c.1200 and early 13th-C chancel chapels; fine sedile in chancel and priest's doorway

PRESTON PATRICK, CUMBRIA, 7 2D
Preston Patrick Hall Hall-house built 14th C with work of c.1500 and later; handsome king-post roofs

PRESTON PLUCKNETT SOMERSET, 2, 2D
Church of St James Medieval church with 19th-C additions has 14th-C chancel and transepts, and 15th-C west tower
Abbey Farm and Barn Fine 15th-C abbey grange with two-storeyed porch and unusual kitchen chimney; adjacent stone barn has original roof

PRITTLEWELL PRIORY, ESSEX, 3, 3C
See Southend-on-Sea

PROBUS, CORNWALL, 1, 2D
Church of St Probus and St Grace 15th- and early 16th-C church restored 19th C has tall west tower built c.1520–30 with battlements and pinnacles

PRUDHOE, NORTHUMBERLAND, 7, 3B
Prudhoe Castle [EH] Extensive Norman castle with inner and outer baileys retains 12th-C keep, fine gatehouse, and 13th-C barbican with upper chapel
Prudhoe Grange, South Street. Mainly 19th-C house with fine 13th-C south doorway;

PULHAM ST MARY, NORFOLK, 4, 4E
Church of St Mary Spacious medieval church restored 1886–7 has 13th-C chancel, west tower, and lavish two-storeyed south porch of 1400s; fine mid 13th-C double piscina

PURSE CAUNDLE MANOR DORSET, 2, 2D
Purse Caundle Manor [HHA] 15th- and 16th-C manor house with additions of 1600s

PURTON, WILTS, 2, 3B
Church of St Mary Church of Norman origin much rebuilt 14th and 15th C retains early 13th-C arcades with later arches, late 14th-C crossing tower, 15th-C chancel, and good west tower; sedilia, Easter Sepulchre, and wall paintings

PWLLHELI, GWYNEDD, 6, 3E
Pennarth Fawr (5 km. / 3 m. E) Small 15th-C hall-house, altered 17th C and restored 1937

PYLE / Y PIL, GLAMORGAN, 6, 4E
Church of St James Church built c.1471 has west tower, south porch, original wagon roof to nave, and late 15th-C font

PYRFORD, SURREY, 3, 1C
Church of St Nicholas Well-preserved Norman church with 16th-C north porch and later bell turret and spire; good medieval wall paintings

QUEEN CAMEL, SOMERSET, 2, 2D
Church of St Barnabas Late 14th-C church with 19th-C work has aisle arcades of c.1360, tall west tower, and later chancel and clerestory; early 15th-C font, and good rood screen and pulpit of c.1500

QUENINGTON, GLOS, 2, 4B
Church of St Swithin Norman church extensively remodelled 1882 with splendid 12th-C carved tympana and north and south doorways

QUIN, CO. CLARE, 12, 3B
Quin Abbey [Dúchas] Substantial ruins of Franciscan friary founded c.1433 and completed c.1450 incorporating remains of late 13th-C castle with round corner towers; church with south transept, slender tower, good windows and tombs, and well-preserved cloister with buttresses and upper dormitory
Church of St Finghin [Dúchas] Plain rectangular church built 1278 to 1285 on west side of river retains triple lancet east window

RAASAY (island off coast of Skye) HIGHLAND (Inner Hebrides), 9, 2D
Church of St Moluag Ruined 13th-C church in Kilmoluag churchyard has late medieval tomb recess in south-east corner
Brochel Castle Remains of late medieval castle occupying defensive site by sea

RABY CASTLE, CO. DURHAM, 7, 3C
Raby Castle [HHA] Impressive castle begun early 14th C, licensed 1378 and remodelled 18th and 19th C with nine towers linked by curtain walling;

gatehouse, great kitchen, and Lower Hall of c.1320 with well-preserved late 14th-C Baron's Hall above

RADBURNE, DERBYS, 5, 4C
Church of St Andrew Medieval church with early 13th-C sedilia and 15th-C north-west tower; good 15th-C monuments

RADCLIFFE, GREATER MANCHESTER, 7, 2E
Church of St Mary, Church Green Medieval church with much 19th-C remodelling retains 14th-C chancel arch, 15th-C tower arch and early 16th-C nave arcades; tower dated 1665
Radcliffe Tower Medieval pele tower situated close to church

RADNAGE, BUCKS, 2, 5B
Church of St Mary 13th-C church rebuilt 14th and 15th C with original central tower (c.1200) and east window; 13th-C wall painting

RAGLAN, GWENT, 6, 5D
Raglan Castle [CADW] Magnificent late medieval castle with moated Great Tower known as "Yellow Tower of Gwent", built 1430s, beside splendid 15th- and 16th-C fortress palace with two courtyards and handsome four-storeyed gatehouse
Church of St Cadoc Medieval church dating mainly from 15th C with later additions and much 19th-C restoration; carved stone base of 15th-C cross in churchyard

RAHAN, CO. OFFALY, 12, 4B
Churches [Dúchas] Medieval remains on site of important early monastery include large West Church (still used for Protestant worship) with rich 12th-C chancel arch, unique circular east window and nave of mainly 1732; ruined church nearby rebuilt 1400s incorporates fine 12th-C west doorway

RAHAN CASTLE, CO. DONEGAL, 11, 3B
See Dunkineely

RAHINNANE (Dingle Peninsula), CO. KERRY, 12, 1C
Castle [Dúchas] Castle built 15th or 16th C using ringfort as bawn

RAHOLP (5.5 km. / 3 ½ m. SW of Srangford), CO. DOWN, 11, 5C
Raholp Church Restored remains of simple early Christian church survive within ringwork of rath; some good early gravestones

RAINHAM, GREATER LONDON, 3, 2C
Church of St Helen and St Giles Well preserved late Norman church with later medieval, 18th- and 19th-C additions has good original windows, chancel arch, west tower and north doorway; medieval wall painting and 15th-C brasses

RAINHAM, KENT, 3, 3C
Church of St Margaret Early 13th-C church reworked 14th C has long chancel and north chapel, broad north aisle and crown-post roofs; good 14th-C oak chest, 15th-C screen and medieval wall painting

RAIT CASTLE (4 km. / 2 ½ m. S of Nairn), HIGHLAND, 9, 4D
Rait Castle * Well-preserved remains of rare surviving rectangular hall castle built c.1300 and altered 16th and 17th C with round south-west tower, unvaulted basement and long upper hall

RAM'S ISLAND (8 km. / 5 m. W of Glenary via Sandy Bay) CO. ANTRIM, 11, 5B
Round Tower Island (bird sanctuary) in Lough Neagh houses remains of Round Tower on site of early monastery

RAMSBURY, WILTS, 2, 4B
Church of the Holy Cross Medieval church has 13th-C chancel enlarged 1400s, 14th-C west tower, embattled aisles, 15th-C arcades, clerestory and north (Darrell) chapel; remains of fine 9th-C crosses, coped stones and good monuments

RAMSEY, CAMBS, 4, 2E
Ramsey Abbey [Gatehouse – NT] Abbey School. Manor house built c.1600 and alterered 19th C incorporates mid 13th-C Lady Chapel and gatehouse of original abbey founded c.969; monument to Ailwin of c.1230 (in gatehouse)
Church of St Thomas of Canterbury Former hospitium or guesthouse built c.1180–90, used as church from 13th C, retains Norman chancel, arcading and west doorway; 13th-C font

RANTON, STAFFS, 5, 3C
Church of All Saints Church built 13th C with mid 18th-C brick chancel
Ranton Abbey Surviving 15th-C west tower of abbey founded c.1150

RANWORTH, NORFOLK, 4, 5D
Church of St Helen Medieval church with embattled nave, west tower, and tall

chancel and tower arches; fine screen of
c.1419, rood loft and painted cantor's desk

RAPHOE, CO. DONEGAL, 11,3B
Cathedral of St Eunan Cathedral church
built mainly 17th and 18th C and restored
from 1892 on site of early monastery
retains fine 13th-C sedilia and piscina
in chancel; two pieces of carved lintel
of late 9th or early 10th C, and fragments
of late 15th-C sculpture

RATASS, CO. KERRY, 12,2C
Church [Dúchas] Early church with
12th-C chancel and restoration of
c.1700 retains good flat-headed
west doorway

RATHALDRON CASTLE
      CO. MEATH, 11,4D
See Navan

RATHCLINE CASTLE (2 km. / 1 ¼
      m. S of Lanesborough, on shore of
      Lough Ree), CO. LONGFORD, 11,3D
Rathcline Castle Scanty remains of late
medieval castle with enclosure and
two towers, reworked and enlarged
early 1600s

RATHFRAN, CO. MAYO, 11,2C
Friary (or Rathfran Abbey) [Dúchas]
Remains of Dominican friary founded
1273 with long 13th-C church altered
1400s, foundations of cloisters, and
16th-C domestic buildings incorporating
part of original sacristy

RATHGALL (6.5 km. / 4 m. E of Tullow,
      Co. Carlow), CO. WICKLOW, 12,5B
Hill Fort [Dúchas] Fine stone fort built
probably early Christian period with three
concentric walls (central one later)

RATHMACKNEE,
      CO. WEXFORD, 12,5C
Castle [Dúchas] Well-preserved,
picturesque ruins of 15th-C castle
consisting of five storeyed tower
house enclosed by near complete
five sided bawn

RATHMICHAEL,
      CO. DUBLIN, 11,5E
Church and Round Tower [Dúchas]
Remains of 12th- or 13th-C church rebuilt
1500s on early monastic site has unusual
early Christian grave slabs attached to
south wall; stump of Round Tower to
south-west

RATHMORE, CO. MEATH, 11,4D
Rathmore Church [Dúchas] Remains of
manorial church built 15th C by Plunkett

family (similar to those at Killeen and
Dunsany) with three-storeyed tower
to north of chancel; triple sedilia with
original ceiling, good carved octagonal
font, and fine reconstructed Plunkett
altar tomb with effigies and niches
Rathmore Castle Ruined tower house
built probably early 1300s

RATHMULLEN,
      CO. DONEGAL, 11,3A
St Mary's Friary [Dúchas] Remains
of church and conventual buildings
of Carmelite friary built 1400s and later,
converted to fortified house c.1617

RATHO (Edinburgh), LOTHIAN, 8,3E
Church of St Mary (Parish Church), Baird
Road [SCS] Norman church with two
17th-C north aisles and south aisle added
c.1830 retains part of 12th-C
doorway, and 15th-C window in east wall;
13th-C tomb slab in south porch
commemorates one of Knights
Hospitaller who then held Ratho

RATHUMNEY CASTLE
      CO. WEXFORD
Rathumney Castle Castle built 13th or
14th C with two-storeyed central hall
and living rooms with fireplaces

RATTIN CASTLE (5 km. / 3 m.
      WSW of Kinnegad),
      CO. WESTMEATH, 11,4D
Rattin Castle Ruins of large and severe
tower house built probably mid 1300s

RATTLESDEN, SUFFOLK, 3,4A
Church of St Nicholas Large 14th-C
church with double hammerbeam roof
with angels (nearly all 19th-C); ornate
14th-C aumbrey in chancel and octagonal
font with ogee arches

RATTOO 1.5 km. / 1 m. SE of Ballyduff),
      CO. KERRY, 12,2C
Church and Round Tower [Dúchas]
Well-preserved Round Tower and remains
of small 15th-C church, survivors of early
monastery; ruined late medieval abbey
nearby

RAUNDS, NORTHANTS, 4,1E
Church of St Mary Church of Norman
origin has west tower begun c.1225 with
tall broach spire, 13th-C south chapel
and 14th-C arcades; fine east window of
c.1275, 15th-C clock dial on tower and
wall paintings

RAVENSCRAIG CASTLE,
      FIFE, 8,3D
See Pathhead

RAY, CO. DONEGAL, 11,3A
High Cross [Dúchas] Tall and plain
10th-C cross survives on ground before
ruins of post-medieval church

READING, BERKS, 2,5B
Reading Abbey Surviving fragments of
12th-C Cluniac abbey include 12th-C
arches of abbey mill, late 13th-C inner
gatehouse and range of 15th-C hospitium
Church of St Laurence Norman church
enlarged c.1196 and rebuilt 15th to 16th C
retains nave south doorway, early 13th-C
north chapel arcade and 15th-C west
tower; good brasses

REASK (Dingle Peninsula),
      CO. KERRY, 12,1C
Cross-Pillars [Dúchas] Fine collection of
cross-decorated slabs (many in Heritage
Centre in Ballyferriter) includes one in
situ with finely carved ornament
(between 7th- and 10th-C)

RECULVER, KENT, 3,4C
Reculver Towers [EH] Surviving late
12th-C two-towered west front of former
7th-C St Mary's Abbey on prominent
cliff-top site; remains of early Saxon
church (founded 669, demolished 1809)
excavated 1926–7

RED BAY (2.5 km. / 1 ½ m. S of
      Cushendall, at foot of Glenariff),
      CO. ANTRIM, 11,5A
Castle Attractive promontory site with
remains of medieval motte and bailey
castle, stone tower, and fragments of
castle built 1561

REDBOURN, HERTS, 3,1B
Church of St Mary Norman church with
14th and 15th-C additions has original
nave, north aisle arcade and west tower;
14th-C Easter Sepulchre and fine rood
screen of c.1478

REDENHALL, NORFOLK, 4,4E
Church of St Mary Medieval church has
14th-C chancel and arcades, fine west
tower begun 1460 with flushwork
panelling, and two-storeyed north
porch; double eagle lectern of c.1500

REDGRAVE, SUFFOLK, 4,4E
Church of St Mary the Virgin 14th-C
church with 15th-C clerestory,
hammerbeam roof to nave, and
west tower added c.1800; 14th-C
font and good sedilia

REEPHAM, NORFOLK, 4,4D
Church of St Mary Medieval church with
later restoration retains 13th and 14th-C

four-bay arcades, and fine monument to
Sir Roger de Kerdiston (d.1337)

REIGATE, SURREY, 3,2D
Church of St Mary Medieval church much
restored 19th C with fine nave arcades of
c.1200, 14th-C south chapel, and early
15th-C aisles and tower; sedilia and
piscina of 1300s

RENFREW, STRATHCLYDE, 10,5C
Renfrew Old Parish Church [SCS]
Church with sanctuary of 1862 containing
two good late medieval monuments

REPTON, DERBYS, 5,4C
Church of St Wystan Remarkable survival
of Saxon chancel and vaulted crypt in
cruciform church rebuilt 13th to 15th C;
west tower completed 1340
Repton Priory (Repton School Museum)
Ruins of Augustinian priory (founded
1172), now part of Repton School, include
church and ornate 15th-C Prior Overton's
Tower

RESTALRIG (Edinburgh),
      LOTHIAN, 8,3E
Parish Church [Chapel – HS] Late
medieval collegiate church much renewed
1836 retains vaulted hexagonal undercroft
of St Triduana's Chapel built c.1477–87

RESTENNETH, TAYSIDE, 8,3C
Restenneth Priory [HS] Impressive
13th-C choir and nave of priory probably
founded later 12th C by David I with tall
square tower begun 1000s (upper stage
12th or 13th-C); fragments of monastic
buildings

RESTORMEL, CORNWALL, 1,3D
Restormel Castle [EH] Mainly late 13th-C
circular castle with curtain wall of 12th or
early 13th C

RHIW, GWYNEDD, 6,3B
Plas yn Rhiw [NT] Medieval manor house
with 16th and 18th-C additions

RHOSSILI, GLAMORGAN, 6,3E
Church of St Mary the Virgin Medieval
church much restored 1800s with plain
west tower; lavish late 12th-C doorway
within south porch

RHUDDLAN, CLWYD, 6,4A
Rhuddlan Castle [CADW] Medieval
castle begun 1277 on concentric plan by
River Clwyd and slighted 1648 has inner
ward with well-preserved circular towers
and double towered gatehouses
Town Plan and Defences Surviving parts

of Norman bank and ditch defences and 13th-C town plan

Church of St Mary Church of *c*.1300 with 15th-C north nave and 19th-C additions retains original chancel and doorway to north (blocked and reset); good medieval slabs and monuments include that to William de Freney, Archbishop of Rages (d. *c*.1290)

Parliament House, Parliament Street. Building incorporates late 13th-C doorway to High Street, probably from castle

Abbey Farm (1 km. / ½ m. SE) Farm buildings on site of Dominican friary founded *c*.1258 incorporate medieval fragments

RHULEN, POWYS, 6,5D
Church of St David Simple and unusual church of *c*.1300 with south porch and timber belfry to west

RIALTON, CORNWALL, 1,2D
Manor House Surviving main range of late 15th-C monastic house (now farmhouse) has good first-floor hall windows and holy well in courtyard

RICCALL, N. YORKS, 7,4E
Church of St Mary Church of Norman origin with 19th-C work retains west tower built *c*.1170–90, rich south doorway of *c*.1190, early 13th-C arcades, late 13th-C chancel and north chapel; medieval cross shaft in churchyard

RICHARD'S CASTLE, HEREFS, 5,2D
Church of St Bartholomew Church of Norman origin rebuilt 14th and 15th C has detached bell tower of *c*.1300 and original nave with early 14th-C south arcade and aisle; carved coffin lid of 1200s

RICHARDSTOWN CASTLE
   CO. LOUTH, 11,4D
See Stabannan

RICHMOND, N. YORKS, 7,3D
Church of St Mary Medieval church much restored 19th C retains arcades of 12th and 13th C, west tower built *c*.1400, and vaulted south porch; good 15th-C black marble font and early 16th-C stalls
Greyfriars Tower, Queen's Road. Surviving tower of 15th-C church of Franciscans has tall arches and fine parapet with pinnacles
Richmond Castle [EH] Remains of imposing castle begun 1071 with 11th-C Great (Scolland's) Hall, curtain wall, towers, and tall well-preserved keep of *c*.1150–*c*.1180

RICKINGHALL INFERIOR
   SUFFOLK, 4,4E
Church of St Mary Medieval church retains Norman round tower with octagonal upper stage of early 1300s, 14th-C chancel, south aisle, and two-storeyed south porch

RIDDLESDEN, W. YORKS, 7,3E
Tithe Barn (at East Riddlesden Hall – NT) Large barn of *c*.1640–50 with king-post roof (see p. 255)

RIEVAULX ABBEY, N. YORKS, 7,4D
Rievaulx Abbey [EH] Spectacular ruins of important 12th-C Cistercian monastery enlarged 13th C survive in beautiful wooded valley

RILLINGTON, N. YORKS, 7,4D
Church of St Andrew Church of Norman origin with north arcade of *c*.1200, north chapel, and 15th-C west tower; early 13th-C font and important wall painting of *c*.1370

RINGHADDY (8 km. / 5 m. NNE of Killyleagh), CO. DOWN, 11,5C
Church and Castle Remains of medieval church and tower house

RINGLAND, NORFOLK, 4,4D
Church of St Peter Church with 13th-C west tower, early 14th-C arcades and chancel, and late medieval clerestory; splendid hammerbeam roof with bosses and ribbed coving

RINNDOWN,
   CO. ROSCOMMON, 11,3D
Castle and Fortifications [Dúchas] Impressive peninsula in Lough Rea houses remains of polygonal castle begun *c*.1227 with later alterations, towered wall with gateway in centre, and remnants of town fortified 1251; nearby remains of small 13th-C church (formerly part of Hospital of St John the Baptist)

RIPLEY, N. YORKS, 7,3D
Church of All Saints Medieval church rebuilt after *c*.1395 with clerestory and top of west tower added 1567; five-bay arcade and priest's dwelling above part of south chapel; fine tomb chest and effigies of *c*.1369; base of weeping cross in churchyard
Ripley Castle [HHA] Mid 16th-C house rebuilt *c*.1780 retains 15th-C gatehouse

RIPLEY, SURREY, 3,1D
Church of St Mary Mainly 19th-C church retains late Norman chancel with lavish string course

RIPON, N. YORKS, 7,3D
Ripon Cathedral * Cathedral founded as monastic church *c*.660; early Saxon crypt (672, one of oldest in Europe) survives beneath 12th- to early 13th-C rebuilding; chapter house of same date had Lady Chapel (now Library) added above in l14th C; medieval furnishings include crossing screen and choir stalls (much restored) with magnificent series of thirty-four misericords (late 15th-C)

RIPPINGALE, LINCS, 4,1C
Church of St Andrew Medieval church with six-bay arcade of *c*.1300, long and wide south aisle, 15th-C clerestory and west tower; coving to rood loft survives, and good monuments include mid 13th-C effigy of deacon
Cross, East Street Fragment of 14th-C cross

RIPPLE, WORCS, 5,3E
Church of St Mary Spacious church built late 12th to early 13th C with medieval and 18th-C additions retains original transepts, late 13th-C chancel, and crossing tower; font of *c*.1300 and carved 15th-C misericords

ROCESTER, STAFFS, 5,3B
Church of St Michael Medieval church restored 19th C has 13th-C west tower and well-preserved cross in churchyard

ROCH, DYFED, 6,2D
Castle Small fortified medieval tower overlooking St Bride's Bay, converted into house during early 20th C

ROCHDALE, GREATER MANCHESTER, 7,2E
Church of St Chad Medieval church with extensive 19th-C additions has 13th-C arcades and 14th-C tower arch; parts of original 15th-C stalls and screens

ROCHE, CORNWALL, 1,2D
St Michael's Chapel Remains of remarkable granite chapel licensed 1409, set on imposing cliff
Church of St Gonard Church much rebuilt 19th C contains fine Norman font with carved snakes and angels' heads

ROCHE ABBEY, S. YORKS, 5,5A
Roche Abbey [EH] Remains of Cistercian abbey founded 1147 (now in 18th-C land-scaped setting) include monastic buildings and church with transepts of *c*.1170

ROCHE CASTLE,
   CO. LOUTH, 11,4C
See Kilcurry

ROCHESTER, KENT, 3,3C
Rochester Castle [EH] Mighty tower keep of Norman Castle begun *c*.1127, tallest in England; forebuilding and curtain walls also survive
Rochester Cathedral * Cathedral begun 1076–1108 on Saxon site; present building of mainly 12th C with 13th-C crypt, presbytery, choir and transepts;
Temple Manor [EH], Strood (2 days notice required) Manor house of Knights Templar built 1200s

ROCK, NORTHUMBERLAND, 7,3A
Church of St Philip and St James Norman church with extensive 19th-C additions retains original corbel table and fine chancel arch; 12th-C cross slab
Rock Hall (now youth hostel) Hall-house of 13th or early 14th C with later medieval and 17th- to 19th-C remodellings

ROCK, WORCS, 5,2D
Church of St Peter Norman church built 1170 with medieval additions has original projecting north doorway, fine chancel arch with carved capitals, and 15th-C west tower; Norman font

ROCKFLEET or CARRIGAHOWLEY,
   CO. MAYO, 11,1C
Castle [Dúchas] Fine 15th- or 16th-C tower in picturesque setting by Clew Bay

ROCKINGHAM, NORTHANTS, 4,1E
Rockingham Castle [HHA] Norman motte and bailey castle reconstructed 1276–91 with impressive 16th-, mid 17th- and 19th-C additions retains gatehouse, keep and remains of hall

RODEL / ROGHADAL (Harris)
   WESTERN ISLES
   (Outer Hebrides), 9,1D
St Clement's Church [HS] Cruciform early 16th-C church restored 1780s and 1873 with imposing west tower and small transepts; late medieval font, graveslabs, and fine collection of 16th-C monuments to MacLeods

ROMALDKIRK, CO. DURHAM
Church of St Romald Norman church with medieval additions retains late 12th-C arcades, south doorway, 14th-C chancel with double piscina, transepts, and 15th-C tower; Norman font

ROMSEY, HANTS, 2,4D
Romsey Abbey Cruciform Norman abbey church with early 11th-C rood sculpture from previous Saxon building

ROMSLEY, WORCS, 5,3D
Church of St Kenelm Norman church
remodelled 14th C has 12th-C nave and
chancel, south doorway with tympanum
of c.1150 and 15th-C west tower

ROODSTOWN CASTLE,
       CO. LOUTH, 11,4D
See Stabannan

ROSCAM, CO. GALWAY, 12,3A
Church and Round Tower [Dúchas]
Remains of Round Tower (possibly
unfinished) and 15th-C parish church
on early monastic site enclosed by
massive cashel

ROSCOMMON,
       CO. ROSCOMMON, 11,3D
Roscommon Castle [Dúchas] Remains of
imposing quadrangular castle built 1269,
reworked by 1280 and extensively altered
after 1578 with splendid twin-towered
gatehouse on east and gatetower on west
Friary (Roscommon Abbey) [Dúchas]
Church of Dominican friary founded
1253, consecrated 1257 and much reworked
c.1453; effigy of Felim O'Conor (carved
1290–1300) survives in chancel
on later 15th-C tomb with warrior
figures on front

ROSCREA, CO. TIPPERARY, 12,4B
Roscrea Castle [Dúchas], Castle Street.
Stone castle built c.1280 with 16th- and
17th-C alterations retains curtain wall
with corner towers and imposing
gatetower
St Cronan's Church and Round Tower
[Dúchas] Site of monastery houses
impressive west gable of 12th-C church
demolished 1812 with fine doorway,
flanking blind arcades, and pediment
above with carved figure (possibly
St Cronan); nearby Round Tower
(shortened 1798) and 12th-C High
Cross with good ornament
Friary [Dúchas], Abbey Street
Fragmentary remains (parts of chancel,
bell tower, and north nave arcade) of
church of Franciscan friary founded
before 1477 and mainly demolished
c.1800 survive as gateway to parish
church begun 1844; carved pillar
nearby (possibly 8th-C cross-shaft)

ROSLIN (10 km. / 6 m. S of Edinburgh),
       LOTHIAN, 8,3E
St Matthew's Chapel (Rosslyn Chapel) *
[SCS] Handsome private collegiate
church built c.1450 with ornate stone
carving (only choir completed) retains
tall clerestory, east walls of transepts,

spacious tunnel-vaulted interior with
fine arcades, rib-vaulted east chapels,
and sacristy at south-east corner;
north entrance to churchyard
incorporates medieval work
(possibly from castle)
Rosslyn Castle [LT] Remains of 15th-C
castle on impressive elevated site by River
North Esk include part of late medieval
bridge, fine west range, and habitable
16th- to 17th-C east range

ROSS CASTLE, CO. KERRY, 12,2D
See Killarney

ROSS CASTLE,
       CO. WESTMEATH, 11,3D
See Finnea

ROSSERK, CO. MAYO, 11,2C
Friary (or Rosserk Abbey) [Dúchas]
Remains of Ireland's best-preserved
Franciscan friary (founded c.1460 or
earlier) include church with south
transept and rich west doorway, and
conventual buildings; fine double piscina
in chancel has good carvings including
unique depiction of Round Tower

ROSS ERRILLY, CO. GALWAY, 12,2A
Ross Errilly Friary [Dúchas] Substantial
and well preserved mainly late 15th-C
buildings of Franciscan frisry founded
c.1351 include church with fine windows,
double south transept and tower added
1498, and beautiful cloister to north with
original arcades; refectory with reader's
desk and kitchen retaining interesting
fish or water tank

ROSSLYN CASTLE AND
       CHAPEL, LOTHIAN, 8,3E
See Roslin

ROSS-ON-WYE, HEREFS, 2,2A
Church of St Mary Medieval church much
rebuilt 1743 with 13th-C chancel arch, fine
north aisle windows, early 14th-C south
porch, west tower and 15th-C Markye
Chapel
Rotherwas Chapel [EH] Simple medieval
chapel with open timber roof and 18th- or
19th-C west tower

ROSYTH, FIFE, 8,3E
Rosyth Castle 15th-C tower house, now
part of 20th-C dockyard, retains vaulted
upper hall remodelled 1635

ROTHERFIELD GREYS,
       OXON, 2,5B
Greys Court [NT] 16th-C house with
18th-C alterations set amid remains of
semi-fortified house (licensed 1347)

ROTHERHAM, S. YORKS, 5,4A
Church of All Saints Spacious church
begun c.1410 retaining 14th-C chancel and
restored 1873–5 has tall crossing tower and
octagonal spire, transepts, south chapel
built 1480, and chancel clerestory of
1508–12; choir stalls of 1452
Bridge Chapel Medieval bridge has
chapel begun c.1483 with simple interior
and vaulted crypt

ROTHESAY (Isle of Bute),
       STRATHCLYDE, 10,4C
Rothesay Castle [HS] Remarkable, well-
preserved castle built probably c.1200 on
circular plan (unique in Scotland); high
curtain walls fortified with round towers
later 13th C, shell of chapel in courtyard,
and imposing Great Tower or gatehouse
projecting into moat begun c.1500 by
James IV and comleted by James V
St Mary's Chapel [HS] Remains of late
medieval chancel of parish church survive
beside High Kirk of 1796; two fine
canopied tombs (13th to 14th-C)

ROTHLEY, LEICS, 5,5C
**Church of St Mary and St John the
Baptist** Spacious medieval church with
chancel and restoration of 1877–8 retains
13th-C north arcade, early 14th-C aisles,
and 15th-C west tower and clerestory;
Norman font, 15th-C screen and good
tomb chest of c.1486
Rothley Temple (now Rothley Court
Hotel) Former 13th-C hall of Knights
Templar rebuilt as house 16th to 19th C;
well-preserved chapel of mid 1200s with
timber roof

ROTHWELL, NORTHANTS, 5,5D
Church of the Holy Trinity Spacious
church built late 12th and 13th C with 15th-
and 17th-C reworking has aisles and
chancel chapels of c.1200, early 13th-C
rib-vaulted crypt, and fine chancel arch of
c.1280–90; 13th-C font, sedilia and piscina

ROUS LENCH, WORCS, 5,3E
Church of St Peter Norman church rebuilt
13th and 19th C with original north and
south doorways, chancel arch and north
arcade; splendid seated Christ of
c.1140–50 above south doorway

ROWALLAN (5 km. / 3 m. N of
       Kilmarnock), STRATHCLYDE, 10,4C
Rowallan Castle [HS] (not currently
accessible to public) Handsome castle
with ruined tower house built 15th C,
roofed 16th-C hall block with later
alterations, and fine mid 16th-C twin
round towers flanking entrance

ROWLSTONE, HEREFS, 2,1A
Church of St Peter Norman church
retains original nave, chancel arch with
carved capitals and south doorway with
fine tympanum depicting Christ in Glory

RUARDEAN, GLOS, 2,2A
Church of St John the Baptist Church
built c.1110 with west tower and south
porch; Norman south doorway with
carved tympanum of c.1150

RUDBAXTON, DYFED, 6,2D
Church of St Michael 13th-C church
retains west tower and later medieval
south aisle with low arcade; spectacular
Howard Memorial dates from 17th C

RUDFORD, GLOS, 2,3A
Church of St Mary Early Norman church
with later additions retains narrow
vaulted chancel, and original south and
west doorways; 14th-C double piscina
and font

RUFFORD, LANCS, 7,2E
Old Hall [NT] Late 15th-C hall-house with
additions of 1662 and 19th C retains lavish
original hall with five-sided bay window,
timber roof, moveable screen between
spere posts, and walls with quatrefoil
decoration

RUFFORD ABBEY, NOTTS, 5,5B
Rufford Abbey [EH] Remains of 17th-C
house built on lower parts of cloisters of
Cistercian abbey founded 1146; well-
preserved lay-brothers' frater and
axial night stair

RUSCO TOWER (4.5 km. / 2 ¾ m. N
       of Gatehouse of Fleet), DUMFRIES
       AND GALLOWAY, 10,5E
Rusco Tower Rectangular tower house
built c.1500 and restored 1975–9 with
remains of 17th-C extension

RUSHDEN, NORTHANTS, 4,1E
Church of St Mary Mainly 15th-C church
has transepts, west tower with recessed
spire, south and north chapels, strainer
arch, and panelled roof; screens and
much 15th-C stained glass

RUSHEN ABBEY,
       ISLE OF MAN, 6,1A
See Ballasalla

RUTHIN, CLWYD, 6,5A
Ruthin Castle Ruins of 13th-C castle in
grounds of 19th-C house **Church of St
Peter** Church begun 1310 with 14th-C
south aisle and extensive 18th- and 19th-C

restorations retains rich late medieval camberbeam roofs

The Old Cloisters Cloisters of college founded 1310, used as warden's residence 16th C, and much altered early 1800s

National Westminster Bank Timber-framed former courthouse of 1401, restored as bank 1925–6

RUTHVEN, GRAMPIAN, 8,3A
Church Surviving north and west walls of medieval church with good military effigy of c.1400 in canopied recess

RUTHWELL, DUMFRIES AND GALLOWAY, 7,1B
Ruthwell and Mount Kedar Church [Cross – HS] Medieval church with 19th-C additions and recasting of 1906 contains famous tall stone cross (probably early 8th-C) ornamented with superb relief sculpture

RYAL, NORTHUMBERLAND, 7,3B
Church of All Saints 12th-C chapel of ease restored 1870 has 13th-C chancel arch; medieval cross slabs in west wall

RYCOTE, OXON, 2,5B
Rycote Chapel [EH] Well-preserved chapel founded 1449 has west tower, wagon roofs, 15th-C pews and stalls, and 17th-C fittings

RYE, E. SUSSEX, 3,3E
Church of St Mary Norman church with medieval remodelling has transepts, 13th-C arcades, chancel chapels, crossing and low tower redone 15th C; sacristy built 1400s with priest's room above
Ypres Tower 13th-C former castle used as prison from 1518 until early 19th C
Medieval Buildings; Good medieval buildings include 14th-C Chapel of Austin Friars, and 15th-C Fletcher's House, Flushing Inn, Mermaid Inn and Old Hospital

RYHALL, RUTLAND, 4,1D
Church of St John the Evangelist 13th-C church remodelled 14th and 15th C has original chancel arch, tower and arcades, aisles and chancel of mainly c.1400, and 15th-C roofs; fine double sedilia of c.1330–40

SADDELL, STRATHCLYDE, 10,3C
Saddell Castle [LT] Well-preserved tower house built 1508 on shore looking towards Arran with first-floor hall and 18th-C outbuildings
Saddell Abbey Fragmentary remains of Cistercian abbey founded c.1164 with splendid collection of carved grave slabs

SAFFRON WALDEN, ESSEX, 3,2A
Church of St Mary the Virgin Large and ornate medieval church much rebuilt c.1450 to c.1525 and 19th C has 13th-C crypt and 15th-C west tower; original roofs and late medieval brasses
Castle Fragments of 12th-C castle keep
Youth Hostel, Bridge Street. Fine timber-framed house of c.1500 with oriels and screen
Medieval Houses Timber-framed buildings in Bridge Street, Myddelton Place, King Street, High Street and Church Street

ST ALBANS, HERTS, 3,1B
Cathedral and Abbey Church of St Alban* Cathedral built 1077–88 with medieval and much 19th-C rebuilding retains original work in transepts, 11th-C crossing with brick tower, nave enlarged late 12th to early 13th C and rebuilt 1300s, and east end started 1257 with early 14th-C Lady Chapel; shrine of St Alban erected c.1302–8 and reconstructed 1800s has timber watching loft; good medieval screen, reredos, chantry chapels, and wall paintings
Cathedral Precinct Scanty remains of monastic buildings with Norman slype, parts of cloisters, and gatehouse built 1360s
The Fighting Cocks Inn Medieval timber-framed inn, possibly former monastic building
Church of St Michael Church of Saxon origin with tower and west end added 1898 retains late 10th- or early 11th-C walls, early 12th-C north aisle, 13th-C Lady Chapel, and 15th-C nave roof
Church of St Stephen Medieval church with early Norman work, early 13th-C south chapel and 15th-C timber additions including bell turret on frame; 15th-C font
Clock Tower Handsome medieval clock tower built 1403–12
The White Hart, Holywell Hill Late medieval timber-framed building

ST ALDHELM'S HEAD, DORSET, 2,3E
St Aldhelm's Chapel Small late 12th-C building with central pier, four rib-vaults, and pyramidal roof

ST ANDREWS, FIFE, 8,3D
Church of St Regulus (St Rule's Tower) [HS] Remarkable 11th- or early 12th-C shrine church with tall west tower built as landmark for pilgrims

Cathedral Church and Priory [HS] Remains of fine 12th- to 13th-C cathedral reworked late 1300s (once largest in Scotland) with adjacent chapter house, warming house, reredorter, and refectory undercroft; Cathedral Museum houses excellent collection of early Christian and medieval monuments found on site
Precinct Wall [HS] Well-preserved medieval wall surrounding priory land with early 16th-C alterations, gates and thirteen surviving towers
St Mary's Church, Kirkheugh [HS] Scanty foundations of small, early church excavated 1860 survive on edge of cliff behind cathedral
St Andrews Castle [HS] Remains of late 14th-C castle used as episcopal palace with 16th-C alterations and additions; interesting bottle dungeon hollowed out of rock
St Salvator's College, St Andrews University, North Street. College founded 1450 reconstructed 1683–90 and 19th C retains tall 15th-C gate tower, and chapel built 1450–60 with apse; fine tomb of Bishop Kennedy
Blackfriars Chapel [HS], South Street. Surviving apsidal-ended north transept of church of Dominican convent begun c.1515
Church of the Holy Trinity, South Street. Church begun 1411 and totally reconstructed 1907–9 retains 15th-C west tower
St Leonard's Chapel (now part of school), South Street and The Pends. Former collegiate chapel begun c.1400, extended c.1512 and curtailed c.1837 with interior restored 1948–52
Deans Court, North Street Early 16th-C courtyard house remodelled late 1500s and converted to hall of residence 1931

ST ASAPH / LLANELWY, CLWYD, 6,4A
St Asaph Cathedral * Smallest cathedral church in England and Wales with 18th- to 20th-C remodelling (particularly choir) retains nave and transepts built c.1310–20, and crossing tower of 1391–2; 13th-C effigy of bishop, good west doorway and window, and splendid late 15th-C canopied stalls (sole surviving set in Wales)
Church of St Kentigern and St Asaph Medieval double-naved church with 15th- and early 16th-C work; good timber roofs

ST ATHAN, GLAMORGAN, 1,5A
Church of St Tathan Cruciform church of c.1300 with later 14th-C rebuilding and 15th-C wagon roofs retains crossing tower; south transept fitted as burial chamber has

fine canopied recess with monument
East Orchard Manor Ruins of seven medieval structures including large hall block, detached chapel, and early 15th-C farm buildings

ST AUSTELL, CORNWALL, 1,3D
Church of the Holy Trinity Medieval church has handsome tower of c.1480 with lavish figure sculpture in niches and two-storeyed south porch; nave interior much restored 1872; good carved Norman font, 12th-C pillar piscina, original wagon roofs, and some early 16th-C bench ends

ST BEES, CUMBRIA, 7,1C
Church of St Mary and St Bega Late Norman church of Benedictine nunnery has original crossing and lavish west doorway of c.1160; 13th- to 15th-C additions and crossing tower of 1855–8; good 14th-C monuments

ST BRIAVELS, GLOS, 2,2A
Church of St Mary Church of Norman origin with work of 13th and 19th C retains original south arcade, clerestory, crossing arches and fine 13th-C chancel; Norman font
St Briavel's Castle [EH] Norman castle retains imposing defensive gatehouse of c.1292–3 and altered hall range

ST BRIDES MAJOR, GLAMORGAN, 6,4E
Church of St Bridget Church of Norman origin much restored 1851 retains 12th-C chancel arch, chancel rebuilt 14th C, and 15th-C tower; good incised slab of 1330s

ST BRIDES-SUPER-ELY / LLANSANFFRAID-AR-ELAI GLAMORGAN, 1,5A
Church of St Bride Modest medieval church has Norman outer arch to south porch, 12th-C south doorway, and late 15th-C image niche in east window (all reused and introduced during restoration of 1849)

ST BURYAN, CORNWALL, 1,1E
Church of St Berian Large mainly late 15th- to early 16th-C church restored from mid 18th C, formerly collegiate, retains four-stage 14th-C tower; splendid rood screen much renewed 19th C runs across nave and aisles

ST CATHERINE'S ORATORY (1.5 km. / 1 m. NW of Niton), ISLE OF WIGHT, 2,4E
St Catherine's Oratory [EH / NT] Lighthouse built 14th C on island's highest point

ST CLEARS, DYFED, 6,3D
Church of St Mary Magdalene 12th-C
church of Cluniac priory has fine Norman
chancel arch with carved capitals and
circular font

ST CLEER, CORNWALL, 1,3D
Church of St Clarus Medieval church with
north arcade of c.1400 and fine west
tower retains Norman north doorway;
13th-C font
Holy Well Attractive 15th-C building with
pitched roof and arcading
King Doniert's Stone [EH] (1.5 km. / 1 m.
NW) Two fragments of carved 9th-C cross
Cross (on St Cleer Common, nr Minions)
9th-C Celtic Christian cross

ST COLUMB MAJOR,
    CORNWALL, 1,2D
Church of St Columba Imposing early
14th-C church with later medieval
remodelling retains transepts and
four-stage west tower with ground floor
open to north and south; octagonal font
of c.1300, early 14th-C piscinas, and
15th-C bench ends

ST CROSS, HANTS, 2,4D
See Winchester

ST CYBI'S WELL, GWYNEDD, 6,3B
See Llangybi

ST DAVID'S, DYFED, 6,2D
Cathedral Late Norman Cathedral with
13th-C tower and presbytery, much
enlarged 14th-C; several early Christian
carved crosses of 7th to 11th C; handsome
late 12th-C nave has oak ceiling of c.1540;
splendid 14th-C rood screen, 15th-C choir
stalls with misericords, fine tall canopied
Bishop's Throne and rare ornate wooden
sedilia; behind high altar, Bishop
Vaughan's Chapel with fan tracery
of 1508–22
Bishop's Palace [CADW] Impressive
mainly 14th-C ruins of 12th- to 15th-C
Bishop's Palace built round large
courtyard, including hall with richly
decorated porch and fine traceried
windows, and imposing façades crowned
by distinctive multi-arched parapets
supported by lively carved corbels
City Cross (In city centre) 14th-C
preaching cross, heavily restored 19th C
St Non's Well [CADW] (1.5 km. / 1 m. W)
Ruins of medieval chapel of indeterminate
date beside holy well with stone vault
dating from 18th C
St Justinian's Chapel (3 km. / 2 m. W)
Simple rectangular structure built
probably 1509–22 to replace earlier chapel

ST DOGMAELS, DYFED, 6,3D
St Dogmaels Abbey [CADW] Ruins of
cruciform church of Norman Abbey,
founded 1115 on site of Celtic clas church
but remodelled 13th C and further altered
14th to 16th C; surviving medieval monastic buildings include cloister, chapter
house and infirmary

ST DONATS / SAIN DUNWYD
    GLAMORGAN, 1,5A
St Donat's Castle (Atlantic College)
Norman castle remodelled c.1300 to early
1600s and 20th C retains 12th-C Mansell
Tower, outer gatehouse of c.1300,
concentric curtain walls and late 15th-C
great hall; fine medieval features
introduced from 1925 include refectory
roof of c.1320 in Bradenstoke Hall
Church of St Donat Church of Norman
origin reworked early 14th to early 16th C
retains 12th-C chancel arch and medieval
lectern; 15th-C cross in churchyard
Rectory (N.of church) Remains of large
late medieval rectory

ST DOULAGH'S, CO. DUBLIN, 11,5D
Church and Cross [Dúchas] Vaulted
13th-C church entered through building
of 1864 and altered 15th to 16th C has
steeply-pitched stone roof, attic room,
and "Hermit's cell" to west (supposedly
burial place of founder, St Doulagh) with
tower above; well to north-east covered
by octagonal medieval building

ST ENDELLION, CORNWALL, 1,3C
Church of St Endellienta 15th-C church
with three-stage tower, wide nave and fine
south doorway; stone tomb chest of
c.1400 and contemporary stoup
inside south door
Roscarrock Surviving part of medieval
house includes upper room with oriel
windows and timber roof of cruck
construction

ST EWE, CORNWALL, 1,2D
Church of All Saints Church with 13th-C
work and good 14th-C west tower and
south aisle; Norman font and important
medieval rood screen with lavish cornice

ST FAGANS, GLAMORGAN, 2,1B
Church of St Mary Medieval church
enlarged 1859–60 with fine early 14th-C
work including triple sedilia and piscina,
and chancel with 15th-C wagon roof;
tower rebuilt 1600s
Castle and Museum of Welsh Life *
Collection of reconstructed buildings
from Wales (some medieval) housed in

grounds of 20th-C museum and castle
built c.1590 within 13th-C walls of
predecessor

ST FILLANS, TAYSIDE, 8,2D
Dundurn Parish Church [SCS] Church
built 1879 near Loch Earn contains fine
medieval stone font

ST FLORENCE, DYFED, 6,3E
Church of St Florentius Cruciform late
Norman and early medieval church with
south transept tower
Carswell House [CADW]
(1.5 km. / 1 m. E) Late 14th- to 15th-C stone
farmhouse has hall with decorative fireplace above vaulted ground floor kitchen;
living room with large hearth and huge
chimney built against gable end
West Tarr House Similar medieval
farmhouse nearby

ST GERMANS, CORNWALL, 1,3D
Church of St Germanus Norman priory
church rebuilt 13th to 16th C and 19th C
retains original west front with two towers
and impressive west portal; font of c.1200,
13th-C chancel and 15th-C south aisle and
porch

ST ISSEY, CORNWALL, 1,2D
Church of St Ida Medieval church rebuilt
1891 contains late 14th-C reredos by
'Master of St Endellion' with stone panels
originally forming part of tomb chest

ST IVE, CORNWALL, 1,3D
Church of St Ivo Church consecrated 1338
with additions of 15th to 16th C has
original windows, west tower, chancel
and wagon roofs; piscina, triple sedilia
and fragment of 14th-C St Christopher

ST IVES, CAMBS
Church of All Saints Large church built
mainly c.1450–70 with some 13th-C work
including fine double piscina
Bridge Six-arched bridge of c.1415 with
tiny two-storeyed Chapel of St Lawrence
half way across

ST IVES, CORNWALL, 1,1E
Church of St Ia Church of 1410–34 altered
c.1500 with four-stage west tower and
gables to east; unusual 15th-C font and late
medieval lantern cross in churchyard

ST JOHN'S POINT,
    CO. DONEGAL, 11,2B
Ballysaggart Friary, Fanegaragh Scanty
remains of Franciscan Tertiary house
founded probably late 1400s with
traceried east window

ST JOHN'S POINT (3 km. / 2 m. SSW
of Killough), CO. DOWN, 11,5C
Church [EHS] Fine small church probably
built 10th or 11th C (used as chapel during
medieval period) with flat-headed west
doorway and antae

ST KEW, CORNWALL, 1,3C
Church of St James Spacious church with
west tower, high nave, and ceiled wagon
roofs; much 15th-C stained glass including
north-east window dated 1469; 15th-C font
and cross head

ST LEVAN, CORNWALL, 1,1E
Church of St Levan Medieval church built
into hillside has north transept, 15th-C
south aisle, west tower, and south porch;
fine Norman font and base of rich rood
screen

ST MACDARA'S ISLAND
    (boat trips from Carna by private
    arrangement only),
    CO. GALWAY, 12,2A
Monastic Church [Dúchas] Primitive
rectangular church (restored late 20th C)
with steeply-pitched stone roof, antae and
flat-headed doorway survives on site of
monastery founded 6th C; remains of
pilgrimage stations nearby with early
Christian slabs

ST MARGARET-AT-CLIFFE,
    KENT, 3,5D
Church of St Margaret Well-preserved
Norman church of c.1140 has clerestoried
nave, high chancel and tower arches, and
wide chancel; ornate west doorway of
c.1150

ST MARGARET'S, HEREFS, 5,1E
Church of St Margaret Church of
Norman origin with original chancel arch
and splendid well-preserved rood screen
of c.1520

ST MARTIN-BY-LOOE,
    CORNWALL, 1,3D
Church of St Keyne and St Martin Church
much rebuilt 15th C retains Norman north
doorway, early 14th-C lower stages of west
tower, and ceiled wagon roofs of 1440s;
good Norman font

ST MARY BOURNE, HANTS, 2,4C
Church of St Peter Norman church
enlarged during medieval period
contains splendid Norman carved
Tournai marble font and early
14th-C effigy of knight

ST MELLONS / LLANEIRWG
(Cardiff), GLAMORGAN, 2, 1B
Church of St Mellon Large 14th-C church
with later remodelling has original
chancel arch, nave with south aisle,
south chapel extended 15th C with fine
image niche, south tower, and wagon
roofs; late medieval benches to nave

ST MICHAEL'S MOUNT (accessible
by causeway from Marazion at low
tide), CORNWALL, 1, 1E
St Michael's Mount [NT] 12th-C
Benedictine priory, dramatically sited on
rocky island off Marazion, converted to
private house 17th C; surviving medieval
work includes 14th-C church

ST MONANS, FIFE, 8, 3D
St Monans Parish Church, Braehead
[SCS] Handsome church built 1362–70 on
dramatic cliff top site and restored 1826–8
retains vaulted choir (restored again 1961),
low crossing tower and transepts;
consecration crosses and 14th-C
sedilia, piscina and aumbry

ST MULLIN'S, CO. CARLOW, 12, 5C
**Early Christian and medieval Monastic
Site** [Dúchas] Buildings on site of
monastery founded 7th C (now set in
graveyard) include stump of Round
Tower, small oratory (St James's Chapel),
carved granite High Cross, and medieval
St Mullin's Abbey church

ST NEOT, CORNWALL, 1, 3D
Church of St Anietus Mainly 15th-C
church retains 14th-C west tower, south
aisle of c.1425 and fine south porch;
important 15th- and early 16th-C stained
glass restored c.1830; 10th-C cross shaft
in churchyard
Cross Early 11th-C carved cross on
Temple Moor
Bridges Two 15th-C bridges, one crossing
River Warleggan and the other River Fowey

ST NEOTS, CAMBS, 3, 1A
Church of St Mary Large mainly 15th-C
church with impressive west tower begun
1489; lavish roofs in nave, aisles and
chapels; 15th-C screens

ST NINIAN'S CAVE (Physgill, on coast
6.5 km. / 4 m. SW of Whithorn),
DUMFRIES AND GALLOWAY, 10, 4E
St Ninian's Cave [HS] Cave by Luce Bay,
possibly retreat of St Ninian, with incised
crosses of 8th or 9th C

ST OLAVE'S PRIORY,
NORFOLK, 4, 5D
St Olave's Priory [EH] (2 km. / 1¼ m. N

of Haddiscoe) Remains of 13th-C
buildings of Augustinian priory founded
c.1216 and converted to house 16th C

ST ORLAND'S STONE (in field near
Cassans Farm, 7.5 km. / 4½ m. W of
Forfar), TAYSIDE, 8, 3C
St Orland's Stone [HS] Early Christian
slab with good carved work

ST OSYTH, ESSEX, 3, 4B
Priory Remains of priory established
c.1127 (remodelled 16th to 18th C) include
13th-C cellarer's range and refectory,
complete late 15th-C gatehouse, and
ornate early 16th-C bishop's lodging
Church of St Peter and St Paul; Church
of Norman origin has 13th-C chancel,
14th-C west tower and early 16th-C
nave with unusual brick arcades and
piers; hammerbeam roof to nave;
St Clair's Hall 14th-C house altered
16th C; remarkable aisled hall

ST PIRAN'S, CORNWALL, 1, 2D
Oratory Small early church of 6th or 7th C
set in Penhale Sands, rediscovered 1835
Church of St Piran 11th-C church rebuilt
c.1462 and later engulfed by dunes; parts
of building moved 1804 and re-erected at
Perranzabuloe include arcade, west tower
and font

SAINTS ISLAND, CO. LONGFORD
All Saints Priory Picturesque remains of
Augustinian priory established before
1244 on island in Lough Ree include small
aiseless church with good lancets in south
wall and 15th-C east window

ST VIGEANS (1 km. / ½ m. N of
Arbroath), TAYSIDE, 8, 4C
St Vigeans Sculptured Stones Museum
[HS] Museum in converted cottages
contains remarkable and extensive
collection of Pictish and early Christian
sculptured stones; Drosten Stone has
rare Hiberno-Saxon inscriptions
St Vigean's Church [SCS] Handsome
church rebuilt 1100s on mound
(consecrated 1242) with 15th-C
remodelling and extensive 19th-C
restoration

ST WINNOW (5 km. / 3 m. S of
Lostwithiel), CORNWALL, 1, 3D
Church of St Winnow Church of Norman
origin with late medieval remodelling and
additions survives in beautiful position by
River Fowey; 15th- and early 16th-C
stained glass in east window of south
aisle, interesting carved bench ends,
and rood screen restored 1907

SALFORD, GREATER
MANCHESTER, 5, 3A
Ordsall Hall Timber-framed hall-house
retains original hall in 15th-C south range
with bay window, spere truss, and spere
posts at dais end; late 16th-C quatrefoil decoration and additions of 1639 and 19th C

SALFORD PRIORS, WARWS, 5, 3E
Church of St Matthew Norman church
with medieval additions has original
north doorway with tympanum, west
tower enlarged 15th C, 12th-C south arcade,
and chancel rebuilt 13th C; 14th-C three-
light window in nave with fine tracery

SALISBURY, WILTS, 2, 4D
Cathedral * Cathedral built 1220–c.1266
and restored 18th and 19th C retains lancet
windows, low retrochoir and Lady Chapel,
east transepts, crossing tower with upper
level and remarkable spire begun 1334,
main transepts, and ten-bay nave with fine
north porch and lavish west screen façade;
part of former pulpitum or stone rood
screen of c.1235–50 in north-east transept
and excellent monuments
Cathedral Buildings Well-preserved
rib-vaulted cloisters of c.1270–c.1300 with
library above east walk added 1445; octagonal chapter house of c.1279–c.1300 with
central pier, big windows and fine sculpture
Cathedral Close Fine cathedral close with
remains of 14th-C wall, four surviving
gates, Bishop's Palace of c.1220 and
c.1460–1500 with later additions, and
numerous 17th- to 19th-C houses
incorporating medieval work
Church of St Edmund, Bedwin Street.
Surviving parts of former collegiate
church begun 1407 with west tower rebuilt
1653–5; late 18th-C north addition and
chancel and south chapel of 1865–7;
13th-C font
Church of St Martin Church built 14th to
early 16th C with west porch, good ceiled
wagon roofs, and north and south chapels
retains chancel of c.1230 and 13th-C tower
with 14th-C upper level; 15th-C lectern
Church of St Thomas of Canterbury,
St Thomas Square. Church rebuilt 15th C
and restored 1800s has south tower of
1400–5, fine north and south chapels built
c.1450, three-storeyed vestry, and rich
interior with wall paintings; 13th-C corbel
table in chancel
John à Port's House, 8 Queen Street.
Timber-framed wool merchant's house
built c.1450 with oversailing upper level
Poultry Cross Hexagonal cross of 15th C
with upper parts added 1853
House of John Halle, New Canal

Remains of wool merchant's house built
1470–83 behind cinema facade of 1881
include original hall with fine timber roof
St Nicholas Hospital, St Nicholas Road
Remains of 13th-C hospital altered
1498–1501 and restored 1854
Medieval Buildings Medieval buildings
include 14th-C inn on south of courtyard
of 19th-C Red Lion Hotel (Milford Street),
timber-framed former Old George Hotel
(High Street) with 14th-C roof to hall, and
15th-C Pheasant Inn (Salt Lane)
Bridge Bridge built c.1230 and reworked
1771 crosses branches of River Avon;
remains of 13th-C chapel on island
Crane Bridge 15th-C bridge widened
19th and 20th C

SALLE, NORFOLK, 4, 4D
Church of St Peter and St Paul Well-
preserved 15th-C church has tall west
tower, vaulted porches, transepts and
good roofs; 15th-C font and canopy,
rood screen, stalls and brasses

SALLEY ABBEY, LANCS, 7, 5E
See Sawley

SALTFLEETBY, LINCS, 4, 2B
Church of All Saints Church of Norman
origin with medieval rebuilding has wide
south aisle of c.1300 with good roof and
stone reredos, and 15th-C north front;
good late medieval screens

SAMLESBURY, LANCS, 7, 2E
Salmesbury Hall * Preston New Road;
Timber-framed hall-house of 1325 with
long range built c.1545 and 19th-C
additions and alterations; 15th-C hall
retains two original dais end doorways
and timber roof

SANCREED, CORNWALL, 1, 1E
Church of St Sancredus Medieval church
with west tower, 15th-C south aisle, north
transept, and good font; two important
Saxon crosses with rich carving survive
in churchyard

SANDAL MAGNA, W. YORKS, 7, 3E
Church of St Helen Cruciform church
built mainly 14th C with crossing tower,
transepts, 15th-C aisles and south chapel;
19th-C west end; 15th-C screen to chapel

SANDBACH, CHESHIRE, 5, 2B
Sandbach Crosses [EH], Market Place.
Parts of two 9th-C crosses with elaborate
carved decoration

SANDIACRE, DERBYS, 5, 4C
Church of St Giles Church of Norman
origin rebuilt 14th and 15th C with original

nave and south doorway, 13th-C west tower and 14th-C chancel; fine triple sedilia and piscina of c.1342–7

SANDRIDGE, HERTS, 3, 1B
Church of St Leonard Norman church restored 1886–7 with late 12th-C nave arcades, 13th-C tower arch, and handsome late 14th-C chancel; Norman font and fine stone rood screen

SANDWICH, KENT, 3, 5D
Church of St Clement, Knightrider Street. Church of Norman origin with medieval remodelling retains original central tower, 13th-C chancel, and 15th-C nave with carved angels to roof; fine font of 1400–6
Church of St Mary the Virgin, Strand Street. Church of 12th-C origin remodelled c.1200 and early 1400s, damaged 1668, has short chancel, broad nave and north aisle
Church of St Peter, Market Street. 13th-C church damaged 1661 with 18th-C work retains much of original interior with clerestory; late 13th-C monument to knight and good tomb chest with effigies of c.1360
St Bartholomew's Hospital, Deal Road. Surviving 13th-C chapel of hospital founded 1217 with good monument to knight of c.1250
Town Buildings Town retains many good medieval buildings and remains including Fisher Gate of late 14th-C origin

SANQUHAR, DUMFRIES AND GALLOWAY, 10, 5D
Parish Church of St Bride Church built 1822–4 contains fine early 15th-C statue of bishop in porch and effigy of priest of c.1500
Sanquhar Castle Ruins of medieval castle with 16th-C west range and restoration of 1890s include late 14th-C south-west keep and mid 15th-C lord's gatehouse lodging

SAUL (3 km. / 2 m. NE of Downpatrick), **CO. DOWN, 11, 5C**
St Patrick's Graveyard Graveyard on site of early monastery, traditionally place of Patrick's landing and first church ("Patrick's Barn"), has two fine mortuary houses (one used as mausoleum); good cross-carved stones in graveyard and Church of Ireland church

SAWLEY, DERBYS, 5, 4C
Church of All Saints Church has Norman chancel arch to good late 13th-C chancel, 14th-C work, and late medieval west

tower, clerestory and south aisle; unusual chantry chapel divided from chancel by solid stone screen holds monuments to Bothe family

SAWLEY, LANCS, 7, 3D
Salley Abbey [EH] Ruins of Cistercian abbey founded 1147

SCALFORD, LEICS, 5, 5C
Church of St Egelwin the Martyr 13th- and 14th-C church with good five-bay arcades and 15th-C clerestory; chancel built 1845; two early 14th-C tomb recesses

SCARBOROUGH, N. YORKS, 7, 5D
Church of St Mary Late 12th and early 13th-C church reworked 1800s has original crossing tower rebuilt 1669, clerestory, outer north aisle of c.1350, and four south chapels added 1380–97
Scarborough Castle [EH] Remains of impressively situated Norman castle include curtain walling, keep built between 1158 and 1169, 13th-C barbican, round towers, and three medieval chapels

SCARCLIFFE, DERBYS, 5, 4B
Church of St Leonard Church with Norman south doorway, 13th-C west tower rebuilt 1842, and post-medieval additions; excellent 13th-C effigy of woman and child (probably Constantia de Frecheville, d.1175) and medieval parish chest

SCATTERY ISLAND / INIS CATHAIG (accessible only by boat), **CO. CLARE, 12, 2B**
Round Tower and Churches [Dúchas] Remains of medieval buildings on island in Shannon Estuary (site of monastery founded 6th C) include fine tall Round Tower, fragments of early Church of the Hill of the Angel, cathedral (or collegiate church of SS Mary and Seanan) altered 13th or 14th C, and 14th-C Church of the Dead

SCOTNEY, KENT, 3, 3D
Scotney Castle [Gardens - NT] Remains of handsome 14th-C castle with circular corner tower and part of gatehouse survive in picturesque setting with moat; fragments of attached house built c.1635

SCOTSTARVIT TOWER (3 km. / 2 m. S of Cupar), **FIFE, 8, 3D**
Scotstarvit Tower [HS / NTS] Handsome well-preserved tower house of c.1500 with attic added 1627

SEAFIN CASTLE (nr Ballyroney, 9 km. / 5½ m. NE of Rathfryland), **CO. DOWN, 11, 5C**
Seafin Castle Remains of stone castle built 1252 to succeed earlier motte and bailey castle at Ballyroney

SEAHAM, CO. DURHAM, 7, 3C
Church of St Mary Church with late 7th- or early 8th-C nave, early 13th-C chancel and low tower; fine double piscina

SEAMER, N. YORKS, 7, 5D
Church of St Martin Large Norman church retains original nave, chancel, and west tower with early 13th-C bell stage; late medieval north chapel and vestry

SEATON, RUTLAND, 4, 1D
Church of All Hallows Church of Norman origin with medieval and 19th-C work retains fine original south doorway and chancel arch, arcades of late 12th to early 13th C, and late 13th-C tower; sedilia, piscina and aumbries of late 1200s

SEATON DELAVAL NORTHUMBERLAND, 7, 3B
Church of Our Lady Small Norman church with 19th-C work has good early 12th-C chancel and sanctuary arches, and west doorway with tympanum; 14th-C piscina and effigy

SEDBERGH, CUMBRIA, 7, 2D
Church of St Andrew Clerestoried church of Norman origin with medieval rebuilding retains original north doorway, early 13th-C arcades in spacious interior, chancel chapels, and west tower

SEDGEFIELD, CO. DURHAM, 7, 3C
Church of St Edmund [OCT] Medieval church has fine 13th-C nave with three-bay arcades, chancel arch of c.1290, transepts, crossing, and imposing 15th-C west tower; rich woodwork added 1630s

SEFTON, MERSEYSIDE, 5, 1A
Church of St Helen Spacious church of 15th to early 16th C retains 14th-C west tower and north chancel chapel; fine late medieval interior with original screens

SEIRKIERAN, CO. OFFALY, 11, 3E
Monastic Site [Dúchas] Extensive site of monastery founded by St Ciaran has early gravestones, part of good 10th-C High Cross, church ruins, and remains of Round Tower; modern Protestant parish

church incorporates earlier work (eg. figures in gable)

SELBORNE, HANTS, 2, 5D
Church of St Mary Church much reworked in 19 C has four-bay Norman arcades and 13th-C south door with iron work

SELBY, N. YORKS, 7, 4E
Selby Abbey Church of Benedictine abbey begun c.1100 and rebuilt early 20th C has Norman west portal, north porch, central tower, nave of 12th and 13th C with gallery and clerestory, and chancel built c.1280–c.1340; 14th-C sedilia, screen and fine 15th-C font cover with crocketed spire

SELHAM, W. SUSSEX, 3, 1E
Church of St James 11th-C church with 19th-C work retains original north doorway and fine chancel arch with unusual carved capitals

SELLING, KENT, 3, 4D
Church of St Mary Norman church much restored 1841–6 has chancel, chapels, transepts and central tower all of c.1190, nave and aisles rebuilt c.1300, and 15th-C work; fine east window with complete stained glass of 1299–1307 and 14th-C wall paintings

SELWORTHY, SOMERSET, 1, 5A
Church of All Saints Mainly 15th-C church retains west tower with 14th-C base; splendid south aisle dated 1538; spacious interior with wagon roofs

SEMPRINGHAM, LINCS, 4, 1C
Church of St Andrew Norman church with medieval additions and work of 1788 and 1868–9 retains 12th-C nave, north arcade, and south and north doorways; 15th-C crossing tower; fine mid 13th-C scrollwork on south door

SETON (2.5 km. / 1½ m. N of Tranent), **LOTHIAN, 8, 3E**
Church of St Mary and the Holy Cross (Seton Collegiate Church) [HS] Medieval church with side walls of ruined nave (probably 13th-C), foundations of chapel built c.1434 below south transept, fine chancel with three-sided apse and sacristy built c.1470–78, and transepts and crossing added c.1513–45; low tower with unusual spire; good piscina and 15th-C effigies

SHAFTESBURY, DORSET, 2, 3D
Shaftesbury Abbey Scarce remains of Benedictine nunnery include 13th-C

crypt, medieval floor tiles of church, and precinct walls

Church of St Peter Mainly 15th-C church rebuilt 16th to 18th C retains west tower, west porch, arcades and crypt

SHANAGOLDEN,
CO. LIMERICK, 12, 2C
Manisternagalliaghduff Abbey [Dúchas] Old Abbey House (3 km. / 2 m. E); Mainly 13th-C remains of rare surviving medieval Augustinian nunnery in secluded valley with church and cloister; remains of gatehouse and unusual pigeon house survive nearby

SHANDWICK (10 km. / 6 m. S of Tain), HIGHLAND, 9, 4D
Shandwick Cross-Slab (Clach a'Charridh) Tall cross slab dating from 8th or 9th C with good carved work

SHANID, CO. LIMERICK, 12, 2C
Castle [Dúchas] Fragmentary ruins of early 13th-C polygonal keep and curtain wall built on earlier motte and bailey

SHAP, CUMBRIA, 7, 2C
Shap Abbey [EH] Ruins of 13th-C and later buildings of medieval Premonstratensian abbey founded late 12th C

SHEEPSTOWN (2 km. / 1¼ m. W of Knocktopher), CO. KILKENNY, 12, 4C
Church [Dúchas] Plain 12th-C church with original west doorway and later additions

SHEFFIELD, S. YORKS, 5, 4A
Bishop's House * Norton Lees Lane, Meersbrook Park. House of c.1500 with stone base, timber-framing, and 17th-C work

SHELTON, NORFOLK, 4, 4E
Church of St Mary Well-preserved brick church of c.1487 with wide arcades and two-storeyed south porch; 14th-C west tower

SHELWICK, HEREFS, 5, 2E
Shelwick Court [LT] House with front of c.1700 contains remarkable medieval great chamber on upper floor with timber roof of c.1400 (roof reused from elsewhere, possibly solar cross-wing of nearby hall)

SHENLEY CHURCH END, BUCKS, 2, 5A
Church of St Mary Church of Norman origin retains fine late 12th-C chancel, crossing, south arcade of c.1200, and

14th-C north arcade and clerestory; good 13th-C sedilia

SHEPTON MALLET, SOMERSET, 2, 2C
Church of St Peter and St Paul Church possibly of Saxon origin rebuilt 1837 has early arcade with 12th-C capitals, late 14th-C west tower, and spendid 15th-C panelled wagon roof with bosses; double piscina of c.1235 and late medieval stone pulpit
The Shambles Unusual 15th-C timber-framed shed

SHERBORNE, DORSET, 2, 2D
Abbey Church Mainly 15th-C abbey church restored 19th C retains Saxon and Norman work, and 13th-C Lady Chapel; fine south front begun c.1420–30 and choir vault of c.1450; glorious late 15th-C fan vault above nave and crossing
Church of All Hallows (to west of abbey) Remains of medieval church on Saxon site
School 17th- and 19th-C school incorporates remains of monastic buildings including cloisters of c.1350–70, abbot's hall and 15th-C abbot's lodging
Almshouse of St John the Baptist and St John the Evangelist Well-preserved almshouse built 1437–48 and restored mid 1800s; chapel retains original stained glass, chancel screen and altarpiece
Conduit Early 16th-C hexagonal conduit built using lavatorium of abbey cloister
Sherborne Old Castle [EH] Ruins of castle built 1107–1135 and converted as mansion 1590s include gatehouse, keep and courtyard block
Town Buildings Some good early 16th-C buildings include Manor House and The Julians (now Dorset County Library)

SHERBURN-IN-ELMET, N. YORKS, 7, 4E
Church of All Saints Spacious late Norman church has original west window, four-bay arcades, west tower of c.1200 with later top, and chancel rebuilt 13th C; rare 15th-C carved cross head

SHERE, SURREY, 3, 1D
Church of St James Mainly 13th-C church retains early Norman central tower with later spire, south chapel of c.1200 lengthened c.1300, and chancel enlarged c.1400; fine font of c.1200, early 13th-C chest, and late medieval brasses

SHERINGHAM, NORFOLK, 4, 4C
Church of All Saints Upper Sheringham Green; Medieval church with west tower of c.1300 has 14th-C font and beam which originally supported its cover; 15th-C screen and rood loft parapet; benches with poppyheads and figures of animals on arms

SHERKIN ISLAND (by boat from Baltimore), CO. CORK, 12, 2E
Farranacouth Abbey [Dúchas] Surviving church and eastern part of domestic wing of Franciscan friary founded 1460 or 1470; sacristy and tower added after 1537

SHERSTON, WILTS, 2, 3B
Church of the Holy Cross Church of Norman origin with medieval rebuilding has 12th-C north arcade, 13th-C crossing arches, north transept, chancel restored 19th C, and 15th-C south side; tall central tower added 1730

SHIFNAL, SHROPS, 5, 2C
Church of St Andrew Substantial church of Norman origin with 13th- to 15th- and 19th-C additions retains south transept doorway of c.1190–1200, 13th-C nave aisles and two-storeyed porch; crossing tower rebuilt c.1300

SHILLINGTON, BEDS, 3, 1A
Church of All Saints Mainly 14th-C ironstone church with east turrets and west tower; good screens and brasses

SHIPDHAM, NORFOLK, 4, 4D
Church of All Saints Church of Norman origin retains priest's doorway of c.1190, 13th- and 15th-C west tower with later lantern, and 14th-C north arcade; fine wooden lectern of c.1500

SHIPLEY, W. SUSSEX, 3, 1E
Church of St Mary Simple early Norman church with additions of 1893 has large central tower, good tower arches, and short chancel; fine 13th-C wooden reliquary

SHIPTON MOYNE, GLOS, 2, 3B
Hodges Barn * Late medieval barn converted to house 1939, formerly belonging to (now lost) manor house of Hodges

SHIPTON-UNDER-WYCHWOOD, OXON, 2, 4A
Church of St Mary Church of Norman origin with medieval rebuilding retains tower of c.1200–50 with octagonal spire, early 13th-C chancel arch, and nave arcades of 1200s; 15th-C font and good stone pulpit

The Shaven Crown Inn 15th-C hostelry has central hall with timber roof

SHIRBURN, OXON, 2, 5B
Church of All Saints [CCT] Church of Norman origin rebuilt 1200s and 1300s with extensive 19th-C work has 13th-C nave arcades and west tower with 18th-C upper stage
Shirburn Castle Moated castle licensed 1377 with corner towers, gatehouse, and extensive 18th- and 19th-C alterations

SHOBDON, HEREFS, 5, 2E
Shobdon Arches Much damaged and renewed remains of mid 12th-C priory church with splendid carved chancel arch of c.1130, two doorways and tympana

SHOREHAM-BY-SEA, W. SUSSEX, 3, 1E
See New Shoreham and Old Shoreham

SHORWELL, ISLE OF WIGHT, 2, 4E
Church of St Peter Mainly 15th-C church remodelled 17th C has early 13th-C south doorway, west tower and original pulpit

SHOTTERY (1.5 km. / 1 m. W of Stratford-upon-Avon), WARWS, 5, 4E
Anne Hathaway's Cottage * Picturesque thatched medieval cottage built 15th C with work of c.1600 (family home of Anne Hathaway before her marriage to William Shakespeare)

SHOTTESBROOKE, BERKS, 2, 5B
Church of St John the Baptist Large cruciform church built 14th C and reworked 15th C; tomb recesses in north transept, font and fine brasses of 14th C

SHOTWICK, CHESHIRE, 5, 1B
Church of St Michael Church of Norman origin rebuilt 14th and 15th C retains original south and chancel doorways, and west tower of c.1500; 15th-C nail studded door

SHREWSBURY, SHROPS, 5, 2C
Church of St Mary [CCT] Norman church with medieval and 19th-C rebuilding has 12th-C west tower with later octagonal spire, transepts, and fine early 13th-C arcades and south porch; stained glass includes 14th-C Jesse window
Old Church of St Chad, Princess Street. Remains of Saxo-Norman church much damaged 1788 with 12th-C south chancel chapel

Abbey of the Holy Cross * Benedictine abbey church founded c.1080 with medieval and 19th-C additions has transepts and nave of c.1100, fine late 14th-C west window, and three-storeyed north porch; Norman pillar piscina and remains of 14th-C shrine of St Winifred
Refectory Pulpit (S of E end of abbey nave) Tall octagonal pulpit of early 1300s, formerly part of monastic buildings
Shrewsbury Castle *, Castle Street Remains of Norman castle reworked 1790 and 1926 include gateway built c.1200 and 13th-C hall heightened 1600s
Vaughan's Mansion Remains of early 14th-C building with post-medieval alterations
Abbot's House, Butcher Row. Early 16th-C timber-framed house with shops to ground floor and overhanging upper levels
Town Walls Tower [NT] (open by written appointment only) Watchtower built 14th C overlooking River Severn

SHUTE, DEVON, 2, 1E
Shute Barton [NT] Unfortified medieval manor house begun 1380 and completed late 16th C

SIBSEY, LINCS, 4, 2C
Church of St Margaret Norman church with medieval and 19th-C rebuilding has original north doorway, 13th-C west tower with later bell stage, and south porch of 1699; part of medieval cross in churchyard

SIBTHORPE, NOTTS, 5, 5B
Church of St Peter Medieval church has 13th-C west tower, fine 14th-C chancel with rich Easter Sepulchre, and 18th-C nave
Dovecot Large circular dovecot built 13th or 14th C

SIDBURY, DEVON, 2, 1E
Church of St Giles Church of Norman origin rebuilt 15th and 19th C retains original west tower (spire 1884) and chancel; plain Saxon crypt discovered 1898 and early 13th-C nave and transepts; 12th-C statues in west wall and medieval wall paintings and wagon roofs

SILCHESTER, HANTS, 2, 5C
Church of St Mary 13th-C parish church with painted wall decoration of masonry and flowers (c.1300 or earlier)

SILKSTONE, S. YORKS, 5, 4A
Church of All Saints Mainly 15th-C church with lively exterior, west tower built after 1479, vestry and good roofs; work of c.1200 and early 14th-C south doorway; rich 16th-C screens

SINGLETON, W. SUSSEX, 2, 5D
Weald and Downland Open Air Museum * Collection of reconstructed medieval and later buildings including 15th-C timber-framed hall-houses

SIZERGH, CUMBRIA, 7, 2D
Sizergh Castle [NT] 14th-C pele tower at core of mainly 16th-C house

SKELBO CASTLE (3 km. / 2 m. NW of Embo), HIGHLAND, 9, 4C
Skelbo Castle 13th-C castle in defensive position by Loch Fleet retains original curtain walling and 15th-C keep

SKELLIG MICHAEL (accessible by boat, weather permitting; trips from Valentia or Derrynane by private arrangement only), CO. KERRY, 12, 1D
Monastic Site [Dúchas] Well-preserved remains of early Christian monastery dramatically set on island in Atlantic probably occupied from 9th to 12th or 13th C include six beehive huts, two oratories, and ruined church of St Michael (possibly 12th-C); good gravestones and crosses

SKELTON, N. YORKS, 7, 4D
Church of St Giles Small and lavish church built c.1247 and restored 1814–18 has rich south doorway, lancet windows, and double bellcote; good piscina in chancel

SKENFRITH, GWENT, 2, 2A
Church of St Bridget or St Bride 13th-C church with later medieval additions has chancel arch with dog-tooth ornament and double-roofed pyramidal timber belfry on low stone tower; magnificent 15th-C embroidered cope survives in north aisle
Skenfrith Castle [NT / CADW] Castle built 1219–32 has circular tower keep and curtain wall with round towers surrounding quadrangular bailey

SKETRICK ISLAND, CO. DOWN, 11, 5C
Sketrick Castle [EHS] (accessible via causeway) Remains of large tower house built probably mid 1400s on island off coast of Strangford Lough

SKIPNESS, STRATHCLYDE, 10, 3C
Skipness Castle and Chapel [HS] Remains of modest early 13th-C hall castle much rebuilt and enlarged later 1200s with curtain wall; fine tower house added early 1500s incorporating medieval keep; ruined chapel built c.1275–1325 near sea shore houses fine grave slabs

SKIPSEA, E. RIDING OF YORKS, 7, 5D
Skipsea Castle [EH] Earthworks of Norman motte and bailey castle

SKIPTON, N. YORKS, 7, 3E
Church of the Holy Trinity Mainly 15th-C church restored 17th C with west tower, clerestory, chancel chapels and good roofs retains work of c.1350; rood screen of 1533
Skipton Castle * Norman castle rebuilt early 14th C with 16th- and mid 17th-C additions has imposing gatehouse and round towers

SKIPWITH, N. YORKS, 7, 4E
Church of St Helen Church of Saxon origin has original tower arch, west tower with 15th-C bell stage, two-bay north aisle of c.1190, fine chancel built c.1300, and 16th-C clerestory; 13th-C ironwork to south door and early 14th-C stained glass in chancel; medieval grave slabs on churchyard wall

SKIRLAUGH, E. RIDING OF YORKS, 7, 5E
Church of St Augustine Ornate church built c.1401–5 has west tower, tall nave and chancel, buttresses, pinnacles, and good windows

SKREEN, CO. MEATH, 11, 4D
Church of St Columba [Dúchas] Dramatic ruins of late 15th-C church on elevated site with imposing west tower and long nave; fragments of carved work include 14th-C panel with effigy of bishop
Skreen Castle Medieval tower house with attached 18th-C dwelling and extensive mid 19th-C alterations

SLADE, CO. WEXFORD, 12, 5D
Slade Castle [Dúchas] Remains of impressive castle with fine late 15th- or early 16th-C tower to north and fortified house added 16th or early 17th C; annexes possibly related to 18th-C salt works

SLANE, CO. MEATH, 11, 4D
Slane Abbey [Dúchas], Hill of Slane Remains of Franciscan monastery or college built 1512 on impressive early site; parish church built 1513 with fine west tower survives to south-west
St Erc's Hermitage Late medieval church with tower and attached anchorite cells set in grounds of Slane Castle; Apostles' Stone of late 14th or early 15th C to north-west has carved figures and Crucifixion
Church of St Patrick 18th-C church retains medieval doorcase and monuments on outer walls re-used from Stackallen and Painestown churches
Slane Bridge Fine late medieval bridge of thirteen arches widened 18th or 19th

SLAPTON, NORTHANTS, 5, 5E
Church of St Botolph Medieval church with 13th-C west tower and many 14th- and 15th-C wall paintings (restored 1971)

SLEAFORD, LINCS, 4, 1C
Church of St Denys Medieval church with 14th-, 15th- and 19th-C remodelling has fine late 12th- to early 13th-C west tower with broach spire; ornate 14th-C aisle fronts and splendid traceried windows
Vicarage Timber-framed vicarage of 15th C with jettied upper floor and 19th-C wing

SLEBECH, DYFED, 6, 2D
Church of St John Ruined medieval church of monastic house founded 12th C by Knights Hospitaller, adapted as parish church during 16th C

SLIGO, CO. SLIGO, 11, 2C
Sligo Abbey [Dúchas] Abbey Street; Remains of Dominican friary founded 1252/3 (rebuilt c.1416) include original 13th-C church with tower, south aisle and south transept added 15th to 16th C, 13th-C sacristy and chapter house, and 15th-C cloister and domestic buildings; fragments of 14th- or 15th-C rood screen (partly reconstructed), well-preserved finely carved 15th- or 16th-C high altar, and excellent O'Crean tomb (1506) with traceried canopy and figured panels to front

SLIMBRIDGE, GLOS, 2, 2B
Church of St John Church of mainly 13th C retains nave built c.1200 with fine capitals to arcades, west tower with recessed spire, two-storeyed sacristy, and chancel with 14th-C triple sedilia

SLOUGH, BERKS, 3, 1C
Church of St Laurence, Upton. Church of Norman origin retains original nave, central tower and fine chancel with painted rib-vault; south aisle rebuilt 1851; Norman font and 15th-C sculpture of Trinity
Upton Court Late 15th-C manor house with spiral staircase and three original oak doorways

SMAILHOLM (10 km. / 6 m. NW of Kelso), BORDERS, 7, 2A
Smailholm Tower [HS] Exceptionally well-preserved plain, five-storeyed tower house and barmkin built mid 15th C on rocky outcrop by small loch

SMARMORE CASTLE, CO. LOUTH, 11, 4D
See Ardee

SMEETH, KENT, 3, 4D
Church of St Mary Early Norman church retains original chancel arch, and west and south doorways; north aisle and chapel added c.1200; 19th-C tower;
Evegate Manor Stone manor house built mid 14th C

SNAITH, E. RIDING OF YORKS, 7, 4E
Church of St Laurence Embattled church of Norman origin has 13th-C west tower and doorway, 14th-C chancel and vestry, and arcades renewed 15th C

SNAPE, SUFFOLK, 3, 5A
Church of St John the Baptist Late medieval church with ornate south porch and richly carved font with donors' inscription

SNETTISHAM, NORFOLK, 4, 3C
Church of St Mary 14th-C church has west front with fine window, clerestory, transepts, and east (former crossing) tower with tall spire

SNITTERFIELD, WARWS, 5, 4E
Church of St James Church built early 14th to 15th C with original nave and aisles, west tower and clerestory; chancel of c.1300 rebuilt after 1858; 14th-C octagonal font

SOBERTON, HANTS, 2, 5D
Church of St Peter and St Paul Norman church enlarged late 12th and early 13th C has wall paintings of c.1300

SOCKBURN, CO. DURHAM, 7, 3C
Church of All Saints (in grounds of Sockburn Hall) Ruins of mainly 13th-C church with museum made c.1900 out of 15th-C Conyers Chapel containing major collection of Saxon and medieval sculpture

SOHAM, CAMBS, 4, 3E
Church of St Andrew Cruciform church of Norman origin has early 14th-C chancel and late 15th- to early 16th-C west tower and remodelling; good wall panelling

inside north porch, fine late medieval timber roof to nave, and parclose screen

SOLIHULL, W. MIDLANDS, 5, 3D
Church of St Alphege Spacious church mainly built late 13th and early 14th C retains chancel and fine north chapel with vaulted undercroft of pre-1300, crossing tower with 15th-C top, and arcades of 1535; late medieval stone reredos in south aisle

SOMERIES CASTLE, BEDS, 3, 1B
See Luton

SOMERSHAM, CAMBS, 4, 2E
Church of St John Unrestored 13th-C church with arcades, piscinas and 14th-C west tower; clerestory and nave roof of 1400s

SOMERTON, SOMERSET, 2, 2D
Church of St Michael Spacious 13th- to 15th-C church retains original octagonal south tower with later upper stage, north transept, embattled clerestory, and fine early 16th-C panelled roof

SOMERTON CASTLE, LINCS, 4, 1C
Somerton Castle Remains of circular angle towers of castle licensed 1281 and enlarged 17th C

SOMPTING, W. SUSSEX, 3, 1E
Church of St Mary the Virgin Saxon church rebuilt 12th C by Knights Templar preserves several pieces of Saxon sculpture; famous for only surviving "Rhenish helm" roof in Britain (c.1040–60)

SOOKHOLME, NOTTS, 5, 5B
Church of SS Peter and Paul Simple Norman chapel with original chancel arch and east windows

SOUTH ACRE, NORFOLK, 4, 3D
Church of St George Medieval church with late 13th-C north chancel chapel and 15th-C west tower; fine hammerbeam roof to nave; Norman font, 14th-C screen and good brass of c.1384

SOUTHAMPTON, HANTS, 2, 4D
Church of St Julian (French Church), Winkle Street Church originally part of hospital founded c.1190, much remodelled 1861
Church of St Michael Church of 11th-C origin with medieval and 19th-C additions retains original tower arches, aisles and 13th-C chapels rebuilt late 14th to 15th C, and late medieval upper parts to tower; black Tournai marble font of c.1170 and two fine 15th-C lecterns

Tudor House Museum *, Bugle Street. Medieval town house built mainly 1491 to 1518 with 18th- to 20th-C alterations
Waterhouse, corner of Commercial Road and Water Lane. Stone waterhouse of early 14th C built by Franciscan friars
Gates and Town and Castle Walls Impressive and remarkably well-preserved gates and walls built mainly c.1360–85 as urban defences include Bargate retaining archway of c.1180–1200
Medieval Merchant's House [EH] 13th-C merchant's house and shop with reconstructed interior
Medieval Buildings Good medieval buildings include: King John's House and Canute's Palace (12th-C merchant's houses, now ruinous), Wool House (14th-C stone warehouse), and The Red Lion and Duke of Wellington Inns (late medieval houses)
Church of St Mary, Swaythling (N.Southampton) Church of Norman origin much reworked 19th C retains good late 12th-C chancel arch and late 15th to early 16th-C west tower

SOUTH BRENT, DEVON, 1, 4D
Church of St Petrock Church of c.1436 restored 19th C with Norman crossing tower at west end; circular Norman font

SOUTH CHURCH, CO. DURHAM, 7, 3C
Church of St Andrew Auckland Spacious church made collegiate 1290s has west tower, transepts, fine two-storeyed south porch (13th-C), and 15th-C alterations and additions; fragments of important late 8th to 9th-C carved cross assembled 1931, late 13th-C piscinas, and chancel stalls of 1416–17
East Deanery Former prebendal houses of collegiate church built 13th or 14th C form three sides of courtyard; later alterations and restoration as house c.1980

SOUTH ELMHAM ALL SAINTS SUFFOLK, 4, 5E
Church of All Saints [CCT] Norman church with later remodelling retains original round tower and nave with 14th-C south arcade

SOUTH ELMHAM ST CROSS SUFFOLK, 4, 4E
Church of St Cross Church of Norman origin with 12th-C north and south doorways, 14th-C west tower, south porch and chancel
Minster Surviving remains of ruined Saxon church with wide nave

SOUTHEND-ON-SEA, ESSEX, 3, 3C
Prittlewell Priory * (now museum) Surviving fragments of Cluniac priory founded c.1110 (rebuilt 18th C) include refectory of 1170 and two-storeyed west range of cloister with prior's quarters; good 15th-C roofs

SOUTH KYME, LINCS, 4, 1C
St Mary and All Saints Church rebuilt 1888 incorporating parts of 12th-C Augustinian priory has south porch and fine Norman doorway; Saxon carving of 7th to 8th C and 12th-C grave cover
South Kyme Tower Remains of four-storeyed tower house built between 1338 and 1381

SOUTH LEIGH, OXON, 2, 4A
Church of St James Norman and 15th-C church with original chancel rebuilt 1871–2 and three-stage west tower; late Norman pillar piscina and 15th-C wall paintings (restored 1872)

SOUTH LOPHAM, NORFOLK, 4, 4E
Church of St Andrew Church of Saxon origin retains fine crossing tower of c.1120, Norman north doorway, 14th-C chancel, and 15th-C clerestory

SOUTH LUFFENHAM, RUTLAND, 4, 1D
Church of St Mary Church of Norman origin with medieval additions retains late 12th-C north arcade, 13th-C south arcade, and chancel arch of c.1300; 14th-C exterior and tomb chest

SOUTH NEWINGTON, OXON, 2, 4A
Church of St Peter ad Vincula Late Norman church remodelled c.1300 has two original bays of north arcade, west tower of c.1290–1300, early 14th-C chancel, and 15th-C porch; fine medieval wall paintings

SOUTHOVER, E. SUSSEX, 3, 2E
See Lewes

SOUTH PETHERTON, SOMERSET, 2, 2D
Church of St Peter and St Paul Medieval church retains tall 13th-C crossing tower with later octagonal upper part, fine crossing vault and arches, and 14th- to 15th-C transepts; good medieval monuments
King Ine's Palace Manor house built 15th C and remodelled 1800s with fine

bay window on south front
Petherton Bridge 15th-C bridge incorporates fragments of two medieval effigies

SOUTH QUEENSFERRY, LOTHIAN, 8, 3E
Priory Church of St Mary of Mt Carmel Hopetoun Road [SCS]; Church of former Carmelite friary built c.1441 and restored 1890 with tunnel-vaulted chancel, south transept, and low crossing tower; traces on west wall of nave demolished c.1820; good 14th-C aumbry, sedilia and piscina

SOUTHROP, GLOS, 2, 4B
Church of St Peter Church of c.1100 rebuilt 13th, 14th and 19th C with Norman north and south doorways and chancel arch, and south transept of c.1300; richly carved font of c.1180

SOUTH SCARLE, NOTTS, 4, 1B
Church of St Helen Church of Norman origin with much medieval rebuilding retains fine 12th-C two-bay arcade, and 13th-C south arcade and chancel; double piscina and 15th-C screen

SOUTH STONEHAM (Southampton), HANTS, 2, 4D
Church of St Mary [OCT] Norman church with medieval and later additions has fine late 12th-C chancel arch and Purbeck marble font

SOUTH WALSHAM, NORFOLK, 4, 5D
Church of St Mary 15th-C church retains original screen with donor's inscription and many bench ends with poppyheads; late 14th-C font with carved tracery

SOUTHWARK, LONDON
See London

SOUTHWELL, NOTTS, 5, 5B
Southwell Minster Important and impressive Norman cathedral with extensive 13th-C additions retains original west towers with pyramidal roofs reworked 1880, nave, crossing tower and transepts; east end rebuilt 1234 to c.1260 and ornate chapter house of c.1290; fine pulpitum of c.1320–40
Bishop's Palace 18th-C house remodelled 1907–9 incorporates 14th- and 15th-C palace of Archbishops of York

SOUTH WINGFIELD, DERBYS, 5, 4B
Wingfield Manor [EH] Picturesque ruins of large mid 15th-C mansion unoccupied since 1770s

SOUTHWOLD, SUFFOLK, 4, 5E
Church of St Edmund Handsome church built after c.1430 has four-stage west tower and fine south porch with flushwork decoration; lofty clerestory and hammerbeam roofs restored 1867; 14th-C chest, 15th-C font and rich screens and stalls

SOUTH WRAXALL, WILTS, 2, 3C
Church of St James Medieval church with 19th-C additions retains west tower and stair turret of c.1300 with saddle-back roofs, good south porch and chapel; mid 15th-C tomb chest
South Wraxall Manor Late medieval manor house with rich 16th- and 17th-C additions has original hall range with porch and bay windows
Manor Farmhouse 14th-C hospice enlarged 17th C with original hall and chapel

SPALDING, LINCS, 4, 2D
Church of St Mary and St Nicholas Church built c.1284 remodelled 14th to 15th and 19th C has transepts, tower, late medieval clerestory and south porch; good 15th-C hammerbeam roof with angels
Medieval Buildings Medieval buildings include: Prior's Oven (Sheepmarket); Abbey Buildings (Priory Road); Ayscoughfee Hall of late 15th or early 16th-C origin

SPALDWICK, CAMBS, 4, 1E
Church of St James Church of Norman origin with medieval additions retains 12th-C north doorway, late 13th-C chancel with good tracery, south arcade built c.1300, tall west tower of mid 1300s, and 16th-C south aisle

SPARSHOLT, OXON, 2, 4B
Church of the Holy Cross Mainly 14th-C church retains south doorway and 13th-C west tower; lavish scrollwork on north door, unusual 13th-C wooden screen, and good 14th-C monuments

SPEDLINS CASTLE (3.5 km. / 2 ¼ m. N of Applegarth), DUMFRIES AND GALLOWAY, 7, 1B
Spedlins Castle Rectangular tower house built c.1500 and restored 1988–9 with upper floors added 1605

SPILSBY, LINCS, 4, 2B
Church of St James Medieval church remodelled 14th to 16th and 19th C retains Willoughby Chapel of c.1350 and 16th-C tower; fine 14th- and 15th-C monuments to Willoughby family

Market Cross Medieval market cross of possibly 14th C

SPOFFORTH, N. YORKS, 7, 3E
Spofforth Castle [EH] Remains of large fortified house licensed 1308 with fine west front and 15th-C work; interesting undercroft built into rock

SPRATTON, NORTHANTS, 5, 5D
Church of St Andrew Norman church with medieval additions retains fine original west tower and south doorway, 12th- and 13th-C arcades, and north chapel built 1495–1505; 14th-C sedilia, reredos niche and good monuments

SPROXTON, LEICS, 4, 1D
Church of St Bartholomew Church of Norman origin restored 1882–3 has 13th-C west tower with late 14th-C upper storey, and 15th-C nave roof with fine corbels; complete Saxon cross in churchyard

SPYNIE (3 km. / 2 m. N of Elgin), GRAMPIAN, 8, 3A
Spynie Palace [HS] Remains of fine medieval castellar palace built 14th C for Bishops of Moray include gatehouse and massive David's Tower of c.1470–80

SAINTS ISLAND, CO. LONGFORD, 11, 3D
All Saints Priory Picturesque remains of Augustinian priory established before 1244 on island in Lough Ree include small aisleless church with good lancets in south wall and 15th-C east window

STABANNAN, CO. LOUTH, 11, 4D
Roodstown Castle [Dúchas] (2.5 km. / 1 ½ m. W) Handsome, well-preserved tower house built probably mid 1400s
Dromin Church (2.5 km. / 1 ½ m. S) Remains of late medieval church on site of 6th-C monastery
Richardstown Castle (1.5 km. / 1 m. SW) Tall tower house built 14th or 15th C with post-medieval additions and conversion to country house

STACKPOLE ELIDORE (CHERITON), DYFED, 6, 2E
Church of St James and St Elidore Norman and medieval church retains vaulted transepts with squints and fine 14th-C tomb effigies

STAFFORD, STAFFS, 5, 3C
Church of St Mary Early 13th-C church much restored and rebuilt 1841–4 has original nave, north transept with north

doorway of c.1310–20, and octagonal crossing tower with 15th-C top; fine and unusual Norman font
Church of St Chad, Greengate Street Norman church with extensive 19th-C additions retains retains four-bay nave, arcades, clerestory, crossing arches, and 15th-C central tower

STAINDROP, CO. DURHAM, 7, 3C
Church of St Mary Large church of Saxon origin with medieval additions retains original 10th- to 11th-C nave, west tower, and aisles built c.1170–80; fine medieval screen and monuments

STALBRIDGE, DORSET, 2, 2D
Market Cross Near complete cross of later 1400s with lavish carved work; cross head early 1950s copy

STAMFORD, LINCS, 4, 1D
Church of All Saints Medieval church with 13th-C blind arcading to exterior, rich south arcade of c.1230, early 16th-C north-west tower, and south chapel; double piscina and good brasses
Church of St George Mainly 15th-C church rebuilt 17th and 19th C retains 13th-C arcades with 14th-C capitals; good nave roof and late medieval font
Church of St John the Baptist Early to mid 15th-C church has north-west tower and good roofs with carved angels; screens and 15th-C brasses
Church of St Martin Medieval church rebuilt c.1460–c.1485 with west tower, vaulted south porch, and north rood stair turret; early 14th-C font and 15th-C stained glass
Church of St Mary Late 13th-C church much rebuilt 15th C and restored 19th C with original west tower, and chancel and chapel arches; north chapel with panelled ceiling of c.1485 contains good carved figure of c.1330
St Leonard's Priory Surviving remains of church of Benedictine cell founded c.1100 and rebuilt 1833 with original north arcade and rich 12th-C west front
Browne's Hospital, Broad Street. Hospital built 1475–6 and extensively remodelled 1870 retains 15th-C south range incorporating two-storeyed chapel with good medieval stained glass and almsbox
Medieval Buildings Medieval buildings include those on Barn Hill, St Mary's Street, and St Mary's Hill; 13th-C Brazenose Gate
Town Walls Pattern of medieval town walls followed in street plan, with remains visible in West Street

STAMULLEN, CO. MEATH, 11, 4D
Former Parish Church Ruins of large late medieval church; attached Preston Chantry Chapel houses richly carved Cadaver monument (probably mid 15th-C) and double slab altar tomb of *c.*1540

STANDISH, GLOS, 2, 3A
Church of St Nicholas Well-preserved early 14th-C church has east window of *c.*1340, west tower with tall spire, and wide nave with diverse roof bosses

STANFORD, NORTHANTS, 5, 5D
Church of St Nicholas Church of mainly *c.*1300–50 retains five-bay arcades, good roof with bosses, and west tower; extensive collection of early 14th- to 16th-C stained glass

STANION, NORTHANTS, 4, 1E
Church of St Peter Medieval church with 13th-C chancel, north chapel and south porch, and 15th-C arcades and west tower; sedilia and rich wall painting of 1400s

STANSFIELD, SUFFOLK, 3, 3A
Church of All Saints Medieval church has nave built *c.*1300 with 14th-C west tower, chancel and iron bound chest
Purton Green Farm [LT] Aisled hall of late 13th C with 16th-C alterations

STANTON FITZWARREN, WILTS, 2, 4B
Church of St Leonard Norman church with north tower added 1631 and 19th-C remodelling retains important 12th-C font carved with eight vices and virtues, and pillar piscina

STANTON HARCOURT, OXON, 2, 4A
Church of St Michael Norman church remodelled 13th C has north and south doorways of *c.*1150, central tower with 15th-C bell stage, chancel of mainly *c.*1250, and Harcourt Chapel built *c.*1470; unusual mid 13th-C screen, and part of shrine of St Edburg made 1294–1317; good monuments and roofs
Stanton Harcourt Manor [HHA] Remains of medieval house include well preserved late 14th-C Great Kitchen with fine roof of 1485, and Pope's Tower built *c.*1460–71

STANTON LACY, SHROPS, 5, 2A
Church of St Peter Spacious crucifom church of Saxon origin with much original and Norman work, and early 14th-C crossing tower and chancel

STANTON ST JOHN, OXON, 2, 5A
Church of St John the Baptist Norman church with late 12th-C north arcade and chancel arch, fine chancel of *c.*1300, and 15th-C west tower; screens of 1400s and early 16th-C bench ends in chancel

STAPLEFORD, NOTTS, 5, 5C
Church of St Helen Church has 13th-C nave, aisles, chancel, and west tower with early 14th-C bell stage; good east window of *c.*1290 or 1300; tall cross shaft in churchyard (probably *c.*1050)

STAPLEFORD, WILTS, 2, 3C
Church of St Mary Norman church much rebuilt 14th C has late 12th-C south arcade with painted scrolls in arches, north tower built 1300s with upper levels added 1674, and 15th-C clerestory; Norman font

STAPLEHURST, KENT, 3, 3D
Church of All Saints Norman church reworked 1800s retains elaborate south door with 11th-C ironwork, 13th-C arcade to south chapel, stone south porch, and 15th-C west tower; good late medieval panelling to tower roof

STEBBING, ESSEX, 3, 3B
Church of St Mary the Virgin Complete mid 14th-C church has west tower with lead spire and splendid stone rood screen of *c.*1340–50

STEEPLE ASHTON, WILTS, 2, 3C
Church of St Mary Handsome 15th- and early 16th-C church with four-stage west tower, rich battlements and pinnacles, and fine stone vaults to aisles, chapels and chancel

STEETLEY, DERBYS, 5, 5A
Chapel Ornate Norman chapel roofed and restored *c.*1880 has nave, chancel and vaulted apse

STEETON HALL (2.5 km. / 1½ m. SSW of Sherburn-in-Elmet), N. YORKS, 7, 4E
Steeton Hall [Gateway – EH] Late medieval castle with later rebuilding retains part of original work, and complete gatehouse of *c.*1360

STEVENTON, OXON, 2, 4B
Church of St Michael Mainly early 14th-C church with south porch tower retains 13th-C pier to south arcade; 15th-C brass
Priory Cottages [NT], 1 Mill Street (Great Hall in South Cottage only, by written appointment) Two timber-framed cottages converted out of former monastic

buildings (possibly guest hall); one contains priory's original great hall

STEVINGTON, BEDS, 3, 1A
Church of St Mary Church retains Anglo-Danish west tower with 15th-C top, south doorway and south arcade of *c.*1300, 14th-C chancel chapels, and later medieval nave clerestory and roof; unusual early 16th-C bench ends and screen

STEWKLEY, BUCKS, 2, 5A
Church of St Michael Largely original Norman church of *c.*1140–50 with lavish zig-zag decoration in nave, vaulted chancel and central tower and on west front

STEYNING, W. SUSSEX, 3, 1E
Church of St Andrew Ambitious late Norman church with 16th- and 19th-C alterations retains west tower arch of *c.*1100, four bays of nave built 1170–80, and clerestory; 12th-C font
Grammar School School founded 1614 has 15th-C wings originally part of hall of Fraternity of Holy Trinity

STEYNTON, DYFED, 6, 2D
Pill Priory (3 km. / 2 m. W) Surviving chancel arch and fragmentary ruins of small 13th-C priory standing by roadside in private garden

STILLINGFLEET, N. YORKS, 7, 4E
Church of St Helen Norman church with medieval and 19th-C work has fine original south portal and door with ironwork of *c.*1160, 13th-C west tower with top added 1400s, and Moreby Chapel founded 1332

STIRLING, CENTRAL, 8, 2D
Stirling Castle [HS] Large, important and powerful castle built mainly 15th and 16th C, spectacularly set on volcanic rock, has remains of late medieval forework with gatehouse (truncated 18th and 19th C) and Prince's Tower, Great Hall built *c.*1500 for James IV, Royal Palace of *c.*1540, and Chapel Royal of mainly 1594; extensive post-medieval additions and alterations
Old Town Wall, Corn Exchange Road / Albert Place. Remaining stretch of medieval town walling
Old Bridge [HS] Attractive bridge built 15th or early 16th C (partly reworked 1749) crosses River Forth
Church of the Holy Rude, St John Street [SCS] Fine medieval church built mainly 15th and 16th C has five-bay nave begun

*c.*1415, choir with apse of earlier to mid 1500s, and plain west tower; original oak roof to nave and former piscina from Cambuskenneth Abbey (now font) in north chapel

STOBO (6.5 km. / 4 m. W of Peebles), BORDERS, 7, 1A
Stobo Kirk [SCS] 12th-C church much restored 1863 has original nave and chancel, tower with upper part rebuilt 16th C, and work of 1991; north transept or Chapel of St Mary of *c.*1460 contains incised slab with chalice and inscription to priest Robert Vesey (d.1473)

STOCKTON, WILTS, 2, 3C
Church of St John the Baptist Church of Norman origin retains 12th-C north arcade and west tower, 13th-C chancel, early 14th-C south arcade, and late medieval clerestory; unusual wall between nave and chancel; Norman font and good early 14th-C monument to lady

STOGUMBER, SOMERSET, 1, 5B
Church of St Mary Medieval church has embattled 14th-C south-west tower, south porch, rich early 16th-C north aisle, and good wagon roofs; octagonal font and stone pulpit

STOGURSEY, SOMERSET, 2, 1C
Church of St Andrew Former church of Benedictine priory founded *c.*1100 rebuilt 12th, 15th and 19th C retains original crossing tower and arches, chancel aisles built *c.*1180–5, and early 15th-C nave; Norman font
Castle Scanty remains of late 13th- or early 14th-C moated castle

STOKE-BY-NAYLAND, SUFFOLK, 3, 4A
Church of St Mary Spacious medieval church with early 14th-C north chapel, south porch rebuilt 19th C, ornate four-stage west tower of mid 15th C, brick north porch and carved south and west doors; 15th-C font, chapel screens, and brasses
Giffords Hall (3 km. / 2 m. NE) Hall-house built after 1428 and altered early 18th and late 19th C retains brick gatehouse, timber-framed ranges, and splendid hammerbeam roof to hall

STOKE CHARITY, HANTS, 2, 4C
Church of St Michael Norman church with medieval additions retains two bays of 11th-C north arcade and lavish chancel arch; mid 13th-C wall painting and many good medieval monuments

STOKE D'ABERNON,
SURREY, 3,1C
Church of St Mary Church of Saxon origin poorly restored 19th C retains work of c.1190, rib-vaulted chancel built c.1250, and Norbury Chapel of c.1490; fine medieval brasses and stained glass

STOKE DRY, RUTLAND, 4,1D
Church of St Andrew Church of 12th-C origin with medieval and 17th-C rebuilding retains finely carved shafts of chancel arch built c.1120, 13th-C west tower and 14th-C arcades; east windows of chancel and south (Digby) chapel of c.1300; 15th-C rood screen with coving for loft, and good wall paintings

STOKE GOLDING, LEICS, 5,4D
Church of St Margaret Well-preserved church enlarged c.1280–90 with wide, rich south aisle and south chapel; north side remodelled 1320–40; fine early 14th-C east window, double piscina and font

STOKE POGES, BUCKS, 3,1C
Church of St Giles Norman church enlarged 1200s with aisles and arcades, north transeptal tower, and addition at east of chancel; fine 14th-C south porch and nave roof; brick Hastings Chapel added c.1560; rare surviving bronze base of altar cross (c.1480)

STOKE PRIOR, WORCS, 5,3E
Church of St Michael Late 12th- and early 13th-C church with original north arcade, chancel arch, south doorway and 13th-C chancel; 15th-C octagonal font

STOKE ROCHFORD, LINCS, 4,1C
Church of St Mary and St Andrew Norman church with medieval and mid 19th-C additions retains north arcade of c.1140, early 13th-C south arcade, and 15th-C north and south chapels; good medieval monuments

STOKE ST GREGORY,
SOMERSET, 2,1D
Church of St Gregory Medieval church with fine crossing and octagonal tower of c.1300, transepts, and much 15th-C work

STOKESAY, SHROPS, 5,2D
Stokesay Castle [EH] Splendid fortified house, one of best preserved in country, has fine Great Hall of c.1270–80, towers, and early 17th-C gatehouse
Church of St John the Baptist Medieval church rebuilt mid 17th C with Norman south doorway and 15th-C chancel and west tower

STOKE-SUB-HAMDON,
SOMERSET, 2,2D
Church of St Mary Norman church with medieval rebuilding retains 12th-C chancel, nave, north doorway with carved tympanum, and north tower with rib vault of c.1190; double piscina of c.1300 and panelled 15th-C nave roof; late medieval cross in churchyard
Priory [NT] 14th-C buildings for priests of lost chantry chapel of St Nicholas

STONE, BUCKS, 2,5A
Church of St John the Baptist Norman church rebuilt 13th, 14th and 19th C retains original south doorway, 13th-C chancel and transepts, and early 14th-C west tower; carved Norman font and good 15th-C brass

STONE, KENT, 3,3C
Church of St Mary the Virgin Medieval church with fine late 13th-C interior has tall rib-vaulted chancel with splendid wall arcading of c.1260, good chancel arch, early 14th-C west tower, and north chapel added c.1527; wall paintings of late 1200s and early 15th-C brass

STONEACRE, KENT, 3,3D
See Otham

STONELEIGH, WARWS, 5,4D
Church of St Mary Norman church has north doorway with carved tympanum, west tower with 15th-C top, wide nave, and lavish chancel arch; post-medieval north and south chapels; Norman font
Stare Bridge Fine late medieval bridge with cutwaters
Stoneleigh Abbey 18th-C house incorporating features of 12th-C Cistercian abbey; mid 14th-C gatehouse

STOPHAM, W. SUSSEX, 3,1E
Church of St Mary 11th-C church with 15th-C work retains original nave, chancel, and west tower rebuilt c.1600; reredos recess of c.1200 and 15th-C brasses
Stopham Bridge Fine medieval bridge rebuilt 1423 has cutwaters and central arch of 1822

STOTTESDON, SHROPS, 5,2D
Church of St Mary Medieval church has Saxon west doorway with Norman tympanum, 11th-C west tower with early 16th-C upper level, 12th-C north arcade, and chancel built 1300s; lavish carved font of c.1160

STOUGHTON, W. SUSSEX, 2,5D
Church of St Mary Cruciform 11th-C church altered 13th C has lavish interior with original chancel arch; south transept converted to tower 14th C

STOURHEAD, WILTS, 2,2C
See Stourton

STOURTON, WILTS, 2,2C
Church of St Peter Mainly 15th-C church with west tower and clerestory retains early 14th-C four-bay arcades; effigy of lady of c.1400
Bristol High Cross, grounds of Stourhead [NT] Tall cross of 1373 erected in gardens 1765 has niches, stone figures and central pinnacle
St Peter's Pump (2 km. / 1 ¼ m. NW of house) 15th-C structure moved from Bristol 1766 with statues, ogee arches, and pinnacle

STOW, LINCS, 4,1B
Church of St Mary One of the largest surviving Saxon churches built early or mid 11th C on cruciform plan with mid 12th-C nave and fine late Norman chancel restored 1851; 15th-C tower above crossing; two 13th-C coffin lids and font

STOWE-NINE-CHURCHES
NORTHANTS, 5,5E
Church of St Michael Church with much work of 16th, 17th and 19th C retains tall Saxon west tower and Norman north doorway; effigy of c.1287

STOWLANGTOFT, SUFFOLK, 4,4E
Church of St George [OCT] Late 14th-C church with flushwork decoration has exceptionally fine carved bench ends, stalls and misericords, and wall painting of St Christopher; early 14th-C font

STRADE, CO. MAYO, 11,2C
Friary [Dúchas] Ruins of friary founded for Franciscans but transferred 1252 to Dominicans include mainly 15th-C church with 13th-C chancel; splendid canopied tomb in south wall (carved c.1475) with excellent figure sculpture and fine 15th-C altar reredos or tomb frontal; good medieval tombstone in vaulted sacristy

STRANRAER, DUMFRIES AND
GALLOWAY, 10,4E
Castle of St John, Charlotte Street. Tower house built c.1510, reworked c.1600 and 1821–2, and converted to visitor's centre 1988–90

STRATA FLORIDA, DYFED, 6,4C
Strata Florida Abbey [CADW] Ruins of important 12th-C Cistercian abbey, renowned medieval centre of Welsh scholarship; magnificent carved west doorway to cruciform late 12th- to early 13th-C church; 14th-C choir and transept chapels with decorative medieval tiles; fragmentary remains of monastic buildings include cloister and chapter house

STRATFORD ST MARY,
SUFFOLK, 3,4A
Church of St Mary Spacious church built 15th to early 16th C and remodelled 19th C has west tower, tall clerestory, and rich north front with chancel chapel, aisle and porch
Priest's House (W of church) Timber-framed priest's house of c.1500

STRATFORD-UPON-AVON,
WARWS, 5,4E
Church of the Holy Trinity Medieval church retains 13th-C transepts, crossing tower heightened early 1300s, and handsome 15th-C chancel; original ceiling with bosses to mid 14th-C south aisle; misericords of c.1500
Gild Chapel Chapel Street. 15th-C gild chapel with west tower, four-bay nave and plain chancel; medieval wall paintings
Clopton Bridge Bridge built c.1480–90 with toll-house tower added 1814
Grammar School Timber-framed building with overhanging upper level built 1417 as guildhall
Almshouses Almshouses of c.1427 with jettied upper storey and later alterations
White Swan Hotel, Rother Street. Timber-framed building of 15th C with 16th-C wall paintings
Anne Hathaway's Cottage: See Shottery

STRELLEY, NOTTS, 5,5B
Church of All Saints Mainly 14th-C church retains transepts, south porch and spacious chancel endowed 1356; near complete late 14th-C rood screen, and fine 15th- and early 16th-C monuments in chancel

STRETHALL, ESSEX, 3,2A
Church of St Mary Saxon church retains original nave, 11th-C chancel arch, 15th-C chancel and west tower; brass to priest made 1400s

STRETTON SUGWAS, HEREFS, 5,2E
Church of St Mary Magdalene Church built 1877–80 incorporates Norman west

doorway and fine tympanum depicting Samson and Lion; 15th-C tiles in vestry and good monument

STUDHAM, BEDS, 3,1B
Church of St Mary Medieval church consecrated 1220 has four-bay arcades of *c.*1210–20 with good capitals, west tower, and Norman bowl to font

STUDLAND, DORSET, 2,3E
Church of St Nicholas Unusually complete Norman church with rib-vaulted tower and square chancel

STUDLEY ROYAL, N. YORKS, 7,3D
Church of St Mary [EH] 19th-C church designed by William Burges in Early English style, built 1871–8 with highly decorated interior (see p. 213)

SUDBURY, SUFFOLK, 3,3A
Church of St Gregory Medieval church rebuilt 1300s and *c.*1485 retains 14th-C arcades, west tower, and south porch with attached chapel; late 14th-C font with splendid medieval cover
Church of St Peter [CCT] Spacious 15th-C church restored 1859 and 1968 has vestry below chancel, tall five-bay arcades, two-storeyed porch, and west tower built *c.*1460–85
Church of All Saints, Church Street. 15th-C church with west tower, north aisle of *c.*1459, attached two-storeyed vestry, and good roofs; ornate parclose screens
Medieval Buildings Several good medieval buildings include: 15th-C Chantry and Salter's Hall (Gainsborough Street); Old Moot Hall (Cross Street); former Chapel of St Bartholomew of priory founded *c.*1115 (off Melford Road)

SUDELEY, GLOS, 2,3A
Church of St Mary Church of *c.*1460 with interior of *c.*1859–63 retains original external appearance; 13th-C stained glass
Sudeley Castle [HHA] Handsome 15th-C castle rebuilt *c.*1572 and 19th C with gateway of *c.*1442, towers, fine original church and mid 15th-C barn

SUENO'S STONE,
    GRAMPIAN, 8,2A
See Forres

SULGRAVE, NORTHANTS, 5,5E
Sulgrave Castle Remains of Norman castle with early 11th-C timber hall discovered during excavations of 1967–72

SUNDON, BEDS, 3,1B
Church of St Mary Mainly 14th-C church with 13th-C arcades to fine interior, west tower, south transept, and clerestory with round windows; 13th-C font

SUTTON, CAMBS, 4,2E
Church of St Andrew Well-preserved church built *c.*1366–88 has imposing west tower with octagonal upper level and two-storeyed south porch; large east window of *c.*1370
The Burystead House rebuilt 18th C has early 14th-C chapel of two storeys; double piscina and wooden roof

SUTTON, HUMBERSIDE, 7,5E
See Hull

SUTTON-AT-HONE, KENT, 3,2C
Church of St John the Baptist Early 14th-C church reworked *c.*1615 and 1862 retains fine original east window and piscina
St John's Jerusalem [NT] Surviving 13th-C chapel of Commandery of Knights Hospitaller with 17th- and 18th-C work

SUTTON BINGHAM,
    SOMERSET, 2,2D
Church of All Saints Simple Norman church of nave and chancel with 13th- and 14th-C work retains original north doorway and chancel arch; Norman font and fine wall paintings of *c.*1300

SUTTON BONNINGTON,
    NOTTS, 5,5C
Church of St Michael Medieval church retains 14th-C north nave arcade with seats built round piers; 14th-C font has three projections for book, salt and candle used in rite of baptism

SUTTON COURTENAY, OXON, 2,4B
Church of All Saints Medieval church retains late 12th-C responds to chancel arch, west tower with 15th-C top, 13th-C chancel, wide nave with mainly 14th-C arcades, and handsome two-storeyed brick south porch; Norman font, good monuments and screens
Norman Hall Plain, rectangular manor house built *c.*1190–1200 with fine south doorway and good timber roof
Manor House Large, handsome house with 17th-C work incorporates medieval remains in south and east ranges
The Abbey Courtyard house reworked 1800s, formerly grange of Abingdon Abbey, retains 14th-C ranges and original great hall

SUTTON UPON DERWENT
    E. RIDING OF YORKS, 7,4E
Church of St Michael Norman church with east arches of arcades built *c.*1160–80 and 14th-C lower stage of tower; part of richly carved Saxon cross shaft and medieval grave slabs

SUTTON VALENCE, KENT, 3,3D
Sutton Valence Castle [EH] Remains of small Norman keep built 12th C to defend important medieval route

SWAFFHAM, NORFOLK, 4,3D
Church of St Peter and St Paul Mainly 15th- and early 16th-C church reworked 18th and 19th C with transepts, rich south porch, west tower, and fine north front; double hammerbeam roof with angels

SWAFFHAM PRIOR, CAMBS, 3,3A
Church of St Mary Church of Norman origin retains west tower with original octagonal stage and 13th-C sixteen-sided upper level; 15th-C arcades and clerestory, and chancel of 1878
Church of St Cyriac Church rebuilt 1809–11 has 15th-C west tower with octagonal upper stage
Baldwin Manor Timber-framed house of early 16th C with overhanging upper storey and carved bressumer

SWALCLIFFE, OXON, 5,4E
Church of St Peter and St Paul Church of Saxon origin has early 13th-C south aisle, south porch, and west tower with 15th-C upper levels; good 14th-C wall paintings
Manor House House remodelled 16th and 19th C retains 13th-C service wing, and hall and solar rebuilt 1397–1423
Tithe Barn Fine tithe barn built *c.*1400 with two gabled porches

SWANSEA / ABERTAWE
    GLAMORGAN, 6,4E
Swansea Castle [CADW], Castle Square Surviving fragments of medieval castle include late 13th-C hall-parlour range with fine arcaded parapet added *c.*1332, north-east tower much altered and later used as prison, and ruins of curtain wall

SWANTON MORLEY,
    NORFOLK, 4,4D
Church of All Saints Spacious church built *c.*1378 with low chancel, four-bay arcades, tall clerestory and west tower

SWAYTHLING, HANTS, 2,4D
See Southampton

SWEETHEART ABBEY, DUMFRIES
    AND GALLOWAY, 7,1B
See New Abbey

SWIMBRIDGE, DEVON, 1,4B
Church of St James Mainly 15th- and 16th-C church retains wagon roofs with bosses and celures; splendid late medieval screen

SWINE, E. RIDING OF YORKS, 7,5E
Church of St Mary Surviving 12th-C clerestoried choir of church of Cistercian nunnery has four-bay arcades, north chapel, and west tower rebuilt 1787; early 16th-C stalls with misericords and fine medieval monuments of between *c.*1370 and *c.*1410

SWINESHEAD, BEDS, 4,1E
Church of St Nicholas Impressive 14th-C church has west tower with 15th-C upper parts, west porch, and 19th-C work; fine chancel contains angle piscina, sedilia and rich Easter Sepulchre

SWINGFIELD, KENT, 3,4D
St John's Commandery [EH], Densole Well-preserved 13th-C chapel reworked as house 16th C retains piscina and fine timber roof

SWORDS, CO. DUBLIN, 11,4D
Swords Castle [Dúchas] Remains of five-sided archbishop's manorial castle altered 13th to 15th C with gatehouse, 14th-C chapel, and imposing tower at north angle (formerly Constable's quarters)
Round Tower [Dúchas] Round Tower in grounds of Church of Ireland church marks site of early monastery; adjoining 14th-C steeple of medieval church

SWYNCOMBE, OXON, 2,5B
Church of St Botolph Early Norman church with 19th-C work has apsidal east end and bellcote; wall paintings discovered 1850

SWYNNERTON, STAFFS, 5,3C
Church of St Mary Church of Norman origin with medieval rebuilding retains two original doorways in tower, 13th-C chancel and nave arcades; fine seated Christ of *c.*1260–80 and 15th-C screen

TAGHADOE, CO. KILDARE, 12,5A
Round Tower [Dúchas] Tall possibly incomplete Round Tower, sole survivor of early Christian monastery

TAGHMON,
   CO. WESTMEATH, 11, 3D
See Portneshangan

TAIN, HIGHLAND, 9, 4D
St Duthus Chapel, Chapel Road. Ruined rectangular chapel built possibly early 13th C survives in 19th-C cemetery
St Duthus Memorial Church, Castle Brae Well-preserved former collegiate church built 15th C and much restored 19th-C situated in graveyard close to ruined church of c.1300; 13th-C font

TAKELEY, ESSEX, 3, 2B
Church of the Holy Trinity Spacious church of Norman origin with 13th-C chancel, early 14th-C south aisle, and 15th-C west tower; fine tall font cover of c.1500

TALGARTH, POWYS, 6, 5D
Church of St Gwendoline Church of 13th-C origin restored 1873 has north vestry, nave rebuilt c.1400, 15th-C south porch with earlier stoup, and tall west tower; late 13th-C cross slab
Great Porthaml Late medieval house with later rebuilding retains fine hall roof above ceiling and 16th-C gate tower

TALLANSTOWN, CO. LOUTH, 11, 4D
Louth Hall Large mansion on elevated site with 18th- and 19th-C work incorporates medieval tower house (possibly built 1300s)
Philipstown Church (1.5 km. / 1 m. N) Remains of attractive late medieval church retaining stoup with carved head
Thomastown Castle / Knock Abbey (2.5 km. / 1½ m. NW) 14th-C keep reworked 1858 and c.1923 with attached 18th-C house supposedly occupies site of abbey founded 1148

TALLEY ABBEY, DYFED, 6, 4D
Talley Abbey [CADW] Scant remains of unfinished cruciform church of austere late 12th-C Premonstratensian abbey, completed with shortened nave during 13th C; chancel used as parish church from 16th to 18th C

TAL-Y-BONT, GWYNEDD, 6, 4A
Cochwillan Old Hall * (1.5 km. / 1 m. S) Medieval farmhouse of c.1450 contains Great Hall with splendid hammerbeam roof

TAMLAGHTARD
   CO. LONDONDERRY, 11, 4A
See Magilligan

TAMWORTH, STAFFS, 5, 4D
Church of St Editha Large church of Saxon origin with much 14th- and some 19th-C rebuilding retains two Norman crossing arches, 13th-C north porch, and 14th-C crypt; late medieval west tower with twin spiral stairs
Chapel of St James (Spittal), Wigginton Road. Small chapel of hospital founded 13th C has late Norman north doorway
Castle * Norman shell keep with tower on east side encloses 17th-C buildings

TANSOR, NORTHANTS, 4, 1E
Church of St Mary Norman church with 13th- and 14th-C work retains 12th-C aisles and chancel of late 1200s; Norman tower with 13th-C upper parts; font of early 1300s

TANTALLON CASTLE (3 km. / 2 m. E of North Berwick), LOTHIAN, 8, 3E
Tantallon Castle [HS] Remains of castle of enclosure built c.1370 on impressive headland site with massive south-west curtain wall retaining mid and outer towers, and part of domestic north-west range

TATTERSHALL, LINCS, 4, 2C
Church of the Holy Trinity Former collegiate church begun 1469 has west tower, clerestory, and huge windows in transept; 15th-C nave pulpit, and stone pulpitum erected 1528; good brasses
Tattershall College [EH] Remains of college founded 1439
Tattershall Castle [NT] Complex moated castle begun 1434–5 retains monumental brick keep with fine chimneypieces and vaulting

TAUNTON, SOMERSET, 2, 1D
Church of St Mary Magdalene Large medieval church has double aisles, rich south side with porch dated 1508, and tall elaborate west tower of c.1488–1514; good 15th-C font
Church of St James Spacious medieval church with 19th-C rebuilding and restoration has fine west tower, five-bay arcades, and rich 15th-C font
Grammar School, Corporation Street. Former grammar school built c.1480 and remodelled c.1520 and 1905 survives among municipal buildings
Castle (now museum) Norman castle with 13th-, 17th-, 18th- and 20th-C remodellings retains original north and west ranges, and houses important stone reredos of c.1380 (originally in Wellington church)

TAVISTOCK, DEVON, 11, 4D
Tavistock Abbey Remains of important Benedictine abbey include late 12th-C gatehouse altered 19th C, medieval hall, and parts of cloister

TAWSTOCK, DEVON, 1, 4B
Church of St Peter Church of Norman origin altered early 14th, 16th and 18th C retains tall crossing tower with timber rib vault; wagon roofs and fine monuments

TEMPLE, LOTHIAN, 8, 3E
Old Parish Church Well-preserved but roofless late 14th-C church with basic plan and good window tracery; west part rebuilt after 16th C using 12th-C stonework; original gable cross now on gatepier of churchyard

TEMPLE BRUER, LINCS, 4, 1C
Temple Bruer Remains of Norman church of Templar preceptory restored late 19th C include tall late 12th-C tower with vaulted ground floor

TEMPLE CRONAN,
   CO. CLARE, 12, 2B
Church of St Cronan [Dúchas] Small 12th-C church with 15th-C work and good original carved heads; gabled stone-built St Cronan's Bed to south-east

TEMPLECRONE,
   CO. DONEGAL, 11, 3A
See Dungloe

TEMPLECROSS,
   CO. WESTMEATH, 11, 3D
See Ballynacarrigy

TEMPLE DOUGLAS ABBEY
   CO. DONEGAL, 11, 3A
See Garton

TEMPLENAGALLIAGHDOO
   CO. MAYO, 11, 1C
See Errew Abbey

TEMPLERUSHIN,
   CO. FERMANAGH, 11, 3C
See Holywell

TEMPLETOWN, CO. LOUTH, 11, 5C
See Grange

TENBY, DYFED, 6, 3E
Tenby Castle On rocky headland above harbour, fragmentary remains of 12th- to 15th-C castle, including barbican and watch tower
Town Walls Surviving stretches of medieval town walls with seven towers and one gate

St Mary's Church Church splendidly rebuilt during 15th-C retains tower of original 13th-C building
Plantagenet House Early 15th-C house
Tudor Merchant's House [NT], Quay Hill Fine surviving town house built late 1400s has original roof trusses and remains of early wall paintings
Church of St Lawrence, Gumfreston (1.5 km. / 1 m. W) Small late Norman and medieval church with tall transept tower has traces of wall paintings

TENTERDEN, KENT, 3, 3D
Church of St Mildred Medieval church with interior much restored c.1864–6 retains 13th-C chancel, 14th-C nave, and fine west tower built c.1449–c.1495; good 15th-C font,

TERMONFECKIN, CO. LOUTH, 11, 4D
Termonfeckin Castle [Dúchas] Three storeyed tower house built 15th C and reworked 1641 retains fine corbelled vault in upper chamber
High Cross [Dúchas], St Fechin's Churchyard. Complete medieval cross with carved work (the cap-stone at top is in the form of a miniature church)

TEVERSAL, NOTTS, 5, 4B
Church of St Catherine Church of Norman origin remodelled 13th, 14th and 17th C has original south doorway

TEWKESBURY, GLOS, 2, 3A
Abbey Church of St Mary Church of Benedictine abbey consecrated 1121 retains fine mid 12th-C west front with recessed arch, crossing tower of c.1150, nave with imposing arcade piers and 14th-C vault, and ambulatory with chapels of 1300s; handsome Beauchamp Chapel of c.1430 with stone screen; presbytery contains stained glass of 1340–4; magnificent collection of monuments
Abbey Precinct [Gatehouse – LT] Remains of abbey buildings include Abbey House (possibly original guest house or abbot's lodging), late medieval gatehouse restored 1849, and barn (barton)
King John's Castle, Mythe Road. Medieval building associated with abbey reworked 17th and 19th C
34–50 Church Street 15th-C terrace of small houses incorporating shops
Medieval Buildings Good medieval town buildings include: 15th-C Cross House (Church Street); Black Bear Inn, Clarence House and early 16th-C Old Fleece Inn (High Street)

THAME, OXON, 2, 5B
Church of St Mary 13th-C cruciform church reworked 14th C, 15th C and 1889–97 retains original transepts, chancel (c.1220), and five-bay arcades (c.1260); good medieval screens and brasses
Thame Park 18th-C house incorporates early 16th-C abbot's lodgings of Cistercian abbey founded 1138; early 14th-C chapel north-west of house (remodelled 1836)
Prebendal House House restored 1836 and 20th C has well-preserved chapel of c.1250, solar enlarged 1300s, and 15th-C hall
The Birdcage Half-timbered 15th-C inn with jettied upper floor and 19th-C alterations

THAXTED, ESSEX, 3, 3A
Church of St John the Baptist Mainly 14th- and 15th-C church with arcades of c.1340, ornate north porch of c.1445 and tall late 15th-C steeple; flat pitched roofs and fragments of medieval stained glass
Guildhall 15th-C guildhall with exposed timber-framing, open ground floor and two overhanging upper storeys
Medieval Buildings Good medieval houses survive close to Guildhall

THEDDLETHORPE, LINCS, 4, 2B
Church of All Saints Handsome church of Norman origin extensively reworked late 14th C has west tower and spacious interior with five-bay arcades; ornate reredos niche, rood screen and font

THETFORD, NORFOLK, 4, 3E
Priory of Our Lady [EH] Surviving remains of church, monastic building and 14th-C gatehouse of Cluniac priory founded 1103–4
Church of the Holy Sepulchre (The Canons) [EH], Brandon Road. Ruins of Augustinian priory church of St Sepulchre founded c.1139
Nunnery Remains of Benedictine nunnery of St George founded c.1160, now forming part of farm
Blackfriars Grammar School, London Road. 19th-C school incorporates remains of friary founded 1335
Bell Hotel, King Street. Timber-framed building of early 1500s with overhanging upper floor
Warren Lodge [EH] Remains of two-storeyed 15th-C tower house, probably former home of priory's gatekeeper

THIRSK, N. YORKS, 7, 3D
Church of St Mary Handsome church begun c.1430 has west tower, tall clerestory, two-storeyed south porch, chancel above

vaulted crypt, and fine openwork battlements; good 15th-C brass and wagon roof

THOCKRINGTON NORTHUMBERLAND, 7, 3B
Church of St Aidan Norman church with 13th-, 17th- and 19th-C work retains original tunnel-vaulted chancel with arch, and apse arch in east wall

THOMASTOWN, CO. KILKENNY, 12, 4C
Church of St Mary [Dúchas] Ruins of church founded late 13th C with chancel used until 1809; head of High Cross in churchyard

THOMASTOWN CASTLE CO. LOUTH, 11, 4D
See Tallanstown

THOOR BALLYLEE 8 km. / 5 m. NE of Gort), CO. GALWAY, 12, 3B
Thoor Ballylee (or Ballylee Castle) [Dúchas] (museum) Four-storeyed 16th-C tower house picturesquely set by stream, made famous as home (together with adjoining cottage) of poet W. B. Yeats during 1920s

THORNBURY, GLOS, 2, 2B
Church of St Mary Mainly 15th-C church with 19th-C additions has chancel of c.1340, large windows in nave and clerestory, and tower of c.1540; late 12th-C font and c.1325 piscina and triple sedilia
Thornbury Castle Manor house begun c.1511 and restored 1854 with well-preserved west front and south range

THORNEY, CAMBS, 4, 2D
Church of St Mary and St Botolph Partly surviving nave of abbey church built c.1085–1108, restored 1638 as parish church, with Norman angle turrets on tall west front; east end added 1840–1

THORNHAM PARVA, SUFFOLK, 4, 4E
Church of St Mary Thatched Norman church retains north and south doorways, short west tower, and 14th-C chancel; splendid retable of c.1300 and 14th-C font

THORNHILL, DUMFRIES AND GALLOWAY, 10, 5D
Nith Bridge Cross Shaft Tall, very well-preserved early cross shaft with excellent carved work

THORNHILL, W. YORKS, 7, 3E
Church of St Michael Medieval church has west tower, east end and window of

1499, and nave and aisles added 1877; north (Savile) chapel built 1447 retains original roof, good stained glass and monuments; fragments of Saxon crosses of c.850
Manor House Ruins of moated 15th-C manor house
Lees Hall (3 km. / 2 m. WNW) Timber-framed house of early 15th C restored 1962–4 has stone base and good hall roof

THORNTON, BUCKS, 2, 5A
Church of St Michael Medieval church rebuilt c.1850 retains exceptional mid 15th-C alabaster effigies and brasses

THORNTON, LEICS, 5, 4C
Church of St Peter Medieval church with aisles of c.1300, 15th-C clerestory and west tower, and chancel built 1864; 15th-C octagonal font and base of rood screen

THORNTON ABBEY, LINCS, 7, 5E
Thornton Abbey and Gatehouse [EH] Remains of Augustinian abbey founded 1139 include octagonal chapter house of 1282–c.1308, church, and imposing brick gatehouse of 1360s and 1380s with carved decoration

THORNTON CURTIS LINCS, 7, 5E
Church of St Laurence Church built 1200-1300 with broad chancel, nave and aisles, and good south doorway; ironwork of c.1200 to south door and of c.1325–50 to north door; black Tournai marble font

THORPE SALVIN, S. YORKS, 5, 5A
Church of St Peter Norman church retains original south doorway, chancel arch, arcades, west tower with 15th-C upper part, and 14th-C chancel; splendid Norman font with carved scenes

THREAVE CASTLE (5 km. / 3 m. W of Castle Douglas), DUMFRIES AND GALLOWAY, 10, 5E
Threave Castle [HS / NTS] Remains of moated castle on island in River Dee with massive tower house built c.1370, 15th-C curtain walls and gatehouse; excavations of 1970s showed castle was originally part of larger complex

THREECASTLES, CO. WICKLOW, 11, 4E
Castle [Dúchas] Sole survivor of three medieval castles consists of probably early 14th-C rectangular keep with well-preserved fireplace on second level

THREEKINGHAM, LINCS, 4, 1C
Church of St Peter Church of Norman origin with 13th- and 14th-C work retains west tower, 13th-C font and good effigies of c.1310

THURGARTON, NOTTS, 5, 5B
Priory Church of St Peter 13th-C church of Augustinian priory founded 1119–39 with later remodelling retains original west portals, west porch and doorway, north-west tower, and south arcade

THURLBEAR, SOMERSET, 2, 1D
Church of St Thomas [CCT] Norman church much altered 15th C and c.1864 has original aisle arcades of c.1100

THURLBY, LINCS, 4, 1D
Church of St Firmin Saxo-Norman church with medieval additions retains original tower with 14th-C upper stage and rood loft staircase; Norman cross, 13th-C font, and good medieval grave covers

THURLES, CO. TIPPERARY, 12, 4E
Church of St Mary, St Mary's Avenue Protestant church retains tomb of Edmund Archer (possibly c.1520) with effigies and finely carved figures of saints
Castles Remains of 15th-C Black Castle and Bridge Castle

THURLESTONE, DEVON, 1, 4E
Church of All Saints Medieval church with unusual 15th-C tower and embattled south porch; double piscina in chancel

THURSLEY, SURREY, 3, 1D
Church of St Michael Small church of Saxon origin poorly restored 19th C retains Norman work and chancel arch of c.1270; unusual late 15th-C timber cage in nave supporting central belfry; font of pre-1100

THURSO, HIGHLAND, 9, 4B
Old Church of St Peter, Wilson Lane Remains of medieval church rebuilt c.1500 with 12th- or 13th-C chancel (Forss Vault), early 17th-C transeptal south "aisle", east tower, and transeptal north "aisle" added 1664

TIBBERAGHNY, CO. KILKENNY, 12, 4C
Cross-pillar [Dúchas] Carved cross-pillar (possibly 9th-C) on site of early monastery

TICKENCOTE, RUTLAND, 4, 1D
Church of St Peter and St Paul Norman church almost completely rebuilt 1792 retains remarkable unrestored chancel arch of c.1160–70 and rib-vaulted chancel with carved boss; font of c.1200

TICKENHAM, SOMERSET, 2, 2B
Church of St Quiricus and St Julietta Early Norman church with 13th- to 15th-C additions retains 11th-C nave and chancel, fine chancel arch of c.1100, and early 13th-C aisles and south chapel; 13th-C monuments, font of c.1300 and 14th-C stained glass
Tickenham Court Well-preserved manor house with hall of c.1400 and solar wing built c.1500

TICKHILL, S. YORKS, 5, 5A
Church of St Mary Fine church of 13th-C origin much rebuilt 14th to 16th C has west tower, tall nave with clerestory, wide arcades, and north and south chancel chapels
Tickhill Castle Remains of Norman castle with early 12th-C gatehouse refaced 1400s

TIDESWELL, DERBYS, 5, 4A
Church of St John the Baptist Church of c.1320–80 has west tower, two-storeyed south porch, and fine chancel with original sedilia and east window; good effigies and brasses of 13th to 15th C

TIDMARSH, BERKS, 2, 5B
Church of St Laurence Church retains excellent Norman south doorway and fine 13th-C polygonal apse; 19th-C bell turret with shingled roof

TIHILLY, CO. OFFALY, 12, 4A
Church and High Cross [Dúchas] Good, unusual High Cross with carved work, early gravestone and remnants of medieval church mark site of early monastery

TILBROOK, CAMBS, 4, 1E
Church of All Saints Mainly 14th-C church with west tower, north chapel, north vestry, and chancel with angle piscina; north aisle and arcade of c.1190; 12th-C cross in south porch and fine 15th-C screen with ribbed coving

TILTY, ESSEX, 3, 3B
Church of St Mary the Virgin Surviving gate chapel of Cistercian abbey founded 1153 has 13th-C nave, big early 14th-C chancel with fine east window, south porch added 1600s, and 18th-C belfry; good sedilia and piscina in chancel

TIMAHOE, CO. LAOIS, 12, 4B
Round Tower and Church [Dúchas] Well preserved Round Tower (probably 12th-C, all that survives of early monastery) with richly carved doorway above ground level; fragments of 15th-C church converted into small castle early 1600s

TIMOLEAGUE, CO. CORK, 12, 2D
Friary [Dúchas] Remains of plain buildings of large Franciscan friary founded 1240 or 1312 include church with early 16th-C tower and alterations and well-preserved claustral buildings

TINTAGEL, CORNWALL, 1, 3C
Tintagel Castle [EH] Ruins of impressively set 12th- and 13th-C castle associated with Arthurian legend, built on site of Celtic monastery probably founded 6th C
Tintagel Old Post Office [NT] Small 14th-C stone manor house used as post office during 19th C
Church of St Merteriana Norman church with later medieval additions

TINTERN (7 km. / 4½ m. N of Fethard), CO. WEXFORD, 12, 5C
Tintern Abbey (Minor) [Dúchas] Ruined church of Cistercian abbey founded c.1200, daughter house of Welsh counterpart, retains nave, crossing with 15th-C tower, altered south transept, and chancel; parts of building converted to domestic use after 1541 (traces of post-medieval work in process of being cleared)

TINTERN, GWENT, 6, 5E
Tintern Abbey [CADW] Impressive, well-preserved ruins of fine 13th- and 14th-C buildings of Cistercian monastery founded 1131 in lovely Wye Valley; splendid abbey church of 1269–1301 with fine early 14th-C west front, good windows and carved work
St Mary's Church Ruins of 13th-C church largely rebuilt 19th C

TINTINHULL, SOMERSET, 2, 2D
Church of St Margaret 13th-C church with later medieval additions retains part of base of stone rood screen; early 16th-C bench ends with blank tracery and flowers

TIPTOFTS MANOR HOUSE (2.5 km. / 1½ m. WSW of Wimbish), ESSEX, 3, 3A
Tiptofts Manor House Rare surviving manor house of c.1350 with original aisled hall

TISBURY, WILTS, 2, 3D
Church of St John the Baptist Spacious church of Norman origin with later remodelling retains late 12th-C crossing arches, early 13th-C two-storeyed north porch, transepts, central tower with upper stage added 1762, and late 14th-C nave arcades; fine 15th-C wagon roof to nave
Place Farm Fine surviving house, barn, and gatehouses of 14th- and 15th-C grange of nunnery of Shaftesbury

TITCHFIELD, HANTS, 2, 5D
Church of St Peter Saxon church with medieval rebuilding retains original west porch heightened as tower 1200s, 12th-C west doorway, south chapel of c.1320, and fine 15th-C north aisle; south aisle added 1867
Titchfield Abbey (Place House) [EH] Ruins of Premonstratensian abbey founded 1232 and converted to mansion 1542 include entrance to chapter house, and parts of nave incorporated in big 16th-C gatehouse
Tithe Barn 15th-C barn with good timber work

TITCHMARSH, NORTHANTS, 4, 1E
Church of St Mary Medieval church has 13th- and 14th-C arcades, and splendid 15th-C west tower; late medieval font

TIVERTON, DEVON, 1, 5C
Church of St Peter Medieval church extensively rebuilt 19th C and restored 1985–6 retains lavish south porch and Greenway Chapel of 1517
Tiverton Castle [HHA] 14th- to 17th-C manor house retains substantial remains of original south range, gatehouse and circular tower
Greenway's Almshouses Almshouses founded 1517 and rebuilt 1731 and 19th C retain ornate chapel with porch

TIXOVER, RUTLAND, 4, 1D
Church of St Mary Magdalene Norman church with medieval and later remodelling has imposing west tower and early 12th-C tower arch; late 12th-C south doorway altered 13th C; 11th- or early 12th-C grave marker at back of piscina

TODDINGTON, BEDS, 3, 1A
Church of St George Embattled 13th-C church rebuilt 15th and early 16th C with crossing tower; elaborate 15th-C stoup in north porch

TOLLER FRATRUM, DORSET, 2, 2E
Church of St Basil Simple medieval church retains fine relief of c.1125–50 and carved Norman font

TOLLERTON, NOTTS, 5, 5C
Church of St Peter 13th-C church rebuilt c.1812 and 1908 retains rare Norman shaft piscina

TOLQUHON (6.5 km. / 4 m. E of Old Meldrum), GRAMPIAN, 8, 4B
Tolquhon Castle [HS] Castle built mainly 1584–89 with ornate gatehouse incorporates ruined 15th-C Auld or Preston's Tower

TONBRIDGE, KENT, 3, 3D
Tonbridge Castle Remains of Norman motte and bailey castle include imposing gatehouse of c.1300 with portcullis room and upper great hall
Medieval Buildings Many good medieval buildings survive in town centre

TONG, SHROPS, 5, 3C
Church of St Bartholomew Mainly 15th-C church has five-bay arcades, crossing tower with octagonal upper level, and Vernon Chapel of 1515; screens, misericords, and many fine medieval monuments

TOPCLIFFE, N. YORKS, 7, 3D
Church of St Columba Church built 1855 contains fine 14th-C brass

TORBRYAN, DEVON, 1, 5D
Church of the Holy Trinity [CCT] 15th-C church has west tower, projecting chancel, and rood loft staircase on north; fine screen and some original stained glass

TORPENHOW, CUMBRIA, 7, 1C
Church of St Michael Church of Norman origin with 17th-C alterations retains chancel arch and doorway of c.1170, late 13th-C east window in chancel, and three-bay arcades

TORPHICHEN, LOTHIAN, 8, 2E
Preceptory Church [HS] Late 12th-C church of house of Knights Hospitaller consists of crossing with tower and vaulted transepts remodelled 1400s; traces of demolished nave and chancel

TORQUAY, DEVON, 1, 5D
Torre Abbey Gatehouse * 14th-C gatehouse of Premonstratensian abbey founded 1196

TORRE ABBEY GATEHOUSE, DEVON, 1, 5D
See Torquay

TORTHORWALD, DUMFRIES AND GALLOWAY, 7, 1B
Torthorwald Castle Imposing ruin of mid 14th-C tower house with 15th-C interior and remodelling

TORTINGTON, W. SUSSEX, 3, 1E
Church of St Mary Magdalene (also known as St Thomas) [CCT] Modest 12th-C church retains south doorway and chancel arch of c.1140, early 13th-C south aisle, and bell turret; Norman font

TORY ISLAND (12 km. / 7 ½ m. N of Horn Head), CO. DONEGAL, 11, 3A
Monastery Ruins [Dúchas], West Town Surviving remains of two churches, two crosses, and unusual Round Tower with sea shell mortar

TOTNES, DEVON, 1, 5D
Totnes Castle [EH] Large Norman motte and bailey castle with ruined shell keep rebuilt early 14th C

TOTTERNHOE, BEDS, 3, 1B
Church of St Giles Large mainly 15th-C church with low west tower and north vestry; fine nave roof and carved angel of c.1500
Castle Remains of medieval motte and bailey castle occupying impressive site

TOUREEN PEAKAUN CO. TIPPERARY, 12, 3C
Church, Crosses and Slabs [Dúchas] Site of early monastery in enchanting Glen of Aherlow contains small 12th-C church with simple flat-headed doorway; several early Christian crosses and grave slabs survive in and around building

TOWYN, GWYNEDD
See Tywyn

TREDINGTON, WARWS, 5, 4E
Church of St Gregory Church built c.1000 with much medieval rebuilding retains arcades of c.1160, south doorway of c.1200, chancel consecrated 1315, and fine 14th-C tower; good screen and benches

TRELLECH / TRELLECK, GWENT, 6, 5E
Church of St Nicholas Early medieval church rebuilt 14th C with large aisled nave and west tower; graveyard contains almost complete 15th-C preaching cross on massive base with five steps

The Virtuous Well (at S end of village) Late medieval holy well in small stone enclave

TRELOWARREN, CORNWALL, 1, 2E
See Mawgan-in-Meneage

TREMATON CASTLE (1.5 km. / 1 m. SW of Saltash), CORNWALL, 11, 4D
Trematon Castle Impressive remains of finely-set medieval castle include excellent 13th-C gatehouse, walls of inner bailey, and shell keep; house built on site 1808

TREMEIRCHION, CLWYD, 6, 5A
Church of Corpus Christi (formerly Holy Trinity) Simple medieval church with north transept added 1864 has good timber roof; late 13th-C effigy of knight, sepulchral slabs, and fine late 14th-C canopied monument to Dafydd ap Hywel ap Madog
St Beuno's College 19th-C Jesuit college with head of good 14th-C churchyard cross in entrance court

TRENT, DORSET, 2, 2D
Church of St Andrew Early 14th-C church with 19th-C additions has south tower and 15th-C chancel; fine screen, 14th-C monuments, and bench ends of c.1500
The Chantry Small, lavish early 16th-C chantry with moulded windows and projecting chimneybreasts

TRESCO (Scilly Isles), CORNWALL, 1, 3E
Tresco Abbey 13th-C arches and walling from church of Benedictine priory of St Nicholas survive in sub-tropical gardens of 19th-C house

TRETOWER, POWYS, 6, 5D
Castle and Court [CADW] Ruins of castle with circular shell keep of c.1150 and parts of 13th-C bailey stand close to fine late medieval manor house; 15th-C timber gallery, great hall of c.1470, gatehouse, curtain wall built c.1480, and 16th- and 17th-C additions

TRIM, CO. MEATH, 11, 4D
Trim Castle [Dúchas] Remains of monumental castle with keep built c.1220 or earlier on unusual Greek-cross plan, and traces of great hall; extensive mid 13th-C perimeter wall enclosing bailey with towers, town gate, and Ireland's only complete surviving barbican gate and tower
St Patrick's Cathedral [Dúchas] Church built 1801 retains good five-storeyed

tower of former 15th-C building with walls of ruined chancel to east; sculptural fragments in tower vestibule include 14th-C slab with Crucifixion; bowl and shaft of carved 15th-C piscina / font at back of nave
St Mary's Abbey (Yellow Steeple) [Dúchas] Splendid seven-storeyed ruined tower, all that survives of church of Augustinian abbey
Talbot's Castle Substantial medieval building, probably original refectory of abbey with tower added to west c.1415, converted to school 1700s and remodelled c.1909; rare oriel window or gallery survives at south-east of drawing room
Sheep Gate [Dúchas] Remains of sole surviving gate of town's extensive medieval defences
Trim Bridge Bridge of four arches probably built mid 1300s crosses River Boyne
Newhaggard Castle Gatehouse (2 km. / 1 ¼ m. W) Remains of late medieval tower with unusual machicolation on south wall

TRIMLESTOWN CASTLE (3 km. / 2 m. W of Trim), CO. MEATH, 11, 4D
Trimlestown Castle Remains of substantial medieval house built probably 1400s by Trimlestown River and modernised c.1800 include two-storeyed barrel-vaulted hall with corner tower to north-west

TRISTERNAGH ABBEY CO. WESTMEATH, 11, 3D
See Ballynacarrigy

TROTTON, W. SUSSEX, 2, 5D
Church of St George Plain church built mainly c.1300 retains 13th-C tower and good roof; wall painting of c.1380 and fine medieval monuments
Bridge Good early 15th-C bridge with five arches and cutwaters

TRULL, SOMERSET, 2, 1D
Church of All Saints Medieval church with late 13th-C west tower and much 15th-C work; good rood screen with tympanum and splendid wooden pulpit of c.1500 with carved figures of saints

TRUMPAN, HIGHLAND, 9, 2D (Skye and Lochalsh) (Inner Hebrides)
Church Ruined medieval church in graveyard with two 15th or 16th-C grave slabs

TRUMPINGTON, CAMBS, 3, 2A
Church of St Mary and St Michael Mainly early 14th-C church renewed 19th C with work of c.1200 and west tower and chancel of c.1300; good 13th-C brass (second oldest in England)
Green Man Inn Medieval public house retains original king-post roof

TRUNCH, NORFOLK, 4, 4C
Church of St Botolph Church of late 14th C with west tower, four-bay arcades, and hammerbeam roof to nave; splendid double-level font canopy and screen dated 1502

TUAM, CO. GALWAY, 12, 3A
Cathedral [Dúchas] Cathedral built 1861–3 incorporates barrel-vaulted chancel of small church of c.1170–80 (nave lost in 1767 fire) with splendid chancel arch (broadest in Ireland) and east window and additions of c.1312; carved shaft of 12th-C High Cross in south nave aisle; remains of Temple Jarlath (church of Premonstratensian abbey) survive to north-west
Market Cross [Dúchas] Cross reassembled from scattered, finely carved 12th-C fragments

TUAMGRANEY, CO. CLARE, 12, 3B
Church [Dúchas] Simple medieval church rebuilt 969 (probably oldest still in use in Ireland) with eastern part added 12th C; carved head at top of east gable supposedly represents St Cronan

TULLAHERIN, CO. KILKENNY, 12, 4C
Church and Round Tower [Dúchas] Tall Round Tower and remains of church with early nave and 15th-C chancel and rebuilding

TULLIALLAN CASTLE, FIFE, 8, 2E
See Kincardine-on-Forth

TULLIBARDINE (10 km. / 6 m. SE of Crieff), TAYSIDE, 8, 2D
Tullibardine Chapel [HS] Unusually well-preserved and unaltered collegiate chapel founded 1446 and rebuilt c.1500, used as mausoleum for Earls of Perth; fine roof and heraldic detail

TULLY AND LAUGHANSTOWN CO. DUBLIN, 11, 5E
Church and Crosses [Dúchas] 12th- or 13th-C church with wide chancel and remains of earlier nave contains early Christian grave slabs; plain High Cross and finely carved cross (probably 13th-C) survive nearby

TULLYLEASE, CO. CORK, 12, 2C
Church and Gravestones [Dúchas] Remains of medieval church (formerly part of Augustinian priory on early monastic site) with 12th-C work, 13th-C south door and 15th-C chancel; fragments of good early gravestones incorporated into chancel walls including particularly fine (possibly 8th- or 9th-C) cross-inscribed slab

TUNSTALL, LANCS, 7, 2D
Church of St John the Baptist 13th-C church extensively rebuilt 1415 with fine two-storeyed porch

TUNSTEAD, NORFOLK, 4, 4D
Church of St Mary Spacious mainly 14th-C church with west tower, and good sedilia and piscina; unusual raised platform and vaulted chamber in chancel; rood screen and beam survive; mid 14th-C ironwork on south door

TUQUOY, ORKNEY, 9, 5A
See Westray

TURLOUGH, CO. MAYO, 11, 2C
Round Tower [Dúchas] Well-preserved Round Tower marks site of early monastery

TURRALOSKIN, CO. ANTRIM, 11, 5A
Pillar Stone Early cross-carved pillar stone

TURTON, LANCS, 7, 2E
Turton Tower * Chapeltown Road; Original pele tower built probably 15th C with 16th-, 17th- and 19th-C additions and remodelling

TURVEY, BEDS, 3, 1A
Church of All Saints Church rebuilt 13th to 15th C with Anglo-Danish nave and west tower; 19th-C chancel; 13th-C ironwork and early 14th-C painting of Crucifixion
Bridge 13th-C bridge extensively rebuilt 1795 and 1820s

TUTBURY, STAFFS, 5, 4C
Tutbury Castle Remains of Norman castle with medieval, 17th- and 18th-C additions include simple 12th-C chapel, north-east gateway of early 1300s, and 15th-C towers
Church of St Mary Former church of priory founded 1080s retains early 12th-C arcades, elaborate west front of c.1160–70, 14th-C south tower, and chancel and apse added 1866

TWIZEL, NORTHUMBERLAND, 7, 2A
Twizel Bridge Fine 15th-C single-span stone bridge

TWYFORD, BUCKS, 2, 5A
Church of the Assumption Norman church with rich original south doorway and chancel arch, 13th-C west tower, and 15th-C tower top, nave roof and benches

TWYWELL, NORTHANTS, 4, 1E
Church of St Nicholas Norman church remodelled c.1300 has original north and south doorways, early 13th-C south aisle, and unusual Easter Sepulchre in chancel

TYWYN / TOWYN, GWYNEDD, 6, 4C
Church of St Cadfan 12th- and early 13th-C cruciform church on 6th-C monastic clas site, much altered late 19th-C, retains Norman nave arcades and deeply-splayed clerestory windows; St Cadfan's Stone of 7th to 9th C, four-sided pillar with Welsh inscription, and two 14th-C tomb effigies

TYDD ST GILES, CAMBS, 4, 2D
Church of St Giles Church of Norman origin reworked 19th C has 12th- and 13th-C six-bay arcades, fine detached tower begun early 1200s with later upper stages, and 14th-C west front

TYDD ST MARY, LINCS, 4, 2D
Church of St Mary Norman church with later chancel, brick clerestory and west tower; 15th-C font; part of 14th-C cross in churchyard

TYNAN (5 km. / 3 m. N of Middletown) **CO. ARMAGH, 11, 4C**
Village Cross [EHS] Village cross (made up of two different crosses) with reworked head of open ringed form survives from early Christian monastery
Crosses Three good High Crosses survive in grounds of Tynan Abbey; Terrace Cross (removed c.1844 from Tynan churchyard) and Island and Well Crosses (removed from early monastic site at Glenarb, Co. Tyrone)

TYNEMOUTH, TYNE AND WEAR, 7, 3B
Tynemouth Priory and Castle [EH] Castle walls, late 14th- to early 15th-C gatehouse, and imposing barbican enclose ruins of Benedictine priory founded c.1090 on Saxon monastic site; fragments of priory church with east end of c.1190 and 15th-C Percy Chantry

TYNINGHAME, LOTHIAN, 8, 4E
Church of St Baldred Richly carved remains of ambitious mid 12th-C church survive in grounds of 19th-C Tyninghame

House and include chancel and apse arches, and apse vault shafts

TYRRELLSPASS CO. WESTMEATH, 11, 3D
Castle Imposing tower house begun c.1410, well converted as residence later 20th C; fragment of effigy brought from ruins of Castlelost

UDNY (7.5 km. / 4½ m. E of Oldmeldrum) **GRAMPIAN, 8, 4B**
Udny Castle Large, dramatic keep built 15th C and altered 17th C and later (still occupied) with vaulted first floor hall

UFFINGTON, OXON, 2, 4B
Church of St Mary Church of c.1250 restored 1677–9 has crossing tower, three handsome porches, and three chapels with large piscinas

UFFORD, SUFFOLK, 3, 4A
Church of St Mary Church of Norman origin retains arcade of c.1200 with later west bays, south porch with flushwork decoration, and fine roofs; splendid font cover of c.1480 reaches nave roof

ULLARD, CO. KILKENNY, 12, 5C
Church and High Cross [Dúchas] Early monastic site houses remains of 12th-C church (altered 1400s) with good sculpted work above doorway; 9th- or 10th-C High Cross with carved biblical scenes survives nearby

UPHALL, LOTHIAN, 8, 2E
Church of St Nicholas Ecclesmachan Road. Norman church with later enlargement and extensive restoration of 1878 retains 12th-C south doorway to nave

UPHILL, SOMERSET, 2, 1C
Old Church of St Nicholas [CCT] Norman church has central tower with 15th-C upper level

UPLEADON, GLOS, 2, 2A
Church of St Mary Medieval church with 12th-C nave and north doorway, unusual timber-framed west tower added c.1500, and 19th-C chancel

UPMARDEN, W. SUSSEX, 2, 5D
Church of St Michael 13th-C church with lancet windows, plain tower and good interior; piscina of 1200s

UPPER HEYFORD, OXON, 2, 4A
Barn Tithe barn (west of church) built c.1400 for New College, Oxford

UPPINGHAM, RUTLAND, 4, 1D
Church of St Peter and St Paul Medieval church extensively rebuilt and enlarged 1860–1 with 14th-C arcades and west tower; four fine pieces of Norman sculpture dating from c.1200

UPTON CRESSETT, SHROPS, 5, 2D
Church of St Michael [CCT] Norman church with 13th- and 19th-C additions retains original chancel arch and south doorway; Norman font
Upton Cressett Hall [HHA] (by appointment only, part available for letting) Brick-built medieval manor house with handsome gatehouse and 14th-C great hall

URCHFONT, WILTS, 2, 3C
Church of St Michael Medieval church with transepts of c.1300, fine rib-vaulted chancel of early 1300s, late 14th-C west tower, arcades and aisles; 13th-C font

URQUHART CASTLE (2.5 km. / 1½ m. SE of Drumnadrochit), **HIGHLAND, 8, 1B**
Urquhart Castle [HS] Remains of dramatic motte and bailey castle (one of largest in Scotland) begun 13th C on promontory by Loch Ness include north tower of mainly early 16th C and gatehouse added after 1509

USK, GWENT, 6, 5E
Priory Church of St Mary Surviving nave and crossing tower of Norman monastic church with medieval additions including 13th-C north aisle and ornate 15th-C north and west porches; fine traceried 15th-C rood screen carved with vines, roses and foliage extends across full width of building
The Castle House * Medieval gatehouse converted into dwelling during 19th C; Norman keep, 13th-C "Garrison" Tower and other ruins of 12th- to 14th-C castle survive in garden

UYEA (island off S. coast of Unst), **SHETLAND, 9, 1A**
Chapel Remains of church built possibly 12th C with late medieval sacristy at west end

UZMASTON, DYFED, 6, 2D
Church of St David (or St Ishmael) Medieval church, partly rebuilt 19th-C, with saddleback tower

VALLE CRUCIS ABBEY, CLWYD, 6, 5B
Valle Crucis Abbey [CADW] Well-preserved remains of Cistercian abbey

founded 1201 include church with impressive gabled west front and good west doorway, barrel-vaulted sacristy, and 14th- or early 15th-C chapter house, slype, and reredorter; important set of sepulchral slabs; only surviving monastic fish pond in Wales
Eliseg's Pillar [CADW] (0.5 km. / ¼ m. NW) 9th-C pillar cross re-erected 1779 on burial mound

VOWCHURCH, HEREFS, 2,1A
Church of St Bartholomew Simple church of Norman origin rebuilt mid 14th C and refitted c.1613 with timber bell turret of c.1522

WADWORTH, S. YORKS, 5,5A
Church of St John the Baptist Church of Norman origin with 13th- and 14th-C reworking has original blank arcading to south porch and south aisle, north arcade of c.1190–1200, and 14th-C south chapel with unusual east window; good medieval monuments

WAINFLEET ALL SAINTS, LINCS, 4,2C
School Brick school founded 1484 has imposing west front with window and three-storeyed towers

WAKEFIELD, W. YORKS, 7,3E
Cathedral * Medieval church (cathedral from 1888) rebuilt 18th C and 1858–74 on site of Saxon building retains nave arcades of 12th to 14th C, chancel arcades built c.1450–75, and fine 15th-C west tower with tallest spire in Yorkshire; east end enlarged 1904
Bridge Chapel Impressive chapel (one of only four surviving in England) built c.1350 on medieval bridge much restored 19th C; rich parapet, stair turret, and sacristy below

WAKERLEY, NORTHANTS, 4,1D
Church of St John the Baptist [CCT] Church of Norman origin with medieval rebuilding retains fine original chancel arch with carved capitals, 14th- and 15th-C arcades and west tower; late 13th-C font
Bridge Medieval bridge of five pointed arches

WALLINGFORD, OXON, 2,5B
Church of St Leonard Norman church with west tower and south arcade added 1849 retains apse and original carving
Castle Remains of medieval motte and bailey castle in grounds of 19th-C house
Wallingford Bridge Medieval bridge rebuilt 1751 and 1809

WALMER, KENT, 3,5D
Church of St Mary, Church Street Norman church with good original chancel arch and south doorway
Walmer Court Ruins of Norman house survive next to St Mary's Churchyard

WALPOLE ST PETER, NORFOLK, 4,2D
Church of St Peter Church built mainly c.1350–c.1440 retains west tower, rood stair turrets, and two-storeyed porch; fine chancel with vaulted passage

WALSALL, W. MIDLANDS, 5,3D
Church of St Matthew Church built mainly 1820–1 retains medieval crypt beneath chancel; font and 15th-C stalls with fine set of eighteen misericords

WALSHESTOWN CASTLE (nr Strangford), CO. DOWN, 11,5C
Walshestown Castle Remains of late medieval tower house and bawn

WALSINGHAM ABBEY, NORFOLK, 4,4C
See Little Walsingham

WALSOKEN, NORFOLK, 4,2D
Church of All Saints Late Norman church with medieval additions has original arcades with zig-zag embellishment, and 13th-C west tower and south porch; octagonal font and good screens

WALTHAM ABBEY, ESSEX, 3,2B
Waltham Abbey [Gatehouse and Bridge – EH] Surviving parts of abbey founded 1030 include church of Holy Cross with impressive early 12th-C nave, 14th-C south chapel (now Lady Chapel) and west tower of 1556–8; remains of late 12th-C cloister, 14th-C gatehouse and bridge

WALTHAM CROSS, HERTS, 3,2B
Eleanor Cross Tall and lavish Eleanor Cross begun 1291 (one of three surviving crosses marking resting places of body of Eleanor, Queen of Edward I, on route to Westminster Abbey) with canopied niches and pinnacle and much 19th- and 20th-C restoration

WALTON-ON-THE-HILL, SURREY, 3,2D
Church of St Peter 15th-C flint church with 19th-C additions retains finely carved lead font of c.1150–60, and good late medieval piscina and triple sedilia

WANBOROUGH, WILTS, 2,4B
Church of St Andrew Medieval church rebuilt 14th and 15th C has fine hexagonal

tower open to crossing beneath, four bay nave arcades, and west tower begun 1435

WANSFORD, CAMBS, 4,1D
Church of St Mary Church of Saxon origin has south doorway of c.1200, 13th-C west tower and north arcade, and chancel of 1902; fine Norman font with carved figures (possibly c.1120)

WARBLINGTON, HANTS, 2,5D
Church of St Thomas à Becket Church of Saxon origin rebuilt late 12th to early 13th-C has central tower with 19th-C spire, north porch and dormer windows
Castle Ruined octagonal turret from gatehouse of former moated castle built 1514–26

WARBOYS, CAMBS, 4,2E
Church of St Mary Magdalene Church rebuilt 1832 retains Norman chancel arch, arcades of early 1200s, and fine 13th-C west tower with broach spire; 12th-C door knocker to chancel

WARDEN, NORTHUMBERLAND, 7,2B
Church of St Michael Cruciform church with additions of 1765 and 19th C retains Saxon west tower and 13th-C transepts; Saxon and 13th-C cross slabs; 7th-C hammerhead cross in churchyard

WARDLEY, RUTLAND, 5,5D
Church of St Botolph Late Norman church with 14th-C west tower and broach spire and later medieval additions; chancel rebuilt 1871

WARDLEY HALL, LANCS, 5,2A
See Worsley

WARDOUR, WILTS, 2,3D
Old Wardour Castle [EH] Ruins of castle licensed c.1393 and altered 1578 with imposing east front and hexagonal courtyard

WARE, HERTS, 3,2B
Church of St Mary Embattled church built 14th and 15th C with later restoration has five-stage west tower, south porch, clerestoried nave, and transepts; fine stone font of late 1300s with figural carving
The Priory Building with 16th- and 17th-C work incorporates remains of medieval house of Franciscans
Place House 14th-C timber-framed manor house altered 16th and 17th C and restored 1974–5

WAREHAM, DORSET, 2,3E
Church of St Mary Church of Saxon origin much rebuilt 1841–2 has chancel with 14th-C sedilia and double piscina, 14th-C chapel and 15th-C west tower; Norman lead font, monuments of pre-1300 and fine windows
Church of St Martin Saxon church with north aisle of c.1200 and 16th-C south tower; traces of 12th- and 15th-C painting
Church of the Holy Trinity Medieval church with 14th-C nave and chancel, and early 16th-C west tower

WARFIELD, BERKS, 2,5B
Church of St Michael 14th-C church with 15th-C west tower and north arcade, remodelled 1872–5; fine nave roof and 15th-C screen and rood loft

WARKWORTH, NORTHUMBERLAND, 7,3A
Church of St Laurence Norman church with medieval and 19th-C additions has original north wall, fine vaulted chancel, and west tower added c.1200; 11th-C monuments and effigy of c.1330
Warkworth Castle [EH] Extensive remains of Norman and medieval castle include gatehouse, towers in curtain wall, and well-preserved three-storeyed keep remodelled 15th C
Warkworth Hermitage [EH] (accessible only by ferry) Unusual cave hermitage cut into cliff has chapel and sacristy of c.1330 and 15th-C domestic block
Bridge 14th-C bridge with cutwater and rectangular tower at south end

WARMINGTON, NORTHANTS, 4,1E
Church of St Mary Church built c.1180–c.1280 with west tower, clerestory and vaulted timber roof; chancel restored 1865; carved 13th-C corbel and good reredos

WARNDON, WORCS, 5,3E
Church of St Nicholas 12th-C church with fine timber-framed west tower, north and south doorways, and timber porch; fragments of medieval stained glass

WARNFORD, HANTS, 2,5D
Church of Our Lady Church of Saxon origin with medieval rebuilding retains large tower of c.1175 and body of c.1210; Saxon or 13th-C sundial in south porch
King John's House Imposing remains of early 13th-C hall range of former house

WARTNABBY, LEICS, 5,5C
Church of St Michael Mainly 13th-C church retains double bellcote on west

tower and fine south arcade with original painting in arches; benches of c.1500

WARTON, LANCS, 7, 2D
Church of St Oswald Medieval church rebuilt 19th C with early 14th-C sedilia, 15th-C north arcade, chancel and west tower
Old Rectory [EH] Medieval stone rectory with remains of 14th-C hall and domestic offices to rear

WARWICK, CUMBRIA, 7, 2B
Church of St Leonard Church built c.1870 retains lavish 12th-C apse with arched recesses, and tower arch (original chancel arch) of c.1130

WARWICK, WARWS, 5, 4E
Church of St Mary Church with west tower, nave, and transepts built 1698–1704 retains large Norman rib-vaulted crypt, chancel finished 1392, chapter house with apse, and sumptuous Beauchamp Chapel of 1443–1464; fine Beauchamp monuments and sculpture
Warwick Castle [HHA] Large and dramatic medieval castle with 17th- to 19th-C additions retains 13th-C work in living quarters, 14th-C Caesar's Tower, Clock Tower and Guy's Tower, and 15th-C Bear and Clarence Towers; old bridge built c.1374–83
Town Walls Remains of 14th-C town walling
West Gate Fine Norman town gate with medieval and 19th-C work and Chapel of St James above
East Gate Gate built before 1426 with St Peter's Chapel (1788) above
Brome Place, Bridge End. Good late medieval timber-framed house
Lord Leycester's Hospital *, High Street. Hospital founded 1571 by Earl of Leicester occupies late medieval buildings of guilds of Holy Trinity and St George with 16th- and 19th-C additions

WATCHET, SOMERSET, 1, 5B
Church of St Decuman Spacious mainly 15th-C church with west tower and rich south aisle retains 13th-C chancel; tiles of 1200s and good wagon roofs

WATERFORD, CO. WATERFORD, 12, 4C
The French Church (or Grey Friars) [Dúchas] Remains of church of Franciscan friary founded c.1240 (used as part of Holy Ghost Hospital after 1545) with big 15th-C tower
Reginald's Tower [Dúchas] (museum),

The Quay. Imposing 12th- to 13th-C circular tower by River Suir remodelled 15th C and reworked 19th C as prison
Christchurch (or Trinity) Cathedral Cathedral built 1770–9 retains medieval crypt and monuments including superbly carved tomb of James Rice (after 1487)

WATERPERRY, OXON, 2, 5A
Church of St Mary Church of Saxon origin with medieval rebuilding and enlargements has tall original arch to 13th-C chancel; 15th-C brasses and good stained glass

WATER STRATFORD, BUCKS, 5, 5E
Church of St Giles Church of Norman origin remodelled 1828 has fine original sculpture in tympana of south doorway and north chancel doorway

WATTON, E. RIDING OF YORKS, 7, 5E
Watton Abbey Surviving 14th- and 15th-C prior's lodgings of Gilbertine priory founded c.1150; impressive west front with turrets and two-storeyed bay window

WAVERLEY ABBEY, SURREY, 2, 5C
Waverley Abbey [EH] Ruined 13th-C buildings of England's first Cistercian monastery (founded 1128)

WEALD AND DOWNLAND OPEN AIR MUSEUM, W. SUSSEX, 2, 5D
See Singleton

WEARE GIFFORD, DEVON, 1, 4B
Weare Gifford Hall Late medieval manor house with splendid 15th-C hall roof

WEAVERTHORPE, E. RIDING OF YORKS, 7, 4D
Church of St Andrew Plain early 12th-C church has original west tower, nave, chancel, and south doorway with tympanum and sundial; Norman font

WEEK ST MARY, CORNWALL, 1, 3C
Church of the Nativity of St Mary Medieval church has late 14th-C south aisle, 15th-C north aisle, and tower with carved figures
The College [LT] Surviving part of school founded 1506 (one of first schools founded by woman) and dissolved 1548
See also: Penhallam

WEETING, NORFOLK, 4, 3E
Church of St Mary Medieval church remodelled 19th C with round tower, and 14th-C chancel and north arcade
Weeting Castle [EH] Remains of moated

Norman manor house with medieval additions

WELLINGBOROUGH, NORTHANTS, 4, 1E
Church of All Hallows Mainly 13th- and 14th-C church with Norman south doorway, west tower of c.1250–1300, and arcades of c.1300; 15th-C roofs, screens and misericords

WELLINGTON, HEREFS, 5, 2E
Church of St Margaret Late Norman church with medieval work has original west tower, chancel arch, and north and south doorways; 13th-C piscina and fine roof to north aisle

WELLOW, SOMERSET, 2, 2C
Church of St Julian Well-preserved medieval church with chancel rebuilt 1890 retains good west tower, south porch and roofs; early 14th-C font and wall paintings of c.1500

WELLS, SOMERSET, 2, 2C
Wells Cathedral * Cathedral built in mainly two phases c.1180–1240 and c.1290–1340; 13th-C west front adorned with nearly four hundred statues; crossing strainer arches of c.1338–48; 14th- and 15th-C towers; 14th-C chapter house; 15th-C cloisters
Bishop's Palace [HHA] Impressive remains of fortified bishop's palace restored 1800s include great hall of c.1280, chapel of c.1285–90, mid 14th-C gatehouse and 15th-C stone barn
Deanery 15th-C deanery with alterations and fenestration of c.1700 retains fine hall with original fireplace, screen and oriel window
Vicars' Close Mid 14th-C terraced housing built to provide lodgings for Vicars Choral with hall of c.1348
Church of St Cuthbert 15th-C parish church has sculptured fragments of original transept reredoses
Nova Opera, Market Place. Even row of houses on north side of Market Place, originally Bishop Bekynton's "new work" of c.1450, retain good medieval work
Bubwith Almshouses, Chamberlain Street Almshouses founded 1436 out of bequest of Bishop Bubwith with good roof to chapel and much early 17th-C and later alteration

WELSHPOOL / Y TRALLWNG, POWYS, 6, 5B
Church of St Mary or Cynfelyn Church refounded c.1250 and restored 19th C retains imposing 13th-C west tower

heightened 1773–7, chancel and two-storeyed south porch added c.1350, and wide 16th-C arcades

WELSH ST DONATS / LLANDDUNWYD, GLAMORGAN, 1, 5A
Church of St Donat Church built 15th and early 16th C with big west tower, plain interior, and original roofs; good 13th-C font and stoup by south door

WELWICK, E. RIDING OF YORKS, 7, 5E
Church of St Mary Medieval church has 13th-C tower arch, four-bay arcades of 1300s, and chancel enlarged 14th C with good tracery; elaborate tomb of c.1340–50 in south wall, 15th-C font and screen

WEMYSS CASTLE (1 km. / ½ m. SE of Coaltown of Wemyss), **FIFE, 8, 3D**
Wemyss Castle Medieval castle with 16th- to 19th-C additions and reconstruction begun 1930s retains two 15th-C towers

WENHASTON, SUFFOLK, 4, 5E
Church of St Peter Norman and medieval church containing rare painting of Last Judgement of c.1520, formerly above chancel arch behind figures on rood screen

WENTWORTH, CAMBS, 4, 2E
Church of St Peter Medieval church rebuilt 1868 retains Norman north and south doorways, 13th-C chancel with double piscina, and west tower built 1300s; fine Norman figural carving of priest

WEOBLEY, HEREFS, 5, 1E
Church of St Peter and St Paul Church of Norman origin has original south doorway, late 13th-C chancel, 14th-C arcades and tall north-west tower; good medieval coffin lid, font and effigies
Medieval Buildings Many good 14th- and 15th-C timber-framed houses in Broad Street, High Street and Meadow Street

WEOBLEY CASTLE, GLAMORGAN, 6, 3E
See Llanrhidian

WEOLEY CASTLE, W. MIDLANDS, 5, 3D
See Birmingham

WEST ACRE, NORFOLK, 4, 3D
Church of All Saints Mainly 15th-C church remodelled 17th or 18th C retains 14th-C west tower; 13th-C carved panel in north porch

Priory Remains of Augustinain priory founded *c.*1100 with 14th-C flint gatehouse, and fragments of church and chapter house

WEST BOLDON,
TYNE AND WEAR, 7,3B
Church of St Nicholas Church of mainly early to mid 13th C has west tower with fine spire, south porch, and three-bay nave arcades; two early 14th-C effigies of priests

WEST BROMWICH,
W. MIDLANDS, 5,3D
Manor House, Hall Green. Moated manor house restored and converted to public house and restaurant mid 20th C retains early 14th-C Great Hall, 15th-C wings, and 16th-C gatehouse

WESTBURY, WILTS, 2,3C
Church of All Saints 14th- and 15th-C church restored 1800s has transepts, crossing tower, north and south chapels, two-storeyed south porch with good vault, and fine west front

WESTBURY-ON-TRYM,
SOMERSET, 2,2B
See Bristol

WEST CHILTINGTON,
W. SUSSEX, 3,1E
Church of St Mary Unrestored Norman church renewed 19th C retains 12th-C chancel arch, north doorway, 13th-C south chancel chapel, and later central bell turret; good wall paintings of 12th and 13th C

WESTDEAN, E. SUSSEX, 3,2E
Church of All Saints Norman church has original nave and west tower with early 14th-C upper stage
Rectory Late 13th-C house with hall and solar
Charleston Manor Manor house retains south wing of *c.*1200 with upper hall; medieval barns and circular dovecot

WESTERLEIGH, GLOS, 2,2B
Church of St James Medieval church much rebuilt 1400s retains 13th-C north doorway and priest's doorway to south chapel, good 15th-C west tower with rich parapet, and wide south aisle; late medieval stone pulpit

WEST HADDON, NORTHANTS, 5,5D
Church of All Saints Medieval church with early 13th-C arcades and south doorway, and 14th-C west tower; carved Norman font of *c.*1120

WESTHALL, SUFFOLK, 4,5E
Church of St Andrew Norman church with original west and south doorways, west tower added *c.*1300, and nave and chancel of mid 14th C; good roofs and font

WESTHAY, SOMERSET, 2,1C
Cross Farm 16th-C painting depicting crude foliage survives on stud and plank panelling of screen which originally divided hall from parlour

WEST HENDRED, OXON, 2,4B
Church of the Holy Trinity Unrestored 14th-C church with original west tower; medieval tiles in nave and chancel

WEST HOATHLY, W. SUSSEX, 3,2D
Church of St Margaret Church built mainly 12th to early 13th C with 14th-C south aisle and late medieval west tower carrying shingled broach spire
Priest House * North Lane (museum); Timber-framed hall-house built early 1400s
Tickeridge Medieval house with later rebuilding and additions retains fine 14th-C work to interior

WEST HUMBLE, SURREY, 3,1D
Chapel Scant remains of simple late 12th-C flint chapel

WEST LAVINGTON, WILTS, 2,3C
Church of All Saints Medieval church renewed 19th C retains north arcade of mainly *c.*1200, 13th-C south arcade, early 14th-C west tower, and rich 15th-C south chapel

WESTLEY WATERLESS,
CAMBS, 3,3A
Church of St Mary Medieval church with 13th-C chancel, 14th-C south doorway and nave, and 16th-C bell tower; good brasses of *c.*1325 and 15th-C octagonal font

WEST MALLING, KENT, 3,3D
Church of St Mary Early Norman church enlarged 13th C with nave reworked 18th C and 1900–1 retains original tower with later spire; 13th-C sedilia in chancel
Malling Abbey Ruins of Benedictine nunnery founded *c.*1090 include tower of abbey church with late medieval octagonal top stage and angle turrets, and 15th-C gatehouse with projecting chapel; fine 13th-C cloister arcades incorporated in nunnery re-established 1916
St Leonard's Tower [EH] Small well-preserved keep-tower built *c.*1100 by Gundulf, Bishop of Rochester

WESTMINSTER, LONDON
See London

WESTON, HERTS, 3,2A
Church of the Holy Trinity Norman church with fine original crossing and north transept, and 15th-C nave; Norman lower part of tower with upper level added 1867

WESTON, LINCS, 4,2D
Church of St Mary Mainly 13th-C church with 19th-C restoration and rebuilding has fine interior and 15th-C west tower; good 13th-C font
Wykeham Chapel Chapel built 1311 retains good original tracery

WESTON, STAFFS, 5,3C
Church of St Andrew Medieval church with extensive 19th-C work retains imposing 13th-C tower, arcades and chancel arch

WESTON ZOYLAND,
SOMERSET, 2,1C
Church of St Mary Medieval church with 14th-C chancel, four-stage west tower, late 15th- to early 16th-C embattled south side, and splendid nave roof; octagonal 15th-C font

WEST PENNARD,
SOMERSET, 2,2C
Court Barn [NT] 15th-C barn restored 20th C with good roof

WESTRAY, ORKNEY, 9,5A
Pierowall Church [HS] Remains of medieval church mostly rebuilt in 17th-C
Westside Church, Tuquoy [HS] Roofless remains of 12th-C church

WEST STOW, SUFFOLK, 4,3E
Saxon Village Site Reconstruction of Saxon village settlement in occupation *c.*400–650 on excavated site

WEST TANFIELD, N. YORKS, 7,3D
Church of St Nicholas Mainly 15th-C church restored 1859–60 with tower and north chapel retains south doorway of *c.*1200 and late 13th-C north arcade; good medieval monuments
Marmion Tower [EH] Surviving 15th-C gatehouse of castle with fine oriel window

WEST WALTON, NORFOLK, 4,2D
Church of St Mary [bell tower – CCT] Church built *c.*1240 has splendid detached bell tower, and fine interior with original arcades and clerestory; wall paintings of *c.*1240–50 and mid 13th-C effigy of priest

WESTWELL, KENT, 3,4D
Church of St Mary 13th-C church with fine rib-vaulted chancel, stone chancel screen and rich tower arch of *c.*1250; Norman font and 14th-C piscina and triple sedilia

WESTWOOD, WILTS, 2,3C
Church of St Mary Church built mainly 15th to early 16th C with fine west tower, stair turret, pinnacles and gargoyles retains 13th-C chancel; 15th-C font cover and good stained glass (chancel)
Westwood Manor [NT] Fine well-preserved manor house of 15th C, *c.*1515–30 and early 17th C

WETHERAL, CUMBRIA, 7,2B
Wetheral Priory Gatehouse [EH] 15th-C gatehouse of Benedictine priory founded *c.*1100

WEXFORD, CO. WEXFORD, 12,5C
St Selskar's Church (or Selskar Abbey) [Dúchas] Remains of church of Augustinian priory of SS Peter and Paul (founded 13th C) with tower built possibly 1300s and mainly 15th-C double nave; ruined 19th-C church on site of chancel
Town Walls Surviving fragments of 14th-C town wall (eg. part by St Selskar's churchyard) and West Gate

WHALLEY, LANCS, 7,2E
Church of St Mary Mainly 13th-C church with fine roofs and 15th-C west tower; splendid stalls of *c.*1420–30 with carved misericords; shafts of three Saxon crosses in churchyard
Whalley Abbey [Outer Gatehouse – EH] Remains of Cistercian abbey first consecrated 1306 with early 14th-C outer gateway, parts of cloister and church, and late 15th-C inner gateway; mainly 19th-C abbot's lodging retains 13th-C masonry

WHALTON,
NORTHUMBERLAND, 7,3B
Church of St Mary Magdalene Church of Saxo-Norman origin remodelled early 13th C has 11th-C west tower and 13th-C nave and chancel north arcades; south porch added 1908; cross slab of 1200s
Old Rectory Medieval house with 18th- and 19th-C work retains west wing of 1300s or 1400s

WHAPLODE, LINCS, 4,2D
Church of St Mary Norman church with original arcades, chancel arch, and fine south and west doorways; 13th-C tower;

part of Norman grave cover and 13th-C coffin lid; fragment of 14th-C cross in churchyard

WHARRAM PERCY VILLAGE,
N. YORKS, 7,4D
See Wharram-le-Street

WHARRAM-LE-STREET,
N. YORKS, 7,4D
Church of St Mary Medieval church with restoration and additions of 1862–4 retains Saxon tower with late 11th- to early 12th-C top
Wharram Percy Deserted Village [EH] (1 km. / ½ m.S) Earthworks of deserted medieval village and dramatic remains of Church of St Martin

WHISSENDINE, RUTLAND, 5,5C
Church of St Andrew Medieval church restored 19th C has spacious late 13th-C interior, 14th-C transepts and tall west tower; roof dated 1728

WHISTON, NORTHANTS, 5,5E
Church of St Mary Early 16th-C church has ornate west tower with gargoyles, south porch and good roofs; 15th-C font

WHITBY, N. YORKS, 7,4C
Whitby Abbey [EH] Picturesque ruins of abbey church rebuilt after c.1220 on early site with fine east end, arcades, gallery and clerestory; remains of late 11th to early 12th-C slype and medieval cross
Church of St Mary Norman church with extensive 18th- and 19th-C additions retains original chancel, nave, south doorway, and tower with 13th-C bell stage

WHITCOMBE, DORSET, 2,2E
Church Medieval church rebuilt 16th and early 20th C has Norman south doorway in nave and 13th-C octagonal font; fragments of two Saxon cross shafts and 13th- to 15th-C painting

WHITE CASTLE, GWENT, 2,1A
White Castle [CADW] Moated 12th- and 13th-C castle has rectangular Norman keep and Inner Ward remodelled 1260s with towers and gatehouse and Outer Ward with curtain wall

WHITECHURCH
CANONICORUM, DORSET, 2,1E
Church of St Candida Mainly 13th-C church retains Norman south doorway, fine early 13th-C carved capitals and 15th-C west tower; Norman font and stone shrine of St Wite

WHITE ISLAND (in Lower Lough Erne, N of Castle Archdale), CO. FERMANAGH, 11,3B
Church Ruins [EHS] Ruins of small church repaired 1840s and restored 1958 with south wall retaining re-erected late 12th-C window and good doorway with carved capitals
Sculpted Stone Figures [EHS] North wall of church houses eight remarkable figures found between 1840 and 1958 (probably dating from 9th to 11th C); particularly fine figure of bishop or abbot with crozier and bell

WHITEKIRK (5.5 km. / 3 ½ m. SE of North Berwick), LOTHIAN, 8,3E
St Mary's Parish Church [SCS] Attractive church of 12th-C origin, restored after 1914, with tunnel-vaulted stone chancel built 1439 and 15th- or 16th-C crossing tower; tithe barn and historic graveyard

WHITE LADIES, SHROPS, 5,3C
White Ladies Priory [EH] Ruins of small late 12th-C priory church with some original windows and doorways

WHITFIELD, KENT, 3,4D
Church of St Peter Saxon church with 12th- and 19th-C work retains original nave and chancel; sanctuary of c.1200 remodelled 1894

WHITFORD / CHWITFFORDD, CLWYD, 6,5A
Church of St Mary Church built mainly 19th C contains good 6th-C pillar stone, 13th-C sepulchral slabs, and early 14th-C cross slabs
Maen Achwyfan Cross [CADW] (1.5 km. / 1 m. WNW) Fine, well-preserved late 10th- or early 11th-C slab cross with primitive carving

WHITHORN, DUMFRIES AND GALLOWAY, 10,4E
Whithorn Priory and Museum [HS] Surviving nave and eastern crypts of important priory church and cathedral built mid 12th C to house relics of St Ninian; substantial 13th-C, 15th-C and later alterations; inscribed stones and crosses (c.450–900) displayed in museum
St Ninian's Priory Parish Church [SCS] Church built 1822 incorporates part of priory dormitory in east wall
Pend Arch, George Street. Altered 15th-C priory gatehouse

WHITTINGEHAME,
LOTHIAN, 8,3E
Whittingehame Tower Three-storeyed tower house built late 15th or early 16th C with post-medieval work

WHITTLESEY, CAMBS, 4,2D
Church of St Mary Medieval church has 13th-C chancel arch, chancel of mainly c.1300 (enlarged 1400s), 14th-C south porch, and impressive mid 15th-C crocketed spire to tower
Church of St Andrew Mainly 14th-C church with later medieval west tower and arcades; original roofs to chancel, chancel chapels, and nave

WHITTON,
NORTHUMBERLAND, 7,3A
Whitton Tower 14th-C tower house or vicar's pele with adjoining house of mid 1800s

WHITWELL, DERBYS, 5,5A
Church of St Lawrence Norman church rebuilt c.1300 to c.1350 retains original nave and west tower with late medieval top; good corbel table to chancel and nave; rich niche and sedilia in chancel

WICKHAMBROOK, SUFFOLK, 3,3A
Church of All Saints Church built mainly 14th C with west tower and fine chancel
Giffords Hall Handsome hall-house built c.1480 and enlarged 20th C

WICKLOW, CO. WICKLOW, 11,5E
Church of St Thomas [Dúchas] 18th-C Protestant church incorporates fine mid 12th-C doorway in porch
Friary (or Abbey) [Dúchas] Fragments of small Franciscan friary founded c.1279 include part of nave and arch of 15th-C tower

WIDCOMBE, SOMERSET, 2,2C
See Bath

WIDDINGTON, ESSEX, 3,2A
Prior's Hall Barn [EH] Fine 15th-C aisled barn with open timber roof

WIDFORD, OXON, 2,4A
Church of St Oswald 13th-C church on site of Roman villa has fragment of mosaic flooring, 13th-C font, wall paintings dating from 14th and 15th C, and late medieval piscina and pulpit

WIGGENHALL ST GERMANS,
NORFOLK, 4,3D
Church of St Germaine Medieval church with 13th-C west tower and 15th-C

four-bay arcades; fine set of early 16th-C benches

WIGGENHALL ST MARY
MAGDALENE, NORFOLK, 4,3D
Church of St Mary Magdalene Large brick church with stone tower of 13th and 14th C has 14th-C arcades, clerestory and sanctus bellcote

WIGGENHALL ST MARY THE
VIRGIN, NORFOLK, 4,3D
Church of St Mary the Virgin [CCT] Mainly 15th-C church with brick nave, aisles and chancel retains near complete set of early 16th-C benches with carved ends

WIGMORE, HEREFS, 5,2D
Church of St James Early Norman church restored 1864 with wide nave, 14th-C chancel, west tower and 15th-C nave roof
Wigmore Castle [EH] Ruins of Norman border castle with medieval additions include late 13th- to 14th-C walls and towers, baileys, and motte with shell keep
Wigmore Abbey Remains of Augustinian priory founded 1179 include walls of late 12th-C abbey church and 14th-C abbot's lodging with original roof trusses

WILBY, NORTHANTS, 5,5E
Church of St Mary 13th- to 15th-C church rebuilt 19th C has fine tower with flying buttresses and octagonal upper stage

WILHAMPSTEAD, BEDS, 3,1A
Church of All Saints Medieval church with 19th-C additions retains early 14th-C south arcade, and fine 15th-C nave roof with carved bosses; west tower added 1852 and chancel of 1873; good brass of c.1430

WILLINGHAM, CAMBS, 4,2E
Church of St Mary and All Saints Church retains early 14th-C chancel reconstructed 1890s, tower with octagonal spire, and fine north chapel or sacristy; parts of lavish Norman portal in south porch; well preserved late medieval roofs and parclose screens, pulpit, coloured dado of rood screen, and wall paintings

WILLOUGHBY-ON-
THE-WOLDS, NOTTS, 5,5C
Church of St Mary and All Saints Medieval church with 13th-C north chapel, chancel and spire, and 15th-C clerestory; fine 14th- and 15th-C monuments to Willoughby family

WILMINGTON, E. SUSSEX, 3, 2E
Church of St Mary and St Peter Norman church with original chancel, 13th-C south aisle, and later bell turret
Priory 14th-C buildings of Benedictine priory founded before 1100 include Prior's Chapel above porch

WIMBORNE MINSTER, DORSET, 2, 3D
Church of St Cuthberga Church of Saxon and Norman origin restored 19th C has late 12th-C nave and crossing tower, vaulted sacristy and library of c.1350, and west tower built 1448–64; fine hoodmould stops of c.1200 in chancel, 13th-C sedilia and piscina, and brass figure of King Ethelred (c.1440)
Priest's House * (museum) Medieval house with 17th- and 18th-C additions; fine window of c.1500
Lodge Farm [NT], Kingston Lacy Estate. Hall-house built early 1400s, possibly former home of manor's head park keeper, warrener and forester (set within estate of important 17th-C house)

WINCHCOMBE, GLOS, 2, 3A
Church of St Peter Church built c.1465, reworked 1690 and 19th C, has west tower with pinnacles, south porch with upper chamber, and wide nave and chancel; two 13th-C stone coffins and 15th-C piscina and screens
George Hotel Early 16th-C former pilgrims' inn with courtyard, open gallery and later alterations

WINCHELSEA, E. SUSSEX, 3, 3E
Church of St Thomas Surviving early 14th-C chancel and north and south chapels of lost church with rich, spacious interior; vaulted undercroft beneath chancel; good 14th-C monuments
Town Plan and Walls Town laid out 1283 on grid plan with remains of 13th-C walls in North Street
Gates Early 14th-C Strandgate with angle towers, Pipewell Gate rebuilt c.1400, and medieval New Gate
Greyfriars Church Garden of Greyfriars contains ruined chancel of Franciscan church built c.1310–20
Court House High Street. 14th-C stone house with 15th-C alterations and 19th-C restoration

WINCHESTER, HANTS, 2, 4D
Cathedral * Exceptionally long cathedral begun 1079 retains apsed crypt, 11th-C transepts, fine retrochoir of late 12th to early 13th C, 14th-C chancel with upper

levels and wooden vault added early 1500s, and twelve-bay nave mainly rebuilt c.1394 onwards; important Norman font of black Tournai marble, wall paintings of c.1230, early 14-C stalls and misericords and splendid medieval chantries monuments and sculpture; nearby remains of Old Minster (founded mid 7th C, rebuilt 971–994, demolished 11th C), New Minster (built 903) and other buildings, excavated 1962–5
Cathedral Precinct Remains of domestic buildings include remarkable early Norman entrance to chapter house, Deanery (prior's lodging) with porch of c.1230, mid 14th-C Pilgrim's Hall with hammerbeam roof, and 15th-C St Swithun's Gate
Wolvesey Castle (Old Bishop's Palace) [EH] Extensive remains of bishop's palace, principal residence of Bishops of Winchester, with north part of c.1130–40 and much later alteration
Church of St Bartholomew, King Alfred Place, off Hyde Street. Norman church with medieval and extensive 19th-C rebuildings has original south doorway; architectural fragments of c.1130 from Benedictine Hyde Abbey
Church of St John the Baptist Medieval church retains two arcades of c.1200, fine late 13th-C window to south chapel, and south-west tower; 13th-C wall paintings and good 14th-C screen
Church of St Peter Chesil Medieval church converted to theatre later 20th C with 13th-C south arcade and south-east tower
Great Hall, Winchester Castle * Important Great Hall built between 1222 and 1236 (still used as court room) set amongst 19th- and 20th-C offices; Hall contains top of large medieval round table
Town Gates and Walls Remains of 13th-C walls altered 14th and 15th C together with 13th-C Westgate and 14th-C Kingsgate with church above
Winchester College * School founded 1382 with extensive post-medieval additions retains late 14th-C Outer Court with gatehouse, Chamber Court with hall and chapel, and cloister with 15th-C Fromond Chantry Chapel
Hospital of St Cross Hospital founded 1136 has fine cruciform church of late 12th to early 13th C with crossing tower and attached Norman sacristy; ranges around courtyard begun c.1445 contain hall, large gatehouse and brethren's lodgings

Butter Cross, High Street. Early 15th-C cross much reworked 1865
Hyde Abbey Gateway Surviving late medieval gateway of Benedictine nunnery founded 965

WINCHFIELD, HANTS, 2, 5C
Church of St Mary Norman church built c.1170 and restored 1850 retains fine west tower, north and south doorways, and retooled chancel arch with zig-zag decoration

WINDRUSH, GLOS, 2, 4A
Church of St Peter Norman church with work of 14th, 15th and 19th C retains splendid 12th-C carved south doorway and chancel arch; good 15th-C font

WINDSOR, BERKS, 3, 1C
Windsor Castle * Norman and medieval castle much altered at later periods and restored 19th C with original work including lower walls of late 12th-C Round Tower and parts of medieval fortifications
St George's Chapel Chapel begun 1475 has sumptuous fan vaulting and richly carved stalls for Knights of Garter

WING, BUCKS, 2, 5A
Church of All Saints Major Saxon church begun 8th C and extensively rebuilt c.950 with polygonal apse and crypt beneath chancel

WING, RUTLAND, 4, 1D
Church of St Peter and St Paul Norman church remodelled 19th C retains mid and late 12th-C arcades and north doorway

WINGFIELD, SUFFOLK, 4, 4E
Church of St Andrew Imposing medieval church rebuilt 14th to 15th C has west tower, annexe with screens and upper room, and ornate south chapel; good screens and monuments; rood loft stairs survive
Wingfield Castle Castle licensed 1384 with extensive mid 16th-C additions retains original south front with central gatehouse
Wingfield Old College [HHA] Remains of domestic buildings of 14th-C priests' college behind house built c.1760

WINGFIELD MANOR, DERBYS, 5, 4B
See South Wingfield

WINGRAVE, BUCKS, 2, 5A
Church of St Peter and St Paul Medieval church extensively restored 1887 has low

chancel of c.1190 with remains of blank arcading, 13th-C west tower with fine tower arch, and 14th-C arcades

WINSTONE, GLOS, 2, 3A
Church of St Bartholomew Small Saxo-Norman church retains original nave with north and south doorways, and medieval two-stage west tower

WINTERBORNE TOMSON, DORSET, 2, 3E
Church of St Andrew [CCT] Norman church with apsidal chancel, weatherboarded bell turret, and plastered wagon roof

WINTERBORNE WHITECHURCH, DORSET, 2, 3D
Church of St Mary Church with additions of 1844 retains early 13th-C chancel and 14th-C central tower; unusual 15th-C font with corner pilasters and good pulpit

WINTERBOURNE BASSETT, WILTS, 2, 3B
Church of St Katherine Medieval church has 14th-C north arcade and good north transept with rich arches; late 13th-C coffin lid in recess

WINTERBOURNE STEEPLETON, DORSET, 2, 2E
Church of St Michael Saxon and Norman church with early nave and 13th-C spire with pinnacles; important 10th-C sculpture depicting flying angel

WINTERINGHAM, LINCS, 7, 4E
Church of All Saints Norman church restored 19th C retains 11th-C tower with 15th-C upper stage, ornate 12th-C arcades, and 13th-C chancel

WINTRINGHAM, N. YORKS, 7, 4D
Church of St Peter Medieval church has Norman chancel with corbel table, 14th-C aisled nave with arcades, and 15th-C west tower; Norman font and good set of 14th-C stained glass

WINWICK, CHESHIRE, 5, 2A
Church of St Oswald Medieval church much rebuilt 19th C with chancel added 1847–8 retains 14th-C north arcade on later piers and west tower; medieval brasses

WIRKSWORTH, DERBYS, 5, 4B
Church of St Mary Mainly late 13th-C church restored and enlarged 19th C has crossing tower and early 14th-C arcades; carved coffin lid of c.800 and Norman architectural fragments

WISBECH, CAMBS, 4,2D
Church of St Peter and St Paul Church of Norman origin rebuilt 14th to 16th C retains late 12th-C north arcade and early 16th-C north tower

WISLEY, SURREY, 3,1C
Church Simple, well-preserved Norman church with 17th- and 19th-C windows

WISSINGTON, SUFFOLK, 3,4A
Church of St Mary Norman church rebuilt 1853 retains nave, chancel, apse and rich south doorway; fine set of wall paintings of c.1250–75

WISTON CASTLE, DYFED, 6,2D
Wiston Castle [CADW] Ruins of late 12th- to early 13th-C stone keep of well-preserved Norman motte and bailey castle

WITCHAMPTON, DORSET, 2,3D
Abbey House Handsome early 16th-C house, possibly built as parsonage, with 18th- and 19th-C additions

WITHERSFIELD, SUFFOLK, 3,3A
Church of St Mary Mainly late medieval church has carved benches and south door with ring handle in form of two salamanders

WITHINGTON, GLOS, 2,3A
Church of St Michael Church of Norman origin with later medieval and 19th-C additions has original north and south doorways, 13th-C south porch, and mainly 15th-C exterior

WITLEY, SURREY, 3,1D
Church of All Saints Church of Saxon origin with medieval, 17th- and 19th-C work has crossing tower, chancel, and south transept added c.1180–1220; traces of 12th-C wall paintings, good 13th-C font and piscina

WITNEY, OXON, 2,4A
Church of St Mary Church of Norman origin much rebuilt 13th to 15th C has late 12th-C porch, fine central tower of 1200s with octagonal spire, and late medieval clerestory; interior much restored 1865–9

WITTERING, CAMBS, 4,1D
Church of All Saints Medieval church retains primitive Saxon chancel arch, good mid 12th-C north arcade, and late 13th-C west tower; north chapel built early 1300s with tomb recess

WOLFETON HOUSE (0.5 km. / ¼ m. S of Charminster), DORSET, 2,2E
Wolfeton House and Gatehouse (Gatehouse – [LT]) (House open by appointment) Fine medieval and 16th-C house, fragment of courtyard building mostly demolished 19th C; gatehouse built mainly 1500s retains corner towers from earlier building (possibly 14th-C), each with a dovecot in the top

WOLLATON, NOTTS, 5,5B
See Nottingham

WOLVERHAMPTON, W. MIDLANDS, 5,3D
Church of St Peter Medieval church much restored 1852–65 retains late 13th-C crossing, nave rebuilt c.1450–80, and early 16th-C central tower; 15th-C stone pulpit and stalls; fine mid 9th-C Wolverhampton Cross stands outside church

WOODBRIDGE, SUFFOLK, 3,4A
Church of St Mary Medieval church has mid 15th-C north porch and tall west tower with rich flushwork decoration, brick south chapel, and good roof; 15th-C font and rood screen

WOODCHURCH, KENT, 3,3D
Church of All Saints 13th-C church with late medieval enlargement retains spacious interior with fine sanctuary and four-bay nave arcades, lancet windows, tower with shingled spire, and 15th-C north porch; Norman font and good 14th-C brass to priest

WOODFORD, NORTHANTS, 4,1E
Church of St Mary Church of Norman origin rebuilt 19th C has north aisle of c.1200, west tower begun 1250, and rib-vaulted south porch; 13th-C sedilia and piscina, and early 14th-C oaken effigies

WOODHORN, NORTHUMBERLAND, 7,3B
Church of St Mary Church of Saxon origin with exterior and chancel much rebuilt 1842–3 retains two original windows above 12th- and 13th-C arcades; fragments of 11th-C cross, good 13th-C effigy, and medieval cross slabs

WOODLANDS MANOR, WILTS, 2,3D
See Mere

WOODSFORD, DORSET, 2,2E
Woodsford Castle [LT] Handsome surviving range of important

quadrangular fortified manor house licensed 1335 and finished 1370 on bank of River Frome has original upper hall and chapel (well-preserved shelf and drain to piscina) and later additions and restoration

WOODSPRING PRIORY (nr Weston-super-Mare), SOMERSET, 2,1C
Woodspring Priory [LT] Remains of Augustinian priory founded 1210 near mouth of River Severn include mainly 15th-C church with tower (converted for domestic use after 1536), infirmary and great barn; range added 1701 on site of prior's lodging

WOOLPIT, SUFFOLK, 3,4A
Church of St Mary Mainly 15th-C church with spire of 1854 retains 14th-C chancel and south aisle, fine stone-faced south porch built c.1430–55, and hammerbeam roof; rood canopy and carved benches

WOOLSTON (2.5 km. / 1 ½ m. NW of Knockin), SHROPS, 5,1C
St Winifred's Well [LT] Charming medieval timber-framed well chapel (later used as court house and cottage) built above well still visited by pilgrims, supposed resting place of body of St Winifred on its way from Holywell to Holy Cross, Shrewsbury

WOOTTON COURTENEY, SOMERSET, 1,5B
Church of All Saints Medieval church with 13th-C tower and chancel has 15th-C nave, windows with carved hoodmould stops, ceiled wagon roofs and bosses; holy water stoup in south porch

WOOTTON WAWEN, WARWS, 5,4E
Church of St Peter Saxon church with Norman and medieval rebuilding retains original central tower (c.1020) with long-and-short work quoins; original porticus openings can be seen inside

WORCESTER, WORCS, 5,3E
Cathedral Cathedral church of Norman origin restored 1800s retains crypt of 1080s, two western bays of nave built c.1185, and elaborate east end begun 1224 with chancel, east transepts, retrochoir and Lady Chapel; nave of mainly c.1320 and 14th-C crossing tower; monument to King John of c.1230 and splendid Prince Arthur's Chantry begun 1504

Cathedral Precinct Monastic buildings adjoining cathedral include important round chapter house of c.1120–5 with central pillar, 14th and 15th-C cloisters with 11th-C slype and good vaults, mid 14th-C refectory with carving of c.1220–30, lavatorium, and ruins of Guesten Hall built c.1338–9; Bishop's Palace to north (rebuilt c.1730) retains internal work of 1200s; Edgar Tower begun early 14th C and reworked 1800s
Church of St Alban, Deansway. Simple Norman church with 13th and 19th-C work
Church of St Andrew, Deansway Surviving late medieval church tower in public garden with spire reworked 1751
Church of St John in Bedwardine, St John's. Medieval church with 19th-C enlargement retains 12th-C north arcade and 15th-C south arcade
The Commandery *, Sidbury. Complex of late 15th-C timber-framed buildings (originally Hospital of St Wulstan) includes great hall with oriel window and screens passage; early 16th-C wall paintings on upper floor
The Greyfriars [NT], Friar Street. Handsome timber-framed building of c.1480 (originally friary guest house) with 16th-C wings

WORKSOP, NOTTS, 5,5A
Worksop Priory (Church of SS Cuthbert and Mary) Late 12th-C church of Augustinian priory founded c.1120 with much 19th- and 20th-C work retains original twin-towered west front and nave with arcades, gallery and clerestory; long 13th-C Lady Chapel; splendid Norman south door in early 13th-C porch
Gatehouse 14th-C gatehouse with good porch and 15th-C window

WORLINGWORTH, SUFFOLK, 4,4E
Church of St Mary Mainly 15th-C church retains chancel built c.1300, south porch and west tower with flushwork panelling, and double hammerbeam roof; good font with fine tall 15th-C cover

WORPLESDON, SURREY, 3,1D
Church of St Mary Medieval church has 13th-C north chapel, 15th-C nave with earlier arcades, unusual east window, and fine west tower

WORSBOROUGH, S. YORKS, 5,4A
Church of St Mary Norman and medieval church retains fine south door carved with

tracery and inscription commemorating donors

WORSLEY, GREATER MANCHESTER, 5, 2A
Wardley Hall Hall-house of *c*.1500 with extensive later additions retains some timber-framing and original hall in south range (now subdivided)

WORSTEAD, NORFOLK, 4, 4D
Church of St Mary Attractive church begun 1379 with west tower, two-storeyed south porch, earlier chancel, and later clerestory and vestry; good medieval screens and hammerbeam roof

WORTH, W. SUSSEX, 3, 2D
Church of St Nicholas Large cruciform Saxon church has fine interior with tall nave, transepts, and low apsidal chancel; north-east tower added 1871; 13th-C font carved *c*.1300

WORTH MATRAVERS, DORSET, 2, 3E
Church of St Nicholas Norman church retains original nave and chancel, chancel arch of *c*.1130, and 13th- and 14th-C windows; fine tympanum of *c*.1160;

WORTHAM MANOR, DEVON, 1, 4C
See Lifton

WOTTON, GLOS, 2, 3A
See Gloucester

WOTTON, SURREY, 3, 1D
Church of St John Early Norman church restored 19th C retains original tower with pyramidal roof, and 13th-C south doorway and north chapel

WOTTON-UNDER-EDGE, GLOS, 2, 2B
Church of St Mary the Virgin Church consecrated 1283 with much post-medieval alteration has original arcades, wide nave and aisles, 14th-C west tower, and clerestory added 1400s; fine Berkeley Brass of 1392

WRANGLE, LINCS, 4, 2C
Church of St Mary and St Nicholas Mainly 15th-C church retains late 12th-C tower arch, fine 13th-C south doorway, 14th-C arcades and chancel; good stained glass of *c*.1350–70

WRAXALL, SOMERSET, 2, 2B
Church of All Saints Mainly late 14th-C church restored 19th C has Norman south doorway, 13th-C portal to south

porch, and unusual west tower; large font and good late 15th-C tomb chest
Birdcombe Court Medieval manor house with later alterations and wings retains fine four-storeyed porch tower

WRESSLE, E. RIDING OF YORKS, 7, 4E
Wressle Castle Surviving south range of monumental castle built *c*.1380 with Lord's and Chapel Towers and late 15th-C windows

WREXHAM, CLWYD, 6, 5B
Church of St Giles [OCT] Impressive medieval church much remodelled 15th C with north porch, clerestory, camberbeam roof, and chancel with polygonal apse retains 14th-C nave arcades; elaborate early 16th-C west tower with crown, niches and sculpture

WROXALL, WARWS, 5, 4D
Wroxall Abbey Surviving 14th-C north aisle of church of Benedictine nunnery consecrated 1315 with west tower added 1663–4 and 19th-C south chapel; good set of medieval stained glass

WROXETER, SHROPS, 5, 2C
Church of St Andrew [CCT] Church of Saxon origin reworked 18th C retains Norman chancel and west tower with later top; 13th-C chest with ironwork

WYCK RISSINGTON, GLOS, 2, 4A
Church of St Laurence Norman church rebuilt and consecrated 1269 retains fine 13th-C chancel, tower, and tower arch; font of *c*.1200

WYE, KENT, 3, 4D
Church of St Gregory and St Martin Surviving clerestoried nave of 13th-C collegiate church remodelled mid 15th C; chancel and south tower added 1701–6; 15th-C octagonal font
College of St Gregory and St Martin Mid 15th-C college with 18th-C remodelling and 20th-C additions forms three ranges around courtyard; hall roof of *c*.1445

WYKE REGIS (2 km. / 1¼ m. S of Weymouth), DORSET, 2, 2E
Church of All Saints Handsome, little-altered church of 1455 with five-bay arcades and west tower; 15th-C font

WYKEN, W. MIDLANDS, 5, 4D
Church of St Mary Well-preserved Norman church has tower with 19th-C

timber upper stage; Norman font and part of wall painting of *c*.1500

WYMINGTON, BEDS, 4, 1E
Church of St Laurence Mainly 14th-C church restored *c*.1844 and 1920s with ornate double-storeyed south porch; 14th-C wall paintings, sedilia and piscinas; some early brasses and 14th-C Curteys monument

WYMONDHAM, NORFOLK, 4, 4D
Wymondham Abbey Church of Benedictine priory founded 1107 (abbey after 1448) retains Norman nave with arcades, crossing tower of *c*.1440, and west tower begun *c*.1448; late 13th-C corporas case, fine hammerbeam roof with angels, and terracotta monument of *c*.1525
Chapel of St Thomas Becket Long Norman chapel rebuilt 14th and 15th C with hammerbeam roof
Medieval Buildings Some good buildings with jettied upper floors
Market Cross Octagonal wooden market cross erected 1617

WYRE (island SE of Rousay), ORKNEY, 9, 5A
St Mary's Chapel [HS] Roofless remains of small mid 12th-C church restored late 1800s
Cubbie Roo's Castle [HS] Surviving rectangular tower of ruined castle built *c*.1145 with medieval additions

WYSALL, NOTTS, 5, 5C
Church of the Holy Trinity Church of Norman origin with 13th-C west tower, 14th-C chancel, and 15th-C south arcade; font of 1200s and fine 15th-C screen and pulpit

WYTHENSHAWE, GREATER MANCHESTER, 5, 3A
Wythenshawe Hall Hall-house with post medieval additions has early 16th-C timber-framed range with original gables, porch, dais bays and hall
Baguley Hall [EH], Hall Lane. 14th-C timber-framed hall-house with additions of 16th to 19th C retains original doorays to screens passage, and hall with spere truss and timber decoration

YANWATH, CUMBRIA, 7, 2C
Yanwath Hall South front of house has well-preserved 14th-C pele tower and 15th-C hall and kitchen

YARDLEY, W. MIDLANDS
Church of St Edburgha [OCT] 13th-C church enlarged 14th and 15th C with west

tower and spire and fine oak porch; 19th-C additions
Old Grammar School (in churchyard) Late 15th-C timber-framed building with original roof

YARDLEY HASTINGS, NORTHANTS, 5, 5E
Church of St Andrew Norman and medieval church with work of 1880s retains early 13th-C west tower, arcades of *c*.1300, and 14th-C chancel
Manor House Remains of hall range of manor house built *c*.1320–40

YARNTON, OXON, 2, 4A
Church of St Bartholomew Norman church with additions of 13th and 17th C has late 12th-C work in south aisle, 13th-C nave and chancel; font of *c*.1400, 15th-C reredos and bench ends, and much medieval stained glass

YATE, GLOS, 2, 2B
Church of St Mary Mainly 13th-C stone church much rebuilt 1400s has fine three-storeyed west tower, 15th-C chancel arch and good font

YATELEY, HANTS, 2, 5C
Church of St Peter Church of Norman origin has 12th-C north doorway, early 13th-C chancel, and fine late medieval timber-framed west tower; good medieval tiles

YATTON, SOMERSET, 2, 1C
Church of St Mary Late 13th- to early 14th-C church with additions of 15th C has crossing tower, transepts, rich south porch, and wagon roof; tomb recesses of *c*.1325 in north transept and late 15th-C monument in north chancel chapel
Old Rectory Medieval prebendal house retains front built 1400s with two-storeyed porch

YAXLEY, CAMBS, 4, 1E
Church of St Peter Large medieval church retains 13th-C transepts and south doorway and 15th-C arcades, west tower and south porch; unusual 13th-C heart burial in north transept

YAXLEY, SUFFOLK, 4, 4E
Church of St Mary Medieval church retains early 14th-C west tower, lavish north porch with flushwork decoration and pinnacles, and 15th-C nave with fine roof; rood screen and rare sexton's wheel over south door (used to determine day of Lady Fast)

YELVERTOFT, NORTHANTS, 5,5D
Church of All Saints Medieval church
with 14th-C arcades, 15th-C outer south
aisle, and fine tomb chest with alabaster
effigy

YEOLMBRIDGE, CORNWALL, 1,3C
Bridge 14th-C bridge has two pointed
arches with three chamfered ribs

YEOVIL, SOMERSET, 2,2D
Church of St John Spacious late 14th-C
church with west tower, transepts and
chancel chapels retains crypt of c.1300;
good window tracery and brass
lectern of c.1450

YETMINSTER, DORSET, 2,2D
Church of St Andrew Medieval church
with 13th-C chancel and 15th-C west
tower, embattled aisles and north porch;
fragments of Saxon and 15th-C sculpture

YNYS SEIRIOL, GWYNEDD, 6,4A
Monastery (on small island off east coast
of Anglesey) Fragmentary traces of 7th-C
chapel, monks' cells and walled enclosure
of monastery reputedly founded by
St Seiriol

YORK, N. YORKS, 7,4E
York Minster * Large cathedral restored
19th and 20th C retains 12th-C crypt
reconstructed 1300s, 13th-C transepts,
late 13th-C octagonal chapter house
with vestibule, nave with tall arcades of
1291–c.1350, eastern arm built c.1361–1420,
crossing and west towers of c.1407–c.1472,
and 14th- to 15th-C additions to south;
splendid set of medieval tracery and
stained glass (most extensive in England);
pulpitum of c.1475–c.1506

Cathedral Precinct Medieval remains
include Archbishop's Palace with late
Norman arcade and chapel of c.1230–40
much restored 1806–13
St William's College *, 5 College Street
(within cathedral precinct) Former
prebendal house enlarged 1455–67
as house of chantry priests retains
three large medieval halls
St Mary's Abbey Remains of Benedictine
abbey founded 1088–9 include impressive
ruined late 13th-C church, extensive
walling, main gatehouse, and hospitium;
fine 13th-C abbot's house (now King's
Manor, Exhibition Square) with
post-medieval additions; fragments
of excellent monastic buildings and
sculpture survive in Yorkshire
Museum
Church of All Saints, North Street
Church of Norman origin with medieval
rebuilding retains chantry founded 1325,
mid 15th-C west tower, and hammerbeam
roof to chancel; fine set of 14th- and
15th-C stained glass
Church of St Martin cum Gregory,
Micklegate Medieval church now used for
exhibitions, etc. with tower of 1844 retains
arcades of c.1200 and 15th-C north chapel,
clerestory and roof
Church of St Mary Bishophill Junior
Church with medieval additions has
Saxon west tower with Roman work and
late 12th-C north arcade; fragments of
Saxon cross shaft
Church of St Mary Castlegate Church of
Saxon origin with Norman, 15th- and
19th-C rebuilding retains mid 12th-C
piers in north aisle and late medieval
west tower; dedication stone of c.1020

Church of Holy Trinity Micklegate
Surviving part of 13th-C nave of former
priory founded 1089 with chancel added
1887 and west front of 1902–4
Medieval Churches Other churches with
good medieval work are: All Saints
Pavement; St Cuthbert (Peaseholme
Green); St Denys (Walmgate);
St Margaret (Walmgate); St Helen
(St Helen's Square); St Martin le Grand
(Coney Street); St Michael Spurriergate;
St Sampson (Church Street); Holy Trinity
Goodramgate [CCT]
Clifford's Tower [EH], Clifford Street.
Fine tower of 1250–75 on steep motte
with 17th-C rebuilding and remains of
medieval castle walling
City Walls Impressive and well-preserved
city walls begun c.1250 and restored
19th and 20th C, the most complete in
England, retain 12th- to 14th-C gates
or bars
Guildhall, St Helen's Square. Guildhall
built 1447–8 and damaged 1900s
St Leonard's Hospital, Museum Street.
Ruins of medieval hospital include 13th-C
passage, vaulted undercroft and chapel
Merchant Taylor's Hall Hall of craft guild
with exterior rebuilt c.1672 and 1715 retains
hall of c.1400 with good roof
Merchant Adventurer's Hall *, Fossgate
(museum) Fine and well-preserved early
15th-C hall of guild of mercers and
merchants (one of best medieval
guildhalls in Europe) with stone
chapel licensed 1411, two-naved
undercroft, and hall with
timberwork above
St Anthony's Hall, Peaseholme Green
Guildhall built 1446–53 and enlarged later

15th C with timber-framed upper level
and 17th-C brickwork
Cottages, Goodramgate. Timber-framed
cottages built c.1320 for chantry priests

YOUGHAL, CO. CORK, 12,3D
Church of St Mary [Dúchas] Good
cruciform parish church built c.1250
replacing earlier building has alterations
of 15th to 16th C and much 18th- to 19th-C
work; unusually long chancel and big
early 13th-C tower near north-west corner;
14th-C font, effigies of early 1300s
(Thomas Paris and Matheu le Mercer),
and 15th-C tomb of Thomas Fleming
Town Walls [Dúchas] Remains of
medieval town walls (among best
preserved in Ireland) re-fortified 1642
North Abbey [Dúchas] Scanty remains
of church of Dominican friary
founded 1268
Medieval Buildings Medieval remains in
Main Street are much altered 15th-C
Tynte's Castle (formerly Walsh's Castle)
and restored 15th to 16th-C gable of
St John's House (hospital founded
1360)
Molana Abbey (or Dairinis Priory)
[Dúchas] (actually Co. Waterford)
Remains of Augustinian priory refounded
late 12th C on site of 6th-C monastery on
island in Blackwater include rectangular
church with fine lancet windows and
claustral buildings

YOULGREAVE, DERBYS, 5,4B
Church of All Saints Crenellated church
of Norman origin with original arcades
and tall 15th-C west tower; font of c.1200
with projecting stoup and good 14th- and
15th-C monuments

Outside Period

BATH, SOMERSET, 2, 2C
Aquae Sulis / Roman Baths Museum *
Famous, well-preserved and much
excavated remains of Roman spa founded
in Flavian times using local springs
renowned for their therapeutic qualities
consist of five baths (Great Bath, oval and
circular baths particularly fine) and two
swimming pools with associated
hypocausts; traces of adjacent
Temple of Sulis

BRACO, TAYSIDE, 8, 2D
Ardoch Roman Camp Complex of
earthworks on site of large Roman camp,
used as base for about 40,000 soldiers
during 2nd C AD

BURGH CASTLE, NORFOLK, 4, 5D
Burgh Castle [EH] Impressive surviving
walls of Roman fort built late 3rd C AD
to defend coast (probably evacuated
c.407–8, excavated 1958–62) with
bastions and traces of Norman
work

CAERLEON (nr Newport),
GWENT, 2, 1B
Caerleon Roman Fortress [CADW]
Important and remarkably well-preserved
remains of extensive Roman fortress
(originally known as Isca) established AD
75 by Second Augustan Legion include
splendid ampthitheatre, barrack blocks
(only examples currently visible in
Europe), and fine bath house
(covered by modern buildings);
finds from many excavations
displayed in town museum

CAERWENT, GWENT, 2, 2B
Caerwent Roman Town [CADW]
Remaining traces of buildings and
parts of wall of Roman town occupied
1st – 4th C AD

CARLOWAY / CARLABHAGH
(Lewis), WESTERN ISLES, 9, 2C
Carloway Broch Substantial remains of
circular broch with internal courtyard,
built late c.100 BC – c.AD 200 on
prominent site amid moorland

CHYSAUSTER ANCIENT
VILLAGE (4 km. / 2 ½ m. NW of
Gulval) CORNWALL, 1, 1E
Ancient Village [EH] Remains of
deserted Romano-Cornish village
with well-preserved houses

DOONE FORT (3 km. / 2 m. S of
Navan in Lough Doon),
CO. DONEGAL, 11, 2B
Doone Fort Well-preserved fort of
roughly oval shape (possibly 5th-C)
dramatically set on its own island
rising out of lake

DUN AENGUS, ARAN
ISLANDS (Inishmore),
CO. GALWAY, 11, 1E
Dun Aengus [Dúchas] Remains of
extensive stone fort (possibly 8th or
7th-C BC, restored 1881) spectacularly
situated on edge of cliff by Atlantic
consists of three concentric walls and
traces of fourth

GRIANAN OF AILEACH,
CO. DONEGAL, 11, 3A
Grianán of Aileach [Dúchas] Fine
roughly circular hill fort close to Loughs
Swilly and Foyle (date uncertain, possibly
6th-C), extensively reworked 1874–8,
has big stone wall with chambers, and
terraces to inside

GURNESS, ORKNEY (Mainland), 9, 5A
Broch of Gurness [HS] Substantial
remains of broch built probably c.100 BC
to AD 100 and remodelled perhaps 2nd or
3rd C AD on cliffs overlooking Eynhallow
Sound (uncovered by 1930 excavation)
consist of drystone-walled tower with
internal courtyard in enclosure defended
by three ditches and ramparts; traces of
houses built over enclosure in late Iron
Age period; two probably Pictish houses
removed from site in 1930s survive rebuilt
immediately to west

HADRIAN'S WALL, CUMBRIA /
NORTHUMBERLAND /
TYNE AND WEAR, 7, 2B
Hadrian's Wall [EH] [World Heritage
Site] Stretches of wall together with link-
ing forts and milecastles begun AD 122–23
by Emperor Hadrian, which ran between
present Bowness-on-Solway and
Wallsend-on-Tyne to mark off boundary

of Roman Empire from northern tribes
beyond; sites of particular interest
include Chesters, Corbridge and
Housesteads

MAES HOWE (Stenness)
ORKNEY (Mainland), 9, 5B
Chambered Cairn [HS] Interesting
megalithic cairn (c.2900–2800 BC) set
amid ancient complex of henges and
standing stones consists of turf-covered
mound on circular platform enclosed by
ditch and bank; internal passage (partly
reconstructed) leads to main chamber
with 12th-C runic inscriptions and
other carvings on walls, small side
cells, and 20th-C roof

MIDHOWE BROCH (island of
Rousay), ORKNEY, 9, 5A
Midhowe Broch [HS] Remains of
drystone-walled broch built probably
2nd C BC on promontory site defended
on landward side (east) by massive stone
rampart with ditches; internal court of
broch converted to two semicircular
houses perhaps 2nd C AD; traces of
possibly 1st-C AD group of houses
within enclosure

MOUSA (small island),
SHETLAND, 9, 1B
Mousa Broch [HS] Exceptionally well-
preserved and tall drystone-walled broch
built 1st C AD on promontory site of now
uninhabited island with rampart on
landward side; unusually thick wall
encircles small courtyard with traces
of work of possibly 3rd or 4th C AD

NEWGRANGE (8 km. / 5 m. SE of
Slane), CO. MEATH, 12, 5E
Newgrange [Dúchas] One of Britain's
best known prehistoric monuments
(c.3100 BC), this imposing roughly
circular, great chambered mound with
retaining kerb-stones and magnificent
corbelled roof contains main passage
orientated towards rising sun of winter
solstice and three burial niches, that to
right bearing beautifully carved roof;
many stones with fine geometrical
designs; twelve pillar stones survive
just outside kerb

RECULVER, KENT, 2, 4C
Roman Fort [EH] (Regulbium) Remains
of probably 3rd-C Roman fort (partly

destroyed by sea erosion) survive on
impressive cliff top site in country park

ST ALBANS, HERTS, 3, 1B
Verulamium Museum * Site of Roman
town of Verulamium (founded soon
after AD 43, altered 2nd and 3rd C) with
fragments of basilica, theatre and walls
houses museum containing fine
collection of excavated remains
including mosaics from domestic
buildings

SILCHESTER, HANTS, 2, 5C
Roman City Walls and Amphitheatre
[EH] Surviving outline and fortifications
of Roman town; archaeological finds
housed in Calleva Museum on site

SKARA BRAE (1 km. / ½ m. S of
Sandwick) ORKNEY
(Mainland), 9, 5B
Skara Brae Historic Village [HS] Well-
preserved farming settlement on south
side of Bay of Skaill, occupied from
c.3100 BC to c.2500 BC, consists of group
of six originally semi-subterranean,
self-contained houses linked by passages;
remarkable built-in stone furniture;
remains of four earlier houses at east
and south; detached workshop to west

STAIGUE, CO. KERRY, 12, 1D
Staigue Fort [Dúchas] Impressive fort of
uncertain date or purpose set in peaceful
valley consists of circular wall (partly
reconstructed 1800s) surrounded by
bank and ditch

STONEHENGE (3 km. / 2 m W of
Amesbury), WILTS, 2, 3C
Stonehenge [EH] [World Heritage Site]
World-famous circle of massive sarsen
stones and lintels orientated on rising
and setting sun, last in sequence of
monuments supposedly erected between
c.3000 and 1600 BC (purpose uncertain),
survives in centre of prehistoric
landscape with earthworks and
burial mounds

TRE'R CEIRI, GWYNEDD, 6, 3B
Tre'r Ceiri (Town of the Giants) Walled
early Celtic settlement on hilltop site
with remains of 150 stone dwellings
occupied until c. AD 400

Glossary

AISLE. A lateral portion of a building, particularly a subsidiary space running parallel to the nave of a church (on either or both sides) and usually separated from it by arches or columns.

ALMONRY. A place at which alms for the poor are distributed, usually referring to a room or building in a monastery specifically for this purpose.

AMBULATORY. In a large church, an aisle-like walkway around the interior of the east end of the building, passing behind the main altar.

ANCHORAGE. The cell or retreat of an anchorite (a person who has withdrawn from the world to live a solitary religious life).

APSE. A semicircular or polygonal projection in a building, often referring to the east end of a church.

ARCADE. A row of arches supported on columns or piers.

ARCH. A curved construction of stone or brick used to span an opening and carry a structure above it, the wedge-like blocks (voussoirs) of which it is made being held together by mutual pressure and supported only from the sides. The term is applied also to similar forms used decoratively (see blind arcading) rather than structurally. See also ogee, stilted arch, strainer arch. *Fig 1*

ASHLAR. Stonework laid in regular courses, with flat, even surfaces and right-angle joints, as opposed to rubble masonry of roughly-cut stones of differing shapes and sizes.

AUMBRY. A secure place in a church for the storage of sacred vessels and other valuable items, usually consisting of a wall recess or cupboard near the altar.

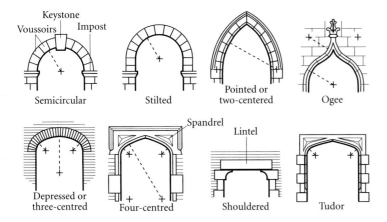

1. *Arches*

BALLFLOWER. An ornamental motif featuring a small globular shape enclosed within a three-petalled stylised flower; it was much used in the 14th century in decorative carving, typically in long rows in the hollows of mouldings. *Fig. 2*

BALUSTER. A small supporting post, usually somewhat bulbous in shape.

BARBICAN. A tower or other structure forming an outer defence guarding the approach to a castle or fortified town.

BARREL VAULT. A vault with an uninterrupted semicircular section, like that of a tunnel (tunnel vault is an alternative name). *Fig 11*

BARTIZAN. A small turret projecting (usually by means of corbelling) from the junction of two walls, often at the top of a tower.

BAR TRACERY. See tracery.

BASILICA. A term originally applied to a type of ancient Roman meeting hall, typically oblong in shape and divided into a central nave and flanking aisles by rows of columns, and subsequently applied to early Christian churches built on a similar pattern.

BASTLE OR BASTEL HOUSE. A small defensible farmhouse characteristic of the northern counties of England (particularly Northumberland), with a byre for animals on the ground floor and living accommodation above; most of the surviving examples date from about the 16th century.

BASTION. An outward projection (generally semicircular or polygonal) from the wall of a fortification that allows defenders to fire along the length of the wall; a bastion is usually flush with the top of the wall rather than rising above it like a tower.

BATTER. The slope of a wall that is thicker at the bottom than it is at the top.

BATTLEMENT. A defensive parapet at the top of a wall with an indented outline formed by raised sections alternating with spaces; the raised sections are called merlons and the openings are called embrasures or crenels, hence the term crenellation for the upper part of the battlements as a whole.

BAWN. In Ireland, a walled enclosure for cattle attached to or near a house or castle.

Billet

Beakhead

Nailhead

Dogtooth

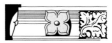
Ballflower

Fleuron

2. *Moulding Enrichments*

BAY. A vertical division of a building or part of a building, usually one marked by some regularly repeated constructional feature or unit of design, such as a row of arches, columns or windows; thus a church nave with four arches along each side and corresponding windows above is described as having four bays.

BEAKHEAD. A decorative motif featuring a grotesque bird's head with a prominent beak (or sometimes a beast's head with a prominent tongue); it was much used in Romanesque architecture for the enrichment of mouldings. *Fig. 2*

BEEHIVE HUT. A type of primitive stone building, circular in plan and decreasing in diameter as it rises, forming a shape rather like a beehive.

BILLET MOULDING. A moulding featuring short cylindrical or rectangular blocks ("billets") spaced at regular intervals; it was popular in Romanesque architecture. *Fig. 2*

BLIND ARCADING (OR BLANK ARCADING). A row of shallow arches attached to a wall as a decorative motif rather than piercing it structurally.

BLIND TRACERY. See tracery.

BLOCK CAPITAL. See capital.

BOSS. An ornamental projection, roughly circular in shape and often richly carved, at a point where two or more ribs intersect in a vault; the term is also applied to similar knoblike projections used elsewhere, for example at the end of mouldings.

BROACH. See spire.

BUTTRESS. A solid, upright mass of stone or brick built against a wall to strengthen and support it, often specifically to resist the outward pressure exerted by an arch or vault. Various names are given to buttresses used at the outer corners of buildings (notably of church towers). Angle buttresses are two that meet at an angle of 90 degrees on adjacent walls; a clasping buttress is a block-like one that encases ("clasps") the whole corner; a diagonal buttress is one that projects diagonally from the corner; and set-back buttresses are similar to angle buttresses but positioned just inwards from the corner, so that they do not touch one another. See also flying buttress. *Fig. 3*

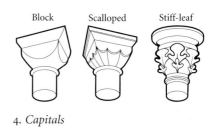

4. *Capitals*

CABLE ORNAMENT. A moulding imitating the twisting strands of a length of rope.

CAPITAL. The topmost part of a column, pilaster or pier, forming a transition between the shaft and the horizontal or arched feature it supports. Capitals are often carved in various distinctive forms. These include the block capital (or cushion capital), a simple type much used in Romanesque architecture, which starts as a rectangular block at the top but has the lower edges rounded to effect a transition to the circular shaft; the scalloped capital, a development of the block capital in which the lower part, instead of being smoothly rounded, is cut into a series of vertical flutes, producing an effect resembling the fan-like shape of a scallop shell; and the stiff-leaf capital, characteristic of the Early English period, which is decorated with luxuriant stylized foliage. *Fig. 4*

CASHEL. In Ireland, a type of ancient fort with a circular stone wall.

CEILED. A term applied to an interior surface, particularly the underside of a roof, that has been overlaid or lined with wood or plaster.

CELURE. A richly decorated area of a church roof over the rood or main altar.

CHANCEL. The east end of a church containing the main altar; in a cross-shaped church it generally refers to the whole of the building east of the crossing and it is sometimes separated from the western part (nave) by a chancel screen.

CHANTRY CHAPEL. A small chapel in or attached to a church endowed for saying Masses for the soul of the founder of the chapel or for the souls of other specified people.

CHAPEL OF EASE. A small place of worship built for the use of parishioners who live remote from their parish church.

CHAPTER HOUSE. A building attached to a cathedral or monastery in which meetings of the governing body ("chapter") are held.

CHEVET. A term, adopted from French, for the east end of a Gothic church with an apse and ambulatory – a type more common in French architecture than English.

CHEVRON. A zig-zag pattern, often used decoratively in Romanesque architecture.

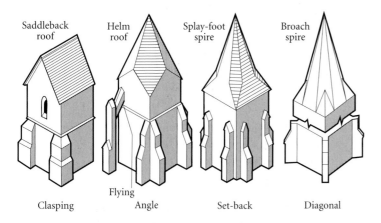

3. *Church Roofs, Spires and Buttresses*

5. *Castles*

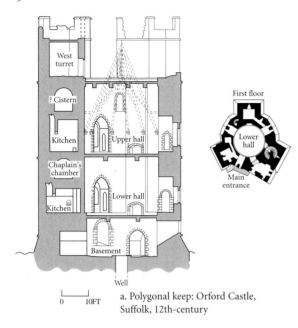

a. Polygonal keep: Orford Castle, Suffolk, 12th-century

West turret

? Cistern

Kitchen

Upper hall

Chaplain's chamber

Lower hall

Kitchen

Basement

Well

0   10FT

First floor

Lower hall

Main entrance

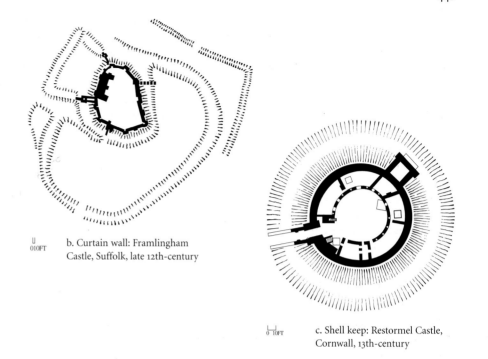

b. Curtain wall: Framlingham Castle, Suffolk, late 12th-century

010FT

c. Shell keep: Restormel Castle, Cornwall, 13th-century

0 10FT

d. Concentric castle: Beaumaris Castle, Angelsey, late 13th- to early 14th-century

0 10FT

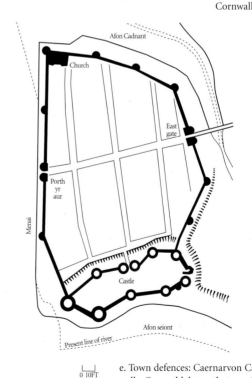

e. Town defences: Caernarvon Castle and town walls, Gwynedd, late 13th- to early 14th-century

Afon Cadnant

Church

East gate

Porth yr aur

Menai

Castle

Afon seiont

Present line of river

0 10FT

CHOIR. The part of a church occupied by the singers who perform or lead the musical parts of services. It is usually in the eastern limb of a cross-shaped church and in architectural contexts the term "choir" is often loosely used as a synonym for "chancel"; however in large churches the choir often includes part of the nave.

CHOIR STALLS. Sets of fixed, enclosed seats arranged in parallel rows in the choir of a church, usually of wood and often very elaborately carved, occupied by the clergy during services; the clergy stood for the major part of services, so the underside of each seat typically had a bracket ("misericord") against which the elderly or infirm could lean for support when the seat was tipped up.

CLAS CHURCH. In Wales, a type of Celtic monastic church built up to about 1200, generally simple in plan and decoration.

CLERESTORY. The upper part of the main longitudinal walls of a church, above the aisle roofs, pierced with a row of windows.

CLOISTER. A covered passageway around an open, usually square space (known as the cloister garth); cloisters are found particularly in monasteries, connecting the church with various other buildings.

CLUSTERED COLUMN. See column.

COB. A mixture of clay and chopped straw (and sometimes other materials such as gravel and sand) used as a walling material in vernacular buildings.

COLLAR BEAM. In a wooden roof, a horizontal beam connecting a sloping rafter on one side to a similar rafter on the other side.

COLUMN. An upright, fairly slender supporting member, usually consisting of a base, a cylindrical (often slightly tapering) shaft and a spreading capital at the top. A clustered, composite or compound column (or pier) is one in which a number of very slender columns or shafts are grouped together (often around a central core) to form a combined support.

COMPOSITE COLUMN. See column.

COMPOUND COLUMN. See column.

CONCENTRIC CASTLE. A castle having two circuits of walls arranged more or less concentrically, the inner one higher and stronger than the outer. *Fig. 5*

CORBEL. A bracket projecting from the face of a wall to support a parapet, beam or other horizontal member. A corbel table is a projecting course of masonry resting on a line of such brackets. Corbelling refers to the use of a series of courses of stone or brickwork, each one projecting slightly more than the one beneath it, to support a feature such as an oriel window or to form a kind of rough arch or dome.

COSMATI WORK. A type of geometrical decoration using coloured marbles and mosaic, popular for architectural enrichment and adorning various types of church furnishing in Italy in the 12th and 13th centuries; Italian craftsmen in the medium worked in Westminster Abbey.

CREDENCE. A small ledge, shelf or table positioned near the altar in a church to hold the bread and wine used in the Eucharist.

CRENELLATION. See battlement.

CROCKET. In Gothic architecture, a leaf-like projection used at regular intervals to embellish sloping surfaces, such as those of canopies and pinnacles.

CROSSING. In a cross-shaped church, the central area formed by the intersection of the nave, chancel and transepts; the crossing is often surmounted by a tower.

CROWN POST. In a wooden roof, a vertical post standing centrally on a transverse beam (tie beam) and supporting other timbers; unlike a king post, it does not rise to the apex of the roof. *Fig. 6*

CRUCKS. Pairs of heavy timbers (individually called blades), rising usually from ground level and inclining inwards, which together with other pairs form the framework of certain types of vernacular buildings.

CRYPT. An underground or partly sunk chamber beneath the floor of a church, typically used to house tombs or relics; crypts in large churches sometimes also contain altars.

CURTAIN WALL. In a castle or other fortification, a perimeter wall, usually linking various towers. *Fig. 5*

CUSHION CAPITAL. See capital.

CUSP. See quatrefoil.

DAGGER. A tracery motif resembling a stylised dagger with a very broad, leaf-like blade and a rounded handle; it was much used in the 14th century. A curved dagger of this type is called a mouchette. *Fig. 10*

DECORATED. See Gothic.

DIAPER. A grid-like pattern of small repeated units used as architectural enrichment – carved, moulded or painted.

DOG-TOOTH. A decorative motif consisting of a series of small units like four-pointed stars, each one rising pyramid-like in the centre; it was popular for the enrichment of mouldings in the 13th century. *Fig. 2*

DONJON. See keep.

DORTER. A dormitory in a monastery.

DRAGON BEAM. In a timber-framed building, a beam projecting diagonally from the corner of an upper storey to support the joists when two adjacent sides are made to overhang the storey below (see jetty). A dragon post is a carved bracket beneath a dragon beam.

DRIPSTONE. See hood moulding.

EARLY ENGLISH. See Gothic.

EASTER SEPULCHRE. A representation of Christ's tomb used in Easter ceremonials; originally Easter sepulchres were temporary structures, but from about 1300 they often took the form of permanent additions to the fabric of churches in England, typically consisting of a carved recess in the north wall of the chancel.

FAN VAULT. A type of arched ceiling in which concave cone shapes, overlaid with ribs, radiate from the wall towards the apex of the vault, producing an effect like a series of opened fans; such vaults were one of the most distinctive features of the Perpendicular style. *Fig. 11*

FERETORY (OR FERETRUM). A shrine for a holy relic; by extension the term is also applied to the place in a church where such a shrine is kept.

FLEURON. A stylised flower, typically square in shape, used as architectural decoration, for example to enrich mouldings. *Fig. 2*

FLUSHWORK. A type of decorative external stonework, found mainly in East Anglia, in which pattern is created by contrasting smooth stonework with areas of knapped (split) flints, which are darker and more variegated in appearance.

FLYING BUTTRESS. A type of external reinforcement used to help support the vaults of large Gothic churches; it consists of a stone arch (or section of an arch) connecting the upper part of a wall to a buttress that stands apart from the wall rather than up against it like a conventional buttress. *Fig. 3*

FOIL. See quatrefoil.

FRATER. An alternative term for refectory – the dining hall of a monastery.

FREESTONE. Any fairly fine-grained stone that can be cut or sawn in any direction and is therefore suitable for carving and masonry.

GALILEE. In a major church, a large porch or chapel at one of the main entrances (usually the one at the west end).

GARDEROBE. A privy in a castle, sometimes built into the thickness of a wall.

GARGOYLE. A projecting waterspout on the roofline of a building carved in the shape of a grotesque human or a monstrous beast, the rainwater emerging through the mouth.

GOTHIC. The style of architecture prevalent in Europe in the late Middle Ages, characterized most obviously by the use of pointed arches. English Gothic architecture is conventionally divided into three phases (using terminology coined by the architect Thomas Rickman in a book published in 1817): Early English (*c.*1175–*c.*1275), Decorated (*c.*1250–*c.*1350), and Perpendicular (*c.*1330–*c.*1530).

GROIN VAULT. A square or roughly square vault formed by the intersection of two barrel vaults (the groins being the edges or ridges created at the points of intersection). *Fig. 11*

GRUBENHAUS (plural GRUBENHÄUSER). A German term (literally "sunken building") for a type of small Dark Ages structure in which the floor was a metre or so below the outside ground level; such buildings may have been used mainly for storage rather than as dwellings.

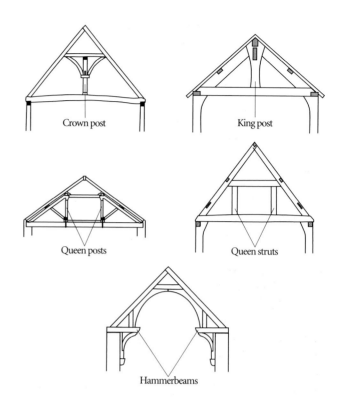

Crown post   King post

Queen posts   Queen struts

Hammerbeams

6. Wooden Roofs

HAGIOSCOPE. See squint.

HALF-SHAFT. See shaft.

HAMMERBEAM ROOF. A type of wooden roof characterized by a series of short horizontal beams ("hammerbeams") that project from opposite walls and support an arching superstructure. *Fig. 6*

HELM ROOF. A steep, spire-like roof over a tower, with four lozenge-shaped faces meeting at a pointed apex. Such roofs are sometimes referred to as Rhenish helms, as the type was popular in the Rhineland. *Fig. 3*

HOOD MOULDING. A projecting moulding over a window, door or arch, serving to divert the flow of rainwater; alternative terms are dripstone and label, the latter generally being applied to rectangular rather than curved mouldings. A label stop is an ornamental termination at each end of the moulding.

IMPOST. The part of a wall, column or pier on which the base of an arch rests, often taking the form of a projecting mould.

INTRADOS. See soffit.

JESSE TREE. A representation of Christ's genealogy in which names or images of his ancestors are arranged like the branches of a tree, growing

7. Monastic Buildings

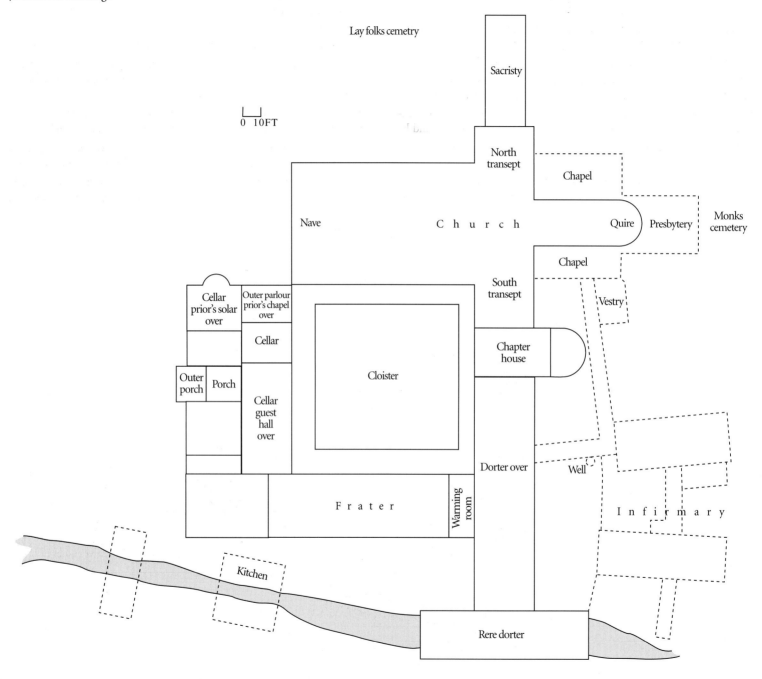

Lay folks cemetry

0 10FT

Sacristy

North transept

Chapel

Nave

C h u r c h

Quire   Presbytery

Monks cemetery

Chapel

South transept

Vestry

Cellar prior's solar over

Outer parlour prior's chapel over

Cellar

Outer porch

Porch

Chapter house

Cloister

Cellar guest hall over

Dorter over

Well

I n f i r m a r y

Frater

Warming room

Kitchen

Rere dorter

a. Norman: Castle Acre Priory, Norfolk, 11th to 12th century

from a recumbent figure of Jesse (father of King David); Jesse trees were found in various forms of medieval art, including painting, sculpture, window tracery and stained glass.

JETTY. A projecting part of a building, overhanging the storey below; the term is also applied to the joists that support the projection.

JOISTS. Horizontal, parallel timber beams that support flooring.

KEEL MOULDING. A moulding with two convex curves meeting in a central ridge, so that in profile it looks rather like the keel of a ship.

KEEP. The largest and strongest tower of a castle, usually centrally situated and more or less independent of the other defences, so it could be used as a final refuge in times of siege; it is also called a donjon.

KEYSTONE. See voussoir.

KING POST. In a wooden roof, a vertical post standing centrally on a transverse beam (tie beam) and connecting it to the apex. Pairs of similar

vertical posts placed symmetrically on a tie beam are called either queen posts or queen struts. Queen posts reach to the sloping sides of the roof, whereas queen struts support a secondary transverse beam, parallel to the one on which they stand. *Fig. 6*

LABEL AND LABEL STOP. See hood moulding.

LADY CHAPEL. A chapel dedicated to the Virgin Mary (Our Lady), usually situated at the east end of a church, behind the main altar, as an extension to the chancel or an aisle.

LANCET. A tall narrow window with a plain pointed head without any tracery, one of the most characteristic features of the Early English style.

LANTERN. A part of a church tower containing windows, or, more generally, any elevated structure that admits light to an interior below.

LAVATORY (or LAVATORIUM). A room or place for washing, particularly in a monastery; typically it consisted of a stone trough in the cloisters,

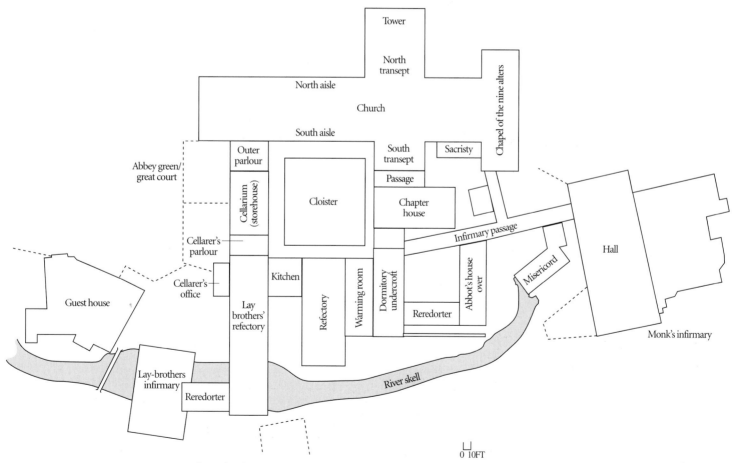

b. Medieval: Fountains Abbey (Cistercian), North Yorkshire, late 12th- to 13th-century

8. *Church Plans*

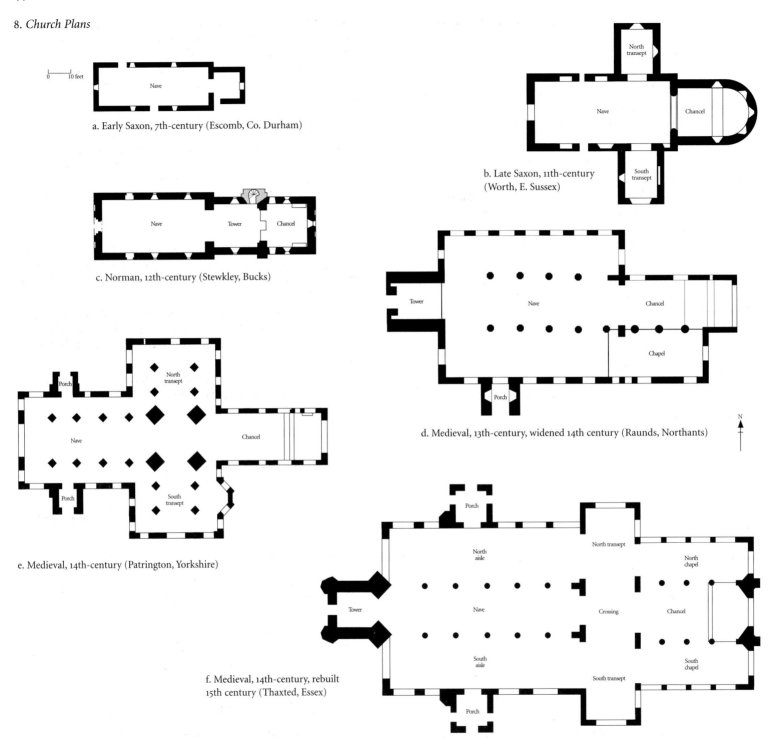

0   10 feet

a. Early Saxon, 7th-century (Escomb, Co. Durham)

b. Late Saxon, 11th-century
(Worth, E. Sussex)

c. Norman, 12th-century (Stewkley, Bucks)

d. Medieval, 13th-century, widened 14th century (Raunds, Northants)

N

e. Medieval, 14th-century (Patrington, Yorkshire)

f. Medieval, 14th-century, rebuilt
15th century (Thaxted, Essex)

near the refectory, in which monks washed their hands before and after eating.

LAVER. A washbasin with a hole for draining.

LEPER'S SQUINT. See squint.

LESENE (also called PILASTER STRIP). An upright strip of stone projecting slightly from a wall surface, characteristic of Anglo-Saxon architecture; lesenes are similar to pilasters but have no base or capital.

LIERNE. A subsidiary, largely decorative rib in a vault, not connected to either the springing point on the wall or the central boss. *Fig 11*

LIGHT. See mullion.

LINTEL. A horizontal beam of stone or wood lying across the top of an opening, such as a doorway, and usually supporting the wall above. *Fig 1*

LONG-AND-SHORT WORK. A treatment of the outer corner of walls typical of Anglo-Saxon architecture, in which flat slabs of stone alternate with upright ones.

LOUVRE. A structure on a roof that allows smoke and steam from a fire to escape but keeps out rain, sometimes in the form of a little turret with slatted sides.

LUCARNE. A small window in a spire.

MEURTRIÈRE. See murder hole.

MACHICOLATIONS. In fortifications, a series of openings in a projecting parapet through which defenders could drop missiles onto attackers at the foot of the wall below; from the later Middle Ages they were sometimes used for decorative effect rather than defensive purposes.

MISERICORD. A term used in architecture with two entirely distinct meanings: (1) a bracket or ledge on the underside of a hinged seat to give support to someone standing (see choir stalls); (2) a room in a monastery in which certain relaxations of the rule were allowed, such as the eating of meat. In both senses the word derives from the Latin "miserere" (have pity).

MOTTE AND BAILEY CASTLE. A type of fortification much used by the Normans after their conquest of England in 1066, featuring a stockade or tower on a natural or artificial mound (motte) linked by an inclined bridge to a courtyard (bailey) defended by a palisade and ditch; such castles were essentially temporary wooden structures, but many of the mottes remain, some of them supporting later stone structures (see shell keep).

MOUCHETTE. See dagger.

MOULDING. A band of ornament used in various architectural contexts, for example to accentuate or enrich the outline of a door or window. There are many distinctive types of moulding characteristic of different styles and periods. *Fig 2*

MULLION. A vertical strip (of stone or other material) dividing a window into upright panels called lights (a window with four mullions has five lights). A similar horizontal strip, at right angles to a mullion, is called a transom.

MURDER HOLE. In military architecture (specifically in the entrances to fortifications), a small opening in a roof or wall through which a musket

9. Cathedral Plans

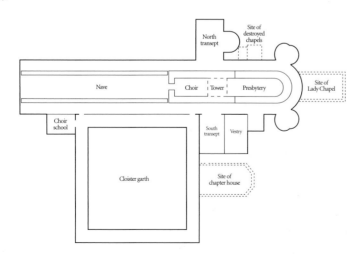

a. Norman: Norwich Cathedral, Norfolk, late 11th- to early 12th-century

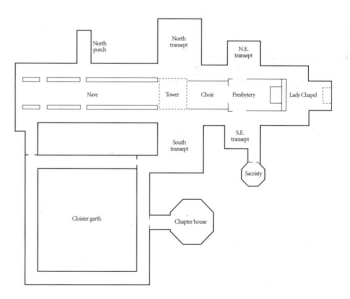

b. Medieval: Salisbury Cathedral, Wiltshire, 13th-century

could be fired or objects could be dropped on attackers. The term "meurtriere" (French for murderess) is used in the same way.

NAILHEAD. An ornamental motif in the form of a row of pyramidal studs, resembling the heads of a series of nails; it was much used on mouldings in the Norman and Early English periods. *Fig 2*

NARTHEX. A vestibule or portico at the main entrance of a church, particularly one stretching across the full width of the building.

NAVE. A term applied to the western limb (generally the largest section) of a church, as opposed to the eastern limb (the chancel), and also to the central division of the western limb, as opposed to the aisles that generally flank it.

NEEDLE SPIRE. See spire.

NICHE. A shallow vertical recess in a wall, often containing a sculpted figure or some other decorative feature.

NODDING OGEE. See ogee.

NOOK SHAFT. See shaft.

NORMAN. See Romanesque.

OGEE. A double curve in which one part is convex and the other concave, like a letter S. An ogee arch has two such curves, meeting in a point at the apex; a nodding ogee is such an arch in which the apex projects forwards (as if nodding its head). *Fig 1*

ORIEL. A bay window projecting from an upper storey and overhanging the wall below.

PALISADE. A row of wooden stakes forming a defensive wall.

PARCLOSE. A screen partitioning off a chapel from the main body of a church or enclosing an object such as an altar, shrine or tomb.

PELE TOWER (or PELE). A small fortified building, characteristic of the English-Scottish border, intended for protection against raiders rather than to withstand a siege; the term is hard to define with precision and is often used fairly loosely, sometimes being applied to non-tower-like structures (wider or longer than they are high) that could rather be described as bastels.

PENTICE. A subsidiary structure, generally with a sloping roof, attached to the wall of a large building and typically serving as a shelter, covered walk or porch.

PERPENDICULAR. See Gothic.

PIER. A substantial vertical supporting member of stone or brick, thicker than a column.

PILASTER. A flat, column-like vertical strip attached to a wall and projecting slightly from it; pilasters are often used decoratively rather than structurally. See also lesene.

PINNACLE. A pointed decorative termination common in Gothic architecture, for example at the top of buttresses.

PISCINA. A small stone basin with a drain, for washing the vessels used in the Mass or Communion; usually it is set in a niche on a wall near the altar (sometimes grouped with sedilia), but it can also be mounted on a column.

PLATE TRACERY. See tracery.

POPPYHEAD. A carved ornament of foliage, flowers and sometimes figures surmounting the end of a church pew or stall.

PORTCULLIS. A heavy grating used as part of the defences of a gateway; when the gate was open it was kept raised, but it could be quickly lowered in grooves in case of attack.

PORTICO. A large, formal entrance porch, usually with a roof supported by columns.

PORTICUS. In Anglo-Saxon architecture, a small subsidiary room or space leading off the main body of a church; the plural of the word is the same as the singular.

PRESBYTERY. The area of a church containing the main altar, at the eastern end of the chancel.

PULPITUM. In a large church, a stone screen separating the nave from the choir, often surmounted by an organ loft.

PURLIN. In a wooden roof, a longitudinal timber that helps to support the sloping rafters.

QUATREFOIL. An ornamental motif consisting of a stylized flower head with four rounded leaves radiating from a common centre (rather like a four-leaved clover); a similar motif with three leaves (or "foils") is called a trefoil. Both are commonly found in tracery and other forms of decoration. Each of the points formed where the foils intersect is called a cusp.

QUEEN POST. See king post.

QUEEN STRUT. See king post.

QUOINS. The stones or bricks forming an external corner of a building, particularly when they are emphasized (as by size, colour or texture) to give visual reinforcement to the corner.

RAFTERS. Inclined timbers that form the slope of a roof.

REREDORTER. A group of privies situated at the back of the dormitory (dorter) in a monastery.

REREDOS. An altarpiece occupying the wall behind the altar; it may take any of various forms, such as a screen or mural.

RESPOND. A half-column or similar feature bonded into a wall and supporting an arch, often at one end of a row of arches.

RETABLE. An altarpiece placed directly on an altar, often in the form of a small painting.

RETICULATED. A term meaning "net-like" applied to tracery in which a repeating pattern of interlocking shapes produces a mesh effect. *Fig 10*

RETROCHOIR. In a large church, the area behind the main altar.

RHENISH HELM. See helm roof.

RIB. A projecting band of stone or brick on the surface of a vault, dividing the vault into various compartments (or "cells"); ribs may be either structural (particularly in the form of intersecting arches crossing from side to side) or ornamental. *Fig 11*

RIDGE BEAM. A horizontal timber running along the apex of a roof.

RIDGE RIB. A central rib running along the apex of a vault, either lengthwise (longitudinal ridge rib) or from side to side (transverse ridge rib). *Fig 11*

ROLL MOULDING. A moulding that is more or less semicircular in section.

ROMANESQUE. The style of architecture prevalent in Europe in the 11th and 12th centuries, characterized most obviously by massiveness of construction and the use of round-headed arches. Romanesque architecture in the British Isles is often described as Norman architecture, as it was largely introduced as a consequence of the Norman conquest of England in 1066.

ROOD. An Anglo-Saxon word for cross or crucifix, referring in architectural contexts to a large carving of the Crucifixion standing or hanging in the nave of a church; almost all roods in British churches were destroyed during the Reformation, but there are plentiful examples of the rood screens on which many of them stood, separating nave from chancel (they are now sometimes known as chancel screens or choir screens). Above the rood screen there was sometimes a gallery known as a rood loft, which was used by lay singers during services.

ROSE WINDOW. A large circular window filled with petal-like tracery. A similar type is the wheel window, in which the tracery has more definite spokes radiating from a centre. Both types are used most commonly in the end walls of large churches, particularly the nave and transepts.

ROUND TOWER. In Ireland, a type of tall circular, usually free-standing tower, slightly tapering towards the top and surmounted by a conical roof, built on monastic sites from about the 10th to the 12th century; such towers were evidently used mainly as belfries but also for storing valuables and as places of refuge in times of danger.

RUBBLE MASONRY. See ashlar.

SACRAMENT HOUSE. A secure cupboard in a church for holding the consecrated bread used in the Eucharist.

SACRISTY. A room in or attached to a church in which are kept the vessels and vestments used by priests during services.

SADDLEBACK ROOF. A term applied to a simple pitched roof, with two gable ends, when such a roof surmounts a tower. *Fig. 3*

SADDLEBARS. Narrow horizontal iron bars used to support the leaded panels of a window; corresponding upright bars are called stanchions.

SCALLOPED CAPITAL. See capital.

SCREEN. A partition separating one part of an interior space from another; in churches it refers to various types of fixed barrier, usually of wood but sometimes of stone or metal, that separate areas of different function or liturgical significance. They vary from light railings to huge, richly decorated architectural structures. See parclose, pulpitum and rood.

SCREENS PASSAGE. In a large medieval house, a passage between the great hall and the kitchen area, separated from the hall by a screen.

SEDILIA. A series of stone seats (usually three) placed on or set into the south wall of the chancel of a church (often grouped with a piscina) for the use of officiating clergy during the singing of certain parts of the Mass; the singular (rarely used) is sedile.

SGRAFFITO. A form of decoration made by scratching through plaster to reveal a differently coloured layer underneath.

SHAFT. A term applied to the trunk or central portion of a column, between the base and the capital, and also (in the context of medieval architecture) to a slender column-like form attached (sometimes in groups) to a wall or other surface. A nook shaft is a shaft in this second sense situated in the internal angle formed by the meeting of two surfaces. A half-shaft is one that projects only partly from the surface to which it is attached.

SHEILA-NA-GIG. A carving of a woman with lewdly displayed genitals – a fertility symbol found on churches, notably in Ireland.

SHELL KEEP. A roughly circular or polygonal stone ring wall around an open central courtyard, replacing the original wooden palisade at the top of the motte in a motte and bailey castle. *Fig. 5*

SHINGLES. Wooden (usually oak) roof tiles; they were in common use until the end of the Middle Ages, when – because they posed a fire hazard – they generally gave way to clay tiles.

SLYPE. A passage or covered way, particularly one in a cathedral or monastery connecting the chapter house with the transept.

SOFFIT. The visible underside of any architectural member, such as an arch, balcony or cornice (the underside of an arch can also be called the intrados).

SOLAR. A term for an upper chamber, usually applied specifically to a private room for the lord in a medieval house.

SOUTERRAIN. An underground passage or chamber.

SPANDREL. A triangular area with one or more curved sides, such as the surface between two adjacent arches. *Fig 1*

SPIRE. A tall structure, tapering upwards to a point, surmounting a tower or roof, particularly of a church. A needle spire is a very slender one, with a base that starts well inside the parapet of the tower. A broach spire is one that is square in plan at the base but becomes octagonal at a slightly higher level, the transition being effected by sloping triangular faces (broaches) at the base. A splay-foot spire is similar to a broach spire in that it is square at the base and octagonal for most of its height, but the transition is effected by four of the sides tapering to a point at the base. *Fig 3*

SPLAY. A sloping surface cut into a wall, usually referring to a window that is wider on the inside than on the outside or vice versa.

SPLAY-FOOT SPIRE. See spire

SQUINT (also called HAGIOSCOPE). A small oblique opening in a wall or pier in a church to allow people whose view would otherwise be obstructed to see the altar during services. The term "leper's squint" is sometimes applied to openings of this kind in the external wall of a church, from the belief that they were used to give confession or Communion to lepers or other people who were not allowed to enter the building. However, their purpose is uncertain and they may well have been used for more mundane purposes, such as ventilation.

STALLS. See choir stalls.

STANCHIONS. See saddlebars.

STEEPLE. The tower and spire of a church considered together, although the term is often loosely applied to the spire alone.

STIFF-LEAF CAPITAL. See capital.

STILTED ARCH. An arch (usually semicircular) in which the sides are vertical for a certain length before the curved profile begins, giving the effect of a normal arch raised on stilts. *Fig 1*

STOUP. A container for consecrated water, usually consisting of a stone basin set into a wall near the entrance of a church.

STRAINER ARCH. An arch inserted between two walls, as for example in the nave of a church, to prevent them leaning inwards.

STRINGCOURSE. A moulding or band of masonry running horizontally along a wall.

STRIPWORK. A type of ornamentation characteristic of Anglo-Saxon architecture in which thin slabs of stone are embedded into a surface to form geometrical patterns.

STUDS. In a timber-framed building, the subsidiary upright timbers, in between the main posts.

TIE BEAM. In a wooden roof, a transverse beam (generally the lowest horizontal member) stretching from side to side and preventing the walls being pushed outwards.

TIERCERON. A subsidiary vault rib, stretching from the main springing point to an off-centre point (rather than the central boss) on a ridge rib. *Fig 11*

TIMBER-FRAMING. A method of construction in which the walls of a building are constructed of interlocking wooden beams, with the spaces between the beams filled with another material, such as brick or plaster.

TRABEATED. A term characterizing a structure built using a post-and-lintel system (uprights supporting cross beams), as opposed to one that is arcuated (using arches).

TRACERY. An openwork pattern of stone (or less commonly brick) embellishing a window (usually only the upper part of the window), one of the most characteristic features of Gothic architecture; by extension, the term is applied also to similar ornament used in other contexts, for example to decorate a wall ("blind tracery") or furniture. There are two basic types of tracery: plate tracery, which is the earliest kind (originating in about 1170) and was comparatively short-lived; and bar tracery, which was first used in France in the 1220s and developed into many different varieties over the next three centuries. In plate tracery, the effect is of an area of flat, solid stone perforated with openings (generally simple geometrical patterns); in bar tracery, thin strips of stone (usually branching out of the mullions) are arranged into meshwork or other patterns. *Fig 10*

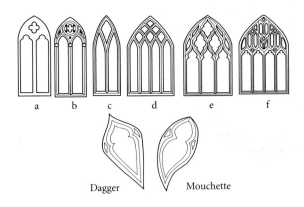

a. Plate tracery   d. Intersecting tracery

b. Geometrical bar tracery   e. Reticulated tracery

c. Y-tracery   f. Panel tracery

10. *Tracery*

TRANSEPTS. In a cross-shaped church, the pair of wings projecting at right angles to the main body of the building that form the "arms" of the cross; some major churches (for example Lincoln and Salisbury Cathedrals) have two sets of transepts.

TRANSOM. See mullion.

TREFOIL. See quatrefoil.

TRIBUNE. A term that has been applied to various raised areas in a building, including the slightly elevated apse characteristic of early Christian basilicas.

TRIFORIUM. In the interior of a large church, a middle "storey" above the arcade and below the clerestory; the triforium is often a narrow elevated passageway, but sometimes it is a "blind" storey, treated purely decoratively.

TRUSS. In a wooden roof, a number of timbers grouped together to form a rigid frame spanning the building from side to side; a series of such trusses placed at regular intervals, typically one to each bay of the building, support longitudinal timbers that in turn support the rafters.

TUNNEL VAULT. See barrel vault.

TYMPANUM. The (usually semicircular) space between the lintel of a door and an arch over it, often used as a field for sculptural decoration, particularly in Romanesque architecture.

UNDERCROFT. An underground or partly underground chamber, generally used as a synonym for crypt but sometimes applied to space used for storage.

VAULT. A roof or ceiling (usually of stone) the construction of which is based on the principle of arches spanning the space covered from side to side. See barrel vault, fan vault, groin vault, and also lierne, rib and tierceron. *Fig 11*

VESICA. An ornamental motif consisting of an upright almond shape.

VOUSSOIR. One of the stones or bricks that form the curve of an arch. They are usually a truncated wedge in shape, tapering towards the inner edge, but in less sophisticated work they may be ordinary oblong shapes ("non-radial voussoirs"), with the plaster instead worked into wedges. The central voussoir is called a keystone. *Fig 1*

WAGON ROOF. A wooden roof with multi-angled arch-like trusses, giving an appearance similar to the series of hoops over which the canvas is stretched in covered wagons.

WALL PLATE. A timber laid along the top of a side wall of a building, from end to end, as part of the construction of a roof; the lower ends of the rafters are attached to the wall plate, and in certain types of roof, other timbers, such as tie beams, are secured to it.

WHEEL WINDOW. See rose window.

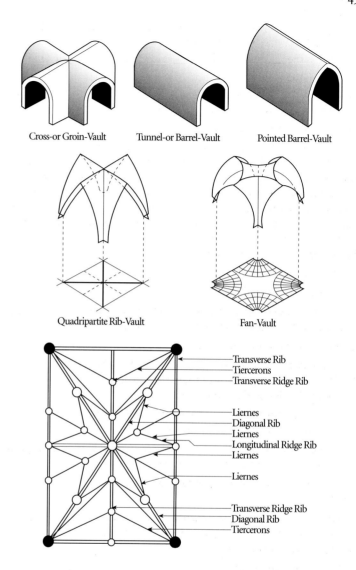

Cross-or Groin-Vault   Tunnel-or Barrel-Vault   Pointed Barrel-Vault

Quadripartite Rib-Vault   Fan-Vault

Transverse Rib
Tiercerons
Transverse Ridge Rib

Liernes
Diagonal Rib
Liernes
Longitudinal Ridge Rib
Liernes

Liernes

Transverse Ridge Rib
Diagonal Rib
Tiercerons

11. *Vaults*

Some suggestions for further reading

ENGLAND

Nikolaus Pevsner and others, *The Buildings of England*, 46 vols, Harmondsworth, 1951–74, followed by an ongoing programme of reprints, revisions and new expanded editions, currently edited by Bridget Cherry.

Nikolaus Pevsner and Priscilla Metcalf, *The Cathedrals of England: Midland, Eastern and Northern England*, Harmondsworth, 1985.

Nikolaus Pevsner and Priscilla Metcalf, *The Cathedrals of England: Southern England*, Harmondsworth, 1985 (this and the preceding volume feature expanded, extensively illustrated versions of the entries on cathedrals from the individual, county-by-county volumes of *The buildings of England*).

Francis Bond, *Gothic Architecture in England*, London, 1905.

J. Charles Cox and Alfred Harvey, *English Church Furniture*, London, 1907.

Francis Bond, *Screens and Galleries in English Churches,* London, 1908.

J. Charles Cox, *The English Parish Church*, London, 1914.

F. E. Howard and F. H. Crossley, *English Church Woodwork*, London, 1917 (2nd edition, 1927).

A. W. Clapham, *English Romanesque Architecture. Before the Conquest*, Oxford, 1930.

A. W. Clapham, *English Romanesque Architecture. After the Conquest*, Oxford, 1934.

E. W. Tristram, *English Medieval Wall Painting: The Twelfth Century*, London, 1944.

E. W. Tristram, *English Medieval Wall Painting: The Thirteenth Century*, 2 vols, Oxford, 1950.

George Zarnecki, *English Romanesque Sculpture 1066–1140*, London, 1951.

Hugh Braun, *English Mediaeval Architecture*, London, 1951.

L. F. Salzman, *Building in England Down to 1540: A Documentary History*, Oxford, 1952.

Graham Hutton, with photographs by Edwin Smith, *English Parish Churches*, London, 1952.

George Zarnecki, *Later English Romanesque Sculpture 1140–1210*, London, 1953.

Olive Cook, with photographs by Edwin Smith, *English Cottages and Farmhouses*, London, 1954

E. W. Tristram, *English Wall Painting of the Fourteenth Century*, London, 1955.

John Betjeman, ed., *Collins Guide to English Parish Churches*, London, 1958 (new edition, 1993).

Olive Cook, with photographs by Edwin Smith, *English Abbeys and Priories*, London, 1960.

Alec Clifton-Taylor, *The Pattern of English Building*, London, 1962 (4th edition, 1987).

Margaret Wood, *The English Mediaeval House*, London, 1965.

Olive Cook, with photographs by Edwin Smith, *The English House Through Seven Centuries*, London, 1968.

Graham Hutton and Olive Cook, with photographs by Edwin Smith, *English Parish Churches*, London, 1976.

Colin Platt, *The English Medieval Town*, London, 1976.

Richard Harris, *Discovering Timber-Framed Buildings*, Princes Risborough, 1978 (3rd revised edition, 1993).

Gerald Cobb, *English Cathedrals. The Forgotten Centuries: Restoration and Change from 1530 to the Present Day*, London, 1980.

Cecil A. Hewett, *English Historic Carpentry*, Chichester, 1980.

Colin Platt, *The Parish Churches of Medieval England*, London, 1981.

Colin Platt, *The Abbeys and Priories of Medieval England*, London, 1984.

Janet Backhouse, D. H. Turner and Leslie Webster, ed., *The Golden Age of Anglo-Saxon Art 966–1066* (catalogue of exhibition at British Museum), London, 1984.

George Zarnecki, Janet Holt and Tristram Holland, ed., *English Romanesque Art 1066–1200* (catalogue of Arts Council of Great Britain exhibition), London, 1984.

Cecil A. Hewett, *English Cathedral and Monastic Carpentry*, Chichester 1985.

Sarah Crewe, *Stained Glass in England c.1180– c.1540*, London, 1987.

Jonathan Alexander and Paul Binski, ed., *Age of Chivalry: Art in Plantagenet England 1200–1400* (catalogue of Royal Academy exhibition), London, 1987.

Edwin Smith and Olive Cook, *English Cathedrals*, London, 1989.

Anthony Quiney, *The Traditional Buildings of England*, London, 1990.

Leslie Webster and Janet Backhouse, ed., *The Making of England: Anglo-Saxon Art and Culture AD 600–1500* (catalogue of exhibition at British Museum), London, 1991.

Elizabeth Eames, *English Tilers*, London, 1992.

Richard Marks, *Stained Glass in England during the Middle Ages*, London, 1993.

Alec Clifton-Taylor and A. S. Ireson, *English Stone Building*, London, 1994.

Adrian Pettifer, *English Castles: A Guide by Counties,* Woodbridge, 1995.

Philip Lindley, *Gothic to Renaissance: Essays on Sculpture in England*, Stamford, 1995.

Stephen Friar, *A Companion to the English Parish Church*, Stroud, 1996.

IRELAND

Alistair Rowan, *The Buildings of Ireland: North West Ulster, The Counties of Londonderry, Donegal, Fermanagh and Tyrone*, Harmondsworth, 1979.

Christine Casey and Alistair Rowan, *The Buildings of Ireland: North Leinster*, Harmondsworth, 1993.

[Christine Casey, *The Buildings of Ireland: Dublin, City and County*, in preparation]

Brendan Lehane, *The Companion Guide to Ireland*, London, 1973 (revised edition, 1985).

John Hunt, *Irish Medieval Figure Sculpture, 1200–1600: A Study of Irish Tombs with Notes on Costume and Armour*, 2 vols, Dublin, 1974.

Lennox Barrow, *The Round Towers of Ireland*, Dublin, 1979.

Maurice Craig, *The Architecture of Ireland, From the Earliest Times to 1880*, London and Dublin, 1982.

Department of the Environment for Northern Ireland, *Historic Monuments of Northern Ireland*, Belfast, 1983 (revised edition, 1987).

Lennox Barrow, *Irish Round Towers*, Dublin, 1985.

Peter Harbison, *Guide to the National and Historic Monuments of Ireland* (includes northern counties), Dublin, 1992.

Everyman Guide to Ireland, London, 1995.

Jacqueline O'Brien and Peter Harbison, *Ancient Ireland from Prehistory to the Middle Ages*, London, 1996.

ISLE OF MAN

Manx National Heritage, *The Ancient and Historic Monuments of the Isle of Man*, Douglas, 1973.

SCOTLAND

Colin McWilliam with Christopher Wilson, *The Buildings of Scotland: Lothian (except Edinburgh)*, Harmondsworth, 1978.

John Gifford, Colin McWilliam and David Walker, with Christopher Wilson, *The Buildings of Scotland: Edinburgh*, Harmondsworth, 1984 (revised 1988 and 1991).

John Gifford, *The Buildings of Scotland: Fife*, Harmondsworth, 1988.

Elizabeth Williamson, Anne Riches and Malcolm Higgs, *The Buildings of Scotland: Glasgow*, Harmondsworth, 1990.

John Gifford, *The Buildings of Scotland: Highlands and Islands*, Harmondsworth, 1992.

John Gifford, *The Buildings of Scotland: Dumfries and Galloway*, Harmondsworth, 1996.

[Frank Arneil Walker, *The Buildings of Scotland: Argyll, Bute and Stirling*, in preparation]

David MacGibbon and Thomas Ross, *The Castellated and Domestic Architecture of Scotland*, 5 vols, 1887–92 (reprinted 1990).

David MacGibbon and Thomas Ross, *The Ecclesiastical Architecture of Scotland*, (3 vols, 1896–7).

J. G. Dunbar *The Historic Architecture of Scotland*, 1966 ("second edition", effectively a different book, titled *The Architecture of Scotland*, 1978).

Christopher Tabraham, *Scottish Castles and Fortifications*, London, 1986.

Stewart Cruden, *Scottish Medieval Churches*, Edinburgh, 1986.

Anthony New, *A Guide to the Abbeys of Scotland*, London, 1988.

Anna Ritchie, *Picts*, Edinburgh, 1989.

Anna Ritchie, *Viking Scotland*, London, 1993.

Richard Fawcett, *Scottish Architecture from the Accession of the Stewarts to the Reformation, 1371–1560*, Edinburgh, 1994.

Richard Fawcett, *Scottish Abbeys and Priories*, London, 1994.

Mike Salter, *Old Parish Churches of Scotland*, Malvern, 1994.

Martin Coventry, *The Castles of Scotland*, Edinburgh, 1995 (revised 1997).

Christopher Tabraham, *Scotland's Castles*, London, 1997.

Richard Fawcett, *Scottish Cathedrals*, London, 1997.

Ian Armit, *Celtic Scotland*, London, 1999.

WALES

Richard Haslam, *The Buildings of Wales: Powys (Montgomeryshire, Radnorshire, Breconshire)*, Harmondsworth, 1979.

Edward Hubbard, *The Buildings of Wales: Clwyd (Denbighshire and Flintshire)*, Harmondsworth, 1986.

John Newman, *The Buildings of Wales: Glamorgan (Mid Glamorgan, South Glamorgan and West Glamorgan)*, Harmondsworth, 1995.

[Thomas Lloyd, Julian Orbach and Robert Scourfield, *The Buildings of Wales: Dyfed (Cardiganshire, Carmarthenshire and Pembrokeshire)*, in preparation]

[John Newman, *The Buildings of Wales: Gwent*, in preparation]

Elizabeth Beazley and Peter Howell, The *Companion Guide to North Wales*, London, 1975.

John B. Hilling, *The Historic Architecture of Wales*, Cardiff, 1976.

Peter Howell and Elizabeth Beazley, *The Companion Guide to South Wales*, London, 1977.

A. J. Taylor, *The Welsh Castles of Edward I*, London, 1985.

Lesley Macinnes, *Anglesey: A Guide to Ancient and Historic Sites on the Isle of Anglesey*, Cardiff, 1989 (revised 1994).

Mike Salter, *Old Parish Churches of Gwent and Glamorgan*, Malvern, 1991.

Mike Salter, *Old Parish Churches of Mid-Wales*, Malvern, 1991.

Sian Rees, *Guide to Ancient and Historic Wales: Dyfed*, London, 1992.

Elizabeth Whittle, *Guide to Ancient and Historic Wales: Glamorgan and Gwent*, London, 1992.

Mike Salter, *Old Parish Churches of North Wales*, Malvern, 1993.

Mike Salter, *Old Parish Churches of South-West Wales*, Malvern, 1994.

Helen Burnham, *Guide to Ancient and Historic Wales: Clwyd and Powys*, London, 1995.

Frances Lynch, *Guide to Ancient and Historic Wales: Gwynedd*, London, 1995.

Lindsay Evans, *The Castles of Wales*, London, 1998.

GENERAL

Francis Bond, *Fonts and Font Covers*, London, 1908.

Lawrence Stone, *Sculpture in Britain: The Middle Ages*, Harmondsworth, 1955 (revised 1972).

H. W. Macklin, *Macklin's Monumental Brasses*, rewritten by John Page-Phillips, London, 1969.

M. D. Anderson, *History and Imagery in British Churches*, London, 1971.

Christina and Bamber Gascoigne, *Castles of Britain*, London, 1975.

Paul Johnson, *The National Trust Book of British Castles*, London, 1978.

Gerald Randall, *Church Furnishing and Decoration in England and Wales*, London, 1980.

R. W. Brunskill, *Traditional Buildings of Britain: An Introduction to Vernacular Architecture*, London, 1981 (new edition, 1992).

James Campbell, ed., *The Anglo-Saxons*, London, 1982.

Colin Platt, *The Castle in Medieval England and Wales*, London, 1982.

Alastair Service, *The Buildings of Britain: Anglo-Saxon and Norman, A Guide and Gazetteer*, London, 1982.

Eric Fernie, *The Architecture of the Anglo-Saxons*, London, 1983.

Bryan Little, *Architecture in Norman Britain*, London, 1985.

R. W. Brunskill, *Timber Building in Britain*, London, 1985 (2nd edition, 1994).

Charles Thomas, *Celtic Britain*, London, 1986.

Peter and Jean Hansell, *Doves and Dovecotes*, Bath, 1988.

Paul Johnson, *Castles of England, Scotland and Wales*, London, 1989.

NADFAS (Patricia Dirsztay), *Inside Churches: A Guide to Church Furnishings*, London, 1989 (revised 1993).

Colin Platt with photographs by Anthony Kersting, *The Architecture of Medieval Britain: A Social History*, New Haven and London, 1990.

R. W. Brunskill, *Brick Building in Britain*, London, 1990.

Henry Thorold, *Collins Guide to the Ruined Abbeys of England, Wales and Scotland*, London, 1993.

Lloyd and Jennifer Laing, *Celtic Britain and Ireland*, London, 1995.

Plantagenet Somerset Fry, *Castles of Britain and Ireland*, London, 1996.

David Robinson, ed., *The Cistercian Abbeys of Britain: Far from the Concourse of Men*, London, 1998.

Index